BODY STAR SIGNS

BODY STAR SIGNS

What your body shape and your stars say about you

Bel Hislop and Jane Oakley

VERMILION
LONDON

First published 1994

1 3 5 7 9 10 8 6 4 2

First published in the United Kingdom
in 1994 by Vermilion,
an imprint of Ebury Press, Random House,
20 Vauxhall Bridge Road, London SW1V 2SA

Random House Australia (Pty) Limited
20 Alfred Street, Milsons Point, Sydney
New South Wales 2061, Australia

Random House New Zealand Limited
18 Poland Road, Glenfield
Auckland 10, New Zealand

Random House South Africa (Pty) Limited
PO Box 337, Bergvlei, South Africa

Random House UK Limited Reg. No. 954009

A CIP catalogue record for this book
is available from the British Library.

Editor: Emma Callery
Design: Roger Walker
Illustrations: David Downton

ISBN 0 09 178391 7

Typeset by Pure Tech Corporation, India
Printed in Great Britain by Clays Ltd, St Ives plc

CONTENTS

PEAR BODY TYPE

HOURGLASS BODY TYPE

RECTANGLE BODY TYPE

TRIANGLE BODY TYPE

INTRODUCTION

This book is the first to combine two unique systems of personality analysis. The connection between body shape and disposition is startlingly new, and partly based on scientific findings, while astrology is as ancient as civilization itself. Together these become the Body Star Sign system which opens up a whole new way of looking at ourselves, our working and emotional lives, and the way we interact with others and the world. The results have been illuminating in a completely new way. The effects extend right through every area of our personality and life. It gives us the means to understand ourselves better and make the most of all the qualities we have and the aspirations we may hold. It brings us acceptance of the self.

For a start, astrology as a system of personal potential and predictor of future trends has now become so respectable it is virtually mainstream. It has always had a central part to play in the Eastern cultures where treaties are signed, governments are inaugurated and marriages arranged according to the positions of the planets. But even here, in the more sceptical West, astrology's star has been steeply in the ascendant. The last decade or so has seen astrologers used to predict stock market movements, help international companies choose their top personnel and give advice on fortuitous times for big deals and aquisitions to be made.

In President Reagan's term of office we even had the most important and successful democracy in the world run on the dictates of an astrologer's advice. This was a democracy whose birth already had been stage managed to occur, on July 4 1776, when the planets were deemed to be at their most propitious for the future of a great and prosperous new country. There are now enough people who have seen astrology working in their lives, in their companies and even their presidencies, for this art to have well and truly earned its campaign medals.

It is the Body-type theory, however, which is truly revolutionary. The idea that there are distinct links between personality and body shape came to Bel and Jane through Bel's work as a personal and style consultant with thousands of women. She knew that there are different female body types, which she categorized into four distinct types to which all women belong – called Pear, Hourglass, Rectangle and Triangle. It soon became clear through her work, however, that these four body types signify much deeper differences in women than merely what style of clothes suited them best.

Important scientific papers (see Science Research below) showed that there are powerful physiological differences between women with different body shapes and patterns of fat distribution. The scientists divide women's body shapes into two distinct types, the 'gynoid' and the 'android'. The gynoid shape is the classic female, bottom-heavy, shape with a pronounced waist and curvy hips. This type falls naturally into two sub-divisions, the Pear and Hourglass. The Pear has narrower shoulders than hips, always retains a waist and flattish tummy, and always has less fat above the waist than below. The Hourglass has balanced shoulders and hips and has fat equally distributed on bust and hips, but always retains a waist.

The other scientific type is the android, which is a top-heavy shape with a weight distribution more similar to a man's. Again this can be sub-divided into two distinct types, the Rectangle and inverted Triangle. The Rectangle has balanced shoulders and hips but little or no waist. She puts on weight from the tummy up rather than from the hips down. The Triangle has broader shoulders than hips. She too puts weight on her upper body but has a waist, flat bottom and *straight* hips which taper towards the thighs.

The scientific evidence showed, for instance, that the gynoid body shapes are more protected by their female hormones from heart disease and diabetes than the android shapes. Latest research shows they get pregnant more easily too. These differences in female body shape affect women's propensity to disease, to their chances of motherhood, their metabolisms, their need for exercise, even the way they age. But, in addition, it became obvious to the authors that there were even more profound character traits exhibited by women in each of the four body shapes.

When working with Bel's clients, discussing their careers, lives, clothing style – related to body shape – the authors discovered that the Pear and Hourglass shapes have a different way of relating to others and the world from the Rectangle and Triangle. This was confirmed by the evidence of an extensive questionnaire which found that the Rectangle's and Triangle's need for vigorous exercise, for instance, correlated with their greater need to express themselves vigorously through their work. That their competitiveness in the gym was translated to their approach to life. They are more dynamic, more ambitious, more egotistical and emotionally detached than their curvy-hipped sisters.

The Pear and the Hourglass are just as capable of carving brilliant careers for themselves in the outside world, but they do it differently and in different metiers – and a career is less likely to be their top priority over family and love. These are basically relating women who make the workplace into a supportive, family-type environment. They promote others more readily than themselves and if forced to compete in highly competitive, traditionally masculine arenas, like bond-dealing, hospital medicine or at the Bar, find it a much greater emotional strain than it is for the naturally competitive, top-heavy shapes of Rectangle and Triangle.

In fact the authors' thesis is that it is mainly the android-shaped women who will be attracted to these professions. And mostly it is they who will manage to succeed in areas where the rules are all made by men – and the qualities admired are assertive detachment, the traditional male values. This explains why Mrs Thatcher, an extreme android in body shape, thrived in the most competitive and ruthless of professions.

The tough survivors in Hollywood, too, tend to be the android shapes, like Roseanne Barr, Cher, Glenn Close, Joan Crawford, Mia Farrow, Katherine Hepburn, Diane Keaton, Madonna, Demi Moore, Dolly Parton, Maggie Smith. The gynoid shapes, on the other hand, are just as successful, but less single-minded, less personally ambitious and more relationship-orientated: they find the ruthlessness and continual self-promotion of Hollywood hard to bear. Just think of the emotional upheavals, or the eventual withdrawal into a private life, for actresses such as Brigitte Bardot, Jessica Lange, Marilyn Monroe, Michelle Pfeiffer, Isabella Rossellini, Julia Roberts. The Pear and Hourglass types tend to be less willing to sacrifice everything for success in their careers and value their emotional lives more, even at the expense of their careers.

It is also interesting to note that in the highest levels of women's sport, where race times have got closer to the men's, and in women's tennis, for instance, where success is more to do with big hitting power and a single-minded dedication to winning, the android body shapes predominate. Steffi Graf, Sally Gunnell, Liz McCoughlan, Yvonne Murray, Martina Navratilova, Gabriela Sabatini, Monica Seles, are all this shape.

The gynoid women enjoy all sports and excel at them too, up to a certain level, bringing much more grace and good humour to the game. The last Wimbledon Ladies champion who was a curvy gynoid type was Maria Bueno whose grace around the court, during her reign in the sixties, was legendary, but she could never have hit a ball as hard as Steffi or Martina. The real first league of sportswomen today are all either Rectangle or Triangle body types.

This is not just because their physiques, big broad shoulders and straight male-type hips, make them able to run faster and hit harder, but dispositionally too the Hourglass and Pear types have not got the killer instinct necessary to win against enormous competition. They are not as prepared to be ruthless, single-minded and necessarily aggressive in order to get that cup or medal. They don't care so desperately that they are first and the best.

Pear and Hourglass women with power exercise it in a very different way. Hillary Clinton, a Pear type, has a brilliant brain and yet has given up her lawyer's practice to support her husband in Washington. Deservedly, she's been put in charge of reforming the US health system. This is close to her heart as a crucial area of care which impinges on every individual's life, when they are at their most vulnerable. But when her daughter Chelsea is ill or her father is dying, she is quite prepared to drop everything to nurse them both, as she has shown. Her priorities are different, not better, from that of the more self-motivated android body types.

Our research with thousands of women established that these four different body types express their energies differently – have a different style – at work, in love, in dressing to suit their shapes and personalities, in diet and exercise needs. If understood, these dispositional differences can allow women to accept more easily their natural character and abilities, and their own way of dealing with the world. We have seen it confirm for women what they really feel about themselves, releasing them from the need to conform to some external construction of how women should feel or be.

Along with this research into the revolutionary body type theory came the realization that combining body shape with the ancient system of astrological star signs provided a deeper insight into individual personality and motivation. A questionnaire sent out to more than 400 of Bel's clients, equal numbers of each body type, conclusively confirmed the sense of putting these two systems together.

The body shape disposition is *always* the overriding factor, but the characteristics of the star signs add their own intensifying or contradictory energy. With the combining of these energies, we have produced 48 different categories of personality, each unique to itself, yet part of the whole.

THE YIN AND YANG OF LIFE

This combining of energies is best explained using the ancient Chinese philosophical concept of Yin and Yang energies. In this context, Yin is seen as female in a responsive, sensitive, intuitive way. It creates through synthesis. It is an energy which conserves and constructs. It is highly sensitized to the responses of others. If we are all boats afloat on the sea of life, then the Yin person is not a sealed vessel. Water continually seeps in and flows out.

It is similarly too limiting to think of Yang energy as masculine. It rushes outwards, rather than receives: it needs to impress itself on the world. It is dynamic, self-centred and creates through assertiveness – and sometimes destruction and re-creation. Its powerful ego insulates it against the influences of others. Afloat on the sea of life, the Yang person is a much more sealed vessel, able to plough her or his own path through the water, without much moisture seeping in or leaching out.

The body types and star signs can both be categorized in this way, and their combinations can be expressed in a formula of Yin and Yang energies:

Pear: Yin+
Hourglass: Yin
Rectangle: Yang
Triangle: Yang+

Cancer, Scorpio, Pisces: water signs – Yin+
Taurus, Virgo, Capricorn: earth signs – Yin
Gemini, Libra, Aquarius: air signs – Yang
Aries, Leo, Sagittarius: fire signs – Yang+

The body star sign energies

	Pear	*Hourglass*	*Rectangle*	*Triangle*
Aries (Yang+)	Yin+/Yang+	Yin/Yang+	Yang/Yang+	Yang+/Yang+
Taurus (Yin)	Yin+/Yin	Yin/Yin	Yang/Yin	Yang+/Yin
Gemini (Yang)	Yin+/Yang	Yin/Yang	Yang/Yang	Yang+/Yang
Cancer (Yin+)	Yin+/Yin+	Yin/Yin+	Yang/Yin+	Yang+/Yin+
Leo (Yang+)	Yin+/Yang+	Yin/Yang+	Yang/Yang+	Yang+/Yang+
Virgo (Yin)	Yin+/Yin	Yin/Yin	Yang/Yin	Yang+/Yin
Libra (Yang)	Yin+/Yang	Yin/Yang	Yang/Yang	Yang+/Yang
Scorpio (Yin+)	Yin+/Yin+	Yin/Yin+	Yang/Yin+	Yang+/Yin+
Sagittarius (Yang+)	Yin+/Yang+	Yin/Yang+	Yang/Yang+	Yang+/Yang+
Capricorn (Yin)	Yin+/Yin	Yin/Yin	Yang/Yin	Yang+/Yin
Aquarius (Yang)	Yin+/Yang	Yin/Yang	Yang/Yang	Yang+/Yang
Pisces (Yin+)	Yin+/Yin+	Yin/Yin+	Yang/Yin+	Yang+/Yin+

The body type is always the predominant influence but the star sign has an important modifying effect. For instance, an extreme Yang+ Triangle type will be particularly forceful if she is also an Aries, itself a Yang+ influence. But these energies will be in harmony – just rather too much for everyone else! If that Yang+ Triangle woman was also an extremely Yin+ star sign like Pisces, then her forcefulness is modified, her feeling side is more marked. But she may feel that there are conflicts and contradictions in her character as a result. Whatever her star sign, if she is a Triangle body type then she remains a Yang+ personality.

In relationships between men and women there is also a balance and an attraction between the Yin individual and the Yang. This is a book which deals with women's body shape and the connection with personality. Whether a man is Yin or Yang is not so closely tied to his shape. (Many body builders with exaggeratedly inverted Triangle body shapes, for instance, are in fact Yin.) But he is as easily identified to the practised eye.

The Yang male is a forceful, relatively self-confident and self-centred individual. He has a hardness about his looks and his character which is lacking in the gentler, kinder, more feeling Yin man. His attitudes to himself and to life are more in the traditional mould. Not quite me Tarzan, you Jane, because he intellectually accepts all the theories on the necessary independence and equality of women, but in his heart he wants to be the main provider and protector – and his woman to be his.

He does not naturally want to talk much about feelings and motivation and psychological niceties. He'd rather get on with doing. The Yang man is an adventurer in life and work. He thrives on risk and danger. He is not as interested in conservation as in progress and is not afraid of destroying something in order to achieve something better. He has ambitions to make a name for himself in some way, to leave his mark on the world.

Neither does he care much how he looks. He will barely manage to run his fingers through his hair and shave (Bob Geldoff doesn't even manage that), and will wear something until it drops. However, he is ambitious and if it's necessary for him to conform and wear a uniform (like a suit for a city banker) to get where he wants, then he will go the whole hog. But he does not enjoy shopping or poring over tie racks or sock counters.

Among his number are Richard Branson, Sean Connery, Gerard Depardieu, Harrison Ford, Bob Geldoff, Paul 'Crocodile Dundee' Hogan, Paul Newman, Prince Philip and Van Morrison – and in sport, most of the Lions and the All Black rugby packs.

The Yin man is the New Man. He is civilized, imaginative and sensitive to the needs and feelings of others. He will be more nurturing towards his children, even when tiny, than the more Yang women are. He puts the needs of his family on a par with his own personal ambitions. He enjoys the company of women, the conversation of women. He is patient with children, old people and pets.

The Yin type of man may well hold down one of the toughest jobs, can be among the most successful men in his profession, but he will be more concerned with the personal, more truly sympathetic towards his friends, colleagues and family. He is not a ruthless operator and is less dynamic and aggressive in his management style than a Yang man will be.

The Yin man prefers creating and consolidating to initiating and destroying. He does not thrive on adrenalin and would pass on the bungee jumping, preferring to spend the evening talking with friends. Part of his greater awareness of others means that he also cares – much more than the Yang man does – about what people think of him. He also cares how he looks, likes clothes and is as likely to be checking himself out in the mirror as you are.

Among his number are Nicholas Cage, Prince Charles, Tom Cruise, Daniel Day-Lewis, Tim Robbins and John Travolta.

It is worth remembering that only a Yang male could say, as Texan Steve Wyatt did at a banquet he attended with Fergie (a Yin), 'I sit with mah woman' (when she wasn't even his woman), and only a Yin man could call Yang Princess Diana 'Squidgy'!

In relationships between the sexes, both Yin and Yang energies need each other to be complete. The excitement is in the differences. They complement each other perfectly. Yin fertilizes

Yang, while Yang energizes Yin (although a Yang woman with a Yin man can feel that it is she who makes the decisions and pushes her softer-hearted man into doing things. The situation is made all the more difficult by the awareness that by being a woman in the driving seat she is going against the prevailing culture). But it is the right personal combination for the Yang woman and the Yin man. She energizes him and he brings a sensitivity and nurture to the relationship. Two Yins together make for great sympathy and soul-matery, but risk stagnation. Two Yangs together make for competition, clashing energy, lack of nurture, and one having to admit defeat. Neither is good neither is bad, both are essential forces in life.

This is also true in friendships and creative partnerships. Yin Dawn French (Hourglass) and Yang Jennifer Saunders (Rectangle) make for a brilliant comedy duo and are in private good friends. When Jennifer teamed up with someone else for the hit comedy *Absolutely Fabulous* she chose another Yin Hourglass, Joanna Lumley. The creativity between the two energies is palpable.

THE FRUITION

This is revolutionary material and it has far-reaching effects in freeing women to be more truly themselves, less influenced by the crude pronouncements on how individuals should behave based purely on whether they are men or women. It is liberating for men too. For just as there are forceful Yang women so too there are sensitive, empathic Yin men.

These insights combined with the modifying factors of astrological signs provide a fascinating, entertaining, and at times profoundly true, addition to astrological lore. It answers all those queries when someone will say, 'But I've never felt I was a real Leo, I've never been that much of a show-off' (she's probably a Pear/Leo) or 'I'm nothing like as wishy-washy as Pisces is so often shown to be!' (she's probably a Triangle/Pisces).

It will help you understand yourself better, your ambitions and interaction with others and the world. This book will show women how best to deal with working and personal relationships, how to express their personalities in clothes and accessories, and recognize their individual dietary and exercise needs.

There is something profound and real in this extraordinary field of body shape/personality and no one else before has made the correlation. But above all this book will be FUN – we all like categorizing ourselves and others, and here we have 48 possibilities. The interest will not only be in our own personality type, but those of our friends, family and work mates – and enemies! It will be enormously revealing and illuminating along the way. Helping all of us to find our full potential, a potential which is uniquely ours, independent of society's view of us as women, lovers, workers and mothers.

THE SCIENTIFIC RESEARCH

The scientific findings as to the significance of female body type are far reaching in their application and importance for women. One of the early scientific papers which alerted other researchers to the correlation between body shape and metabolism was published in 1983 in the Journal of Clinical Investigations by researchers at the University of Gothenburg, Sweden. They divided 670 women into two basic body types; those who put weight on predominantly above the hips and those who put on weight predominantly on the lower hips, bottom and thighs.

The researchers found that women with upper body adiposity had a predominance of large fat cells which reacted differently from the smaller fat cells characteristic of women with lower body adiposity. But most remarkably they found a significant increase in metabolic aberrations leading to diabetes and heart disease among the top-heavy android type compared with the bottom-heavy gynoid type.

In this Gothenburg paper's own words: 'The present study reports on extensive metabolic and morphologic investigations in 930 obese men and women. The data clearly showed that the men as a group were more susceptible than women to the metabolic aberrations induced by moderate obesity. *However, women with a typical male abdominal type of obesity, also had a metabolic risk profile resembling that of men.* When taken together, the results stressed the importance of the regional distribution of the adipose tissue to the metabolic aberrations that are seen in the obese state.'

The researchers believed that the most likely regulator of whether a woman is an android or a gynoid type is the sex-hormones. So it would seem that a gynoid-shaped woman's metabolism is more protected and influenced by female hormones than the top-heavy android body shape, with male-type fat distribution.

This might explain why, with the volunteer dieters for Bel's bestselling book *The Body Breakthrough*, the Pear- and Hourglass-type women put on weight more readily from puberty onwards, and put on significantly more in pregnancy, although the Rectangle-type women, even more than the Triangles, caught up with them from their thirties onwards. In a subsequent questionnnaire it was remarkable to see how different was the average weight gain in pregnancy for the four body types, (a time when one's hormones completely take over). The gynoid types put on over 30lbs weight on average with each pregnancy, compared to an average of only 19lbs for the android shapes. Some of the Pear types noticed that their weight began to go up before they were even certain they were pregnant, as if the increased female hormones had sent the body immediately into a safety-first conservation of supplies.

A well-regarded paper published in 1982 from researchers at the Medical College of Wisconsin suggests that 'sites of fat distribution [in women] provide a diagnostic tool to predict abnormalities in glucose and lipid metabolism.' Most of these researchers use the ratio between waist measurement and hip measurement to determine whether a woman patient has a propensity of upper body fat or lower body fat (the closer the measurements are, the more 'apple-shaped' and therefore the more upper body fat: whereas a classic 'pear-shape' will have a waist measurement significantly smaller than her hip measurement, an indication of lower body fat.)

A follow-up to the Gothenburg paper in 1984 suggests that women with increased upper body fat should reduce their weight, and would subsequently reduce certain specific risks to their health – but that further research was necessary to check the extent of this causal relationship: 'Our findings suggest that studies of reduction of body weight and concomitantly of the ratio of waist to hip circumference in subjects in whom this index is increased are urgently needed. The effect of such intervention should be studied with respect to risks for cardiovascular disease.'

An extensive 1988 paper, 'A Weight Shape Index for Assessing Risk of Disease in 44,820 Women', extended the findings of the previous researchers. This study involved the researchers at the Medical College of Wisconsin again but this time with the collaboration of women on a sensible slimming programme with an American non-profit making slimming club. The women were divided into two age groups; 19,947 women in the 20–35 years group were investigated for correlation between body fat distribution and menstrual abnormalities, and 24,873 women in the 40–59 years group were investigated for the prevalence of chronic diseases, diabetes, gall bladder and heart.

The paper claimed: 'Upper body fat predominance results in an increased risk of diabetes, hypertension, gall bladder disease and menstrual abnormalities.'

Most recently, a fascinating paper was published in February 1993 in the *British Medical Journal* from a team of researchers in Holland investigating the connection between body fat distribution in women and their fertility. They monitored 500 women who had come to the clinic wanting to become pregnant through artificial insemination (their partners being infertile). The researchers used the same waist/hip ratio as before to differentiate those women who put weight on in a gynoid pattern of fat distribution from those with an android pattern.

They found a marked increase in a woman's fertility if she was 'hippy' with a marked waist (the Pear and Hourglass type) as opposed to a woman who had a closer ratio between her waist and hip measurement (Rectangle and Triangle). The differences were even more marked if a woman who put weight predominantly on her tummy and the top half of her body (Rectangle or Triangle) got so overweight that her waist and hip measurement were almost the same, then '[she] would have difficulty in becoming pregnant'.

The researchers ended this remarkable study with the conclusion: 'Body fat distribution in women of reproductive age seems to have more impact on fertility than age or obesity'. In other words, a woman's body type seems to be significant in determining her experiences in ever wider areas of her life.

REFERENCES

Kissebah, Ahmed H et al, 1982: Relation of Body Fat Distribution to Metabolic Complications of Obesity. *Journal of Clinical Endocrinology and Metabolism* Vol 54, No.2 pp254–259.

Krotkiewski, Marcin et al, 1983: Impact of Obesity on Metabolism in Men & Women: Importance of Regional Adipose Tissue Distribution. *Journal of Clinical Investigations* Vol 72, September 1983, pp1150–1162.

Lapidus, Leif et al, 1984: Distribution of Adipose Tissue and Risk of Cardiovascular Disease and Death: a 12 year follow up of participants in the population study of women in Gothenburg, Sweden. *British Medical Journal* Vol 289, 10th November 1984, pp1257–1261.

Alfred A Rimm, Arthur J Hartz and Mary E Fischer, 1988: A Weight Shape Index for Assessing Risk of Disease in 44,820 Women. *Journal of Clinical Epidemiology* Vol 41, No 5, pp459–465, 1988

Boukje M Zaadstra, Jacob C Seidell et al, 1993: Fat and Female Fecundity: Prospective study of effect of body fat distribution on conception rates. *British Medical Journal* Vol 306, 20 February 1993.

QUESTIONNAIRE

WHICH BODY TYPE?

Here's your chance to decide which body type you are and then you can put it together with your star sign and turn to the relevant pages in the book to find out the personality characteristics which apply to you – in life, in work, in style and in health. You will also for fun, be given a dream lover, a fantasy job and a style treat. We hope you'll emerge knowing more about yourself and liking what you see.

For each question, please read alternatives carefully and tick one answer in the boxes at the right hand side

BODY SHAPE

1 Please look at yourself in a mirror, without your clothes, and face-on. Do you have a body shape with:
a shoulders and hips of similar width, with little or no waist? [C]
b shoulder and hip of similar width, with a defined waist? [B]
c shoulders narrower than hips, with a slim waist? [A]
d broader shoulders with tapering hips and a waist? [D]

2a Now look at yourself sideways. Is your bottom:
a flat and tucked in? [C&D]
b a more rounded curve? [A&B]

2b Still looking sideways, do you carry most weight:
- a in front of you on bust, tummy and spare tyre (roll of fat above waist)? [C&D]
- b behind you, on bottom? [A]
- c equally front and back, on bust and bottom? [B]

3 Now looking at yourself from the back, do you have noticeable 'saddlebags' (curvy deposits of fat on the outer thighs)?
- a No [C&D]
- b Yes [A&B]

4 With a tape measure, measure your waist and then the *biggest* part of your hips. Is your hip measurement:
- a MORE than 25cm (10in) bigger than your waist? [A&B]
- b LESS than 25cm (10in) bigger than your waist? [C&D]

WEIGHT DISTRIBUTION

5 Still looking at yourself in the mirror, face-on and then side-on. When you put on weight is it more noticeable:
- a in your face-on body profile, *ie* you get *wider*? [A&B]
- b in your side-on body profile, *ie* you get *deeper*? [C&D]

6a When you are/were very slim and put on those *first* 3kg (7lb) of weight, where was it most noticeable:
- a *lower* hips and thighs, and a bit on tummy? [B]
- b tummy and spare tyre? [C]
- c *lower* hips and thighs? [A]
- d tummy, upper chest and face? [D]

6b When you are more than 3kg (7lb) overweight, where does your excess weight accumulate:
- a on tummy, upper chest, upper arms, *upper* hips, *ie* just below waist, and inside thighs, BUT retaining a waist? [D]
- b most on *lower* hips and thighs, little on top half of body? [A]
- c pretty much all over, ie on bust and predominantly on hips, BUT retaining a waist? [B]
- d on tummy, spare tyre, bust, back and *upper* hips, losing what little waist you might have had? [C]

7 If you were to put on 3kg (7lb) would you get noticeably fatter in the face?
a Yes [C&D]
b No [A&B]

8 If you were to put on 3kg (7lb) would your hands and feet get noticeably more fleshy?
a Yes [B&C]
b No [A&D]

ENERGY LEVELS AND EATING PATTERNS

9 Regardless of demands of work, children, etc, when naturally are you most *mentally* energetic?
a slow to get going, most *creative* energy at night [C]
b physical energy levels pretty constant all day, *creative* energy increases from afternoon into evening [A]
c brightest in the morning, early to bed [D]
d spurts and slumps of *creative* energy throughout the day [B]

10 Regardless of the social and work demands in your life (and when you're not on a diet), which best describes your natural eating habits:
a like to snack through the day [B]
b irregular or erratic meal times, no heavy meals at night [D]
c healthy appetite – start eating can't stop [C]
d can go for quite a long time without food, seldom binge [A]

EXERCISE

11 How sporty were you as a schoolgirl?
a keen to get out of the gym periods and ferocious hockey matches – not at all competitive but happy to play tennis and rounders [A]
b very sporty and enthusiastic, loved athletics, team sports, etc, likely to enter for as many events as possible on Sports Day [C]
c sporty and very competitive, not so keen on team sports but good at individual athletic events, competitive tennis/squash/gymnastics and dancing [D]

d pretty easy-going either way, good at team sports, not very competitive, more interested in the camaraderie [B]

12 If you want to lose weight, do you:
a go on a diet and not worry about increasing your exercise? [A]
b go on a diet and *think* about doing more exercise but not be very enthusiastic about it? [B]
c go on a diet and work out a practical plan for doing more regular exercise – and intend to keep to it? [C]
d you're already doing quite a bit of exercise, so you go on a diet and increase your exercise even more? [D]

13 When you're engaged in a vigorous programme of exercise and sport would you get depressed and put on weight if you gave it up?
a Yes [C&D]
b No [A&B]

Now add up all the capital letters in the boxes you have ticked.
A predominance of As and you're a **PEAR** type
A predominance of Bs and you're an **HOURGLASS** type
A predominance of Cs and you're a **RECTANGLE** type
A predominance of Ds and you're a **TRIANGLE** type

If you have no clear predominance of any one letter, then add up just the ticks from the *Body Shape* and *Weight Distribution* sections. They are more accurately indicative of your body type.

Finally, check your own physical characteristics against the checklist over the page which will help to clarify your type (but obviously not everyone will conform to *all* the characteristics of their type). The four body types, however, apply to all women, whatever their race or nationality.

If you have passed the menopause and your shape has thickened, particularly around the waist – a Triangle type, for example, can become more like a Rectangle – then answer the questions as if for your original shape and turn to the appropriate body star sign.

THE FOUR BODY TYPES

These illustrations show you exactly where each body type is most likely to put on weight.

The Pear

has narrower shoulders than hips
has less fat above the waist than below
always has a waist and flattish tummy
has curvy hips and thighs

If you:

- put weight predominantly on your *lower* hips, bottom and thighs
- have a small bust in proportion to your hips
- have delicate shoulders and neck
- rarely put weight on your shoulders and face

then you are a Pear Type

The Hourglass

has balanced shoulders and hips
has fat equally distributed on bust and hips
retains a waist, however heavy she gets
always has a curve to her hips however thin she gets

If you:

- put weight on all over, but particularly on *lower* hips and bottom
- have a rounded bosom and rounded bottom
- always keep your waist
- have basically *rounded* limbs

then you are an Hourglass Type

The Rectangle

has balanced shoulders and hips
has *not* got a sharply defined waist, even when slim
has a strong and sturdy body often with slim legs
has straight hips and a flattish bottom

If you:

- have lean legs and a flattish bottom which gets fatter and squarer from the waist down
- put weight on torso, predominantly on stomach, spare tyre, breasts, upper back and upper hips
- lose what little waist you have when overweight (become more of a 'cube' than a Rectangle)
- become *deeper*, ie put weight on the front
- have basically *straight* limbs

then you are a Rectangle Type

The Triangle

has broader shoulders than hips
has a waist and *straight* hips which taper towards thighs
has a narrow pelvis and a flat bottom
has lean lower legs

If you:

- look top heavy when you put on weight
- put weight on predominantly above the hip bone; on tummy, chest, face, spare tyre, upper arms, *upper* hips and *inner* thighs
- have straight hips which get boxy when overweight
- get fleshy and squarer in the back and chest when overweight

then you are a Triangle Type

THE FOUR BODY TYPES

PEAR

(Yin+)

IN LIFE

This body type is the one most dominated by her female hormones. She is the most Yin of all. Deeply feeling and sympathetic to the pleasures and pain of others, it is as if the Pear type sometimes has no strongly defined boundaries, that every experience, every suffering person or thing penetrates her inadequate defences. She is that boat afloat on the sea of reality who is not properly sealed, and too open to the elements.

Relationships matter most to the Pear type. Even at work, she relates to others rather than focusing solely on her own ambitions. She has a ready sympathetic imagination for the lives and experiences of other people and will often forget her own self in the nurturing of them. The Pear type finds it very hard to keep her heart out of every situation. She can do what has to be done, in emergencies she can be the calmest and the most stable, but it all takes a greater emotional toll from her.

She likes to deal in subtleties, aware always of the results of her actions on others. She can be accused of not being straightforward enough, too oblique and opaque, but this is often due to the fact that she does not see the world as black and white. She is far too aware of all the shades in between. There are also some things which are too terrible for her to contemplate, and so she prefers to evade or ignore, something which can be incomprehensible to the more robust Yang body types. She has great physical stamina but emotionally is drained by having to deal with the tragic, the heartless and the cruel sides of life in a way which Rectangle and Triangle types will never really understand.

The Pear type does not like to make a spectacle of herself. She is much more circumspect in public than her more Yang sisters. Far too aware of the opinions and rights of others, she is sometimes over-conscientious about not offending or inconveniencing neighbours, colleagues and friends. She does not want to draw attention to herself but can deal with the limelight when it happens to swing her way. Great at promoting others, she feels little need to push herself to the fore. This may seem falsely modest to the Yang women, who like to live their lives at the top, but quite genuinely the Pear type has a different agenda which does not rely on public acclaim.

She wants to live a full emotional life as well as do work which she loves and is good at. If that brings her fame and riches all well and good – although most Pears could do without the fame – but she will never be happy sacrificing her private life for the material rewards of success.

IN WORK

She is happiest working in a creative family-type environment where colleagues pull together as a team, mutually supportive – without that sense of politicking with everyone looking out only for themselves. Tough, unpleasant atmospheres wear her down emotionally and take more out of her than out of the other three body types. She is a great team player, and is equally happy to be the leader, but will not step on anyone's hands to get there. She can lack focus and discipline, being too easily distracted by the wider issues in every situation. She is particularly concerned always with the human costs.

More intuitive than the other three body types, the Pear type has instincts and hunches which can be unnerring if she allows herself to follow them through. Human character and motivation fascinate her more than the plain facts of any situation. She deals in the personal rather than the ideological, is someone who can appreciate the broad brush characterization of society, but who values most the experiences of the individual.

The Pear type can be just as successful and high profile in the world as any of the other body types, but she does it at a greater cost to herself. It hurts her much more to give up the privacy and personal life which real worldly success so often demands. She finds it hard to be tough, misunderstood and disliked. She is not likely to choose the aggressive more male-dominated careers, in the City for instance, or the high-pressure life of a heart surgeon. She is actually constitutionally incapable of being a Mrs Thatcher (a Triangle type), who so completely chanelled her energies into one single-minded ambition, that children and husband and friends barely got a look in on her life.

IN LOVE

This is what makes the world go round for the Pear type. She will be attracted to a Yang kind of man to complement her Yin-ness. She is attracted to a man's ability to deal competently with the world, and offer her a few more skins as protection. She is not at all drawn to young pretty men in the way that her Yang sisters are. She finds them boyish and in need of mothering, rather than desirable. It is the confident man, who may even be rather unreconstructed, who catches her eye. Marlon Brando rather than Lawrence Olivier, Sean Connery rather than Jeremy Irons.

Our questionnaire found that the Pear type is more likely than any of the body types to want to have children – and is just as ready to love any child, as her own, who comes into her care. She is also the one type who finds it hardest to leave her children to the care of others when they are young. Her sensitivity and empathy towards the vulnerable is intensified with childbirth. She knows that when she is an old lady it will not be her material achievements which she will savour but the relationships she has made, with her men, her children, her family and friends. Those always matter most to her: if she *had* to choose between family and career, her family would come first every time.

Sex matters very much to the Pear type as an expression of feeling. She finds it almost impossible to detach it from affection and commitment. She is the furthest from the traditionally 'masculine' view, that it can happily exist outside the bounds of love, or even liking, which is a view with which some of her practical Yang sisters can sympathize. Our questionnaire showed her desiring more sex than the other body types, the predominance of her female hormones perhaps meaning she is less likely to be distracted from making love by the demands of work and desire for power in the world. The Pear type finds sex more exciting than power.

IN STYLE

The classic Pear has smaller shoulders and torso than hips. Meryl Streep and Miranda Richardson are two actresses with this body type. Her face rarely puts on weight and her shoulders, back and neck always have a slim, delicate look to them. Whatever her size, a Pear-shaped woman will always have a waist and this needs emphasizing. The basic principle of style is that she should wear clothes which have the same or similar line to her body line. So jackets and tops should be shaped to the waist unless she's very overweight when she may feel happier in something less fitted. But even so, Pear women should keep that jacket in a soft and draping fabric, like wool crepe, silk or linen.

Generally speaking then, jackets should have soft, rounded shoulder pads, curvy lapels, curved rather than angular hemlines, and be softly fitted to the waist. Fabrics should not be too crisp, Pears should keep away from gabardine, but fine wools, silk, linen and 'peach skin' viscoses and rayons are fine. Suede is always preferable to leather. Blouses and tops in delicate, feminine fabrics like fine laces, chiffon, organza and fine cottons all suit the Pear type.

Straight skirts are always a problem for the Pear-shape woman, even if she is slim. The straightest Pears should go in a skirt is a tulip-shaped skirt with a couple of soft pleats easing from the waist to the hips. Otherwise a gathered or a riding skirt will be most flattering.

The same is true about trousers. The straight-hipped, masculine-cut jeans or trousers are much too big on the waist and tight across the lower hips and top of thigh. Much more flattering to her are trousers with a couple of soft pleats from the front waistband easing into loose legs which taper to the ankle. Again, soft fluid fabrics are best, nothing too stiff or military.

Pear types have disproportionately delicate shoulders in relation to their wider hips, and some padding at the shoulder, even in blouses, helps balance the Pear body shape, whatever her size. But all details in clothing and accessories should tend towards the curve rather than the straight – collars, lapels, handbags, belt buckles.

Jewellery for a Pear-shaped woman follows the same line as

her body and her clothes. Keep detail curvy: any chain links or beads should be round or oval rather than geometric and flat; curb-link bracelets rather than brick-link for instance. Because she tends to have slim shoulders and neck, necklaces are very pretty on her – and pearls look fabulous on both the curvy shapes, the Pear and the Hourglass. Again, brooches should have swept, curvy lines rather than be too geometric. Organic images – flowers, leaves, wings, crescent moons, serpentine squiggles – all have the necessary curve for this type. Watches should have round or oval faces and not be too big in the face, or heavy in the bracelet or strap, unless she is big-boned.

It is important to check that the colour of her clothes suits her too. She can hold each item under her chin in front of a mirror and look at what it does to her skin and hair. If wearing it intensifies and enlivens her own colouring then that is a colour that is right for her individual skin tones. If she looks washed out or sallow, or her hair loses colour and dark rings seem to appear under her eyes, then she is getting it wrong. To give a garment greater versatility choose a neutral colour; for example, black, navy, charcoal, pewter, cream, grey or taupe.

It is as important also to bear in mind colour, line and scale when choosing jewellery as it is when choosing clothes. She can hold the piece she likes next to her skin to check that the colours are flattering. Cool skin tones are much better with silver metal and cool (blue-based) colours, while warm skin tones are flattered by gold metals and warm (yellow-based) colours. The scale or size of jewellery will depend on her bone size and height. If she is over 167cm (5ft 6in) tall and has large bones (wrists measuring 16.5cm [6 1/2in] or more) then she needs large, substantial pieces. If she is between 160 and 167cm (5ft 3in and 5ft 6in) with medium-sized bones (wrists 14–16.5cm [5 1/2–6 1/2in]) then large but delicate pieces suit her best, or medium-sized if they are more chunky in design. If she is petite, 160cm (5ft 3in) or less, with small bones (less than 14cm [5 1/2in]) then small scale jewellery is best.

Style Treats

In each body star sign there is a style treat to suit that personality. By reading all the style treats pertaining to your body type you will discover how to build up a wardrobe to best suit your shape. The style treats for the Pear body type are found on pages:

75, 83, 91, 100, 110, 119, 128, 138, 148, 158, 168, 177.

IN HEALTH

The Pear type has a steady energy which tends to be at its lowest in the morning and peak in the evening. Strenuous exercise does not appeal to her, although exercises enhancing suppleness and grace do, ie yoga, Callanetics, and relaxed swimming. If a Pear-shaped woman has a basically sedentary job, does no formal exercise and is content with her life, her metabolism can become rather sluggish. Introduce some emotional drama, however, whether falling in love or being suddenly catapulted into the limelight at work – or having to deal with unpleasant office politics – and this type's metabolism can be so energized with excitement or anxiety that she can lose half a stone in a week. Doing more exercise, walking, swimming, floor exercises, also keeps this type of metabolism burning.

It was shown in the trials run by Bel for her book *The Body Breakthrough* that the Pear type will lose weight best and feel most happy and energetic (and therefore more likely to stick to the regime) if she follows her natural metabolic rhythm and food preferences. Less energetic in the morning, the Pear type is better having a very light or non-existent breakfast (a piece of fruit at the most) and then having her main meal at lunchtime, with a lighter meal in the evening. The best foods for her are plenty of low-fat protein (like cottage cheese or white fish), unrefined carbohydrates (like baked potato, wholemeal bread, brown rice), with almost limitless salad and vegetables, and generous amounts of fruit.

Even though Pear-shaped women tend not to be natural athletes, and exercise is not absolutely essential to their fitness or well-being (as it is for the Rectangle and Triangle types), exercise does help everyone to lose weight and feel better. Half an hour's brisk walking uses up 180 calories, for instance, and by boosting the basal metabolic rate for a few hours after the exercise has ceased it thus continues to help burn more calories. Exercise also helps to tone up muscles and increase suppleness and strength.

There is also an undeniable 'feel good' factor to exercising which cannot be ignored. If a Pear-shaped woman does some exercise which suits her body type and disposition it undoubtedly lifts the spirits, makes her generally more positive about herself, more in tune with her body – and less likely to neglect and abuse it with junk food or other excesses. Swimming twice a week, or walking an extra mile to work or the shops every day, running up stairs rather than taking the lift, all will help keep Pears healthy, happy – and slim.

SOME PEAR-TYPE CELEBRITIES

Actresses

Hayley Mills (Aries)
Candice Bergen (Taurus)
Sally Anne Howes (Cancer)
Meryl Streep (Cancer)
Josie Lawrence (Gemini)
Virginia McKenna (Gemini)
Anne Bancroft (Virgo)
Patricia Hodge (Libra)
Julia Roberts (Scorpio)
Jenny Agutter (Sagittarius)
Lee Remick (Sagittarius)
Susannah York (Capricorn)
Jane Seymour (Aquarius)
Eleanor Bron (Pisces)
Miranda Richardson (Pisces)
Imogen Stubbs (Pisces)

Singers

Kate Bush (Leo)

Writers

Mary Shelley (Virgo)
Naomi Wolf (Scorpio)
Marina Warner (Scorpio)

Icons

Isadora Duncan (Gemini)
Hillary Clinton (Scorpio)

THE FOUR BODY TYPES

HOURGLASS

(YIN)

IN LIFE

Here is a balanced body type, with a leaning towards being Yin rather than Yang, but this woman can straddle both sides of the divide. She still puts relationships at the centre of her life but they are less dominatingly so. She can keep her feeling nature on the back burner while she concentrates on her career, but she is always aware that there is a deep emotional side to her which wants to make partnerships, and have a family. Because she has both the desire to make a career in the world and the need to have a family she can get rather out of balance if she denies either side. Practical woman as she is, she is best suited to successfully managing her life so that she can have it all.

More focused on the outside world than the Pear type, less insulated from the demands of others than the Rectangle and Triangle, the Hourglass is best in situations where her talents with people and her good instincts can find expression. She is gregarious and good in any team situation: her sympathy for the positions and feelings of others makes her cooperative and sensitive. She has not got a driven, ruthless side, although she may develop a dogged workaholism when other aspects of her life are unsatisfactory and the whole thing gets out of balance.

She can be very determined to get her own way, but unlike the Yang body types she may be less than straightforward about doing it. She is not as easy with confronting people and things as a Rectangle type can be, and so in difficult situations she may retreat into secretiveness and emotionalism which is incomprehensible to the forthright Rectangle. She needs to try and keep both the feeling and the rational side balanced, neither neglected in favour of the other.

IN WORK

She can excel anywhere where she doesn't have to work in complete isolation or in a cut-throat atmosphere of high stress and competition. Our research showed that dehumanized, high-stress situations exhausted and demoralized the Yin body type much sooner than the Yang, some of whom thrive on the excitement of the fight. Intuitive, sensitive to the feelings and atmospheres around her, the Hourglass type is usually a calming influence in any working environment.

Once she has a family she is less likely to sacrifice all to the good of the job, in fact if she does she will suffer emotionally. For the Yin body types need to have their emotional lives pretty much central in order to feel happy and to function properly. If she hasn't got enough people to nurture at home then she will nurture her friends and colleagues. She is terrific at assessing other people's strengths and helping them to express themselves better. There is much less self-centredness in the Yin body types than the Yang, they are better at sharing the glory, and being pleased at the success of others. They are generally less protected from the world by their own ego.

When an Hourglass woman gets to the top of her profession she brings a very different feel to the place than the more Yang type women do. There is a sense of concern for others and a softer approach generally. It may lack dynamism and entrepreneurial appreciation of risk (unless a real Yang character, male or female, has some important input). Anita Roddick, founder and head of Body Shop, is an Hourglass and has attempted to keep the vast organization in a family-type set-up. The business side is now managed by her Yang husband, who sees that the competitive, business-like edge remains. Although Body Shop is too big to be truly intimate, this atmosphere is what many Hourglass bosses attempt to bring to their companies.

IN LOVE

Love sits at the centre of the Hourglass type's life on a seesaw with Work. In a battle between the two, love and family would win, but it wouldn't be quite such a foregone conclusion as it is with the Pear type. The Hourglass type needs an emotional life and is likely to find her partner and settle down sooner rather than later. It is the Yang kind of man who catches her imagination. Not perhaps the most unreconstructed Gerard Depardieu types but the less extreme, like Harrison Ford for instance, would do nicely. If her need for a loving relationship is not satisfied in a close partnership, then she needs to express this side of herself with a loving circle of friends.

Children and family life bring her much pleasure and she ideally manages to juggle caring for them in an involved way with continuing her working life, even if only part-time until they're older. Our questionnaire was full of Hourglass type women managing to have both sides of life, although on the verge of exhaustion much of the time. She is not happy handing her children over full-time to someone else to bring up. But similarly she is not so ready to give up all her outside ambitions.

As with the Pear, sex is an important part of the Hourglass's expression of her emotional nature. She is less likely to be able to separate it from love and tends to see it as part of the whole commitment. She may go into a sexual relationship thinking she's not in love, but she is likely to quickly bond and feel that suddenly she is.

IN STYLE

The most flattering clothes for any body type are those which follow the natural lines of one's body. The Hourglass has a balanced shape, with shoulders and hips of equal width, with fat equally distributed on breasts and hips and always with a marked waist. Unlike the Rectangle and Triangle shapes, the Pear and Hourglass types have hips which are curvy, not square, and both are prone to putting weight on the lower part of their hips and top of thighs. This is the classic female shape (Marilyn Monroe is a curvy version and Cindy Crawford a less extreme one). When slim/ish, this is the easiest to dress in the widest range of styles. Hourglass-shaped women must always bear in mind that they look best in clothes which have curve and fluidity.

Jackets and tops are most flattering if they have a slightly fitted waist, or are worn with a good belt to emphasize the waist. If she wears shoulder pads then they should be narrow and rounded, rather than heavy and straight. Similarly, the weight of fabric is important; cloths should be light and fluid, never heavy and uniform-like. Silks, linens, light wool crepes, good quality viscoses, soft cottons all look lovely on this shape.

Trousers and skirts should also be curved in shape over the hips. If an Hourglass-shaped woman is very slim, then narrow, stretchy skirts and leggings can look very sexy on her curvy body. But usually she is flattered more by skirts and trousers with some soft pleating into the waistband to give a bit of easing over the hips and to make sure the waist is small enough. Tulip shaped skirts, fine pleats, or riding skirts are a good look on this shape.

All detail should be kept balanced – curved details with crisper fabrics; straight lines for lapels, jacket hems and collars should always be balanced with softer fabrics. Style detail and weight of fabric need to be complementary so the overall impression is feminine and soft.

If she is relatively slim, the Hourglass body type is the easiest to dress in a wide variety of styles when she puts on weight because she puts on weight in a balanced way all over. What was once an hourglass becomes more a cottage loaf. As a result, she does not want to emphasize her waist so much because it only over-emphasizes the curves on either side. In this case, a straighter style jacket in a distinctly soft, fluid fabric like a washed silk, can be very flattering if worn over a skirt and blouse secured with a belt. It is a mistake to try and camouflage herself completely in a shapeless garment, much better to hint at the waist she still has.

Accessories are always important and should be pretty with curvy rather than geometric detail – shoes with almond-shaped rather than sharply chiselled toes, a soft handbag rather than a big square Kelly bag, and rounded rather than pointed collars and lapels, unless softened by a fluid fabric. A string of pearls will always flatter these Yin shapes, and Pear- and Hourglass-shaped women also look good in lace collars and chiffon scarves. Everything should be light and fluid.

It is important to check that the colour of her clothes suits her too. She can hold each item under her chin in front of a mirror and look at what it does to her skin and hair. If wearing it intensifies and enlivens her own colouring then that is a colour that is right for her individual skin tones. If she looks washed out or sallow, or her hair loses colour and dark rings seem to appear under her eyes, then she is getting it wrong. To give a garment greater versatility choose a neutral colour; for example, black, navy, charcoal, pewter, cream, grey or taupe.

It is as important also to bear in mind colour, line and scale when choosing jewellery as it is when choosing clothes. She can hold the piece she likes next to her skin to check that the colours are flattering. Cool skin tones are much better with silver metal and cool (blue-based) colours, while warm skin tones are flattered by gold metals and warm (yellow-based) colours. The scale or size of jewellery will depend on her bone size and height. If she is over 167cm (5ft 6in) tall and has large bones (wrists measuring 16.5cm [6 1/2in] or more) then she needs large, substantial pieces. If she is between 160 and 167cm (5ft 3in and 5ft 6in) with medium-sized bones (wrists 14–16.5cm [5 1/2–6 1/2in]) then large but delicate pieces suit her best, or medium-sized if they are more chunky in design. If she is petite, 160cm (5ft 3in) or less, with small bones (less than 14cm [5 1/2in]) then small scale jewellery is best.

Style Treats

In each body star sign there is a style treat to suit that personality. By reading all the style treats pertaining to your body type you will discover how to build up a wardrobe to best suit your shape. The style treats for the Hourglass body type are found on pages:

188, 196, 205, 214, 224, 233, 243, 252, 263, 273, 283, 292.

IN HEALTH

An Hourglass-type woman, who puts weight on her hips and thighs rather than around her waist, has certain medical advantages (see Introduction). Less likely to suffer from heart disease, hard aerobic exercise is not a necessary part of any fitness regime for her. This is lucky because although an Hourglass-shaped woman is naturally quite sporty she prefers games like tennis and activities like walking, swimming and dancing to serious workouts in the gym. Yoga is also a good way of exercising her body type as it keeps her supple and her back strong.

It was shown in the trials run by Bel for her book *The Body Breakthrough* that an Hourglass type benefitted enormously from eating three regular meals a day, eliminating the snacks she is so prone to, and cutting down on stimulants like coffee and alcohol. When it came to losing weight this regime was essential.

Her best meals were rich in fruit and raw vegetables, protein came from fish and chicken, eggs and low-fat dairy products. A full four-week diet and exercise plan tailormade for the Hourglass body type can be found in *The Body Breakthrough*.

In outline, it was found that a breakfast that consisted of fruit with muesli or another kind of cereal was a good start to the day. Snacking is a weakness of this body type and so no more eating until lunch when lots of salad or lightly cooked vegetables, with some protein, can be eaten to keep the energy up. Supper is again a balanced meal with pasta and salad or protein and vegetables, and a piece of fruit for pudding. Hourglass-shaped women are often good cooks and they will soon find ways to work out delicious variations on these basic good rules for slimness and health.

Exercise is another area where balance and moderation pay off. But the Hourglass-shaped woman is not going to gravitate naturally into highly competitive areas of sport like sprinting, speed swimming or gruelling circuit training in the gym or in the advanced aerobics class. In desperation she may turn to these extreme measures but she is more naturally at home doing low-impact work, dancing, yoga and Callanetics. She is always going to be curvy-hipped and trying to turn herself into a narrow-hipped athlete will only result in starvation and destruction of her natural good looks. Just think of the Boticelli Venus arising from the waves and you have the embodiment of this classic female shape, the Hourglass.

SOME HOURGLASS-TYPE CELEBRITIES

Actresses

Emma Thompson (Aries)
Jessica Lange (Taurus)
Michelle Pfeiffer (Taurus)
Natasha Richardson (Taurus)
Marilyn Monroe (Gemini)
Isabella Rossellini (Gemini)
Kathleen Turner (Gemini)
Gina Lollobrigida (Cancer)
Melanie Griffiths (Leo)
Pauline Collins (Virgo)
Julie Andrews (Libra)
Brigitte Bardot (Libra)
Catherine Deneuve (Libra)
Olivia Newton-John (Libra)
Kim Basinger (Sagittarius)
Sissy Spacek (Capricorn)
Geena Davis (Aquarius)
Greta Scacchi (Aquarius)
Holly Hunter (Pisces)
Elizabeth Taylor (Pisces)
Joanne Woodward (Pisces)

Singers

Diana Ross (Aries)
Ella Fitzgerald (Taurus)
Kylie Minogue (Gemini)
Sade (Capricorn)
Maria Callas (Sagittarius)
Kiri te Kanawa (Pisces)

Television

Selena Scott (Taurus)
Paula Yates (Taurus)
Julia Somerfield (Cancer)
Anna Ford (Libra)

Celebrities

Joanna Lumley (Taurus)
Naomi Campbell (Gemini)
Jerry Hall (Cancer)
Jean Shrimpton (Scorpio)
Oprah Winfrey (Aquarius)

Royalty

Princess Anne (Leo)
Princess Margaret (Leo)
Duchess of Kent (Pisces)

THE FOUR BODY TYPES

RECTANGLE

(YANG)

IN LIFE

This is the first of the Yang body shapes and this woman is correspondingly more concerned with self and the impressing of that self on the outside world. She is a mover and shaker. She gets things done. Sometimes with some insensitivity to the feelings of others, but then she argues, if one has to always be considering others one wouldn't do anything at all. She is robust and forthright and knows what she wants from life.

From the research we did it was obvious that Rectangle and Triangle types may take some time, sometimes as late as their thirties and forties, to really come into their own. As the Yang woman is still at some odds with the traditions of our culture, when she is young she may feel that she ought to be other than she is, that she ought to try and be more unselfish, more focused on the needs of others and not on herself. But she doesn't necessarily want to care for others. She isn't feminine in the traditional sense of the word. Love and family matter to her, but not at the expense of herself, and her place in the world.

The Yang energy sees the world spread out before her and wonders with excitement, what is there here for me? How can I make my mark? The Yin energy sees the world spread out before her and wonders with some awe, what I can do for it? And often is too daunted by the reply. The Rectangle energy is impulsive and self-motivated. She is ambitious and unembarrassed by the fact. She operates through action, rather than reflection. She is insulated enough against the demands of others to be able to carve her way to the top of whatever she chooses to do.

IN WORK

This is at the heart of the lives of most Rectangle types. She positively needs a larger platform for her ambitions than the home and hearth. She likes being in charge yet is a Trojan member of any team. One only has to think of the number of Rectangle-type women on all those school governing boards and committees. She is a terrific committee woman, working for an improvement in circumstances for others and providing the necessary focus for her own energies and the need for a platform for her views.

In the workplace, Rectangle types are hard working, have physical stamina and personal ambition. They can combine a robust, uncomplicated friendliness with their drive to succeed and be respected and much liked members of any company.

Rectangle types are best working where there is some chance of the limelight alighting on them. They are not likely to blush unseen for long. Prestige and status matter to them in a way that don't concern the Yin body types so much. But the Rectangle type is also very unsqueamish about getting her hands dirty and mucking in. She has the breadth of shoulder to carry responsibility and that is just what she does so well.

IN LOVE

There are always some problems for the Rectangle type. She feels that she is going against traditional type by being the forceful, forthright personality that she is, a Yang woman in a society where Yin women embody the feminine ideal. (Although, modern woman is meant to be the ambitious superwoman type who manages to be everything at once.) But she must be true to herself, this is the only way that she will find happiness and fulfilment. Her ideal partner in life is a Yin male, kind and sensitive, imaginative about others and supportive of her. A Nigel

Havers type rather than a Jack Nicolson, a Garry Lineker rather than a Gazza.

Our research shows that more Yang women than Yin decide not to have children, or leave it so late while they pursue their careers that they find they have missed the boat. If the Rectangle type does have children then her family matters enormously to her, and she will fight to defend it to the end. She will be the first to admit that she is not really cut out for full-time hands-on nurturing of little babies and is more likely to be roaring back to work, at least part-time, as soon as she can. She can leave the empathic nurturing of the children, the patient listening to childish tales of woe, to her Yin husband or a kind mother's help, while she gets on with expressing her energy and ambitions in the outside world.

If she does decide to look after her children herself, full-time, then she makes motherhood into a career. She may even go in for a really big family, so that she has a really big job to absorb that ambitious energy. Motherhood then becomes her business which she runs very efficiently, doing everything right, like Suzuki violin lessons, extra language coaching, lots of sports (which she might well join in, being naturally sporty) and grown up conversation at table. Even so, she will be the first to admit that she is not a natural nurturer, her mothering is more practical and active. She risks, however, visiting her own frustrated ambitions upon her children and becoming one of those pushy, bossy mothers who don't just let their children be.

She is practical too about sex. She has a healthy interest and enjoys it as an answer to her physical needs. If it's within a loving relationship that's great, but it does not have to be. She is more able to separate sex from love when she needs to. Just as for many men, it is often her work which matters more and creams off most of her creative energy.

It is quite interesting to ponder the different ways that Princess Diana and the Duchess of York came up against the Establishment. For the Duchess of York (an Hourglass type), her unforgiveable sin was sexual. For the Princess of Wales (a Rectangle type), hers was ambitions above her station. She wanted a Court of her own and to be able to continue her high profile work. One was brought down by sex and unwise libido, the other was wounded by her desire for the very highest status work, rather than love.

IN STYLE

With a Rectangle body shape, a woman's hips and shoulders are similar in width and she does not have a marked waist. (Princess

Diana, Vanessa Redgrave and Glenn Close are slim versions of this type, Victoria Wood, Cilla Black and Jennifer Saunders the more generous examples). Unlike the Pear and Hourglass, a Rectangle's hips are not curvy but straight. Also, when she puts on weight she becomes 'deeper' rather than wider, putting weight on the front of her body – on her tummy, spare tyre and bust – and becoming more of a cube than a rectangle. Her legs remain slim however heavy she gets.

The basic principle of style is that one wears clothes which have the same or similar line to one's body line. So the most flattering line for jackets and tops for a Rectangle-shaped woman are straight cut, without a marked waist and no curvy details in seams and lapels. Square shoulders suit her better than curved, and she needs clothes which look as if they've been well tailored in a good fabric. She should keep to the crisp, strong fabrics like gabardine, worsted wools and heavy silks. Crumpled linens and thin silks, which suit the Pear and Hourglass, can just look messy and unbecoming on the Rectangle body shape.

Skirts and trousers are much more flattering to this shape if they continue this geometrical look, straight and tapering to the hem. There should be only crisp pleating and no gathering into the waistband. Keep the profile straight and lean.

The Rectangle type is not prone to putting on weight when young, but the pounds might appear more in her middle years. If she is very overweight she may feel more at ease wearing softer fabrics and less tailored skirts, but she should limit the softness in the skirt to well-pressed pleats, rather than gathers, and keep her jackets and tops straight in shape and detail. But even if she feels too big for narrow profile dressing it's worth her trying a straight skirt or narrow-legged trousers with a loose tunic top or straight loose jacket. She will be amazed to find how flattering this can be to all variations within this Rectangle body shape.

Scooped necklines are not flattering to this shape so Rectangles should keep to shirt style, boat, square or V-necks. Flimsy fabrics like organza, chiffon, soft silks and lace are too soft and can look frumpy or cheap on her. Unless she has very straight shoulders, square shoulder pads in everything from jackets to T-shirts add elegance and sharpness to her style.

A Rectangle type should also keep all her clothes and accessory detail geometrical rather than curvy – necklines, lapels and jacket edges, belt buckles and handbags. Jewellery, too, is more flattering to this shape if it reflects this angularity of line; square, triangular or rectangular earrings rather than round, flat-link bracelets and necklaces, or torques rather than curvy links. Nothing should be too filigree or fussy.

It is important to check that the colour of her clothes suits her too. She can hold each item under her chin in front of a mirror and look at what it does to her skin and hair. If wearing it intensifies and enlivens her own colouring then that is a colour that is right for her individual skin tones. If she looks washed out or sallow, or her hair loses colour and dark rings seem to appear under her eyes, then she is getting it wrong. To give a garment greater versatility choose a neutral colour; for example, black, navy, charcoal, pewter, cream, grey or taupe.

It is as important also to bear in mind colour, line and scale when choosing jewellery as it is when choosing clothes. She can hold the piece she likes next to her skin to check that the colours are flattering. Cool skin tones are much better with silver metal and cool (blue-based) colours, while warm skin tones are flattered by gold metals and warm (yellow-based) colours. The scale or size of jewellery will depend on her bone size and height. If she is over 167cm (5ft 6in) tall and has large bones (wrists measuring 16.5cm [6 1/2in] or more) then she needs large, substantial pieces. If she is between 160 and 167cm (5ft 3in and 5ft 6in) with medium-sized bones (wrists 14–16.5cm [5 1/2–6 1/2in]) then large but delicate pieces suit her best, or medium-sized if they are more chunky in design. If she is petite, 160cm (5ft 3in) or less, with small bones (less than 14cm [5 1/2in]) then small scale jewellery is best.

Style Treats

In each body star sign there is a style treat to suit that personality. By reading all the style treats pertaining to your body type you will discover how to build up a wardrobe to best suit your shape. The style treats for the Rectangle body type are found on pages:

303, 313, 323, 335, 343, 354, 364, 374, 384, 393, 403, 414.

IN HEALTH

Because the Rectangle type has a powerful body and is naturally athletic, it positively needs to be exercised vigorously. Many of this type get depressed and feel sluggish if they aren't exercising regularly. Aerobic sports like jogging, speed swimming, competitive squash and tennis, are best suited to this type's physique and temperament. Rectangles would be wise to do some sort of aerobic activity for at least half an hour, three times a week.

If she is seriously overweight, or hasn't exercised for ages, she should get medical advice first and start off slowly, walking briskly and swimming, building up over a few weeks to the more vigorous sports.

From a dietary point of view, the Rectangle type's robustness of constitution is also expressed in a robustness of appetite. This type finds it hard to stop eating once she starts and so needs a diet with some restraining boundaries. There is plenty of anecdotal evidence that greater health and weight loss can be achieved by not mixing, in one meal, food which is a concentrated carbohydrate with food that is concentrated protein, ie meat with vegetables and salad is fine but meat with bread or potatoes is wrong mixing.

A full four-week diet and exercise regime tailormade for this body metabolism is included in Bel's book *The Body Breakthrough*. Volunteers tested the diets and their comments and successes are included in the book.

In short, the best diet for the Rectangle type in the battle to regain that slim figure of her youth, is one which allows for one substantial meal a day, otherwise she feels deprived. A diet that is largely rabbit-food with little protein is not only impossible for her to stick to but can actually deplete her energy and make her pale and ill. A Rectangle-shaped woman tends to be a late-in-the-day type who, if she isn't being forced to get up really early by children or work demands, would naturally be a late starter who then works, or parties, into the night. So her best time for eating her main meal is the evening.

Breakfast and lunch should be light, low-fat meals, ie fruit and a little muesli for breakfast; lunch should be something like a salad and baked potato, or a pitta bread filled with humous and lettuce, tomato and a few slices of avocado. No snacking during the day, and then for supper a proper protein and vegetables main meal (grilled fish, steak, or chicken), with a low-fat, low-carbohydrate pudding like yogurt and fresh fruit.

But the key to maintaining that youthful Rectangle figure is exercise and lots of it. This is one of the messages that came through loud and clear in the research done for *The Body Breakthrough*: the Rectangle and Triangle body types (the Yangs) thrive on hard *aerobic* exercise, at least three times a week. So a Rectangle needs to make sure she is in the swimming pool, on the running track, tennis court or in the aerobics class at least twice, preferably three times, a week for at least half-an-hour's energetic action.

SOME RECTANGLE-TYPE CELEBRITIES

Actresses

Penelope Keith (Aries) Shirley MacLaine (Taurus)

Toyah Wilcox (Taurus)
Helena Bonham-Carter (Gemini)
Susan Sarandon (Libra)
Roseanne Barr (Scorpio)
Jodie Foster (Scorpio)
Whoopi Goldberg (Scorpio)
Stefanie Powers (Scorpio)
Bette Midler (Sagittarius)
Vanessa Redgrave (Aquarius)
Patricia Routledge (Aquarius)
Glenn Close (Pisces)
Julie Walters (Pisces)

Singers
Montserrat Caballé (Aries)
Barbra Streisand (Taurus)
Jessye Norman (Virgo)
Dame Joan Sutherland (Scorpio)
Tina Turner (Sagittarius)
Liza Minelli (Pisces)
Nina Simone (Pisces)

Writers
Barbara Cartland (Cancer)
AS Byatt (Virgo)
Lady Antonia Fraser (Virgo)
Fay Weldon (Virgo)
Jackie Collins (Libra)
Germaine Greer (Aquarius)

Celebrities
Ruby Wax (Aries)
Cilla Black (Gemini)
Claire Rayner (Pisces)

Sport
Steffi Graf (Gemini)
Sally Gunnell (Leo)
Martina Navratilova (Libra)
Chris Evert (Sagittarius)

Royalty
Queen Elizabeth II (Taurus)
Princess Diana (Cancer)
Queen Mother (Leo)
Princess Michael of Kent (Capricorn)
Princess Caroline of Monaco (Aquarius)

THE FOUR BODY TYPES

TRIANGLE

(YANG+)

IN LIFE

This body type is the most extreme Yang of the four and as such she is the most focused, the most in need of her own powerbase from which she can make her mark on the world. For that is what she wants to do above all else. She is a perfectionist and has to be the best at anything she tackles.

There are two physical types within the overall categorization of the Triangle body shape, a female body with shoulders wider than her hips. The first is the sportier androgynous figure with strong shoulders and well-developed muscles, like Princess Stephanie of Monaco, and the second is the slighter, more prepubescent look, epitomized by Mia Farrow. Although superficially they seem to be such different body types they are versions of the same, and each shares the same indomitable will, the desire for visible success in the outside world, the need to win.

This woman, however, may take a long time to recognize her innate power and need for success and an external powerbase. Our research showed many Triangle types confused, when they were young, by how different they felt from what was expected of them by parents, school and society at large. Many went along with undemanding jobs, or married young to get out of a stifling situation at home. But only in their maturity did some of them really come into their own and accept that she had a driving ambition to express herself in the world. She wanted to be someone. She wanted power.

IN WORK

Without a doubt, work and the independence and status it brings is at the centre of this woman's life. Public success more than her private life is what drives her on. From our questionnaire it was obvious that the Triangle type is essentially an individualist. She is not at her best in a team, finds relating to more than one person at a time difficult, and prefers to work alone, at her own pace and with her own ideas and priorities.

Many of our top female bosses are Triangle types: this woman is the best equipped of all to focus on her goal and reach her destination. But her single-mindedness and lack of natural sympathy with employers and colleagues often makes her unpopular in the process. She is tough, does not waste time on worrying about other peoples' feelings and doesn't really mind what others think of her. Above all she wants the top job and can outface and outgun the men.

Whether she is a professional dancer, a plumber or a commodity broker, the Triangle type is often very highly skilled technically and gets a great deal of pleasure from her skill. She is not a slapdash, intuitive sort of person and rather brings skill and terrific hard work and dedication to everything she undertakes. When the Triangle type really comes into her own, she is proud to be thought tough. She recognizes that to get on in a masculine world, a woman has to be twice as smart and three times as ambitious as any of the men. In the highly competitive masculine professions, like commodity broking, heart surgery, high finance and the Bar, our surveys found that the successful women are almost all Yang body types, and the most successful of all are likely to be the Triangles. But they are also likely to have sacrificed a home life in the process. Unlike Yin women, for whom gruelling, high-stress work demands a much greater emotional cost, the Triangle type thinks that on the whole, work and self-fulfillment matter more than relationships and others.

IN LOVE

The Triangle type often finds relationships and intimacy difficult. It isn't top of her priorities, although when she's young she may think that love is all she wants. If she marries and has children early, then when all her natural ambition starts to surface it can only be expressed in her domestic life, which is uncomfortable for her and for her family. Her need for a powerbase can then result in her having more children and using them as her way of being different, and best in the world. Or she drives them on to be what she wanted to be, the prima ballerina, the top pianist, the actress or showjumper, the academic powerhouse. It is much better, as she probably realizes, that she gets out and does all that for herself. Her children will be happier with an easy-going nurturing dad or au pair than a driven, frazzled mother.

From our questionnaire it was clear that the more obvious pattern for Triangle types is to leave settling down until much later than the other types. She is usually too busy getting on with her career to turn her mind to motherhood. In fact, of all the four body types, the Triangle is the most likely to choose not to have children at all. Only 25 per cent of our questionnaire Triangle-type respondees, of childbearing age, had had children, and of those who had not, a surprising number over the age of 36 were 'still thinking about it'.

When this happens with a Triangle type, it is her work which carries all her creative energies and if that is ever taken away from her she can be devastated. So it can only be wise for the Triangle type to guard against pursuing one thing too single-mindedly at the expense of everything else in her life.

The man for a Triangle type woman is most successfully a Yin, nurturing, kind sort of man who will soothe all her stresses away after a grinding time at the office/studio/hospital/law courts. She may be drawn to a flashy, Yang sort with whom she crosses swords, but for a long term view two Yang types can only end in tears – or separate lives.

Madly interested, and matter-of-fact, about sex early in her life, it is likely to become sublimated to work as the success bug takes over later on. From the questionnaire and interviews we conducted it was noticeable how many Triangle types are not very much at ease in their own bodies. Their drive for perfectionism and dislike of female flesh can make some chronically dissatisfied, punishing the flesh with diets and gruelling workouts. With some of these women, sex can become more a currency than a spontaneous expression of feeling. Power matters to Triangle types and to some, power is more exciting than sex.

IN STYLE

The basic principle of style is that you wear clothes which have the same or similar line to your body line. So a Triangle-shaped woman, whatever her size, should keep everything angled and sharp in order to look her best – and slimmest. Her jackets and tops should have straight, angular shoulders and should taper from shoulder to waist. Similarly, skirts and trousers should be narrow, tapering into the hem or ankle. Any gathers can make her look heavy or dowdy. The Triangle type often has good athletic legs and looks best in short skirts, jeans or leggings (but they must be made of a substantial fabric which keeps its lean shape and doesn't bag or wrinkle).

For Triangle-type women, fabrics need to be close woven and crisp – too soft and crumpled like linen and she can look a mess. Gabardines, wool, crisp cottons and heavy silk all look smart and sharp enough. Shiny materials like leather and satin also suit the Triangle type really well. All details on clothing and accessories – lapels, jacket edges, belt buckles, shoes, handbags and necklines – need to be angular rather than curvy (a scoop neckline can make her look very broad and heavy in the shoulder).

Scale can be particularly important with Triangle types. A small Triangle (less than 157cm [5ft 3in] tall) should stick with short jackets and knee-length skirts. She can wear longer jackets but only with short skirts, or longer skirts but only with short jackets. Details like lapels, buttons or weight of fabric should not overpower her, and she needs to be careful that sleeves and skirts are not too long.

The taller Triangle-type woman (over 165cm [5ft 6in]) does not have the same problems. She can wear shorter and longer skirts or jackets. She just has to be careful to keep well away from anything remotely frilly or curvy and fabrics which are too soft and gauzy. Both Princess Stephanie and Gabriella Sabatini look magnificent in their simple, mannish sports clothes and sharp casual clothes, but terrible the moment they put on girly frocks or dress up in the classic flouncy ball dress. Sheath dresses or sharp separates are far more flattering.

It is important to check that the colour of her clothes suits her too. She can hold each item under her chin in front of a mirror and look at what it does to her skin and hair. If wearing it intensifies and enlivens her own colouring then that is a colour that is right for her individual skin tones. If she looks washed out or sallow, or her hair loses colour and dark rings seem to appear under her eyes, then she is getting it wrong. To give a garment greater versatility choose a neutral colour; for example, black, navy, charcoal, pewter, cream, grey or taupe.

It is as important also to bear in mind colour, line and scale when choosing jewellery as it is when choosing clothes. She can hold the piece she likes next to her skin to check that the colours are flattering. Cool skin tones are much better with silver metal and cool (blue-based) colours, while warm skin tones are flattered by gold metals and warm (yellow-based) colours. The scale or size of jewellery will depend on her bone size and height. If she is over 167cm (5ft 6in) tall and has large bones (wrists measuring 16.5cm [6 1/2in] or more) then she needs large, substantial pieces. If she is between 160 and 167cm (5ft 3in and 5ft 6in) with medium-sized bones (wrists 14–16.5cm [5 1/2–6 1/2in]) then large but delicate pieces suit her best, or medium-sized if they are more chunky in design. If she is petite, 160cm (5ft 3in) or less, with small bones (less than 14cm [5 1/2in]) then small scale jewellery is best.

Style Treats

In each both star sign there is a style treat to suit that personality. By reading all the style treats pertaining to your body type you will discover how to build up a wardrobe to best suit your shape. The style treats for the Triangle body type are found on pages: 425, 435, 446, 458, 467, 478, 487, 498, 510, 521, 531, 541.

IN HEALTH

The best diet for a Triangle-shaped woman is a low-fat diet. With a reduced fat, reduced sugar and increased fibre intake, this diet takes into account the latest findings on healthy nutrition. For her book *The Body Breakthrough* Bel worked from scientific findings and with volunteer dieters and found that the Triangle type tends to need more protein than the other types and should not have too many dairy products. The book outlines the diet and exercise regimes tailormade for the four body type metabolisms.

A Triangle-shaped woman tends to be an early riser whose energy level is at its best in the morning. Consequently, her metabolism deals best with having a hearty breakfast, a main meal at lunchtime, and then only a light evening meal. Such a big breakfast may be difficult to fit in to a busy life but will help keep her energy levels high and her metabolism burning through the day.

Eating a substantial lunch can also cause problems for a

woman working out of the home. A packed lunch, however, with a piece of cold chicken for instance, wholemeal roll, raw carrots, or other salad vegetables, will do very well.

The Triangle type is at her best when doing regular aerobic exercise, ie exercise which raises the heart rate like aerobics, speed swimming, jogging, bicycling, at least three times a week. She tends to be physically well coordinated and energetic dancing, like jazz, or tap, appeal to her too. The most vigorous exercise burns up ten calories a minute, which represents 300 calories for half-an-hour's exercise. But more than the obvious energy-burning advantage of exercise, aerobic exercise like this markedly boosts the metabolism for quite a few hours after you have stopped. It also has the effect for women with this body shape of increasing the general feeling of well-being and fitness.

This body type, then, has great stamina and a steady flow of energy but is obsessional and so runs some risk of overdoing her exercise routines. If she feels she is getting run down, or beginning to injure muscles and sprain joints, she must be careful to give her body time to recover. Vigorous exercise with periods of proper relaxation are essential to her long-term health and happiness.

SOME TRIANGLE-TYPE CELEBRITIES

Actresses

Joan Crawford (Aries)
Bette Davis (Aries)
Annette Bening (Gemini)
Anjelica Huston (Cancer)
Diana Rigg (Cancer)
Greta Garbo (Virgo)
Sigourney Weaver (Libra)
Demi Moore (Scorpio)
Marlene Dietrich (Capricorn)
Maggie Smith (Capricorn)
Laura Dern (Aquarius)
Mia Farrow (Aquarius)

Singers

Cher (Taurus)
Grace Jones (Taurus)
Edith Piaf (Sagittarius)
Annie Lennox (Capricorn)

Sports

Gabriela Sabatini (Aries)
Virginia Wade (Cancer)
Amy Johnson (Sagittarius)

Celebrities

Joan Rivers (Gemini)
Esther Rantzen (Cancer)
Jackie Kennedy Onassis (Leo)
Madonna (Leo)
Margaret Thatcher (Libra)
Georgia O'Keefe (Scorpio)
Princess Stephanie of Monaco (Aquarius)

WHICH STAR SIGN?

21 March – 20 April	Aries
21 April – 21 May	Taurus
22 May – 21 June	Gemini
22 June – 22 July	Cancer
23 July – 23 August	Leo
24 August – 22 September	Virgo
23 September – 23 October	Libra
24 October – 22 November	Scorpio
23 November – 21 December	Sagittarius
22 December – 20 January	Capricorn
21 January – 18 February	Aquarius
19 February – 20 March	Pisces

For those of you born on the cusp, here is the definitive guide as to which star sign you are. The dates and times given opposite and overleaf indicate where each star sign begins for every year from 1930 to 2000. Look along the line for your year of birth until you reach your appropriate month. The first number is the day of the month and the following number with the point is the exact time (in Greenwich Mean Time and expressed as a 24-hour clock) when the sun moves into the astrological sign at the head of the column. For instance, someone born on 20 January 1963 would find that at 18.08 (6.08 pm) on that day the sun moved into Aquarius. If he/she was born at 6.30 pm then that person is an Aquarian, but if he/she had been born at breakfast time then the sun would still have been in Capricorn.

YEAR	JANUARY *Aquarius*	FEBRUARY *Pisces*	MARCH *Aries*	APRIL *Taurus*	MAY *Gemini*	JUNE *Cancer*	JULY *Leo*	AUGUST *Virgo*	SEPTEMBER *Libra*	OCTOBER *Scorpio*	NOVEMBER *Sagittarius*	DECEMBER *Capricorn*
1930	20 18.33	19 9.00	21 8.30	20 20.06	21 19.42	22 3.53	23 14.42	23 21.26	23 18.36	24 3.26	23 0.34	22 13.39
1931	21 0.17	19 14.40	21 14.06	21 1.40	22 1.15	22 9.28	23 20.21	24 3.10	24 0.23	24 9.15	23 6.25	22 19.30
1932	21 6.07	19 20.28	20 19.54	20 7.28	21 7.07	21 15.23	23 2.18	23 9.06	23 6.16	23 15.04	22 12.10	22 1.14
1933	20 11.53	19 2.16	21 1.43	20 13.18	21 12.57	21 21.12	23 8.05	23 14.52	23 12.01	23 20.48	22 17.53	22 6.57
1934	20 17.37	19 8.02	21 7.28	21 19.00	21 18.35	22 2.48	23 13.42	23 20.32	23 17.45	24 2.36	22 23.44	22 12.49
1935	20 23.28	19 13.52	21 13.18	21 0.50	22 0.25	22 8.38	23 19.33	24 2.24	23 23.38	24 8.29	23 5.35	22 18.37
1936	21 5.12	19 19.33	20 18.58	20 6.31	21 6.07	21 14.22	23 1.18	23 8.10	23 5.26	23 14.18	22 11.25	22 0.27
1937	20 11.01	19 1.21	21 0.45	20 12.19	21 11.57	21 20.12	23 7.07	23 13.58	23 11.13	23 20.06	22 17.16	22 6.22
1938	20 16.59	19 7.20	21 6.43	20 18.15	21 17.50	22 2.04	23 12.57	23 19.46	23 16.59	24 1.54	22 23.06	22 12.13
1939	20 22.51	19 13.09	21 12.28	20 23.55	21 23.27	22 7.39	23 18.37	24 1.31	23 22.49	24 7.46	23 4.58	22 18.06
1940	21 4.44	19 19.04	20 18.24	20 5.51	21 5.23	21 13.36	23 0.34	23 7.26	23 4.46	23 13.39	22 10.49	21 23.55
1941	20 10.34	19 0.56	21 0.20	20 11.50	21 11.23	21 19.33	23 6.26	23 13.17	23 10.33	23 19.27	22 16.38	22 5.44
1942	20 16.23	19 6.47	21 6.11	20 17.39	21 17.09	22 1.16	23 12.07	23 18.58	23 16.16	24 1.15	22 22.30	22 11.40
1943	20 22.19	19 12.40	21 12.03	20 23.31	21 23.03	22 7.12	23 18.04	24 0.55	23 22.12	24 7.06	23 4.21	22 17.29
1944	21 4.07	19 18.27	20 17.49	20 5.18	21 4.51	21 13.02	22 23.58	23 6.46	23 4.02	23 12.56	22 10.08	21 23.15
1945	20 9.54	19 0.15	20 23.37	20 11.07	21 10.40	21 18.52	23 5.45	23 12.35	23 9.50	23 18.44	22 15.55	22 5.04
1946	20 15.45	19 6.09	21 5.33	20 17.02	21 16.34	22 0.44	23 11.37	23 18.26	23 15.41	24 0.35	22 21.46	22 10.53
1947	20 21.32	19 11.52	21 11.13	20 22.39	21 22.09	22 6.19	23 17.14	24 0.09	23 21.29	24 6.26	23 3.38	22 16.43
1948	21 3.18	19 17.37	20 16.57	20 4.25	21 3.58	21 12.11	22 23.06	23 6.03	23 3.22	23 12.18	22 9.29	21 22.33
1949	20 9.09	18 23.37	20 22.48	20 10.17	21 9.51	21 18.03	23 4.57	23 11.48	23 9.06	23 18.03	22 15.16	22 4.23
1950	20 15.00	19 5.18	21 4.35	20 15.59	21 15.27	21 23.36	23 10.30	23 17.23	23 14.44	23 23.45	22 21.03	22 10.13
1951	20 20.52	19 11.10	21 10.26	20 21.48	21 21.15	22 5.25	23 16.21	23 23.16	23 20.37	24 5.36	23 2.51	22 16.00
1952	21 2.28	19 16.57	20 16.14	20 3.37	21 3.04	21 11.13	22 22.07	23 5.03	23 2.24	23 11.22	22 8.36	21 21.43
1953	20 8.21	18 22.41	20 22.01	20 9.25	21 8.53	21 17.00	23 3.52	23 10.45	23 8.06	23 17.06	22 14.22	22 3.31
1954	20 14.11	19 4.32	21 3.53	20 15.20	21 14.47	21 22.54	23 9.45	23 16.36	23 13.55	23 22.56	22 20.14	22 9.24

YEAR	JANUARY *Aquarius*	FEBRUARY *Pisces*	MARCH *Aries*	APRIL *Taurus*	MAY *Gemini*	JUNE *Cancer*	JULY *Leo*	AUGUST *Virgo*	SEPTEMBER *Libra*	OCTOBER *Scorpio*	NOVEMBER *Sagittarius*	DECEMBER *Capricorn*
1955	20 20.02	19 10.19	21 9.35	20 20.58	21 20.24	22 4.31	23 15.25	23 22.19	23 19.41	24 4.43	23 2.01	22 15.11
1956	21 1.48	19 16.05	20 15.20	20 2.43	21 2.13	21 10.24	22 21.20	23 4.15	23 1.35	23 10.34	22 7.50	21 21.00
1957	20 7.39	18 21.58	20 21.17	20 8.41	21 8.10	21 16.21	23 3.15	23 10.08	23 7.26	23 16.24	22 13.39	22 2.49
1958	20 13.29	19 3.49	21 3.06	20 14.27	21 13.51	21 21.57	23 8.51	23 15.46	23 13.09	23 22.11	22 19.29	22 8.40
1959	20 19.19	19 9.38	21 8.55	20 20.17	21 19.42	22 3.50	23 14.48	23 21.44	23 19.09	24 4.11	23 1.27	22 14.34
1960	21 1.10	19 15.26	20 14.43	20 2.06	21 1.34	21 9.42	22 20.28	23 3.34	23 0.59	23 10.02	22 7.18	21 20.26
1961	20 7.01	18 21.17	20 20.32	20 7.55	21 7.22	21 15.30	23 2.24	23 9.19	23 6.43	23 15.47	22 13.06	22 2.20
1962	20 12.58	19 3.15	21 2.30	20 13.51	21 13.17	21 21.24	23 8.18	23 15.13	23 12.35	23 21.40	22 19.02	22 8.15
1963	20 18.54	19 9.09	21 8.20	20 19.36	21 18.58	22 3.04	23 13.59	23 20.58	23 18.24	24 3.29	23 0.49	22 14.02
1964	21 0.41	19 14.57	20 14.10	20 1.27	21 0.50	21 8.57	22 19.53	23 2.51	23 0.17	23 9.21	22 6.39	21 19.50
1965	20 6.29	18 20.48	20 20.05	20 7.26	21 6.50	21 14.56	23 1.48	23 8.43	23 6.06	23 15.10	22 12.29	22 1.41
1966	20 12.20	19 2.38	21 1.53	20 13.12	21 12.32	21 20.34	23 7.23	23 14.18	23 11.43	23 20.51	22 18.14	22 7.28
1967	20 18.08	19 8.24	21 7.37	20 18.55	21 18.18	22 2.23	23 13.16	23 20.13	23 17.38	24 2.44	23 0.05	22 13.16
1968	20 23.54	19 14.09	20 13.22	20 0.41	21 0.06	21 8.13	22 19.06	23 2.03	22 23.26	23 8.30	22 5.49	21 19.00
1969	20 5.38	18 19.55	20 19.06	20 6.27	21 5.50	21 13.55	23 0.48	23 7.44	23 5.07	23 14.11	22 11.31	22 0.44
1970	20 11.24	19 1.42	21 0.57	20 12.15	21 11.38	21 19.43	23 6.37	23 13.34	23 10.59	23 20.04	22 17.35	22 6.36
1971	20 17.13	19 7.27	21 6.38	20 17.54	21 17.15	22 1.20	23 12.15	23 19.15	23 16.45	24 1.53	22 23.14	22 12.24
1972	20 22.59	19 13.12	20 12.22	19 23.38	20 23.00	21 7.06	22 18.03	23 1.03	22 22.33	23 7.42	22 5.03	21 18.13
1973	20 4.48	18 19.01	20 18.13	20 5.31	21 4.54	21 13.01	22 23.56	23 6.54	23 4.21	23 13.30	22 10.54	22 0.06
1974	20 10.46	19 0.59	21 0.07	20 11.19	21 10.36	21 18.38	23 5.30	23 12.29	23 9.59	23 19.11	22 16.39	22 5.56
1975	20 16.37	19 6.50	21 5.57	20 17.06	21 16.24	22 0.27	23 11.22	23 18.24	23 15.55	24 1.06	22 22.31	22 11.46
1976	20 22.25	19 12.40	20 11.50	19 23.03	20 22.21	21 6.25	22 17.19	23 0.19	22 21.48	23 6.58	22 4.22	21 17.35
1977	20 4.15	18 18.31	20 17.43	20 4.58	21 4.15	21 12.14	22 23.04	23 6.01	23 3.30	23 12.41	22 10.07	21 23.23
1978	20 10.04	19 0.21	20 23.34	20 10.50	21 10.09	21 18.10	23 5.01	23 11.57	23 9.26	23 18.37	22 16.05	22 5.21
1979	20 16.00	19 6.14	21 5.22	20 16.36	21 15.54	21 23.57	23 10.49	23 17.47	23 15.17	24 0.28	22 21.54	22 11.10

YEAR	JANUARY Aquarius	FEBRUARY Pisces	MARCH Aries	APRIL Taurus	MAY Gemini	JUNE Cancer	JULY Leo	AUGUST Virgo	SEPTEMBER Libra	OCTOBER Scorpio	NOVEMBER Sagittarius	DECEMBER Capricorn
1980	20 21.49	19 12.02	20 11.10	19 22.23	20 21.42	21 5.47	22 16.42	22 23.41	22 21.09	23 6.18	22 3.42	21 16.56
1981	20 3.36	18 17.52	20 17.03	20 4.19	21 3.40	21 11.45	22 22.40	23 5.39	23 3.06	23 12.13	22 9.36	21 22.51
1982	20 9.31	18 23.47	20 22.56	20 10.08	21 9.23	21 17.23	23 4.16	23 11.16	23 8.47	23 17.58	22 15.24	22 4.39
1983	20 15.17	19 5.31	21 4.39	20 15.51	21 15.07	21 23.09	23 10.05	23 17.08	23 14.42	23 23.55	22 21.19	22 10.30
1984	20 21.05	19 11.17	20 10.25	19 21.39	20 20.58	21 5.03	22 15.59	22 23.01	22 20.33	23 5.46	22 3.11	21 16.23
1985	20 2.58	18 17.08	20 16.14	20 3.26	21 2.43	21 10.45	22 21.37	23 4.36	23 2.06	23 11.22	22 8.51	21 22.08
1986	20 8.47	18 22.58	20 22.03	20 9.13	21 8.28	21 16.30	23 3.25	23 10.26	23 7.59	23 17.15	22 14.45	22 4.03
1987	20 14.41	19 4.50	21 3.52	20 14.58	21 14.10	21 22.11	23 9.06	23 16.10	23 13.46	23 23.01	22 20.30	22 9.46
1988	20 20.25	19 10.36	20 9.39	19 20.45	20 19.57	21 3.57	22 14.52	22 21.54	22 19.29	23 4.45	22 2.12	21 15.28
1989	20 2.07	18 16.21	20 15.29	20 2.39	21 1.54	21 9.53	22 20.46	23 3.47	23 1.20	23 10.36	22 8.05	21 21.22
1990	20 8.02	18 22.14	20 21.20	20 8.27	21 7.38	21 15.33	23 2.22	23 9.21	23 6.56	23 16.14	22 13.47	22 3.07
1991	20 13.48	19 3.59	21 3.02	20 14.09	21 13.21	21 21.19	23 8.12	23 15.13	23 12.49	23 22.06	22 19.36	22 8.54
1992	20 19.33	19 9.44	20 8.49	19 19.57	20 19.13	21 3.15	22 14.09	22 21.11	22 18.43	23 3.58	22 1.26	21 14.44
1993	20 1.23	18 15.36	20 14.41	20 1.50	21 1.02	21 9.00	22 19.51	23 2.51	23 0.23	23 9.38	22 7.07	21 20.26
1994	20 7.09	18 21.23	20 20.29	20 7.37	21 6.50	21 14.49	23 1.42	23 8.45	23 6.21	23 15.37	22 13.07	22 2.24
1995	20 13.02	19 3.12	21 2.16	20 13.23	21 12.35	21 20.36	23 7.31	23 14.36	23 12.14	23 21.33	22 19.03	22 8.18
1996	20 18.54	19 9.02	20 8.04	19 19.11	20 18.24	21 2.25	22 13.20	22 20.24	22 18.01	23 3.20	22 0.51	21 14.07
1997	20 0.44	18 14.53	20 13.56	20 1.04	21 0.19	21 8.21	22 19.17	23 2.21	22 23.57	23 9.16	22 6.49	21 20.08
1998	20 6.48	18 20.56	20 19.56	20 6.58	21 6.07	21 14.04	23 0.57	23 8.00	23 5.39	23 15.00	22 12.36	22 1.58
1999	20 12.39	19 2.48	21 1.47	20 12.47	21 11.54	21 19.50	23 6.46	23 13.53	23 11.33	23 20.54	22 18.26	22 7.45
2000	20 18.25	19 8.35	20 7.37	19 18.41	20 17.51	21 1.49	22 12.44	22 19.50	22 17.29	23 2.49	22 0.21	21 13.39

THE TWELVE STAR SIGNS

ARIES 21 MARCH – 20 APRIL
RULER: MARS, FIRE SIGN (YANG+), CARDINAL

The sign of the Pioneer and the Gladiator. Likely to be: courageous, headstrong, fast-moving, straightforward, assertive, energetic, idealistic and optimistic. But can be: irresponsible, thoughtless, overbearing, aggressive, reckless, self-centred and tactless.

Some Aries Celebrities (with Body Types)

(The two extreme body shapes, the Pear and the Triangle, can be difficult to recognize from film or photograph, and ideally need to be identified by seeing the person in the flesh. So some of these Hourglasses may be Pears and vice versa and similarly some of the Rectangles may be Triangles, and vice versa. The historical figures are identified from portraits and are informed guesses.)

Actresses

Jane Asher (Triangle)
Julie Christie (Hourglass)
Joan Crawford (Triangle)
Bette Davis (Triangle)
Hannah Gordon (Rectangle)
Penelope Keith (Rectangle)
Ali MacGraw (Triangle)
Debbie Reynolds (Hourglass)
Emma Thompson (Hourglass)
Ruby Wax (Rectangle)

Presenters/Personalities

Joan Bakewell (Triangle)
Elle Macpherson (Triangle)

Singers

Pearl Bailey (Rectangle)
Montserrat Caballé (Rectangle)
Diana Ross (Hourglass)
Dusty Springfield (Rectangle)

Writers

Maya Angelou (Rectangle)
Sheila Kitzinger (Rectangle)

Sport

Clare Francis (Triangle)
Gabriela Sabatini (Triangle)

Power & Politics

Lucretia Borgia (Rectangle)
Catherine de Medici (Rectangle)

TAURUS 21 APRIL – 21 MAY
RULER: VENUS, EARTH SIGN (YIN), FIXED

The sign of the Realist and Conservator. Likely to be: trustworthy, affectionate, practical, sweet-natured, unpretentious, honest, sexy, and patient. But can be: obstinate, lazy, greedy, mercenary, know-all, unimaginative, plodding and possessive.

Some Taurus Celebrities (with Body Types)

Actresses
Francesca Annis (Hourglass)
Candice Bergen (Pear)
Cher (Triangle)
Audrey Hepburn (Hourglass)
Glenda Jackson (Rectangle)
Grace Jones (Triangle)
Jessica Lange (Hourglass)
Maureen Lipman (Rectangle)
Joanna Lumley (Hourglass)
Shirley MacLaine (Rectangle)
Geraldine McEwan (Pear)
Michelle Pfeiffer (Hourglass)
Sian Phillips (Rectangle)
Natasha Richardson (Hourglass)
Zoe Wanamaker (Rectangle)
Toyah Willcox (Triangle)
Paula Yates (Hourglass)

Music
Ella Fitzgerald (Hourglass)
Jane Glover (Rectangle)
Dame Nellie Melba (Rectangle)
Rosalind Plowright (Rectangle)
Barbra Streisand (Rectangle)
Tammy Wynette (Hourglass)

Ballet
Darcey Bussell (Hourglass)
Margot Fonteyn (Hourglass)

Personalities
Selena Scott (Hourglass)
Shirley Temple Black (Hourglass)

Writers
Rachel Billington (Hourglass)
Daphne du Maurier (Triangle)
Barbara Taylor Bradford (Rectangle)

Power
Catherine the Great (Rectangle)
Queen Elizabeth II (Rectangle)
Lady Emma Hamilton (Pear)
Helena Kennedy QC (Rectangle)
Golda Meir (Rectangle)
Florence Nightingale (Triangle)
Eva Peron (Triangle)
Mrs Mary Robinson – Irish President (Triangle)

GEMINI 22 MAY – 21 JUNE
RULER: MERCURY, AIR SIGN (YANG), MUTABLE

The sign of the Communicator and Entertainer. Likely to be: talkative, versatile, observant, quick-witted, sociable, multi-talented, amusing and well-informed. But can be: superficial, unfeeling, fickle, weak-willed, argumentative, manipulative and gossipy.

Some Gemini Celebrities (with Body Types)

Actresses

Eileen Atkins (Rectangle)
Linda Bellingham (Rectangle)
Annette Bening (Triangle)
Helena Bonham-Carter (Rectangle)
Cheryl Campbell (Hourglass)
Joan Collins (Hourglass)
Josie Lawrence (Pear)
Virginia McKenna (Pear)
Marilyn Monroe (Hourglass)
Nanette Newman (Rectangle)
Beryl Reid (Rectangle)
Isabella Rossellini (Hourglass)
Jane Russell (Triangle)
Brooke Shields (Hourglass)
Kathleen Turner (Hourglass)
Billie Whitelaw (Hourglass)
Penelope Wilton (Rectangle)

Singers

Cilla Black (Rectangle)
Judy Garland (Triangle)
Gladys Knight (Triangle)
Peggy Lee (Rectangle)
Kylie Minogue (Hourglass)
Alison Moyet (Rectangle)
Suzi Quatro (Triangle)
Nancy Sinatra (Triangle)

Sport

Zola Budd (Triangle)
Steffi Graf (Rectangle)
Jenny Pitman (Rectangle)

Power & Influence

Joan Rivers (Triangle)
Duchess of Windsor (Triangle)
Queen Victoria (Rectangle)

Beauties

Naomi Campbell (Hourglass)
Isadora Duncan (Pear)

Writers

Catherine Cookson (Rectangle)
Margaret Drabble (Rectangle)
Margaret Forster (Triangle)
Françoise Sagan (Triangle)

CANCER 22 JUNE – 22 JULY
RULER: MOON, WATER SIGN (YIN +), CARDINAL

The sign of the Nurturer and Collector. Likely to be: compassionate, hard-working, sympathetic, supportive, intuitive, protective, public-spirited and inspired. But can be: cranky, insecure, depressive, devious, prejudiced, moody, evasive and defensive.

Some Cancer Celebrities (with Body Types)

Actresses
Genevieve Bujold (Hourglass)
Leslie Caron (Hourglass)
Olivia de Havilland (Hourglass)
Anjelica Huston (Triangle)
Gina Lollobrigida (Hourglass)
Kelly McGillis (Pear)
Pauline Quirke (Rectangle)
Diana Rigg (Triangle)
Jennifer Saunders (Rectangle)
Prunella Scales (Hourglass)
Barbara Stanwyck (Triangle)
Meryl Streep (Pear)

TV Personalites
Sue Lawley (Rectangle)
Esther Rantzen (Triangle)
Julia Somerfield (Hourglass)

Singers and Musicians
Debbie Harry (Rectangle)
Anne-Sophie Mutter (Hourglass)

Writers
Barbara Cartland (Rectangle)
Monica Dickins (Rectangle)
Molly Keane (Rectangle)
Fay Maschler (Pear)
Iris Murdoch (Rectangle)
Dilys Powell (Rectangle)
Mary Wesley (Triangle)

Sport
Annabel Croft (Rectangle)
Pam Shriver (Rectangle)
Virginia Wade (Triangle)

Fashion
Jerry Hall (Hourglass)
Betty Jackson (Rectangle)

Temporal power
Princess Diana (Rectangle)
Empress Josephine (Pear)
Emmeline Pankhurst (Triangle)

LEO 23 JULY – 23 AUGUST
RULER: SUN, FIRE SIGN (YANG +), FIXED

The sign of the Director and Prima Donna. Likely to be: warm-hearted, generous, honourable, forthright, candid, optimistic, brave, creative and chivalric. But can be: extravagant, despotic, bombastic, arrogant, egotistical, ostentatious, patronizing and opinionated.

Some Leo Celebrities (with Body Types)

Actresses
Rosanna Arquette (Hourglass)
Lucille Ball (Rectangle)
Coral Browne (Rectangle)
Geraldine Chaplin (Triangle)
Susan George (Rectangle)
Melanie Griffiths (Hourglass)
Barbara Jefford (Rectangle)
Anna Massey (Triangle)
Helen Mirren (Rectangle)
Frances de la Tour (Rectangle)
Mae West (Triangle)
Shelley Winters (Rectangle)

Singers
Janet Baker (Rectangle)
Sarah Brightman (Hourglass)
Kate Bush (Pear)
Whitney Houston (Triangle)
Madonna (Triangle)

Writers & Illustrators
Sally Beaumann (Hourglass)
Emily Brontë (Pear)
Dorothy Parker (Triangle)
Bernice Rubens (Triangle)
Posy Simmonds (Hourglass)
Jacqueline Susann (Triangle)

Public Power
Rt Hon Lord Justice Butler-Sloss (Rectangle)
Barbara Mills (Director of Serious Fraud Squad) (Rectangle)
Sue Slipman (Director National Council Single Parent Families) (Triangle)
Shirley Williams (Baroness Williams) (Rectangle)

Fashion
Coco Chanel (Triangle)
Iman (Hourglass)

Sport
Jo Durie (Rectangle)
Sally Gunnell (Rectangle)

Royalty
Princess Anne (Hourglass)
Princess Margaret (Hourglass)
Queen Mother (Rectangle)
Jacqueline Kennedy Onassis (Triangle)

VIRGO 24 AUGUST – 22 SEPTEMBER
RULER: MERCURY, EARTH SIGN (YIN), MUTABLE

The sign of the Craftswoman and Analyst. Likely to be: articulate, discerning, honest, reliable, sensual, kind, self-effacing, humorous and sincere. But can be: nit-picking, querulous, pedantic, obsessive, interfering, prudish, fastidious, unconfident and a hypochondriac.

Some Virgo Celebrities (with Body Types)

Actresses
Lauren Bacall (Rectangle)
Anne Bancroft (Pear)
Ingrid Bergman (Rectangle)
Jacqueline Bisset (Triangle)
Pauline Collins (Hourglass)
Greta Garbo (Triangle)
Sophia Loren (Hourglass)
Alison Steadman (Rectangle)
Raquel Welch (Hourglass)

Writers
AS Byatt (Rectangle)
Agatha Christie (Rectangle)
Shirley Conran (Rectangle)
Lady Antonia Fraser (Rectangle)
Elizabeth Longford (Hourglass)
Alison Lurie (Triangle)
Jessica Mitford (Rectangle)
Penelope Mortimer (Rectangle)
Mary Shelley (Pear)
Edith Sitwell (Rectangle)
Alice Thomas-Ellis (Hourglass)
Fay Weldon (Rectangle)

TV
Kate Adie (Rectangle)
Pamela Armstrong (Hourglass)

Fashion
Twiggy (Rectangle)
Zandra Rhodes (Triangle)

Singer
Jessye Norman (Triangle)

Power
Queen Elizabeth I (Triangle)
Mother Teresa (Rectangle)

LIBRA 23 SEPTEMBER – 23 OCTOBER
RULER: VENUS, AIR SIGN, (YANG), CARDINAL

The sign of the Artist and Diplomat. Likely to be: charming, discreet, fair, reasonable, aesthetic, friendly, civilized, attractive and humane. But can be: indecisive, dishonest, narcissistic, lazy, ineffectual, unreliable, manipulative and all things to all men.

Some Libra Celebrities (with Body Types)

Actresses
Julie Andrews (Hourglass)
Brigitte Bardot (Hourglass)
Sarah Bernhardt (Rectangle)
Catherine Deneuve (Hourglass)
Angie Dickinson (Rectangle)
Britt Ekland (Triangle)
Carrie Fisher (Triangle)
Lilian Gish (Triangle)
Patricia Hodge (Pear)
Lillie Langtry (Hourglass)
Emily Lloyd (Hourglass)
Anna Neagle (Rectangle)
Susan Sarandon (Rectangle)
Sigourney Weaver (Triangle)
Catherine Zeta Jones (Hourglass)

Music
Linda McCartney (Rectangle)
Olivia Newton-John (Hourglass)

Sport
Martina Navratilova (Rectangle)
Maria Bueno (Hourglass)

Writers
Jackie Collins (Rectangle)
Elizabeth Gaskell (Rectangle)
Doris Lessing (Rectangle)
Katherine Mansfield (Triangle)
Jan Morris (Rectangle)
Lisa St Aubin de Terain (Pear)

Political
Betty Boothroyd (Rectangle)
Edwina Currie (Rectangle)
Melina Mercouri (Triangle)
Emma Nicholson (Rectangle)
Marie Stopes (Triangle)
Margaret Thatcher (Triangle)

Personalities
Judith Chalmers (Rectangle)
Anna Ford (Hourglass)
Dawn French (Hourglass)
Donna Karan (Hourglass)
Mavis Nicholson (Rectangle)
Anneka Rice (Rectangle)
Angela Rippon (Rectangle)
Duchess of York (Hourglass)

SCORPIO 24 OCTOBER – 22 NOVEMBER RULER: MARS/PLUTO, WATER SIGN (YIN+), FIXED

The sign of the Creator and Restorer. Likely to be: creative, self-sacrificing, passionate, perceptive, profound, loyal, trustworthy, heroic and undaunted. But can be: suspicious, intolerant, tempestuous, jealous, obsessive, withdrawn, resentful, and always right.

Some Scorpio Celebrities (with Body Types)

Actresses

Roseanne Barr (Rectangle)
Bo Derek (Triangle)
Linda Evans (Triangle)
Sally Field (Hourglass)
Jodie Foster (Rectangle)
Whoopi Goldberg (Rectangle)
Goldie Hawn (Hourglass)
Mariel Hemingway (Triangle)
Lauren Hutton (Triangle)
Grace Kelly (Hourglass)
Vivien Leigh (Hourglass)
Demi Moore (Triangle)
Tatum O'Neal (Rectangle)
Joan Plowright (Rectangle)
Stefanie Powers (Rectangle)
Julia Roberts (Pear)
Jaclyn Smith (Hourglass)
Sean Young (Triangle)

Singers

Petula Clarke (Pear)
Cleo Laine (Hourglass)
Joni Mitchell (Triangle)
Dame Joan Sutherland (Rectangle)

Sport

Nadia Comaneci (Rectangle)
Billie Jean King (Rectangle)

Art

Dame Elizabeth Frink (Rectangle)
Georgia O'Keefe (Triangle)

Writers

Beryl Bainbridge (Rectangle)
Nadine Gordimer (Triangle)
Naomi Wolf (Pear)
Sylvia Plath (Hourglass)
Marina Warner (Pear)

Power and Icons

Marie Antoinette (Hourglass)
Tina Brown (Hourglass)
Hillary Clinton (Pear)
Indira Gandhi (Rectangle)
Jean Shrimpton (Hourglass)
Anna Wintour (Triangle)

Business

Anita Roddick (Hourglass)

SAGITTARIUS 23 NOVEMBER – 21 DECEMBER RULER: JUPITER, FIRE SIGN (YANG+), MUTABLE

The sign of the Adventurer and Philosopher. Likely to be: frank, stimulating, energetic, tolerant, expansive, generous, visionary and wise. But can be: restless, indiscreet, rash, profligate, overinflated, immature, superficial and insensitive.

Some Sagittarius Celebrities (with Body Types)

Actresses
Jenny Agutter (Pear)
Kim Basinger (Hourglass)
Gladys Cooper (Rectangle)
Judi Dench (Hourglass)
Jane Fonda (Rectangle)
Bette Midler (Rectangle)
Lee Remick (Hourglass)
Pamela Stephenson (Hourglass)

Writers
Jane Austen (Rectangle)
Edna O'Brien (Rectangle)
Christina Rossetti (Hourglass)

Music & Dance
Joan Armatrading (Rectangle)
Maria Callas (Hourglass)
Dame Alicia Markova (Triangle)
Sinead O'Connor (Triangle)
Edith Piaf (Triangle)
Elizabeth Schwarzkopf (Hourglass)
Tina Turner (Rectangle)

Sport & Travel
Chris Evert (Rectangle)
Amy Johnson (Triangle)
Dervla Murphy (Rectangle)

CAPRICORN 22 DECEMBER – 20 JANUARY RULER: SATURN, EARTH SIGN (YIN), CARDINAL

The sign of the Administrator and Builder. Likely to be: responsible, discliplined, ambitious, high-minded, trustworthy, distinguished, industrious, philosophical and persevering. But can be: lofty, dogmatic, snobbish, social-climbing, gloomy, disapproving, inhibited, conventional and joyless.

Some Capricorn Celebrities (with Body Types)

Actresses
Kirstie Alley (Hourglass)
Peggy Ashcroft (Hourglass)
Dyan Cannon (Triangle)
Capucine (Triangle)
Marlene Dietrich (Triangle)
Faye Dunaway (Triangle)
Ava Gardner (Triangle)
Diane Keaton (Triangle)
Sarah Miles (Triangle)
Victoria Principal (Hourglass)
Maggie Smith (Triangle)
Sissy Spacek (Hourglass)
Tracy Ullman (Rectangle)
Susannah York (Pear)

Singers & Dancers
Joan Baez (Triangle)
Shirley Bassey (Rectangle)
Grace Bumbry (Rectangle)
Marianne Faithfull (Rectangle)
Janis Joplin (Rectangle)
Annie Lennox (Triangle)
Dolly Parton (Triangle)
Sade (Hourglass)

Writers
Simone de Beauvoir (Rectangle)
Suzy Menkes (Rectangle)
Dorothy Sayers (Rectangle)
Susan Sontag (Rectangle)

Artists
Barbara Hepworth (Rectangle)

Political pioneers and personages
Joan of Arc (Triangle)
Raisa Gorbachev (Rectangle)
Sylvia Pankhurst (Rectangle)
Joan Ruddock (Rectangle)

Royals
Princess Alexandra (Rectangle)
Princess Michael of Kent (Rectangle)

Power
Eve Pollard (Lady Lloyd) (Triangle)
Helena Rubinstein (Triangle)

AQUARIUS 21 JANUARY – 18 FEBRUARY
RULER: URANUS, AIR SIGN (YANG), FIXED

The sign of the Innovator and Revolutionary. Likely to be: original, perceptive, free-spirited, cerebal, humanitarian, unconventional, truthful, fascinating and fair. But can be: chilly, absent-minded, rebellious, rude, unpredictable, stubborn, uncooperative and perverse.

Some Aquarius Celebrities (with Body Types)

Actresses

Tallulah Bankhead (Triangle)
Claire Bloom (Hourglass)
Sinead Cusack (Rectangle)
Geena Davis (Hourglass)
Laura Dern (Triangle)
Mia Farrow (Triangle)
Farrah Fawcett (Hourglass)
Zsa Zsa Gabor (Triangle)
Nastassia Kinski (Triangle)
Kim Novak (Hourglass)
Charlotte Rampling (Triangle)
Vanessa Redgrave (Rectangle)
Patricia Routledge (Rectangle)
Greta Scacchi (Hourglass)
Jane Seymour (Pear)
Cybill Shepherd (Hourglass)
Jean Simmons (Hourglass)
Janet Suzman (Rectangle)

Singers & Dancers

Eartha Kitt (Triangle)
Yoko Ono (Rectangle)
Anna Pavlova (Pear)
Renata Tebaldi (Triangle)

Writers & Adventurers

Colette (Triangle)
Ruth Rendell (Rectangle)
Freya Stark (Triangle)
Virginia Woolf (Triangle)

Feminists

Betty Friedan (Rectangle)
Germaine Greer (Rectangle)
Helen Gurley Brown (Triangle)
Mary Quant (Triangle)

Foodies

Josceline Dimbleby (Hourglass)
Pru Leith (Rectangle)

Personalities

Christie Brinkley (Hourglass)
Oprah Winfrey (Hourglass)

Royalty

Queen Beatrix of the Netherlands (Pear)
Princess Caroline of Monaco (Rectangle)
Princess Stephanie of Monaco (Triangle)

PISCES 19 FEBRUARY – 20 MARCH RULER: NEPTUNE, WATER SIGN (YIN+), MUTABLE

The sign of the Synthesizer and Translator. Likely to be: sensitive, empathic, mystical, poetic, selfless, open-minded, charitable, generous-hearted and wise. But can be: vague, whimsical, hypercritical, over-emotional, pernickety, helpless, self-protective and escapist.

Some Pisces Celebrities (with Body Types)

Actresses
Ursula Andress (Triangle)
Drew Barrymore (Rectangle)
Eleanor Bron (Pear)
Shakira Caine (Hourglass)
Glenn Close (Rectangle)
Lesley-Anne Down (Hourglass)
Jean Harlow (Triangle)
Holly Hunter (Hourglass)
Isabelle Huppert (Hourglass)
Lynne Redgrave (Hourglass)
Miranda Richardson (Pear)
Imogen Stubbs (Pear)
Elizabeth Taylor (Hourglass)
Julie Walters (Rectangle)
Joanne Woodward (Hourglass)

Dancers
Leslie Collier (Rectangle)
Sylvie Guillem (Triangle)
Antoinette Sibley (Rectangle)

Singers
Elkie Brooks (Hourglass)
Kiri te Kanawa (Hourglass)
Vera Lyn (Rectangle)
Liza Minnelli (Rectangle)
Elaine Paige (Triangle)
Nina Simone (Rectangle)

Writers & Artists
Elizabeth Barrett Browning (Pear)
Penelope Lively (Rectangle)
Claire Rayner (Rectangle)
Vita Sackville-West (Triangle)

Politics
Virginia Bottomley (Hourglass)

Saints
Duchess of Kent (Hourglass)

delicate shoulders and neck

always retains her waist

smaller bust size than hip size

gains weight mostly on lower hips, bottom and thighs

pronounced curve on top, outer thigh

PEAR

ARIES

(Yin+/Yang+)

MOTTO:

Somewhere the sun is shining

IN LIFE

Here we have the two extremes of body shape and star sign. The Pear shape is ultra-feminine – the Yin+ influence is basic to this character, making her intuitive, receptive to the feelings of others, flexible and relationship-orientated. And Aries, as the modifying characteristic, is ultra-masculine. As a fire sign, Aries is already Yang+, but as a cardinal fire sign it is the most Yang of them all. It is essentially to do with outrushing energy, with action rather than contemplation, with assertion rather than receptivity. Such polarity of influences is bound to cause some confusion.

An Aries woman is naturally full of energy and will want, above all, to impress herself on the world. She is an individual, self-motivated and self-centred. However, the Pear-shape woman is a much more subtle and intuitive being. This combination can cause a clash in ambitions, and a confused message being broadcast to friends and lovers, but it also energizes the Pear-type temperament and deepens and refines the Arien energy. One moment the Pear/Aries woman is impetuously rushing into an adventure – a new business scheme, an eight-week trek through the Himalayan foothills, or a new love affair with an unsuitable man – and the next she is pulling back, suddenly concerned for her colleagues, her cats should she be away from home too long, or the wife and children of the man she thinks she's in love with.

Pear/Aries is always on the move. If she isn't actually physically rushing from one project to the next, or from one friend to another, her mind is racing with various plans, thoughts and adventures. The Pear-type influence may make her slightly more

reflective and more aware of interests other than her own, but she is not likely to become entirely laid back and sybaritic. There will be plenty of irons in the fire for her to juggle.

There is something larger than life about Aries, she is simple, big-hearted, absolutely without malice and expecting the best of everyone. The Pear-type subtlety and understanding of others makes Pear/Aries more aware that there are people unlike herself, that there are cheats and liars in this world, that she can get burned. It might mean she's just as optimistic but slightly less naive than she might otherwise be. Her intellectual energy burns as brightly as ever, just with a little more profundity and understanding of human psychology.

Although the energies of her body type and star sign tend to be opposed, they come together to great effect in Pear/Aries with a sense of outrage at unfairness and cruelty. Aries is a born crusader and the Pear type is naturally a truly sympathetic woman who can meet others and share in either their happiness or distress. Together these two influences can produce a most humanitarian character who has both the emotional depth and the forcefulness to act to change things. Pear/Aries cannot pass by on the other side of the street. She will leap to anyone's aid, offering practical help and emotional support.

Pear/Aries has ideals which she sometimes does not know how to translate into reality. She has so much energy and ability, but the real world can be rather separate from her dreams and she finds it hard to connect the two: to bring the dream to life or make the work embody the ideal. The Pear type adds an ability to take a longer view, to plan for the future instead of just living, and acting, in the present. This can make Pear/Aries more cautious than other Aries body types, but more effective in the end. There may be slightly less energetic action but more solid result, slightly less inflated optimism about life, love and work – but a more realistic recognition of the importance of all these features existing in harmony.

Her Pear-type nature also gives Pear/Aries a greater ability to work alongside others in a collaborative effort, without always having to be in charge, leading from the front (and sometimes unaware of the dangerous dissent in the ranks!). But, there are other times when these contradictory energies of Yin+ and Yang+ do not harmonize, rather they pull in different directions.

This can be disconcerting for Pear/Aries, and for those who work with her and love her. Does she want to conquer the world, overwhelming all opposition and playing the warrior queen, or is she heading for a caring, sharing role in work and life, supporting her man and mothering her children? It must be said this combination, for all its contradictions, comes up with the least aggressive, most sympathetic Aries woman you could meet – and conversely, one of the most assertive Pear-shaped women you are likely to come across. Here is a woman full of surprises.

IN WORK

Pear/Aries women are never dull. They have energy enough to spare and just when they seem to be getting on to a very high horse indeed, bossing the world and his wife, they have a capacity to suddenly snap out of egotistic mode and into a sympathetic awareness of the effect they are having on others. This can make for an invincible talent in any work that involves a sensitivity to people, combined with great will, energy and courage.

Pear-shaped women are brilliant at synthesizing ideas, encouraging people and promoting others. They are naturally the feelers and carers who make working situations into supportive networks where hierarchy and competition are less important than harmony and good feeling. Aries women, however, are competitive with a capital C and like winning at anything they undertake – even if it's just the school fête cake stall. They can be brash, self-promoting, enthusiastic and tough, but in this intriguing combination of Yin+ body-shape and Yang+ star sign, the self-motivated drive of the Aries is transformed into an ability to collaborate creatively, to embrace the interests of others and consider the welfare of the group or community.

Pear/Aries woman needs variety and likes working within energetic organizations. Imaginative, frightened by grinding routine, she craves a sense of adventure, however small, and that feeling that at any moment the unexpected might happen. Her passport is always kept up to date and to hand. Foreign currency has a greater erotic charge for this woman than diamonds.

Working on a magazine or in a television company would provide the Pear/Aries woman with the variety she needs and scope for her interest in action and ideas. Running a travel agency, employment bureau, or organizing the PR of a multinational company all have their attractions. Aries characteristically does not like anything to be longterm, or involve a great deal of profound thought and research. They are spontaneous people who want immediate results and instant gratification. 'I want it now' is their classic saying. For the Pear/Aries woman, however, the overriding influence of her body shape makes for some interesting modifications to this most precipitate of characters. 'I want

it now' becomes more readily, 'Let's get/do/see it as soon as possible, what do you think?'. Less uncompromising, less bulldozing and more responsive, the fabled energy and initiative is still there, but in a less raw state.

The nurturing side of the Pear-shape woman allied with the adventurousness and drive of the Aries star sign can produce women who pioneer better conditions for others worse off than themselves. Prison educator, overseas aid worker, nurse, provide possible outlets for this imaginative energy. These women have a sympathy for the underdog, and for animals in general, and working with animals is a possibility. Anything offering variety, activity, new projects, new ideas, unexpected situations and lots of people to care about – and occasionally dazzle – will keep Pear/Aries happy.

Ideal Fantasy Job

Editor of *Time Out* (an entertainments listing magazine, managed as a cooperative venture). The lack of strict hierarchy in a magazine like this appeals to her egalitarian Pear side, the variety and excitement of being absolutely up-to-the-minute with all the news and events would give her Aries side a buzz. Pear/Aries would make a boss who did not stand on ceremony, cared little for status but was always interested in new ideas – and would be terrific fun.

IN LOVE

The double Yin effect of the Pear body shape means that for this woman relationships matter most of all. Everything is seen in personal terms and the 'significant others' in her life, her family, husband, children, are all at the forefront of her priorities and thoughts. Even when she is young, she will not have a breezy attitude towards sex, she will fall in love early and be ill at ease with the idea of playing the field, switching from boyfriend to boyfriend, her feelings disengaged. A close and lasting relationship which embraces having children is likely to be pretty high on her agenda.

But then when you add that Aries mix, you have something more complicated altogether. Aries is the leading astrological sign, the baby of the horoscope, and is sometimes likened to the archetypal baby in character. Centre of attention, naturally self-obsessed, not in the sense of being selfish, but just finding it hard to realize that needs other than their own exist, they delight everyone with their curiosity and enthusiasm for life.

In the knotty area of love, however, the Aries need for excitement and romance can lead them a little astray. This is where the one-man-girl approach of the Pear can help this personality settle down enough to make that commitment to love, family and domesticity, but woebetide the man who thinks, having wooed his Pear/Aries woman, that he can settle into a nice, easy routine with a good and placid wife. Life for her will always have to consist of some adventure and so even in marriage, hung about with children, the Pear/Aries woman needs to keep her dreams, and her life its surprises.

The man for her has to be basically Yang, as a contrast to her basically Yin self. Someone whose energy is focused on the outside world, proactive and more self-centred than she is, he is less sensitive to the needs of others but more able to drive his ideas and ambitions through obstacles and antagonisms. Because of her own Yang+ overlay from her Aries star sign, the man for Pear/Aries cannot be too much of the unreconstructed male because that aspect of her character will not appreciate being tucked under his big hairy arm.

When they become mothers, many Pear-shaped women are overwhelmed by their feelings for their children and find it more satisfactory to postpone their careers and stay at home and care for their babies themselves, particularly in the earliest years when they are most vulnerable. This decision is not quite so unequivocal for the Pear/Aries woman, however, who might rebel against all the domesticity and lack of excitement – after the novelty has worn off.

She will be passionate about her children, but some of that Aries competitiveness will start to rear its head as she compares her little offspring with others – is she walking sooner? talking better? will she get into that school with the entrance exam even parents fail? All that Aries energy and egocentricity, however strongly modified here by body shape, is going to have to go somewhere and it is safest and most healthy for her family if it is channelled out of the home. A continuing career, even if only part-time until the children are at school, is a must for this most caring but ambitious mum.

Pear/Aries has lots of friends. She is a sympathetic shoulder to cry on as well as a woman with get-up-and-go who is willing to try new schemes, go to new places, and taste whatever life has to offer – as long as it doesn't impinge on her duties to her loved ones.

Ideal Lover

David Attenborough, a Yang enough male to complement the highly female side of the Pear/Aries woman, but not too unreconstructedly

so. The Aries part of this combination will object to being bossed about and treated like the little woman, and she'd never get such insensitive behaviour from the divine David. He'd also provide enough adventure and surprises, although she'd have to be careful that the adventures and surprises weren't only to be found in his life, while she was expected to keep the home fires burning.

IN STYLE

The Pear/Aries woman can find it difficult working out her attitude to clothes, and the kind of dressing that suits both her body and character. Just as there is a contradiction of energies in her personality, given her extreme Yin body shape and her extreme Yang sun sign, so too there is an ambivalence in the way she chooses to express herself in the world.

Her body shape demands soft, feminine clothes but this can be a little at odds with the Aries side of the equation. Fire sign women anyway are often not very interested in the detail of dressing and clothes. The pleasures of experimenting with cloth and cut and colour, the sensuous *feel* of the thing, pass them by, although they like the *effects* that clothes can produce – signalling status, drawing attention, making statements, doing a good job keeping them warm or dry.

The Aries woman, then, has not got the time or the will to sort out a complex *modus operandi* for her wardrobe, but she likes her clothes to work. In addition, the Pear/Aries possesses a greater interest in dressing to suit her looks and individual body shape, although she can feel uneasy with the necessary softness of the clothes that suit her best. The sporty, outdoorsy, masculine Aries element sometimes rebels and she will put on the straight-leg jeans and big, hairy, checked cowboy shirt (more suited to her Rectangle-shaped friends) and not mind that they look slightly at odds with her softer body shape.

Perhaps the answer to the problem of how best to dress a Pear/Aries, with all the natural contradictions this combination implies, is to dress more casually and sportily if she feels that suits her personality best. But she must always bear in mind the central principles of style and detail that suit the Pear type. This helps Pear/Aries make the right decisions, and so end up with a wardrobe where everything suits her, most things go with other things, and there are no expensive – or even cheap – mistakes. For more specific information see In Style on page 28.

Style Treat

Sports clothes that are becoming to Pear-shaped women are very dificult to come by. If she is buying new tennis gear, for instance, she shouldn't depress herself by trying on those straight-legged shorts (leave them to Martina) she will look much better in a pleated or divided skirt, or a tennis dress with a fitted bodice and a skirt gathered over her hips.

As an Aries type of Pear, she is more likely to be sporty than anyone else of her body type and so it might be a useful treat to find herself a tracksuit that really suits her shape. Tracksuits are difficult garments to wear with much glamour at the best of times (although they do look passable on the slim Rectangle type of body, with her narrow hips and straight slim legs). The more curvy, female shape such as that of the Pear should go for trousers in a fluid jersey or other soft fabric that isn't too bulky. The classic sweatshirt top is not very flattering as it hides her shape and turns her into a blob with emphasis drawn to her widest bit, the hip. Much better is a fitted vest or body which shows the Pear type's neat upper torso. Tucked into loose trousers, the whole under an open zip-up tracksuit top (not too heavyweight fabric). This may well be the Pear/Aries' answer to the ubiquitous and largely unflattering sweater-top tracksuit. Try it and see.

IN HEALTH

Pear/Aries has generally good health with rapid powers of recuperation. What ailments she has will probably centre on the head, the traditional part of the body ruled by Aries. Headaches when stress levels get too great – driving, combative Mars is the ruling planet of this star sign – sinusitis and hay fever are typical problems. Digestive upsets are also a possiblity for this type. She should learn how to slow down, meditate, allow time for herself. But apart from the occasional accident due to her impetuousity, this combination is seldom in the doctor's surgery.

Among all the four body types, Pears are the luckiest in a few respects. They may not have the lean hips and thighs of a born athlete, but there is overwhelming scientific evidence that their shape, dominated by its female hormones, protects them from the masculine diseases of heart attacks and diabetes. A further advantage for the Pear and Hourglass shapes has been highlighted by recent research in Denmark (see Introduction). This showed that hippy shapes with marked waists, what is called the 'gynoid' pattern of weight distribution, are more likely to conceive than

the Rectangle and Triangle shapes, whose hips are closer in measurement to their waists.

In order to stay healthy generally, it is necessary to take some consideration of diet and exercise. In her research for her book *The Body Breakthrough*, Bel found that each body type has a metabolism which is unique to their type, and different from the other three types. Her team of volunteers tested diets and exercise plans tailormade for their body types, and the results, together with a four-week diet and exercise plan for each body type, were published in the above mentioned book. For more specific information on diet and exercise see In Health on page 29. However, as far as exercise goes, with a Pear/Aries some of the information on page 29 might need a little revision. Here we have a very competitive, extreme Yang overlay, and although you are unlikely to find your Pear/Aries woman heading the scrum in a women's rugby match, you may well find her playing a mean game of tennis. Aries like to win and are unlikely to relinquish all their competitive spirit and claim that playing the game matters more.

CELEBRITY PEAR/ARIES

Hayley Mills is an actress who embodies both the qualities of this body star-sign. She has narrow, delicate shoulders, is soft-looking and classically womanly and yet, particularly as a child actress, has the puppy-like energy and enthusiasm of her Aries sign.

Fire sign women have a straightforwardness that makes them seem more jolly good sorts or one of the boys, able to drink, ride and swear with the best of them. With Hayley, this straight-talking side is modified by the personality which her extreme Yin body shape brings to bear, so she is more of a subtle mix, happier to play wife and mother, less of a good fella.

PEAR/ARIES PROFILE

Mary is a forty-year-old client of Bel's. She is a Pear/Aries who gives the impression of being very gentle, motherly, nurturing and low-key, but it became clear that she could be pretty tough when she had to be. She outfaced the social services department where she worked when she wanted to go back to half-time working arrangements after having her two youngest children. 'They wanted to give me the days which were the busiest in the department (which would have meant in effect working full-time for part-time pay and perks) and I had asked to work the days which fitted in with my arrangements. At first I was hurt at being taken for a ride, but then I thought No, this matters to me. I work well and will be very reliable and fair in my treatment of them, the least I need is fair treatment in return. I was suddenly quite prepared to take them to arbitration if I had to'.

Mary said she needed to work, for financial as well as personal reasons, but she could only contemplate leaving her children on a part-time basis and even so found it terribly hard to leave her baby: 'I had to drag myself away from her. I felt awful going and thought about her all the time. To make myself feel a bit better I looked for someone who would be really loving to her, a real mother-substitute and not just a child-minder. I cared more that she was happy than that I wasn't threatened in my position as mum.'

Her dress sense was interesting and showed all the confusion one would expect given the mixed messages of her body shape and star sign. She wore soft gathered skirts and culottes, some in floral prints and good colours for her colouring BUT all her blouses, jackets and cardigans were straight in their lines, imparting a uniform-like rigidity and completely hiding her waist and the delicacy of her shape. Wearing clothes which contradicted her own body lines and appeared to be wearing her instead of vice versa, reduced Mary's appearance to a shapeless blur rather than enhancing her best points. But having seen the difference that a belt made, or the right curvy jacket, she felt some of her old confidence return.

Mary is a real Pear personality in that she enjoys the sensuality of clothes, the fun of experimenting and combining outfits, but she also has the more practical, impatient Aries side, a side which also loves novelty of any kind and gets bored with always having to make do with the same old things.

IN HOPE

Pear/Aries can be a confusion of energies, ambitions and messages which drives everyone, including herself, up the wall. But she has the potential to be a wonderfully well-rounded character with the sensitivity, quick feeling and awareness of others conferred by her body shape allied to the energy, spontaneity and sheer drive of her star sign.

PEAR
TAURUS
(Yin+/Yin)

MOTTO:
Rome was not built in a day

IN LIFE:

Here we have someone who is practical, affectionate, utterly reliable and earthily sexual. The Pear/Taurus is likely to be a super cook, a capable gardener, a brilliant mother AND great in bed. In all these nurturing areas, both body shape and star sign are in harmony and the Pear/Taurus woman is seen as God's gift to man by the more conventional Yang kind of bloke who wants a feminine, sexy woman to take care of the relational areas of life while he gets on with conquering the world. Comfort, security and stability really matter here, and there are many men who appreciate just that.

Taureans have a legendary love of music and are meant to have beautiful singing voices – we have not been able to conduct an extensive survey on this but certainly most of the Taureans we know sing, and they at least think their voices wonderful. Art, too, especially the kind you can feel and touch – like good furniture, paintings, carpets and sculpture – has its attractions for the traditional Pear/Taurus. And traditional is right; you are unlikely to find anything too modern, uncomfortable, or whimsical in a Taurus home.

There is also another less cosy side to Taurus. As an Earth sign, she also has a will to power – nothing too obvious, like Leo's drive for fame and queenship, nothing too passionate like Scorpio's, but a need nevertheless to be in control and to have things done her way. And kind and charming as she is, sensitive also to other people's feelings, it is very hard to get her to change her mind.

This need for power is expressed in the realm of the emotions and family life. A Pear/Taurean wants to be at the emotional centre of her family or team at work. Although she is a loving, nurturing figure sometimes she is too much the nerve centre of the organization, through which every decision and process has to pass. She can be a benign dictator – quite wonderfully benign in fact, encouraging the talents and aspirations of her children/employees, working long hours to secure everyone's success and happiness. But she is bad at delegating, too quick to know what's going on, too certain she is right, with too much influence over what others do and think. The trouble is that she is remarkably competent and is better at most things/more often right about most things – but she would be even cleverer if she allowed a little more autonomy to others and relaxed a bit more herself.

Pear/Taurus is highly sensual. Although she has great self-control, her love of food, her affectionate physical nature, her tactile response to people and things – she likes touching and stroking – is evident once you know her better. Practical and matter-of-fact, she needs to see things and touch them to know they are real. She can sometimes be too earthbound – romance and fantasy isn't a top priority in her life – and more imaginative types will find her materialist attitude to life leaves something to be desired. When her true love compares her to a summer's day, she is more likely to think of the reality of rained-off picnics and mud underfoot than of cloudless skies and the darling buds of May.

Loving and loyal, she is rooted in the good things of the earth, and bases her philosophy of life on what she would call the common-sense view. She is good to others and they will be good to her. She believes that the world will reflect back what she gives out to the world. She is courageous and strong-minded, but would never choose to be a loner. Although she is better equipped than many Pear types to be self-sufficient if she has to, naturally she needs to love and be loved and values the affection of her friends and family.

IN WORK

The Pear/Taurus is not afraid of work. She has great endurance and can work solidly and consistently at whatever task she sets her mind to. She is good at recognizing the qualities of others and encouraging and promoting them, but a strange loss of faith overcomes her when faced with the need to do the same for herself. The Pear/Taurus can stay far too long in one job where she holds the whole edifice together, controls everything in her

quiet, efficient way – but does not ask for, and barely receives, any real recognition for her achievement. This can make her resentful as she sees less able but more pushy and light-hearted people leap-frogging over her in the career structure.

This inability to push herself forward makes the Pear/Taurus woman remain too often in a supportive role to a boss who is half as bright and four times less diligent. This woman can excel at anything that demands intelligence, attention to detail, determination and loyalty and although she may well stay in a subservient position for what other star signs consider to be far too long, her ability to endure can have its rewards. Having bided her time she may suddenly find there is a palace coup and she is the right person in the right place at the right time – and at last her latent power can be exercised. She has a perfectionist side which can make her nit-picking and impatient with those who don't think or approach their work in the same way as her. She has to fight her tendency to feel she is always right.

Her Pear body shape makes her a sympathetic, intuitive, feeling person who will do anything for those in pain or need, with a real ability to understand others: the Taurus element adds tenacity and strength of mind and a solid, down-to-earth rootedness which means the Pear/Taurean is a tower of strength in caring professions, like nursing and therapy. She can walk the difficult tightrope between feeling genuine compassion and becoming too subjectively involved.

Pear/Taurus would also make an excellent teacher. Intelligent, strong-minded, yet sympathetic to the problems that other people may suffer in trying to learn, she would be particularly gifted with children with special needs. She is a fine mixture of soft heart and strong will, which all children respect and respond to well.

Pear types often find it very hard to promote themselves or their work aggressively and are better doing that for others. Hence their success in careers as editors in publishing, or as art or literary agents. With her talent for business, Pear/Taurus would also make a good go of running an art or craft gallery. Commerce is always attractive to the hard-working, diligent Taurus who enjoys making money and turning it into solid possessions, but the influence of this combination's body shape means that the really arid, competitive field of high finance is not a fertile field for the Pear/Taurus.

Music is a great love and talent which can be turned into a career. Pear/Taurus might find that she wants to work in a professional orchestra or choir. She is a great team player and enjoys being part of a group of people. Because she is not a great egoist, it would be harder for her to be a soloist, unless she is pushed or promoted by a mentor who is more hard-headed and ambitious than she naturally is.

Ideal Fantasy Job

A child care guru like Penelope Leach. (This is a fertile area for Taureans, both Dr Spock and Dr Hugh Jolly were born under this affectionate but dogmatic sign.) Pear/Taurus is certainly opinionated (in the nicest possible way!) and once she has some babies of her own she is nowhere more opinionated than over how best to bring up children. She has a very good practical yet intuitive approach to most things, and is a naturally good and loving mother: so what better job than sharing some of her insights with other less naturally gifted and generally more confused parents?

IN LOVE

The Pear/Taurus excels at love. Amorous, sensual rather than ecstatic, this combination of body shape and star sign makes for a woman who is unlikely to complain of a headache at bedtime. She loves the whole seduction routine, the delicious meal, the candlelight, the kisses and stroking, the uncurling by the fire – Taureans are very tactile people and if their loved ones are not available for a cuddle they will be cuddling their pets, or teddies. The Pear/Taurus likes a Yang man who will take charge sexually.

The only thing which can deflect her from her sensual life is if she succumbs to her other weakness and becomes too much the weary – and dreary – workaholic. It is important for this woman not to deny herself the essential nourishment of cooking, caring for her loved ones, fresh air, music and gardens.

And most important, perhaps, for her emotional and spiritual wellbeing is her creation of a family. We have found that Pear- and Hourglass-type women tend to reach puberty earlier than their Rectangle and Triangle friends and thoughts of settling down and having children begin to rear in their minds sooner. Taurus adds a more practical, materialistic attitude, however, which makes it unlikely that Pear/Taureans will be child brides, but they are likely to have found themselves their mate and begun to make their nest before their thirties.

As a mother, this combination really comes into its own. Loving, patient, practical, the Pear/Taurus will be very tempted to stay at home and look after her babies, particularly when they are young. Only financial hardship will drive her out of the home.

If she has the security she craves then her family and house will be buzzing with happy industry.

This is basically a traditional woman who needs a traditional type man – with a big chest to lean on occasionally and broad shoulders to support the family and household. She will stand beside him, earn money if and when she needs to, keep him well-fed, sympathetically supported and happy in bed. She will go back to work when the children no longer need her full-time, but in the meantime they come first, and she will make the most of her time with them.

Ideal Lover

Someone really Yang for this double Yin woman, grisled Sean Connery or burly Gerard Depardieu, both men whose testosterone runs a bit wild and who like their women womanly – preferably in their bed when not in the kitchen. Depardieu is on the face of it an unlikely sex symbol, big, bear-like, overweight, tatooed and an ex-jailbird, but he is an unpretentious man and best of all for a Pear/Taurus, he loves gardening. In his case, tending his vineyard...and drinking the results. The perfect man for her!

IN STYLE

Pear-shape women have an inherent delight in clothes and jewellery, they like the sensuality of cloth, the pleasures of colour and enjoy the creative experimentation involved in putting various garments and accessories together. Taureans, however, often finds this sort of imaginative thought and experimentation a bit of a bore. Their sense of style is quite decided; they dress well, in good quality clothes and are at their best with an understated, elegant look. If they keep it simple, like Candice Bergen or Audrey Hepburn, they can rank among the best-dressed women in the world.

BUT, boy, can they go off the rails when they strike out and try to be adventurous in their dressing. A classic example of a Taurean woman who frequently goes over the top and can look amazingly tacky is Cher (a Triangle/Taurus).

So you see, by combining the natural flair of the Pear with the interest in good quality and a strong sense of style of the Taurus, we have probably the most stylish Taurean here, with a good instinct for colour and clothes which makes her unlikely to stumble into any style pitfalls.

Before buying new clothes, however, it is useful to know a few style pointers which help Pear/Taurus make the right decisions, and so end up with a wardrobe where everything suits her, most things go with other things, and there are no expensive – or even cheap – mistakes. We don't all share the same body shape and an outfit that looks fantastic on one person can look dreadful on somebody else. This is not just a matter of slenderness. Wearing clothes which suit her body shape, rather than hiding her good points and drawing attention to her bad, can make Pear/Taurus look positively slimmer and more attractive and authoritative. For more specific information, see In Style on page 28.

Style Treat

Good quality accessories really are important and if money is short then by buying a really beautiful pair of shoes, scarf or handbag, it lifts not only one's spirits but the general stylishness of one's whole outfit. Pear/Taurus could think about buying herself a really good leather or suede bag. She should choose carefully.

For her shape she shouldn't go for anything too hard and angular – those big square bags in patent crocodile are much too hard-edged and aggressive for her looks and style. She should keep the lines soft – she may be drawn to suede for this reason – and go for quality. Pear/Taurus will probably want a versatile bag which she can take virtually anywhere, one which will go with most things. It is best, therefore, to stick with the neutral colours, like black, brown, navy, taupe, pewter or grey. It need not cost a bomb, but if she finds one which she really likes she should not be afraid of spending more than she would normally. It will be a great investment which upgrades her whole look.

If she uses a briefcase for work, then she shouldn't use a handbag as well because it makes her look too cluttered and unprofessional. Pear/Taurus should choose a briefcase in a soft leather, rather than a hard boxy one.

IN HEALTH

The traditional areas of physical weakness for Taureans are their throat and glands. As a result of their inability to let things go, they are also prone to constipation and back problems. They are often dragging the whole of their pasts with them, as a great stone ball attached to their ankles. Encouraging her spiritual life, whether through conventional religions or through art and music and meditation, can be a liberating experience for the often burdened Pear/Taurus.

Among all the four body types, Pears are the luckiest in a few respects. They may not have the lean hips and thighs of a born

athlete, but there is overwhelming scientific evidence that their shape, dominated by its female hormones, protects them from the masculine diseases of heart attacks and diabetes. A further advantage for the Pear and Hourglass shapes is that they are more likely to conceive than the Rectangle and Triangle shapes (see Introduction).

In order to stay healthy generally, it is necessary to take some consideration of diet and exercise. In her research for her book *The Body Breakthrough*, Bel found that each body type has a metabolism which is unique to their type, and different from the other three types. Her team of volunteers tested diets and exercise plans tailormade for their body types, and the results, together with a four-week diet and exercise plan for each body type, were published in the above mentioned book. For more specific information on diet and exercise, see In Health on page 29.

CELEBRITY PEAR/TAURUS

Candice Bergen is a Pear/Taurus who shows much of the characteristic qualities of this combination. She looks at her best in simple, fluid, uncluttered clothes. She has a definite feeling of softness and gentleness, even in her famous American TV role as Ms Murphy Brown where she plays a dynamic career woman with a baby.

In her personal life she values her family life highly, is a great cook, and is married to the French film director Louis Malle. After he had his recent open heart operation, she realized just where her priorities lay. Although she had won three Emmys for her part in this series, she has asked the producers to cut down the importance of the character of Murphy Brown and build up other characters so that she is not needed so consistently for filming and can spend more time with her husband of thirteen years and their seven-year-old daughter.

In the cutthroat competitiveness of Hollywood, the caring, unselfish man or woman, ready to give up her own shots at fame to be with a loved one is considered either a saint or mad. Candice is a rarity in this profession for being so down-to-earth, kind and thoroughly grown-up. So thoroughly Pear/Taurus in fact.

PEAR/TAURUS PROFILE

Maria is a Pear/Taurus who is maternal and capable in her approach to everyone and everything. She genuinely cares for people and will listen to their troubles and has a great deal of natural insight and tolerance. But she is not sentimental and with a practical streak wants to see some tangible movement and progress. Above all she enjoys the pleasures of intellectual conversation, is radical and individual and interested in everything from politics to quantum physics to art, music and literature. She has attracted a loose and wide-ranging group of friends and is the organizer and inspiration of an informal salon. 'I like nothing better than to have a group of people round my table all talking animatedly. I love to think that I have brought them together and somehow provided the soil out of which something interesting and satisfying can grow'.

Her talent for giving informal dinner parties which embrace a range of people of every age and background, old friends and those she is as yet barely acquainted with, verges on genius. Everyone in her compass feels loved and cared for, and somehow special. The elegant and always delicious meals she produces from a tiny kitchen unite people around her table. 'I do prefer to give parties rather than to go to them. I suppose then they are in my hands and can be as I want them to be. I lie in bed after everyone has gone home and I feel that I have created something as creative as a play or poem. I feel powerful and happy then.' In this way the Taurus need for power, her love of good things, food and company finds expression in the most benign way.

IN HOPE

The Pear/Taurus woman has so many good qualities and is so naturally the best friend, the reliable worker and the good wife and mother, it would be a pity if she allowed her strong sense of duty, her protective impulses and her natural endurance of hardship and hard work to overburden her spirit. She must not forget that doing things just for the fun of it is also necessary and valuable. Her spiritual nature can also be too readily forgotten in the everyday demands of the physical and material world. Working out some scheme for exploration, and time that is just for her, away from the daily round, might re-energize a tired spirit.

> 'Gather ye rosebuds while ye may,
> Old Time is still a-flying,
> And this same flower that smiles today
> Tomorrow will be a-dying.'

PEAR
GEMINI

(Yin+/Yang)

MOTTO:

If you can't ride two horses at once, you shouldn't be in the circus

IN LIFE

My, oh my, we have a zany one here. The deeply feeling and intuitive disposition bestowed on the Pear/Gemini by her body shape is shaken up and stirred by that monkey-puzzle of a star sign. Gemini is always noticeable; ruled by Mercury, the messenger of the gods, she is an arch communicator – chatting away, endlessly curious, her thoughts flitting over a wide range of interests. Gemini is often accused of superficiality because of her vast array of general knowledge, which she easily displays, but sometimes with a lack of any real depth, or understanding. As an air sign there is also an emotional coolness associated with this sign. There is a cerebral detachment which can be hurtful to more sensitive or feeling souls. But this is often a protective shield for a character who is so uncertain in the emotional arena that she cannot risk being dragged in to the unknown by the feelings of others.

This is where the conflicts in this fascinating combination begin. The Yin+ side of this equation makes her an emotionally sensitive being for whom relationships matter above all. So with the Pear/Gemini it is her Pear-type deeper feelings which threaten the light, detached Gemini side. This can make for a marked split in her life: she may operate at work in a cool, intellectual way and then allow her emotions their full expression at home, or in her interests and hobbies.

Or it could be that the pattern of her whole life splits into two. Gemini is a sign which is traditionally identified with the young, it is the third sign of the zodiac and is ruled by the eternally youthful Mercury. The Pear/Gemini may well find that in her youth she is cool and detached, curious about everything, not settling easily to solid work or committed relationships, enjoying talk, travel and lots of laughs. Like the eternal child, she remains distinctly self-centred and not very aware of the needs or feelings of others.

Then as she grows up, her strong feeling nature starts to make itself felt. She wants to spend more time in really *understanding* subjects or people. She no longer needs to flit from one thing to the next. She discovers how much she enjoys listening as well as talking, and how important people and relationships are in her life.

There will, however, always be a problem integrating these two elements. Sometimes she will retreat into her cerebral self, and seem cut off from the feeling side of life, quite cool – at times even ruthless – but it is in an attempt to protect herself from the emotional centre which threatens to overwhelm her. When Pear/Gemini is in one of these detached Geminian phases, she can suddenly be surprised and overwhelmed by the force of her feelings when they are activated by some tragedy among her friends or family, or by falling passionately in love, or perhaps by childbirth and the making of her own family.

She is lighthearted and sociable and a delight in any social situation. Pear/Gemini combines the communicative fluency of her star sign with the intuitive sympathy and affection for others that comes with her body type. Friends and family matter to her, and at work or at play she is happier making human connections rather than being hell-bent on winning and flattening the opposition.

Ideas and the intellectual life fascinate her, but she is more realistic and humane in her application of theories to life. Pear/Gemini will never be an idealogue who imposes systems on people and situations, quite oblivious or dismissive of the human costs. She can get carried away verbally, arguing for her point of view, even against enormous odds. But she can just as sincerely argue for the opposing view the next night. She is adaptable, amusing, and never as dogmatic as she seems. She is always open to persuasion.

Pear/Gemini has great nervous energy and this combination of opposites, the feeling and thinking, in one character can cause extra stress and strain. It helps if she recognizes these two elements and gives enough space and voice to each side of her nature.

IN WORK

Here Pear/Gemini displays some of her temperamental duality. Variety, communication, no routine please, chatters the Yang Gemini in this combination; something worthwhile, meaningful and closely involved with people, murmurs the Yin+ body shape. Insensitivity and restlessness are going to be less of a problem for this Gemini combination and she is likely to be a great success in any work involving verbal teamwork with others. Something in the communications industries immediately springs to mind. For instance, Pear/Gemini would be very happy and would do well working in a creative team on a magazine or newspaper. Journalism, PR, advertising – as long as it was not too individually competitive and cut-throat – are all people businesses where flair, ideas and empathy with others are crucial qualities.

The Yin+ body shape in this combination gives the bright and breezy Gemini some much needed emotional ballast – it allows her to empathize with other people, to synthesize the ideas and energies of the whole team, without being just self-centredly driving on her own. The Pear/Gemini may find herself drawn into the caring professions, but more in the communicative, talking area – like therapy – than the practical hands-on experience of dealing with the muck and tears.

With all that emphasis on quicksilver thinking and clever talk, the law – particularly the Bar – has always been a traditional career for Gemini people.

But this area can be tough, competitive and unfeeling and so less of a happy place for the Pear/Gemini and rather more suited to the Rectangle/ or Triangle/Gemini woman. The Pear/Gemini is better with work which does not demand such single-minded drive that her personal life comes a poor second. Being a solicitor, perhaps, or a legal advisor, where her personal skills, as well as her intellectual abilites, are also brought to the fore would suit her well.

The Pear/Gemini has great social skills and can manage to suss out and respond in the right way to each person that she meets and with whom she has to deal. The Yin+ body shape gives her great powers of sympathy and intuition and the Yang of her Gemini star sign brings an outgoing nature and enormous pleasure in parties and meetings where conversation holds sway. The Pear/Gemini could have the makings of a terrific hostess – welcoming, charming, intelligent, witty, always with a deep sense of sympathy and feeling for others.

Ideal Fantasy Job

Roving Ambassador for the United Nations. There would be lots of travel, loads of variety and the Pear/Gemini's undoubted negotiating skills, and her gift with people, would be utilized to the full. The caring side of this combination could also be expressed, as she negotiates for more aid or peace initiatives across the world – but she would have to be at one stage removed from the too distressing daily round of poverty and disease.

IN LOVE

What a difficult woman to categorize and what a difficult one to please. Her dual nature can cause the most trouble to a Pear/Gemini in the realm of the heart. She sometimes cannot work out whether she's the coolest customer in the world, who would rather keep herself protected from that dark abyss of feeling, or whether she's heart and passion personified, only needing to find the man of her dreams to give up all this toil in the commercial world. She can swing between swearing celibacy is best and planning to settle down in a cottage with a large-chested man, to grow flowers, write poetry and make jam. And while she is trying to work out whether she's Ms Cool or Ms Uncool, Pear/Gemini can try out some pretty odd fellows along the way.

When it comes to the important decisions about love and family, the Pear/Gemini must never forget that her Yin+ body shape makes her at base a feeling, emotional woman. Her energies will be expressed all over the place, especially when she is young, but at heart she is drawn towards making a home, being a mother and – when the time is right – she will find that she focuses much of her creative energy on that goal. This does not mean to say that when she has children she will be happy to be at home full-time. Her need for change and variety will never go away, but may be sublimated during her children's early years.

She will be an amusing, energetic, affectionate mother who will never become too emotionally demanding or cloying with her man or their children. In marriage, she is in need of some space for herself, and cannot bear having too many emotional demands being made on her and being leant upon too heavily and for too long. She will want to suddenly toss her mane and head for the hills, if not in reality then in spirit at least.

But the Yin+ side of this combination means she is likely to wish to be the main carer for her children, probably feeling that

no one else (apart perhaps from closest family) will ever extend the sympathy and quality of care to them that she would herself. Although she may well work part-time and leave her children for short periods in the care of others, it is probable that she will find it very hard to go back to full-time work with the old verve. Something very profound will have happened to her emotions.

Ideal Lover

This combination likes to laugh and so a witty, bright kind of man would seem in order. But he also has to be a Yang kind of guy for it is the basic character of one's body shape which tends to categorize the kind of men who turn us on. The Pear/Gemini has a Yang star sign but a Yin+ body shape and when it comes to sex appeal she is much more likely to go for her opposite. So hunky, but witty and amusing – how about Harrison Ford? Particularly in *The Mosquito Coast* where he wears gold-rimmed glasses, sweat and stubble and looks intellectual and manly. She could have terrific conversations with him in between the mad cap schemes and the passionate tumbles.

IN STYLE

This woman will have a wardrobe full of clothes, to suit her multifarious character and moods. Pear types tend to love clothes and experiment with various garments and accessories – they really like shopping and so naturally accumulate a range of clothes, frills and furbelows. Ally this characteristic to the Gemini's curiosity, and her love of change and need for variety, and you have wardrobes bursting with stuff.

The Pear/Gemini woman is able to swing from looking utterly unaware of her appearance one day to being transformed into the most glamorous, interestingly-dressed woman the next. You will never be sure how you will find her when you drop by for coffee – she may be slopping around in some old jersey the cat has been wearing and pyjama bottoms she's burnt holes in with an experiment with bleach, or she may be dressed up to the nines in a snakeskin print silk body with a wrap skirt and silver Navajo belt. She is always full of surprises.

Before buying any more clothes, however, it is useful to know a few style pointers which help Pear/Gemini make the right decisions, and so end up with a wardrobe where everything suits her, most things go with other things, and there are no expensive – or even cheap – mistakes. We don't all share the same body

shape and an outfit that looks fantastic on one person can look dreadful on somebody else. This is not just a matter of slenderness. Wearing clothes which suit her body shape, rather than hiding her good points and drawing attention to her bad, can make Pear/Gemini look positively slimmer and more attractive and authoritative. For more specific information, see In Style on page 28.

Style Treat

Pear/Gemini has a quirky individuality about her clothes and likes expressing herself through them. She should buy herself the hat of her dreams – AND WEAR IT! It can be anything from the most modest little cloche hat to a theatrical artist's beret.

Whatever her choice, she should make sure the style is not too mannish or severe. Any kind of headgear for her body type should be soft and feminine. So if she chooses a more masculine style, like a top hat, then the fabric and dressing of it has to be softer such as velvet with a curly brim and netting round the crown.

IN HEALTH

Traditionally, the Gemini personality is meant to be prone to respiratory problems. Smoking is obviously an even worse idea for this type than for most. She really needs to make sure that she gets plenty of fresh air, preferably on leisurely country walks. The beauty of nature calms the Pear/Gemini down and reminds her that things continue to change and evolve even when she's not doing anything about it.

Nerviness is another traditional weakness of this sign and although the Yin+ body type makes for a less frantic, flitting personality, it also means she is more sensitive to atmosphere and feelings than she may think. A Pear/Gemini can become very overwrought when work or her emotional life goes wrong. She can easily go off the emotional rails and become quite unbalanced for a while. She needs calm, strong friends and a stable secure environment. Walking, meditation, or any other activity which draws her forces back into herself, restoring her own energies, is very necessary in her busy life.

The Pear/Gemini woman can be as extreme about food, diet and exercise as she is about everything else. Often not too bothered with food (this is not the most sensual of signs), she will more often than not pick at yogurt, cheese and any leftovers standing at the fridge. This means she does not necessarily get enough of the good things, and is probably drinking too much

coffee – and smoking too. She may then decide to do something about her weight/health and go on a killer regime where she is only eating grapefruits and is attempting to force herself into becoming a marathon runner.

It is no wonder that these plans, usually dreamed up by her cerebral side on the spur of the moment – and taking no account of her feeling, feminine side at all – founders after the first week. For a start, Geminis hate routine and although they can be obsessive are not very good at grinding discipline. The fact that Pear-shaped women are not overly keen on organized exercise, also means any cranky, over-the-top exercise regime is even more likely to fall at the first fence.

Among all the four body types, Pears are the luckiest in a few respects. They may not have the lean hips and thighs of a born athlete, but there is overwhelming scientific evidence that their shape, dominated by its female hormones, protects them from the masculine diseases of heart attacks and diabetes. A further advantage for the Pear and Hourglass shapes is that they are more likely to conceive than the Rectangle and Triangle shapes (see Introduction).

In order to stay healthy generally, it is necessary to take some consideration of diet and exercise. In her research for her book *The Body Breakthrough*, Bel found that each body type has a metabolism which is unique to their type, and different from the other three types. Her team of volunteers tested diets and exercise plans tailormade for their body types, and the results, together with a four-week diet and exercise plan for each body type, were published in the above mentioned book. For more specific information on diet and exercise, see In Health on page 29.

CELEBRITY PROFILE

Isadora Duncan was an American dancer who lived from 1878 until her tragic and bizarre death when her scarf got entangled in the wheels of a car in Nice and killed her when she was only forty-nine. She was a Pear/Gemini and exhibited many of that combination's qualities. She was thrilled by ideas but basically had an emotional approach to her dancing and to life which gave her an enormous charismatic appeal and influence.

She was the pioneer of free dance, as opposed to the classical ballet: she developed a simple system of movement 'springing from the soul'. The magic and sincerity of this, the free sensuality of her dancing, the generosity of her character, captured the imagination of Europe.

Isadora believed that through noble movement people could lead better lives. Her passionate nonconformity extended into her personal life. She had many interesting men as lovers and produced babies by a few of them. She cared deeply for her children and never really recovered after a terrible accident in Paris when two of them were drowned.

She is remembered for her womanly, soft body and the sensuality, emotionality and freedom of her dancing.

PEAR/GEMINI PROFILE

Susie is an accountant in her thirties and has always known that there are two distinct sides to her nature. As a child she felt very strongly about things but chose to express her feelings more to her horse and in riding on her own than to friends or family. When she was 16, her first important relationship came to an end and she suffered a great deal over that. This caused her a lot of pain and for the next two decades she protected herself in relationships by never becoming too emotionally involved. During this part of her youth the cool, detached side, predominated.

Susie would attract men who liked her uncomplicated, toughish exterior, but then were nonplussed and alarmed when she let her guard down and showed the extreme vulnerability and emotional side of her nature. 'I was in my thirties and a relationship came to an end. He had been someone who admired my careerist side but could not deal with my emotions – a side which I also wasn't used to expressing. I felt devastated, out of all proportion really to the relationship.'

The long-neglected feeling side of her character now reared its head and Susie found she did not care any more about pursuing this all-consuming career. She had been thinking for some time that what she enjoyed most about her job was dealing with the young recruits who joined the company, teaching them, overseeing their work and listening to their problems. 'I had this great turnaround in my life. I began to find great pleasure in my women friends. Also, and most importantly, there was one man who had always remained there for me, through thick and thin. I had cried on his shoulder so many times, and always gone to him as my best friend. He'd always recognized and loved my emotional side which I felt I had protected for so long.' She realized that she *did* want to be married and have children and that she couldn't envisage life without this man.

She is now married to him and runs a consultancy business from home advising individuals and companies on their finances,

taxes and accounts. She is very keen to have children. 'I feel much calmer, more identified with my softer side. More able to be myself really. I still get highly strung and obsessional about work, but it's all in better balance. My relationships sit at the centre of my life and I'm much happier.'

IN HOPE

Those who love Pear/Gemini may sometimes hold their heads and moan. She has so many faces and no one, perhaps not even herself, ever knows which of them is going to greet the day. The husband of a Pear/Gemini wailed, 'I don't know about two faces, it feels more like 102 : I love about 99 of them but those other few – Oh, God, eech!' She has a great range of qualities and abilities, the capacity to love with imagination and compassion, the intellectual energy to explore new ideas and charm new people.

Byron was an Aquarian, an air sign like Gemini, and he realized the necessity of communicating not just words and ideas, but feelings. In his great poem *Don Juan* (who must have been a Gemini) he wrote:

'All who joy would win
Must share it, – Happiness was born a twin'

PEAR
CANCER

(Yin+/Yin+)

MOTTO:
Home is where the heart is

IN LIFE

The Pear/Cancer woman is a deeply sensitive, intuitive and mysterious being. She has a strong defence mechanism, and like the crab (the symbol of the sign), has a hoary old shell that puts off predators and protects – and without which the vulnerable little body inside would die. This self-defence can make Pear/Cancer seem remote and cool at times. It can mean that at her most weak and vulnerable, she retreats into her shell and finds it hard to emerge, admit her weakness and ask for help. This recoil from unnecessary exposure of her deepest feelings can make Pear/Cancer seem brusque and contrary when in reality she is trying to protect herself from the debilitating mood swings from elation into deep despair which characterize her sign.

She has to be careful when she is in that state of Cancerian melancholy not to cast too much of a wet blanket over the spirits of the others who work and live with her, for Pear/Cancer unhappiness turns not to rage and ranting, nor even to poetic despair, but more to a damp and chilly gloom which is hard to ignore. This can be one of the ways these complex people draw attention to themselves, by absenting themselves from the throng and withdrawing into dumb misery.

The crab metaphor seems to be a particularly appropriate one, for there is something sideways in the way that Cancerians approach issues, particularly if they are difficult or delicate matters. The Pear body shape adds another helping of Yin+ to this already over-feeling nature and makes this character even more unstraightforward in her approach. You can wound a Pear/

Cancer deeply and never know, because she is unlikely to confront you with her hurt. Much more her style is to retreat and absorb. This can have all sorts of unhappy consequences. Misunderstandings abound, moodiness is another possibility and the Pear/Cancer can make herself ill with the weight of unexpressed emotion. Tenacity, however, is a quality which you will find plenty of in a Pear/Cancer. In its positive mode this means she is loyal until the tenth of never, she may go all moody on you but she won't give up on you.

The Moon is the ruler of Cancer and people born under this sign share something of that lunar mystery, the changeability of its nature and the powerful influence on apparently unrelated forces, like the world's tides, women's reproductive cycles, and sensitive people everywhere. A prominent Moon in a horoscope is interpreted as bestowing a certain sensitivity to and success within the public eye. This influence can be seen very clearly in certain Cancerians who have an almost supernatural ability to intuit the needs and fantasies of the time, producing books, films, music and personalities which are just right. When you consider that Ingmar Bergman, Iris Murdoch, George Orwell, Emmeline Pankhurst, Proust, Ken Russell, Meryl Streep and the Princess of Wales are all Cancerians, one can see how each has become synonymous with his or her time.

The Pear/Cancer may be open to nameless fears and quirks of imagination which can constrain her in her everyday life. For instance, she is enormously emotionally attached to her home and will spend much time, creative energy and money making it just how she wants it: comfortable, usually conservatively furnished, and pretty. The idea of an intruder contaminating this sacred place, threatening the family which matters more to her than anything, can make her lie awake at night. Burglar alarms have a great appeal to the Pear/Cancer: home and safety are key words in her credo.

Allied to tenacity is possessiveness and an inability to throw things away. This character does not like to let anyone or anything go – ex-lovers, grown children, old magazines – all are clung on to, always very subtly and sometimes beyond what is sensible or sane. But when it moves into the pyschological and old wounds and feelings are chewed over and over, neither jettisoned or transformed into something new, it can be a terrible burden for the already over-burdened Pear/Cancer.

She is, however, the most feeling and generous-hearted of women. If someone is in trouble, her hypersensitive recognition of their needs is wonderfully soothing and reassuring. She longs always to relate, to make emotional connections, to heal the wounded and unhappy. This hypersensitivity to feeling and to the unconscious generally makes Pear/Cancer highly creative in her life and work. She has deep imaginative resources to call on and will express herself through music or art, or just by making her surroundings beautiful and being the best cook in her circle of friends.

IN WORK

The Pear/Cancer's genius is in understanding others and dealing with the public at large. She can seem rather remote and inscrutable, even chilly, at times, but that is only when the old crabby shell has been pulled back on to protect her sensitive self from criticism or failure. Sensitive to others, nevertheless she is capable of being focused, conscientious and as hardnosed as any business woman. Commerce and business appeal to her, she likes making money, and she can run a really successful company, especially one which relies on gauging public taste and response.

Pear/Cancer makes a gifted teacher, drawing all children to her with her kind, intuitive personality. She delights them with the depth of her understanding of her subject and the imaginative ways in which she puts ideas and feelings across. History holds a particular appeal for her because of her great interest in the past.

Artistic and hard-working, anything centred on the house, garden and home bring out the best in Pear/Cancer. She is almost invariably a good cook and her idea of bliss is to have a large table groaning with food and a crowd of family and friends sitting around, appreciating the delicious meal and basking in her hospitality. Interior decorating, restoration of houses, household management and catering are all attractive careers for this organized and talented woman.

From houses and history to antiques and books is but a short journey and there are likely to be more than a fair share of Pear/Cancers in the antiques trade and working in secondhand books and publishing. Her flair at understanding what the public wants and needs can make her astute at recognizing trends; her valuing of tradition and the past means she enjoys discovering unloved old pieces of art and furniture and bringing them back to life. The nurturing impulse of the Pear unites with Cancer's maternal qualities and produces a character who loves restoring everything.

Because a Pear/Cancer takes criticism very personally, she can be afraid of putting herself into a situation where she may be

publically criticized or made to look a fool. Combined with an almost pathological love of privacy, this means that the limelight is not her natural habitat. But her positive side is so hardworking and effective, so tuned into the feelings, thoughts and motivations of others, that she makes an excellent team worker. Because she can pick up on the general trends of fashion and ideas in the world at large she can be enormously successful where any work involving the public is concerned.

Ideal Fantasy Job

Producer of a television programme dealing with antiques would use many of these Pear/Cancer attributes. The love and enthusiasm for the past and for antique artefacts and works of art means she would never grow cynical or bored with the job. Her organizational skills and good memory are also essential assets. Then her unerring ability to sense the public's needs makes her a successful producer of any television show where she can use her intuitive ideas to come up with a winning formula.

IN LOVE

Here we have a double Yin+ personality and that spells Relationships with a capital R. Relating to others, loving others, bringing out the best in them and caring for their physical and emotional needs can all be enormously satisfying to a Pear/Cancer woman. She is all-woman in the sense of being deeply feeling, more than averagely sensual and interested in sex, passionate about her children – and anyone else's who need comfort and care – and perfectly happy to uphold the family, her husband and the whole emotional centre of home. The word HOME carries great resonance for this woman. It is the centre of her being, even if she is a single working woman living alone.

She is likely to be quite a conservative kind of woman who values the status quo and enjoys being a wife and mother. She is proud of her talents which make her such a compelling homemaker – her children's friends use her house as a home from home (sometimes a better home than home) because there is always a welcome and good food to be had. Her own friends know they can always turn to her when they need a shoulder to cry on.

A Pear/Cancer woman is very good at listening to others and sympathizing with their pleasures and griefs, but she will be more reticent about her own private life. There is a veil that protects her privacy which is rarely drawn back except in extremis. On those rare occasions, her friends who have always thought her the calmest, most well-organized and placid of people may be alarmed at the extent of a Pear/Cancer's distress when things go wrong in her personal life.

This depth of feeling and basic vulnerability means the Pear/Cancer woman is attracted to a solid, loving, protective kind of man. She needs reassurance and as a double Yin+ woman will find the Yang range of men to her liking. These are the men who will not interfere too much with her domain at home – she is not too keen on the New Man who is as adept in the kitchen as she is, and spends as much time cooing over the babies. She prefers to be queen in her castle and let him be king in his. She will certainly admire him and support him in return for his love and protection from a sometimes cruel and alarming world. Her natural business sense means that they could readily run a company together, preferably from home. As long as her partner was dynamic and entrepreneurial and needed superb, intelligent back-up and ideas from his Pear/Cancer, their business and personal success would be assured.

Ideal Fantasy Lover

Mel Gibson is the sort of all-male man who gives the impression he is made for protecting the home and his family from marauders. The Pear/Cancer will feel very safe with him around, and she will be free to get on with the rearing and caring that suits her character so well. As an important aside, a man like Mel would surely appreciate the sort of womanly sexuality which this woman emanates, even in her butcher's apron and with flour on her nose.

IN STYLE

Bel has been amazed at how many of her Pear/Cancer clients love silk next to their skin. All said luxurious silk underwear was almost an essential in their wardrobe. Even if dressed in the oldest, tattiest clothes, the knowledge that she was wearing a beautiful set of peachy silk underwear made her feel incredibly sexy. So the sensuous Yin+ Pear and the sensitive Yin+ Cancer come together in an orgy of delicious underwear. This combination of qualities produces a woman who loves clothes, likes shopping for them, running the fabric through her fingers, planning what will go with what. She may be practical and capable in most of what she does but she wants to do it in good quality, understated clothes that make her feel a million dollars. She is not bothered with designer names, status has little part in her approach to dressing.

Before buying any more clothes, however, it is useful to know a few style pointers which help Pear/Cancer make the right decisions, and so end up with a wardrobe where everything suits her, most things go with other things, and there are no expensive – or even cheap – mistakes. We don't all share the same body shape and an outfit that looks fantastic on one person can look dreadful on somebody else. This is not just a matter of slenderness. Wearing clothes which suit her body shape, rather than hiding her good points and drawing attention to her bad, can make Pear/Cancer look positively slimmer and more attractive and authoritative. For more specific information see In Style on page 28.

The Pear/Cancer's appreciation of the past means she may well have a few bits of clothing or jewellery from her Grandmother, or bought in a secondhand shop – beautiful organza blouses, an antique paisley shawl perhaps, a velvet smoking jacket, an embroidered belt. She will love not only the beauty of the garment and how well it enhances her own feminine looks, but will delight in the delicacy of the workmanship, the quality of the fabric, the uniqueness of the whole thing.

Style Treat

A particular treat for a Pear/Cancer might well be to go to an auction of old clothes and textiles and find something beautiful to wear, or something which she can convert or make up into a stunning garment. She should be careful to choose styles and fabrics that are soft and feminine and therefore more flattering for her body shape. Pear/Cancer's skills often extend to dressmaking and such a collection of wonderful clothes and materials from ages gone by will inspire her to produce something unique and beautiful.

IN HEALTH

Pear/Cancer women have a tendency to take on too much. They think they have endless emotional energy for every needy person who passes their door. They will come to anyone's aid, particularly if they are children who seem to be neglected or unhappy. They too readily identify themselves as the mother to the world and can exhaust their hearts and bodies in the process.

An old American proverb expresses the Pear/Cancer dilemma rather well: 'There is no slave out of heaven like a loving woman; and of all loving women, there is no such slave as a mother.' It is important for her health and the happiness of all those who love her that she realizes that she cannot afford to become enslaved to her sympathies and ready emotions. Pear/Cancer can be prone to stomach ulcers through worry. She also may have problems with circulation, and the whole lymph system will be extra sensitive to imbalances in the body.

But just as her powerful emotions can sometimes defeat the strength of her body, so too they can heal her from seeming hopeless and chronic conditions. Positive energy is therefore crucial for this combination.

The Pear/Cancer woman will be prone to putting on weight, largely because she is such a good cook, so interested in food and enjoys the sensuality and conviviality of eating with those she loves. She may well decide that she enjoys food too much to bother about the extra pounds which arrive with the years – and if she has a Yang male for a husband or partner he is unlikely to complain as she gets curvier.

Among all the four body types, Pears are the luckiest in a few respects. They may not have the lean hips and thighs of a born athlete, but there is overwhelming scientific evidence that their shape, dominated by its female hormones, protects them from the masculine diseases of heart attacks and diabetes. A further advantage for the Pear and Hourglass shapes is that they are more likely to conceive than the Rectangle and Triangle shapes (see Introduction).

In order to stay healthy generally, it is necessary to take some consideration of diet and exercise. In her research for her book *The Body Breakthrough*, Bel found that each body type has a metabolism which is unique to their type, and different from the other three types. Her team of volunteers tested diets and exercise plans tailormade for their body types, and the results, together with a four-week diet and exercise plan for each body type, were published in the above mentioned book. For more specific information on diet and exercise, see In Health on page 29.

CELEBRITY PEAR/CANCER

Meryl Streep immediately springs to mind as a very characteristic Pear/Cancer whose natural habitat is not the glitz, superficiality and competitiveness of Hollywood. She is an actress with enormous emotional reserves which allow her to identify profoundly with the characters she plays. Her job demands that she exposes herself as an actress, but in true Pear/Cancer fashion, she fiercely protects the privacy of her own self and her family. You would never find her giving a tell-all interview to the media, or stage-managing a stunt to promote herself.

The double Yin+ quality of this combination is so well expressed by Meryl's aura of feminity which is very different from the doubly ambitious, double Yang+ qualities of a Triangle/Aries actress like, for instance, Joan Crawford of whom it was said 'She is much given to good works once they have been glamourized, and would not step on the hands of another girl grasping at a straw – except under exceptional circumstances. Nobody with a life such as that lived by the Queen of Hollywood today would do anything different.'

Well, Meryl Streep has been the queen of Hollywood and she did do things differently. Although she could be difficult to work with it was more due to her intensity of feeling for the part, and her conscientious perfectionism, her fear of being criticized – or worse still ridiculed – which made her withdrawn and sometimes gruff. She expresses all the paradoxes of this complicated character of Pear/Cancer.

She has a powerful maternal quality which made motherhood the most important thing in her life (she had her fourth child at the age of 44 which is pretty dedicated maternalism). But it also provided her with the depth of experience which could summon the extraordinary force of grief which made her deadly choice between her children in *Sophie's Choice* almost unbearable to watch. The belief that human relationships would always matter more than her own performances meant she could take time off from her early career to nurse the actor John Casale as he died slowly of cancer.

PEAR/CANCER PROFILE

Barbara is a Pear/Cancer in her thirties. She has three children and has enjoyed the experiences of pregnancy, birth and motherhood so much that she has trained to become a National Childbirth Trust tutor. She became a brilliant teacher – highly sympathetic, intuitive and yet practical too, always aware of the needs of the mothers and babies who passed through her hands. 'In many ways I wish I'd trained as a midwife. I am fascinated by the importance of the experiences of pregnancy and birth. A woman's future feelings about herself, her body and the baby she has produced can be set up by this crucial experience'.

Barbara recognized quite early that in order to function fully in the outside world she needed to love someone and be loved herself. Without a loving relationship she felt diminished and only half alive. Yet in typical Pear/Cancer fashion she found it very hard to confide any of this to her friends or family. At her worst moments of melancholy she would disappear from view and could only be winkled out of hiding by her most persevering friends.

'I love working from home. It is the centre of my life in every sense.' Pretty, comfortable, the kitchen is always in use for children's suppers, friend's meetings, coffee and biscuits for the prospective parents who come to lessons there. Working from home, happy at home, everyone from her children through to her students always know where to find her and that there will be a welcome whenever they drop by.

Occasionally, though, she is in an emotional crisis: 'I just have to withdraw into myself and close the door on the world. I know it's difficult for others to deal with, but it's the way I am.' Barbara has gone to therapists on and off over the years to try to deal with this dark, damp cloud which spasmodically descends.

Like every Pear/Cancer, Barbara never allows anyone whom she has loved ever to leave. An ex-husband still hangs around, old boyfriends drop by on their way somewhere else, friends are there for life, the women and babies she has helped with her childbirth classes become an extended family and she will share their joys and sadnesses as if they were her own.

'There is a tragic paradox to motherhood; it requires the most intense, unselfish love on the mother's side, and yet it is the same love which must help the child grow away from the mother, to become fully independent.' And no one recognizes that better than Pear/Cancer.

IN HOPE

Cranky, caring, imaginative, possessive, the Pear/Cancer is the mother of the world and the mirror of others. She needs to find a way of conserving that well of emotional energy which she believes almost to have no end. It isn't bottomless and she risks a collapse of her physical or mental health unless she finds a way of focusing more on her own needs – and extending that legendary nurturing genius to herself. She should learn to live for the present, still her fears and let the future take care of itself:

> 'Present joys are more to flesh and blood,
> Than a dull prospect of a distant good.'

PEAR
LEO

(Yin+/Yang+)

MOTTO:

Don't hide your light under a bushel

IN LIFE

The Pear/Leo, the Yin+ body shape with the Yang+ star sign, is a whole enigmatic bundle of fun. When you have different energies, as you have in this combination, it is worth remembering that the body shape is the underlying influence, the star sign the modifier. So here we have a basically feeling, intuitive, other-orientated woman with an energetic, self-promoting, outgoing overlay.

The best result is a confident, wonderfully warm-hearted, people-person who inspires everyone with her love of life and her understanding of others. She will be less headstrong than the average Leo, more able to see the consequences of her actions and therefore less likely to get herself into sticky corners which she has to back out of in an ungainly way – hurting her Leonine pride in the process. She is capable of achieving much, but in a less trumpetted, flashy way than the other other Leo body types. She is also less of a laugh, less reckless, less transparent and more discreet in her ways.

But there is a more negative side of the Pear/Leo which she has to watch out for and put in its place. The secret which the Leo is so good at hiding, even from herself, is that she isn't so brash and confident and secure as she likes to make out. She can be a terrific showman and part of her show is herself as this irresistible life force – after all isn't the sun her ruler, and the king of the jungle her beast? Now, when the Leo persona is mixed with the much more reflective, self-effacing and receptive Pear body shape your Pear/Leo can see too readily behind the mask of utter confidence and natural rulership with which the mighty Leo protects herself.

This can result in a loss of confidence – a hanging back just when circumstances demand a going forward in hope.

The Pear/Leo woman loves company. She naturally gravitates towards the centre of any group, she has an instinctive authority but will not be very direct in expressing it. There'll be no dancing on the tables, no impersonations of Mae West (a Triangle/Leo). This more subtle operator will draw attention with the warmth of her personality, her interest in others and her own quiet intelligence.

So many royals occupy the Leo's den, it's not surprising there are some snarls and one-upmanship. The Queen Mother (Rectangle/Leo), Princess Anne and Princess Margaret (both Hourglass/Leos) have to share their sign with that American royal, Jacqueline Kennedy Onassis and the self-proclaimed queen of heaven, Madonna (both Triangle/Leos). The Pear/Leo, however, would never want so high a profile or so much self-reflecting glory. Her warmth and charisma is a more personal and interior thing. She is happy enough to be loved and admired by her family, friends and work colleagues – she doesn't hanker after world celebrity. But she is a Leo, nevertheless, and Leos need to be centre stage, even if the stage is only her own domestic hearth, the local neighbourhood watch committee or an office of three.

How the world perceives her matters to Pear/Leo. Her Yin+ body type makes her very sensitive to the reactions and feelings of others and her Leo pride and sense of self means she wants to appear memorable and noble in status and spirit. Pear/Leo has an instinctive ability to look and behave true to the fantasy of her own personality. There is a filmstarry side to all Leos and Pear/Leo is no exception. She is aware of her audience and is skilful at projecting that image of warmth, intelligence, style, classiness – a combination of her best qualities, those she wants displayed to the admiring crowd. She is a great romantic and is herself the heroine of the fantasy.

Pear/Leo does need to be appreciated. A few highly flattering remarks work wonders (you can't overdo the hyperbole as far as she's concerned), she loves glamorous presents and is most appreciative of any special treats like racing at Ascot or centre court men's final at Wimbledon. If it's glamorous, classy and sought after then nothing is too corny for this youthful and enthusiastic soul.

Whatever her circumstances, Pear/Leo is blessed with a basically positive attitude to life, a generous heart and an idealistic but at times naive spirit. The Pear/Leo character does not bear anyone malice and cannot understand the malice in others. This

means that there are times when she is shocked or disillusioned by the pettiness of those who envy her or bear the world a grudge. But it is worth remembering that ancient saying that the greatest are those who do not lose their childlike heart, that thinking the best of people brings out the best.

IN WORK

Any Leo feels the world is her oyster (most of the time). The Pear/Leo is slightly less inflated but more able to read the reactions of others and fit her ambitions into the scheme of things – for she is less wrapped in her own ego. This robs her of some of that Leonine blind optimism, but it also provides her with the realism to assess her own abilities and focus fully on what she wants to do and how best to do it.

Fame is a snare for Leos generally, sometimes deflecting them from contemplating the substance of what they should be doing. The longing for fame is less likely to get in the way of the Pear/Leo's true interests, and rather than seek it she may find it comes to her, with all its mixed blessings. So Pear/Leo will find herself, perhaps unwittingly, somewhere centre stage, although not necessarily in the limelight. She would be marvellous in many professions. In the business world she would work well in any area where client contact is important. She is unlikely to flourish in a solitary position where she meets no one during the day, but called upon to give presentations, to synthesize ideas and write policy reports, to deal with personnel: in all these the Pear/Leo will flourish.

Despite her need for company, the Pear/Leo woman makes a good writer – more in the fields of human interest journalism, biography and fiction perhaps than comedy scripts or technical analysis. She cannot manage happily to be alone for days on end, but will work among her family and take breaks when she will go shopping or sit chatting in some nice brasserie with friends. This combination does not produce the self-denying ascetic. Life is predominantly for living in the Pear/Leo's book.

Pear/Leo has a large and generous heart and the hardships of others will move her to tears, but she is not at her best dealing one to one with the really desperate and down and out. The Pear part of this equation makes her take everyone's suffering far too personally and empathically so that the whole world seems to be full of wounded and dying people. The Leo part feels too acutely her own impotence in allaying the misery of others, and powerlessness is not a feeling that any Leo can come to terms with.

Pear/Leo may have idealistic plans for a better world, but she is happier at one remove, planning the political campaign, organizing the aid, publicizing the plight. She can bring her moral energy to bear on other people and situations and is able to use her personal charm and persuasion to change attitudes and influence leaders. She is not likely to be single-minded and tough enough to grab the leadership herself.

The law (and probably laying down the law too) is a traditional Leonine occupation. There is something in this sign which values the great national traditions and likes to uphold the structures of civilization. Pear/Leo likes to belong to the Establishment. She also enjoys the flamboyant dressing-up still involved in various activities. A barrister's wig and robes would appeal to her theatrical side, although she would not find dealing with the masculine prejudices in that profession quite so much fun. Instead, she is more likely to end up with her own solicitor's practice, or running a legal advice bureau. People matter first and her happiness is not something Pear/Leo willingly sacrifices for material success.

Pear/Leo's artistic side needs a practical outlet and she may well find this in gardening – but on quite a grand scale. Gazebos and pergolas hung with wisteria, for instance, combines the Pear/Leo's love of the romantic with the grand. Or how about making and decorating wonderful cakes, exploring new ways of using paint on walls to give luxurious finishes, or making jewellery out of real gold and semi-precious stones? Everything she does has to have a sense of style and luxury about it – and draw a little attention at the same time. Even a Pear/Leo likes to create a bit of a stir, a ripple of applause.

Ideal Fantasy Job

Successful novelist – Pear/Leo has a snobbish side and she is unlikely to want to be a tacky bestselling novelist in the bonkbuster mode. But a great novel that wins an award and sells a few hundred thousand copies to discriminating souls would do very nicely. As a more discreet Leo than most, Pear/Leo would just like the esteem of her peers and bothers less with the adoration of the crowd.

IN LOVE

The Pear/Leo woman is first of all a Yin+ female, and this means relationships are the most important things in her life – relationships with her family, her friends, her lover or husband – and

most of all with her children. She has a great capacity for feeling, for nurturing and compassion, all intensified by the warm fire of her star sign. As a Yin+ woman she will be attracted most readily to the Yang end of the male spectrum; Richard Gere rather than Daniel Day Lewis, Paul Newman rather than Jeremy Irons.

The Yang male may not be terribly good on the empathy and nurturing side of human life – except when he has to – but he is decisive, straightforward and active, and he makes the running in any sexual affair. The Pear-shape woman is not naturally a pursuer, she prefers to be pursued. The Pear/Leo has the added quality of needing to be respected. Leos are insistent on this. Never forget that she is basically a queen, even if it's only in her backyard, and she does not like to be taken for granted over too long a period of time – she certainly does not care for any rude or dismissive treatment from either her man or the children. So although she likes the idea of being pursued and taken by a hunk of a man – he has to do it *respectfully* which may prove quite a test!

The Pear/Leo woman might have a bit of a tussle over her conflicting desires to look after her children herself (particularly when they are young), and her more Leonine need for a wider stage than the four walls of her house, a larger audience than her family. Yin+ women quite genuinely believe there is no one who will love and care for their children in the empathic, sensitive and unselfish way that they can – and they are probably right. This causes them a great deal of grief when they attempt to fulfill the other side of themselves which demands some work or life away from the home, and some sort of handing over of the daily care of the children to another. A Pear/Leo woman would be perfectly happy if it is her partner (as long as he is imaginative, caring and *gentle* towards them), mother or sister taking over the child care, but she would worry herself sick over less trustworthy and intimately connected people.

Working from home, however unsatisfactory and fragmented, or a part-time job may be the best compromise for the first years for a worried Pear/Leo mother. Being a full-time mother and expressing all her energy and warm-heartedness and creativity with her children may be the other path that she takes. Everything this woman does is done wholeheartedly and that is the secret of her success.

The lucky children of this mother will never doubt they are loved. They will have memories of the most marvellous parties, both for the children and their parents, and will be encouraged

early to be independent and fearless in a world that is represented to them as largely benign.

Ideal Fantasy Lover

Someone rich, someone full of energy and excitement, someone who will enhance her life with his own life force – Britain's best-known business man and billionaire, Richard Branson. As the boss of Virgin, his bitter battle over British Airways dirty tricks campaign would have warmed the cockles of a Pear/Leo's heart. Motivated by excitement and challenge, Branson could never be boring or predictable. Pear/Leo has such a rich fantasy life in which she is always the heroine – in Richard Branson she would have a real live hero, warts and all.

IN STYLE

Just as the Pear/Leo is likely to be the softest, most intuitive and unegotistical of all Leos, so she is likely to be the most attention-seeking dresser among all the Pears. Cool colours and understated styles just aren't exciting enough for her Leonine personality. She is terribly drawn to animal prints, leopard, giraffe or tiger – rather than a shaggy old lion – but certainly the call of the wild is answered in her, if only with a chiffon scarf.

As well as wearing clothes, Pear body types tend to love shopping for them and the whole creative effort of putting new things with old. The Pear/Leo woman is no exception to this rule, she will have wardrobes full of clothes but they will just be slightly more look-at-me in style. The Pear/Leo may be a little more discreet than the Rectangle/Leo, for instance, but she will still see herself as the *femme fatale* one week and the prairie girl the next. She will adapt looks to suit herself, from films or *Vogue*, or from a friend whose style she admires.

There will always be a stir of excitement when a Leo woman of whatever body type arrives at a party dressed in her best. She's naturally a bit late as it is, but in addition she's not a woman who slips unnoticed into the room. If by some abberation she is wearing an understated little number you can be sure that there will be something attention-grabbing about her looks – her hair may be in an Ivana Trump beehive, her jewellery may be a version of the Crown Jewels – or that discreet black dress may be completely backless as far as her bottom.

Before buying any more clothes, however, it is useful to know a few style pointers which help Pear/Leo make the right decisions, and so end up with a wardrobe where everything suits her, most

things go with other things, and there are no expensive – or even cheap – mistakes. We don't all share the same body shape and an outfit that looks fantastic on one person can look dreadful on somebody else. This is not just a matter of slenderness. Wearing clothes which suit her body shape, rather than hiding her good points and drawing attention to her bad, can make Pear/Leo look positively slimmer and more attractive and authoritative. For more specific information see In Style on page 28.

Style Treat

It has to be something luxurious, it has to look expensive, how about a really beautiful, animal-print, leather organizer for Pear/Leo, to keep track of all those friends and associates – and to start the jottings of that prize-winning novel? She could match it up with a really nice fountain pen and she'll have something that will be useful, last for decades and get better with the years.

IN HEALTH

Pear/Leo health tends to be good. There is a great deal of endurance in this sign. The fluctuating energy levels of the Leo are modified by the more stable, long-term energy of the Pear, so there is not so great a need for this lion to flop under a tree for half the day after each exertion.

In the whole area of food, too, the Pear has a modifying influence which can only be for the good. Leos bring their appetite for life to the table and are known as naturally BIG eaters. It's not that they are greedy so much as desirous to partake of everything on offer – experiencing as much as possible is their creed. The Pear/Leo, however, is more likely to resist the second helpings, the extra piece of crackling on the pork, that after-dinner choc, which may have seduced her Rectangle/Leo sister. This also means she is less threatened by the sort of weight gain which can creep up on the Rectangle women, particularly in middle-age.

So as a Leo, her health is likely to be best as a Pear/Leo, protected by her shape from the classic Leo area of weakness, the heart. Among all the four body types, Pears are the luckiest in a few respects. They may not have the lean hips and thighs of a born athlete, but there is overwhelming scientific evidence that their shape, dominated by its female hormones, protects them from the masculine diseases of heart attacks and diabetes. A further advantage for the Pear and Hourglass shapes is that they are more likely to conceive than the Rectangle and Triangle shapes (see Introduction).

The joints can be an area for concern for many Leos and keeping down the weight is crucial in not putting more strain than necessary on knees and hips.

In order to stay healthy generally, it is necessary to take some consideration of diet and exercise. In her research for her book *The Body Breakthrough*, Bel found that each body type has a metabolism which is unique to their type, and different from the other three types. Her team of volunteers tested diets and exercise plans tailormade for their body types, and the results, together with a four-week diet and exercise plan for each body type, were published in the above mentioned book. For more specific information on diet and exercise, see In Health on page 29.

A Pear/Leo may sometimes feel that she takes on too much. It's part of her nature to do so, but she has the steady energy and emotional resources to cope with a great deal over a long period of time. There is an exuberance and optimism about her which can carry her through the difficult times, and the Yang+ of her star sign will protect the more sensitive, receptive Yin+ Pear from getting too overwhelmed by feeling, for herself and everyone else. It is always necessary though for the Pear/Leo to take some time off from life to re-energize her great batteries. She will know how best to do this, whether through spiritual retreat, doing something artistic, or travelling to a far off land. But she should work something like that into the year's plan.

CELEBRITY PEAR/LEO

Emily Brontë, sister of Charlotte and Anne, author of the passionately over-the-top romantic masterpiece *Wuthering Heights*, was born 20 August 1918. She was intensely attached to the moorland landscape around Haworth where she lived in isolation with her sisters, father and brother Branwell. She had a most enigmatic, almost mystical character, and is now recognized as a poet of masterly power, whose voice is uniquely her own.

Emily Brontë's profound emotional depths and her dark yet realistic imagination produced her poetry and the extraordinary *Wuthering Heights*. This shocked and alarmed critics of her day with its dark brooding intensity, but her portraits of Catherine Earnshaw and Heathcliffe and her evocation of the wild and beautiful moors have haunted succeeding generations of readers and cinema-goers.

It is no accident that *Wuthering Heights* is so often filmed and remains so long in the memory. The theatricality of its Leo author is all there in the Gothic setting, the-larger-than-life characters,

the vast stage on which they strut and weep, playing out the run of human passions, cruelty, folly and inevitable tragedy. Emily isolated herself more from human company than did Charlotte, she was more attached to the moors and to home, yet she set out with a grandeur of vision to make her mark on the world: to give us Cathie and Heathcliffe and the extraordinary haunting pile of Wuthering Heights.

PEAR/LEO PROFILE

Janet is a young theatrical costumier. Ever since she was a small girl and had been taken to see an amateur production of *The Wizard of Oz* she had wanted to be involved with drama and the stage, so when she left school she went on to train as an actress. 'I loved the team work, the over-the-top emotion, all that darling this and darling that really appealed to me. But I realized I was less happy on stage and preferred to work on the production and directing side.'

She enjoyed casting and then encouraging and bringing out the best in the actors: 'But directing jobs for anyone new to the game were few and far between, and for a woman who was not good at being really pushy they were even more elusive.' Then fate intervened in the form of an unexpected pregnancy. Janet knew immediately that she wanted to keep this baby more than anything, even though its father and she were not a couple and she had very little means of support.

After her son's birth the chances of directing receded even further and so Janet decided to use her other great interest, design, textiles and dress making. She was lucky to be able to offer herself in place of a friend who had to drop out through illness dressing the productions at a small repertory company. Here she learnt her trade, with her baby Josh by her side in the dusty backstage.

'Right from the beginning I knew that I couldn't leave Josh. I couldn't even leave him in order to work full-time for better money in some more sensible profession. I think the fact that it was just me for him made me even more protective than I would have been naturally. Anyway, it had to be a job where he could come with me.'

Janet feels she has managed to reconcile the two parts of her Pear/Leo nature – the need to be a good loving mother to her baby, a promoter of others through her work and personal life, and the Leo side where she needs to have her work recognized, and some applause – if only in passing.

IN HOPE

Pear/Leo has great emotional warmth, optimism and a genius in communicating with others, in subtle as well as straightforward ways. She will always be the friend whose presence is like the sun coming up; she is the wife and mother whose absence is like taking the fire from the hearth. This ability to communicate feeling is a gift which can find a wider purpose. She should think where best it can be focused, after she has given those she loves all that they need.

Here is this particular genius being expressed by a fellow Pear/Leo, Emily Brontë, in the closing lines of her *tour de force*:

'I lingered round them, under that benign sky: watched the moths fluttering among the heath and harebells; listened to the soft wind breathing through the grass; and wondered how anyone could ever imagine unquiet slumbers for the sleepers in that quiet earth.' Start practising!

PEAR
VIRGO

(Yin+/Yin)

MOTTO:

The race is not to the swift nor the battle to the strong

IN LIFE

Never flashy nor boastful, always hard working, discriminating and sometimes self-effacing to a fault, Pear/Virgo may be overlooked in a crowd, or taken for granted by her boss or friends – but not for long. She may be made of the stuff which produces saints (Mother Theresa is a shining example of Virgo saintliness) but she also has an unmistakeable strength of mind and certainty as to what she is and where she's going (Queen Elizabeth I, Savanarola, Sam Goldwyn and Ivan the Terrible were all Virgos too and no one's going to accuse them of turning the other cheek).

Pear/Virgo is a finely balanced combination, a double Yin sign, and her depths and qualities are largely beneath the surface, only to be revealed to those lucky enough to really know or be loved by her. For a start she has a look of delicate, enigmatic feminity about her; she is graceful, modest in demeanour – in an attractive way that suggests quiet confidence and self-containment – and her eyes are likely to be remarkably beautiful with an almost childlike clarity. She retains her youthful look all her life and continues to be active, quick and graceful in her movements long after her contemporaries may have settled into the easy chair of middle age.

Mercury, the messenger of the gods, the planet of intelligence and communication, rules Gemini and Virgo, but here in Virgo he is more grounded by being attached to an earth sign. Pear/Virgo is not going to be zany and multi-facetted in the way Pear/Gemini can be, she is not going to flit among snippets of fascinating

information like an intellectual butterfly – she is going to be interested only in what is useful. She is in her element in any sphere where communication is involved, and she is likely to be a talker on anything from the latest book review she's read, to the strange taste exhibited by the new neighbours down the street, to the state of the Stock Market. Being a Pear, she has a marked empathy with the thoughts and feelings of others, and with her natural Virgoan discrimination – which notices and grades everything – she can be as astute a judge of character or situation as anyone.

Virgo is well-known as the critic of the zodiac, and this great discriminatory skill, the ability to classify to the subtlest degree, can become nit-picking and overly critical in personal relationships. If it gets out of hand this positive talent will produce a nagging, negative, fussy, never satisfied personality whom people with thin skins or susceptible temperaments choose to avoid. The basic Pear type qualities will make her kinder and more imaginative about the feelings of others, but it can also increase Virgo's susceptibilty to self-doubt and melancholy.

Pear/Virgo is also a great synthesizer. She likes evaluating people and things and then putting them together with their complementary partners and elements to form a creative whole. This is one of the positive aspects of the Virgo talent for discrimination. She recognizes the subtlest shifts in qualities and meaning and makes a gifted expert in a number of fields which require a fine eye or ear – picture restoring, instrument tuning, collecting of all sorts – the possibilites are endless.

Pear/Virgos also need to be needed, they like to be useful and the idea of service can be a sacred one in their philosophy of life. Not typically ambitious, she lacks the single-mindedness necessary for the pursuit of a single goal, but is much happier as the brains behind the throne, advising, working out strategy, encouraging and counselling.

Virgo often gets a bad press in the character analyses of popular astrology – who wants to be told that they are always so clean and tidy and obsessed with detail and hygiene? Who needs to have their sexual attractiveness impugned by the rumours of chastity, prudery and self-denial? None of this is true – and yet all of it is true: these qualities are merely the other side of a character marked by its talent for discrimination and need for order. Whether the order is internal or external depends on the individual's focus.

The Pear element in the Pear/Virgo combination adds a freer, more instinctive drive to this practical Virgoan energy. There is

likely to be more disorder in the Pear/Virgo's home than in the average Virgo's; there is likely to be more sensual expression of sex in what *can* be a very sexual sign – if and when everything else is *just right*. So Pear/Virgo is more relaxed, more in touch with feeling – both positive and negative – more easily relating to others, less perfectionist in the end than the other Virgo body types.

IN WORK

It will be a rare Pear/Virgo who is top of some tree that has required pushiness, ruthlessness and single-minded effort to climb. This woman is realistic and wise. She knows precisely what her talents are and is most unlikely to inflate them to herself, or others—unlike the fire signs, for instance. She does not aspire, or naturally reach for the top. Above all she wants to do useful things to the best of her ability.

She also recognizes that life has all sorts of other parts to it which matter as much to her alongside a career. She is likely to want to be a mother, and do that well. Pear/Virgo often has a great facility with her hands and a love of craftwork – it's more useful than fine art and therefore appeals more.

As a gifted watcher and commentator on the activities of others she makes a brilliant journalist and, with the input of her Pear-type depth of feeling and imagination about other people's lives, she has the qualities to become a writer. Virgo is one of the signs which predominate in the horoscopes of writers – from the giants of Dante, Tolstoy and Goethe to HG Wells, DH Lawrence, Agatha Christie, Shirley Conran *et al*.

She is great at organization and can be happy and useful running a business or an office. Kind to employees, an excellent member of any team, she is good at delegating and giving clear, logical instructions. She always knows how to behave and look appropriate for the job. There will be no wild-goings on at the office party, although she may be quite uninhibited at home.

The Pear/Virgo is one of the most dependable women you could meet, whether she's your friend who has promised to sit in for you at the shop while you go to the dentist, or she's the administrative director of your multi-national company whose 20-page report you need by lunchtime – and you know she is beginning to go down with the 'flu. You may get a few moans afterwards, and she may take a day off work to recover, if it was a particularly nerve-wracking effort – for she is a natural worrier and her nerves can easily be wracked – but she will never let you down.

Statistician, strategist, systems-maker, chess player, teacher, botanical classifier, librarian, craftswoman, gardener – these are all areas where this quietly capable woman can turn her hand to great effect. Her crafts will be useful rather than ravishing, her garden more likely a well-planned vegetable plot than a wilderness garden, her library efficient and well-run rather than quirky and mysterious, but she will be a hardworking team-mate, a fair boss and a thoroughly honest and trustworthy employee.

Ideal Fantasy Job

Designing and planting an Elizabethan herb garden. This would satisfy a Pear/Virgo on many different levels: the research is just what she excels at; the intricacy of design which gives her all the delights of doing a jigsaw (a favourite occupation) but using living plants; the usefulness of the enterprise combined with beauty; the closeness to the earth and living things.

IN LOVE

Pear/Virgo has to get over this public characterization of Virgos as somehow asexual, or certainly virginal and nit-picking. Nothing should be further from the truth. Virgo is an earth sign and as such has a healthy and uncomplicated sensuality. The problem can be that the discriminatory, some may say fussy, side of Virgo can mean that she is easily put off by things not being quite right – her man is wearing socks which clash with his shoes, he doesn't smell squeaky clean, he's arrived just as she is trying to puzzle out the last clue in her crossword.

She can cause herself, and those who love her, some anguish in this drive for perfection which leaves her unappreciative of the very real and good qualities with which the necessarily imperfect are blessed. Here the Pear side of the equation comes to her aid because a Pear-type woman is a sensual, feeling woman. With her, sexual desire flows outwards from the body and is not particularly controlled from the head, so she is often not too fussy about the external *niceties* of her man and isn't put off by the odd whiff or food stain. Now the Pear/Virgo is going to be more fussy than most Pears but less fussy than most Virgos, so somewhere in between we find a woman who can get to grips with the good-enough human male.

This is a fortunate thing because the Pear/Virgo woman is very happy as a wife and mother. She is drawn to the protective, masculine end of the male spectrum (where you also find the

rougher, grubbier lot who don't care much for appearance – theirs at least). She is a double Yin woman and she naturally gravitates towards a rugged chest.

She will be a practical and devoted mother to children whose clothes will always be whiter than white and whose meals will be properly planned and properly balanced. Although the rest of us know that the families on television ads are not like ours in real life, the Pear/Virgo is quite capable of creating a family which is. Her children will have polished, smiling faces, they will practise their musical instruments and their bedrooms will remain a delightful amalgam of unscribbled-on wallpaper, a floor clear of toys, beds neatly made, and their unstained clothes folded in their individual drawers. The kitchen gleams, even though a delicious meal has just been prepared; the golden labrador has a shiny coat and does not smell, and her husband may well be the simple, contented, manly kind.

One thing you can be pretty sure of is that the Pear/Virgo woman is no swinger. Her feelings go deep, she is naturally faithful, and her Virgo star sign means she is, above all, realistic. If she's got a domestic set up that is good enough, then she will work at maintaining it. You won't find her wasting time or energy dreaming of the man on a horse who might just turn up when she takes the right sort of bath. Dreaming is not her forte. And if she is careful and aware of the demoralizing effect on others, she can even make nit-picking and nagging a thing of the past.

She is a woman who attracts good friends. Loyal, practical and sympathetic, she is always there in a crisis or emergency. She is very good at putting other people's needs first when necessary (and sometimes when not absolutely necessary) and would never be just a fairweather friend. The practical reasonableness of the Virgo is united with the affectionate sympathy of the Pear body type.

Ideal Fantasy Lover

It has to be the young Sean Connery. He's certainly Yang enough for this double Yin woman, and his down-to-earth, no-nonsense approach to all the hype and frippery of Hollywood would appeal to this equally down-to-earth personality. All that diving into shark-infested seas too kept him clean and polished enough. He is, of course, a Virgo himself and shows an admirable grasp of finances and investment – he is said to be one of the most financially shrewd actors in Hollywood and as such is one of the richest. None of this would go amiss in the Pear/Virgo's book.

IN STYLE

This woman is perfectly happy to blush unseen. She is never going to be a flashy dresser, you will not come across her at a party wearing fishnet tights, snakeskin boots – or even a plunging neckline. Instead, she prefers really classy clothes which are cool and understated, and made in the finest cloth and with the most delicate and well-made detail. The fluid tailoring and superb fabrics of Jean Muir and the curvier versions of Armani all would suit her to a T. She will not be happy in a jacket with fraying button-holes or a skirt with a crooked seam. Although she may have to shop in chain stores, she will search diligently for the style and garment which has a classy simplicity about it. Most likely she will teach herself to sew so that she can have her clothes exactly the way she likes.

Nothing in excess would be her motto, and with the Pear/Virgo's quiet, transparent-skinned beauty it is the best way to flatter her feminine looks. Clothes in a really dramatic style, or heavy or shiny fabric will only end up wearing her, eclipsing the light that shines out of her clear eyes.

Before buying any more clothes, however, it is useful to know a few style pointers which help Pear/Virgo make the right decisions, and so end up with a wardrobe where everything suits her, most things go with other things, and there are no expensive – or even cheap – mistakes. We don't all share the same body shape and an outfit that looks fantastic on one person can look dreadful on somebody else. This is not just a matter of slenderness. Wearing clothes which suit her body shape, rather than hiding her good points and drawing attention to her bad, can make Pear/Virgo look positively slimmer and more attractive and authoritative. For more specific information see In Style on page 28.

Style Treat

Good quality, classic chic, wearability, are all words which have some resonance when a Pear/Virgo is considering her wardrobe. As a treat she could try to buy herself a good jacket that will add great style to anything she puts it with. If you have to choose where you spend your money, remember that a jacket is the most difficult item of clothing to make and so its qualities really matter.

Make sure that everything is right about this jacket. Pear/Virgo must keep in mind all the style pointers for her shape discussed on page 28. She should feel terrific just by slipping it on. If it's a really good jacket it is an investment which will transform

a Pear/Virgo's wardrobe and give her confidence every time she wears it.

Being a Virgo, she will want versatility, particularly if the jacket has cost quite a bit. It is best, therefore, to choose a neutral colour (black, navy, taupe, pewter, grey or brown, or white or cream for summer).

IN HEALTH

Virgos are notorious hypochondriacs – and when they are not paging through *The Family Doctor Book of Symptoms*, worrying that they have some fatal disease – they are ever health conscious, pouring over the vitamin catalogues and wondering whether to give up meat. They are more likely than most to stock up on disinfectant every time they go to the supermarket – those ads which show animated germs marching out of the plughole to threaten innocent children go straight to their heart.

A Pear/Virgo is not as bothered as the other Virgoan body types, but she will have a fully-stocked bathroom cupboard with herbal as well as pharmaceutical remedies, just in case. The nervous system is always going to be the area of weakness for this sign. She is a worrier and when she gets particularly stressed is prone to digestive upsets and extreme fatigue. The Pear/Virgo actually has great stamina and if she can keep this nervousness in hand there is nothing much which brings her down.

Among all the four body types, Pears are the luckiest in a few respects. They may not have the lean hips and thighs of a born athlete, but there is overwhelming scientific evidence that their shape, dominated by its female hormones, protects them from the masculine diseases of heart attacks and diabetes. A further advantage for the Pear and Hourglass shapes is that they are more likely to conceive than the Rectangle and Triangle shapes (see Introduction).

When it comes to diet and exercise the Pear/Virgo's motto could well be 'enough is as good as a feast', for she is unlikely to be a greedy eater, she knows when she has had enough. Similarly, she is unlikely to overdo the exercise, but will be less of a couch potato than her more sybaritic Pear sisters. Pear/Virgo is always doing something, she likes being busy and thinks that she gets enough exercise during her daily toil.

In order to stay healthy generally, it is necessary to take some consideration of diet and exercise, however. In her research for her book *The Body Breakthrough*, Bel found that each body type has a metabolism which is unique to their type, and different from the other three types. Her team of volunteers tested diets and exercise plans tailormade for their body types, and the results, together with a four-week diet and exercise plan for each body type, were published in the above mentioned book. For more specific information on diet and exercise, see In Health on page 29.

CELEBRITY PEAR/VIRGO

Anne Bancroft made Mrs Robinson the teenage male fantasy for a generation who saw Dustin Hofmann in *The Graduate*. There she played the sophisticated friend of his parents who seduced the gauche boy Dustin and set him on the road to manhood and responsibility. She is an actress of quiet emotional power and dignity. The last thing you will get from her is histrionics and blab-it-all interviews to the press.

Her early career in cinema gave her very little chance to show her emotional range; the parts were largely two-dimensional bit parts in one-dimensional gangster movies and Westerns. Anne Bancroft then turned to the stage and made the part of Annie Sullivan in *The Miracle Worker*, the partially-blind teacher to the deaf, dumb and blind Helen Keller, triumphantly her own. All her quiet Pear/Virgo passion was expressed here and she won an Oscar for Best Actress in 1962 for her part in the film version.

Anne Bancroft has been married to the seriously wacky director, Mel Brooks, for nearly 20 years: he says she is the Beauty to his Beast and obviously relies heavily on her emotional equilibrium, kindness and solid good sense.

PEAR/VIRGO PROFILE

Kelly is PA to a charismatic chairman of a public company in the City and she is absolutely indispensable. 'I've worked with John for five years now, and really I run his life. I enjoy being able to use all my organizational side – and my judgement too. He often asks me what I think about anything from his business decisions to what presents he should get his children. I really like the whole big business side of the job, although I'd hate to have his job. He has so little time for anything else, hardly ever sees his family and just lives in the office.'

Kelly left school wanting to be a craftswoman and went and did a course in bookbinding, which she loved, but there wasn't enough work for her to be able to live so she went back to college

to learn word processing and business studies. 'I was lucky, I went as a temp to John's office while his PA was on holiday and then when she decided to leave just a few months later he offered me the job. I think he knew that I was really good at all the back-up things he needed. I am a bit of a perfectionist. I like to have everything in it's place, in my head at least! I organize my boss's working diary, brief him before meetings, advise him where I think he's overlooked something important. I feel it's a creative job and that John and I work as a team, so his success is also mine. Every day is different and I really look forward to going in.'

Kelly is in her mid-twenties and wants to be married and have a family sometime in the future. 'But it's hard finding the right man. I come from this close-knit family where we all get on. My Mum's a real mum in that she's always been around for us kids. She's gone back to work now, but she really put us first when we were at home and I think that's how I would like to bring up my children. With that kind of love and security.'

She has a quiet confidence about her. She doesn't need to draw attention to herself, but in a group she is often the calm centre in the storm, watching, thinking, remembering. 'I can only be happy if I'm working with people I like and feel that there is friendship there. John is a really good boss because he gives me all the feedback from meetings and so on, and lets me participate in the running of the company. I think I have just the sort of job for me.'

IN HOPE

With all these admirable qualities of sympathetic kindness, pragmatism, good sense, patience and discrimination, why is the Pear/Virgo so hard on herself, ever seeking for perfection? The essence of being human is in not being perfect – it is our frailties which bring us closer to others in a shared recognition of ourselves. Somerset Maugham (a very imperfect Aquarian) encapsulated a fear others feel about this goal, ' Perfection has one grave defect: it is apt to be dull'.

The other great defect is that it means Pear/Virgo is often disappointed in others and in life. This critical, discriminating, classifying spirit can be a boon and a bane. Dr Samuel Johnson, Virgoan genius observer of men, made that famous comment, on hearing that an unhappily married man had married again immediately on the death of his first wife: it is the triumph of hope over experience. Perhaps the Pear/Virgo too should go on venturing hopefully – and occasionally make a leap of faith, even against the odds.

PEAR
LIBRA
(Yin+/Yang)

MOTTO:
To understand is to forgive

IN LIFE

Relationship is the key word for both the Pear type and the Libran type, but there are two very different expressions of relationship at work here. The relationship that occupies the mind and life of the Yin+ Pear is to do with loving and feeling, to do with personal relationships between lovers, friends, parents and children. The relationship which is central to the Yang Libra is in the realm of thinking and ideas. She is fascinated by the balancing of light and shade in that picture over there, the connection between theory and practice. Human connections matter very much too, but they are more the light airy connections of friendship and romance than of passion.

In Pear/Libra there will be times when the feeling Yin+ side dominates and she will tap into a great understanding of the lives and motives of others. She understands, sometimes without the need for words, the thoughts and feelings of others and will be able to offer them selfless consolation. At other times, the more cerebral Libra will predominate with her ready sympathy but greater detachment; she will be able to bring her analytic approach to the situation, however personal and emotional that may be.

For a woman with a star sign which is signified by the scales and who values balance, the strongly feeling disposition of her Pear body type can be disconcerting. Just when she feels she can deal coolly and intellectually with a problem, she will find her heart begins to beat a different message from her head: the deliberations become less clear cut as her feelings are engaged.

This heart might interfere, for instance, with the rational decision to cut the workforce in a recession-hit business – how can you make someone redundant whose wife has just had a baby, and who's so keen to work and get on?

The Yin+ heart may take the Libra head in too deep when it comes to relationships too. Suddenly the casual flirtation is a do-or-die love affair, when her Libra side would have preferred it to stay light and fun. Friendships will last longer and matter more. Feeling will sometimes overwhelm reason.

There is no getting away from it, for any Libran and for the Pear/Libran as much as any, Appearance Does Matter. And that is not just appearance in the narrow sense of glossy looks, fancy clothes and a brand new coupe – although those things are valued highly by her. It is also the appearance, the appropriateness of things, which matter: this is less an expression of vanity than of this need for balance, for getting it right.

The Pear/Libra is not going to be at the forefront of any garish activity, any jarring protest, or any shocking stunt. She is much more the one who brings disparate elements together, who blends and looks for connections. This can make for a certain blandness in her personality, but she is restful to be with and inspires calm in others.

Pear/Libra is basically a really *nice* person, who cares about people and is concerned deeply about fairness and justice. Nothing will throw her more off balance than a sense of injustice. In a world where corruption, selfishness, violence and injustice are endemic she can spend much of her time feeling terribly bereft of the harmony she so craves.

But don't be fooled by the Miss Goody-Two-Shoes side of this personality – she, like everyone else, has her shadow side. This can be one of the areas of weakness for a Pear/Libra: how she is regarded by her friends, passing acquaintances and the world at large matters very much to her. She can make herself very unhappy trying to please everyone all of the time, without any sense of what she needs in order to please herself – at least for part of the time. At her most insecure, she will find herself agreeing to things she doesn't approve of, saying things she doesn't believe, doing things she doesn't want to do, all in the vain hope of pleasing her audience.

There are more public figures in the sign of Libra than in any other and this need and ability to please is one of the reasons they are there: Julie Andrews, Brigitte Bardot, Judith Chalmers, Anna Ford, Clive James, Julio Inglesias, Cliff Richard, all have a sweet willingness, and a quiet, unflashy charm in the pleasing. Pear

types are the least publicity-minded of them all preferring to express that same charm and sweetness in the more private arenas of home, family and work.

IN WORK

A Pear/Libran, like all Librans, has great aesthetic taste. She is unhappy in ugly surroundings, and noise and disharmony grate on her nerves. She is not at ease either in the grimmer or grottier areas of life – both actual dirt or moral sleeziness puts her off very quickly. So she needs to look for work in areas which involve the arts, communication or the clarity and purity of facts – research or the pure harmonies of mathematics have their real attractions for this type.

Beauty is one of the qualities awarded to this star sign and it is true that most Librans, either male or female, do have a symmetry to their looks which has a classic beauty of its own, regardless of the individual combination of features. With a star sign ruled by Venus, associated with Aphrodite, certainly beauty and aesthetics generally attract the Pear/Libra. She may well find herself drawn to fashion design, styling for photographers, or being a photographer or artist herself. Television and radio are also areas where the Pear/Libra can excel with her ability to relate so well to people, allied to her natural intelligence and charm.

There is an impressive line-up of Libran actresses, Catherine Deneuve (Hourglass), Susan Sarandon (Rectangle) and Sigourney Weaver (Triangle) to name but a few, and the stage and film worlds seem to attract this starry personality. Pear/Librans are rarer than the more focused and ambitious body types like Rectangle and Triangle, but those there are, like Patricia Hodge, will bring a particular emotional depth and sympathy to the parts they play.

The arts in general are a good place for Pear/Libra to be found. She may have the ability to make a career out of being an artist, a painter, photographer, musician or writer, although she might find the solitariness of these kinds of professions hard to bear. She would make an excellent agent for artists, nurturing them with her affectionate, nurturing Yin+ side, and dealing decisively with the business and contractual aspects of their work with her cerebral Yang Libra side. Her charm would be no disadvantage in her negotiations with the buyers. She is the kind of woman who would fight for her clients' interests where she would shy away from asserting her own rights.

Because of her genuine charm and willingness to please, a Pear/Libran has to be aware of not appearing to bow whichever

way the wind is blowing, to appear superficial or fickle or lacking in true opinions of her own. This longing for everyone and everything to be in harmony can make her back off from a situation where there is discord or disagreement of any kind. Confrontation can be a very traumatic thing for her. So work where she has to fight for every concession and argue every idea through brick walls of opposition will exhaust her emotionally and make her ill.

Pear/Libra is the ultimate team player and would be an intelligent and unifying element in any workplace where she could express her ability to relate ideas to principles, people to other people, and weigh up the merits of one plan against those of another. Diplomatic, with excellent taste, she will very rarely put a foot wrong and could only be criticized really for not being decisive enough, or pushy enough, when the time comes. Even-tempered, civilized and calm, the Pear/Libra comes closer than most combinations to being all nice things to all people, liked by most and loathed the least.

Ideal Fantasy Job

Style Consultant to Richard Branson and his Virgin empire. Here she could let her impeccable good taste smarten up the Branson image and improve on the aesthetics of his airline and megastores. Good funds, friendly people, international clientele – a chance to use all her talents in a non-competitive environment. Pear/Libra's need for fair play in everything would mean she'd be particularly happy working in such a non-hierarchical set-up as Virgin, where everyone has some say. And boss Branson is Yang and will appreciate her discreet and sympathetic Yin-ness (but then wouldn't he make even Ruby Wax seem discreet and self-effacing?).

IN LOVE

The French writer Saint-Exupery could have been expressing the philosophy of a Pear/Libran when he wrote 'Mankind is a knot, a web, a mesh into which relationships are tied. Only those relationships matter.' And the relationships which are most tightly tied into that mesh and which matter more than anything are the relationships she makes with her man and her children.

This woman is not likely to want to go through life without experiencing the central relationship of motherhood. When she has been overwhelmed with the passions that this tiny creature rouses in her cool intellectual self, Pear/Libra will struggle to remain that balanced, detached self. But she will find the Yin+ part of her personality will predominate – and continue to predominate – probably until that small, dependent being is beginning to detach his or herself a little and settle happily into school.

Pear/Libra is an intellectual combination and even though the emotional side of her is strong, even though she may well be happier remaining a pretty much full-time mother while her children are dependent, she will be busy keeping her mind active – and playing stimulating verbal games and reading stories to her children.

This mother is likely to have clean, well-turned out, pretty children – no snotty noses and grubby bibs on her kids. Their manners will also be something which exercise her. Appearance and the social niceties are important to a Pear/Libran and you are not going to find her in a torn, food-stained dress surrounded by a gaggle of rowdy, down-at-heel children.

Her high standards of good looks and pleasant manners extends to her choice in men. Her Yin+ body type means she is drawn instinctively to the Yang kind of man, but not too rough round the edges and not too pongy at the armpits! She needs him to be strong and decisive. Although the legendary Libran indecisiveness is more an ability to see all sides of the coin allied, in the Pear/Libra, to a desire not to hurt anyone's feelings, with a good Yang bloke she can be protected from this anxiety and can let him make some of the decisions. He can hurt a few feelings too, if need be, although not in front of her.

Friends will be queueing up to come round. Pear/Libra is sympathetic and good fun. Her house will always look nice and comfortable and she'll be the perfect hostess in whatever situation she finds herself, from Embassy Wife to tea for two by the fire.

Ideal Fantasy Lover

Robert Redford. He is quiet, well-behaved, and *seriously* good looking – although he says his looks have been a burden to him as an actor and he has increasingly sought to express himself behind the camera as a director of movies. He is not just a handsome face, he cares enormously about the state of America, has always been a Democrat, and campaigns on the environment and for injustices against individuals who have no voice.

He is pretty balanced between Yin and Yang, but enough on the Yang side for a Yin+/Yang woman, who has the modifying Yang overlay of her cerebral star sign. He is thoughtful for her intellectual side but glamorous too in his entirely cool and civilized way. He will allow her space and needs it for himself.

No Screaming Lord Such for this woman, but a little bit of forcefulness in a sun-browned, lean, fit body (and a remarkably unvain one too) never goes amiss.

IN STYLE

This is where Pear/Libra comes into her own. She has a strongly developed aesthetic sense and will have a distinct style of her own. Whatever she wears she will look wonderful, because of her natural ability to harmonize and balance colours, shapes, accessories. You will never see a Pear/Libra wearing a ghastly combination of garments or colours – unusual, arty mixes perhaps, but even then she is more naturally attracted to a look that is romantic and feminine, than something shockingly odd or bizarre.

Pear/Libra is physically graceful and wears her clothes with a style and confidence which also helps create this feeling of elegance. Traditionally, Librans are meant to be attracted to light, romantic clothes, and this is particularly suitable as a way of dressing for the Pear-shape version of this sign.

Embroidery, beadwork, fancy bits and pieces, jewellery and accessories, all are used by her creatively to embellish her basic look. The beautiful hippy with daisies entwined in her hair, drifting through a field of poppies in a flowered organdie dress is the archetypal picture of a young Pear/Libran – although being a person who always dresses appropriately she is just as likely to turn up in a suit, albeit curvaceous and softly tailored, should the occasion demand.

Before buying any more clothes, however, it is useful to know a few style pointers which help Pear/Libra make the right decisions, and so end up with a wardrobe where everything suits her, most things go with other things, and there are no expensive – or even cheap – mistakes. We don't all share the same body shape and an outfit that looks fantastic on one person can look dreadful on somebody else. This is not just a matter of slenderness. Wearing clothes which suit her body shape, rather than hiding her good points and drawing attention to her bad, can make Pear/Libra look positively slimmer and more attractive and authoritative. For more specific information see In Style on page 28.

Style Treat

Now that dresses are back in fashion – and this is a garment that can really suit the Pear/Libran character and shape – she could try and find herself a beautiful dress with a fitted bodice and narrow sleeves, flowing out to a gathered or flared skirt. The fabric

should be light and fluid so that it gently clings to her body as she moves. It is interesting how different the right dress makes you feel. Graceful, womanly, grown-up, desirable – these are all qualities which the Pear/Libran woman can express when she feels like it.

A good dress can be much more versatile than one might think, especially if it is in a neutral colour. With accessories it can then be dressed up or down. Pear/Libra might want to put a curvy jacket over the top and give it a more business-like look, or add some glamorous costume jewellery – a necklace and some earrings perhaps – and make it more dressy for evening. A scarf can also be effective in giving a completely new look.

IN HEALTH

The Pear/Libran is quite a physically relaxed sort of woman. She does not go in for frenetic bursts of energy but burns steadily, even languidly, and then can have moments of peaceful, almost meditative calm. Health weakspots for her are the kidneys and the skin. The kidneys' activity as a purifier can be seen at work metaphorically in the Libran personality who can put too much strain on herself by trying to remove all the troublesome, unsightly and gritty elements in life. Perhaps by relaxing that drive to harmonize and balance, especially in areas where this can only bring heartbreak and disappointment, will take the pressure off the Pear/Libra.

It is a sorry sight when any Libran gets really out of balance – it panics her and drives her to extremes of behaviour and emotion which are unnatural and unnerving. Proper eating habits, regular rest and some planned breaks from concern for others will help get her back into equilibrium.

Among all the four body types, Pears are the luckiest in a few respects. They may not have the lean hips and thighs of a born athlete, but there is overwhelming scientific evidence that their shape, dominated by its female hormones, protects them from the masculine diseases of heart attacks and diabetes. A further advantage for the Pear and Hourglass shapes is that they are more likely to conceive than the Rectangle and Triangle shapes (see Introduction).

In order to stay healthy generally, it is necessary to take some consideration of diet and exercise. In her research for her book *The Body Breakthrough*, Bel found that each body type has a metabolism which is unique to their type, and different from the other three types. Her team of volunteers tested diets and exercise

plans tailormade for their body types, and the results, together with a four-week diet and exercise plan for each body type, were published in the above mentioned book. For more specific information on diet and exercise, see In Health on page 29.

CELEBRITY PEAR/LIBRA

Patricia Hodge is everything a Pear/Libra should be, and more. Beautiful, in that quiet elegant way, she is so far from vulgar you don't even expect her to use the word. She dresses impeccably, knows her body and chooses soft, fluid clothes which enhance her narrow, shapely torso and disguise her broader hips. Jean Muir is one of the designers she wears and those intelligent, grown-up, subtly sexy clothes mirror Patricia Hodge's style perfectly.

Her life also runs true to Pear/Libra influences. Surprised by joy with the births of two sons, when she was over 40 and had almost given up on being able to have children, she has been determined that they belong centrally in her life. 'There'd never been a moment when I hadn't been passionate about children.' She has now returned to theatre work – specifically because it means she works while her babies sleep and then is there when they are awake – she says the toughest aspect of working again is leaving her boys each evening.

Patricia Hodge's success is to do with her remaining exactly herself and not trying to become some overtly glamorous film star who sacrifices everything on the altar of fame. 'The best thing I've ever done in my life wasn't having Alexander (her first son), but having Edward for him. I find the dimension of there being a second child quite extraordinary. Suddenly you're a total family unit.' Hers is an apparently civilized, balanced way of life, with family and work in equal bloom and her natural modesty and intelligence rewarded with a lapful of riches, which you feel she never quite expected.

PEAR/LIBRA PROFILE

Cassie is now a student reading History of Art at Manchester University. It seems a very appropriate subject because she is beautiful in a smooth-skinned classic way which makes her look as if she has just stepped out of an 18th-century Italian painting. When she was at school she was very popular and much preferred her friendships with her girlfriends and going out with them to getting on with her work. 'I was heading for terrible "A" level results and I don't know what job, if any, I wanted to do but then suddenly something clicked in my head and I decided to work.' She did well enough to go to university and really began to enjoy the work. The subject matter satisfied all her aesthetic interests and her love of setting everything in its historical and artistic place.

Cassie's relationship with her boyfriend, a particularly good-looking specimen of manhood, and her friendships are the central springs of her life. 'I really don't like argument and confrontation, and have to steel myself if there ever is anything that I have to have out with my parents or boyfriend. Mum and her boyfriend enjoy arguing, but they exasperate me and I just have to walk out of the room.' She finds it very hard watching the news because she wishes that the whole world would get along in a kinder more civilized way, but as yet she has no desire to do anything to change it herself.

IN HOPE

The Pear/Libran will have a character that is a marvellous combination of feeling and intellect: she will find personal happiness and intellectual fulfilment in both worlds if she allows the full expression of her own nature. The main obstacle to this could be her overriding craving for approval, which can, if it gets out of hand, undermine her own sense of self and personal esteem, and turn her into a narcissist wanting others to mirror her, telling her she is the fairest, the brightest, the best.

It is hard for a Pear/Libra to do, but it may be worth while caring less for the form and valuing more the substance – don't wait till the music is right, just get on with the dance.

PEAR

SCORPIO

(Yin+/Yin+)

MOTTO:
Knowledge is power

IN LIFE

Don't let the Pear/Scorpio's unassuming manner let you think you've got a little mouse on your hands – if she is a mouse then she's a mouse that occasionally roars. Scorpio is ruled by the mysterious Pluto, planet of transformation and regeneration, and the sign is one of creation and achievement. The Pear side of this combination may make this woman's main arena the emotions and personal relationships, but create and transform is what she is on earth to do. Pear/Scorpio is on a spiritual journey and nothing she does is trivial.

A double Yin+, this woman's feelings go deeper than most people can even imagine. She hides them well. She can appear the most capable woman, with an ability to get on with life, but scratch her hard enough, or go to her in trouble, and you will find a wealth of sympathy and emotion of which those outside her closest circle have little idea.

Because Scorpio is a water sign, the element of feeling and sensitivity, and because this is united in a body type which is receptive and has an overriding need for relationship, the Pear/Scorpio woman puts her heart and soul into everything she undertakes. She is loyal to the end. No one will lose her as a friend (there may be times they wish they could!) – unless they do something that she takes as an unforgivable betrayal, like harming her children or covetting her man, and she will turn from them for good. She is understanding about most of the frailties of others because she is so aware of her own, but betrayal of love and trust is something she cannot live with. She recognizes the

world as a difficult and lonely place, and she needs to have significant connections with other people. Her relationships with her family and friends make the safety net that reinforces her confidence; and catches her should she fall. Scorpio always has a risky path to walk in life. Scorpio labours under one of the worst presses in the zodiac. Sex-mad, brooding, vengeful, she is portrayed in the older books as a delux model of the Borgias. It has to be said that with extreme provocation and in the face of real cruelty to someone or thing weaker, or gross abuse of power (that really gets her), she can surprise everyone who knows her as an otherwise easy, pacific sort of person. Then you might see a Pear/Scorpio angry, with those Plutonic deathray eyes that stun at twenty paces!

More enlightened commentators, however, don't make these exceptions into rules and they point to the out-of-the-ordinary sweetness and compassion in the sign. This is particularly true of a Pear/Scorpio. She is the softest face of this formidable sign. There is a genuine empathy in all Scorpios for the suffering of others. But Pear/Scorpio has the intuitive imagination and the lack of ego to forget her own suffering in the face of the need of someone she loves – or even a passing stranger who catches at her heart. She has a reverence for life and finds it hard even to throw away a plant that is ailing or unwanted. It is not for nothing that John Keats and St Augustine were Scorpios – although the sign also harbours powerful cannon like Picasso, Martin Luther, Charles de Gaulle, Nehru and Indira Ghandi.

Love really matters to this combination. But it's not lighthearted, flirtatious love, although she can flirt along with the best of them. It is that deep spiritual connection which two people make for life which interests her most. It is love for her man, passionate love for her children, and love for her friends and work. She has a creative ability to pull new life out of catastrophe. The phoenix rising from the ashes is another symbol of Scorpio's nature, and Pear/Scorpio can survive the worst crises. But at a cost. She is hypersensitive, with her feelings and nerves not properly insulated from the outside world. She has her collapses, but they are after the event and in private.

Although Scorpio generally likes to be in charge, Pear/Scorpio is the least dominant of all the Scorpios. In any situation, she is aware of the rights and feelings of the other people involved and, although she likes to have her voice heard and treated with respect, she is less likely to steamroll her opinions through. The Yin+ body type means she is aware of her power but it is internalized. She does not need to flaunt it and rarely wants to test it

against others. Above all she needs to make a difference, to make things better, kinder, fairer – if only among her nearest and dearest.

Large scale virtues and equally large scale vices make this sign as far from wishy-washy as you can get. In the Pear, however, the iron will is tempered by real concern for others, the drive for power becomes more a dawdle round the back roads, although like all Scorpios, Pear/Scorpio is not receptive to being bossed about or trampled over. She will smile and give in and be the sweetest of little women – but only up to a point; the mouse will transform into the eagle – the other creature that symbolizes Scorpio – and with proper pride and courage she will draw herself up and unfurl her wings.

IN WORK

Here the Pear/Scorpio can show the real penetration of her insights and understanding. She is ideally suited to research work, from female private eye to historian in the Bodleian Library. Her Pear-type disposition makes her empathic towards others and able to work harmoniously in a team, but her Scorpio side means she enjoys directing the way the team should go. Furthermore, because of her almost telepathic understanding of human nature and motivation, she can often be right.

The Pear/Scorpio woman is not afraid of hard work and won't consider any task beneath her. She doesn't stand on her dignity and will muck in with the rest. External hierarchies of power do not impress her and she has her own agenda – to work on what she wants to the best of her ability, and not mind too much the criticism, both good and bad, that may come from others. Scorpios are notoriously immune to flattery: they are sure of their own worth and the quality of what they do (and it isn't necessarily a very high opinion) and they do not depend much on the opinions, real or inflated, of others.

Ideas interest her, particularly those to do with the hidden streams of human character. She is intrigued by what it is that makes an individual unique, where is the spring of the human spirit, what has brought us to this place and where will our journey take us? Scorpio is the sign of the prophet. The spiritual side of life is real to her. It is also the sign of the psychoanalyst and Pear/Scorpio would particularly bring a profound understanding and sensitivity to bear on such work. Although it is hard for Scorpio not to be intensely involved, Pear/Scorpio is good at recognizing the individuality in others and letting them be.

Investigational journalism, the uncovering of injustice and fighting the good fight, are all Pear/Scorpio characteristics. But the Pear influence modifies the more evangelical zeal and means the knight-in-shining-armour side of her personality is called forth less often than, for instance, might be the case with her Rectangle/Scorpio friend.

There is an obsessional side to all Scorpio characters which can be destructive as well as constructive. The better side of this can be seen in whatever area of work she is in – when the Pear/Scorpio sets her sights set on anything, she will work on through to the end, however long it takes and however much it costs her personally. She is very bad at giving up on things – when sometimes giving up is just what she ought to learn to do.

The less productive side of her obsessiveness shows on the few occasions when Pear/Scorpio's emotional life goes off the rails and she cannot eat or work or sleep until she has understood the situation and worked the hurt out of herself. In such situations she is impenetrable. But then the phoenix arises from the dust and the transformed self emerges wiser and more resilient.

Ideal Fantasy Job

Discoverer of Byron's autobiography, not burnt after all by his publisher John Murray, but whisked off the fire by his clerk and kept in hiding under the floorboards of his house. Modern day Pear/Scorpio takes up a floorboard in search of a leak and discovers the decaying leather bag with the precious handwritten manuscript – and all the secrets of one of Britain's greatest Romantic poets whose life was so wild that he was dubbed 'mad, bad, and dangerous to know'.

IN LOVE

For the Pear/Scorpio woman there is no two ways about it: love is everything. Now this is love in all its guises. There is seldom any mild liking involved with this character. She is a loyal and passionate friend, although she is not naturally gushy and given to flattery, and some of her friends may not know how much she cares until they are in trouble. Love as an emotion can be extended to her work. If she is lucky enough to find something which truly expresses her talents and her feelings, then that work is included in the creative relationship too.

Then there is the more conventional focus for love, although Pear/Scorpio is seldom very conventional in her way of expressing it – for a Pear/Scorpio's love for a man is nothing less than a

grand passion. One only has to see the transformation in Julia Roberts, a classic Pear/Scorpio, now she's found her hunky Yang male, country singer Lyle Lovett. This combination produces a woman who cannot abide a cool, indifferent kind of relationship, a cool and indifferent kind of man – she would rather be at war than frozen in some ice-box of a relationship. She is emotionally generous and will offer a good deal to the man she loves. He may appear to the outside world to be the most ordinary of mortals, but to a Pear/Scorpio who loves him he is special and worth it all.

All this intensity of feeling can be a bore, however. Pear/Scorpio has a need to transform herself and others, which can prove troublesome in her closest relationships. She falls in love with someone, imbuing him with romantically enhanced qualities which she then sets about encouraging in the real (but obstinately unchanging) lover. When she realizes that her beloved male is actually slightly more human than heroic, the disappointment can be traumatic for them both. She has to learn a hard lesson.

This double Yin+ woman is deeply female in a primitive kind of way and she responds on the deepest levels to a rather primitive masculinity in the men she goes for: broad forearms, big shoulders, utter disregard for his own appearance and an uncritical pleasure in her physical form. As long as the sex is good enough – straightforwardly passionate and warm – Scorpio/Pear will forgive quite a lot of unreconstructed maleness (lounging around with the lads, single-minded workaholicism, a general lack of refinement and sensitivity of emotion). She would rather he was a better behaved version of the Yang male, like Harrison Ford for instance, but she can put up with a Marlon Brando or Van Morrison even in his later, more corpulent years.

The one bugbear in her book is sexual jealousy. This is as difficult for her to live with as it is for her lover. But it is very real and anyone who gets deeply involved with a Pear/Scorpio (and there is no other way to be sexually involved with her) shouldn't underestimate the power of her feelings. Sex is not a dalliance for her, nor is it mere entertainment – one night stands don't exist in her personal diary. For a Pear/Scorpio, sex has a deep spiritual component and it is this which she feels binds her and her man beyond time and place. When he takes that sort of commitment lightly, or otherwise devalues it, she feels that he has struck at the very centre of her being.

But the deepest feeling of all is reserved by a Pear/Scorpio for her children. For them she will go through fire if she has to. She may possess a sense of having a larger destiny somewhere in the world, but when these children are young she will feel that

she alone is sensitized to their needs and she cannot leave them in the care of someone less responsive than herself. She also gets a great deal of pleasure from watching them grow and providing a safe haven for that to happen. The other ambitions in her life will have to fit in around that fundamental core.

This doesn't mean she's necessarily a wonderfully good mother. She is empathically sensitive to the feelings and needs of her children, she is fair and generous in her support, but she has to guard against being too directive. She is sometimes distracted with the maelstrom of her own emotions. But her great virtue as a mother is her rock solid integrity, her appreciation of her children's individuality, and the fact that they always know where they are with her. They can say anything, do anything, be anything, and she may be forceful in her disapproval, but will never stop loving them.

To a lesser extent her friends know this too. She is most at ease with women and is likely to have a sisterhood of friends, all as strong-minded as herself, who bring a supportive good humour to each other and the general vicissitudes of life.

Ideal Fantasy Lover

Bruce Springsteen singing 'Born in the USA', raunchy-voiced, sweating, dressed in jeans and a crumpled shirt with its sleeves rolled roughly up, and his eyes narrowed from squinting into the sun (or is it the stage lights?).

Perhaps not a man with whom to have meaningful conversations on the purpose of life, but surely a man to rock and roll with.

IN STYLE

Pear/Scorpio is a combination which produces a love of clothes and a particular sense of style. The sensual feel of the fabric, the fluid cut of the cloth, the sense of theatre and mystery, these are the influences which you find in a Pear/Scorpio wardrobe. As far as style goes, a Pear/Scorpio's individuality owes very little to any convention of fashion or appropriate behaviour, and shows little regard for others. The Pear/Scorpio is first and foremost expressing herself, experimenting with creative possibilities, imaginatively recreating garments, and possibly causing a stir.

A Pear/Scorpio will be found browsing at sale time – she enjoys a bargain – or looking at the better quality designer clothes, fingering the luxurious fabrics, and occasionally spending much more than she can afford on an item that makes her feel

a million dollars. She is not overly influenced by the passing fads of fashion but will wear old favourites until they drop.

Before buying any more clothes, however, it is useful to know a few style pointers which help Pear/Scorpio make the right decisions, and so end up with a wardrobe where everything suits her, most things go with other things, and there are no expensive – or even cheap – mistakes. We don't all share the same body shape and an outfit that looks fantastic on one person can look dreadful on somebody else. This is not just a matter of slenderness. Wearing clothes which suit her body shape, rather than hiding her good points and drawing attention to her bad, can make Pear/Scorpio look positively slimmer and more attractive and authoritative. For more specific information, see In Style on page 28.

Style Treat

It may seem odd to suggest as a treat for the slightly dramatic Pear/Scorpio something so timelessly classic as a double row of good pearls, but this is a piece of jewellery which suits most Pear and Hourglass types so well that pearls should be a staple part of their wardrobe. Cultured pearls need not be too expensive if you buy them secondhand, or at a jewellery auction, taking the free advice of the experts who are on hand. If cultured pearls are too expensive there are beautiful faux pearls to be bought in any big department store. Try the baroque ones, they are particularly becoming to Pear/Scorpio's style and looks.

It is important for a Pear/Scorpio to realize that there are a range of different colour pearls and that certain shades are much more flattering to her skin than others. They can be silvery, cool white, through ivory to cream, then there are the pink, grey and almost black pearls. She should really look carefully at them against the skin of her neck and face. Then she will see which ones have a real lustre on her skin, making it look more flawless and glowing – the effect that pearls are meant to have.

IN HEALTH

A Pear/Scorpio woman can suffer from a high degree of emotional tension when things go wrong in her life. The very intensity of her reactions mean that she suffers far more from the ordinary vicissitudes of life than others would ever think – than even she sometimes realizes. She can give the impression of being a tough, controlled kind of person, but this protective façade hides something much more sensitive which shrivels when people treat her unjustly, or reject her affection. This takes its toll on her digestive system and can give her nervous diarrhoea and stomach ulcers.

Among all the four body types, Pears are the luckiest in a few respects. They may not have the lean hips and thighs of a born athlete, but there is overwhelming scientific evidence that their shape, dominated by its female hormones, protects them from the masculine diseases of heart attacks and diabetes. A further advantage for the Pear and Hourglass shapes is that they are more likely to conceive than the Rectangle and Triangle shapes (see Introduction).

In order to stay healthy generally, it is necessary to take some consideration of diet and exercise. In her research for her book *The Body Breakthrough*, Bel found that each body type has a metabolism which is unique to their type, and different from the other three types. Her team of volunteers tested diets and exercise plans tailormade for their body types, and the results, together with a four-week diet and exercise plan for each body type, were published in the above mentioned book. For more specific information, on diet and exercise, see In Health on page 29.

CELEBRITY PEAR/SCORPIO

Hillary Clinton, first lady of the United States, without whom there would be no Democratic presidency this time around, is a Pear/Scorpio of immense and subtle power. True to type, she has taken the most cruel criticisms of her looks, marriage, character, dress sense and morals, with stoicism and dignity. This naturally private woman has accepted the public humiliations of having her husband, with whom she was once – and may be still – passionately in love, shown to have been a philanderer. She has had his prowess in bed discussed on nationwide television by a glammed-up super-bimbo (this would have been particularly agonizing for a Pear/Scorpio to whom sex is intensely personal); and has been criticized for being a wimp or a conniver for standing by him and reinstating his public credibility with her passionate defence of their right to have frailities in the marriage like anyone else. She would have just as surely been criticized for being a cold and selfish woman if she had told him to take a walk.

BUT she has not stood sweetly by while her only child, daughter Chelsea and at a sensitive age, was cruelly attacked and ridiculed in the media for her lack of beauty. Here the fierce protective maternal streak of the Pear/Scorpio lashed out and a total news blackout was put on any coverage of her daughter. She wanted her protected at all costs from this crippling attention.

Hillary was a brilliant law student when she met the golden boy Clinton. Much has been made of her transformation (in true Scorpio fashion) from slightly dowdy, bespectacled academic to beautiful blonde, contact-lens wearing political wife. No Scorpio shirks at doing what has to be done to achieve the larger good, and Hillary wanted a Democratic presidency, she wanted a Clinton presidency, and she knew that her collaboration was a crucial part of that ambition.

She and her husband have achieved it, although at times there appeared to be tremendous odds against them. But she is not the type of woman to be submissive for long. She does not want to dominate, but she needs an arena for her own power, and her husband, in entrusting to her the overhaul of the health system in the States, has given her one of the most difficult and important jobs in the administration. She has set to it with a will – and with an unorthodox approach in that she has wanted to talk to everyone involved, particularly the small people who use it and try to make it work at ground level. It is obvious that Hillary is true to her double Yin character and really cares about the plights of individuals.

Although much is made in the press of her ambition, Hillary Clinton has never sacrificed her husband's or child's interests for her own. When the fact that she had retained her maiden name became an issue while her husband was running for Governor, she gave it up even though she is a feminist and was already established as a lawyer in that name. When Clinton became Governor she worked in a practice in his own state, rather than choose to make much more money and more of a name for herself in a practice in one of the major East or West Coast towns. And she began her case for the new health care plan to the powerful Ways and Means Committee with these words: '. . . more importantly for me, I'm here as a mother, a daughter, a sister, a woman . . .'. You would never get an extreme Yang woman, a Mrs Thatcher for instance, ever defining herself in that relational way – let alone claiming those identities with pride.

Now that he is president, her Pear/Scorpio loyalty has meant that she has not dropped the friends of their more modest days. She is a striking example of a woman who has used her power to promote others, to achieve ideals, and forge through change – that she in the process is herself promoted is only to be expected. Her friends and family have no doubt that it is still true that her family comes first. She expressed her real priorities in a speech during the election: 'What power wouldn't I trade for a little more time with my family? What price wouldn't I pay for an evening with friends?'

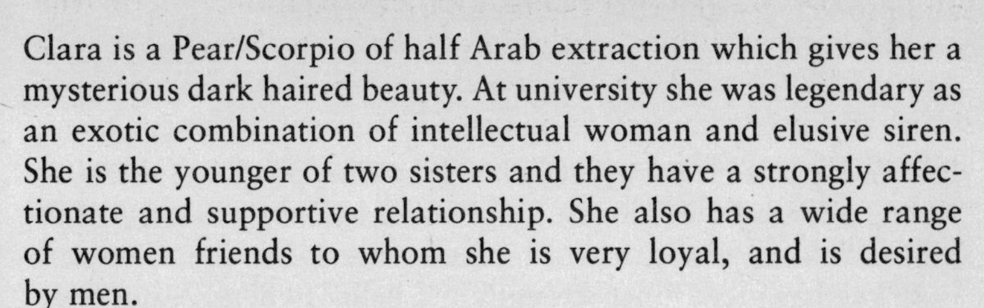

PEAR/SCORPIO PROFILE

Clara is a Pear/Scorpio of half Arab extraction which gives her a mysterious dark haired beauty. At university she was legendary as an exotic combination of intellectual woman and elusive siren. She is the younger of two sisters and they have a strongly affectionate and supportive relationship. She also has a wide range of women friends to whom she is very loyal, and is desired by men.

Leaving with a first class degree she was immediately offered a job as features editor of a glossy magazine and continued her intellectually glamorous life, the quiet centre around whom people hovered and men buzzed. She was offered a part in a film by a besotted film director she went to interview, but knew that that sort of life was not for her. 'I didn't want that sort of distraction. I don't want fame. I was already writing a book which I wanted to have time to finish and I was going to get married. Those two things mattered much more.'

She married young, a journalist who was posted to San Francisco, so she left behind her world and went with him for two years. She spent this time in the university library at Berkeley researching her book. She had a child ('the most momentous event of my life'), but the marriage was already strewn with rocks; her husband was hardly ever with her and she suspected he was off with other women, although he always denied it and always came back to her.

With great sadness, Clara decided that she could not go on living with a man she could not trust and she came back to England with her baby and started life on her own, anew. 'It was hard and lonely, and I felt a terrible failure leaving the marriage like that. But it was nice to get back into something of the artistic and literary life I had left behind. And of course I had my daughter who I could look after virtually full-time because I worked at night and from home.'

But there was always a need for a partner to love and be loved by and for ten years she searched for the right one, feeling always that her first priority was the happiness of her daughter. Although she was regarded by her friends as the attractive, intellectual face of feminism she confounded everyone by falling madly in love with a not particularly intellectual, great hunk of manhood. 'I've just always liked big-hearted, rock-solid, masculine men who don't buckle at the knees if you happen to want to rest your head occasionally on their chest.' Her female friends – and the artistic male ones – offered her all the empathy in the

world, but her new husband made her feel all-woman, desirable and protected – and that she found irresistible.

IN HOPE

Pear/Scorpio can be overwhelmed by the power of her own feelings, can become obsessed and out of balance when any of the pillars of love, family, friendship and work show signs of crumbling. She has great inner strength and belief in herself, but is not so good at showing her vulnerability and sensitive spirit. She is driven by the need to find the real thing in life, the truth behind the veil, but bad at letting others see the truth behind her own veil: a veil that implies so much strength that the tenderness which she needs can seem redundant. Keats, a fellow Scorpio, recognized this characteristic need to get to the heart of things – and to allow others to get to the heart of Scorpio – 'Scenery is fine – but human nature is finer.'

PEAR

SAGITTARIUS

(Yin+/Yang+)

MOTTO:

Every cloud has a silver lining

IN LIFE

The contradictions in this character are fascinating. The extreme Yin body shape with the extreme Yang star sign can give Pear/Sagittarius moments when she doesn't know if she's coming or going, laughing or crying, setting off on an adventure or curling up like a cat by the fire. Generous, gifted, compassionate and wise, there is a wacky element too to this character which will mean she can suddenly make a joke too far, fool around just too much and end up flat on her face – in a cow pat for good measure.

Sagittarius is the third and most volatile of the fire signs and brings to this combination a questing, adventurous quality. In Pear/Sagittarius this may not manifest itself in the more obvious way by making her the eternal back-packer with the physical world as her oyster. It is more likely to be that her intellect and spirit is on an eternal quest, enjoying new discoveries, meeting new people, working out new theories – as well as planning those more tangible explorations of coral island or inland sea.

She is a great talker and likes to communicate her newest enthusiasms or tell the latest jokes she's just heard. Like all Sagittarians, she can put her foot in it because she talks before she thinks. She is also accident-prone and when she's not tripping over her own toes she's delicately crunching other people's.

Of all the Sags, however, the Pear/Sagittarius is the most sensitive to the feelings of others and is likely to suffer terrible agonies when she realizes the full import of something she has just said. There is absolutely nothing malicious in these faux pas, it comes more from a natural exuberance and naivety, and poor

Pear/Sagittarius suffers more at what she has said in an unguarded moment than the more robust Rectangle/ and Triangle/ Sagittarians might.

Lucky old Pear/Sagittarius too. These women have a natural intuition as to who is worth knowing, which contacts should be pursued. Now it has none of the calculated social climbing of the Capricorn, or the more flashy celebrity-seeking of the Leo, but it is an opportunism all the same, an impulsive taking up of any chance that comes her way to further her ideas, her career, her experiences of life.

Sagittarians are interested in the higher pursuits of mind and soul, in philosophy, belief systems, and religion in an idealistic, theoretical way. With such Sagittarians as William Blake, Flaubert, Nostradamus, Rilke, Mark Twain, Laurens Van der Post, and the guru of the 'orange people' Bhagwan Shree Rajneesh as examples, you can see the range of prophets and thinkers that shelter under these Sagittarius skies.

Fire signs can often feel ill at ease in their bodies, there can be a lack of identity with their physical selves, and none more so than the expansive Sagittarius. This is to do with this sign's reluctance to have limitations and constraints put on her fantasies and ideas. However, the Yin body types, like the Pear and Hourglass, tend to identify particularly closely with their bodies and so, when the two contradictory elements are united in Pear/Sagittarius, there can be confusion. A client of Bel's says she sometimes feels so much more tomboyish and sporty than she looks, with her ultra-feminine body shape, and that she can still be surprised by the difference.

At worst, the emotional sensitivity and need for relationships of the Pear-type influence can be frustrated by the lack of reality which can be the negative side of Sagittarius's unsettled nature. When these contradictory impulses take hold there can be an unhappy mix where both the heart and mind are frustrated by the impulses of the other.

At best, though, the sensitivity and depth of feeling from the Pear type adds substance and profundity to the adventurous and philosophical nature of Sagittarius. In addition, the Pear body type influence can be excellent in grounding a character which can become too flippant and rootless. The energy of the Yang+ star sign also enlarges and enlivens the intuitive and emotional world of the Yin+ body type and so provides the impetus to make permanent relationships. While another body type Sagittarian might keep on rolling, never to gather moss, a Pear/Sagittarius is drawn to a more settled life, and will contemplate children and family – although not perhaps with the alacrity with which her Pear/Cancer sister might, for instance.

IN WORK

Pear/Sagittarius can turn her talents to a wide range of work. One thing it cannot be is routine. A nine-to-five filing job will not last very long with a personality who is on a quest, who needs intellectual change and the possibility of movement. She feels happiest in a freelance capacity, or employed in an unorthodox organization where the employees have a degree of autonomy and can plan their day and work to their own rhythm.

Anything outdoors has an immediate plus for a personality who loves open skies and long vistas. Horticulture, working with animals (particularly horses), lying under a tree contemplating the universe, each has its attractions.

Then there is the more verbal side of exploration – the research, writing and publishing of books – all these suit a combination which is fired by ideas and their dissemination. The Pear side of this combination produces a greater diplomacy and ability to fit in with others and work alongside them as members of a team than might otherwise be expected in a Sagittarian.

Teaching is also an ideal career for this personality which combines the love of true knowledge, as opposed to just facts, with a sympathy and feeling for people, particularly the young. Pear/Sagittarius can be inspiring in her enthusiasm for things. She will always bring a sense of adventure to the classroom or lecture hall. Traditionally, Sagittarius is meant to be a sign which confers an ability with languages. Certainly, the Pear/Sagittarius's fascination with cultures other than her own leads on to the study of the related languages, and this may be another fruitful area for her teaching skills.

With a natural feeling for justice and the placing of individual persons and situations into a wider scheme of things, the Pear/Sagittarius may be drawn to work within the disciplines of the law and theology. However, it is likely that she is not single-minded and ambitious enough to be happy making the necessary sacrifices in her private life to be a success as a woman in such predominately male professions.

The intuitive strength and emotional depths that the Pear body type brings to the intellectual questing, innate in this star sign, makes Pear/Sagittarius particularly talented in investigating and making sense of the human psyche. Perhaps not ideally suited to be a therapist – too much sitting around indoors in darkened

rooms – she is much more inclined to be able to synthesize psycho-analytic theory and write the next chapter in the practice of that art.

Ideal Fantasy Job

Philosopher, intuitive thinker and pycho-analysis guru, like Jung. In an area such as this, the mind and emotion meet to create a whole system of the personality that is illuminating and takes account of the individuality and spirituality of mankind.

IN LOVE

Here some of the contradictions of the Pear/Sagittarius may be most critically expressed. One part pulls towards relationships, anchorage, care for beings other than oneself. The other part of the combination pulls towards voyage, exploration, freedom. How best to reconcile these two energies?

It seems that one way out of the conundrum is to pursue the Sagittarian dream when young – travel, changing jobs, changing men (although the Pear-type element makes a string of casual sexual liaisons less likely). Then when the wanderlust, or just running with the flow of ideas and experience, begins to diminish a bit, the Pear-type desire starts to assert itself. Later in the day than most Pears, earlier than most Sagittarians, the Pear/Sag will decide that someone special to love and be loved by, that a dog perhaps and even a few barefoot children – if not exactly roses round the door – sounds rather nice and worth some sacrifices. So the Pear/Sagittarius may come late to settling down.

Love is likely to be a central priority but not the only motivation in her life. The pleasures of children will be in the teaching of them, and showing them the world and its wonders – maternal as Pear types are, their Sagittarian side makes them impatient and not good at staying still or tied down for long. When it comes to the dilemma of work and children, there are two paths. She will either be a full-time mother during the earliest years, retaining her adventurousness and insisting on taking her children along with her, or she will drag herself away from them and return to part-time work. She is likely to feel claustrophobic if made to stay within four walls with the constant tie of small dependent beings, however passionately she loves them.

Friendship matters very much to her. She will have a circle of both men and women friends with whom she has adventures and escapades. Pear/Sagittarius is an active labrador dog kind of personality with a feline curl-up-by-the-fire-with-a-good-book kind of temperament. The enthusiastic side which runs pantingly after sticks sometimes predominates, then the sensual, reflective, cat-like side takes over. Her friends are never quite sure whether an invitation to Sunday lunch will involve a huge meal and then a lazy stretch in the garden with the papers, or a picnic lunch, rucksacks to the ready, and a bicycle ride to a prehistoric monument 15 miles away.

These totally opposed energies of Yin+ and Yang+ make for confusions as to what kind of man she is attracted to. Her body type is really the deepest significator of temperament and so ideally the Pear/Sagittarius is attracted to a Yang sort of guy – decisive, assertive, his energy directed outwards into the world. But for a Sagittarian, he cannot be too overbearingly Yang because otherwise he will antagonize that extreme Yang star sign who does not care too much for being directed in life. A well-balanced, easy-going, assertive man who is also sensitive enough to see when to give in, or offer help, would be the dream man for a Pear/Sagittarius – but where to find him?

Ideal Fantasy Lover

Kevin Costner would just about fit the bill, especially if he's dancing with wolves. That outdoorsy, breezy masculinity is just down this woman's street, particularly as it's allied to a philosophically correct, idealistic view of the natural world and the spiritual values of the people in it. He is *just* Yang enough for her but has a more sensitive, empathic side than one would expect from one of the more extreme examples of Yangness like, for instance, Arnie Schwartzenegger.

IN STYLE

Pear types like clothes, the whole creative, sensuous part of dressing, the feel of the cloth, the experimentation with different looks, colours, accessories. But Sagittarius, like the fire signs generally, is not too bothered with the whole palaver. Something classy, good-looking and usually casual and easy to wear is her only real concern. For special occasions a fantasy element may creep in to brilliant effect – or not, depending on whether the experiment works. Just as Sagittarius can make social gaffes, so too can she make the odd sartorial mistake (traditionally they are known as the scruffiest of all the signs of the zodiac).

Luckily, the Pear element brings in a greater awareness of the effect she has on others, and so those lime green flares are likely to stay in the Sale rack. In fact, this sensitivity to cloth, colour and romance means that Pear/Sagittarius can go to town when she dresses up for a special occasion.

Anything romantic or in period with a fitted bodice, bare shoulders and full skirt looks great on this figure, although the Sagittarius part of this combination may not feel quite at ease in filmy organza, bows and furbelows. Something a little more quirky and individual, like an evening get-up similar to a modified cavalier's costume, with soft velvet fashioned into loose breeches and a fitted jacket, for instance, might suit her tomboyish side better.

Before buying any more clothes, however, it is useful to know a few style pointers which help Pear/Sagittarius make the right decisions, and so end up with a wardrobe where everything suits her, most things go with other things, and there are no expensive – or even cheap – mistakes. We don't all share the same body shape and an outfit that looks fantastic on one person can look dreadful on somebody else. This is not just a matter of slenderness. Wearing clothes which suit her body shape, rather than hiding her good points and drawing attention to her bad, can make Pear/Sagittarius look positively slimmer and more attractive and authoritative. For more specific information see In Style on page 28.

Style Treat

For the active side of Pear/Sagittarius's life a good pair of trousers is a great investment. However, it is hard finding trousers which really flatter the Pear-shape figure. Most of the time they are cut too straight in the leg and so she ends up with a pair which are far too baggy in the tummy and waist area and then tight across the lower hip and thigh. Pear/Sagittarius should look out for a designer who understands the curvy-hipped figure and who produces trousers with the necessary drape at the lower hips, as outlined in the style pointers above.

Once she has found a pair that are well-cut for her shape she should perhaps consider going back to the same designer next time, because it might save all the time and demoralization of trying on all those straight-legged trousers which are so unflattering to her shape. The most versatile trousers will be in a neutral colour that goes with most of the jackets and tops in her wardrobe – navy, black, brown, taupe, pewter and grey.

IN HEALTH

This sign is ruled by Jupiter and there is always a danger of expansion, inflation and excess where this planet is to be found. Sagittarians can overdo things in a big way, always hasty, often over-indulgent in food and wine, their livers and digestive systems are apt to cause problems. The other traditional areas of disease are the hips, gall bladder, and joints which are prone to rheumatism. Luckily a Pear/Sagittarius woman also has great recuperative powers and is unlikely to languish on her sickbed for long. There is always too much going on and life within four walls quickly palls – even quicker if she's stuck in bed.

Among all the four body types, Pears are the luckiest in a few respects. They may not have the lean hips and thighs of a born athlete, but there is overwhelming scientific evidence that their shape, dominated by its female hormones, protects them from the masculine diseases of heart attacks and diabetes. A further advantage for the Pear and Hourglass shapes is that they are more likely to conceive than the Rectangle and Triangle shapes (see Introduction).

In order to stay healthy generally, it is necessary to take some consideration of diet and exercise. In her research for her book *The Body Breakthrough*, Bel found that each body type has a metabolism which is unique to their type, and different from the other three types. Her team of volunteers tested diets and exercise plans tailormade for their body types, and the results, together with a four-week diet and exercise plan for each body type, were published in the above mentioned book.

Diet may be rather a sore point for the Pear/Sagittarius, however, because she can be a marvellous cook and quite an enthusiastic eater. She's also not likely to bother over-much about her weight: she is not the vainest of women and has more important things to occupy her mind. She may find herself gently expanding from being a small pear into being a big bell. She can reassure herself, however, with the fact that large, bottom-heavy women are a good deal healthier than large, top-heavy women (see the science section in the Introduction). She is likely to live long and well. For more specific information on diet and exercise, see In Health on page 29.

PEAR/SAGITTARIUS CELEBRITY

Jenny Agutter, the delightful elder sister in *The Railway Children* who became everyone's favourite child actress, lives up to all the expectations of her Pear/Sagittarius character. She has all the good humour, modesty and independence of the combination and enjoyed her young adulthood as a free spirit shuttling between London and Hollywood when the mood or work took her. She was perfectly happy, never played the game of the grand Hollywood star, was always her own woman, but she knew she was searching for the man to settle down with. But not yet.

Then at 37, just as her friends were beginning to think it would never happen, she met and fell in love with a Swedish hotelier ten years her senior. Suddenly togetherness held enormous appeal, but it still mattered to this Pear/Sagittarius that she could continue her adventuring way of life – if most of it was now in the mind. 'We found we had so much in common: we both love travel, food, and theatre, art, adventure, excitement, exploring new places' – only now she would be sharing these classically Sagittarian things with someone else.

As a Pear type she is basically a maternal, deeply feeling woman; as a Pear/Sagittarius having found her man she was impatient to get on with having children at last – and intended to bring them up in the same informal, outdoorsy, sensible way that she had grown up. Luckily she produced her first baby without any trouble and was so delighted with wifehood and new motherhood that she virtually gave up films to be with her son full-time. 'This is the sort of thing I want to do now – a day's work here, a day's work there', and her child goes everywhere with her. 'I've waited so long for my baby, I don't want to miss a second of him', she explains with her unaffected honesty and enthusiasm.

PEAR/SAGITTARIUS PROFILE

Laura is in her early thirties. She is a soprano, singing with several choirs and solo, and she often travels to sing at music festivals in Europe, America and the States. The freelance nature of her work and the variety involved in singing different pieces in different concert halls often in different countries suits her temperament very well indeed. If she could choose any job in the world she wouldn't change anything about what she does.

She married in her late twenties and knows that children are very much part of her and her husband's plans. But when to choose to take time off from work? 'As a freelance singer, I've always got that feeling that I can't turn down work, that perhaps there will be much less for me when I re-enter the circuit. Should I wait until I'm better established? It's such a hard thing to choose – and there's that other unknown quantity; I'll be changed emotionally by the whole thing, will I be able to leave my baby to fly off to same distant engagement?'

All her life Laura has felt a certain tension between the obviously female, sexual, nurturing side of her personality and the masculine star sign which gives her a breezy, at times over-the-top exuberance, and a restless, questing, youthfulness. She is a highly sympathetic woman with a number of close women friends. Intuitive and imaginative about the lives of others, she is fascinated by the dynamics in relationships, including her own.

'I think my Sagittarian side is what comes out most in my singing.' It's essentially an act of communication, for her, not of ego. Because her body type gives her an underlying Yin+ disposition, she can communicate a particular depth of feeling in her music which makes her voice extraordinarily moving. Most interestingly, Laura sings best when she is singing for someone she identifies with and cares about. 'I sing best at a festival when I know and like the organizer and want it to be a success for him or her too.'

As far as clothes go Laura also recognizes a distinct split in her style personality. She loves clothes made from fine fabrics; soft, romantic cloths like velvets, silk, fine wools. She is an excellent dressmaker and makes all her concert clothes. It is here that the over-the-top side of her Sagittarian self gets expressed in lovely dresses in jewel-rich colours. Her face has rather an Elizabethan beauty and certainly her body shape too is well-suited to that period's style – small tight bodices, rich fabrics, bejewelled corsages and flowing skirts. Shoes, a great weakness for all Yin characters, are her particular indulgence. 'I cannot get enough of them – purple suede ankle boots were my obsession while I was singing in Japan.'

IN HOPE

This union of opposites can be the most happy blend of complementary abilities and strengths. The enriching of experience with feeling, the enlivening of everyday life with vision and adventure. Virginia Woolf expresses well this forward-looking spirit: 'If we didn't live venturously, plucking the wild goat by the beard, and trembling over precipices, we should never be depressed, I've no doubt; but already should be faded, fatalistic and aged.'

PEAR

CAPRICORN

(Yin+/Yin)

MOTTO:

Softly, softly, catchee monkee

IN LIFE

Capricorn is a mysterious and misunderstood star sign. She is not just a straightforward mountain-goat toiling up the rocky slopes of worldly ambition, shrewd, down-to-earth, hard-working; she is also a seeker after the alchemy in life. This is not due to emotional and mystical elements in her character, it is much more a need to understand the hidden forces, the streams of energy that govern our lives. Capricorns have to be in control and so, on the profoundest level, they need to know what it is they have to control.

The Pear qualities deepen the mystery of this sign and internalize some of that legendary urge for betterment. She desires to improve herself, to know more, understand more deeply, to be a better person. She brings a force of emotion to an earth sign which is not at ease in the sphere of feeling, and this can make for mental or emotional collapses when her feeling side breaks through the Capricorn control. The power of feeling that she tries to keep just below the surface can alarm a Pear/Capricorn, because everything in her astrological nature is terrified by loss of control.

Pear/Capricorn can turn ideas into reality. She is not a dreamer nor does she indulge in inflated fantasies of wealth and fame. She has the vision but also the capacity for dogged hard work to attain her goal. Not easily distracted or deflected, she tends to put on blinkers when she has to – luckily the Pear side of this combination makes her less willing to cut herself off from the emotional part of her life. Pear/Capricorn allows time for family and friends: her self-sufficiency is not quite so sufficient.

Structure and tradition is also important to Capricorn. She likes hierarchies and knowing where she belongs. She also likes to know where she intends to end up. Setting her sights on the higher peaks of her goals, from where she will be able to survey her achievement, gives a sense of seriousness and purpose to everything she does. You are unlikely to hear her say, 'Let's just do it for the hell of it', or 'Mosey over and we'll eat ice-cream, watch a video and just goof around'. Wasting time, hanging out and whistling on street corners watching the world go by are not attractive alternatives for this woman.

The Pear element in this combination makes this appreciation of tradition and structure focus less on the power structures of the business and professional worlds and more on the family. All well and good, if she belongs to a socially important family, or has married into one, but if not she will have aspirations to better herself and her family in this life. Manners matter to her, not so much through her fastidiousness, as may be the case with a Virgo mother, or her aesthetic sense as may be the case with a Libra, but because good manners are a sign of class and breeding and stand one in good stead in the outside world.

Private education too is likely to be more important to the Capricorn mother than to most. This is undoubtedly partly to do with her genuine valuing of education – and being disciplined herself she prefers the more traditional approaches to it – but the main attraction of private education is that she recognizes it as one of the important steps in a ladder of opportunity and worldly achievement that Pear/Capricorn wants to climb and wants her children to be able to climb.

Capricorns traditionally have a very hard time being children. They either have physically tough childhoods or emotionally deprived ones. Even in good loving homes a Capricorn child can feel at odds with the other children in his family or school. They are not at ease being children, often give the impression that they are old beyond their years and will prefer the company of their grandparents, for instance, to that of other children.

As teenagers their sense of isolation can become more acute because the Capricorn nature does not readily play the wild, irresponsible, giddy goat, and isn't naturally gregarious . There is a consolation for all the difficulties of their youth, however, for Capricornians really come into their own during and after middle-age. Then they magically become younger in outlook, outstripping in energy many of their contemporaries who are heading for the slippers and TV dinner. At last they learn how to relax more and enjoy the fruits of all that hard labour. They are

even known to kick up their heels and become almost frivolous at the Derby and Joan dances.

When you look at a list of Capricorn celebrities you see people with terrific staying power: Joan Baez, Shirley Bassey, Humphrey Bogart, Pablo Casals, Marlene Dietrich, Marianne Faithfull, Anthony Hopkins, Dolly Parton, Maggie Smith, Mao Tse Tung. For none of these has middle age been in any way a drawback, and for some it was the age when their lives began to take off. For Pear/Capricorn the best years are always yet to come.

IN WORK

Here we have a Trojan worker. She has true grit and stamina and she can toil – long after Leo the lion, for instance, has collapsed under a shady tree for a nap, or the mischievous Gemini twins have decided on a shopping spree to cheer themselves up. Capricorn woman has that mountain-goat hardiness which means she sets her sights and does not get put off by the stoniness of the ground or the tiredness of her bones.

Pear/Capricorn may be slightly more relaxed than most Capricorns but she is still going to make the most of every minute of her day. If she finds time for a gossip with a friend, she will bring her knitting with her so she can do that at the same time; if she's ill off work with the 'flu, she will decide to take advantage of the spare time and paint the hall as she recuperates. When she travels she never just stares out of the window enjoying the sights or letting her mind wander in some delicious daydream, she is reading something useful or writing letters or planning the next day's schedule.

An organizer and an achiever she may be, but the Pear part of this character is a softening, intuitive, feeling influence which can deflect some of the more single-minded energies of its star sign. She becomes more human, but less focused and more confused about where she's going and what she should be doing. Education is a natural area for her talents. She has a good intuitive rapport with children, she genuinely cares about the passing on of knowledge and understands so well herself the necessity of having all the tools possible for progress in an increasingly competitive and difficult world.

Pear/Capricorn may also be a great storyteller and this might be an area where she wants to make a career for herself. She may express this ability through writing fiction or biography, where her strong narrative sense draws the reader on. Her sense of order and structure is a very necessary gift for any writer. Or she may choose to translate the storytelling gift to the stage where she either performs her own scripts or brings alive the stories of others.

The appreciation of structure can lead the Pear/Capricorn into the world of music, either playing the instruments or administrating the orchestra or concert hall. She has a love of nature and would make an excellent horticulturist or landscape gardener. Pear/Capricorn's greatest ability is in being able to turn ideas into reality. She recognizes the necessity of each step along the way. She is neither daunted by the slowness of the progress nor the magnitude of the task ahead of her. Where other signs like Gemini, perhaps, or Sagittarius, have tons of ideas but little endurance, make lots of noise, have a good laugh and a rap with their admiring friends, Pear/Capricorn can plan and then methodically work from the foundations up. She will toil until she ultimately stands at the top and surveys the world.

A great trait of the earth signs is reliability. If Pear/Capricorn says she will have that report on your desk by five o'clock that evening you can be sure that it will be there. Similarly, there is no hyperbole in this sign, no inflated optimism and wishful thinking, if she says something is possible it is: if she says there isn't a snowball's chance in hell, then you know not to venture there without your heatshield.

Ideal Fantasy Job

Estate Manager of a royal property. All the excellent administrative ability of Pear/Capricorn would be united with her sense of tradition and hierarchy. Her love of nature and the countryside would also be sated to the full.

IN LOVE

For the Pear temperament, relationships are central to life, but Capricorn traditionally finds such things difficult – giving in, letting go, and freely expressing her feelings is not her natural way. Capricorn has a reputation as a celibate sign, yet when she does let rip there is a distinct sexuality there – as with all earthy signs. This allied with the Pear sensuality will make for a very sexual being, if only she can let some of that guard slip long enough.

Pear/Capricorn is serious, and sex for her is serious. She is not likely to have gone through a promiscuous period in her youth and is usually controlled enough to select her men quite carefully.

His status does matter – she is the sensible one who is more likely to choose the conductor than the first violinist. Ever practical and conscious, she knows that when it comes to commitment she is choosing the man who will father her children, and therefore ideally he should be respectable, well-bred and with prospects.

When it comes to sexual attraction, she is drawn to the more Yang men who are busy pursuing status and fortune in the outside world. She does not mind the late nights when she is home alone, or the weekends when he has to go on leadership workshops or play golf with the boss. She sees it as all for the good of the family and she will do her bit in keeping the home fires stoked and burning.

When she allows her barriers to come down, the emotions that the Pear disposition brings to this combination run very deep. Love and motherhood can be an alarming experience for the controlled Capricorn because of the very intensity and uncontrolled nature of the feelings which are stirred up. Pear/Capricorn is a passionate woman and her family matter more to her than anything, but she is full of conflict about how she expresses her own ambitions alongside her real desire to bring her children up properly. Both ideals matter so much and she is likely to drive herself very hard to fulfil both demanding areas of her life.

The Pear/Capricorn home is likely to be an orderly hive of activity. Lounging, half-dressed kids, television blaring and plates of half-eaten baked beans on the floor are her idea of hell. Her children will be traditionally well-dressed (for as long as she has any say over the matter), they will practise their instruments, talk properly and eat family meals round the dining room table, with good damask napkins and candles on Sunday. There will be country walks and reading after tea.

Fellow Capricorn AA Milne, creator of Pooh Bear, expressed the seriousness with which he approached even nursery life, a sentiment with which a Pear/Capricorn woman would absolutely agree. The safe and gentle world of Pooh Corner would find an echo in her aspirations for her own family life: '*When We Were Very Young* is not the work of a poet becoming playful' AA Milne explained, 'it is the work of a light-verse writer taking his job seriously even though he is taking it into the nursery. It seems that the nursery, more than any other room in the house, likes to be approached seriously.'

Ideal Fantasy Lover

James Woods is an actor who combines a sexy Yangness with enough brains to satisfy any aspirational Capricorn. He won a full scholarship to the Massachusetts Institute of Technology, a prestigious scientific hothouse, where he read for a degree in political science. His look of a lean, hungry wolf allied to the nervous energy and emotional intensity he brings to his screen roles in films such as *Best Seller* and *The Cop* makes him an unlikely but powerful sex symbol to discriminating women. A Pear/Capricorn woman would never feel unsafe or insecure with him about.

IN STYLE

Capricorn women are notable for their fine faces with that strong bone structure that stands up so well to age. You only have to think of Marlene Dietrich, Faye Dunaway, Sade, Maggie Smith, Ava Gardner and Annie Lennox to get the picture. Pear/Capricorn will have slightly softer features than the classic androgynous beauty of a Triangle/Capricorn like Annie Lennox, for instance, but she will have notable cheek bones and striking looks.

There are two sides to Pear/Capricorn which will express themselves through dress. She especially likes clothes which are classy and look expensive in an unfussy, unflashy way. If she can afford it she is naturally drawn to designer clothes which have a distinctive signature to them. Chanel, always so recognizable, is a favourite. Never anything vulgar, or over-the-top, but the particular style of, say, a Vivienne Westwood dress for special occasions (her Elizabethan-style boned corset-bodices are so becoming to the Pear shape) suits the distinction in the Pear/Capricorn personality. If the occasion demands it, there will be no woman better or more appropriately dressed than a Pear/Capricorn.

Conversely, the earthy, practical Capricorn side means that when she is home, working or digging around in the garden or shepherding her children, then she is likely to be completely casual in a pair of trousers and a T-shirt with plimsolls on her feet.

Before buying any more clothes, however, it is useful to know a few style pointers which help Pear/Capricorn make the right decisions, and so end up with a wardrobe where everything suits her, most things go with other things, and there are no expensive – or even cheap – mistakes. We don't all share the same body shape and an outfit that looks fantastic on one person can look dreadful on somebody else. This is not just a matter of slenderness. Wearing clothes which suit her body shape, rather than hiding her good points and drawing attention to her bad, can make Pear/Capricorn look positively slimmer and more attractive

and authoritative. For more specific information see In Style on page 28.

Style Treat

Capricorns are traditionally meant to be attracted to leather. With a Pear shape the softer suede is a much more flattering version, so for a Pear/Capricorn a suede skirt makes a super treat. If she prefers, one of those good quality 'suede' fabrics make a fine alternative. A riding or circular-shaped skirt would be the most flattering style, a wraparound for only the slimmest of Pear hips.

For greatest versatility it is a good idea for Pear/Capricorn to choose a neutral colour that goes with the rest of her wardrobe – black, navy, brown, pewter, taupe or olive. It can be dressed up or down with what she wears with it.

A great look is made when a suede skirt is teamed with a small curvy jacket, blouse and belt. This will pass well enough as a distinctive business look. Or teamed with a small-checked shirt, waistcoat and ankle boots she can make a more informal, cowgirl look. For evening, the skirt teamed with a glamorous or frill-fronted blouse, with necklace and earrings, will give her an outfit which will go happily to any but the most formal of occasions.

IN HEALTH

Capricorn is meant to rule the skin and the tendons, ligaments and joints – the knees in particular. This makes Pear/Capricorn prone to aches and pains, sprains, arthritis and skin complaints. She is more likely to have a chill than a fever, and may be prone to periods of melancholy. But, the cheering part is that Pear/Capricorn's health, like that of all Capricorns, gets better with age. Stamina improves, optimism begins to break through, and contrary to the rest of the population, she suffers less and less from general colds and ailments as she gets older. A cheerful and robust old age can be expected with widened horizons, more travel and a bit more fun – just when everyone else is reaching for their zimmer frames.

Also, among all the four body types, Pears are the luckiest in a few respects. They may not have the lean hips and thighs of a born athlete, but there is overwhelming scientific evidence that their shape, dominated by its female hormones, protects them from the masculine diseases of heart attacks and diabetes. A further advantage for the Pear and Hourglass shapes is that they are more likely to conceive than the Rectangle and Triangle shapes (see Introduction).

In order to stay healthy generally, it is necessary to take some consideration of diet and exercise. In her research for her book *The Body Breakthrough*, Bel found that each body type has a metabolism which is unique to their type, and different from the other three types. Her team of volunteers tested diets and exercise plans tailormade for their body types, and the results, together with a four-week diet and exercise plan for each body type, were published in the above mentioned book.

As far as exercise goes, a Pear/Capricorn woman is naturally on the run through the day. Her own sense of purpose and inability to waste time means she is not likely to spend the afternoons on a sofa reading a magazine and eating chocolates – unless it's work and she's in an ad for Milk Tray. Her Pear metabolism makes it less essential for her to do formal exercise three times a week for her own well-being, as the Rectangle and Triangle types need to do, but she may well work a dance or tennis class, or yoga into her busy week. Yoga is particularly good for this star sign because of the propensity for her joints to stiffen up and become less flexible. The more high-impact aerobics, squash and road running are not really her thing at all. For more specific information on diet and exercise, see In Health on page 29.

CELEBRITY PEAR/CAPRICORN

Susannah York has always been attractive both in person and personality. Her few good films, *Tom Jones*, *A Man For All Seasons*, *They Shoot Horses Don't They?* (for which she won an Oscar nomination) and *Images*, among them, showed her ability to convey poignant feeling and flirty capriciousness. She has had her Capricornian ambition somewhat curtailed by her Pear-type motherliness which meant she was around as much as possible to bring up her two children, largely on her own. She loves working in America (where she has been particularly well appreciated) but her attachment to home and family and friends held her back: 'I could get more work if I lived in California but it always seemed a heavy price to pay.'

PEAR/CAPRICORN PROFILE

Marisa is in her mid-thirties and a very successful radio producer. 'I know it's a job that many people would love to have, but it took great perserverance and a good deal of luck to end up doing what I'm doing.' She doesn't add that talent is also necessary because she's naturally modest and doesn't make a song and dance about what she achieves.

When she was a schoolgirl and very unhappy she decided, with no help from family and not much from school, that she was going to get herself to Oxford. 'I hadn't got quite the right qualifications so I turned up and argued my case with the appropriate authorities.' She was accepted to read Politics, Philosophy and Economics. This was the beginning of her fortunes turning. 'It was the first time I began to feel I belonged anywhere. I was happy and made a number of very good friends. It was a wonderful time.'

Nevertheless, she always felt a bit of an outsider. 'Everyone else seemed to be so much more successful at the game of life than I was. I felt I was a loose wheel rolling haphazardly from one near miss to another. There was never any shortage of boyfriends, but they were always those exciting, unbalanced, macho men who risked their lives in various madcap schemes. I wanted to find someone who would love me for who I was, not what I represented. I was wanting to settle down, I realize now, but I was choosing men who seemed to have all the right qualifications – except the most important ones of all, maturity, trustworthiness, and the ability to love.'

Everytime she felt she had found the right man it was as if she set her goal and then attempted to climb to it – she poured out her deep well of emotion, she was sexy, funny, intelligent, endlessly sympathetic and tried to do everything to please. Then when this didn't work, the full wave of despair would wash over her. 'Why do I need so much to be part of a couple that I will do anything to try and persuade some man that I am right for him?'

Today, while all the emotional dramas are being played out in her life, and she feels she is on the brink of the abyss, Marisa manages to continue with her work as imaginatively and efficiently as ever. She is seldom idle. She has decorated her pretty small house herself in the spare time she has in between running a passionate and troubled love life, and writing and recording radio programmes. She is intelligent, sexy, warm, highly successful in a glamorous profession, surrounded by friends who think she's great, but she feels there is an overwhelming hole in her life where she wants a good, warm, loving man to be.

Her Pear-type nature has a tremendous drive towards relationships and her own hard upbringing makes her even more vulnerable to the dream of the perfect family. But her dogged Capricorn side means too that she sets her sights and then nothing can deflect her. Given the strength of the hopes she has riding on this kind of effort, when she fails it is no wonder she suffers the emotional collapses that so alarm her earthy, practical Capricornian side.

IN HOPE

Relationships are difficult for Pear/Capricorn women, but they are also absolutely central to their lives. Of all the Capricorn types, she is least likely to want to be self-sufficient and live a single, work-dominated life. All that determination to achieve, so characteristic of this sign, can become focused on this one particular area of experience and her failures can cast her into gloom. Perhaps she should try to widen her focus, concentrate less on the goal and enjoy more the journey and the landscape along the way.

> Is it so small a thing
> To have enjoyed the sun?
> To have lived light in the spring,
> To have loved, to have thought, to have done?

Matthew Arnold could have been addressing the anxious, driven, unrelaxed Capricorn with that verse – and he might have added sometimes when you take your eyes off the goal, good things sneak up on you unawares. Perhaps the Pear/Capricorn woman can get what she needs without necessarily seeking it.

PEAR

AQUARIUS

(Yin+/Yang)

MOTTO:

Love thy neighbour as thyself

IN LIFE

Here we have an extreme body/mind polarity, difficult for the Pear/Aquarius woman to reconcile. 'You don't know how hard it is to be a Pear/Aquarius' one of Bel's clients wrote on her questionnaire. The trouble is that she is caught between powerful forces which will always pull her in opposing directions and at times make her feel that she is either betraying her heart or neglecting the dictates of her head. But if she manages this difficult task of synthesizing both, she will have a mind that is humanized by intuition and affection, and a heart which is disciplined and aware, completely free of sentimentality and any claustrophobic possessiveness.

Aquarius is the last of the air signs, and is the most complex, fixed, and impersonally intellectual. Ideas, inventions, analysis, are her field of expertise; groups of people, humanity in general, rather than individuals and their small, suffering lives, concern the Aquarian most. This star sign gives her a computer-fast mind that would normally care not one whit about the opinion of others, because its own originality and far-sightedness belongs in the impersonal realm of tomorrow.

BUT for a Pear/Aquarius, the influence of her body shape, the most Yin of all four, means she relates to others much more emotionally than an Aquarian with a Yang body shape would. She cares very much about other people's responses, her heart and highly developed intuition make personal connections and prevent her intellect from dealing with the world in such a cut and dried manner. In the end, relationships – particularly her family relationships – matter more than anything.

There is a distinct individualism about Pear/Aquarius woman. She does not naturally respect tradition or automatically wish to prop up the status quo. Accepted truths are not necessarily her truths – and truth does matter to her. Being a fixed sign, however, she can be very dogmatic about what those truths are and, despite her own resistance to being made to accept anybody else's authorized version, she can appear over-zealous in her attempts to convert and reform others to her way of thinking. However, the contrary tensions of the body shape in this combination can rear their heads, causing confusion. 'You want to be different,' a Pear/Aquarius client explained, 'you want to be elsewhere, to be doing something else entirely, but then there is this side which needs to conform, to be dutiful, and think about others . . . nothing is black and white, it would be so much easier if it was.'

Yet out of this intellectual questioning and freedom from convention and restraint springs a strong creative urge which can express itself in anything she does. Experimental writers like James Joyce, Gertrude Stein and Virginia Woolf were leaders of the Modernist movement and were all inspired Aquarians, as were William Burroughs, Byron and Colette, individualists everyone. Revolutionary scientists like Charles Darwin, Thomas Edison and Galileo also show that flaring creative spark.

Pear/Aquarius is always open to new ideas and alternative approaches – sometimes too much so, and then the influence of her Pear body type can provide a good emotional base. Inspiration rooted in reality, experimentation but with a human face, this is how the two polarized influences can flow together in this one personality.

Helpless, Pear/Aquarius will never be. She is strong-minded, independent and – in a subtle way – a law unto herself. Her profoundly female nature is disciplined and runs deep, you won't see it expressed in surface fluffiness and flirtatiousness. But it will make her a terrific, loyal and supportive friend, to friends and lovers alike. She is not a suffocating, possessive person: she likes space in her life and will allow it in the lives of those she loves.

When she does manage to integrate the unconventional, rapier-sharp intellect of this combination with the deep feeling, womanly self, Pear/Aquarius becomes a fascinating combination of cool and warm, rationality and emotion, self-will and supportiveness of others. But it is a continual struggle for her not to slip into self-protective detachment or highly-strung guilt. This star sign and body type represent two completely unalike forces, but successfully harnessed they can be creative on a grand scale.

IN WORK

Pear/Aquarius is more concerned with the personal and emotional than the average Aquarius, but she is also more focused on the world at large than the average Pear. She is likely to be drawn to humanitarian causes, caring deeply for human rights, opportunities for women, for instance, and giving a voice to children and their issues.

Not necessarily drawn to the practical, hands-on approach to improving society, Pear/Aquarius is more likely to turn to discussion, protests and dissemination of information through writing, broadcasting or documentary filming. Aquarius is ruled by the eccentric and revolutionary planet Uranus, the same planet which traditionally indicates all the wonders of modern technology, like television and radio transmission, telephones, computers and faxes. These are all likely to play their part in the broadcasting of Aquarius's ideas for a new order, a better future.

In the same spirit, teaching of computer, science, technology and anything new in the areas of the arts and humanities holds a definite attraction for the Pear/Aquarius. That quick, inquiring mind enjoys the world of ideas and here, in teaching, this is united with the nurturing side, so important to the Pear body type. For all Aquarians, there is a real sense that the important concerns are so much larger than the individual, that the future awaits. As a Pear/Aquarius there is more of a sense of the needs and feelings of the individual, but she still has her gaze on some vision of the future. The passing on of knowledge to the next generation really matters to her and she has the imagination and enthusiasm to inspire her students with her ideas.

Trying to understand more about the human mind and its motivations is another area of fruitful work for this combination. Psychology and anthropology fascinate her. On more esoteric levels she may be attracted to studying alternative religions, astrology and astronomy; anything which allows that mankind belongs in a wider and deeper system than the purely material one in which most of us operate most of our days. Her rational mind is always there as a constraint on the more extreme elements of practice and belief, but she is remarkably free of the inhibitions and prejudices which make more traditionally minded people close their minds to anything unorthodox.

Alternative methods of healing are also an area where the Pear/Aquarius woman can express her appreciation of ideas which run counter to accepted practice but which have their own truth. Osteopathy, acupuncture, reflexology, aromatherapy, all suit the individualist, humanitarian part of this combination, while the intuition and empathy characteristic of her body type encourages her ability to diagnose and heal.

Whatever Pear/Aquarius does she does with discipline. This is not someone who skives off early or makes promises she does not keep. She is not a soft, indulgent kind of woman, although the Pear influence makes her more sympathetic and responsive than would otherwise be the case. Anything demanding a rigorous intelligence, a willingness to work with ideas and an ability to deal kindly with people will suit her well.

Ideal Fantasy Job

Producer of an avant-garde arts programme on television. This would give Pear/Aquarius all the scope she needs to explore the latest ideas, and to put them across to the viewers in quirky and original ways. She may find she much prefers being the brains behind the programme rather than the presenter in front of the cameras. Pear/Aquarius does not seek casual fame.

IN LOVE

Here the Pear/Aquarius journey is not going to be a smooth one. Love for this woman is not a simple matter. Her fundamental Yin+ nature means she is sexually attracted to the Yang man in all his ambitious, self-centred glory. Show her a James Dean or the young Marlon Brando and she will feel suddenly a little weak about the knees. She might even have a momentary longing to put her independent and capable head upon his hairy chest. Certainly the sexual chemistry between the Yin+ woman and the Yang male works a treat.

But this Pear-type woman is also an Aquarius and that is a star sign which finds intimate human relationships a little difficult. It means she is no starry-eyed romantic and she is practical. She is not good at playing for long the adoring woman to her macho man, a man who basically appreciates his woman best when she's expressing herself in the kitchen, the nursery and the bed. He is less enthusiastic when she's on her soapbox, or frantically rushing from pillar to post trying to fit in her work, her community activities and her care of him and the children.

So although she may fall heavily for an unreconstructed sort of guy, she really needs a slightly 'newer' version: not quite Yin (they are the men for her Yang sisters) but a little more capable of

running his life without all the traditional wifely support, and of mucking in with the domesticities when she needs him to. This woman is practical enough to realize that the qualities which make a good husband and father can be rather different from those which set her heartbeat racing. Basically pretty independent and needing her space, she has a struggle to reconcile her pragmatic and idealistic sides with her desire.

Children too can cause the Pear/Aquarius more than her fair share of anxiety and guilt. As a Pear she would not really contemplate the possibility of not having children, for being a mother and very involved in the upbringing of her children is the central pole of her emotional nature. Although she is this disciplined, cerebral star sign, when her children are born she is prone to all the profound emotional upheavals which change her self and her life for ever.

She may be surprised by her passion for them and her great sympathy for their vulnerability and dependence. But, much as she loves them and enjoys caring for them, her Aquarian nature naturally sets her eyes on a wider horizon than the one bounded by her four walls.

More emotional than the other Aquarius women, she will have her man and her children at the centre of her priorities, but they will be having to share the action with a whole galaxy of other interests and concerns. There will be the fund-raising events for school, her weekly class on esoteric philosophy, the monthly meetings of the local branch of Greenpeace who meet at her house, and – no little matter – her work.

If a Pear/Aquarius goes back to any sort of work when her children are still young she will go to enormous trouble to get someone wholly trustworthy, preferably a member of the family, to help look after them. There will be no casual, informal arrangements for this mother. She will not be happy leaving her children with anyone who is not either a member of her family, or someone she makes into a member of her family – by choosing her carefully and treating her with affection and respect.

So determined to do everything well, so certain that her own energies are limitless, the Pear/Aquarian can exhaust herself in the process. She can be rigid and stubborn, thinking she is always right so that no one can ever tell her when she needs a break, where she may be going wrong. Everyone, those she loves, work colleagues, neighbours, can be ignored in the headlong drive she has to be the good mother/wife/career woman/neighbour. Sometimes all she needs is a week off duty from everything to get herself back again to the basics that matter. To take some of the advice of that old song would do her no end of good – grab your coat and grab your hat, leave your worries on the doorstep, just direct your feet to the sunny side of the street. And lean against a wall there, whistling.

Ideal Lover

Must be a man of ideas as well as having a distinctly Yang sex appeal. The playwright Arthur Miller still has a phenomenal physical and sexual presence, and has endless intellectual credentials. Through his plays he is a protester against dehumanization and loss of individuality. A Pear/Aquarius woman would relate to that. She would never grow tired of him, although he might not be so good in the 'new man' department. But he's unorthodox enough perhaps for that not to matter too much.

IN STYLE

Aquarian style is quirky. They are not greatly influenced by fashion, what other people are wearing or thinking. They are often ahead of time, or certainly out of time, and follow their own tune in such matters. They like to look different from everyone else, because they sometimes feel that they are from another planet anyway. This means that an Aquarian can look anything between an absolute mess to madly artistic, or extraordinarily distinguished. If you think of the distinctive style – or lack of style – of these famous Aquarians you will begin to get the picture: Dame Edna Everage, Zsa Zsa Gabor, Yoko Ono, Vanessa Redgrave, and Virginia Woolf.

But when it comes to the style of a Pear/Aquarian you have a slightly less off-the-wall approach. A Pear type likes clothes, she appreciates the feel of the cloth and the inherent pleasure in wearing beautiful clothes in lovely fabrics. She is still not likely to be much moved by the dictates of fashion generally but will at least attempt to put together a look that reflects her own personality and does not draw too much derisory attention to her. But she will be individual in the choice of garments and colours she mixes together. 'I'd never have thought that that pink and orange would go so well together, but they do. You are brave!' are the sorts of things which Pear/Aquarians get used to hearing from their good friends – and ironically from their not-so-good-friends.

Fast thinking, lightning in her decision-making, it helps Pear/Aquarius to know a few style pointers for her shape which help her to make the right decisions, and so end up with a wardrobe where everything suits her, most things go with other things, and

there are no expensive – or even cheap – mistakes. We don't all share the same body shape and an outfit that looks fantastic on one person can look dreadful on somebody else. And this is not a matter of slenderness. Wearing clothes which suit her body shape, rather than hiding her good points and drawing attention to her bad, can make Pear/Aquarius look positively slimmer and more attractive and authoritative. Femininity with strength, curve with character, fluidity with form, sums up the style of clothing which suits a Pear/Aquarius woman best. For more specific information, see In Style on page 28.

Style Treat

Accessories really are an area for creative expression for the Pear/Aquarius woman and a good treat could well be a beautiful silk scarf in a dramatic colour which suits her colouring and sets off her beauty.

What you wear next to your face is the most important garment of all. It either enhances or detracts, depending on whether it's a colour that tones in with your natural colouring or drains colour from it. For instance, a natural redhead with warm skin tones would look much more vibrant if she wore a scarf of a soft luminescent orange or strong coral colour. Similarly, a white skinned, dark haired woman with Elizabeth Taylor's cool colouring would look even more vivid with an intense blue scarf. But each scarf would look terrible on the other.

Without a full individual consultation it is hard to know exactly what any individual's full range of suitable colours are, but you can experiment yourself by looking at your skin colour in a good natural light while you hold the scarves you are most interested in under your chin. Watch your eye colour become more vivid, and your skin glow when you have the right colour. When you see that happen, buy yourself a good scarf in that colour and learn to tie it in different ways on your old and favourite jackets and blouses to ring the changes.

IN HEALTH

Pear/Aquarius has no glaring health weaknesses. The ankles and circulatory system are traditional areas of trouble, so sprains, varicose veins and hardened arteries are worth keeping an eye on. The Pear/Aquarius is not a great eater. She is not one of the overweening sensualists among us, nor is she naturally a lazy sybarite whose idea of hard work is rousing herself from the recumbent position on a sofa, strolling over to the fridge and then back to s-t-r-e-t-c-h over and switch on the telly. Pear/Aquarius is much more likely to be grabbing a sandwich as she gets in from work, eating it on the hoof as she baths the kids, throws on her slouchy trousers and gets ready for the meeting due at her house that evening. (She also has to skim read the last 200 pages of a report in the ten minutes left to her.)

Among all the four body types, Pears are the luckiest in a few respects. They may not have the lean hips and thighs of a born athlete, but there is overwhelming scientific evidence that their shape, dominated by its female hormones, protects them from the masculine diseases of heart attacks and diabetes. A further advantage for the Pear and Hourglass shapes is that they are more likely to conceive than the Rectangle and Triangle shapes (see Introduction).

But if she wants to lose weight (and childbearing can leave Pear and Hourglass shapes with about a stone extra to lose), then it makes sense to follow a diet which is tailormade to her body type's metabolism. In order to stay healthy generally, it is necessary to take some consideration of diet and exercise. In her research for her book *The Body Breakthrough*, Bel found that each body type has a metabolism which is unique to their type, and different from the other three types. A team of volunteers tested diets and exercise plans tailormade for their body types, and the results, together with a four-week diet and exercise plan for each body type, were published in the above mentioned book. For more specific information on diet and exercise, see In Health on page 29.

CELEBRITY PEAR/AQUARIUS

Jane Seymour is an actress who has shown all the quirky individualism of the Aquarius character combined with the emotional and family-centred nature of the Pear type. She has two children, Katie and Sean, but is no longer married to their father. The break up of the marriage was particularly traumatic for her and the children, but after a lot of heartache she has married again, to James Keach. 'At home with my family I'm just myself; a wife and a mother. And that's what's really important to me. Years ago, when I was younger and more experienced, I used to think my career was, but I was wrong. Today, without a doubt, I put my family before my job.'

Her career successfully continued with a variety of meaty parts in various series, including *Medicine Woman* and films made for TV. It is quite obvious that her relationships come first for her,

that she lacks the ruthlessness and single-minded ambition to propel her from a beautiful, averagely-talented actress to a beautiful, averagely-talented star. And obviously, even when working, she feels she does best if she has a good relationship with her director. Her new husband directed *Medicine Woman* with happy results, 'Some of my best work has been done with him directing. He knows how to get that something extra out of me, because I love and trust him.'

Jane Seymour knows exactly how to flatter her feminine, small waisted figure. She looks her best in period costume, or in evening dresses with bare shoulders, a fitted bodice, nipped-in waist and full skirts. Otherwise she wears T-shirts or lacy shirts tucked into a longish, full or riding skirt, the whole cinched in with a dramatic belt.

A surprising number of actresses are Aquarians: Carol Channing, Sinead Cusack, Mia Farrow, Zsa Zsa Gabor, Nastassia Kinski, Eartha Kitt, Charlotte Rampling, Vanessa Redgrave, Greta Scacchi, Cybill Shepherd, Jean Simmons, Janet Suzman, the list goes on and on. They all have a distinct individuality about them and a feeling of cool and clear intelligence.

PEAR/AQUARIUS PROFILE

Trisha is a young woman in her twenties, an avante garde playwright who wants to explore the collective unconscious by having three or four actors on stage following the haphazard thought patterns we all have but occasionally intersecting with others. While she works on trying to get her work staged, she earns her subsistence money doing the lighting for a local rep company. Material wealth has never mattered to her, her greatest pleasures are sitting among a group of friends discussing their artistic projects, their plans for setting up touring theatre companies to take theatre out to the people who don't usually see it. Trisha says, 'I can't think of any work that could make me happier than bringing theatre and ideas to people, making them think, entertaining them for a while and perhaps leaving them changed in some fundamental way.'

She feels that she was always 'different' from her friends at school. At college, she was less satisfied with the status quo and was horrified when student friends said they'd vote Conservative because their family always had. Trisha went on marches for peace, human rights, women's issues of all kinds. She had lots of friends with whom she would talk and argue into the night. However, she did find it hard to reconcile her radical ideas with her emotional needs which seemed to her, when she was younger, to be rather shockingly conventional.

When she fell for a boy she went overboard, hook, line and sinker. 'I immediately began dreaming of marriage and babies. I loved him to bits and felt I wanted to do anything to make him happy.' She hasn't married yet, but is still puzzled by her ambivalent idea of the man who's right for her: 'I never went for those sorts of guys who were meant to be more sympathetic, shared the chores and were great to gossip to. For me it was always the driven yet intelligent type, busy on working out his own destiny. I didn't want hours of sweet and sensitive wooing, I wanted the more primitive "I want you – now" approach. It was just their raw masculinity which mattered I suppose. But I also think that sort of man is not ideal husband or father material. There, you see, the rational unromantic side of me.'

IN HOPE

The Pear/Aquarius has a double-headed serpent to control, love and the drive for relationship on one side, intellect and the need for detachment and the impersonal on the other. When the two come together there is the chance of a great enriching of both forces; a humanizing of the intellect, a rationalizing of the heart. Pear/Aquarius, perhaps more than most combinations, can live out in her own life the true meaning of love as explained by the philosopher Erich Fromm: 'Love is union with somebody, or something, outside onself, under the condition of retaining the separateness and integrity of one's own self.' Certainly, Pear/Aquarius is an example of the true thinker with a heart.

PEAR

PISCES

(Yin+/Yin+)

MOTTO:

'Tis better to have loved and lost than never to have loved at all

IN LIFE

The intuitive, romantic star-sign of Pisces will have all these qualities emphasized if she is also a Pear. This combination produces the most 'feminine' of women (Yin+/Yin+) who is terrifically empathic towards others, so much so that she has to guard against sacrificing herself too readily for the happiness or comfort of friends and family. She feels for everyone and everything, animals and plants, the world at large. All who suffer are drawn to her side, but she has to learn that she cannot give unstintingly and needs some unconditional loving in return.

Pisces is the last of the water signs and is the most evolved and complex of all the zodiac. Nobody else will ever quite fathom her, and sometimes she is not very good at understanding her own watery depths. She is ruled by Neptune, god of the seas, with a trident and a shell-shaped chariot drawn by sea-horses. The mystery and romance of this symbol suits this sign quite well. Pear/Pisces may be organizing a garbage collection march in her neighbourhood, or selling fish from a slab at her local market, she may be in old working clothes and her hair pushed into a bobble hat, but there will be an unmistakeable gentleness and femaleness about her aura. There will also be an other-worldliness about her eyes – and it is the eyes which are often most striking in a Pisces. 'Fish eyes' is one cruel description, but more accurate would be to say that her eyes indicate the antiquity of her soul.

Pear/Pisces, more than most, recognizes a spiritual dimension to life. She reaches out to this world herself through religion or mysticism, or through her vivid imagination and fluid creativity. This strong spiritual side makes the Piscean artist able to lift her art on to a different plane, tapping into the most moving and powerful of human emotions. Just think of the genius of Nureyev, Nijinsky and Diaghilev in the world of ballet; of Caruso and Kiri te Kanawa in opera; of Einstein, Victor Hugo, Michelangelo and Renoir. Inspired and inspirational Pisces all.

It can be difficult sometimes for Pear/Pisces to deal with the hard realities of life, the cruelty of individuals, the poverty in the world, the mess of dishes in the kitchen sink. Her strength – and her weakness – is this fluidity, this dislike of working within rigid boundaries. In her book, anything is possible if you dream it, but it can be much more fun to stay in that world of dreams than to actually have to root the dream to earth. It is from this that the warnings of the Pisces' propensity to escape into the world of illusion through drugs and other excesses come.

If we are all afloat on the sea of life, some of us are battleships with impermeable hulls and some of us leaky boats where water flows in and out in equal proportion. But then Pear/Pisces is a sponge. She has no real boundaries which keep out the feelings and needs of others. She has no way of keeping herself contained. She is open to everything and she finds it really difficult to make her boundaries firm, to say 'this far and no further'.

She can only protect herself through shutting herself away, and by escaping through dreams. This can produce in Pear/Pisces a tendency to lethargy, passivity, a sense of being overwhelmed by how much there is to be done. She can sink too readily into the warm bath of daydreams rather than brave the bracing wind of life in the raw. Waiting for something else to happen will only freeze her into immobility and indecision.

The Pisces symbol has two fish swimming in opposite directions, so well representing the indecisiveness of this sign. But it is an indecisiveness born of the rare ability to see all sides of a question, everybody's point of view. Nowhere is this more marked than in the Pear/Pisces. Here her emotional, intuitive nature is further sensitized by the Pear body type which enhances the feeling that everyone is connected, and the happiness of others is her concern. Life will never be black and white for her. Rather, it is a subtle, multi-layered kaleidoscope of feeling, motivation, expectation and aspiration.

IN WORK

Pear/Pisces is the poet, the visionary artist, the carer of children and animals and all vulnerable, powerless people. Sometimes the

tragedies of the world can weigh too heavily on her sensitive spirit and she needs to withdraw more into herself. In an office, Pear/Pisces is the perfect right-hand woman; intelligent, far-sighted, extremely supportive, she is one step ahead of you most of the time – except when her love life is not going well, or her children are ill when she may seem unusually distrait.

High-powered, ruthless working conditions take their toll on her emotionally. This woman has to feel she is in an harmonious environment where her commitment and loyalty are appreciated and returned, and where she is not manipulated by more crass types. Pear/Pisces is extraordinarily receptive to the auras and atmospheres of other people and situations (many are actually psychic) and can be upset, even made ill, by inharmonious or uncongenial working conditions.

Neptune, the ruler of Pisces, is the planet that rules film and film-making. It is remarkable how many actors and actresses belong in this sign. Their sensitivity and fluidity allows them readily to assume the persona of others. Their ability to operate on a more spiritual or higher consciousness also provides them with that extra emotional depth and affecting power. Playing the part of another character particularly allows the Piscean to hide the very vulnerable core of herself.

But a Pear/Pisces is the least self-promoting of all the Pisceans, so she would find the ruthless competitiveness and cold materialism of Hollywood contrary to her talent and personality. Instead, she would prefer to just get on and act in, say, the theatre, art movies, or television. There are three very individual and private actresses who are Pear/Pisces and share these traits: Eleanor Bron, Imogen Stubbs and Miranda Richardson. They are all distinctly female, chameleon-like and elusive – and low profile in their approach to the media circus that so easily consumes members of their profession.

Imaginative writing, music, dancing, these are all areas where Pear/Pisces will feel at home and able to excel. Creative activities allow her to tap the deepest levels of her complex character. As the twelfth and last sign of the zodiac, Pisces is the most removed from the ego, the most spiritually evolved. It contains all the lessons that the eleven star signs before have learned and it is this wisdom which Pear/Pisces can bring to her art. If she cannot make the creative arts her career then she may well make them part of her life by practising them as hobbies in her spare-time.

The healing arts are also a field where Pear/Pisces talents are well-expressed. She is likely to be drawn to the more alternative areas, like osteopathy, acupuncture, reflexology and homoeopathy.

She can be so intuitive and sensitive to others that she finds she has a real gift for healing. She will certainly be skilful at diagnosis. Therapy also is the kind of work where these strong healing qualities can be put to constructive use.

Ideal Fantasy Job

What about being a romantic novelist? Based at home, with an acute brain teaming with ideas and susceptible to romance, what better job for the Pear/Pisces? It will allow her to express all that imaginative and emotional energy in conjuring up her own Saturnine hero – and the melting Piscean heroine who heals the dark man of sorrow with her limitless love (and sexuality). Pisces are meant to be good at managing money and so she will also enjoy sinking her loot into investment trusts and off-shore funds, and watching the stock exchange rise.

IN LOVE

Pear/Pisces is likely to be washed away on a tide of emotion. She has to guard against giving herself up to it completely. She has to be careful not to forget herself in her love and care for her loved ones. With a delicate sensuality, this woman likes to be chosen, and taken – but not too roughly! Pear/Pisces is a natural seductress – and easily seduced herself by the right man giving off the right signals. Pisces has a sixth sense for most things, and which man is for her is one of them.

The man for her is masculine to her feminine, Yang+ to her double Yin. Sex for her is an emotional and spiritual renewal, it's tied up with life and death and rebirth, and she makes her commitment for life. Pear/Pisces makes her man feel overwhelmingly male, and he will respond like magic to her overwhelmingly female self. There will be no urging to slim from the man in her life: he appreciates the Victorian ideal of a beautiful face and shoulders, delicate hands and feet, a tiny waist and child-bearing hips. Small bottoms in jeans are not her (or his) thing.

Her ideal man will be able to give her a few extra skins of protection with his more robust view of the world. He needs to be a responsible sort who readily takes some of the burden off her over-burdened shoulders. She is too willing to carry the world's pain (as well as her neighbour's) and it wears her nerves to a frazzle. But with a broad-shouldered man beside her she can enjoy the necessary luxury of being cared for, being able to let go a little.

Pear/Pisces is passionate about her children and extremely imaginative and sensitive to their needs. Too much so at times,

occasionally she could do with a little more firmness and robustness in her handling of them. Life would seem grey for her without children and if she couldn't have them herself she would happily adopt, being able to love any child who needed it.

She is one of the women who find it traumatic to leave her young children to the care of others; she believes no one else will deal as sympathetically with them as she – and she is probably right. Pear/Pisces is more likely than most to elect to stay at home and look after them herself if she can. One of Bel's Pear/Pisces clients, highly intelligent and a successful career woman before she had her family, explained it this way: 'Before having my first child I was telling everyone I'd be back at work in three months. But as soon as I'd had him I was lost – I couldn't part with him and wouldn't leave him with anyone except family. In spite of great loneliness and feelings of isolation there was no way I could go back to work and leave him. Now I have three children aged seven, five and four and still I have to be the one they come home from school to. But I am now thinking of part-time work which I can fit in with school hours. I will still feel the same until they leave home, I'm sure. Tied by the leg until then!' The Pear/Pisces woman then, much more than a Triangle/Aquarius like Mia Farrow, for instance, is the natural mother of the world.

Friends also bask in the warmth of her care and attention. She will bring everyone into her embrace and make them feel welcome. Pear/Pisces is always taking on too much and then dragging herself back from the brink of collapse – too often with food or drink as an emergency fix, which only ends up exhausting her further. Those who care about her in return have to step in sometimes and forcibly remove her from the caring treadmill.

Ideal Fantasy Lover

Patrick Swayze is an actor and a man of interesting contrasts. There is no doubt about his Yangness, and for a Pear/Pisces there is something irresistible about a big, protective man. His early life was marked by his heavy-drinking, motor-bike roaring, hell-raising. Yet he is essentially a simple, good-hearted boy from Texas, happily married to his childhood sweetheart, on whom he depends, and sensitive (to a point) and sentimental – and used to be a ballet dancer! More gymnastic than graceful for sure.

IN STYLE

Typical Pear/Pisces style has a distinct artistic overlay. She is not going to be happy in anything which is strictly utilitarian, or a uniform-like look that constrains her and is too hard-edged. Dressing is a creative act for her and she will have a wardrobe bulging with anything from gorgeous designer pieces to imaginative and whimsical garments she collected from the jumble and intends to wear in some distinctive ensemble. She does not want her clothes to trumpet her presence in the room, but rather to reflect her romantic, female and mysterious nature, to attract and intrigue. Bel's Pear/Pisces clients all mentioned liking clothes which were 'floaty and feminine'. One went further, 'Yes, I'd love to look and float around like a mermaid, long hair, soft sensuous clothes, gliding mysteriously around . . . feathers, silks, pearls.'

Before buying any more clothes, however, it is useful to know a few style pointers which help Pear/Pisces make the right decisions, and so end up with a wardrobe where everything suits her, most things go with other things, and there are no expensive – or even cheap – mistakes. We don't all share the same body shape and an outfit that looks fantastic on one person can look dreadful on somebody else. This is not just a matter of slenderness. Wearing clothes which suit her body shape, rather than hiding her good points and drawing attention to her bad, can make Pear/Pisces look positively slimmer and more attractive and authoritative.

Ruled by Neptune, the planet of dreams and illusion and the sea, it is worth remembering that this woman is mysterious and female even when she's in the garden dressed in baggy men's trousers and up to her knees in steaming compost. She'll probably have pearls in her ears and her soft whispy hair pulled up into an untidy pony tail and will strike the male who loves her as the most desirable thing he's seen since Snow White. That's the other way that Pear/Pisces' gift for illusion works. For more specific information, see In Style on page 28.

Style Treat

The feet are one of the parts of the body ruled over by Pisces, and Pear/Pisces often have quite small, pretty feet. As her treat she could buy herself a delicate pair of suede shoes in a glowing colour, try purple, or green or aqua, the colours of the sea. Keep to a round or almond toe, small curvy heels and any other detail should be curvy rather than straight.

A pair of ankle boots might well be an even better treat. Practical but pretty, they would keep Pisces' notoriously cold feet nice and warm, and be fun to wear. They can be in suede, which is less practical but softer and more feminine in keeping with Pear

style, or a very soft leather. Better for Pear/Pisces to go for the more romantic styles rather than the Doc Martin look.

IN HEALTH

The Pear/Pisces woman is not drawn to vigorous exercise but she need not feel guilty about her preference for a stroll in the country under milky blue skies. Her body shape is protected from heart disease and diabetes and so intensive aerobic activity (which so improves the health and well-being of the Rectangle body shapes, for instance) is not essential for her. Much more to her liking will be walking, swimming and yoga – all improving her suppleness and stamina. The Pear/Pisces, however, is likely to be super-fertile (see Introduction) which has its own problems.

Traditionally, Pisceans are hypersensitive to drugs and alcohol; old astrology books are full of dire warnings about how easily depraved this sign can become. Things aren't as grim as that but the Pisces metabolism is not very robust and it is best if she moderates her food and drink intake and keeps away from drugs of all types.

In order to stay healthy generally, it is necessary to take some consideration of diet and exercise. In her research for her book *The Body Breakthrough*, Bel found that each body type has a metabolism which is unique to their type, and different from the other three types. Her team of volunteers tested diets and exercise plans tailormade for their body types, and the results, together with a four-week diet and exercise plan for each body type, were published in the above mentioned book.

Pear/Pisces woman will never be highly sporty, competitive or hardy, although she has great endurance and stuck in the desert would outlive any man. She also will never have lean male hips and narrow thighs, but then she is one of those women who is very happy to be a woman. For more specific information on diet and exercise, see page 29.

CELEBRITY PEAR/PISCES

Miranda Richardson embodies so many of the characteristics of this combination. She has an ethereal beauty and a chameleon-like ability to transform herself and enter the personality and life of the character she portrays. She first sprang to prominence piaying Ruth Ellis, the last woman to be hanged, in *Dance With a Stranger* and she not only suffered the exhaustion of her own efforts but also was a mysterious conduit for Ruth Ellis's pain.

Like a true Pear/Pisces, Miranda Richardson has a mystical side which can make her seem superstitious about courting disaster. But she is also open to the forces and influences in her work and life which cannot be measured, and need not be understood. Her acting genius comes into this amorphous area of the unexplained.

Two recent film parts, both of which won her international acclaim, show the range of her portrayals: in *The Crying Game* she played an IRA terrorist with frightening intensity; in Louis Malle's *Damage* she is the betrayed wife driven to the edge of sanity by her grief. This part was paltry and unpromising until Miranda Richardson got imaginative hold of it, 'You should have seen the script' said Leslie Caron (who was also in the film), 'All she had was "Pass the salt" and "Have you brushed your teeth darling?" '. From these crumbs she managed to create the most moving and persuasive character in the whole film. Her Oscar nomination recognized her feat.

As a result of these two critically acclaimed roles, Miranda Richardson is being talked of now as an actress whose range equals that of Anthony Hopkins and Maggie Smith. She has an excellent brain and an extraordinary lack of the usual actor-ego. She also has a real sexual presence which is subtle and unstarry, but all the more powerful for that.

Emotional depth and integrity mark her work. She famously turned down the part of the mistress in *Fatal Attraction*, the part Glenn Close eventually played, because she felt it was regressive and misogynous. She is personally enormously private and elusive – the idea of self-promotion is anathema to her – and she lives as close to living things and the great elemental forces of nature as she can. Gardening, falconry, the countryside all feed her spirit.

PEAR/PISCES PROFILE

Before Sarah-Jane married she worked on the problems page of a woman's magazine. She enjoyed the work, feeling that she was making a difference to some of the unhappy women who wrote in for advice. Then she met and fell in love with Harry, an up-and-coming designer on the magazine. They made a bizarre couple, she with her finely bred good looks and refined manners and he looking like David Bailey, after he had gone to seed. 'Friends were rather surprised by my choice, he was a bit of a rough diamond, but I thought he was madly sexy and exciting.'

Within three months they were married and a month later Sarah-Jane was pregnant. She had always intended to go back to

work but was taken aback at how strongly she felt that she could not leave her little son, and wouldn't be able to trust anyone else to look after him properly. She had a daughter within a year and settled down to care for them full-time. When she discovered Harry was having an affair with a really ambitious journalist on the magazine she was distraught. 'A friend of mine, who was much tougher than me, rather took over my life at that point. She told me I should pack Harry's bags and throw him out.'

Sarah-Jane was so beside herself that she couldn't think straight. She was grateful to be told what to do and followed this advice. 'I still wonder whether it was right. Harry did go. He's such a pig-obstinate man, I know he'd never ask me to take him back. So there I was, my dream of providing a happy family for us all to grow in in shatters, and me now having to bring up two very young children on my own.'

Sarah-Jane thought she'd better try to get her life back on some sort of tracks and went back to work on a sister magazine full-time, leaving her children with a nanny. But she quickly found this situation almost unbearable. Her children missed her terribly, she was sure the nanny was not being as responsive and loving to them as she should be and the work she was doing suddenly seemed trivial. She gave up the nanny and the job and went back to full-time child care in very straightened circumstances.

She knew that she wanted to find another man, because she really missed not having a man to love and be loved by. She also wanted to provide a secure home with a mother *and* father for her children. As she never went anywhere she wondered if this would ever happen. 'It was extraordinary. I met Derek in the school playground. He was collecting a girlfriend's child for her and we got talking. I liked his intellectual, unworldly manner and he was good and kind. I loved him. I find it easy to love people, and I thought this would work out.'

It did work out. He's very Yin for such a Yin woman and there is a lack of energy and excitement in their relationship – they are more soul mates than lovers – but Sarah-Jane has had another baby to cement their relationship.

Sarah-Jane admits that she has no desire to try and pick up the threads of her career, or any career. She might look for some part-time work, but she has been very content to have her family and her children at the centre of her life. 'It is the relationships I have made, my husband, my children, my friends, that matter most to me. As I grow older it is these that I will look on with greatest pleasure, not how many letters I answered for a problem

page, nor the passing excitements of working on a magazine, of independence and the dream of a small and fast-gone fame.'

IN HOPE

Pear/Pisces is so full of talent; soaring imagination, expressive emotion, a strong spiritual dimension, a wealth of brilliant ideas. But too often she is not that creative spirit she could be but a disappointed and lethargic woman whose conversation is full of regrets. The problems for Pear/Pisces are in uniting the dream with reality. 'Everything is a dangerous drug except reality – and that is unendurable', this piece of graffito was probably written by a disillusioned Pisces and it gets to the heart of the dilemma. Hold on to the dream, by all means – that is what sets the Pear/Pisces apart from the duller, less imaginative siblings in the zodiac – but make sure you don't lose the substance by grasping at the shadow.

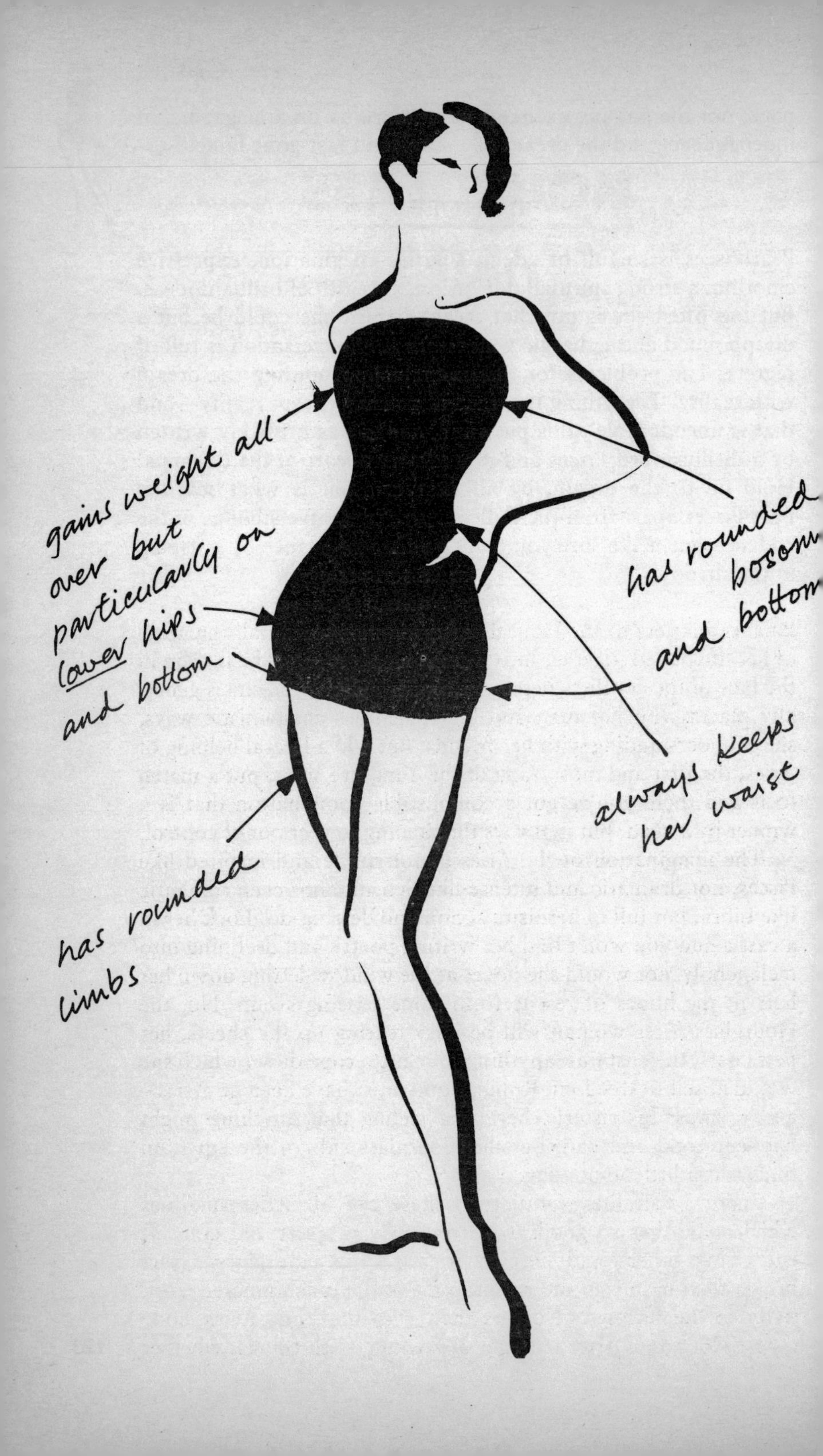
gains weight all over but particularly on lower hips and bottom
has rounded limbs
has rounded bosom and bottom
always keeps her waist

HOURGLASS

ARIES

(Yin/Yang+)

MOTTO:

All things are possible

IN LIFE

Balance matters to the Hourglass-type woman, with all the areas of her life pulled together into a harmonious whole. She is calm in the face of the conflicts between children and career, she is generally placid with her man and his sometimes chauvinistic ways, she is understanding with her friends. But add a liberal helping of Aries, the first and most Yang of the Yang fire signs, put a match to it and there you've got a combustible combination that is a winner by a head, but is always threatening to veer out of control.

The imagination of the Aries is not subtle and inspired like Pisces, nor dramatic and intense like Scorpio, nor even romantic like Libra, but full of heroism, action and derring-do. Lock her in a castle and you won't find her writing poetry and declining into melancholy, nor would she hover at the window letting down her hair in the hopes of rescue from some passing swain. No, the Hourglass/Aries woman will be busy tearing up the sheets, her petticoats, the curtains, anything to make a rope down which she would abseil to freedom. Robin Hood must have been an Aries – and so must his sister! There is a feeling that anything might happen, good and bad, but the Hourglass side of the equation finds this a little unnerving.

Energy, wilfulness, initiative, these are all Aries qualities which make her so good at starting new projects and great at energizing others and making friends. The Hourglass aspect brings staying power and endurance – and a much greater sensitivity to the feelings of others than with the Yang Arien body types: Hourglass/Aries is better at sticking with things, whether

they are a new business scheme or a marriage that is proving rocky or boring. She is more likely to look before she leaps, to think before she speaks, and will hurt fewer feelings.

Hourglass/Aries are the perfect headgirls of this world. She is wonderfully jolly, friendly, enthusiastic. Straightforward and honest, she is brilliant at championing underdogs and picking up the weak and unhappy. Sex kitten she is not, in fact she is completely free of guile and mystery. If she reveals her perfect hourglass body it is done in a wholesome, matter-of-fact – if sometimes giggly – way. Hourglass/Aries has all the female graces bestowed on her by her female shape, but she also has a chappish side, an ability to be one of the boys – for a while at least.

Fire sign women (Aries, Leo, Sagittarius) sometimes feel rather ill-at-ease with their female side. These are star signs of outrushing energy, of assertion, will and ego. Yet Hourglass/Aries has a distinctly female body shape and the Yin disposition which goes with it. She is much softer and more feeling orientated than her Rectangle/ and Triangle/Aries sisters, she is much more able to express the nurturing, intuitive side. But even she can feel that at times her 'female' side is at odds with her 'male'. She can find her enthusiasm for a new project suddenly pall when she realizes she will be away from her husband and children for too long. Or she might be happy working in a great office, full of friends, for a company to which she feels loyalty and gratitude. Then she's head-hunted to go into an alien set-up where she has a chance of being fast-tracked and earning a lot more money, but with uncongenial people, and much less time off. She finds it hard sometimes to work out which are her priorities.

As she gets to know herself and have the confidence to fulfil her true needs and not those pushed on her by others, Hourglass/Aries will always go for the alternative which allows her a full and balanced life. She thrives on action and variety, she will not walk away from a challenge, but she is not happy working so hard that she has no time for other things. Neither is she able to live an emotionally self-contained life. Her relationships and emotional connections are always going to matter to her in the end.

IN WORK

Hourglass/Aries is not at her best as a cog in a wheel. She likes to lead, not so much as a typical Aries perhaps, because her body type makes her a great team player and responsive to others, but she is likely to want to be there out in front, putting her ideas into practice. What she really needs is a challenge. However much she plays the devoted wife and mother she needs to feel that she is bringing about some element of change or progress in the outside world. She may express this need for a cause by working in the offices of a Feed the World charity or becoming a parent/governor at her children's school – or she may actually take her energies into the battlefield and seek some kind of political power or offer herself as an overseas worker for one of the aid agencies. This crusading side of her can take any form, from internal and low profile to external and prominent in the media.

She will be great at anything to do with the public. That fire sign warmth and friendliness is tempered by the kindness and consideration of her Yin body type. That optimistic energy is rooted in reality by the balance and good sense of the Hourglass type. Public Relations, advertising, demonstrating and presenting are all rewarding areas of employment. They need someone with intelligence and enthusiasm and in Hourglass/Aries those qualities are there in triplicate.

Hourglass/Aries is also able to work in situations where emergencies crop up and courageous decisions amd decisive action are necessary. The producer behind the screen in the television newsroom is one such job which demands such quick thinking and nerves of steel. The staff nurse on a busy casualty department of a teaching hospital is another such occupation. Lives are in her hands, and she has the chance to make a great difference to a not insignificant number of people. There is a matter-of-factness about Hourglass/Aries that stands her in good stead in these highly charged situations. She is not likely to panic – neither is she going to get deeply emotionally involved, nor take an instant dislike to a crucial member of the team.

With the imagination and drive that an Aries star sign contributes, and the classic beauty and balanced, affectionate and commonsensical temperament of the Hourglass body, Hourglass/Aries are easily drawn into a career in the theatre or films – either on stage or in the wings.

Hourglass/Aries is a woman of action and contemplation. She has a propensity to foolishly rush in where wise women never go, but she restrains herself just in time to consider a few of the pros and cons – then rushes in anyway. She will help start that new business, or buy that derelict property which needs renovation, or learn Japanese to get that job. Journalism is a good career for Hourglass/Aries because of this crusading zeal, her need for variety and her ability to think on her feet and make decisions fast. She has no lack of courage and would be the one to tie herself to the sacrificial rock in the hopes that she can interview the dragon,

before he claims his thousandth virgin. (Ever optimistic, she thinks the fact that she is not a virgin will put him off incinerating her.)

Ideal Fantasy Job

Running an ailing commercial breakfast television show, and turning the declining figures round. Hourglass/Aries would bring endless optimism and energy to a challenging job, her humane and people-sensitive side (the Hourglass effect) would mean she could handle the rest of the production team well. She would also be pretty good at intuitively knowing the right personality mix and general tone for the presenters to aim for.

IN LOVE

Traditionally, astrology has held that Aries women have a problem with love – they're not very good at being pursued (they'd rather be the pursuer) or accepting (they'd rather be asserting). This is a sign that is ruled by the ultra-masculine planet Mars, representative of war, conflict and strong-arm bully-boys. It is true that Aries does not make for sweet-tempered, submissive women, who wait with patience by the porch door for their man to come home from the war/prison/cattle drive/or pub. But it does produce women who know what they want and are not afraid to work to get it. These are women who like to move on fast to new challenges, and do not suffer fools gladly.

But then, of course, the Hourglass element in this combination feminizes this Yang+ sign. Here in Hourglass/Aries there is an energetic practicality, but also a much more basically female and sexual being. Her Yin body type means she is attracted to a Yang man, but her Aries side makes it difficult if he is too unreconstructed – she doesn't care to be bossed about. Al Pacino, Robert de Niro, Paul Newman, all these masculine men came up in the client questionnaire as being the sort of men for an Hourglass/Aries showing the domination of the Yin body shape, over the Yang+ star sign, when it comes to the basics of sexual attraction.

Hourglass/Aries woman has a strong sexuality, although she is not a particularly subtle or seductive operator. She is much more likely to be straightforward about the whole thing and give herself up with some pleasure to a pretty basic man. Jealousy can be an Aries bugbear, but the balanced Hourglass makes this less of a problem than for the other Arien body types.

This woman is likely to enter into motherhood with the same zest and energy that she brings to everything else she does. Again, the drive for marriage and motherhood is more likely to come from her Yin body type. The classic Aries character can be a little too self-centred to be much interested in the sort of selflessness demanded by motherhood. But Hourglass-type women are much more naturally maternal and, although not as passionate about having children as the Pears, they nevertheless see it as a central part of their lives.

The problems come, however, in the whole complicated area of how to reconcile the Hourglass/Aries' desire for a career with her feelings about children, family and how best to care for them. Hourglass/Aries needs a life in the outside world, desiring action, progress, and crusades, which can be rather cramped by horizons which extend to the school gate. Some of Bel's Hourglass/Aries clients expressed dismay at the loss of status and executive power involved in turning full-time careers into part-time. As they wanted to be home with their children for much of the time, the solution for some of them was to start a new career on a part-time basis.

Ideal Fantasy Lover

As Emma Thompson is a classic Hourglass/Aries, the fantasy lover for this combination has to be the love of her life, Kenneth Branagh. He's certainly Yang enough to make the sexual electricity spark, but he is intelligent and eager enough not to be too bossy. Enormously ambitious, he's already gone further and faster than any other actor/director of his generation.

No one could ever accuse Ken of being lazy, or too modest in his expectations, and this may cause some trouble with a demanding, sexy Hourglass/Aries woman – he just isn't around enough. And isn't in her bed enough. Emma, in her frank talking, foot-in-mouthish way has already mentioned this small problem, 'Ken is too hard-working for sex – well, most of the time, but we're working on it. We'd both enjoy having a family.'

IN STYLE

While the Hourglass/Aries woman has a feminine shape, she has the Yang overlay of her star sign to contend with. Not really terrifically interested in clothes, she can struggle sometimes to get the natural, unconstructed look which she likes best of all. The Yin body types, the Pear and Hourglass, tend to be more interested in clothes than the Yang, they enjoy the creativity involved in putting various garments and colours together, the sensual feel of the cloth. With Hourglass/Aries women there is more interest and flair than with the Rectangle/Aries, for instance, but the whole effort of putting a look together can sometimes seem too much.

This woman on the whole wants classy, understated clothes in which she can feel comfortable. She is not going to be a slavish follower of fashion but can kick the traces over occasionally with a big bold print, or some slightly over-the-top garment, like a tasselled skirt or a pair of thigh high boots. For more specific information, see In Style on page 34.

Style Treat

Evening dress can be difficult for the more casual, informal Hourglass/Aries. Classic Hourglasses look fabulous in those draped, diagonally pleated siren-dresses that so became the movie stars of the fifties, but a modern day Hourglass/Aries might feel this rather dressy for the annual firm dance or the occasional visit to the opera. She might be happier with the more flexible look of separates.

As a treat, she could go in search of an evening jacket in an interesting colour – bright if she can wear bright colours, muted if her colouring requires a softer look. The fabric should be really special: silk, metallic organza, or chamois, mock suede or actual suede. The style needs to be soft and shaped to the waist, nothing too overpowering in the shoulder line. This could then be teamed with a flowing skirt or soft, pleated evening trousers in a silk or good quality viscose. Then Hourglass/Aries will have a look she can ring the changes with, and in which she can go virtually anywhere, feeling great.

It is important to check that the colour of the garment you are buying suits you well. Take it into daylight, hold it under your chin and look at what it does to your skin, eyes and hair. If wearing it intensifies and enlivens your colouring then that is a colour that is right for your skin tones. If you look washed out or sallow, or your hair loses colour and dark rings seem to appear under your eyes, then you are getting it wrong. This sounds a lot of trouble to go to, but it is worth it for it enhances the pleasure you will get every time you wear it.

IN HEALTH

Traditionally Aries rules the head and Ariens are likely to get headaches when stressed. Meditation can only do a busy head-driven person like Hourglass/Aries good and might minimize any risks of headaches when life gets hectic.

She is more likely than most to be accident prone, nothing serious but burns in the kitchen and tripping over shoes in the hall – that sort of thing – and often involving bashing the head in some way. Fevers are more likely to strike than chills, but if ever

Hourglass/Aries is ill she is likely to be very impatient with her invalidism and will throw off whatever it is that ails her fast. She is not the perfect candidate for a chronic disease.

The Hourglass metabolism is a balanced one which is easily thrown off balance by too many stimulants, like tea, coffee, alcohol and cigarettes. These sap her energy and leave her exhausted and reaching for another coffee/drink/fag to perk her up again. Bad eating habits also sabotage her metabolism and leave her a collapse case at the end of the week.

Although it is not imperative for her health that Hourglass/Aries does a great deal of formal exercise, being an Aries means she is more competitive than most Hourglasses and will play a mean game of tennis, and play to win. Exercise anyway does help everyone to lose weight by burning more calories (half an hour's brisk walking uses up 180 calories) and by boosting the basal metabolic rate for a few hours after the exercise has ceased, thus continuing to burn more calories. Exercise also helps to tone up muscles and increase suppleness and strength.

There is an undeniable 'feel good' factor to exercising which cannot be ignored. If Hourglass/Aries does some exercise which suits her body type and disposition it undoubtedly lifts the spirits, makes her generally more positive about herself, more in tune with her body – and less likely to neglect and abuse it with junk food or other excesses. Tennis, swimming, walking an extra mile to work or the shops every day, running up stairs rather than taking the lift, all will help keep Hourglass/Aries healthy, happy – and slim. For more specific information on diet and exercise, see In Health on page 36.

CELEBRITY HOURGLASS/ARIES

Emma Thompson, most decorated and celebrated young British actress, wife of Renaissance Man, Kenneth Branagh, is a classic Hourglass/Aries. Her tomboyish Aries side gives her a genuine and straightforward manner, and something rather clumsy and gallumphing too about the way she walks and talks, happily putting her foot in it while she's at it.

She has a marvellous slim Hourglass body, but very little idea of how best to clothe it, or how best to show off the good clothes that she has rushed out to buy at the last moment, because she has an awards ceremony to attend. She's still terribly English and jolly-hockey-sticks and even when she's dressed in Armani or Caroline Charles there remains about her a sense that she's got scratched knees, a hitched up gymslip and her socks at half-mast.

Not formally trained as an actress, she is nevertheless a wonderfully talented one and has won, before she is 30, the most covetted award of all, the Oscar for Best Actress for her part in *Howard's End*. She seems to take it all in her balanced way. She insists that despite everything else, the most important thing that ever happened to her is 'falling in love with Ken'.

With her English degree from Cambridge, she brings a certain intelligence and seriousness to all she does, but she protests that she also feels deeply. As befits her Hourglass disposition, family life and children are high on her agenda.

HOURGLASS/ARIES PROFILE

Mel is married to a builder who has been out of work for a year because of the squeeze on housebuilding during the recession. 'It's been very hard on him. He's not one to enjoy being at home. He likes his work and the sense that he's looking after his family by earning. Sometimes I look at him and I could cry. I hate to see a good, strong man brought so low.'

She has two children under three, but has decided that she has to get some casual work to help with the family's finances. 'I wanted to do evening work so that Ted was free to look for work during the day, but then could look after the kids when I went out. I thought the best thing was being a barmaid. It's not good pay, and it's sometimes exhausting and you're dealing with some pretty rough types, but it fits in with what I want.'

When Ted is back at work full-time then Mel wants to train to be a nurse. She likes variety and wants to feel that she's doing something worthwhile. Working shifts too she hopes means she can fit in with her wish to see as much as possible of her children.

IN HOPE

Energy, balance and beauty, all are key words for an Hourglass/Aries and they are all possible as long as the impatient, self-centred Aries element in this dynamic combination does not get the bit between its teeth and gallop off after some impossible dream. This drive for novelty, for excitement, for danger, which can lead more extreme Aries into destroying what they have in pursuit of the fantasy of what they want, is fortunately grounded when united with an Hourglass temperament. There is an ancient Chinese proverb which warns against the unreal: 'To believe in one's dreams is to spend all of one's life asleep.'

HOURGLASS
TAURUS

(Yin/Yin)

MOTTO:

Storm makes oaks take deeper root

IN LIFE

In this combination you have balance, stability, strength – and true femaleness. Taurus is seen by many astrological commentators as the archetype of Woman, not the mystical haunting feminity of Pisces, nor the maternal female of Cancer, nor even the magnetic sexual female of Scorpio, but rooted, basic, earthy woman, receptive and creative. The balanced Yin temperament of her Hourglass body type, which deepens her emotional nature and makes relationships more important to her, merely add to these stable, good earth qualities.

Given these sterling characteristics, Hourglass/Taurus woman has two very distinct paths she can travel. She is often beautiful in a serene, harmonious way and her sybaritic side could well become the dominant one. If so, she will be languidly sensuous, dressed in good clothes and seductive in a cloud of perfume. She is the fantasy ideal woman for many men, sexual, receptive, uncritical, uncomplicated. She just needs a good man, a decent income, a comfortable home and access to the kind of material comforts which feature in so much of the advertising in the glossier magazines. Ruled by Venus, this aspect of Taurus/Hourglass woman displays all the pleasure-loving side of the goddess, all the straightforward seductiveness suggested by her name.

Some of the most beautiful women are Hourglass/Taurus, women like Audrey Hepburn, Jessica Lange, Joanna Lumley Michelle Pfeiffer and Natasha Richardson. There is a delicacy and sensuality about their looks which sets them apart.

Don't forget that these Venusian qualities are incorporated in an Earth sign, and so there is that other expression of Hourglass/Taurus temperament – her matter-of-factness and loyalty, her capacity for hard work and an earthy sensuality. She combines all the affectionate, hospitable qualities with the endurance and determination of being a fixed sign. Hourglass/Taurus makes an excellent friend in times of feast or famine. But she is practical above all and will get impatient if a friend in need doesn't quite quickly pull herself together and become once more a friend indeed.

There is a fundamental honesty about Hourglass/Taurus which is much more than not telling lies or cheating the tax man. Her straightforward, realistic character means she sees everything clearly, unclouded by wishful thinking, or the curlicues of fantasy. She can be accused of being unimaginative and materialistic in her thinking but she just tells it as it is. Her intelligence may well be penetrating but it is best employed in understanding and dealing with the real world.

Nothing much fazes Hourglass/Taurus or puts her off. She is not squeamish by nature, does not stand on her dignity and has few illusions waiting to be shattered. Her emotional nature tends to be pretty equable and she may not entirely comprehend the flights of ecstacy and despair of her more volatile friends. But they run to the calm oasis of her house when their lives are overwhelmed by emotional whirlpools or black rocks of despair and they find sanity and solace – and a cup of tea and homemade biscuits too.

There is an underlying force in this personality. She may be naturally placid but she is also very strong. There is in Taurus an undeniable need for power and for it to be in her own hands: she is not satisfied in getting it vicariously through the agency of a husband or lover, or in relationships with her family and friends. This fuels her steady energy for work and solid advancement. She does not easily give up, but neither is she happy taking risks and is not a natural entrepreneur, like the fire signs often are. She is good at building empires but steady and sure is more her way.

But this good constructive drive can become translated, in Hourglass/Taurus, into a dogged, workaholic side which makes her conscientious and perfectionist in everything she does. Not pedantic like Virgo, she nevertheless feels that no one can do it as well as she can – and she's probably right, but she doesn't give anyone else a chance to try. Being a fixed sign, she can go doggedly off course denying her own needs for love and sex and relationship. This sublimation of what is a powerful drive in this woman can make for an embittered, joyless, unnecessarily driven personality. This is only when the Hourglass/Taurus has lost all her natural balance and clarity of vision through submerging her feeling nature to the material.

Luckily, the balancing effect of the Hourglass temperament is always working to bring this personality back into equilibrium, is always tugging at her heart with the need for human contact and loving relationships. It is important that Hourglass/Taurus strives for this perspective, because when all the areas of her life are in harmony she is a happy and successful woman who spreads her creativity and contentment to all those in her compass.

IN WORK

Hourglass/Taurus takes a pride in how much she can take on, how well she manages her family life and working life, how she controls the lot with apparent ease. If she is able to maintain a sense of proportion, a lightness of touch and is willing to relax her high standards just a little, she brilliantly juggles the contrary demands of life. But too easily, the blinkers go on, and the narrow, driven side of this combination can emerge. When this happens, joy, imagination and inspiration sail out of the window. (Taureans are not naturally ecstatic at the best of times so need to conserve what they have.) Dogmatism, exhaustion and self-pity too easily take their place.

Hourglass/Taurus has to strive always to fertilize both areas of her life: to bring a little of the sybarite into the workaholic side; to energize the sensual side with a little of that determination and willingness to work for her own gain. She cannot live through the energies of others but she also needs to replenish her own self. The sort of work which she excels at is fundamentally creative. Music is one area where the Taurean is traditionally talented – if not possessing a beautiful singing voice, she will have a strong musical taste and may well be dedicated and gifted enough to make this her career.

Art and design is also a fruitful area for work. Hourglass/Taurus has an eye for line and colour. If she does not have enough artistic talent herself, she can make a marvellous agent or promoter of other artists. She could also enjoy working in a gallery or shop which sold beautiful *objets d'art*, where she would be wonderfully knowledgable about the artists and their work, and diligent in promoting their interests.

Taurus can be self-contained and finds it hard to remember that others need some praise. But the Hourglass element in this

combination brings a greater awareness of other people's emotional needs and confers on Hourglass/Taurus an ability to get on with colleagues and make them feel appreciated.

There are so many actresses who are Hourglass/Taurus that film and the stage must be another natural area of work for those who enjoy creating a new character in a different world. She is not only likely to be beautiful, but her Yin body type means she is good in team situations and is much less likely to play the temperamental star demanding mega-trailers and executive jets as do some of the more assertive Yang body type actresses, like Sharon Stone and Demi Moore. Hourglass/Taurus wants to be paid a fair wage (and that might well mean as much as the male lead) but she is less concerned with tangible symbols of status and success.

Working literally with the earth, growing things, cultivating plants, designing gardens, is a natural outlet for this personality's nurturing abilities and earthy interests. Managing people also is rather like tending a garden – nurturing their health, cultivating their brains or careers, and this has its own appeal. So personnel work, nursing, teaching and advisory jobs are all areas where this versatile woman will excel. She has the compassion and intuitive awareness of other people's emotions and lives, but is earthed enough herself to maintain an appropriately objective stance.

Ideal Fantasy Job

All the practical, business, organizational and caring skills of the Hourglass/Taurus would be well used in running her own business offering to troubleshoot for people dealing with sudden domestic emergencies. With her team of skilled craftsmen and willing helpers, she's able to dispatch help to whoever rings her at headquarters – nanny ill? she'll have an ex-nurse round within the hour; pipes burst and you have a meeting at work you can't reschedule? she'll organize the plumber and negotiate the best fee; elderly father's house been broken into? she'll get someone round to make him tea and tidy up the mess for him and wait until you get there. In this way Hourglass/Taurus would be responsible for making the lives of a lot of people easier and happier and building herself a good little business along the way – not much beats that.

IN LOVE

Hourglass/Taurus is made for love. This is a highly physical, sensual combination, very basic, nothing bizarre or fantastical, just good honest love and sex – and lots of it. Earth signs are just that, earthy, basic and matter-of-fact. Hourglass/Taurus has a tenacity and fixity which means she can set her sights on her goal and patiently work towards that end.

This tenacity and endurance is as evident in Hourglass/Taurus's love life as it is in every other aspect of her life. She is not likely to run out on her man, like some impetuous fire sign, or a more detached air sign might. Of all the combinations she is perhaps the most likely to endure a partner's dullness – or his infidelity. She will sit it out and wait for the storm to pass. She will be less hurt than the water signs, less mad than the fire, and less independent than air. She will also be more sensible than any in realizing how little this abberation means and how strong her hold on her man is. She knows he will return – and more often than not she is right, he'd be a fool not to when all his physical comforts are so well catered for, when he finds such security of body and mind in her embrace.

Everything about this woman is wholesome and natural and the most natural outcome of all this love and sex is children. The Hourglass/Taurus woman makes a wonderful mother in a down-to-earth way. She won't be zany, fizzing with ideas and embarrassing in her taste in clothes. She will be loyal, reliable and sympathetic to the feelings of others, and if this means she's rather unimaginative and earthbound that's a small price to pay for always knowing where you are with her.

Her air sign children might rebel against what they see as emotional prejudices and lack of a pure disinterested intellect. But even so they will recognize the absolute rock-steady quality of their Hourglass/Taurus mother's devotion. Family life really matters to her. She is likely to want to be around during her children's childhood. She is practical and will probably turn to part-time work when they begin going to school. She might well think of starting her own business, which she can run from home.

One of her great human qualities is the ability to accept people for what they are. She does not harbour fantasies of what they may become, nor does she promote her children as prodigies or angels or try to change her man into an improved version. She recognizes what she sees and doesn't try to embellish the sometimes mundane detail of her life and the lives of others.

Ideal Fantasy Lover

The man for an Hourglass/Taurus woman has to be Yang – there are no two ways about it. She is at heart an archetypally female woman and she attracts and is attracted to that basically male kind of man who appreciates her body and soul (and it doesn't

bother her too much that it's more the body than the soul which bothers him). Nick Nolte, reformed hell-raiser and hunky hero in *Cape Cod* and *Prince Of Tides*, just about fits the bill. The slight problem of his number of ex-wives can be overlooked by an Hourglass/Taurus – who better to keep him happy and home than a woman of strong resolve combined with a calm and affectionate disposition in a curvaceous body.

IN STYLE

Both Yin elements in this combination are into sensuous fabrics and rich and beautiful clothes. Silks, velvets, embroidery and lace, all attract her eye and strong tactile sense. When it comes to style, however, the Hourglass/Taurus can misjudge things and go suddenly and dramatically over-the-top. Joanna Lumley, actress, writer, and personality, has lots of wonderful Jean Muir clothes, having modelled for her in her youth. She is an intelligent beauty who looks classically elegant and distinguished in such classy clothes. And yet at gala occasions she is much more likely to turn up wearing very tight, very glittery, very tarty clothes.

Hourglass/Taurus is at her best wearing clothes of understated elegance and terrific quality. She has a pleasing symmetry about her face and body and looks classically wonderful rather than fussy or fantastical. She is not going to dress in a variety of moods, express a kaleidoscope of personalities, as her Gemini sister is prone to do. She likes value for money and is happiest buying her good designer clothes at their yearly sales. For more specific information, see In Style on page 34.

Style Treat

For our busy, well-organized Hourglass/Taurus, the perfect accessory would be a beautifully designed miniature portable phone. Then she can be in touch with home, while she's out and about sorting out her business, and can continue her business while she's bathing little Joe or cooking the fish pie for supper.

Ever practical, it also means she is always in touch with home or the emergency services, should she break down on the road at night. She could also come to the aid of any other woman in a similar situation.

IN HEALTH

As long as Hourglass/Taurus does not start burning the candle at both ends, smoke too much, drink too much and forget to have regular meals she will have a tremendously strong constitution which will seldom let her down. She does need to take care of her throat, the part of the body traditionally ruled by Taurus, and she can have trouble with her back – as much because of the pyscho-logical burdens of taking on so much and never easily giving up and letting things go. Taurus is a retentive sign and if you think of the patient ox who is the animal symbol of this sign you can recognize how too easily an Hourglass/Taurus will carry her past and her responsibilities like a great yoke across her shoulders.

Hourglass/Taurus has a tendency to put on weight. She is sensual and likes the good things of life and that includes food. Hourglass types have more delicate metabolisms than Rectangle types, for instance, and are more easily thrown out of balance by irregular eating habits and too many stimulants. If she wants to eat sensibly and lose weight along the way, her best bet is to follow a diet which takes into account these metabolic characteristics. For more specific information on diet and exercise, see In Health on page 36.

CELEBRITY HOURGLASS/TAURUS

Michelle Pfeiffer is an Hourglass/Taurus beauty who has amazed Hollywood by virtually turning her back on her career, for the time being at least, to care for a baby she has adopted. What has surprised her friends all the more is that she gets so much pleasure from looking after the baby herself: 'She's at her happiest when she's burping her, changing her nappies and when she's bouncing the baby on her knee.' Her sister confirms this Hourglass/Taurus trait: 'Michelle's always been a super-caring person, a care-taker of friends and family. I think this child means a lot more to her than the movie career.'

Paula Yates is perhaps the most archetypal of Hourglass/Taurus celebrities. As a lonely only child from a broken home (with a celebrity father) she attached herself very young to the wild man of rock, Bob Geldoff. Grunge-glamorous long before it was fashionable and rawly sexual, he was the most Yang bloke she could have found: Bob on the impulse to be a Yin man 'I always read that men have got to be taught that it's OK to express themselves. Fuck Off! I mean, Freud got it wrong . . .'

Rumour has it that the young Paula caught his attention with her sexual enthusiasm and then wouldn't go away. She had made her choice of man and she was going to stay. Pregnancy and three babies eventually cemented the relationship, but Paula carried the domestic responsibilities (with the help of a nanny) while Bob

continued to help save the world. She seemed to accept this as her role and set to it with a will. Her children were going to have the perfect, secure, loving family that she had always longed for and never had herself.

In a typical Hourglass/Taurus down-to-earth way she saw this as providing all the emotional and material comforts – wonderful, traditional Christmases, a Kate Greenaway vision of cosy, innocent childhood surrounded by animals, toys and open fires (properly fire-guarded) and toasted crumpets for tea.

HOURGLASS/TAURUS PROFILE

Lisa is a freelance book designer who works from home, 'I like my home, and enjoy setting up my studio here and having this nice secure feeling of everything under one roof.' Her house is comfortable and arty in a restrained way. Redolent of comfort and good taste, her rooms have nothing contrived about them nor are they over-neat.

She is married to David, an investment banker who works long, hard hours. 'I was attracted firstly to his enormous forearms! I saw him working in the garden next door – this was about five years ago – and he looked more like a gamekeeper than a banker. And very sexy in his rolled up sleeves, his old muddy jeans and with tousled, greenfly flecked hair. I fancied being Lady Chatterley to his Mellors and was rather disappointed when I saw him all trussed up for work in his dark suit.'

She wants to have children in the next three years, if possible, and has dreams of moving to the country, although David's job would have to change – or he'd commute – if that was to become reality. 'I think I've always thought I'd have children and that they would be one of the main pleasures in my life. I think I'd try and keep up some freelance work, but you never know 'til you have them quite how you do feel, and whether you're going to be much interested in struggling on with a part-time job. I'm not good at doing anything in a half-hearted manner. I would be driving myself at two o'clock in the morning and then getting ratty with the children the next day. I do picture David and me with rosy kids round the AGA, a kitchen garden bursting in at the kitchen door. But what it'll be like if I get to that stage I don't know.'

Lisa is happy with her lot. She has no wild ambitions and impossible dreams but is centred on the basic foundations of home, hearth and relationships, and is pleased to be her sort of woman: 'I think of David and me as equal but different and it is

that difference which supplies the sexual excitement in our relationship.'

IN HOPE

Sometimes Hourglass/Taurus can be too predictable and sensible for her own good. She will get her life running smoothly on tramlines and be very hard to deflect into any lighthearted serendipity. It might be fun for her, and shake the complacency of those around her, if she occasionally indulges the other side of her character.

If she's the self-sacrificing, hard-working kind of Hourglass/Taurus, perhaps she should spend the whole day pampering herself in a beauty salon, or a week-end in a health farm. On the other hand, if she's the sybaritic, lounging around type who spends enough of her time already looking pampered and beautiful (there are fewer of this type these days) she might find it enriching to put on her dirtiest clothes and toil away clearing and planting wasteland, making barren ground fertile. Hourglass/Taurus woman is naturally someone who encourages things to grow and she is more capable and successful at it than most.

HOURGLASS
GEMINI

(Yin/Yang)

MOTTO:

In skating over thin ice our safety is in speed

IN LIFE

There are so many facets to this combination that it is difficult to pin down the salient features – just as it is difficult to tie down an Hourglass/Gemini woman in full flow, describing an escapade or rushing off to explore some new territory. Gemini is ruled by Mercury, planet of communication, and is known for its quick-silver brain and changeable personality. The symbol for the sign is The Twins which expresses another characteristic of the Gemini personality, a confusion sometimes as to where this person truly belongs, and what she is at her core. Is she rational mind or intuitive soul, is she saint or sinner, intellectual or artist?

Luckily these confusions are centred by the very balanced nature of the Hourglass temperament. Yin body type with Yang star sign here means there are great possibilities for a whole and balanced individual to develop, where the feeling, intuitive side is as strongly represented as the rational and intellectual. The fascination with ideas – and lots of them – is one of the traits of the Gemini which can lead to accusations of her being butterfly-brained or superficial. The Hourglass side of this combination brings in a steadying, deepening quality and consequently a greater interest in sticking with a particular idea or project for longer and exploring its fuller implications.

The other great quality of the Gemini is her ability to change chameleon-like to suit the people she's among and the situation she's in. This makes her a marvellous mimic, actor, saleswoman – and journalist too – for she can appear so sympathetic to whoever she's talking to. But the downside of this changeability is the difficulty she sometimes has in making deep relationships. She is not at ease with intense feelings for anything or anyone. She doesn't care for probing discussions which seek to penetrate the surface of her light and easy manner.

There is a coolness in her temperament, which can be tipped into coldness by her self-protective response to any unfortunate emotional experiences. Here again, though, the Hourglass element in this character adds a nurturing balance, which encourages the Hourglass/Gemini to become more feeling and sympathetic to others, more easy and in need of relationships herself. She realizes life can be more than a series of adventures.

Pear/Gemini, for instance, with that strong pull towards feelings and relationship, is a combination with a real seesawing between heart and mind, between responsibility and freedom. But here with Hourglass/Gemini there is a less extreme polarity, a sense of closer balance which can help Gemini in the area she finds hardest – that of real human connections, of desire, love and enduring commitment. More intense, emotional combinations might find her fickle and heartless at times, but her Yin Hourglass body type brings the fertilizing power of feeling to bear on these quick-change Twins, and makes for a much more compassionate and balanced personality.

Imaginative and social, Hourglass/Gemini is a delight at any party. She's full of life and laughter, lighthearted, always flirtatious, but she's not usually a man-eater and other women's men are safe with her. It's the fun and games that matter more to her than a great passionate affair or any heavy intrigue – or even polishing her ego in the admiration of the opposite sex. She does not care particularly for being restricted or tied down, although the two Yin body types, the Pear and Hourglass, are not as allergic to marriage as the Yang body types allied with this Gemini star sign can be.

This love of variety, this speed and lightness and reluctance to shut the door on other possibilities and tie herself down generally, means Hourglass/Gemini is brilliant at running two (or even more) careers, hobbies, lovers, at once.

IN WORK

Words, communication, people, variety, mix these together and you have all the necessary ingredients for any work or career for Hourglass/Gemini. This leaves the field wide open. Journalism, or any work in television, radio or publishing, is a natural for this woman who loves ideas and has all the necessary skills to

disseminate them. The Hourglass body type gives her a matter-of-factness and sweetness of temperament which can add useful ballast to the airy and inventive, but sometimes lightweight, cast of mind of the Gemini.

Jack of all trades and master of none best describes the variety of talents of Hourglass/Gemini and the ease with which she moves on from one area of interest to another. Boredom and constraint are her two bugbears and she would rather work for a pittance in something which intellectually stimulates her and offers her novelty and challenge than be straightjacketed in a job of numbing tedium which paid her a fortune. She is not as ambitious as other star body signs might be and so there is nothing to stop Hourglass/Gemini kicking up her heels if she feels fenced in or ground down.

The gift of the gab also belongs to Hourglass/Gemini. Combine this talent with her charm and intuitive ability to understand others (the Hourglass element there) and you have a saleswoman *par excellence*. This talent can find expression in anything from the highly paid executive in a top advertising agency who lunches prospective clients, to the charming, well-informed demonstrator of vacuum cleaners at the local department store. She is not in any way dishonest, but she's mighty plausible when it comes to talking people into – and herself out of – anything she sets her mind to.

Ideal Fantasy Job

Playwright-in-Residence. Hourglass/Gemini is not as happy in front of the lights as she is being the brains behind the stage, the individual who creates the play from a mere kernel of an idea and is therefore responsible for making the whole thing happen. Geminis are very happy in theatrical circles. They are so gifted at playing other parts in life, it seems the most fortunate thing if they can bring this natural talent into their work – and get paid for it, however little. Material success is not a top priority for Hourglass/Gemini but intellectual stimulation and creativity are. Here she would be as happy as anyone could be.

IN LOVE

For Gemini, there is more than a grain of truth that in everything it is the journey, not the arrival, that matters. Nowhere is this truer than in the arena of love, sex and marriage. There is some conflict likely in Hourglass/Gemini because of this strong drive in Yin women towards relationship and love. When united with emotional water star signs, like Pisces, Cancer and Scorpio, or with impetuous fire, like Leo and Aries, the Hourglass woman is likely to be propelled by her heart and hormones into quite an early marriage. But here, united with the most airy and unharnessable of signs, there's likely to be a good deal of to-ing and fro-ing.

Gemini woman is naturally rather detached and cerebral, interested more in light romance and friendship rather than passion. In fact, anything that begins to get too intense, possessive and steamy sends her running for the door. However, the Hourglass body type is a much more sensual and sexual being: she is drawn towards love and relationship. The result is a psyche with contrasting pulls.

Flirtatious, enjoying lighthearted games and quickfire banter, the Hourglass/Gemini is at her best during the courtship period of any relationship. She can get a little fed up with the routine and mundanity of life once the honeymoon is over. She needs a man who is Yang enough to excite the Yin body type, but he cannot be in the least boorish or boring. She wants intellectual fireworks, or at least unpredictable change, to keep her interested.

Children are also an area of some ambivalence for the Hourglass/Gemini. For an Hourglass there is a real sense that having children and a family life is one of the main reasons for being on this earth, but the Gemini part of this combination is afraid of being slowed down, tied down, losing her independence. Responsibility, predictability and routine are not her strong suit. Enjoying the company of children, she feels she's more like them sometimes than like the grown-ups. But Hourglass/Gemini is more grown-up than that, and there is a marked difference in attitude to her feelings on the subject as she grows older: 'I do want to have children. At my age [35], if I did have a baby I would give up my career and try to work freelance from home because it would be important to be with a child. Years ago I would have rebelled against this totally, saying I wouldn't give up my job (ie independence) for anything!!' was how one of Bel's Hourglass/Gemini clients expressed the shift.

This combination makes for a loving, sympathetic mother, but one who is pleased to encourage her children's independence from early on. She is unlikely to be still driving them to school when they are 14. Her children will have been taught to ride bikes from an early age and as soon as they had passed their proficiency test they would be pedalling themselves to school if at all possible. She values education and will encourage her children at school and hope they do well, but she is not interested in reflecting any of their glory into her life. She will always have her own busy life to live and would never be happy living vicariously

through someone else; she needs projects on the go, plans to draw up, and people to see. Hourglass/Gemini would end up thoroughly demoralized and depressed if she was isolated from other human company with only the dusters and washing-up for company.

Always ready for any adventure, Hourglass/Gemini is not the sort of woman to stick to a routine and refuse to drop everything in order to go on a spontaneous expedition to the market/cinema/beach/protest march. Her man can either run beside her or leave her to her own enthusiasms, she will be happy with either alternative. Neither is she someone who has to be hand in glove with those she loves. Distance makes the heart grow fonder for Hourglass/Gemini, but because of the Yin influence of her body type it is a very warm and sympathetic heart and the distance isn't very far.

Ideal Fantasy Lover

Brains and/or quirkiness of character are essentials for this woman in her choice of man, along with an uncomplicated maleness. The arrogant and wildly clever film director Spike Lee is an interesting choice. He is the angry young man of American cinema who goes out of his way to show everyone he is his own man. In the process he elicits intense reactions to his films, *She's Gotta Have It* and *Malcolm X* among them, and to himself. He courts enemies among the Academy Awards establishment, and is known as a volatile iconoclast and the most important and politically provocative of American film-makers. All this will appeal enormously to the intellectual side of the Hourglass/Gemini, his intense, arrogant Yangness will appeal to her female Yin self. Dangerous, but exciting.

As an older and less intellectually challenging choice there is always Paul 'Crocodile Dundee' Hogan, who has the necessary humour and devil-may-care approach to life which can only appeal to the freewheeling side of this combination. A man who is willing to sling his swag over his shoulder and head off to the outback at the slightest constraint will be an inspiring companion for this woman. What fun to be had together tickling crocodiles in some steamy billabong – and laughing like kookaburras under the shade of a coolabah tree.

IN STYLE

When young, Hourglass/Gemini will have piles of cheap, fashionable clothes which capture every passing mood of her own and society at large. Flares, catsuits, animal print leotards, diaphanous tea-dresses, big jerseys and lycra leggings, mother's sixties stuff and granny's evening frocks, all jostle together, ready to be combined in some original, quirky way. She loves change and this is readily seen in the clothes she wears. You never know what your young Hourglass/Gemini might be wearing when you next catch sight of her in the High Street.

She is sometimes completely unrecognizable and is just as likely to experiment with her hair colour, style and make-up. Can that sweet blonde teenager in jeans and T-shirt you met at her mother's last week really be the same as this black-haired vamp with the beehive, wearing a velvet dress that seems to have escaped from the set of *Gothic Terror 2*? Youth is a time of experimentation and Gemini, star sign of eternal youthfulness, is going to experiment with a vengeance.

As she grows older, the Hourglass element in this combination begins to exert itself more. This brings an appreciation of good quality clothes, a love of creative dressing, but nothing too extreme. Hourglass/Gemini too, when she reaches her late twenties and early thirties, has worked out better who she is and where she's going. So our maturer woman starts to get together a more coherent style for herself. Her need for variety is expressed in wearing different types of clothes for different occasions. She is unlikely to want to wear her work clothes out in the evening. She is also going to continue to want to experiment with different hairstyles, and is a sucker for the promotions of new lipstick and make-up colours. Variety is still the spice of life for this woman. For more specific information, see In Style on page 35.

Style Treat

The quickest way for any woman to feel rejuvenated and restyled, is to have a super haircut. For Hourglass/Gemini it's probably best if she keeps her hair at shoulder length: this will allow for the greatest versatility. Wear it up for that sophisticated, working woman image, or loosely piled on top for the romantic, dishevelled look. Straight and swingy, it makes her sporty and casual – twisted into a knot, or whisked into a ponytail, and you have a whole new look again. Splash out and treat yourself. Finding the right stylist for a good haircut is essential. If you aren't happy with your current hairdresser, look at other women you know and see who has a particularly good cut. Ask who does her hair and go to see him or her. The best hairdresser isn't necessarily the most expensive, or the one who brooks no discussion, insisting on imposing a certain style on you. Nor is he or she the one who just attempts to do what the client wants, without any experimentation and discussion. The best stylists will look at the texture and quality of your hair, will take into account the shape

of your head and face, your height and way of life. They will discuss the pros and cons and how to maintain the sort of style they suggest, and will only go ahead when you both are happy with the decision.

Just as clothes with curve suit an Hourglass-type woman best, so too do soft, wavy and not too severely short hairstyles. Some Hourglass-type women become very attached to their long hair – although Hourglass/Gemini is probably the least sentimental of all – but anyone over thirty is probably flattered more by hair which doesn't come much below her shoulders. Also, if she is in business, a well-cut, mid-length hair style looks more credible.

IN HEALTH

Gemini rules the main communication network of the body, the nervous system. Overwork and over-anxiety can play havoc with Hourglass/Gemini's wellbeing. Digestive upsets, anxiety, frazzled nerves are all possible when she has been rushing around too much or feeling overburdened with responsibilites. 'Worried sick' is an expression which could well be applied to the distraught Hourglass/Gemini. Therefore, finding ways of relaxing is very important for this combination. Yoga, meditation, long walks in the country, just learning how to turn off from the continual stimuli of life to which she is naturally so responsive.

The chest and lungs can also be susceptible. Hourglass/Gemini might be prone to hayfever and asthma and therefore cutting out smoking is even more of a priority for this woman. And, of course, learning to unwind and relax will be helpful in all these areas.

The Hourglass metabolism is a balanced one which is easily thrown off balance by too many stimulants, like tea, coffee, alcohol and cigarettes. These sap her energy and leave her exhausted and reaching for another coffee/drink/fag to perk her up again. Bad eating habits also sabotage her metabolism and leave her a collapse case at the end of the week. For more specific information on diet and exercise, see In Health on page 36.

CELEBRITY HOURGLASS/GEMINI

There are many beautiful Hourglass/Gemini celebrities among the actress sorority – Marilyn Monroe, in many ways the most extraordinarily lovely to look at, then Joan Collins, Isabella Rossellini, another unique beauty whose face stares out of the Lancôme ads, Kylie Minogue and Brooke Shields.

Kylie Minogue went from being a schoolgirl to world stardom through her part on the hit Australian soap *Neighbours*. She had to put up with all sorts of critical attacks and vilification, particularly as she went through the Geminian chameleon-like changes when she tried to turn herself into vamp on the lines of Madonna. This was a mistake as she has none of the ability of that lady (a Triangle/Leo)to ruthlessly manipulate the media. She remained a sweet kid, youthful and somehow innocent.

Brooke Shields is someone who, rather like Marilyn Monroe, had her beautiful face and body hijacked by the media – and like Marilyn, she was to some extent the victim of other people's ambitions. For years her life as a child and teenager was ruled by her ambitious ex-actress mother who promoted her from babyhood, as this beautiful but unattainable object of desire. From modelling as America's most beautiful baby she came under the scrutiny of the world when she was only 12 and was chosen by Louis Malle to play the child prostitute in *Pretty Baby*.

She remembers her desperate desire for approval, her tight self-control in public which denied any feelings which were inappropriate – above all her terrific lack of confidence in her own worth. The films which followed, such as *The Blue Lagoon* and *Endless Love* seemed to trade on exposing as much of her body as possible. But privately this young actress was struggling with her inability to make deep relationships and was not managing to be naturally sexual at all. In true Gemini fashion she found the initial flirtation stages possible but not the love – 'I fall in love all the time, but it doesn't go any further' she was quoted as saying.

Acting is a great Gemini profession, and Brooke Shields recognizes that through acting she realizes some of the different facets of her personality. Not being long on self-knowledge, many Geminis are blind to their own character, unless it is pointed out to them in clear terms. Scripts and the process of filming does that for Brooke: 'Acting used to be such fun . . . "Who am I Going to Be Today?" . . there are many different facets to my personality that I might never get to realize at all if I didn't have film to do it in.'

Brooke Shields interestingly broke out of the Hollywood fish bowl, putting her career on hold and took herself off to Princeton to do a degree. This search for the intellectual part of herself and a greater balance is a true Hourglass/Gemini thing to do. Perhaps she can now begin to find what she really wants to do with her life, which will make her a better actress and an independent woman in the process.

HOURGLASS/GEMINI PROFILE

Mo is a freelance hairdresser who works on modelling sessions, does occasional work on films and cuts for a group of loyal friends who find her amusing company and always good for a laugh. 'It suits me to never really know where I will be working from one week to the next. A studio will ring me up to book me for a couple of days, then I fit in my private clients and work either at their places or mine. I'm easy.'

She is always changing her own hair and it's a standing joke among the people she works with that you never know if Mo's a blonde, a redhead or a natural turquoise mohican. 'My clothes for work are pretty practical – jeans or leggings with a shirt, or a jersey in winter. But I do realize that I look best in the lighter fabrics and I love belts of all kinds. In fact that's the one thing I collect. I try and get a striking belt from whatever country I visit.'

When she goes clubbing at night she lets rip a bit more, and wears an eclectic mix of styles, never knowing until she walks out of the door precisely how she wants to look that night. Mo has lots of friends, and gets on very well with her women friends, but at 26 she has no desire yet to settle down with a man.

'I love the beginning of a relationship, it's exciting and my adrenaline is running and I lose lots of weight. I am never bored. But then when things start to settle into routine, and the moment he starts to get possessive, I feel a little claustrophobic. "I wanna get outa here" keeps going round in my brain. I know I'll want to have children when I'm older and I'll care very much for them, but just now I'm having a lot of fun. I see myself as whistling, barefoot on the sand, just footloose and fancy-free!'

IN HOPE

Deep in the Hourglass/Gemini psyche is this need to integrate her intellectual free-spirit with her feeling female nature. She resists it when young and then wonders why there is a certain sterility in her life: she's happy while on her adventures but there is always the time in between when she has to come home. There is an old Chinese proverb, the truth of which Hourglass/Gemini recognizes in these bleaker moments of return, 'The mind covers more ground than the heart, but goes less far.' But this Gemini is fortunate in having the deepening, heartening influence of her Hourglass body type, and it is this feeling side which needs, perhaps, to be allowed equal expression in her life.

HOURGLASS
CANCER
(Yin/Yin+)

MOTTO:

A friend in need is a friend indeed

IN LIFE

Here we have the double Yin personality, the feeling woman, whose sympathies extend to everyone who suffers or is in need. The Cancerian influence gives this emotional combination a strong maternal aspect which is expressed with family, friends and in the workplace. There is a genuine caring for others, an ability to work for the general good, a feeling that family matters most of all – and that sense of family is brought into the working environment. This has many positive advantages: Hourglass/Cancer's colleagues are treated as individuals with equal rights; there is a concern for everyone's happiness; there is little hierarchy and even the smallest has a voice. But in times of disagreement, the dissenting voice can be made to feel he/she is committing a kind of emotional betrayal.

Cancer is also a cautious sign, and her Hourglass-type disposition does nothing to embolden this character. Hourglass/Cancer is not dynamically entrepreneurial or a gambler in any way. In fact, she's unlikely even to be a big spender, she is so good at conserving her own assets, and looking after the money and investments of others.

The past matters very much to her and she will hang on to old friends, old jerseys, old books, old everything, for they all have sentimental connotations. She finds it very hard to let things go, is a collector and conserver in the broadest and deepest sense. That tenacious old crab, symbol of the sign, clings on to these past memories, old relationships, every issue of *Vogue* from when her mother first started buying it: or her children whom she finds hard to let go of when it is time for them to make lives of their own.

Hypersensitive, this star sign is ruled by the Moon and intuitively picks up on the waxing and waning of the moods of others close to her. She has her own fluctuating feelings to deal with too. This sensitivity imparts a marvellous mystical imagination which makes the Hourglass/Cancer woman so creative. But at times it also makes her slightly cut off from others who cannot follow where her moods and feelings take her.

She is one of the deepest and subtlest of characters, and one of the most difficult to understand. Not to herself, but to those who are more straightforward. Earth signs are bemused by her profound and largely hidden emotionalism, fire signs bluster at it, and air signs shrug their shoulders and skip away. There is something mysterious and seductive about this now-you-see-me-now-you-don't aspect to Hourglass/Cancer. She can be extraordinarily calm and hardworking and practical, applying herself to a multitude of tasks that would have a less tenacious combination, like Hourglass/Gemini, escaping to the nearest cinema for respite. She can be everyone's perfect mother, sympathetic, loving, and full of imaginative insights.

But then, some hurt, some memory, or even some alteration in the Moon's phase, will cause her to disappear – not physically – but spiritually. Suddenly there is a blank, a personality lost in her own inner turmoil. In fact, sometimes she really does disappear. You'll notice she's not at your usual meeting place, or she stops ringing, or she's evasive when you call. It is just that she is in a melancholy period when she is dealing with her own submerged being.

Hourglass/Cancer has every good quality in the book, they are just strung together in a puzzling and occasionally impenetrable way: sometimes they function all together in wonderful harmony, and then everyone wants to be her friend. At other times these qualities get lost in the high tide of fearfulness, morbid imaginings, and emotional panic, and Hourglass/Cancer is hard put to keep herself going – let alone restore the spirits of others.

IN WORK

Hourglass/Cancer is a collector and a cultivator. The collector side comes out in her love of antiques, of research (particularly historical), and her talent with managing money. All these are fruitful areas in which she can build her career. Running an antiques shop, writing about *objets d'art*, or working as an expert in a big auction house tempt her. Her love of the past and gift with understanding the lives of others outside her experience means that a project collecting first-hand reports of life during

the Great Depression, for instance – and then perhaps writing about that – would also hold her interest over the years it would take to put together. Accountancy and book-keeping, and business in general, also attracts the Hourglass/Cancer with her excellent memory and her ability as a shrewd tactician.

The cultivating side of her character is even more productive in the work field. She is a natural gardener and horticulturist. Sensitive to the individuality of plants, she has brilliant green fingers and knows almost intuitively where best to position them in a garden, be it flower or vegetable. Like Prince Charles – a Scorpio and another emotional, intuitive water sign – she will believe in talking to plants and will wonder why more rational beings should ever think it a sure sign of looniness.

The cultivation and care of children also has a strong appeal for Hourglass/Cancer. This can express itself in anything from teaching to fostering, from paediatric nursing to training to be a speech therapist. In all these occupations, Hourglass/Cancer's highly intuitive nature can read signals others don't even notice and can express support and sympathy just when and where it is needed most.

Catering too attracts this woman because her sensual nature makes her very appreciative of food – its flavour, texture, colour and character in various combinations – and she is often a very fine cook. One of those unflappable, attractive young women, driving round town in her gleaming little van delivering delicious meals for executive lunches might well be your enterprising Hourglass/Cancer. She will be able to gauge just right the tastes of her clients and will unerringly come up with the appropriate menu. She will make it look effortless, but she is likely to have spent some anxious hours over it – she does not ride problems and tension as easily as she appears to.

Although, Hourglass/Cancer does not actively seek the limelight, like more obviously extrovert combinations might, she is quite happy if a bit of it swings her way. With the Moon as ruler, she has an ability to deal with the public at large and although she will project her modest, kind, feminine self, she won't be quite so ill-at-ease with public prominence as she may make out. Jobs where she is a spokesperson, or heads a committee – or even joins the select band of Hourglass/Cancer actresses (who tend to manage to sacrifice their emotional lives as little as possible to their trade) might suit her very well.

Ideal Fantasy Job

Head Gardener at Sissinghurst. This is the castle in Kent, England, where Vita Sackville-West built from nothing a garden of

breathtaking beauty. She made white gardens fashionable and encouraged the informal, sensual, plant-led design which has been taken up so enthusiastically by other gardeners since – with every size of garden.

This job would satisfy all Hourglass/Cancer's love of history and her passion for growing things. She would be excellent at heading a team of women gardeners, would never stand on her dignity, pull rank or insist on any special treatment. They would all muck in together, and the satisfaction of the job, the closeness to nature and the beauty of her surroundings would keep the old Cancerian melancholy at bay.

IN LOVE

In the area of love, sex, marriage and family, Hourglass/Cancer comes into her own. This is a double Yin combination and therefore a primary focus and force in her life is her relationships with others. She is very likely to marry. Deeply emotional, under that hard shell she sometimes displays as protection she is also very conservative and values tradition. Once she has chosen her man, the crab's tenacity comes into play and she will find it very hard to let him go. Bel has two Hourglass/Cancer clients who brought themselves almost to the brink of panic and mental collapse when they thought the men they wanted were about to slip from their grasp – and this was before they married.

Hourglass/Cancer will never be a straightforwardly ruthless character, she is far too sensitive to the feelings and wishes of others, but she is able to get her own way using more oblique methods which can verge on emotional blackmail. She can withdraw into herself, she can collapse in a catatonic state, she can appear terribly vulnerable or fiercely determined, whatever is necessary to achieve what she needs. None of this is an act – as it could be with a more calculating woman. On the contrary, it is the very force of her feelings, the life and death importance of the relationship to her, the power of her fluctuating moods, the ever-lurking melancholy, which can so overwhelm her own self – and any opposition from others.

The strong maternal aspect of Hourglass/Cancer can colour all her relationships, even with a husband or lover. It will either express itself as a need in her to be mothered or, more probably, as a mothering quality in her love for her man. This can cause some confusion in the sorts of men that she attracts and is attracted to. Her Yin Hourglass body type means there is a sexual excitement with a Yang, macho kind of guy. Your Jack Nicolsons and Harvey Keitels we're talking here.

Now these men are not so keen on being mothered by their women – although there are women who feel that's precisely what they should have had more of to make them slightly more civilized and feeling individuals. So if Hourglass/Cancer veers away from these rough diamonds and heads more for the sweeter alternative, not quite Jason Donovan but someone more tractable, she sacrifices along the way the sexual excitement that exists between Yin women and Yang men. But she probably has a more peaceful life.

With whoever she chooses as a mate, Hourglass/Cancer is likely to head straight for motherhood. It takes a very bad experience of childhood and family life, or great personal unhappiness, to make this woman decide against having children. When her baby arrives, all the sympathetic, protective, feeling side of her flows out to this helpless being: she will feel she has come home. Her personal talents combine in the loving and nurturing of this small, dependent creature. All her creativity can be channelled into building a family, the house and the garden.

This does not mean that Hourglass/Cancer will remain so child and domestically centred for ever, but when these small, vulnerable babies need her she will find the bond with them very hard to unravel, and probably will not try. The Hourglass element of this body type, however, helps stabilize her if she goes overboard with an experience like motherhood. She may be emotionally overwhelmed but will not become obsessed.

As her children grow, go to school, and need her less full-time, the typical Hourglass/Cancer mother will be looking for outside stimulus in the form of part-time work, or projects of various kinds. There is no getting away from the fact that this personality needs to be needed, ideally by those closest to her, her children and husband, but also by her friends and colleagues at work. She can therefore become indispensable to them, controlling them benignly through their need of her, an ever-available source of comfort, help and understanding. However, she has to be careful not to sap their independence nor to wear herself out in the process of mothering the world.

Ideal Fantasy Lover

For an ideal fantasy lover, the mothering side of Hourglass/Cancer is deliberately to be ignored. Here is a man who was never made for mothering, and who not even an incorrigible Hourglass/Cancer would dream of trying to pat on the head, kiss on the cheek or chuck under the chin – the glorious greaser, bad-mouthing, sex-mad, Mickey Rourke. When he first entered the acting profession,

he was hailed as the new James Dean and Marlon Brando rolled into one, which means the sort of man most fathers of daughters would have nighmares about.

His huge gleaming Harley Davidson on which he roars to and from the studios has sent less charismatic actors reaching for their crash helmets (Rourke says he'd rather die than wear one of those) and the teens of Paris and Los Angeles copy his black leather jackets and swept back hair. But Hourglass/Cancer could let her fantasies rip, swept off on the back of his Harley to some downtown bar. He is probably mad, most definitely bad and terrifically *dangerous* to know.

IN STYLE

Luxury and understated elegance, these are the words which keep on coming through from Hourglass/Cancer clients: 'all jerseys in cashmere, shoes Italian leather, clothes designer label, classic cuts – with good taste oozing out of everywhere. Pure silk underwear . . .' Everything has to feel good as well as look good, but no flashy consumerism – the Cartier watch is not for her.

Certain clothes of Cancerian women will have emotional connotations which make her very attached to them long after they should have been given to the jumble sale. Those scuffed red shoes, for instance, may make her feel happy every time she puts them on because she first wore them to a party where she danced all night with a man she was in love with. That silk blouse was a present from her mother and so carries all the affection she feels for her. There can be the biography of her life lined up on the hangers in her wardrobe, which is why she often has so many clothes, and can never find the heart to pass some on and throw others out.

The Hourglass element also adds a love of clothes, but this time for less personal reasons. Yin women have a natural delight in the sensuality of clothes, the creative putting together of colours and textures, the trying out of new looks, the experimentation and fooling around. She will work out a look that suits her and then experiment with subtle variations on her main theme. For more specific information, see In Style on page 34.

Style Treat

Hourglass/Cancer is not good at spoiling herself, particularly if she has children or feels she is short of money. She can always find a reason why she shouldn't spend money (unlike a Leo, Pisces or Scorpio for instance who can be very good at finding reasons why they *should*). One of the greatest treats for her is beautiful, luxurious underwear and so when the time comes for her to cheer herself up, or reward herself – or just surprise everyone by acting out of character – she can splash out on something pretty, something feminine, something silk. A bra and pants set, perhaps, or a body in silk and lace. Anything that really feels good next to her skin will make her feel good all day long.

Like her other clothing, her underwear should follow the curve of her body. She looks good in lace and frills, scooped necklines and feminine rather than sporty pants. The wonderful Gossard Wonderbra, remarkably inexpensive and a perennial favourite with mothers and their trendy daughters, is a good bra for many Hourglass shapes, particularly the slenderer one with quite small breasts. Anyone more generously endowed might find this bra does rather *too* much for her figure.

IN HEALTH

The glandular system is an area traditionally ruled by Cancer and Hourglass/Cancer may be prone to putting on weight – not least because she loves her food, but also because of her interest in fine cooking and generally sensual nature, rather than just pure greed. Worry is also a problem for Hourglass/Cancer and this can be too easily internalized where it attacks the lining of the stomach, making her prone to ulcers. Finding ways of releasing these kinds of tensions are important for her health and happiness. It is a different problem from the nerviness of the Hourglass/Gemini for instance, but relaxation, meditation and yoga are just as effective with any of these anxious, or nervous temperaments.

The Hourglass metabolism is a balanced one which is easily thrown off balance by too many stimulants, like tea, coffee, alcohol and cigarettes. These sap her energy and leave her exhausted and reaching for another coffee/drink/fag to perk her up again. Bad eating habits also sabotage her metabolism and leave her a collapse case at the end of the week. For more specific information on diet and exercise, see In Health on page 36.

CELEBRITY HOURGLASS/CANCER

Kelly McGillis is one of those actresses who is brilliant in a part which has some resonance with her own emotional nature, but she is not equipped with the single-minded ambition to drive her way up the stardom ladder in such a ruthless place as Hollywood. Her beauty was first remarked on in *Reuben, Reuben*, and this led to her being cast in the Academy award winning *Witness*,

where her quiet grace and luminous beauty fill the screen as she touchingly portrays the young Amish widow. As any Hourglass/Cancer woman might, she falls deeply in love with the gorgeous city detective, the deeply Yang, Harrison Ford. There have not been any really good parts for her since then.

Marriage to yacht broker Fred Tillman followed and she threw herself into that, delighted to start a family and settle down into marital bliss. She told friends she thought she had the perfect marriage, she was so happy that she abandoned Hollywood to concentrate on her family life. She no longer dressed glamorously and loved going about her business in Key West in Florida, where they ran a business together, without being recognized – just an ordinary mum.

But then a bombshell hit her out of the blue. Her husband was picked up by the police just days after she gave birth to her second child, a daughter. He was apparently trying to pick up a prostitute while she was home nursing her baby.

Hourglass/Cancer is a much more sensitive creature than she ever lets on to the world. Her love and loyalty for her husband, her powerful maternal feelings for her children, her creation of the ideal family life around them all, were all betrayed by that one act. But understand it as she might, the wound probably goes too deep for it ever to be truly forgiven.

HOURGLASS/CANCER PROFILE

Mary finally married her husband, an electronics engineer, after they had both been saving for five years to get their deposit for a house. They were then relocated from London to the Sussex coast where she had three children, very close in age. Money was particularly tight when the children were young: 'I had to do something to bring a little more money into the household so I took up work like cleaning other peoples' houses – where I could take the children with me – oh, and I also worked as a silverspoon waitress in the evenings while my husband babysat.' Later on she turned her talents as a cook to good purpose and catered for dinner-parties for people in the neighbourhood.

Mary has enormous energy, and as soon as her children were at school full-time her working hours outside the home expanded. 'Now that my children have grown up I have taken on the running of a busy office as my full-time day job, then I do small-time market gardening from my big garden at home, where I grow fruit and vegetables for the family's own use and for sale at the local shop.'

Her greatest pleasure is to cook and she makes her own wine, mountains of jam to keep a large extended family and wide circle of friends well-supplied, and she also cooks regular cordon bleu meals for friends. Her children and a growing band of grandchildren are always returning to the fold – and even her middle-aged sisters turn up whenever they can to enjoy the extent of her warm hospitality and delicious food.

Mary's health is where all this energy and industry takes its toll, however. Whenever she overdoes things she gets ill or sprains or strains something but never gives herself enough time off to rest properly and heal her complaining body. She always does recover, though, and the next thing her family knows is that she is learning to tap-dance or has signed up for yet another course – on human biology or advanced book-keeping – and still she goes on giving out the comfort and maternal care.

IN HOPE

'The moon is a friend for the lonesome to talk to', is a line from a Carl Sandburg poem which characterizes the sympathetic nature of this combination, ruled as it is by the moon. Hourglass/Cancer needs to strive for balance, needs to care for herself as well as others, needs to hold back a little bit of that love and energy. Everyone who loves her fears sometimes that she will exhaust herself emotionally – waning, like her ruling moon, to invisibility.

HOURGLASS
LEO

(Yin/Yang+)

MOTTO:

Make hay while the sun shines

IN LIFE

Ruled by the mighty sun, all Leos share a straightforward, sunny temperament, and a big, generous personality which holds few mysteries. Like the sun, she exudes warmth and power although if she does not get her due respect she can sulk, and withdraw behind the clouds. But Hourglass/Leo is not quite so unequivocally Leonine as the Rectangle and Triangle sort; she is less of an irresistible force. Neither is she quite as responsive to the feelings of others as the Pear/Leo. Nevertheless, her female body shape makes her highly intuitive and receptive, and in Hourglass/Leo she has a great combination of sensitivity and power – when she can manage to harness these two influences together in creative harmony.

The trouble can come when this masculine, out-going star sign pulls in a different direction from the more nurturing Yin body type. The terrific energy of the Hourglass/Leo will be focused on home and family as well as work and at times she will feel that the career is just too much (whereas a Rectangle or Triangle/Leo who might feel torn between the two demands would be more likely to want to accommodate the work). The Hourglass/Leo is a fascinating mixture of lioness-on-the-hunt and fire-side cat.

Leos have a brilliant press in the astrological books – and they are not averse to trumpeting it themselves but this is an indication of another side of the Leo character which is not so readily mentioned. They are great fantasists. The world – and themselves as heroes in it – can become wonderfully embellished by their inflated imaginations, and their need for specialness and glory. You just need to look at some of the Leonine celebrities to see how self-made their images are: Lawrence of Arabia, Fidel Castro, Mick Jagger, Madonna, Cecil B de Mille, Andy Warhol and Mae West. You can't get more inflated in ego than that lot.

This makes them great fun to know and most of the time they are life enhancing too, but this self-inflation also masks their own insecurities and can set up a bluff barrier which gets in the way of true intimacy with others. If you're meant to be this magnificent creature, king of the jungle, then how can you admit that you are sometimes depressed, sometimes a failure and at times wonder what is the point of it all?

Hourglass/Leo is not the most self-promoting of lions, but she is likely to have a basically exuberant outlook on life and be at the centre of any social gathering. Her striking good looks (more often than not she has a fine mane of hair – even if it is not worn in golden curls down her back) will draw all eyes upon her as she arrives – just a little too late. Pride of place is important to her. Watch her when a group of people sit down for dinner, unplaced. Hourglass/Leo will gravitate naturally to the head of the table (or the best seat on the right of the host). Although she will not obviously shove anyone else aside, she will gracefully slip her rounded rear into the best seat there, before the rest twig what's up. And she is graceful, so it will all look perfectly natural.

Princess Margaret and Princess Anne are both Hourglass/Leos and they have both found it hard, in their separate ways, to take second, third or fourth place in the grandest hierarchy of all. Hourglass/Leo feels so naturally suited for the job of Queen, or President, or Professor, or Chair, or Excellency – or Divine Goddess – it is no wonder that she bridles slightly at being treated no better than the rest of us. Despite these little peccadillos, she is a most admirable beast, hard-working, energetic, never petty, although sometimes overbearing. She can organize, delegate and manage large-scale plans without blinking an eyelash. She is not so good with trifling detail, or boring administrative jobs, but then that's what she has minions for and she is terrific at delegating work to others.

IN WORK

Hourglass/Leo has a natural authority and although she is not drivingly ambitious and tends to put her personal life before her professional, she makes an excellent boss. She is sensitive enough

to the feelings and needs of those who work with her, but not too sensitive to be able to get them to do what she wants, and to delegate the dull and routine jobs which she finds so difficult. She has enough energy, confidence and vision to see the full extent of any plan and can implement whatever projects and reforms are necessary for its completion. She easily inspires others and likes nothing better than to be at the head of a band of loyal followers. She is popular and works well in a team, and although she likes to be the leader, being an Hourglass/Leo and slightly softer round the edges, she will not make everyone's life difficult if she's not. One of her favourite fantasies is leading her team to victory.

Hourglass/Leo is drawn particularly to two types of job: the glamorous ones, to do with clothes, beauty, the stage, music, art – and the caring ones, teaching or running charities or organizations to help less fortunate people. She can also make an excellent entrepreneur, organizing other people and utilizing their talents and then, with her vision of the whole, bringing everyone together in dynamic interaction.

Being centre of the activity is really important for a Leo and, although the Hourglass side of this combination modifies that egocentricity, the Hourglass/Leo is still going to be happier working where she has her own powerbase rather than merely working in someone else's orbit. There are quite a few kinds of career where this centre-of-operations feature is built in and they are obvious places to make Hourglass/Leo shine. There is the law (but being a barrister offers more autonomy than being a solicitor), the stage, and government at all its levels – although the Hourglass influence in this combination makes her less willing to sacrifice her personal life for something as male-dominated as Parliament, or even the Inns of Court.

One of her few weaknesses is a simplicity and nobility of character which means she finds it very hard to understand deviousness, pettiness and malice in others. She is not well-armed against any underhand attack; and being rather a high profile, exuberant personality she does attract her fair share of detractors. But she can be genuinely puzzled by nastiness in others and has only her own optimism to help her rise above any antagonism sent her way. It does mean that she is not good at jobs involving Byzantine politicking and behind-the-scenes dealing.

Public relations is the Hourglass/Leo's natural habitat. Good with people, positively green-fingered when it comes to publicity and promotion, this is an area where she can be her own boss with her own accounts – and can call upon her wide range of talents, from the executive to creative. Understanding the need

for fantasy so well, she can tap into the dreams and aspirations of others.

Ideal Fantasy Job

Here we have a queen of fantasy and in her bath, full of expensive bubbles, she dreams perhaps of having a position specially created for her – Worldwide Corporate Fundraiser for the Arts Council of Great Britain, no less. It is worth remembering what Mae West, an archetypal Leo (although this time a more formidable Triangle) said when asked in an interview what she'd like to be remembered for. Without any hesitation she said 'Everything!'.

Well this fantasy job would combine everything that an Hourglass/Leo could ever need: a terrific band of devoted staff to do all the boring bits back home while she travels from capital to capital, boardroom to boardroom, splendid restaurant to splendid restaurant. Everywhere she would be centre of attention, and treated with enormous respect – almost royally – cheque books would be taken out, noughts added, smiles, congratulations, APPRECIATION, *ADORATION*. Such a good cause, such a classy cause – and lots of glittery galas and occasions for serious dressing-up. And of course, dreaming among the bubbles, Hourglass/Leo knows she will remain through it all her unspoilt, unassuming, modest self, loved by husband and children.

IN LOVE

Love is a central force in Hourglass/Leo's life. For her, it's not a lukewarm, companionable thing: the theatricality of this woman means that she appreciates bright lights, grand gestures and strong passions. When young, she is prone to fall in love with love itself, with the way it makes her feel, with the lustre it adds to life and the guarantee it gives her of being centre-stage in another person's dream. Well, she had better be made to feel central to his being otherwise she is off to somewhere she's better appreciated.

When she is appreciated there is no one more generous and warm-hearted. She has a natural optimism which carries her through most of the trials and tribulations life has to offer. She is stylish and charismatic, and has a bevy of admirers. Much too strong meat for less confident, hypersensitive souls, and competitive with those who challenge her divine right to rule, she needs friends around her who are her equal – but not too assertively so. Appreciation and admiration are a necessary qualification for any relationship with this woman.

In social situations, the Hourglass/Leo can come over as strong-minded and decisive. She will attract men who like powerful women. But this woman is not as straightforward as she seems. With the Yin influence of her body type, she has an unexpected softness and sensitivity which at times makes her long for a strong protective man. So the men who are initially attracted to this extrovert, forceful exterior can be a bit disconcerted when they find their big strong woman has a more vulnerable and distinctly dependent side.

She is not really in danger of giving up everything for love, but she has moments of thinking she might, and bolting with the man of her dreams to a new life of sun and sea and pomegranates. Because of her Hourglass disposition, the man to set her pulses raçing has to be a Yang male, a Richard Gere or Paul Newman kind of male, but not too overbearing, because no Leo can put up with being taken for granted or bossed around.

The curvy-hipped, Yin-type women have a strong libido (for these women sex is closely allied with feeling and is very much an expression of their deeper selves) so as an Hourglass, combined with a proud and energetic star sign, this combination produces some fireworks. (One longtime married Hourglass/Leo said she liked having sex with her husband twice a week when working, four times a week on holiday – and if we were talking Richard Gere or Robert de Niro then twice a night would be more like it!) But woe-betide any lover of the Hourglass/Leo who treats this woman with less than full respect. Vulgarity or crassness sets her teeth on edge, and liars and two-timers are never forgiven.

Hourglass/Leo is irresistibly drawn to motherhood. The Yin body types are maternal anyway, and Leo is a natural parent – after all, a family is no less than a kingdom, with a benign despot at its head. While she is pregnant she will be making plans to return to work, but she is likely to be taken by surprise with the force of emotion that arrives with her baby. The Yin body types are more dominated by their female hormones and they find it harder to drag themselves away from their young children and hand them over to anyone else. This might well be the scenario for Hourglass/Leo too.

Her need for a larger stage than the one bounded by her garden fence or the school playground, however, will lead her into part-time work, committees, amateur dramatics, fund raising, society hostessing or any other interests and projects which give her some feedback from the outside world. To be a happy lion, Hourglass/Leo must have a chance of an admiring audience beyond her undoubtedly besotted – but fatigued – family.

As a mother, the Hourglass/Leo is terrific. She has empathy and sensitivity towards her children's needs and a good deal of get-up-and-go which energizes the whole family. She can be a little too aspirational, wanting her children to excel at lessons, at playing the violin, captaining the games teams AND being the most popular kids in town, but as long as she has some outside interests then her great energy is deflected from too much interfering concentration on her own family. She is possessive and loyal: everyone will always know where they stand and how much she cares.

Ideal Fantasy Lover

He has to be Yang, for her Yin body type, he has to have status, he has to be sexy, he has to be seriously rich – he has to be Robert de Niro. Known as 'The Emperor' in the business, and titles are appreciated by Hourglass/Leo too, de Niro is the most consummate film actor of his generation.

There is nothing soft or sentimental about the acting or the man. De Niro is tough, ambitious, greatly talented, and now a successful big-time real estate developer and film entrepreneur with a block down in Lower Manhattan where he has a restaurant, film centre and offices. The only possible fly in the ointment is that Robert de Niro is a Leo too – is there room enough for two big cats?

IN STYLE

There is always a theatricality about the Leo personality, a pleasure in dressing up and attracting attention. The Hourglass/Leo should attempt to do this with more fluid, romantic clothes – a velvet hunting jacket, soft hats, softly pleated trousers that emphasize her waist and curve over her hips.

Quality is another big consideration, and unlike the Hourglass/Cancer for instance, the quality – or rather the expense – has to show. Hourglass/Leo likes the best because she is the best, but she also needs her clothes to make that statement to the world. Contrary to popular belief, Leos are not really zany dressers. They certainly like to draw attention to themselves but they are quite conservative and loathe ridicule. You will not find your Hourglass/Leo mincing down the road in platform shoes and a multicoloured jester's suit. She would much prefer that eyes swivel when she passes due to her own personal magnetism – and the 24 carat diamonds sparkling round her throat. She will also express her warm and artistic temperament with marvellous

accessories: knee-high suede boots, good jewellery, and a quality leather handbag.

Also, perhaps surprisingly, Hourglass/Leo is a practical combination and comfort is important to her too. You may well be knocked off your perch at the opera by an Hourglass/Leo in all her peacock finery, but then visit her at home the next day and you may not recognize the woman who comes to the door in her old school tracksuit bottoms and her husband's cricket shirt. For more specific information, see In Style on page 34.

Style Treat

A fringed, soft, suede cowgirl jacket, worn with a riding skirt, and soft suede boots. These are expensive items, but an Hourglass/Leo is more able than almost anyone to get over the shock of the bill and get on with the fun of showing off the goods. Whatever the size of the purchase, however, it is important that she ensures that the garment she's about to buy really suits *her*. The style, for example, needs to be soft and curvy: a jacket that is too straight or made in too rigid a material looks hard and unflattering on this feminine shape.

It is important to check that the colour of the garment you are buying suits you well. Take it into daylight, hold it under your chin and look at what it does to your skin, eyes and hair. If wearing it intensifies and enlivens your colouring then that is a colour that is right for your skin tones. If you look washed out or sallow, or your hair loses colour and dark rings seem to appear under your eyes, then you are getting it wrong. This sounds a lot of trouble to go to, but it is worth it for it enhances the pleasure you will get every time you wear it.

IN HEALTH

Leos traditionally have to care for their hearts, the organ of the body that is ruled by this star sign. Joints too seem to come under Leo's jurisdiction and are prone to stiffening up a bit. Regular, moderate exercise can only safeguard both.

The Hourglass metabolism is a balanced one which is easily thrown off balance by too many stimulants, like tea, coffee, alcohol and cigarettes. These sap her energy and leave her exhausted and reaching for another coffee/drink/fag to perk her up again. Bad eating habits also sabotage her metabolism and leave her a collapse case at the end of the week.

Hourglass/Leo's exuberant appetite does not stop at the fridge door. She enjoys food and can find herself squeezing into last summer's tennis dress, swearing it must have shrunk. So it is even more important for this Hourglass woman that she sticks to a good regime when losing weight. For more specific information on diet and exercise, see page 36.

HOURGLASS/LEO CELEBRITY

Melanie Griffiths couldn't be more classically Hourglass, or more classically Leo. First of all the Leo side. She boasts 'I've got the bod for sin' and doesn't stop telling the press about how much she loves her Don Johnson, how perfect is their marriage (the second time), how wonderful are their children and what a 'fairy-tale princess' she feels in the middle of all this material and emotional wealth. She is careful not to let her children grow up too spoilt, living between Hollywood and Aspen, so she tells them about other children more deprived than them, 'I talk to them about poverty and children who don't have a plane to take them up to Aspen'! It is such a blatant case of pride riding for a fall that one fears for her. But it also exhibits another aspect to the Hourglass/Leo personality; she is utterly transparent, there may be blindness and foolishness even, but there is never any pettiness or malice in this character.

Her lack of discrimination in the films she picks also shows her lack of real calculation and single-mindedness as far as her career is concerned. She first came to prominence in the gossip columns as the sexy blonde daughter of actress Tippi Hedren. Then she followed this with a series of dumb blonde roles in forgettable movies. Her playing a seductive young woman in the sinister *Something Wild* created quite a stir, and then *Working Girl*, with Harrison Ford, gave her real scope to develop her sexy, funny character and gave her a chance to show a sweet strength which has promise for future roles. She got her Oscar nomination for that but no films since have been worth much. Her personal life seems to be of greater interest to her – and the Press. 'I really love working, but I feel I have to make family life my first priority and that means my career is just the icing on the cake . . .' Some icing, some cake.

HOURGLASS/LEO PROFILE

Marisa was born in America but travelled to England when she was a student. In Britain, she was relentlessly pursued by an Englishman, whom she eventually agreed to marry, as much because she was kind-hearted and wanted to put him out of his

misery, than for any positive reasons on her side. That set her fate. She became an Anglo-American, not quite at home anywhere.

A really striking and beautiful woman, she looks rather like Raquel Welch's younger sister. As a young married woman she went and worked for Harrods in their PR department and then when her two children came along, she left full-time employment. However, when they reached school-age, Marisa set up her own small PR consultancy, which she could run from home while bringing up her children, with the help of a succession of au pair girls.

Always opinionated, she believes fervently that a mother's place is in the home, 'I don't think lack of money, or women's frustrated ambitions, or any of these material things are worth a toss in the face of one's children's need for a secure and constant mother figure, who puts their needs first when they are small, and disciplines them firmly and loves them dearly as they grow.' She has been known to tell off other mothers in her street when she thinks they aren't doing their job properly, and more than once has marched into the local pub to haul out her under-age son – and his friend – who were innocently playing the fruit machines in a corner. She will imperiously tell the barman off too for letting them in, and toss her mane of hair at his abuse as she goes.

Also in true Hourglass/Leo style she can look magnificent when she's dressed up with somewhere to go, but when she's home, she'll slope around in the most ill-matched set of clothes which look as if she's pulled them out of the laundry basket in the dark.

One of her many great talents is in giving parties. Any excuse and she's getting out the party hats and blowing up balloons. She can cook up a storm too, and isn't in the least fazed by the idea of catering for 40 people.

Everything Marisa does, she does at the last minute and with enormous energy. A typical day has her zooming off to play tennis, then back with ten minutes to spare before a new client is due to arrive to discuss her proposal. The dog has eczema and so that evening she has an appointment at the vet's, after collecting her daughter's flute from the menders. Then back home to make a casual supper for all 20 members of the choir she belongs to before they repair to the local church hall to practise for the mid-summer concert. Then home to her man, to snuggle in front of the television for an hour. And finally to bed to make mad, passionate love. Marisa says with a shrug, 'I'm not perfect, I'm opinionated, and interfering, but I love my children, I love the men in my life, I love my friends – and I love life.'

IN HOPE

Hourglass/Leo was dealt the royal flush at her birth. She holds a spread of everything necessary for a successful and happy life, and really it's only her own lack of judgement which can ever frustrate that potential. For lack of discrimination is perhaps the one poor card she turned up. It's that which can lead her to value the superficial over the profound, immediate gratification over understanding, and form over substance. In the words of the song, 'You gotta know when to hold 'em, know when to fold 'em, know when to walk away and know when to run. You never count your money while you're sittin' at the table, there'll be time enough to count it when the dealing's done.'

HOURGLASS
VIRGO

(Yin/Yin)

MOTTO:
All that glitters is not gold

IN LIFE

Kindness and goodness are words which fit this character well. Hourglass/Virgo is also honest to the core. This not only means that she does not delude herself, but that she can be trusted to deliver your million quid in cash to the bank. She is not a fantasist, she does not exaggerate even, and she is certainly no good at lying. She knows exactly the measure of her personality and abilities – and she is probably just as unsentimental in sizing up everyone else in her orbit. She may lack vision, imagination and daring, but she is blessed with a great ability to deal with what *is*.

An earth star sign, she is completely at home on the material and physical plane. She knows precisely what is what – and that word 'precisely' is important here. This woman has the finest discrimination in most areas of life. She is sharp on the misuse of language, picks up immediately on that sloppy grammar or mispronunciation, and she is visually acute in judging colour and shape. She will notice the faintest brushstroke when other eyes merely slither over the painting as a whole, on a walk in the country she will read physical signs like animal footprints and discarded feathers and be the first to see the green shoots of spring.

Hourglass/Virgo is the combination which produces the classifiers and synthesizers of the world – art experts and restorers, ornithologists, graphologists, writers and editors, researchers and craftswomen, anything which requires that meticulous eye for detail and that ability to collect and collate. She can, however, become a little obsessional about this need to explain everything and to find it a place in the complicated universe she inhabits.

Virgo is ruled by Mercury, the god of intelligence and communication, and certainly Hourglass/Virgo is interested in communication and knowledge, not so much for it's own sake, but so that she has more bits to put into place in this vast and complex plan. She is really extremely intelligent. It is the quality which shines through her lucid gaze. Her at times practical outlook, however, can mean she judges people or things harshly which do not appear to fit her scheme. She can turn her back on or discard the maverick thoughts, the eccentric people who resist conformity. She is made uneasy by unorthodoxy because she needs to know where she stands, and where everything else around her belongs.

Virgos are meant to be mad keen on tidyness and cleanliness, and this is one of the sticks used to beat her – usually centred on jokes about her making love in rubber gloves and other unfair slurs like that. This liking for everything in its place, however, can be expressed in many as an obsessional concern for putting things in neat piles, stacking things away in cupboards, and hoovering diligently every day. But there may be just as many Hourglass/Virgos whose houses look as untidy as the next person's. In this case she nevertheless knows precisely where everything is, although the process of actually filing everything away has not yet begun (and may never begin).

The sex and cleanliness jokes are really unfair, because Hourglass/Virgo, as a combination of Yin body type and earth star sign, has an extremely healthy libido. It is true that she may notice that incipient pimple on your chin, or wrinkle her nose at the slightly musty smell of your jacket when you're caught in the rain, but it won't put her off – it might put her man off, though, if she cannot resist pointing these small flaws out to him, even in the height of passion.

Her real strengths are expressed through her personal relationships, for she will notice signs and responses in others which more self-centred and exuberant combinations would never see. The slight pallor that tells her you're under the weather, the tightening of your mouth that means you're depressed, none of this goes unnoticed – and good, kind, practical person that she is, she will act on them and do her best to help you and make you well.

But Hourglass/Virgo is not all sweetness and light. She can irritate the life out of her nearest and dearest, her colleagues too, with occasional nit-picking, carping and pettish complaints. Her obsession with detail, her literal and pragmatic mind, her constitutional

inability to take a gamble, may send more spontaneous and expressive characters screaming up the wall with frustration.

When they (and they are usually fire signs) eventually make it back down again they will realize with sympathy that Hourglass/Virgo suffers too. She would sometimes like to be other than she is. But she has a highly-strung disposition which cannot deal with too much chaos and ad-libbing in life. She needs to stand on dry ground and see her path laid out before her. Nothing makes her more anxious than veering off into the steamy jungle without a map, with strange animal and bird calls, possible pitfalls at every step, and poor visibility.

IN WORK

Work is an important part of Hourglass/Virgo's life. She is not happy lazing about doing nothing, she is not a natural playgirl or parasite. She is on Earth to work and to make a difference. If you look at a list of Virgoan writers, for instance, you find a disproportionate number with prodigious outputs over many years of hard labour. Agatha Christie, Antonia Fraser, Dr Samuel Johnson, DH Lawrence, JB Priestley, Mary Stewart, Tolstoy, Fay Weldon, HG Wells, and that biographer of vast lives, Michael Holroyd, are all long-haul writers. Nothing is too much trouble, nothing is too small to bother with, everything is placed in context in the jigsaw puzzle of life.

To those great qualities of discrimination and synthesis, are added the one that matters most of all when it comes to success – diligence. Dr Johnson himself knew this well, 'Few things are impossible to diligence and skill' he intoned, and it is a truth that Hourglass/Virgo knows in her bones, if she works hard enough she will get her rewards.

Working with words is an obvious area in which she can excel. Writing, journalism, television and radio will be a natural home for her. Although she is not likely to push herself forward as the anchorwoman on the television news, or the front-of-camera interviewer in a chat show, Hourglass/Virgo will accept gracefully and do a sterling job if the opportunity is thrust upon her. Her love of classifying makes academic research fruitful and libraries shelter many of these hard-working women, either studying or working.

Book-keeping, statistics, accountancy: all benefit from Hourglass/Virgo's scrupulous, careful nature and love of order. And the teaching professions are where the communicative ruler of this star sign, Mercury, comes into his own. Hourglass/Virgo is sensitive to her pupils' thoughts and feelings, and clear and lucid in her teaching: nothing will be too much trouble for her to do for the class and every lesson will be beautifully prepared and thought through. She will never bore her students with repetitive or waffly material and will genuinely care that they get on well in their studies. If a job is worth doing it's worth doing well is really the motto of Hourglass/Virgo. Sloppy and slapdash she will never be.

Her intelligence is one of the most striking things about an Hourglass/Virgo. But she is often at her best as the conduit for the ideas of others. She refines, sets in context and synthesizes, and is most happy in an intermediary role where she facilitates creation. This is why teaching, broadcasting, interpreting, representing, are all areas where her great abilities are well expressed.

That love of collecting and classifying, combined with a delight in the organic world, can also lead Hourglass/Virgo into horticulture – perhaps more as a plantswoman than a landscape gardener, where her discrimination would help immeasurably in the cultivation of rare breeds of plant and the creation of new colours and strains of existing ones.

Ideal Fantasy Job

Ambassador in Toyko. Japan embodies so many of the qualities which appeal to Hourglass/Virgo: grace and courtesy and the finest discrimination in all areas of life – the art, the gardens, the social mores which are all governed by an ancient and complex set of rules and measurements. It is a formal and yet liberating place where individuals are safer than in any other developed country in the world.

Hourglass/Virgo would quickly learn the rules that govern Japanese life. With her linguistic ability she would manage to master the language better than most other Westerners. And she could take up flower arranging with the other diplomatic women and the Japanese wives, whose lives she would get to understand better.

Being in the privileged position of being a foreigner of high rank she could enjoy all the benefits of this extraordinary society with few of the limitations. In her quiet and unassuming manner, so appreciated by her Japanese hosts, she would strengthen the cultural and trading bonds between her country and theirs and return in modest triumph with a few exquisite pieces of Japanese art to put in her tastefully uncluttered home.

IN LOVE

If you were to meet a young Hourglass/Virgo at a party she would seem very slightly demure, distinctly feminine in a pretty,

unflashy sort of way, and, yes, virginal. But this all belies the fact that hers is an earth star sign, and therefore she is at ease with the physical and carnal sides of human nature. Sex is dealt with in a rather matter-of-fact kind of way although her Yin body type adds a further dimension of sensuality and erotic desire. This combination does not necessarily mean that Hourglass/Virgo has rampaging appetites, or that she is exhibitionist in any way, but that she is a feeling woman and is very likely to have love and the bearing and caring for children firmly on her agenda.

Now she does have this reputation for fussiness and it is not entirely false, but it is due to her natural discrimination and highly developed sense or order and propriety and not to a hopeless pettiness of mind. She will notice that her man has not had a shower before coming to bed, she will recognize that he has put on weight during his holiday, it will irritate her that he doesn't seem to care he's dropped a bit of yolk from his boiled egg down his tie. She can't help it, she wishes sometimes she could, she'd love to be so abandoned to passion or so engrossed in the wood that she didn't notice the trees – and the algae, the bark insects, the oozing of the sap! But that always being right, that nit-picking, is the shadow side of Hourglass/Virgo and she should resist it getting a grip on her.

Ideally, this quiet, affectionate, highly strung woman needs a solid and humorous man to lean on, someone who is confident enough not to mind her occasional ticking off and rattiness when she's overtired, or worried that she can't do her work as well as she'd like to. Her Yin body shape, the Hourglass, means she is attracted to a Yang man, but nothing too coarse and unreconstructed. Too much chest-beating and general groping would grate terribly on her nerves. But someone clever, decisive and powerful would suit her double Yin temperament very well indeed.

There is no real problem in her mind about children. Hourglass/Virgo is naturally maternal. She won't go in for a vast brood, something neat, sensible and manageable, like one of each, would suit her much better. And she will be a loving and well-organized mother who does everything really well, from bringing up baby, to upholstering the three-piece suite in the evening, to baking all the cookies for the Brownies' Open Day, to organizing the supplementary reading scheme at school.

She is also a skilful hostess, making sure everyone has enough to eat and drink, introducing singles to appropriate friends, bringing people together. Here Hourglass/Virgo's skills at uniting disparate elements can make her an inspired matchmaker. The combination of her feeling nature with her intelligence and terrific organizational skills produces the sort of perfect wife and mother who most men, children and family pets appreciate.

Again, like most of the Yin women, caring for her children is a top priority in Hourglass/Virgo's life. She will keep a foot in her working camp, because work does matter to her, but it will probably take a distinctly second place to her first priority, while the children are young, of home and family.

Ideal Fantasy Lover

Well, this is a highly intelligent and a gently humorous woman and so both sides of her nature can be answered in the dream man. He has to be Yang of course for there to be that frisson of excitement, so how about the gorgeous Denzil Washington, whose charismatic good looks and depth of feeling persuaded Richard Attenborough to cast him as Steve Biko, the South African activist killed in police custody, in his moving film *Cry Freedom*? This man is serious and intelligent (subsequently shown to good effect in *Malcolm X*) – both necessary attributes for any Virgo. But he is also seriously sexy and blessed with a sense of humour, as was evident in *Much Ado About Nothing*. Lucky the Hourglass/Virgo who finds a man like this: intelligence, laughter and sexual desire are closely related for this woman.

IN STYLE

Hourglass/Virgo is a woman who likes clothes, who appreciates the feel of cloth, the fineness of the sewing, the interleaving details of design. Her discrimination recognizes the extreme skill and artistry in a Jean Muir frock, for instance, and to wear clothes which have been put together by a team of true craftspeople fills her with delight. She is a true appreciator of detail, skill and design, and will never be happy wearing a shoddily-made garment with a crooked collar, uneven hem and fraying buttonholes.

Hourglass/Virgo's ideal would be to have a few beautifully-made clothes rather than a wardrobe full of cheap and cheerful stuff. She often longs to be a bolder, more experimental dresser, but accepts that she really does feel more comfortable in classy, classic things, with neat collars and fine detail, her look completed with good quality accessories. For more specific information, see In Style on page 34.

Style Treat

Hourglass/Virgo has to stop wishing she could be a more outrageous dresser and go instead for a wonderfully chic and

understated classic look that fellow Virgos like Greta Garbo, Ingrid Bergman and Lauren Bacall have so brilliantly made their own. At its most striking, it is an expensive look. It is the best quality silks, fine wools and cashmere. It is designers like Jean Muir. But Hourglass/Virgo, in her style treat, can take the first step towards this classically feminine look – a twinset. Ideally in cashmere with a simple, classic cut and in a colour that suits her. Sales are good hunting grounds for this most luxurious of materials at slightly less than the gold-dust prices cashmere now commands. If Hourglass/Virgo really cannot afford this luxury, she should try a twinset in fine lambswool.

A twinset is a wonderfully versatile purchase – chic with a wrap around skirt, she could even add pearls. Or worn with jeans for a more casual look she can make it look rather French. Then it can be split up to wear separately under a suit jacket – or the cardigan can double up as a casual kind of jacket itself.

IN HEALTH

Hourglass/Virgo has not got nerves of steel. She may be an earth sign with all the stabilizing qualities that can bring but she is one of the mutable, or changeable, signs too (along with Sagittarius, Gemini and Pisces) and this brings its own struggle with the effort to maintain balance. The nervous and digestive systems are both areas ruled by Virgo, and it is here that she expresses her tensions through over-work and too much worry. Tension headaches, butterflies in the stomach, indigestion, these are a few of the manifestations of what anxiety can do to her system.

She has to be careful not to take on more and more work, more caring for others and ever more responsibility. Hourglass/Virgo does not do things by halves. She may not be a perfectionist but she truly believes that everything she does has to be to the utmost of her ability – whether it's just writing a note to her child's teacher or something crucial, like editing a new English/French dictionary. The balanced Hourglass temperament can help Hourglass/Virgo to keep an essential sense of proportion and equilibrium in her life, but she has to be vigilant and use her great perceptive powers to read the signs in herself, of her health being undermined.

The Hourglass metabolism is a balanced one which is easily thrown off balance by too many stimulants, like tea, coffee, alcohol and cigarettes. These sap her energy and leave her exhausted and reaching for another coffee/drink/fag to perk her up again. Bad eating habits also sabotage her metabolism and leave her a collapse case at the end of the week. For more specific information on diet and exercise, see In Health on page 36.

CELEBRITY HOURGLASS/VIRGO

Pauline Collins is an actress who seems to have confounded all the stereotypes. When she was younger and bringing up her three children with her actor husband John Alderton, she starred in television series like *Upstairs Downstairs* and *Thomas and Sarah*. Always well-respected as an actress and much loved by the public for her down-to-earth, kind, humorous, mumsie image, she seemed to be happily continuing in this rewarding but low-key way. Her children and marriage always her central concern while she worked nice television parts round school holidays.

Then she was cast in the one-woman play *Shirley Valentine* and suddenly people recognized the extent of her acting ability, the depth of the feelings and poignancy, as well as humour, that she could bring to a part. She took *Shirley* to Broadway, to rave reviews and then when Lewis Gilbert decided to make the film, he chose this unassuming actress who looked her age, who had the cuddly cottage-loaf shape of a mother of three teenagers, a woman who was an individual and was never going to play the Hollywood glamour puss game. She was nominated for an Oscar.

Pauline Collins, her childbearing over, her childrearing almost so, now in middle age seems to have the world before her. She has just co-starred with the hunky Hollywood hero Patrick Swayze in *City of Joy*. She is an excellent example of the way an Hourglass/Virgo can get the important things into balance, spread her energies efficiently, and end up almost having it all.

HOURGLASS/VIRGO PROFILE

Paula is a literary agent who works on the fiction side of a large agency in London. 'I fell into this by chance. I read English at Oxford and have always loved anything to do with words and literature. I tried writing my first novel, like most people with my interests I suppose, but I realized this wasn't really for me. When I was working on the university magazine I was much happier recognizing the talents of others and helping to improve their stuff and then getting it printed. I love being a facilitator, I suppose.'

Paula graduated and for a year was without a job. She knew that it might help if she learnt to wordprocess properly so she took a course, and then just as she was finishing this she heard that there was a secretarial/assistant job going at a literary

agency. 'After only a week I knew that this was what I wanted to do. And during the last two years I have learned the trade and now have my own list of authors. I love the feeling that I am nurturing people with talent, that I am putting the right authors with the right editors in the right publishing company. There is something very satisfying in making these creative connections and I take great care to find the best home for each of my author's babies. It may be a cliché, but books are babies in all sorts of emotional ways, and they need almost as careful handling.'

Talking about babies, Paula is thinking about marrying the man she has been living with for a year. He teaches philosophy and roars off to work on a big BMW motorbike. He's not particularly bothered about children, but she hopes that by the time she's 30 they'll be building a family together. She is adamant that she wants to be around for her children and wants to be instrumental in their upbringing and central in their emotional lives, 'but I think that I will probably be able to do what I do part-time, with fewer authors, but devoting just as much time to those I do have.'

She is beautiful in a quiet, English way with translucent skin and fine green eyes. She dresses in a quiet way too, with neat little jackets, soft trousers, blouses with rounded collars. There is something Audrey Hepburn-ish about her style which suits her very well (Audrey Hepburn was a very slim Hourglass/Taurus). She longs to break out sometimes, but knows that leopardskin leggings or a red jumpsuit, for instance, just aren't her style. Even the leathers she has to wear on the back of her man's bike rather overwhelm her with their hardness and lack of flexibility. Her boyfriend was initially drawn to her fragile feminine look but soon learned that soft and feminine to a degree, Paula has her feet on the ground and most surely can look after herself.

IN HOPE

Hourglass/Virgo can be the nicest of women, the kindest and most practical of friends, and the most faithful and endearing of lovers. Worry about getting things right is her great enemy, and lack of vision her great flaw. But this combination of influences gives her the intuition and pragmatism to truly appreciate the central dictum of *The Road Less Travelled*, Scott Peck's bestselling exploration of spiritual growth. 'Life is difficult. This is a great truth, one of the greatest truths . . . once it is accepted, the fact that life is difficult no longer matters.' Once Hourglass/Virgo can genuinely accept this, the small anxieties which depress her spirit fall into their true perspective and she has the energy to move on.

HOURGLASS
LIBRA

(Yin/Yang)

MOTTO:
Love is a many-splendoured thing

IN LIFE

The three central forces of Hourglass/Libra's life are Balance, Beauty, and Relationship. Both body type and star sign characteristics are concerned with balance, with seeing both sides of every picture, a need to maintain all areas of her own life in some sort of equilibrium. Her interest in beauty is not just a concern for her own appearance, although that will always be there (sometimes to excessive degree), but it is an appreciation too of the aesthetics of everything in her surroundings. She likes people to be good-looking, she loves pretty furnishings in her house, pictures on the walls, nothing too dramatic, everything attractive and pleasant and peaceful. This can lead to accusations that Hourglass/Libra is vain and superficial in her judgements, of people particularly, behaving for instance as if beauty is goodness and style is everything. But this is to misunderstand this combination's love of symmetry and form, and the pleasure she gets from bringing everything together into right and pleasing relationship with each other.

The interest in relationship is in the broadest as well as the personal senses of the word. In fact, having an air sign in this partnership means Hourglass/Libra is not so much interested in the sexual and emotional union of two individuals as in the whole interrelation and balance between disparate people and things. Her loves, her friendships, her hobbies and intellectual pursuits are all drawn into her need to relate, one to one – herself with her colleagues, herself with her family, herself with her husband and children. Air signs are basically cerebral and this drive to make

connections is expressed very much in the mind and its thoughts. Music, philosophy, mathematics, for instance, are also expressions of Hourglass/Libra's appreciation of patterns and balance and she can find them very satisfying areas of study for this reason.

This search for harmony, for connections, gives her an ability to find an affinity with some quality or interest in virtually anybody. Introduce her to a stranger and she will have sussed out, within the first few sentences, what they have in common and will have charmed him or her with her genuine interest in making these kinds of positive connections. She does not approach people critically or suspiciously, but with this desire to find something out and to share what they have in common.

This is what makes her a fine diplomat, statesman, arbitrator or negotiator – and hostess. She has a reputation for being charming and putting anyone at their ease. But so good is she at understanding everyone's points of view, seeing both sides of every coin, that Hourglass/Libra can find it hard to make a decision which demands giving greater weight to one interest over another. This is a betrayal of the unity she naturally strives to find. So she is described as indecisive, dithering, even sycophantic, but it is more truly due to her basic need to harmoniously unite things and people.

Of course, personal relationships comes in here and they are very important to the Hourglass/Libra, particularly love, marriage and motherhood. Any relationship for an Hourglass/Libra has to have lots of communication and harmony. She is not happy with explosive, passionate, up and down affairs. Her natural propensity to intellectualize everything may mean that she wants to spend hours with her women friends discussing their relationships (she'll be just as interested in her friends' relationships as she is in her own, she is not a self-centred woman), and hours with her partner doing the same. He may find this analytic approach very difficult to deal with, wishing she'd stop gabbing and worrying and to-ing and fro-ing and just get on with it.

This comes to the other element in this combination which can be very difficult for the Hourglass/Libra to live with, as well as any one who has to deal with her. She tends to be a perfectionist. Virgo, as an earth sign, has not really got the imagination to turn her discrimination into perfectionism, but Libra, an intellectual air sign, introduces a good measure of imagination and day dreams into this characteristic. United with her longing for balance, beauty and harmony, this produces the perfectionist for whom everything and everyone, including herself, is never quite up to the mark. She has in her mind a picture of the ideal friendship, lover, relationship, piece of work, the ideal *her*, and is always trying to match what is with what should be. Being an Hourglass body type makes her a little more balanced, a little more laid back over this than if she was a Rectangle or Triangle, for instance, but there is always this ideal dogging her footsteps and foiling her sense of achievement.

Hourglass/Libra is truly charming and often remarkably beautiful. Julie Andrews, Brigitte Bardot, Catherine Deneuve, Anna Ford, Felicity Kendal and Emily Lloyd all share a certain light-boned, symmetrical beauty. Hourglass/Libra is usually also sympathetic and kind. If she can relax her high aesthetic standards a little and let some of the bad and the ugly at least go through their paces before being dismissed, she might learn a thing or two.

IN WORK

Hourglass/Libra is talented in so many areas that sometimes it is hard for her to choose which career or profession is right for her. She is a marvellous team-worker, supportive, sensitive to every other member in the group and highly intelligent in organizing what work has to be done – and she is always beautifully turned out. She has great interpersonal skills and is probably going to be happiest where she is dealing with other people.

Her innate sense of fairness and justice makes the law and allied professions one of the natural homes for Hourglass/Libra. She may choose to be a solicitor (perhaps she is not tough enough or competitive enough to want to be a barrister). She may do legal aid work, or be a legal advisor to a company, or citizen's advice, or anywhere where she can right wrongs and help people get their just rewards. She would also excel as the perfect negotiator and arbitrator in any organization or dispute, and her sense of justice allied with her tact and diplomacy would ensure that both sides came away satisfied with the outcome.

The beautifying of places and people also appeals to a side of her nature. As a little girl, she may well dream of being a hairdresser, and a number of Hourglass/Libra women will go into that, or being a beautician, as a career. She is quite likely to be drawn into the massage and aromatherapy side of healing: anything which brings inharmonious parts back into harmony is where her interests lie.

The beautifying of places will be expressed by her interest in refurbishing old houses and interior decoration generally.

Hourglass/Libra has a nature which can only be happy in places of pleasing proportion and harmonious atmosphere. Conserving beautiful tracts of countryside might belong under the same umbrella. She is someone who truly feels that 'Beauty is truth, truth beauty, – that is all/Ye know on earth, and all ye need to know'. She would make a fine writer with her taste and feeling for harmonious form. With a good, logical brain she can write anything from reports to political tracts to biography. The softer edge of journalism, writing articles of human interest, would suit Hourglass/Libra rather better than the foot-in-the-door reporting demanded by the tabloids.

The arts are an obvious place for this aesthetic side, all this love of symmetry, harmony and form, to find satisfying expression. In front of the cameras (Anna Ford is an Hourglass/Libra) and behind them, making arts programmes or using her charm and warmth to get the best out of others, Hourglass/Libra is at home in any arena where ideas are the currency and attractiveness and social graces are of value.

Given their beauty and charm, Hourglass/Libra also ends up in front of the cameras on the film set. Brigitte Bardot is the obvious example, but Olivia Newton John and Julie Andrews are other Hourglass/Libra actresses who have made their names in their charming, lighthearted ways. This is not a combination which produces the emotional heavyweights who can bring to their parts a powerhouse of intensity and feeling. The basically airy, intellectual side of Libra does not flourish in the steamy hothouse of the heart.

Ideal Fantasy Job

Hourglass/Libra ideally needs to be surrounded by people she enjoys being with, a job that involves using her considerable intelligence, with proximity to beautiful things – preferably clothes – thrown in, and you've got the ideal fantasy job. Fashion Editor on a daily national newspaper. This demands more intellectual independence than most of the equivalent jobs on the glossies, and she would love all the hectic fun of going to the Collections, working out the messages and advising her readers of what looks will work for them in the season ahead.

The newpaper's offices would provide Hourglass/Libra with a busy, buzzing atmosphere full of interesting ideas and people with whom she could make connections – to be lighthouse keeper with only the sea and the sky for company would be a surefire recipe for Hourglass/Libra despair. But most of all she would be surrounded by clothes of every style and possibility, from every

designer from the grand to the unknown – it came up time and again in the questionnaire that a real passion of an Hourglass/Libra's life is clothes, clothes and more clothes.

IN LOVE

Hourglass/Libra loves romance. She loves the idea of love, and the courtship of love. The excitement of that first shared glance, the gentle flattery, the getting to know each other's minds and thoughts and wishes, the moonlit walks, the candlelit dinners, the trembling kiss, the lingering backward glance. There is a certain romantic fiction quality to her expectations, a sense sometimes that the events which lead up to the bedroom door are more attractive to her than what happens on the other side. She is definitely a woman who likes to be wooed, who likes the mood and the atmosphere to be right.

Only occasionally will she see the charm of the bull-at-the-gate approach for she has a natural preference for a well-dressed lover who can exchange light and witty banter with her, whisk her off to a stylish dinner, and then escort her home. She is neither a zany nor an unconventional woman and she likes the proprieties to be observed. But when they are, and everything is just right, then she can give in to the sensual side of her Hourglass body-type nature. This Yin body type will mean she is naturally attracted to a Yang man, but nothing too unreconstructed and gross. The younger Paul Newman type would have done very well, intelligent, good looking and definitely able to look after himself – and anyone else.

Hourglass/Libra is cool and rational, at least half the time, but the emotional, nurturing side of her Hourglass disposition will quite likely take her unawares when she has children. All her well-laid plans about nannies and returning to work, may well founder – or be put off for a while – as she marvels at the protective passion which grips her on the sight of her small baby. This woman is likely to want to care for her children herself when they are young, but the intellectual, detached side of her character sends her looking to resume some sort of outside interest or part-time career when her children go off to school.

Hourglass/Libra makes a much loved wife and mother. She has a lightness of touch which allows all those in her orbit to have their own space and privacy. She is gregarious and social and the house will probably be full of people and chatter. Her natural Libra interest in others is emotionally deepened and made more sympathetic by the Hourglass body type, and so she is not only a social port of call for friends and neighbours but also a support

in times of emotional storm. She will be up to date on the latest fashions, fiction and theories of human nature – and will always look marvellous.

Ideal Fantasy Lover

Good looks are an essential for the fantasy lover of an Hourglass/Libra, Yangness is too, although nothing too grungy round the edges, and he must have intelligence and humour. Well, we don't know about the last two qualities but the good looks and Yangness young actor, Brad Pitt, has in excess. The all-American good bad boy, he played the sexy pick-up for Thelma in *Thelma and Louise*, with a passion and athleticism which made the audience understand very easily why Thelma (Hourglass/Aquarian) seemed so keen. He has not stopped working since.

An older fantasy lover for Hourglass/Libra could always be the handsome, intelligent and witty Paul Newman. He certainly has it all – and he is still married after more than three decades to beautiful, supportive Hourglass actress, Joanne Woodward. Just before he married her, he had a line in a film in which they both had parts, his as a Southern stud, where he makes this memorable promise to her: 'You're gonna wake up in the mornin' smilin' '. Well, he's won every prize, made countless films, still looks a million dollars – and is worth many millions more, he's sexy as they come – and there's no reason why any woman who loved him wouldn't continue to wake up in the mornin', smilin'!

IN STYLE

Is this female interested in clothes and appearance! Quality, understated, expensive clothes, designer wear; shoes – lots – and 'handmade, just for me'. Jewellery, not cheap and junky, but the expensive, classy kind. A warning to any mother with an Hourglass/Libra daughter, padlock your purse – she's going to be expensive. Get a lock for your wardrobe too, particularly if you have anything really good and classy that you keep for special occasions – she has an unerring eye for the best and is not averse to 'borrowing' anything she thinks she needs. And you may not discover this has happened until you investigate the pile of clothes at the bottom of her bed and find your precious Armani T-shirt cast off with the rest of her gear.

Hourglass/Libra looks wonderful and intends to go on doing so. She loves clothes, combining looks, the feeling of luxury and quality, the classy understatement. She either has or would like to have wardrobes full of lovely clothes in silks, linens and fine wools, simple dresses, curvaceous suits and languid separates, all in classy, coordinating colours – creams, sable, coffee, navy, dusty pink and muted aqua. You won't be bludgeoned into noticing Hourglass/Libra in a gathering, but she will slowly emerge from the throng as one of the most stylish women there. For more specific information, see In Style on page 34.

Style Treat

Hourglass/Libra is likely to use clothes and jewellery as a minor but effective form of therapy. If she's a bit low, or bored, or feeling unappreciated, then experimenting with a new look, with her existing clothes, or going out and buying herself something new can work wonders. As a style treat for this combination, how about a special piece of costume jewellery? These won't necessarily be found on the ordinary displays in department stores, but either locked away in the display cases or from a shop which specializes in individual pieces made by young designers trying to make their way.

Jewellery is important for two reasons; to finish off an outfit and to express one's personality. Hourglass/Libra should bear this in mind when choosing a piece. She should also take into account her colouring, body shape, bone size (see guidelines on page 35) and height. She can try on both gold and silver- coloured jewellery and check which is most flattering next to her skin (see page 35). With a curvy body shape, jewellery, like her clothes, is more flattering if it describes more curved lines than geometrical.

IN HEALTH

For the Hourglass/Libra, it all comes back to balance. As long as she leads a basically balanced life and does not over-indulge the lazy sybaritic side of her character she will remain fit and healthy. Nor must she subject herself to long-term stress by working too hard and denying herself the social, relational side of life which is essential fuel to her soul.

Traditionally, Libra rules the kidneys and lumbar region, and it is possible to see the metaphorical connection between the constant homoeostasis and purifying agency of the kidneys in the body and the drive to harmonize and restore equilibrium which Libra expresses in life. This need in Hourglass/Libra is even more marked, and it is in this attempt to keep everything in balance that she can exhaust herself and make herself ill.

Putting on too much weight can be one of the ways which this stress manifests itself in Hourglass/Libra.

The Hourglass metabolism is a balanced one which is easily thrown off balance by too many stimulants, like tea, coffee, alcohol and cigarettes. These sap her energy and leave her exhausted and reaching for another coffee/drink/fag to perk her up again. Bad eating habits also sabotage her metabolism and leave her a collapse case at the end of the week. For more specific information on diet and exercise, see In Health on page 36.

CELEBRITY HOURGLASS/LIBRA

Brigitte Bardot is the archetypal Hourlass/Libra. Beautiful, feline, girlish, sprung to fame through the ambitions of a man who loved her, Roger Vadim, then shunning the cameras to regain her privacy, allowing only her friends access to her. Her energies were then channelled into righting wrongs over abused animals and the environment.

Olivia Newton-John, another Hourglass/Libra, has ended her career with the same concerns – the environment and how to stop the abuses man is perpetrating upon it dominates her thoughts. Her starring role in *Grease* catapulted her to fame in 1978 and she continued with a gruelling career as a singer and actress until just recently, when in her early forties she was diagnosed as having breast cancer. This she believes was almost entirely to do with the stresses in her own life; 'I was trying to do so many things: I was working for the environment, I had a career, was running a business and I'm a mother too.'

Becoming a mother changed Olivia's perspective on life and her career. She suddenly became much more interested in the environment, because she wanted the world to be a better place for the next generation. She also wished to get back into harmony with nature and possibly move back to a ranch in Australia with her family to live a simpler life. Having worn herself out trying to do too much, she has decided to put her career on hold and spend most of her time with her husband and daughter. This is the rebalancing which is necessary for Hourglass/Libra's happiness and health and Olivia Newton-John has had to learn the hard way, through illness and tragedy: 'Just being with my daughter and husband all the time over these last few months has been like a wonderful reward for me.'

HOURGLASS/LIBRA PROFILE

Denise is an art teacher at a large girls' school. She is extremely pretty and wears romantic, flowing clothes and lots of make-

up, even false eyelashes. She is bubbly and enormous fun, if rather vague, and the girls like her enormously and tend to treat her as one of them. On a field trip to see Salisbury Cathedral, she and her class were caught in a terrific downpour and her pupils were intrigued to see her face quite denuded of make-up and her sleek, sophisticated hair suddenly frizzed up into lots of little ringlets.

'They told me with great delight that I looked about 12 years old (they were sixth formers) and far too young to have cadged a place on the expedition!'

Denise has been married for ten years and has not managed to have children, which is a cause of some grief to her, but she finds consolation of a kind in dealing with her young and lively bunch of pupils. 'I think one of the most attractive parts of my job is the contact with the girls. I love teenage girls, they are so full of wit and fun – and hope for the future. I get a great deal of pleasure from their company and from helping them to make the most of themselves and aim high. Girls so often don't think ambitiously enough and I hope in my small way I help some of the girls here to believe that they can aim for the best and make it.'

Denise is known for her stylish dress sense. Being 'arty' she puts unusual garments together and gets away with it – she's really good at picking up bargains in thrift shops and teaming them with a high quality pair of trousers or jacket and ending up looking not only original but really chic too. 'One of my most successful combinations is an Armani jacket I got secondhand. It's beautiful soft buttermilk crepe and fluid and sexy and I wear it over a series of drifty floral dresses – one is my mother's and that's a cotton lawn and then I have a voile one with nasturtiums printed on it which came from the summer jumble sale at school. I love being creative with clothes, and wouldn't want to dress entirely in old clothes – also as you get older you need to look more structured and definite. But I love really classically beautiful, chic stuff put with something quirky and arty.'

Friendships and love affairs have always been most important to Denise and they have taken up a lot of her thoughts and time. 'I am glad to be married, it leaves me energy to concentrate on other things, my work mainly and my own painting. Of course, there are times when I wish I could fall in love again, that I could find Mr Right, but I know deep down that there is no Mr Right, there is only Mr Almost-Right, or even Mr He'll Do, and the rest is one's imagination and hard work.'

IN HOPE

Hourglass/Libra has a softness in her looks and a gentleness in her character; she can appear too willing to please, too lightweight in her opinions, too blown by the prevailing breeze. For she is eternally in the middle, trying to see both sides, trying to be fair, always ready to mediate and make connections. She is the great composer of the world, bringing others together, making people happy and everything harmonious. If she was in charge of the world we would have justice and friendship and very little aggression. Among all the lotus eating there may not be much progress either.

But this need for everything to be civilized can make Hourglass/Libra suffer in the face of the world's patent brutality and very lack of civility. The famous Libra playwright, Eugene O'Neill, recognized this longing for things to be different, 'Obsessed by a fairy tale, we spend our lives searching for a magic door and a lost kingdom of peace.' Dear Hourglass/Libra needs only to get on with the story she's already living and the room she's already in. The world and the people in it may not be perfect, but it's all we've got – and it's not too bad at that.

HOURGLASS
SCORPIO

(Yin/Yin+)

MOTTO:

Still waters run deep

IN LIFE

Emotional depths, will and transformation are all key qualities of the Hourglass/Scorpio. She is not as she seems. Lively, sunny, sweet-tempered, she hides her deepest feelings and sensitivity to others, to atmospheres, to life, with her well-developed control. No one would ever accuse Hourglass/Scorpio of being wishy-washy or superficial. Things and people matter more to her than to most combinations. She gets emotionally involved in everything she does, she loves with a passion and dislikes with equal intensity. She is not a natural flatterer and she finds it almost impossible to smile and say the right thing to someone she does not care for.

This ability to feel deeply about things is a double-edged sword. On the one hand it means Hourglass/Scorpio is remarkable in her loyalty, her willingness to share someone else's burden and her ability to feel their pain. She can be a rock for anyone to cling to, and a fighter who is fierce in their defence. Her real sweetness of character can be brought forth by the sufferings of others.

But the other side of this intensity means Hourglass/Scorpio can get a bit heavy-hearted when things go wrong. She finds it hard to toss off problems or be frivolous in relationships. She cannot understand the more lighthearted attitudes to love and romance, and brings to them expectations that few mere mortals can match. Loyalty until death, ecstacy, merging of souls may be putting it a bit mildly, but this is a personality who is characterized by an approach to life which is all or nothing.

The force of will can prove difficult too. The positive side means that when Hourglass/Scorpio really puts her mind to something, she can make water come from stone. She does not easily accept that things are impossible or that human ability and energy is limited. She believes in forces beyond the material and can summon them to her own aid. It is this that makes so many Scorpios great and powerful artists, like Richard Burton, George Eliot, Epstein, Dame Elizabeth Frink, Keats, Picasso, Rodin, Dame Joan Sutherland, Dylan Thomas, Turgenev, Vermeer, Voltaire, not a lightweight among them! Faint heart never won anything at all, as far as these personalities are concerned.

But this willpower can mean that Hourglass/Scorpio likes to be in control – not necessarily obviously in charge, but in control. She can turn very obstinate indeed if she is *ordered* to do something, rather than sweetly asked, and although she likes to work in a team, she does like to be one of the significant members of that team whose voice is heard. Hourglass/Scorpio doesn't chatter away, but when she speaks it is usually worth listening. Hourglass/Scorpio is more tractable than the Rectangle and Triangle brand of this powerful sign, but even she and her more amenable Pear/Scorpio sister will resist being pushed around.

She does respect strength, however, and will happily work alongside an equally strong-minded individual, in fact she needs to be surrounded by such equals to really feel she can relax about her own power. Hourglass/Scorpio knows she is strong but she is also all-female and is afraid of appearing too opinionated, too assured and determined – above all she does not want to seem threatening to men or other women. This is a woman's woman who gets on really well with her friends and is often the nurturing sister to a group of them, who come to her for support and love.

Scorpio, like Capricorn, can have a puzzling and off-putting press. In some astrology books there is all this talk of the suspicion, acrimony, and self-destructive urges (after all don't Scorpions sting themselves to death when cornered rather than be captured or killed?), only the really profound astrologers mention the sweetness in her soul. The eagle is the other symbol of Scorpio and that is a bird who can soar higher than almost any other living thing. Scorpio has this capacity too, to leave the material world behind, to forget her own ego, her own self, when she needs to take to the skies. Hourglass/Scorpio has a spiritual strength which brings help to the suffering and hope to the unloved.

Transformation is peculiarly Scorpionic, the phoenix rising from the ashes, and Hourglass/Scorpio understands more deeply than anyone the fact that out of loss and suffering comes rebirth, new life and greater understanding.

IN WORK

Hourglass/Scorpio may well find she has an interest in and particular gift for healing. This may express itself in the orthodox medical professions, as a nurse, psychiatrist or doctor: being associated with birth and death, she would make a wonderful midwife or a deeply caring grief counsellor or worker in a hospice. She will be just as open, however, to the alternative approaches and that may be where her greatest abilities lie. Osteopathy, homoeopathy, herbalism, acupuncture, faith healing, reflexology, aromatherapy are all areas of healing and therapy which may well appeal to this woman. The psychotherapies too are a natural focus for her interests and intuitive, caring, investigative abilities. She really believes in the individual's ability to understand and thereby transform him and herself and it is gratifying to be the conduit for this transformation.

Like all Scorpios, Hourglass/Scorpio is fascinated by any research or investigative work. Being deep in a pile of rare manuscripts in a dusty library can give her a greater thrill than spending the night with a millionaire eating and dancing at 'Annabel's'. Uncovering layers of secret information and recreating stories, she is brilliant at reading between the lines and interpreting the personalities and motivations of those who live only on the page. Her powerful empathy with others can bring events and people back from the dead. This is another expression of her phoenix-like power to raise something anew from the ashes.

The arts is an area where this creative power is naturally expressed. There is a particular empathy for Hourglass/Scorpio with the plastic arts – with sculpture, pottery, and modelling of all kinds. To have Epstein, Elizabeth Frink and Rodin as sculptors of genius and all Scorpios is more than coincidence. There is something directly creative in the union of the artist's spirit with the spirit of the stone or clay, which brings to birth a work of art in embodied form.

Science, metalwork and alchemy, the transforming of base metal into gold, are all traditional areas of expertise for the Scorpio talent. Mad inventors there may be, but Hourglass/Scorpio will more likely take to research work in the labs in areas where the intuitive leap is valued. This woman brings her unorthodoxy and imagination to everything she does.

She also brings great stamina and endurance to any work she believes in. If a job is to be done, Hourglass/Scorpio does not shirk it. She may be tired, it may be routine and menial, but if work has to be produced, and she believes in the project, then she stands neither on her pride nor does she complain but rolls up her sleeves along with the best of them.

Ideal Fantasy Job

Chief producer of a women's radio magazine programme. Hourglass/Scorpio would excel at running a show such as this initiating an intelligent, deeply researched and eclectic range of subjects. She would bring her own balance to the programme – a consummately womanly woman who always values her emotional life and recognizes the passions involved in the bearing and rearing of children, but who is also enormously effective intellectually, and decisive and rigorous in her pursuit of the truth.

In her fantasy, she would win over even more male viewers to the programme, enlarge her rapt female audience, and begin to change people's understanding and tolerance of others' points of view. Hourglass/Scorpio is never happier than when she feels she is transforming herself, or others, for the better. A century and a half ago she would have made a remakable missionary: denied that, she dreams of touching the lives of millions through a humane and intelligent programme, with herself at the helm.

IN LOVE

Here the innate balance of the Hourglass body type comes to the aid of a fundamentally emotionally extreme personality. Scorpio feels Passionately about Friendship and Love. She is wonderful when everything goes along fine, but if a love affair breaks up, particularly through some dishonesty and betrayal, she can go a little overboard with grief and fear of loss. Obsessional thoughts, lack of appetite, lost sleep, irrational suspicions and fear can haunt her – not that you will know anything about it unless you are extremely perceptive, or one of her closest friends, for she will keep her cheerful mask up for the world while her insides are being gnawed at by rats.

But being an Hourglass/Scorpio she tends to be able to keep things in slightly better perspective. She will have lots of friends who, given this rare opportunity, will respond as loyally and supportively to her as she has always been to them (she is on the whole an excellent reader of character and picker of friends). Her amazing powers of recovery will also mean that she will rise, renewed from the ashes of her relationship and turn it to her advantage in the end.

Love and sex are not light matters with her. Hourglass/Scorpio is almost constitutionally incapable of knowingly having a one-night-stand. For her, sex carries a more profound freight than just an expression of a physical need, or a bit of fun, or even a tool for wielding power, or making her feel desirable. It is a union and commitment on a deeper level, an appreciation which she expects her man to share – sometimes to her disappointment.

This double Yin woman is highly sexual and will go for a sexual Yang man. When it comes to basic attraction, she does not mind the rawer, rougher element – Gerard Depardieu, the young Marlon on the waterfront, Van Morrison even. This woman likes her men masterful, someone powerful enough to make it worth giving in to. Of course, as far as living with a man in cosy domesticity with two children and a dog, these more unreconstructed blokes may be a little less of a good thing. But she is more than up to educating them a bit.

Children also bring out her strong feelings of empathy and protectiveness. Hourglass/Scorpio finds it very easy to imagine herself in the tiny bootees of her baby and is sensitive in her dealings with her. She is more likely to look after her children herself, until they get to school age when she will go back to work or study in whatever capacity suits her best. Again, the balance of her body type makes her able to juggle rather more successfully the whole problem of motherhood and career, but if there ever is a clash of interests, her Yin body type means that the family will come first in her priorities. She is not a weak or soppy mother, but her children know just where they stand with her, how much she loves them and how she will do her utmost to defend them, and give them enough freedom to be themselves.

Unorthodox herself, she is not afraid of her children being eccentric and choosing unconventional jobs and careers. An Hourglass/Scorpio client of Bel's explained what she meant, 'It may sound terribly hypocritical but I do mean it – I really just want my children to put energy and enthusiasm into whatever they do and they will get great pleasure and satisfaction in return. If that earns them enough to live on, all well and good, but it is the commitment and outflow of energy – that is all that matters.'

Ideal Fantasy Lover

It just has to be the best screen lover, the man with the hunky body and close-set chocolate eyes, impressive actor and sexy heart-throb – Richard Gere. In fact he has matured and got sexier

with age, particularly now that he has settled down with supermodel Cindy Crawford, become a Buddhist and started making successful films again. He has been as acclaimed as a stage actor as he has on film, but it is for his films, like *American Gigolo*, *An Officer and a Gentleman*, *Pretty Woman* and *Sommersby* that he is best remembered. Notable for the sex scenes, his nakedness – and his excellent acting. An outdoorsy man, he loves the woods and fields: 'My favourite thing in the world is to go into the forest and cut down vines. You know – freeing the trees. I find it tremendously satisfying.' And Hourglass/Scorpio would understand that impulse completely, and join him with the billhook herself.

IN STYLE

Hourglass/Scorpio does not lay as much store on having expensive designer clothes as on having enough lovely clothes of a varied type to allow her to really express herself through what she wears. She is highly creative and enjoys customizing clothes to suit her better, and at the same time making them unique to her. She will change the buttons on a dress, or sew some lace on the collar of an old blouse whose fabric she likes. She is good at adding fancy belts, or a few pieces of striking jewellery to make her look individual and stylish, but not over-the-top in any obvious way.

There is a theatricality to Scorpio which the balanced Hourglass temperament keeps slightly more in check than may be the case for Pear/Scorpio, for instance. But often this controlled personality can be more expressive of her subtle changing moods through her clothes, than she ever is in her talk or everyday actions. One Hourglass/Scorpio known for her distinctive, creative way of dressing, admitted, 'I am extremely changeable and moody and often change my clothes twice, even three times, a day . . . Sometimes I enjoy the androgynous look, although it doesn't often work with me. I also love the archetypal country maiden look, really feminine.' For more specific information, see In Style on page 34.

Style Treat

Hourglass/Scorpio is confident and original enough in her own style to be able to wear a hat and make it seem neither over-dressed nor funny. The right hat can supply that touch of mystery and romanticism which is one of the hidden streams of this character. She could try a soft velvet hat with a medium brim for winter, or a fine, shapely, straw for summer. The real fun comes for Hourglass/Scorpio in dressing the hat herself. There are so many beautiful ribbons now on sale in the large department stores or specialist shops and it is much more economical to buy a plain hat and add your own trimmings.

For the velvet, she could try a brilliant piece of silk which she can wrap, finely pleated, round the base of the crown and then spread the pleats into a small fan at the side. She could add a brooch in a complementary colour, or a spray of feathers, if she felt the fan needed more emphasis. The summer hat could be trimmed with a beautiful shot organza ribbon, and again if she felt creative enough, she could twist more of the ribbon into fabric roses which could be sewn on in clusters. The permutations are endless, and the result is a hat which is unique to the Hourglass/Scorpio who personalized it.

IN HEALTH

Scorpios have a natural physical endurance and are seldom ill. But should chaos arise in her emotional life then the ailments most likely to strike are to do with her nose and throat, and the reproductive organs. So finding an outlet for her intense emotions is a necessary part of her staying well. The Hourglass element adds the propensity for balance, and a *need* for balance, and so it is particularly important that Hourglass/Scorpio eats regularly, gets enough sleep and learns how to relax and get everything into greater perspective. However, her powers of recuperation are strong and she will seldom be down for long.

She may be very good at recognizing symptoms of illness and unhappiness in others but is not so good at doing the same for herself. She should learn how to use her healing powers on herself as much as on others.

The Hourglass metabolism is a balanced one which is easily thrown off balance by too many stimulants, like tea, coffee, alcohol and cigarettes. These sap her energy and leave her exhausted and reaching for another coffee/drink/fag to perk her up again. Bad eating habits also sabotage her metabolism and leave her a collapse case at the end of the week. For more specific information on diet and exercise, see In Health on page 36.

CELEBRITY HOURGLASS/SCORPIO

There are quite a few celebrity Hourglass/Scorpios, for this combination combines great female sensitivity and intuition with drive and determination. Anita Roddick, founder of Body Shop is

one, so is Goldie Hawn and Lulu. The poet Sylvia Plath, and actress/princesses Grace Kelly and Vivien Leigh were also Hourglass/Scorpio – all show the emotional power and creative ability and determination of this character type.

Goldie Hawn is a typical Hourglass/Scorpio actress who puts her family life at the centre of her happiness. 'My family is the most important thing in the world to me. Unless everything is all right at home I am no good in the other areas of my life.' This is archetypal Hourglass/Scorpio double-Yin feeling. She is determined and successful and, at 46, one of the longest lasting Hollywood leading ladies, but as mother of three and devoted to the extremely Yang hunk, Kurt Russell, she still thinks of having another baby – because it's so much fun. Here is one sensible woman with both areas of her life pretty much in balance – and obviously adored by the right sort of man for her.

HOURGLASS/SCORPIO PROFILE

Sarah-Jane is a graphologist who works for big companies who employ her to interpet the handwriting of applicants for their executive positions. She is fascinated by all areas of character analysis, from psychoanalysis through astrology to personality testing. 'Human character and motivation is such a complicated and endlessly intriguing area of research. I love my work and am just as excited when I look at a sheet of new handwriting as I used to be turning seashells over on the shore at home in Cornwall.'

Sarah-Jane has a baby whom she is passionate about. 'No one can tell you what it is like. I was bowled over by my feelings for this little defenceless being and I knew I couldn't leave her.' She manages to do her handwriting analysis and report writing at home and only occasionally has to go into the offices of the businesses who employ her, so she can be the main carer of her baby, and the problems of childcare are more easily solved.

'I do go for rather dynamic, masculine kinds of men, as my partner is, but they aren't so good at being sympathetic and emotionally in tune. I have to tell him what I need from him emotionally and then he'll willingly do his best, but waiting hoping he might get there through intuition would mean I'd die of starvation in the process!'

IN HOPE

Hourglass/Scorpio is an emotional powerhouse whose strength and sensitivity can be used to great creative and destructive – and it's usually self-destructive – effect. The Hourglass part of this equation gives a greater propensity for this intense Scorpio side to be better balanced and less extreme, but it also gives a greater need for this balance. Being off-balance causes more trouble to this woman than to most. Greater self-awareness, less profligate giving of self and feeling to others, more reflection and meditation, all these are safeguards to an intense, powerful but vulnerable character.

Another remarkable Scorpio, the profound thinker and radical theologian, Martin Luther, recognized the precise problem for this passionate temperament: 'The human heart is like a ship on a stormy sea driven about by winds blowing from all four corners of heaven.' Hourglass/Scorpio, therefore, should sometimes head for port to mend the sails and take on fresh provisions – and a good map and compass – before setting out on her voyage again.

HOURGLASS SAGITTARIUS

(Yin/Yang+)

MOTTO:
Distance lends enchantment to the view

IN LIFE

Honesty, perceptiveness, energy, adventure, these are the qualities of this masculine fire sign, united – sometimes not too easily – with the nurturing, other-orientated Yin body type with whom relationships matter and feelings rule. The combined Hourglass/Sagittarius personality makes the Hourglass side more fiery and unpredictable and the Sagittarius more rooted and domesticated, with a definite need for balance in her life. This rooting can be a great boon to a delightful character who readily becomes excessively unrealistic. She can be idealistic with a manner that alternates between being foot-in-mouth and thoroughly over-the-top. In fact, Sagittarians generally are notoriously accident-prone.

When a Sagittarius tells a joke (and she has a great sense of humour) it can all get out of hand – either too rude, or too personal, or too convoluted, just roll Pamela Stephenson (Hourglass/Sagittarius) and Billy Connolly (more-of-a-hunk/Sagittarius) together and you begin to get the picture of Sagittarius humour. Fortunately, the Hourglass element brings a measure of sensitivity to the feelings of others – but it may be too late to save the day. The Hourglass/Sagittarius will at least *recognize* she has made a terrific gaffe when she told the joke about the paraplegic wedding to her cousin whose brother has just had a near-fatal motorbike crash.

Women really like her for her breezy straighforwardness, and generous spirit, although her propensity to put her foot in it can make the more sensitive of them wince – for her and the recipient of her frank comments. Despite her impetuous heart and thoughtless tongue, there is not one ounce of malice in this woman. Men, too, feel at home with her, she has this feminine body shape, and the sympathetic people-orientated disposition to go with it, but she is not seductive like an Hourglass/Pisces can be, nor girlish and flirtatious like the Hourglass/Libra. She can be like one of the boys, although physically so obviously not.

Happy, optimistic, bouncing individuals, the Sagittarius element is also given a precious grounding in emotion and common sense by the qualities of the Hourglass body type. Love and friendship is brought into closer focus, and an empathy with others and a well-developed sensuality are all characteristics of this body type. So we have a personality who is less of a lone traveller and more of a warm-hearted woman who takes on more than she can manage but tries to do everything all the same.

Jupiter rules this star sign and this planet brings a wonderful expansiveness to her character. She is a great communicator; a dour or silent Hourglass/Sagittarius would be a rare sight indeed. More usually you will come across a tall, outdoorsy woman, good looking in a clear-eyed scrubbed way, perhaps in the centre of a crowd, possibly in the middle of some anecdote of slapstick adventure or dubious humour. Although Princess Anne is an Hourglass/Leo (one of the other Yang+ fire signs) there is something similar about the frank, outspoken, no-nonsense quality in this combination's make-up.

Stimulating, full of ideas, highly amusing and enthusiastic, Hourglass/Sagittarius most certainly is. But she can also be clumsy, indiscreet, slapdash, impatient and reckless. Tempers can flare, petulance rear its head, mad risks get taken and stories wildly exaggerated. But this combination rarely sulks and always forgives such failings in others. Open-minded and philosophical to the end, there are unlikely to be any rigid views or dyed-in-the-wool prejudices in this woman's cupboard. Nor are there likely to be skeletons lurking there – any there might have been will have been yanked out long ago and thrown into the street accompanied by a lot of laughter.

Hourglass/Sagittarius can express these two opposite qualities of Yin and Yang+ either in alternating situations or synthesized into a complex but well-balanced personality. The bluff, straight-talking woman, who is keen on adventurous travel and horses, dogs too – and the pursuit of knowledge – can also be the imaginative, feeling woman who empathizes with the suffering of others and offers real practical help and a selfless disregard for her own needs. Multifaceted, always interesting, ever optimistic,

Hourglass/Sagitarius is a character who does not pass through life unnoticed.

IN WORK

Routine is not her strong suit. New ideas, new people, communication, friendship, all these are necessary for Hourglass/Sagittarius to be able to work happily and express some of her talents tangibly. She does not make the perfect employee, because she is not so amenable to being told what to do and to being made to do it within narrow guidelines or time limits. She can also get on her high horse if she sees petty dishonesty and institutionalized apathy. This is when the mouth is likely to shoot off, probably to the wrong person at the wrong time. However, as long as her job has a good deal of autonomy and variety, and her own initiative is required and rewarded, she will stay a few years and make more than her fair share of contribution to the company as a whole.

Hourglass/Sagittarius will certainly always be popular and manage to get on well with most of the people with whom she comes into contact. She just has to watch her impetuosity and enthusiasm otherwise she will be promising deadlines that cannot be kept, or products which haven't yet made it to the shelves. In the end, many Hourglass/Sagittarius women opt for working freelance or for themselves. They have many talents and if they stick at something long enough can make most things successful.

Writing books, teaching and philosophy are the traditional areas of interest for Sagittarius, and certainly the Hourglass element in this character adds a greater sensitivity and awareness of other people's needs and points of view. She will be excellent at communicating her own love of the subject she is teaching or writing about, and will be all the more sympathetically accessible to her students.

Jupiter, as the ruler of Sagittarius, means another traditional area of expertise is the law and theology. Jupiter is meant to impart the just and fair view, the long-term perspective, the propensity to wisdom – either innate or gained through experience. The Yin body type here makes it less likely that Hourglass/Sagittarius is going to be so willing to sacrifice her personal life in order to compete in the male preserves of the Inns of Court or the Church, but she may well seek to express her judicious side as a solicitor, or her theological side in teaching. She may put her intelligence, her natural sense of justice and desire for fair play to practical use in advisory councils, lobbying members of parliament, rallying support for the underdogs in society.

Animals are an eternal weakness for this combination. The symbol for Sagittarius is a centaur – half man, half horse – and it is true that Hourglass/Sagittarius, like the other types of Sagittarians, is often drawn to horses and riding. She loves dogs too, and most animals, the wilder the better for she appreciates the independence and overwhelming sense of freedom that such animals embody. Working with animals may well be a really attractive proposition for her, as a vet, at the stables, or just running her own informal refuge.

Food can be Hourglass/Sagittarius's downfall. Often a wonderfully good cook, she will say that she only became one because she loved eating so much. And there may be some truth in this. Sagittarius, like all fire signs, tends to have a large appetite. You are unlikely to find this healthy Hourglass/Sagittarius disconsolately toying with a lettuce leaf. And you know she is seriously ill if she doesn't make it down for breakfast. All this interest in and enjoyment of both food and drink, can take it's toll on the Hourglass/Sagittarius's naturally slim body and sporty nature. Particularly so if she makes catering a career. She will be a marvellous, sought-after cook, and an increasingly comfortable one – rather more Queen of Puddings than garnish of spring onion!

Communication is Hourglass/Sagittarius's lifeblood and she expresses this need either through lecturing, preaching and broadcasting or writing, acting, and even rallying protestors or support. Enthusiasm and optimism keep her going through others' apathy or disapproval, and a sense of a larger vision and wider perspective helps her inspire others to keep going too. When she has her eyes on the far horizon, she can bear to stick with some of the inevitable drudgery of life and even exercise her philosophical soul.

Ideal Fantasy Job

Rallying people to a good cause, communicating, travelling, changing some status quo in the world: give the Hourglass/Sagittarius these ingredients in a job and you have a happy and successful woman – and a changed world. President of the World Wildlife Organization would suit her well. There are these whales to be saved, governments to be lectured and persuaded, campaigns to be mounted, educational programmes to be started, countries to be seen. She has the energy and the communication skills, she is also likely to be good at languages and will not baulk at learning a few more if that makes her more effective in the field.

Hourglass/Sagittarius is not a woman who is much impressed by hierarchies and status, but she is capable of really making a

difference – and this might be her fantasy platform on which to achieve just that.

IN LOVE

Passionate but changeable, good fun rather than erotic, Hourglass/Sagittarius is a combination of opposing influences where the Yang+ star sign brings an uneasiness with the archetypal images of womanhood – but the Yin body type roots her firmly in them. So this woman alternates between wanting to be footloose and fancy free, planning adventures which do not involve the love of her life, and then sudden realizations of how deep her relationships with friends, lovers and family go, and how important they are to her.

There is a difficulty for Sagittarius in being in her physical body. She tends to be idealistic and finds its limitations hard to bear. She can be so carried away with the fantasy of how she is, her own personal mythology, that reminders of her physical self can bring her up with a a jolt. This is particularly so when this changeable, fiery spirit belongs in a female, Yin body where the sensual and physical demands of her nature are strong – and can be contradictory to the Sagittarian longing for quest, mobility, lost horizons.

Hourglass/Sagittarius can feel that she sometimes has at least two modes of operation – the breezy extrovert one when she's talking up a storm, game for any adventure and restless at the thought of any contraints. Then there is the deeper more feeling side, when her heart seems to swell with sympathy for the world and its suffering people and her own closest relationships take first priority in her life. This latter way of being is more likely to predominate as Hourglass/Sagittarius gets older – she naturally remains youthful and untroubled by responsibilities for longer than most women and is not likely to rush into marriage young.

She has a band of jolly friends, both men and women, who are as lively and adventurous as she is. When they are young they organize house parties in Lombok, or picnics on Mount Etna – although for some these dreams will be more realistically translated into a communal bicycle ride through Northern France (the food is *so* good!). Then as she reaches her thirties, and friends have begun to pair off and settle down, the Hourglass side of her temperament begins to have its say. She wants someone special for herself. Again, choosing what kind of man can be problematic for her. She likes a variety, for their different qualities, she's frightened of narrowing her choices and getting bored.

Hourglass/Sagittarius's Yin body shape means in the most basic area of sexual attraction she will find her knees tremble just a little in the company of the Yang male. These are preferably outdoorsy types – mountain climbers with huge forearms and weatherbeaten faces, or the great intellectual traveller with his total disregard for appearance and other-worldly philosophical expression. Men who are relatively self-contained and used to being in charge give her a thrill.

But that Yang+ star sign means that Hourglass/Sagittarius is not too pleased if she is expected to play the little woman to these hard men. She is sweet and soft and sexy in his arms but she is not compliant or uncomplaining in life. Although the 'new man' is not a sexual turn-on for this woman, a little bit of his consideration and awareness of the female point of view tacked on to one of the 'old men' won't go amiss.

It is probably clear by now that Hourglass/Sagittarius is not naturally domestic. She may be a fine cook, largely because she likes food herself, but she cannot see the point in endless tidying up and cleaning – and she's a spontaneous woman who lives in the present with a dream about the future, and so is unlikely to have the clothes and bedlinen for the next week, ironed and lined up in the airing cupboard ready for use. A frantic rummage through the linen basket and last minute speed washes is more her style.

Motherhood too, is rather a shock to her. She is afraid of having her feet stuck in concrete and young children with their routine needs have a way of doing just that. The Hourglass side of this combination activates maternal feelings and so she will be likely to put off having her own children and making a family a central part of her life. The powerful emotions which can well up and overwhelm a woman as she gazes on her baby holds some alarm for this travelling woman. She recognizes that part of herself which will become so deeply attached, but she is afraid of it because where then is the freedom? the potential to move on? the chance of adventure?

Of course, the only way for Hourglass/Sagittarius to deal with this feeling of panic at horizons closing in, is to see that adventure, quest, and open horizons can be an internal reality as well. If she understands that there is still something new to learn, variety, and freedom, even if physically she may be more rooted to the spot, motherhood itself can be seen as a new and exciting adventure. As long as she has her physical escape routes, and does not get mired in too deadly a routine or too lonely and isolated a life, the days of her children's childhood are a delight to her.

She, sooner than most Hourglass body types, will be seeking part-time work at least. She is unlikely to be able to drag herself away from her children completely, but she will recognize this basic need for some outside stimulation right from the beginning, anything from evening classes, to a women's group to some sort of work – or continuing with her career part-time. She will be a disorganized, amusing, lively and much-loved mum, not awfully good with the physical realities of washing machines and lunch boxes, but full of ideas and enthusiasms and warmth – and always planning that adventure for them all.

Ideal Fantasy Lover

Jack Nicholson, in his younger days a bit too much of a handful for any woman, is now a more sensitive and caring individual without losing one bit of his eccentric, energetic, maniacal charm. Yang, from his toe nails to the top of his balding head, he has never accepted restraints on his acting or in his personal life. Success came to him slowly but when it came he was suddenly among the big box-office stars. His brilliant and dynamic performance in *One Flew Over the Cuckoo's Nest* won him his Oscar.

His acting is always characterized by energy, exuberance and over-the-topness, all qualities with which Hourglass/Sagittarius will feel at home. As the Devil in *The Witches of Eastwick* and The Joker in *Batman* he completely overdid it – and yet still managed to get away with it. Hourglass/Sagittarius would completely sympathize with the freewheeling side of this man, the absolutely unorthodox approach to life, the explosive ideas and excessive enthusiasm. She would never be bored with him, in fact might sometimes find herself thinking longingly of a log fire, a pair of slippers and a nice half-read book. A night in for a change!

IN STYLE

Although Sagittarians can be among the worst dressed women of the zodiac, they can also be pretty smart when they have to be. Wherever they fall on the sartorial scale, they are always individual; there is no fashion slave ready to leap out from this woman's rucksack. However, the Hourglass element in this character brings a greater appreciation of clothes and style than is the case when this sign is combined with the Yang body types. Basically, Sagittarius isn't bothered much with image, she's too busy with her plans and ideas and dreams.

When she does think of her clothes and what to wear she is much happier in informal, individual clothes. Trousers or leggings with distinctive shirts – one client said she longed for a series of English Eccentric silk shirts printed with their bold and witty designs. She has not got the patience or dedication necessary for clothes with coordinating accessories or tight belts, figure-hugging shapes, skirts that ride up when you sit down, or blow over your head with every passing bus, and jackets that only work done up. For more specific information, see In Style on page 34.

Style Treat

A treat for Hourglass/Sagittarius is to go and buy something red. Red is a marvellous colour. It is a fiery colour – a Sagittarian colour. It reflects the cheerful extrovert nature of this combination. It lifts her own and other people's spirits. It makes a definite statement – much as Hourglass/Sagittarius likes making definite statements – something along the lines of 'Yes, I am wonderful, I do make a splash, I am full of life. Isn't it great!'

This treat can be anything from a red scarf or handkerchief to red earrings, a jersey or a tulip-shaped skirt which is the ideal 'straight' skirt for an Hourglass. If she's feeling really triumphant she can splash out on a red dress. (But please don't go the whole hog and add red shoes and handbag as well!)

But remember, there are many shades of red. There are blue reds and orange reds; clear bright reds or muted, blended reds; light or deep reds. It is important to check that the colour of the garment you are buying suits you well. Take it into daylight, hold it under your chin and look at what it does to your skin, eyes and hair. If wearing it intensifies and enlivens your colouring then that is a colour that is right for your skin tones. If you look washed out or sallow, or your hair loses colour and dark rings seem to appear under your eyes, then you are getting it wrong. This sounds a lot of trouble to go to, but it is worth it for it enhances the pleasure you will get every time you wear it.

IN HEALTH

Like all fire signs, Sagittarius can go down rapidly with illness, but has a natural recuperative power and always springs back fast. Traditionally, she is vulnerable to liver disorders, stomach upsets and rheumatism, and problems which arise from the sometimes reckless and certainly over-indulgent way of life. With that possible liver sensitivity it is wise for Hourglass/Sagittarius to be careful not to overdo the drinking. The more sporty Hourglass/Sagittarius women might find some difficulty with their joints, particularly the hips, and should not ignore any aches or pains.

The Hourglass metabolism is a balanced one which is easily thrown off balance by too many stimulants, like tea, coffee, alcohol and cigarettes. These sap her energy and leave her exhausted and reaching for another coffee/drink/fag to perk her up again. Bad eating habits also sabotage her metabolism and leave her a collapse case at the end of the week. For more specific information on diet and exercise, see In Health on page 36.

CELEBRITY HOURGLASS/SAGITTARIUS

The world's greatest – and most tragic – operatic soprano, Maria Callas. She was a lonely, unhappy child who had one extraordinary gift which seemed to be the only thing which attracted the attention and love she so desperately needed. She had a voice. This was all that seemed to matter, first to her drivingly ambitious mother who saw it as a way out of poverty and anonymity – and then to Maria's husband who, 30 years her senior, decided to become her manager and to make her the greatest and most successful singer in the world.

When the young Maria Callas looked at herself in the mirror, she saw someone unloved, unlovely she thought – and she ate for comfort and got quite large, and felt even less valued, less important for herself. All she was was the container for this extraordinary voice, and her body the vehicle for the passionate emotions she could enact on stage. This power made audiences react to her with passion. Her career was a constant struggle, driven by two ambitious people, surrounded by jealousies from others.

Then, at the peak of her powers, she met Onassis. He cared not one jot for opera, he didn't care about her voice, but he seemed to be the first person in her life who responded to her as a person, as a woman. He introduced her to passionate sex, to travel, to fun, to the glamorous high life, all the things that had been denied her in the relentless drive to the top of her profession. Suddenly the female side of her was being fed and she gave up everything she had worked so hard to achieve, for love.

Her audiences and the press did not take kindly to this dereliction of her art. She appeared to be retiring from the world's operatic stages to follow this toad-like philistine around the glamour spots of the world. There were reports that her voice was failing. And in fact Maria was having technical problems with it. Her few performances were interrupted with illness and breakdown. 'There are two people in me, Maria and Callas. I like to think that they go together because in my work Maria is always present. Their difference is only that Callas is a celebrity.'

But, for all practical purposes, as long as her love affair with Onassis lasted, the woman dominated the artist.

After a tempestuous time together, Onassis suddenly went off and married Jacqueline Kennedy. Maria Callas never spoke of this but was shattered by her emotional loss – and the loss now of her voice and her career. She was never again given the right emotional or professional support and had lost the stamina and the right state of mind for performance. She died alone, of a drug overdose.

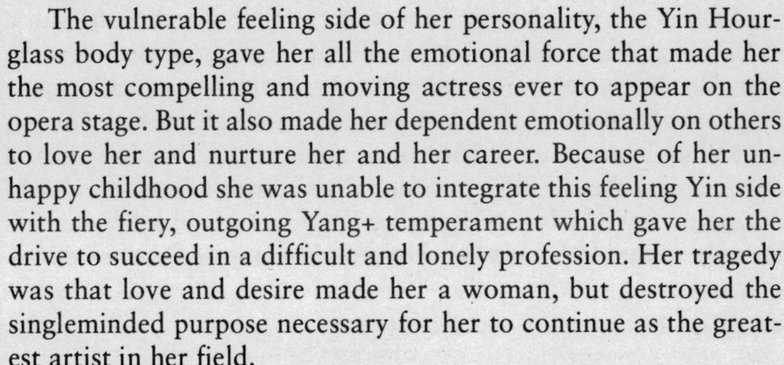

The vulnerable feeling side of her personality, the Yin Hourglass body type, gave her all the emotional force that made her the most compelling and moving actress ever to appear on the opera stage. But it also made her dependent emotionally on others to love her and nurture her and her career. Because of her unhappy childhood she was unable to integrate this feeling Yin side with the fiery, outgoing Yang+ temperament which gave her the drive to succeed in a difficult and lonely profession. Her tragedy was that love and desire made her a woman, but destroyed the singleminded purpose necessary for her to continue as the greatest artist in her field.

HOURGLASS/SAGITTARIUS PROFILE

Sam is a jewellery designer whose energy, general friendliness and warm enthusiasm makes her friends everywhere and influences people. She talks fast, with large expressive hands: 'I'm great at getting commissions. I find I get carried away in my enthusiasm for what I do, and I promise all sorts of things to people, even that I will do pieces that involve new techniques I haven't mastered yet, and then when I get back to the studio and look at what I've been commissioned to do I feel weak. How will I ever do it in the time? Can I manage to set that sort of stone in that particular setting which I so glibly suggested might be right? How can I afford to get the materials? You see I'm not so good at the business side of things and frequently forget to ask for a downpayment. But I do love this work. I see myself expressing organic images in my designs – reflections of the earth and sky and water and trees. I try and give them deeper meanings than just the physical ones of form and material. I hope they are like wearing a bit of this beautiful world pinned to your lapel.'

Her boyfriend is another designer in the same complex of workshops. He works with wrought iron and doesn't say much. She is wildly expressive and he is the strong silent kind who fell in love with her when she rushed into his workshop to ask him to

prize her wrist free from a bracelet she'd made which wouldn't come off. 'He's so big and strong and protective in his own quiet way. I find him a rock around which I swirl.'

'We both love exploring – it doesn't have to be abroad. Every summer for a month we try to just take off without a definite idea about where we're going and what we're doing. We went up into the highlands of Scotland last year. This year I think we'll get to New Mexico and the desert states of the US. I want to investigate the Native American jewellery techniques.'

Sam is tall and slim and most of the time wears jeans and a man's shirt while she's working, with a huge apron tied over the top. On the few occasions when they go somewhere really smart she loves dressing up, but in an eclectic collection which she has picked up from designer friends, or made herself, or altered from secondhand shops. 'I like occasionally showing off my figure and turning a few heads – and getting Dave in a bit of a lather. He's usually so laid back, it's good to see him jumping!'

IN HOPE

Wonderfully optimistic, they are real seekers after silver linings, smilers in the face of doom, followers of the rainbow – and if anyone will find that pot of gold it will be Hourglass/Sagittarius. When she unites the fertilizing power of her Yin feeling nature with the energy and expansiveness of her Yang star sign, this combination can move mountains and create new worlds – even if in her own imagination. There is an old Russian proverb, 'The toe of the star-gazer is often stubbed' and Hourglass/Sagittarius is always stubbing her toe while gazing at the stars or even the slightly distant horizon. This does not make her lower her gaze one wit. Her enthusiasm and good humour is what carries the day and it is her phalanx of friends who sometimes guide her feet over the uneven stones.

HOURGLASS
CAPRICORN

(Yin/Yin)

MOTTO:
The early bird catches the worm

IN LIFE

Advancement, hard work, serious purpose and enduring ambition are the qualities that Hourglass/Capricorn expresses in the material world. Spiritual progress and personal destiny is what she can be about in her internal world. Often she will reap the reward for all this toil in the second part of her life. Hourglass/Capricorn is not at ease as a young person, and often has a hard or unhappy childhood where she feels an outsider, unappreciated and never part of any gang. But then all the hard work and the sense of being a lonely outsider makes way for the beginning of contentment and a feeling of achievement.

This is a profound and puzzling star sign. Popular astrology deals her a dour set of cards: worldly ambition, austerity, discipline, pessimism, snobbishness, high-mindedness. But there is more to this story than that. She is a builder and an achiever. She does not waste time or money. She concentrates resources and uses them where they are most effective. Seldom put off by hard work, disappointment or failure and ever patient, she is always keeping her gaze fixed on the peak towards which she is climbing.

In social situations she can seem solitary and reserved and is not naturally the life and soul of the party or the joker in the pack. This is where the Hourglass element comes to this personality's rescue. Capricorn can find relationships difficult. However, the Yin body type is primarily interested in human relationships and has an empathy and sensitivity towards others which makes her sympathetic and attractive. Hourglass/Capricorn

may at times seem remote but she is far from being an egotistical person whom no one can really reach.

Capricorn is an earth star sign and combined with the Hourglass body type it gives her a strong sexuality which needs expression, otherwise she risks sublimating this energy into work and becoming closed off and embittered. She needs to always keep the balance between the practical and the emotional, the ambitious and the playful. This is where the balancing propensity of the Hourglass type helps her integrate the forces in her life: with Hourglass/Capricorn there is a softer, more feminine, face on the self-discipline and industry of this sign. She is more successful at making friends than Rectangle and Triangle/Capricorn, for instance (although they may be more successful at influencing people). But sympathetic and surrounded by friends as she may be, Hourglass/Capricorn will still have that seriousness of purpose: she will need still to manage people and things.

It is important that Hourglass/Capricorn has an outlet for her managing side. She needs to have some goal to strive for, something to achieve beyond her personal relationships, otherwise she is apt to take over – her children, her husband, her friends. This woman is a winner. Not that anyone might think so to see her in action. There is no flashy speed off the starting post, like some Aries funster. She isn't advertising her success all along the way, like a Leo. She's not promising the moon like some Sagittarian idealist, nor talking up a storm like the Gemini next to her. Hourglass/Capricorn sets her sights and plods on without diversion or self-advertisement.

But like the tortoise, more often than not she gets there before the hare. She reminds herself, 'When you feel how depressingly slowly you climb, it's well to remember that Things Take Time.' She wins out because she is not afraid of long-term goals, of hard work that takes years to be recognized, of all those unfashionable qualities like duty, responsibility, respect for authority. Actually it is this respect for authority which can earn Hourglass/Capricorn a reputation for being a social climber. Because she values success and works so hard herself to climb that mountain, she has a great admiration for anyone who is higher up the mountain than she is. Now with Hourglass/Capricorn this success may be seen in terms of anything from chair of the school governors, to chief buyer in the store she works in. It's not necessarily 'society' in the traditional sense which she aims to emulate, although she will not be immune to the charisma of the odd title here or there.

It is as much to do with admiration for other people's achievements as to do with wanting to have useful or important friends.

Hourglass/Capricorn, however, is likely to insist that her children learn gracious table manners and speak properly so that they can move in any circles without letting her or themselves down. She values traditional virtues and likes order, structure and substantiality. She is the backbone of society, the pragmatist of the world, and is wise and sometimes ironic in the long perspective she can take: mountainous problems shrink to manageable molehills in front of her calm, determined gaze. This is the woman to have on board wherever wisdom, endurance and a steady heart are needed.

IN WORK

This woman never stops work, whether she's at home, in the garden or at the most high-powered management consultancy in the city. She is diligent and hard-working to a fault. Luckily, her Hourglass temperament lightens her up and loosens her belt encouraging her to find time for relationships. The Hourglass side also means she will work well and happily in a team. She is not going to insist that she's in charge although, as a cardinal sign, she does like to lead the way – not in a cavalry charge like Aries (a fire cardinal sign) or with a charm offensive like Libra (air cardinal) – but in a well thought out and executed manner, if a little slow.

Hourglass/Capricorn is at her best in a situation where there is structure and hierarchy. She is much happier knowing what her brief is and where she stands, so that she can focus on where she's going. The Civil Service is an obvious place for some – and it has enlightened policies on part-time work and job sharing. There are such a range of jobs within its huge compass that there is really something for anyone who enjoys the security and focus of a hierarchical set-up. Salaries are good and pensions are still among the best in any company. All these things matter to Hourglass/Capricorn because it is in her middle and old age when life really begins to open out, and money will be needed for all that travelling and exploration and refound youth.

Music and acting are also realms of activity which Hourglass/Capricorn is drawn to and can make into a profession. She has all the dedication and ability for hard work and practice – and she is not easily defeated. She may lack some of the real focused ambition of her Rectangle and Triangle sisters, who will go out and take what they want, but she will make the most of any opportunities which come her way.

Hourglass/Capricorn loves buildings and gardens and may well find herself a job involved with architectural salvage or

restoration of landscape gardens. She has a great love of history and the great traditions and heritage handed down to us. With her sense of the importance of continuity and appropriateness, she will consider it a duty to hand on to the next generation some treasure that has been left to our safe keeping, but in a better state.

This reverence for the past and history can also lead Hourglass/Capricorn into libraries for research. She has all the concentration and intellectual penetration necessary to become a great scholar. Her patience over long stretches of time, her ability to keep her eyes on the goal, means she will always get there in the end. She might want to write up her researches, make scholarly books or blockbusting family sagas, but whatever she puts her mind to she will finish. If success is 90 per cent effort and 10 per cent talent, Hourglass/Capricorn has got it licked every time (with a good deal of talent left over for something else!).

Ideal Fantasy Job

Top society photographer. This involves all the skill and stamina which Hourglass/Capricorn has in excess. Her love of structure and form gives her a great visual eye for composition. She would know just where to position her subject so that the flattering afternoon light burnished her skin and made the stately house in the background glow like Camelot. Hourglass/Capricorn's unerring appreciation of what is appropriate, of how best to behave, would stand her in excellent stead in whatever situation she found herself.

A brilliant manager, a patient and calm operator, a sensitive personality yet a tough businesswoman, it would only be a matter of time before she had inherited Norman Parkinson's shoes. With this admirable woman, there would be no chance of dates being mixed up, negatives messed up, clients embarrassed. Discretion, ambition, efficiency, after all, are her middle names.

IN LOVE

Guarded, cautious and romantic, Hourglass/Capricorn does not leap lightly on the merry-go-round of courtship and love. She longs for it but is ill at ease with the conventional expressions of passion. Control of herself and of her environment is always important, and however close she eventually allows a lover to come, there is always a part of herself which is walled up like a secret garden to which only she has the key.

Hourglass/Capricorn is great at doing things for her friends and loved ones but is not so good at accepting help or gifts from

them. In a way this is also an expression of her need for control – by being the giver rather than the receiver, she remains in control and is never obligated to another. It would allow a greater intimacy with those she loves if she could just allow these roles to be reversed occasionally.

Although Hourglass/Capricorn has a romantic side, she never quite forgets her sensible self enough to throw everything to the winds for the sake of love. Even if she marries young, and certainly if she marries when she's older, she is never going to choose a truly unsuitable man. Marriage has to do with security and good sense, after all this man is going to be the father of her children and possibly the main provider of finance and status for the family. What's the use in running off with that dashingly handsome trapese artist? If he's the circus boss's son it might just be OK, but to protest that you love him more than life itself, that he gives you orgasms every night, and you cannot live without him would not meet with approval as the best reasons to marry.

The Yin element of her body type, united with the earthiness of this star sign, means that when Hourglass/Capricorn allows herself to express it she has a strong sensual side. Slow to ignite, nevertheless it burns steadily and long. When this woman commits herself to anyone or anything it is a true commitment. She is not readily deflected by hardship, routine or unrewarded effort. She is a faithful and deep feeling woman, but these emotional depths are never allowed to get out of hand, to weep or gush all over the place. Her feelings are always constrained by considerations as to what is right and proper, always disciplined, practical and methodical.

Hourglass/Capricorn is the perfect woman for a traditional man in a position of power who needs a thoroughly grown-up, well-behaved wife, who knows just what and what not to say and when to say it. Her quiet womanliness and fine-boned beauty are all bonuses along the way. As far as her own taste is concerned, she appreciates a man with status and power. A title would make her feel she had almost managed to scale that mountain she's been slowly climbing from the moment she could walk. Her Yin body type means she is attracted to a Yang kind of male – Sean Connery, Francoise Mitterand, Sir Bob Geldoff, Prince Philip, Tiny Rowland, Rod Stewart – there's quite a range to choose from.

Marriage and children are also very much on this woman's agenda. She likes the structure and tradition of family life, and she likes the idea of continuing the dynasty – or building one anew. She will be naturally maternal, but sometimes a bit

undemonstrative in showing her love for her man and children. She's more likely to express it by making sure her household runs on oiled wheels; meals on time, clean clothes in orderly cupboards, homework always done, and music lessons attended to.

Hourglass/Capricorn has a prodigious talent for managing everything from a large public company to the gerbil's daily exercise routine. She probably needs to have some part-time or voluntary work, at least, to use up some of this terrific executive ability so that she doesn't drive her family mad organizing them into the middle of next week. Her Yin body type makes her very emotionally attached to her children and highly protective of them, but her need to continue her steady ascent in her career probably means that she will go back to work in whatever capacity she can, when she has assured herself that her children will be all right without her. Naturally, she will make sure she has the very best, the most well organized childcare possible. This mother does not leave anything to chance and does not believe in serendipity.

Ideal Fantasy Lover

Hourglass/Capricorn needs a Yang man, an intelligent man, someone whom she can respect, who works as hard as she does and has depths and complexities which add to his mystery. Sir Anthony Hopkins is an actor of extraordinary power on both stage and screen. Once hailed as the new Olivier, his apocalyptic bouts of self-destructive drinking made him for a time almost unemployable. Then pulling himself out of the hole of alcoholism in the mid-1980s he set stages alight once more.

On screen his intelligent, internalized acting makes him the still centre in the storm of action, emoting from other actors. Nowhere was this more chillingly effective than in *The Silence of the Lambs* when he electrified his audiences across the world with his performance as Hannibal Lecter. This earned him an almost superhuman reputation and an Oscar as best actor.

It is interesting perhaps to note that Sir Anthony is also a Capricorn. So uneasy in his youth, so ambitious and yet out of balance and lacking focus. Grim, pessimistic and single-minded even in the matter of self-destruction, he all but destroyed his chances. But what evidence of the determination and ambition of this sign such that it can bring him virtually back from the dead. At the age of 56, he has not only restored himself triumphantly to the first rank of actors working today, but he has surpassed his earlier self and stands now at the pinnacle of the acting profession. At the top at last – and knighted! And how well such success would become an Hourglass/Capricorn woman.

IN STYLE

Simplicity, stylishness, nothing ostentatious, everything classy: think of the style of such chanteuses as Sade, Marlene Dietrich and Annie Lennox (although the last two are Triangle/Capricorns which makes them more self-consciously concerned with image). Hourglass/Capricorn will not be so concerned with smartness and formality but she will be happiest in clothes which are uncluttered, classic and well-bred. Polo-neck jerseys, well-cut trousers, classic coats (ideally in a Cashmere mix), good quality shoes, simple but expensive-looking jewellery. She will never want to stand out in a crowd because of her wild, zany or flashy clothes – she would much rather be noticed for her quiet elegance and impeccable taste. For more specific information, see In Style on page 34.

Style Treat

A watch can be a fun accessory or a status symbol and for an Hourglass/Capricorn the simple, unadorned status symbol is the one to go for. A good quality watch can last at least for the lifetime of the wearer and this sense of continuity and passing heirlooms on to the next generation appeals to the traditionally-minded Capricorn. If she thinks this way too, then Hourglass/Capricorn should invest in the best watch she can afford, either saving up a bit if need be or buying a good secondhand watch from a reputable auction house or trustworthy secondhand jewellers. Because she has a curvy body, a watch with an oval or round face is more flattering than a rectangular one. For advice on choosing gold or silver and the scale of the watch, see page 35.

IN HEALTH

Hourglass/Capricorn has a good constitution and a stamina which improves with age. Traditionally, Capricornians are meant to really come into their own in their middle and old age. Just as the other more speedy, extrovert signs are running out of steam, dear long-distance Capricorn starts to pull ahead, lighten up and reap her rewards at last. When Hourglass/Capricorn gets past her youth she appears to get younger and fitter with the years.

Her weak areas are her joints, particularly the knees, and tendons and muscles are prone to sprains. Teeth too might be a problem, and skin complaints are more often found among this star sign. But these are all minor considerations in a constitution which is basically very sound and built to last.

Hourglass/Capricorn is not a self-indulgent woman. She is not likely to get carried away with the chocolate box, or suddenly decide to experiment with making ice-cream – and then have to eat the lot because it didn't really work! As a Yin body shape she can be prone to accumulating weight with pregnancy and child-birth, but she has the self-discipline to get it off, if and when she decides to. Whatever this woman might lack, it is not willpower.

The Hourglass metabolism is a balanced one which is easily thrown off balance by too many stimulants, like tea, coffee, alcohol and cigarettes. These sap her energy and leave her exhausted and reaching for another coffee/drink/fag to perk her up again. Bad eating habits also sabotage her metabolism and leave her a collapse case at the end of the week. For more specific information on diet and exercise, see In Health on page 36.

HOURGLASS/CAPRICORN CELEBRITY

One of the most beautiful and stylish women in London, Sade went from being a fashion student to be a singing superstar with songs like 'Your Love is King' and 'Smooth Operator'. She is a perfectionist who has learnt to loosen up a bit, but she is not prepared to sacrifice everything for her singing career.

Typically Hourglass/Capricorn, her philosophy has always been individual and little to do with baldly competitive, single-minded ambition. 'A lot of people are prepared to do a lot of things just to be out there [famous]. I don't do what the others do . . . I don't give a damn if Janet Jackson's at no 1 and I'm at no 10 . . . I'm not that *extremely* different. It's just that there are a lot more things I'm not prepared to do.'

She likes men who are not enslaved to her or her career. A Yin woman, she is attracted to the more Yang male: 'I don't think I could possibly be with a man who followed me everywhere. I'd feel it would degrade him – in my eyes . . . I know that's very old-fashioned. *He* might not mind, but I would.'

HOURGLASS/CAPRICORN PROFILE

Stef is in her late thirties and is a part-time university lecturer in historical studies. She has two children, of four and six, but would like more: 'Yes, I do like to think of having a dynasty, being the matriarch at the head of a large, influential family!' She laughs, but she admits that she likes seeing herself and her children as just part of a greater stream of family stretching both ways in time.

'I am determined that I can both look after my children and continue with my work. They are the most important things in my life and I can't leave them full-time, but I am very organized and can, with help, manage to be there for all the essential bits of their day and do my job part-time. At the moment I'm on sabbatical so that I can research family life in Victorian England for a book I have been commissioned to write. My husband works just as hard as I do and doesn't get back until after eight most nights. He's in business, and so I can't expect much hands-on help from him, but I know he supports my work and the mother's help and I manage the children.'

Stef does show an immaculately well-managed exterior to the world. She is rather beautiful with fine bone structure and always looks smart when she goes out. She allows herself to slop around a bit in leggings and an oversized jersey when she is home for the day, however. Her children are well-behaved and talented – music lessons, homework, tennis and dancing classes, all fitted into their busy day. Her house is comfortable, rather conventional, but attractive and civilized. You know you are not going to find half-eaten biscuits and hamster droppings down the back of her matching sofas!

'I am less frustrated than I used to be at having to slow down my career in order to be with my children. I have relaxed a bit more. I know that it isn't essential that I achieve all I want to by a certain age. I can go on working away, teaching, improving my status in the college, writing books, hopefully sitting on a few committees. Life really can begin at forty. Well, I'd better believe it because I'm banking on that. I am positive that success is 90 per cent hard work, 5 per cent talent and 5 per cent luck. I reckon I've probably got enough talent, I can't do anything about the luck, but I can certainly put in that 90 per cent – in fact, being a woman I'm probably safer putting in 100 per cent, just to make sure.'

Deeply attached to her children, supportive of her husband (who thinks she's superwoman) and terrifically hardworking, Stef has little time for fun and games. 'Something has to give in this busy schedule and I'm afraid I can't bother with reading anything other than what I have to for my research or job. We rarely go out unless it's business, and I never really treat myself with time just to sit and chat with friends or read a magazine. I wouldn't know what to do with myself if I wasn't busy all the time.'

IN HOPE

Hourglass/Capricorn, so wise and disciplined, so hardworking, how much she puts to shame the profligate, laughing, lounging

members of the less practical and consistent star signs. She achieves so much more in this world than those who are distracted along the way, but there is always a sense in Hourglass/Capricorn that in her business-like way she might have missed something of the passing show. Somerset Maugham, an Aquarian and one of those profligate, lounging members of the human race, who nevertheless managed to achieve a fair bit along the way, on one of his discoveries: 'Excess on occasion is exhilarating. It prevents moderation from acquiring the deadening effect of a habit.' Might that not be a heady motto for the most admirable of combinations, the Hourglass/Capricorn, to embroider in needlepoint on a cushion?

HOURGLASS
AQUARIUS

(Yin/Yang)

MOTTO:

Listen to the music of the spheres

IN LIFE

Here we have a balanced Yin body shape united with a balanced Yang star sign. When Hourglass/Aquarius recognizes these two fundamental forces in herself and can integrate both aspects in her life, the feeling nature of her body type will be in harmony with the cerebral nature of this air sign. Both the Hourglass type and the air type strive for balance. At its best, the Aquarian idealism and concern for humanity at large, which can sometimes be rather chilly and dogmatic when she is dealing with the individual piece of humanity in front of her nose, is made more personal and warmly sympathetic by the underlying disposition of a Yin body type. Similarly, this Hourglass-type disposition, so concerned with relationships and individuals, is given a broader scope and wider horizon by the far-sighted, more detached Aquarius overlay in this combination.

Endlessly curious about natural phenomenon and other people, trying always to get at the truth of things, Hourglass/Aquarius is not a conventional woman. She cares little for what people think of her (although this is more extremely true of Rectangle/ and Triangle/Aquarius, for Hourglass/ and Pear/Aquarius are more sensitive to others generally, and therefore to their opinions too). She seems to be dancing to a different tune from the rest of us and sometimes gives off an aura of being on another planet – and rather isolated there. Friends really matter to this combination, but they can find it difficult to get truly intimate with her. The cool and detached side of Hourglass/Aquarius shies away from possessive, cloying relationships and heavy emotional demands.

She can be logical and ruthlessly dispassionate, about something like genetic screening, for instance, where others may be subjective and take a moral or spiritual stance, but then suddenly her Hourglass side will give her a jolt of overwhelming sympathy for someone in trouble, or the terrible plight, perhaps, of the homeless children of Brazil. Her ideas and theories are unclouded by feeling. But her feelings are readily available when she is confronted by the reality of suffering.

Naturally analytic, she notices everything and files it away in her sharp brain for future use. She makes up her own mind about most things. She will ask advice, usually more out of curiosity than a real need for guidance, but always goes her own way. Aquarius is ruled by two contrary energies, Saturn the planet of order and structure and tradition, and Uranus, revolutionary, inventive, inspirational, and this gives an unpredictable element to this combination. No one ever knows where they are with Hourglass/Aquarius all the time – or even most of the time. It is true that she is always reliable when she says she will do something, but she can be difficult to pin down to that initial commitment. She values structure and appreciates the very hierarchies she affects to ignore or undermine, but she does not like personal constraints, is not happy closing down opportunities and possibilities. She truly belongs to the future where all possiblities are as yet unknown.

Although she is such a modern woman in her open-mindedness and need for personal freedom, Hourglass/Aquarius can be maddeningly rigid in her opinions and will occasionally get onto her idealogical high horse and tell everyone what is what. Aquarius is a fixed sign, which makes her at times pretty immoveable on subjects which are of particular interest to her. She is not susceptible either to flattery or down-right bullying. She digs in her toes and refuses to budge.

Alongside this obstinate, I-know-I'm-right attitude is a brain that can quickly skip from one subject to the next, not with the butterfly lightness of a Gemini, but with the high-tec, number-crunching speed of the computer variety. Whirr, click, clunk – and suddenly she has switched from discussing the newest domestic water filtering system to the cycle of drought in Somalia, or to the programme she saw on television last night which traced the increase in the developed world of asthma and other allergic reactions. There is a logical connection between them all, and the deeper significance of these subjects is not lost on her, but can often be lost on her audience. These wider perspectives are what can give Hourglass/Aquarius a reputation for wackiness, which isn't entirely justified.

One thing you can be certain about Hourglass/Aquarius, she is neither as conventional as she can sometimes seem, nor is she as off the wall as she sometimes makes herself out to be. This is a woman who can be brilliantly well-organized as well as occasionally have moments of true inspiration. She is someone to whom friendship really matters, but who also enjoys periods of remoteness and solitariness. She likes being in the centre of things, but needs lots of personal space, too. Her revolutionary side can express itself in anything from joining Greenpeace to actually setting about changing the way we all see the world, like fellow Aquarians, Darwin and Galileo. Or the way we read and write English literature, like James Joyce, Gertrude Stein or Virginia Woolf. Hourglass/Aquarius is not ordinary or predictable.

IN WORK

Ideas, ideals, dealing with humanity at large, rather than the sad individual reality, *thinking* about changing the world, these are areas where Hourglass/Aquarius would be most happy. The dissemination of ideas through newsprint, television, radio and film are all the natural working arenas for this personality who can combine so fruitfully the caring, people-orientated disposition of her Yin body type, with the inspirational, intellectual side of the Aquarius temperament. Hourglass/Aquarius can combine both the logical, factual approach with a fine intuition which makes her able to produce articles/programmes/films which tap into a wider consciousness. She is not naturally parochial, with her eyes fixed on the garden fence or even the national boundary – the world is her brief.

This logical, intuitive approach combined with her profound curiosity about human nature means that Hourglass/Aquarius makes an excellent therapist or analyst. She enjoys putting cause and effect together, and she is detached enough not to get too emotionally involved. Alternatively, rather than hands-on experience, she may prefer to research and write books about the human societies and interpersonal dynamics.

Charity work and work with organizations like Greenpeace and Amnesty International, which aim to create a fairer, more humanitarian and better world, will always attract Hourglass/Aquarius. Whether she just covenants money to such organizations and wishes them well, or actually dedicates her life's work to them, she will always be interested in attempts to alter the status quo and improve the position of the underdog. She can call on the necessary detachment to protect her from being

submerged by the enormity of the tragedies, human cruelties and natural disasters with which she has to deal.

There are many scientists and inventors too in the sign of Aquarius, and how this ingenuity expresses itself in Hourglass/Aquarius is very varied. She may indeed choose a research job with one of the university labs, or work in the research and development side of a large company, but she is just as likely to show her inventiveness in her writing, for instance, if she's a journalist, or in the way she dresses herself, or brings her children up against the prevailing advice of childcare gurus. She does not take kindly to rules for rules' sake, and works everything out to suit herself.

The word 'reform' does not threaten her peace of mind, but rather is music to her ears. Hourglass/Aquarius would be excellent at investigating any traditional practices, from the recruiting procedure of staff at the British Library to looking at how high court judges are appointed. She could write a detailed, closely argued report and then put forward a programme of improvements which would make the whole procedure fairer and more efficient. Work like this is ideally suited to Hourglass/Aquarius talents.

Ideal Fantasy Job

With Hourglass/Aquarian we are talking about a really idealistic job. Something like founder of a New Age University would do. She is interested in alternative education, where skills and traditions other than those honoured by Western culture can be offered to students alongside the conventional ones of sciences and arts. Mythology, astronomy, astrology, psychology, story-telling, Amazon Indian pharmacology, cabinet-making, conservation, herbalism, alternative religions are just part of the knowledge of the world largely ignored by the established schools and institutions. Hourglass/Aquarius would surround herself with thinkers and individualists like herself, and offer to others the chance to develop their own alternative skills – and in the process make some difference to the world.

IN LOVE

The Hourglass/Aquarian's need for freedom and space extends into the realm of the emotions. Passionate, possessive love is too cloying and claustrophobic for Hourglass/Aquarius. She has this Yin body type which makes her dispositionally drawn to making close relationships, having children and making family the centre of her life. But she is also an Aquarian and that gives her a more detached approach to the whole matter. She will be attracted most by a man whose mind responds to hers. She likes to be entertained, kept thinking, to have her horizons enlarged by someone who is interested in a world of ideas, even if it's a different world from hers.

Because of the dictates of her Yin body shape, Hourglass/ Aquarius is more likely to be attracted physically to a Yang kind of man, but not too overbearingly so – he needs to be more balanced towards the Yin side, an 'almost' new man. The raw sexuality of the more extreme versions of Yang malehood might be a little too gross for this cerebral combination.

When she does meet her match she loves with loyalty and sincerity of feeling. She is truthful and rational and not likely to weave great romantic fantasies around her man or the relationship. This is not a woman who is going to skip off one night into the moonlight following some romantic dream – even if he looks like James Dean, writes poetry like Byron and sings like Placido Domingo (all fellow Aquarians).

She may feel some claustrophobia in even the most well-balanced and unoppressive relationships, but can overcome this by making sure that however busy she is there is always time for her intellectual life – be it reading without interruption, or following a course, or planning her everyday projects. Her Yin body type means she will embrace motherhood and be a most sympathetic and loving parent, but she will find the inevitable restrictions on her need for physical and emotional space quite hard to bear at times. This is when Hourglass/Aquarius begins to plan her part-time work, or even the return to full-time work when her children no longer need her so consistently.

The Rectangle/ and Triangle/Aquarius tend to have much less of an ambivalent attitude to babies and work. They know that on the whole they feel better going back to work full-time, that they are frustrated at home with their children, however much they love them. The Hourglass/Aquarius needs her space and independence it is true, but she is more hormonally attached to her children and finds it more difficult to hand them over to a proxy mother in the form of a nanny, childminder or mother's help.

Friends play a large part in Hourglass/Aquarius's life. It's an expression of her need for wider horizons, less concentrated relationships. She will have a number of friends, but only one or two who are really intimate. She is not a woman who naturally wants to discuss endlessly the minutiae of emotions, although she is fascinated by human nature and our place in this world.

Ideal Fantasy Lover

Someone to entertain her, someone who is never boring or too demanding emotionally, but who nevertheless is a Yang bloke, uncomplicated, assertive, unvain – an Hourglass/Aquarian would never feel hedged in or stuck in a rut with the divine Lenny Henry. Creator of the immortal Delbert Wilkins, fast-talking Brixton wide-boy and Theophilus P Wildebeest, the American soul-singer with a studded codpiece and underpants with the studs inside, Hourglass/Aquarius has met her match in creative anarchy.

Lenny is married to ebullient Hourglass actress and comedienne Dawn French and it is obvious he has a most devoted and amatory side, but he would be so busy with his own life that there would be loads of space for Hourglass/Aquarius to be herself and get on with her show. And when they were together there would be lots of love and laughs. Like all Yang men, Lenny likes his Yin women curvaceous so there would be no pressure to go on a diet or change her looks with this guy around. Bliss.

IN STYLE

The strict dictates of fashion mean very little to this woman. Unorthodox in life, she is just as much her own woman when it comes to clothes. Being an Hourglass, a Yin body type, means she is interested in the creative possibilities of clothes – she enjoys the sensuality of them, the zing of unusual colour combinations.

The only style rule that affects Hourglass/Aquarius is the need to look different from everybody else. Now this doesn't necessarily mean that she sets out to wear anything obviously different, like a clown suit or the full cowgirl regalia, in fact more often than not she likes understated, good quality clothes. But she will make them individual to her either by changing certain details, or wearing unusual accessories – or she will put them together in a striking or novel way. When she is putting together a look, lack of fussiness and variety are both important to her. She won't look the same from one week to the next.

Neither will you find this woman in any uniform that makes her indistinguishable from others doing her job – for instance, if she's a secretary in a conventional business like banking, she will not conform to the sensible, smart secretarial garb which is so noticeable on the streets of the City at lunchtime. Even if she is obliged to wear a proper uniform, like at school, Hourglass/Aquarius will have shortened the hem, taken in the blouse, changed the colour of the cardigan, anything which makes her not quite

one of the crowd. For more specific information, see In Style on page 34.

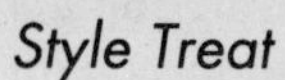

Style Treat

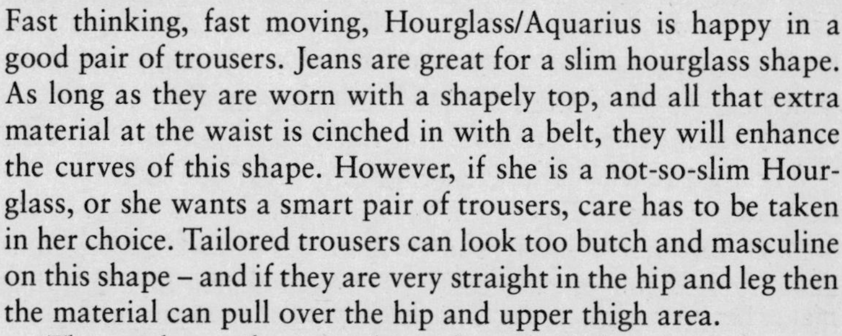

Fast thinking, fast moving, Hourglass/Aquarius is happy in a good pair of trousers. Jeans are great for a slim hourglass shape. As long as they are worn with a shapely top, and all that extra material at the waist is cinched in with a belt, they will enhance the curves of this shape. However, if she is a not-so-slim Hourglass, or she wants a smart pair of trousers, care has to be taken in her choice. Tailored trousers can look too butch and masculine on this shape – and if they are very straight in the hip and leg then the material can pull over the hip and upper thigh area.

The good news for curvy-hipped women is that there are more trousers in the shops cut to flatter this sort of figure. The nineties' look is much softer and more fluid than the 'power dressing' of the eighties. So Hourglass/Aquarius can choose as her treat one of these softer, looser leg trousers in a fluid fabric – light wool crepe, silk, linen, or these better quality viscoses and rayons which hang beautifully. The style, as mentioned above, is most flattering if it follows the lines of her body – a few pleats at the waist so that the waistband is small enough, and there is enough material in the hip and thigh area to skim loosely over the body and give a fluid streamlined effect. She should choose one of the neutral colours for greater versatility.

IN HEALTH

The traditional areas of weakness for an Aquarian are the circulation, and ankles and lower legs. Varicose veins may be a problem, but apart from that and the occasional ankle sprain, perhaps, Hourglass/Aquarius should live a long and healthy life. This is one of the personalities who really needs lots of country air, best got on long walks when she can breathe, and think. She tends to need lots of sleep and a balanced way of life to keep her from becoming frazzled by all the demands on her energies and time.

The Hourglass metabolism is a balanced one which is easily thrown off balance by too many stimulants, like tea, coffee, alcohol and cigarettes. These sap her energy and leave her exhausted and reaching for another coffee/drink/fag to perk her up again. Bad eating habits also sabotage her metabolism and leave her a collapse case at the end of the week.

Of all the Hourglass women, however, Aquarius is the most concerned with healthy eating and is likely to be a frequent

visitor to her local natural food shop, to stock up on the wholemeal bread, herb teas and vitamin pills. She is not naturally greedy but can be rather erratic in her eating habits, grabbing a snack on the run, or forgetting to eat because she's so busy with her work, the family or friends. Balance in everything is the keynote to her maintaining her health. For more specific information on diet and exercise, see In Health on page 36.

CELEBRITY HOURGLASS/AQUARIUS

Geena Davis is an archetypal Hourglass/Aquarian, beautiful in an unusual quirky way, intelligent, feminine and pretty zany which makes her portrayals on screen multi-facetted, individual and strangely touching. The strong-minded but wacky side of her character first sprang to prominence in *Beetlejuice*. Greater acclaim followed with her part as the sexy, slightly dippy, Thelma in the feminist road movie, *Thelma and Louise*. In her mid- thirties, Geena Davis has arrived as one of the most important and successful actresses in Hollywood, but she is an absolute one-off. There is no one like her.

HOURGLASS/AQUARIUS PROFILE

Barbara is a witty, wise-cracking American who has lived in England for the last twenty years. She married an Englishman and had two children, whom she stayed at home to look after. Highly educated and very intelligent, Barbara did not want to go back to work while she was bringing up her children, 'It just seemed right to be looking after them myself, although I was lonely and lost my self-confidence, as far as work and the outside world was concerned'.

When her children were in full-time school, her husband Andy started pushing for her to go back to work again – a move that Barbara resisted for quite a few more years. She resented being pushed about by his wishes and wanted to do something only when she felt ready to do it.

Trained as an Art Historian, she heard on the grapevine that a London museum was looking for some more cataloguing assistants for a huge collection of modern art which had been bequeathed to the nation. Barbara wrote to the museum, was invited to interview, and because modern art is her specialism she was suddenly talking up a storm. She believes that her sheer enthusiasm, and the explosion of the ideas she had been mulling over in her head for years, got her the job – even though she hadn't worked for ten years. 'I love the work. I love tracing the provenances of pictures, establishing their place and position in the various movements, even in some cases establishing their authenticity. I particularly like working with a team. We have so much to talk about and so many laughs. I'm never bored or lonely and just wish I had more hours in the day, because I love being with my children too and just need more time for both these important areas of my life.'

She dresses very eclectically. Fond of bits of ethnic clothing and jewellery, Barbara always looks individual: 'One of my favourite outfits is a pair of harem pants in a very sober grey colour with which I wear a short embroidered jacket, I think from Guatemala, which is butter-yellow cotton with predominantly red appliqués and embroidery all over it to give it a paisley-ish effect. I then wear this silver Coptic cross I bought in Liberty's one extravagant day when I went out to cheer myself up. The whole look is pulled together with a belt in turquoise silk (actually a remnant, again from Liberty's) which works as a kind of cummerbund and emphasizes my waist under the short jacket.'

She dreams of a political set-up where women and women's viewpoints are given much greater influence: 'I believe that nurturing, non-competitive, non-materialistic values are far more necessary now in this world than the old aggressive, acquisitive, conquering qualities which got us to this stage in history. I'd love to see things change radically, but I don't think I'm someone who's good at activating these things. I can only think and hope – and bring my children up in a civilized, rational way to carry these values into the future.'

IN HOPE

Hourglass/Aquarius is a humanitarian and her eyes are always on the distant horizon, her mind more often concerned with large issues beyond the individual. She has an abiding need for fresh air and space, both physical and metaphorical. This is how she restores herself, giving balance to her life. She needs to learn how to integrate this feeling, relational Yin side of her Hourglass body type with the more detached, cerebral Aquarius. Byron, the great Romantic poet – and an Aquarian too – turned for solace to the mystery of the natural world, with a response which she would recognize:

> 'There is a pleasure in the pathless woods,
> There is a rapture on the lonely shore,
> There is society where none intrudes,
> By the deep Sea, and Music in its roar:
> I love not Man the less, but Nature more.'

HOURGLASS PISCES

(Yin/Yin+)

MOTTO:
All for love and love for all

IN LIFE

Imaginative, sensitive and caring beyond anything most people appreciate or understand, after Pear/Pisces, Hourglass/Pisces is the most receptive and sensitive of all the 48 body type star signs. She absorbs the energies of anything she is exposed to. She can mirror whatever situation she finds herself in: if she is with artists, she is highly imaginative and creative; if she is with lawyers, her brain is acute and to the point; if she is with a party crowd she can swing along with the rest. But she is perhaps most herself when her extraordinary depth of sympathetic feeling is called for, with children, sitting with people who are suffering, empathizing with animals, communing with nature. Hourglass/Pisces is an interpreter of everything from great art to the slightest movement of a field mouse.

She has a strong spiritual nature, although it does not need to be expressed in any orthodox way. But the non-material world matters as much to her as the everyday nuts and bolts of existence. This sensitivity to the fluctuating feelings and atmospheres that surround her can mean that she treats truth as a relative thing. When you can see every side of every story, how much more impossible is it to make black and white judgements that have any usefulness or meaning? This means that Hourglass/Pisces can be accused of indecisiveness, even dishonesty at times. But when you appreciate the fineness of her perceptions of feeling and influences then you can see just how impossible it is to draw a straight line and say beyond this point everything is wrong/bad/immoral. Yes, but . . . and what if . . . and well, look at it this way . . . and perhaps, but who can say for sure?

It can be very alarming for a sensitive Hourglass/Pisces to have so many tentacles out in the world being continually stimulated with emotions of pity, love, concern, protectiveness. It is alarming having so little personal barrier to protect herself, and so many Hourglass/Pisces try to be much more organizing and brusque than they really are in an attempt to protect themselves from the extreme flux of feelings to which they are so terribly prone. They can come over as bossy and controlling, but the moment they realize they have stepped over the mark and hurt someone's feelings they are instantly contrite and you see the exceptionally sensitive, caring soul that lies so close to the surface.

Hourglass/Pisces can also go to the other extreme in an attempt to protect her vulnerable self. Sometimes her myriad feelings can just overwhelm her spirit and then she will disappear. Sometimes this is literally, often with a lover in tow for security – and, well, love. This woman lives for love and to love. Or this disappearing trick can be done through manner alone. She can become vague and evasive, not able to meet your questions or give you any answer to even the simplest request. Or she can lose any ability to be rational and detached, and slips into a sentimental, over-emotionalism, which drowns any discussion in a sticky bath of feeling.

Hourglass/Pisces has a boundless imagination, free floating fantasies, a direct line to the unconscious – and this dangerous talent also informs her creative work. But it is a difficult thing for her to live with sometimes – and for those who live with her – for there can be a blurring between what is real and what is only dreamed. Alongside this comes a romanticism which is applied to all areas of life. Perhaps she has a fantasy about her house really being a mysterious castle with a secret garden at the back, or that that man who passes her window every morning on his way to work is really a film director who will one day turn and see her at her desk and know that she has the perfect face for his next romantic heroine (but then perhaps he will – with Hourglass/Pisces anything is possible after all).

IN WORK

The obvious areas for this woman to excel in are the arts. Hourglass/Pisces brings her extraordinary imagination and sympathy to bear on anything which requires an interpretation of another's life – acting, writing fiction and biography, singing and music-making. She is an interpreter of genius, so ego-less that the personalities, wills and intentions of others can be translated through the body and soul of Hourglass/Pisces to moving effect.

A great number of Pisceans are drawn into the artistic professions. Their creations and performances have an extra helping of soul which lifts them onto a different plane altogether. Think of Harry Belafonte, Elkie Brooks, Caruso, Nat King Cole, Kiri te Kanawa and Nina Simone – all these singers are able to make spines prickle and eyes fill with tears. In the world of ballet, the two most legendary male dancers ever, Nijinsky and Nureyev, were both Pisceans, as is the new meteoric star, Sylvie Guillem.

Neptune, the ruler of Pisces, is to do with illusion, fantasy, mysticism and spiritual intuitions – and film and acting come under his jurisdiction. Holly Hunter displays in her acting all of this combination's emotional force and the power of empathy and transformation. The most famous Hourglass/Pisces actress, however, has to be Elizabeth Taylor, whose life and beauty long ago achieved legendary status and whose dosing with drink and medicinal drugs – the two addictions that Pisceans are traditionally warned against – many times nearly cost her her life.

Teaching, for similar reasons, can use this talent to absorb and interpret. An Hourglass/Piscean may well find herself teaching dance, music, acting, history or creative writing – all the areas which particularly rely on the imagination being transmuted into something else. However, Hourglass/Pisces is not very robust emotionally and if she has to battle with unruly, uncouth and disruptive classrooms then she is quickly exhausted and worn to a frazzle.

As a healer, she can tap into some of this empathic energy, but again she has to be careful to try to maintain her balance at all times and not allow herself to become utterly drained in the healing process. Anything from being a nurse or doctor through to osteopathy, hypnotherapy and psychotherapy can engage her interests and make good use of her talents. Beware anything that is hard-nosed and traditionally masculine, with a competitive hierarchical structure – as some sections of medicine are – for these are not congenial to this sensitive spirit.

Hourglass/Pisces has a fine intellect and can work in areas where rational thought and logic are uppermost, but she will bring to this work a strongly intuitive element which may not sit too easily with the way her colleagues make their decisions. She will have hunches which she will want to follow as if they were as cast iron as black and white statistics. Sir James Goldsmith, the legendary business man and financier (and Piscean), has made some of his greatest killings on the stock market and in business by operating on his intuitive hunches, trusted more by him than any computer analysis however far-reaching and intensive.

Because she cares little for the material trappings of life, the conventional flags of progress or success, Hourglass/Pisces can appear to underestimate herself, to lack ambition. She just isn't that interested in the things which preoccupy most of the rest of the population, the nice house in the good neighbourhood, the three-piece suite, the yearly holiday somewhere warm, the promotion and bonus at Christmas, her children's exam results, their places in the school team. Her mind and energies are spent more on the ideas and feelings that run on an alternative but parallel level – does the house have the right atmosphere, can she and her family be happy here? Is the job really satisfying to one's true self? Are the children learning how to deal truthfully with the world, and expressing all their talents – not just the approved academic ones?

Because of this view of the world, Hourglass/Pisces can be an unconventional boss or employee. She may be more concerned with the supportive atmosphere of the work place than with what percentage of the profits come to the staff as bonuses. She will be quite acute enough to work that out, but it will not be as crucial to her as it would be to a Rectangle/Taurus, for instance.

Ideal Fantasy Job

Hourglass/Pisces has a great romantic imagination, loves being taken out of herself, and has a delicate, otherworldly beauty. Prima ballerina in the Royal Ballet is the fantasy of so many young girls and there is every reason why it should still be a fantasy of the grown-up Hourglass/Pisces. The expressing of emotion through the beauty and fluidity of her body, the feminine grace, the dreamlike images, the transporting of herself and her audience into another realm, through imagination, and empathic emotion – all this is attractive to this combination. She has the ability to tap into a spiritual dimension which unites people on the deepest levels.

It is no coincidence that so many of the world's most exceptional ballet supernovae are and were Pisceans. Charlie Chaplin described seeing Nijinsky dance in *L'Après-midi d'Un Faune*: 'The mystic world he created, the tragic unseen lurking in the shadows of pastoral loveliness as he moved through its mystery, a god of passionate sadness – all this he conveyed in a few simple gestures without apparent effort.'

IN LOVE

Sensitive, tender, devoted, these are all words which are true of an Hourglass/Pisces when it comes to love – and really she is

always in love with someone or something. Her emotions are engaged at all times: in everything she does, she feels and makes connections. Her essential need to love and be loved may be so strong that her vulnerability to others frightens her, and the occasional Hourglass/Pisces protects this eager, delicate heart behind a brusque and cool manner. But the real feeling side of her is so close under the surface that it quickly comes welling up.

She is in no way a simple soul. With Aries/Rectangle, for instance, you see what you get, straightforward, completely unmysterious, a blast of pure energy at times – like when the brass section comes in in a symphonic score. Hourglass/Pisces belongs much more in the string section, with a bit of harp and flute – and that almost imperceptible throb of the double bass adding mystery and unknowingness. Nobody ever quite knows how she works, and she is sometimes a mystery even to herself.

Her inability to make cut and dried pronouncements extends into the realm of love. She cannot say that she will love someone for ever, because how can anyone ever be so fixed – and so certain of his fixity? Pisces is a mutable sign, which means she is changeable, transforming, in a deep sense of the word. This fluidity can mean she is accused of deviousness or evasiveness, or all the other less than solid attributes. But this is to misunderstand the extraordinary sympathies of this sign which mean she can in a sense love everybody, just as she can feel for everybody. As a result, she sometimes has to protect herself from all this unbearable emotion by pretending that she loves nobody, and can assume a world-weary cynicism.

The sort of man for this double Yin woman has to be on the Yang side of the spectrum. She may be occasionally drawn to a sympathetic Yin man in an attempt at finding herself a companionable, unstressful relationship, but really for the parnership to have energy and sexual sparks two opposing types are necessary. So, not the gentle, suffering, Daniel Day Lewis type, more the de Niro/Al Pacino/Depardieu type.

Children and family life are bound to be central to Hourglass/Pisces' life. She is deeply feeling and sympathetic and extremely good at seeing life from her children's point of view. She will never be an overbearing, bullying sort of parent, but may be an emotionally exhausted wreck at times. She is so busy caring for every child who crosses her path, sympathizing with their mothers, even suffering with their pets, that she feels she is someone who completely lacks a skin, let alone has a shell to climb into. She will be imaginative with her children, allowing them any amount of their own fantasies and never trampling on their dreams. She is also very artistic and will encourage this self-expression in them.

An Hourglass/Pisces mother finds it very hard to leave her children in the care of others, particularly when they are young. She can just about consider it if she has a sister or mother who she can trust to be as sensitive to their needs as she is herself. An Hourglass/Pisces opera singer with an exceptional voice and a brilliant early career, said if financial considerations did not come into the equation, she'd be happiest staying at home full-time to look after her two children, and possibly even have another two. Such is the emotional commitment and satisfaction that some of these Hourglass/Pisces mothers get from motherhood.

Ideal Fantasy Lover

There are few more quietly sexy and ruggedly good looking actors than Sam Neill. Born in Ireland and brought up in New Zealand he first sprang to public attention playing the handsome young man in love with the spirited heroine in the Australian film, *My Brilliant Career*. Brilliant and rock-like in *Dead Calm*, he gives the impression of being able to protect those he loves – even from psychopaths, supernatural and natural forces. And now from rampaging dinosaurs as well. He starred hunkily in Speilberg's prehistoric Tyrannobuster *Jurassic Park*. All of this is extremely attractive to a Yin woman. He also seems more than capable of providing a waterproof coat and a good few skins for the undefended Hourglass/Pisces.

IN STYLE

The fluidity of this personality means that Hourglass/Pisces will have a variety of looks, dependent on mood and occasion. Sometimes it will be the sweet maid of Buttermere, with lace collars and apron dresses, sometimes the chic city woman with her softly tailored suit and good accessories, sometimes the evening vamp in figure-hugging velvet and diamonds in her hair. There is something very soft and luminously beautiful about this woman's looks. Femininity is writ large in the shape of her body, the grace of her movements, the delicacy of her hands and feet, the gentleness of her manner and look. She is at her best enhancing this mysterious combination of quiet strength and feminine grace, just like the following Hourglass/Pisceans – the Duchess of Kent, Lesley-Anne Down, Liz Taylor, Joanne Woodward (married for ever to divine Newman; the success of the double Yin woman/double Yang man).

Floatiness with layers of diaphanous fabric, or organdie tea-dresses and drifting silk tops, are all looks for which Pear/ and Hourglass/Pisces have a particular fondness. See-through fabrics, or garments without a definite hard edge or hem also reflect the fluidity and imaginative fluctuations of this combination. Really sensitive to colour, she is not likely to go for brave reds and clashingly unusual combinations – it's a rare Hourglass/Pisces who wears orange palazzo-pants with a deep fuchsia shirt. Shimmering ocean colours and pearl-like neutrals are more her line. For more specific information, see In Style on page 34.

Style Treat

Shoes really are her favourite buys, but as a treat perhaps Hourglass/Pisces should turn to that other area that needs emphasis, the Hourglass waist. How about a beautiful belt? A good belt will last for years and so it's worth investing time and money to get a really special one. If she cannot afford some of the striking designer belts, then she can wait for the Sales and go to a shop which has a good selection of super belts and select the one that suits her best.

When choosing she shouldn't forget to take into account her shape, scale and proportions. As an Hourglass, she is best in soft leather or suede and the buckle should be curvy rather than severely angular. As with jewellery, height and bone size also determine the right scale of belt to flatter her most. If she is tall and has medium to large bones then she can look marvellous in a wide belt (7.5–10cm [3–4in]) with a big buckle. If she is petite in both height and bone structure, however, then she should go for something smaller – but not too small and insignificant, a width of 5cm (2in) should be fine.

When choosing her belt, the Hourglass/Pisces should also take her body proportions into consideration. If she has a long body and shorter legs, then a wider belt looks great on this figure and helps create the illusion of a shorter body and longer legs. If, on the other hand, she has longer legs and a shorter torso, her belt should not be too broad, otherwise it may look as if the belt is holding up her bust.

IN HEALTH

Not the most robust of combinations, Hourglass/Pisces easily takes on much too much and ends up emotionally and physically exhausted. She finds it very hard to say no to anyone – particularly to anyone who is suffering or in need. Her already over-sensitive nervous system can be easily overloaded, and matters are made worse by drink or drugs, from caffeine to therapeutic and recreational drugs: traditionally, Pisces is warned against addiction to these things. The Hourglass element of this combination also stresses the need to maintain a balance in her life.

Excess weight is likely to be a bit of a problem for Hourglass/Pisces because this is a most sensuous combination who really enjoys her food. As a highly sensitive and emotional woman, food can become a refuge or therapy when the world gets too much for her. She is also a double Yin dominated by her female hormones which give a predisposition to gain weight and get even curvier. So Hourglass/Pisces should either relax and enjoy her extra curviness (most Yang men really appreciate female flesh) or she has to beware of her propensities. For more specific information on diet and exercise, see In Health on page 36.

CELEBRITY HOURGLASS/PISCES

Best-selling novelist Jilly Cooper is very much a classic Hourglass/Pisces. It is impossible not to like her and be pleased for her success, for she is so obviously the nicest of people. Funny, modest, feminine, self-deprecating, vague and unsophisticated, she has a real ability to achieve what she wants when she focuses her energies in one direction. 'If I wasn't working [10 hours a day] I'd revert to type, and be flibbertigibbeting all over the place.'

Her success started in the late sixties when she began writing humorous weekly coloumns about young married life for a Sunday paper. Fifteen years later she was writing fiction full time and making millions. Her happy marriage featured in every article about her until her husband Leo's longtime and disgruntled mistress went public in a self-justifying, self-pitying article in a national newspaper a few years ago.

Terribly hurt, as only a deeply emotional Hourglass/Pisces can be, but keeping as silent as she could about it (not as silent as she should have been, no doubt), Jilly bore the whole thing with dignity. She just wrote longer books and spent more hours doing it. She says she writes her rumbustious, soft-centred, happy-ending kind of books because she likes to make people happy. She has no pretentions to anything more literary, few pretensions generally. She is now collaborating with a very hunky man on a novel about huskies. Any animals – and rugged men generally – make Jilly go weak at the knees. She deserves a bit of knee-trembling herself, after all the fun she's given her readers over the years.

HOURGLASS/PISCES PROFILE

Wanda is a tall, slender Hourglass/Pisces with clear eyes and the sort of understated beauty which can be so characteristic of this combination. 'I was married to a struggling musician and so had to go out to work, even when my children were young. I really wanted to stay at home with them – I felt they needed me full-time, and I needed that time with them. But circumstances decreed otherwise. I found a nursery school post which meant that at least I could take them with me – and holidays were not going to be a problem.'

Her divorce was terrifically traumatic for her. She felt that she had given so much to the man and the marriage, that she had taken on things – like this job – which she didn't want to do but which she did for them both, the team as she saw it. And now, it was all thrown back in her face. 'I struggled on rather. I was not happy alone, but I knew I had to make the best of it for my children's sake. Then I met John, whose job meant postings abroad for periods of a couple of years at a time. I knew I wanted to get married again, and he was someone I could be a really good friend with – it wasn't an overwhelming passion, but that sort of feeling had hurt me so much in the past.'

Wanda re-trained as a teacher of English as a foreign language so that she could follow her new husband to his postings but could always find some work. 'I think being a single mother was really difficult for me emotionally. I made a conscious effort not to be so sensitive and emotional about things. I think I would have cracked up if I had allowed myself to feel in the intense way I always had. So I shut off and pretended I didn't care so much – but of course I did.'

She can appear quite tough, rather managing and bossy with her family and friends. Yet so thinly disguised is the deeply feeling person underneath this exterior that if a member of her family or a friend points out she does not need to be organized into getting 'sorted out', Wanda is immediately contrite and full of explanations and apologies, realizing instantly how she overstepped the mark of true caring. 'I think it's a very difficult thing to be, an Hourglass/Pisces in this world where we are meant to be so materialistic and out for ourselves, where women are meant to be as ambitious and driven as men. I have tried but it exhausts me – it's just not me. I want to be loved and I want to love. That's what it comes down to in the end.'

IN HOPE

Think of the Pisces symbol of the two fishes, the most vulnerable of all the living creatures of the zodiac, a jungle in which roam

lions and bulls and crabs and goats and rams, and people in various guises. These flitting, almost skinless creatures, floating one moment, then swimming off in opposite directions and disappearing in the ripples and currents of the water – this is the vulnerable, elusive self of Hourglass/Pisces. This is the personality so at home in water, the symbol of the emotions, the unconscious, the maternal. She intuitively knows more than the rest of us, and feels everything. She is most herself when giving of herself. This is a creative act for Hourglass/Pisces. The great romantic and poet, Elizabeth Barrett Browning, herself a Pisces, recognized a central truth about this temperament: 'Who so loves/Believes the impossible.'

gains weight
on face,
neck and
shoulders

gains weight on
torso – stomach
spare tyre,
breasts,
upper back and
upper hips
(love handles)

not much of a waist

flattish bottom
which becomes
squarer with
extra weight

legs stay slimmer
than torso

RECTANGLE

ARIES

(Yang/Yang+)

MOTTO:

Better to wear out than to rust out

IN LIFE

Energy, initiative and the sense of being an individual, these are keys to this dynamic combination. The two Yang energies of body type and star sign unite to produce a powerhouse of a woman. Optimistic, self-reliant and vigorous, she is brilliant at starting things, new schemes, new journeys, new businesses, new relationships. This is the combination of the pioneer and the initiator and with a great rush of energy that is what she does. There is seldom any time for reading the instruction manual, for thinking through the final outcome of this particular move, for looking at the lives of those who it will affect: movement and progress are what matter most.

With Rectangle/Aries, this outflow of energy is expressed through the body. She is a woman of action not contemplation. Her body is the way she communicates and expresses herself and she is likely to be very interested in sport and exercise and keeping herself active. She is certainly not vain and this enjoyment of exercise and fitness is not to do with how she looks so much as to allow her to be what she truly is, a woman of action who is not happy when she has any physical limitations imposed upon her.

Aries is a fire sign and so this combination is easily caught up in the fantasy of this sign – the knight in shining armour is particularly an Aries ideal and it is Rectangle/Aries who rides through life as if she is that knight. She is not in the least interested in playing the traditional role of knight's lady, walled up in a tower fluttering her tiny hand and lacy handkerchief. This

woman is going to be where the action is, and she's quite prepared to shoulder the men aside to get there.

Adventure and chivalric battles for what is right fuel her vision of herself. Ruled by Mars, the most masculine and combative of energies, Aries is the first sign of the zodiac and Rectangle/Aries woman is determined to continue to be first in whatever she undertakes. She is highly competitive, but saved by a terrific sense of humour and an ability not to take herself too seriously.

With all these great, expansive virtues, one of the areas of unease for Rectangle/Aries is her idea of herself as a woman. She is dynamic and executive and yet sometimes lacks sensitivity towards the feelings of others. She is much happier making things happen and energizing others than being sympathetic or nurturing. A double Yang character, she is more at ease in traditionally 'masculine' modes of behaviour. So much so that sometimes she is anxious about how best to express her female self.

This woman likes to lead, she likes to be in control, she cannot bear being patronized as the little woman, or constrained to a stereotype of behaviour. She is not feminine in the traditional sense of the word. Think of the round-the-world yatchswoman and novelist Clare Francis, the opera singer Montserrat Caballe, Valerie Singleton, Dusty Springfield, Ruby Wax and the publicist Lyn Franks – they are all Rectangle/Aries and the words you would use to describe them all are – good sports, great fun, full of energy and ideas, admirable, attractive. But the words beautiful, feminine, even womanly, do not immediately spring to one's lips. Whereas Hourglass/Aries women like Julie Christie, Cherie Lunghi, Diana Ross and Emma Thompson, for instance, have the double Yang star sign, tempered with their Yin body type. They still have that Arien 'Me-First' energy but they are softer in looks and character, and more in tune with the archetypal female in themselves than is the Rectangle/Arien woman.

Rectangle/Aries can be rash and is often foolhardy. It's partly the speed with which she rushes into things, but she also has a temperament which is far happier *doing* things than thinking about doing them. A decorator friend rings up and asks Rectangle/Aries to join her next week on an expedition to France to deliver some furninture to a client there. Rectangle/Aries has a toddler who is not very well and a dog who's about to have puppies. Anyone else would have passed on the invitation. Not her, she takes her small son with her and organizes her sister to come and dog-sit. Spontaneity of action is half the attraction and rising to the challenge is the other half. If she ends up having to find a doctor in France, or organize a flight home early, it doesn't upset her at all – it's just another opportunity to use her energy and ingenuity. She feels more alive and exhilarated by the attempt.

She is great fun, often very funny too. Easily accepted as one of the lads, she has many men friends but is warm and supportive of her women friends too – although she hasn't much patience for endless discussions of the emotional ins and outs of ailing relationships. Give her a cause to fight and she can be a force to be reckoned with: shut her in a room with a neurotic friend and it will be Rectangle/Aries who will be climbing the wall within the hour. Horses for courses, as she may well say, recognizing as clearly as anyone where her limitations lie.

IN WORK

Work outside the home is of central importance to Rectangle/Aries. Her energies can never be properly contained within the family, and if they are forced to be then she will find ways of expressing these creative surges of Must-Do-Now-forcefulness by organizing all the school activities, setting up a neighbourhood bike swap, or starting a choir. PR supremo Lyn Franks expresses this energy exactly when she says, 'Yes of course I loved my husband, my children, my parents, my dog, my house – but that was only when I had time.'

Without challenging work Rectangle/Aries can be a trial – and bossy with it. Just remember what Lucrezia Borgia and Catherine de Medici, both Rectangle/Aries no doubt, got up to when they weren't occupied enough with running armies or scaling precipices.

In her natural state, Rectangle/Aries is full of self-confidence. She believes she can do anything she puts her mind to, and this should be something which involves action and people and being on stage in some guise or other. She likes to win. Politics would seem to be a natural habitat for this woman. Certainly there are more Arien MPs than there are of any other sign – but then, of course, an overwhelming number of those are men. Rectangle/Aries is very well-equipped to take on the masculine dominated professions because she has the confidence, competitiveness and fighting spirit to get her through all the prejudice and stonewalling she will encounter.

Sport and athletics is another area where this great energy and competitiveness can be well used, and of course the Rectangle body type is a strong, athletic type. Even if Rectangle/Aries does not choose sport as a career, she will be most likely to do some

sort of sport or exercise in her spare time because her body type needs it for reasons of health and well-being.

The Army and police are also areas where this straightforward, courageous spirit can thrive. Brigadier Anne Field, one of the highest ranking women in the British Army, is a Rectangle/Aries and there are other women of this combination drawn by the challenge of such a life of courage, teamwork and action. The sense of fighting for a better world is also part of the attraction to the chivalric side of this temperament.

Rectangle/Aries is not very happy for long as a lowly employee in some routine administrative job. Not strong on being told what to do (to be frank, she would rather be telling others what to do), not good at plodding on to the end of dull jobs (she is full of enthusiasm for the start of anything but not a good stayer), not content in sedentary jobs with little action, she is soon bolting for the door. Straightforward in her speech, sometimes tactless, even brash, Rectangle/Aries is not known for her diplomatic skills. She is, however, a born leader and given her head will impress with her energy and executive ability.

Emergencies and difficult situations do not phase her at all. She rises to the occasion and can act decisively and well. In ordinary times of non-emergency she can be rather bossy and overwhelming, but her vices and virtues are all so transparent. She is quite lacking in either side or malice. She is what you see and she says what she thinks – often without a necessary filtering system to prevent her from hurting other people's feelings or making some foot-in-mouth remark. But it is all done without thought and carries no emotional freight. You can be as frank to her and know you are unlikely to hurt her feelings in return.

Ideal Fantasy Job

Head of a head-hunting agency for management consultants. Aries rules the head, in everything she does she leads with the head, above all she likes to *be* head. It is the first sign of the zodiac and she also always wants to be first, so it is appropriate that Rectangle/Aries' ideal job should be as a high-flying head-hunter, finding the right people for the right positions, moving in high circles in the business world – being known as the best in her field.

Having done all the courses – on public speaking, on how to present herself properly, also a style and image session – she can then have fun being legitimately bossy by directing her clients to these various consultants to improve *their* image. And then she can enjoy the pleasure of seeing people she knows are right for

the job being offered the job, sometimes against terrific competition. This woman is herself highly competitive and she likes to win, so winning whichever way gives her a buzz – as does all the corporate entertaining of companies and tendering for work. Rectangle/Aries ARE GO.

IN LOVE

Love is a less easy area of operations for Rectangle/Aries. Any sort of work challenge, fine – but the deeper and subtler emotions are a more difficult matter, especially as it means understanding and accommodating the generally mysterious feelings of someone else.

Being high on fantasy, she is keen on romance, responds brilliantly to the whirlwind courtship, is hot for the chase (and she's as likely to do the chasing as be the chased!). The chivalric ideal is not to be forgotten. It's an attractive fantasy for all Ariens, but for Aries women with the Yang body types (Rectangle and Triangle) it has a particular potency. Romance and challenge are two important ingredients in her relationships, as in life. Rectangle/Aries wants to feel she is righting wrongs, fighting on the side of the great and good, overcoming hardship and obstacles.

She is not someone who longs to be married from the time she is sixteen. There's far too much she wants to do first in the world. But when thoughts do turn to choosing her man, she is quite capable of taking on a divorcé with six children, or a man who has been crippled in a car crash. Her indomitable energy and knight in shining armour side is quick to ride to any rescue, and the man she chooses to marry may be her biggest rescue of all. Not that there is the slightest bit of a martyr or masochist in Rectangle/Aries. Just a big-hearted energy and a belief that nothing is too much for her.

When we said choose, we meant choose – Rectangle/Aries is the woman most likely to ask a man to marry her. She is so decisive and impetuous that when she has made up her mind she doesn't want to wait around a few months hoping he might get round to proposing. Neither is she much good at manoevering him into anything. She meets everything straight on, blurts things out and gallops on.

As a double Yang woman, she can only really be happy with a Yin man. If she was to move in with, let alone marry, a Yang man like Sean Connery or Bob Geldoff, there would be such clashing of egos, so much competitiveness, so many sparks as each tried to push the other around and gain the upper hand, that

it would end in fisticuffs or a sullen temporary defeat for one of them. A Yin man with this woman is the perfect foil for her fieriness and energy which would add dynamic to the whole thing. His sensitivity and imagination would make up for her lack of these, his nurturing would fertilize the relationship and keep it going. He would love and admire her and she would adore him, and turn to him for comfort and support when battling the outside world just got to be too much.

Unmitigated domestic life holds few attractions for her really. She can be bossy and far too impatient to be happy caring for her children full-time. If she ends up without other outlets, all her ambitions and pushiness can become focused on her man and children, with unhappy results for all concerned. She needs outside interests and channels for this extraordinary executive energy – and this usually means working at least part-time, probably ideally full-time.

Rectangle/Aries is a good fun mother to have around. She has lots of energy, is often sporty and ready for anything. She's the sort of mother to take her young children with her on a sailing holiday, or to go pony-trekking in Wales when they are barely toddlers. She does not recognize the limitations and conventions less adventurous mothers might. Fantastic with hearty boys and tomboy girls, she may be rather insensitive and unimaginative in her treatment of her more emotional and introverted sons and daughters, but she is never a mean or malicious person. Any faults are glaringly obvious and easily pointed out and made amends for.

Ideal Fantasy Lover

Tom Hanks is a delightful Yin male who would gladden the heart of a Rectangle/Aries. Subtle and funny, this actor looks eternally boyish and mischievous but in a touching and entirely genuine way. He sprang to fame with *Splash* playing opposite that most Yang of actresses Darryl Hannah, whom he fell in love with both as maid and mermaid. As the lead in *Bonfire of the Vanities* it was not his fault that the film was so disappointing, but although he took a lot of flak for that flop this man still has far to go.

Rectangle/Aries would be a superb partner for him because she would be so businesslike about his career and stop him becoming involved in anything which was not good enough for his talents. Yin-type people are too readily influenced by their feelings for the other people involved, and will agree to do something because they like the person who's asking, or don't want to let someone down. There'd be none of that unbusinesslike

behaviour when it came to work, if Rectangle/Aries woman was around to direct operations.

IN STYLE

Being a double Yang, Rectangle/Aries is not too interested in clothes for clothes' sake. She wants to look good, she wants to look different, but she doesn't want to spend ages shopping for just the right thing to go with that other thing, in just the right size – and then what about the shade? All this thought and reflection and experimentation (which her Yin sisters can turn into a creative act – just *feel* the beauty of this cloth!) tends to bore her to tears. Ideally, she would like to be able to walk into one shop and put a whole wardrobe of snazzy outfits together with a series of well coordinated, smart but unfussy clothes. She cannot be bothered with anything fussy or fiddly or floaty, and this is fortunate because her body type means she is much better suited by good clean lines and geometric detail. She loves bright colours and bold accessories which make a statement. This woman is into making statements. For more specific information, see In Style on page 41.

Style Treat

Rectangle/Aries has a particular weakness for red. So how about a pair of red earrings? For business, however, earrings would be more appropriate in gold or silver. For advice on choosing the right colour if buying gold or silver, see page 43. In business, earrings are as important to a woman as a tie is to a man. As long as they are not dangly or dressy, they give definition to the face and add authority to her working look. Most women who come to style sessions with Bel wear earrings which are too small for their features. Obviously one cannot wear dustbin lids on one's ears for work, but it is possible to go bigger than most women realize. If she has large bones, a large face and is tall then, even for work, Rectangle/Aries should wear large-scale earrings. If, however, she is petite and with small features then obviously smaller earrings are more flattering – anything too large will look as if her face is being worn by her earrings.

The line of this jewellery is also just as important as scale. As with clothes and other accessories, the Rectangle body type needs to keep to the angular – triangular or rectangular earrings, rather than round. Of course, if she is dressed casually then she can either dispense with earrings all together, or wear more zany ones – however the mood takes her.

A bigger treat in the same theme could be a pair of red Chelsea boots to go with her jeans or casual trousers. Rectangle types look great in 501s and tailored, straight-leg trousers. Rectangle/Aries should choose leather for the boots, rather than suede (suede is too soft a look for this type) and square or chisel toes are more flattering to her whole look than the softer round or almond. Again she should make sure that the red is a shade which suits her colouring best.

IN HEALTH

Rectangle/Aries should have a robust constitution. Aries is ruler of the head and so headaches, sinusitis, eye strain and head wounds (from bashing it against brick walls perhaps?) are traditionally most probable. But any illness or complaint is liable to be short-term. This combination is not likely to have chronic lingering diseases, but her impetuosity and lack of pacing herself properly can result in bad eating habits and general fatigue.

Putting on weight will not be a problem when she is young. Bel's research with volunteer dieters for her book *The Body Breakthrough* showed that the Rectangle body shape tended to stay slim when young, but the pounds may begin to pile on a bit in her middle years. This body type has a robust constitution, and she has an athletic body with a strength and solidity about it which is mirrored in the constancy of her energy flow.

When overweight, this type becomes the classic 'apple' shape, mentioned in the scientific papers in this book's introduction. These point out that case histories of tens of thousands of women have shown that this shape is less protected than the Pear and Hourglass from male type diseases, like arteriosclerosis and diabetes. Rectangle/Aries, whose busy life may lead to irregular scrappy meals and snatched periods of exercise and not enough rest, needs exercise and a well-balanced diet for the sake of her health as well as any vanity about her looks. For more specific information on diet and exercise, see In Health on page 43.

CELEBRITY RECTANGLE/ARIES

Ruby Wax is Rectangle/Aries with nobs on. She is the American comedienne whose programmes on television have been characterized by her manic motor-mouth, her energy and wacky humour. Although unbelievably brash, as only a Rectangle/Aries can be, she also has that characteristic transparent niceness. As well as managing an awesome output of work, she has produced two babies and kept a marriage going with a sweetly long-suffering TV producer husband.

Her periods of extreme activity need to alternate with periods of extreme rest when she just takes off for a few days by herself to a hotel where she can't be recognized and just works on restoring herself. She says being a female comic is a hard life, the mental equivalent of coal mining. But it's also obvious that as a Rectangle/Aries she cannot resist the challenge: the harder it gets, the more she fights and wants to win.

RECTANGLE/ARIES PROFILE

Chris is in her late twenties and drives a mini cab from 5pm to 2am. She has a small son of four and a husband who has been made redundant who looks after him while she works. 'This job isn't everyone's cup of tea, it can be lonely and it can be dangerous, but I work for a company who only accepts fares from people who give their name, address and telephone number. We aren't allowed to cruise the streets looking for punters. But it does pay me quite well and I'm never bored. You never know what's going to happen next, where you're going to have to go, who you'll pick up. I've made a few friends this way. People talk, particularly at night.'

Twice she's been involved in unpleasant incidents. Once when one of her fares tried to run off at the lights without paying. Chris leapt out of the car and ran after him: 'I was so angry, I didn't stop to think what I was doing.' Although she's not very tall she is strong and grabbed him by the collar so firmly, he was intimidated into handing over the money he owed her. The other time she had a couple in the car who she didn't realize were drunk. When the man started hitting the woman who was screaming, Chris stopped the car and went to intervene, 'It was then that the woman hit me full in the face and told me to mind my own business. I turned them both out of the car then and there. I've been much more careful not to take on fares who have been drinking heavily. For a start you risk having to clean up their sick in the back of your car. No thank you!'

Despite the risk, she says she would hate to have an ordinary job. She likes being more her own boss, and plans to start her own company in the next two years, run much more efficiently than the one she's currently working for.

She is small and slim and wears jeans or leggings and a shirt for work. 'I have to be comfortable above anything else. I think leggings have been the greatest thing since sliced bread for women like me because they are so easy to wear whatever you're

doing – and can look smart with the right tops. When I go out I like to really dress up – something bright and possibly glittery. I don't mind if I look rather over-the-top, I like standing out in a crowd and Dave likes being proud of me.'

IN HOPE

If in doubt, act. This seems to be the Rectangle/Aries' answer to most of the conundrums of life and there is something quite admirable in this attitude. The great philospher Santayana would seem to agree with her approach: 'Nature drives with a loose rein and vitality of any sort can blunder through many a predicament in which reason would despair'.

There will be very little wingeing from Rectangle/Aries: she is truly someone who picks herself up, dusts herself down and starts all over again. However, there are times when things go wrong and she is so quickly up and off in the opposite direction that she appears not to realize the consequences of some of her actions, or to learn from her mistakes. Perhaps, as the baby of the zodiac, she has to make her own mistakes over and over again, and finally come to some reflection and wisdom in the process. But whatever stage she is in, Rectangle/Aries is one of the great energizers in this world. She is never dull or dire to have around.

RECTANGLE

TAURUS

(Yang/Yin)

MOTTO:

The age of miracles is past

IN LIFE

Here is a personality of enormous strength and stability. Rectangle/Taurus is a balance between Yang body type and Yin star sign – an earth sign – and she stands four-square, practical, rooted in reality and capable of achieving anything she sets out to do. Her only problem is lack of imagination and aspiration. Rectangle/Taurus needs to aim a bit higher. She has all the determination and focus to get where she wants.

One of the facts which Taureans find slightly embarrassing is how many dictators and power-hungry people were born under their sign: Hitler, Lenin and Marx make quite a good start but then when you add Catherine the Great, Cromwell, Sigmund Freud, Eva Peron and Malcolm X you know we are dealing with some real heavyweights here (add the other sort of heavyweights, Henry Cooper, Joe Louis and Sugar Ray Robinson and you've got to be convinced).

Persistence is what these exceptional Taureans share with the less alarming, everyday kind of folk. This, allied to a certain self-containment and an overwhelming strength of mind – which those closest to them might call sheer stubbornness and always-having-to-be-right-itis – and you have an enormously effective being in whatever area of life she chooses to operate.

Rectangle/Taurus is also one of the hardest workers of all the body type star sign combinations. When she puts her shoulder to the wheel she does not stop until the job is done. She may have a good moan along the way, but she is never a shirker. In fact, the opposite is closer to the truth; Rectangle/Taurus can too easily

become a workaholic who narrows down her focus so much that friends, family, hobbies, socializing, holidays, good fun, gossip and fooling about, all get shelved while she answers the relentless call of work. She can become dogged and joyless and put herself on a terrible treadmill, which she doesn't enjoy but does not seem to be able to stop.

The sensual, sybaritic, even lazy, side of Taurus is less evident in the Yang body shapes than with the Yin (the Pear/ and Hourglass/Taurus). She likes good food, fine furnishings and sex, but the practical, outgoing Yang energy makes for a greater sense of realistic, down-to-earth practicality – she is not going to toss her study books into a corner and set off giggling to an early bed, just as she would never buy a beautiful but expensive sofa, for instance, on sight – without first working out how she was going to pay for it and whether she couldn't get one cheaper elsewhere. She is no fool and is not about to rush in where angels or anyone else may fear to tread.

But Rectangle/Taurus can be an absolute angel too. This insistence on sticking with things, on dealing with reality, on being unvarnishedly exactly who she is, means she makes the most loyal and reliable friend and lover. She has a calmness which is a great solace in life's storms. She is practical and will immediately step in to protect and take care of all the administrative and bureacratic details in any crisis. She may not be the most immediately sensitive and sympathetic of people, but she is kindness itself when she recognizes that help is needed, and what it is she can provide.

She is not a nervous woman, nor is she likely to be neurotic. She can sulk a bit and even brood, but not for long. It's too much of a waste of time and effort to keep it up. Rectangle/Taurus holds few illusions about herself and isn't over-romantic about others either. She has a romantic heart but the earthiness of her star sign and the Yangness of her body type keeps any romanticism from getting out of hand. Her inability to flatter and charm sorts the real friends from the hangers-on: her honesty can seem brutal.

She is naturally slow to make up her mind about things. She is not happy with snap decisions and impetuous actions. Nothing anyone can do will make a Rectangle/Taurus hurry an important decision or rush thoughtlessly into something new. However, sometimes when the decision is made, she will implement it speedily, and often without much diplomacy or finesse, and there will be squeals of outrage at her apparent insensitivity.

Rectangle/Taurus likes her home and is keener to entertain there than to gallivant about from pub to bar to nightclub. She is

a great hostess, welcoming and hospitable in her calm, practical way. She can also be a good listener and a highly intelligent and knowledgeable person on a wide range of subjects. Facts impress her and her memory can be excellent. Financial security is another area where she values the tangible. Much as she appreciates how important money is in this world, and a Rectangle/Taurus appreciates this more than most, she is not foolhardy enough, or greedy enough, to risk what she has on harebrained get-rich-quick schemes.

Taurus and Aries, although neighbours in the wheel of the zodiac, could not be more dissimilar in their approach to life. Rectangle/Taurus suffers from an under-estimation of her gifts and powers: she is afraid of risk and the unknown and often stays in jobs and relationships long beyond their sell-by date.

IN WORK

Rectangle/Taurus is worth her weight in gold in any job where reliability, hard work and responsibility are called for. She has a conscientious attitude to everything she does, a great flair for the financial side of business, and is a calming influence and support to other staff. She is obstinate and should never be bullied into doing anything against her will. Although usually placid and slow to anger, when met head on the bullishness of her sign comes to the fore – her nostrils flare, head goes down and steam comes out of her ears. Nobody pushes Rectangle/Taurus around, in fact she is more likely to do the pushing – and she *always* thinks she's right (and often is).

She can be a perfectionist boss who finds it hard to remember to praise her co-workers. Because she is so confident in her own abilities and does not look for compliments and support herself, she forgets that more expressive and less secure individuals thrive on a little encouragement. When an employee, asked why she was leaving, said – you're very tough to work for and stinting in your praise, her Rectangle/Taurus boss replied, 'You think I'm tough on you, but I'm far tougher on myself'. That is such a revealing answer. The driven workaholic side is there, also the misunderstood but stoic element. But perhaps, most noticeable to the unappreciated employee, is Rectangle/Taurus's continued inability to profer sympathy or praise!

She has a down-to-earth appreciation of money and its importance in the world. She also has a good idea of her own worth and is not inclined to work for nothing. There is a story of the great opera singer Dame Nellie Melba (a Rectangle/Taurus) being

asked to dinner by a rich hostess who then suggested that she might 'sing a little song' for her fellow guests. The great Dame replied that it was no trouble to sing a little song, but it was even less arduous surely for her hostess 'to sign a little cheque'?

This woman is a powerhouse in any sort of business. She can be a loyal employee or a reliable and gifted boss. She is not afraid of difficulties and will carry through a job to the end. She may be slow to start and steady as she goes, but she does not run out when things get difficult or boring. She has a great capacity to endure, sometimes too great a capacity to endure and she stays in a job sometimes beyond her own best interests.

Any work to do with the good earth and the human senses is work that will appeal to Rectangle/Taurus. She is often musical, with a lovely singing or speaking voice. The great-voiced Barbra Streisand is a Rectangle/Taurus with all the perserverance too which comes with this combination. The Yang element in this combination means that Rectangle/Taurus might be drawn to the business side of music, managing some aspect of a recording company or working with the bookings of an orchestra – if not actually performing herself.

Similarly, the art world attracts her. Braque, Delacroix, Durer, Gainsborough and Turner are all great Taurean artists, and Rectangle/Taurus with her strong sensual side certainly has the ambition and staying power to put in the focused hard work that is necessary to succeed in such difficult areas. Alternatively, she may find herself on the more administrative side, running an art gallery, or becoming an artists' agent.

Acting is also the domain of the Rectangle/Taurus. This too is a tough profession and the Yang element in this combination helps give her a determination and detachment which stops her being as easily hurt by rejection and the competitiveness of others. Rectangle/Taureans, Glenda Jackson and Shirley MacLaine for instance, are both highly capable personalities with great staying power. One could not accuse either of being sensitive flowers.

The love of the earth can be expressed in gardening, farming, working with green issues, the conservation of buildings, or the architecture of new ones. Rectangle/Taurus needs fresh air and open spaces and she would be very happy walking over the acres which belonged to her, watching the first shoots of spring. Her love of nature would also lead her naturally into protests and organizations aimed at protecting the beauty of unspoiled countryside. Rectangle/Taurus is herself a natural, unspoilt sort of woman, without whiles and guile, and what she lacks, perhaps, in imagination and inspiration she makes up for in good down-to-earth sense and a loyal heart.

Ideal Fantasy Job

Musical director and conductor of a Baroque choir. Rectangle/Taurus can combine her terrific administrative ability with her musical strengths with such a job, she could even sing along with them. She loves being in charge, so selecting which pieces they should perform and then working out her own distinctive interpretations is a real treat. There is a particular thrill for her in conducting a musical group and getting all the individual voices to blend into one effective and harmonious whole. Taurus is not naturally a show-off but the Rectangle side of this combination likes to have a stage on which to operate, so this job, which doesn't elevate her alone but as the director and conductor of a group, gives her the right amount of publicity and acclaim.

IN LOVE

On a physical, sensual level, Taurus is very keen on love. The Rectangle aspect in this combination makes her more practical and action-orientated than sensual and embracing, which means Rectangle/Taurus has a healthy and matter-of-fact appetite for sex. She is unlikely to fall madly in love at first sight, she is not the ecstatic type who claims her soul merges with the other in the act of love. She does not turn every sexual encounter into the love of her life: she calls a spade a spade – and lust is lust. This woman takes it as it comes and she does not romanticize the facts.

She is an earth sign and therefore earthy in her approach to the opposite sex. She sees men in a clear light and on the whole likes what she sees. Her Yang body type means she is attracted to the more Yin kind of man – the Nigel Havers/Warren Beatty type rather than the Sean Connery/Paul Newman Yang version. And she is just as likely to make the first move in the relationship as he is. She knows what she likes and is patient and prepared to wait, but she doesn't play games to get him. Good looks matter to her, she likes a man to be well-dressed and attractive, but she is not a fastidious woman and is unlikely to penalize a man for grubbiness or shabbiness – although most Yin men care very much about their appearance anyway.

Love and family matter to Rectangle/Taurus, but she is unlikely to put them as absolutely central to her life. Work is going to play an important part too and she will find it hard to take much time off in order to have her children and look after them

as babies. She is more likely to return quite quickly, at least to part-time employment. Security matters to her, and that is usually expressed as material security. She wants a nice house and a good income to support her family and their way of life. She is not a casual, fancy-free kind of woman, who will roll up her bedding, tuck a baby under each arm and take off for Katmandu if the mood takes her.

Rectangle/Taurus will organize her working and family life well. Everything will run smoothly, but more for her benefit than for others – she is not very imaginative about other people's needs or points of view. But if these conflicting points of view are pointed out she is always fair and kindly and willing to accommodate them – up to a point. Taurus is a fixed star sign and these fixed signs find it quite hard to compromise. They have to battle with the conviction that they are always right.

She is a good, practical and loving wife and mother. She is loyal to those she loves and to her special and close friends. There is nothing worryingly unpredictable and changeable about her. Everyone always knows exactly where they stand. She can become too narrow in her preoccupations, particularly over work. She can over-work. But she has all the sterling qualities of her star sign, reliability, serenity and realism united with the practical, managerial and out-going qualities of her body type. Queen Elizabeth ll is a Rectangle/Taurus and she epitomizes all these admirable qualities for which British women are traditionally famous. The right woman in any crisis.

Ideal Fantasy Lover

Yang body type women need Yin men otherwise there can be an almighty clash of egos and will, where someone has to lose. Rectangle/Taurus, so appreciative of good looks, can't go far wrong with the heart-throb actor Tom Cruise. He is an actor who has reached superstardom but still has some way to go. He is not one of the hell-raising young Hollywood studs, however, and has shown that his emotional life matters just as much to him.

He was brought up by his mother alongside four sisters, so is sympathetic towards women generally. He is desperate to have a family and, having been married to Australian actress Nicole Kidman for a couple of years without managing to produce a baby of their own, the couple decided to adopt. Tom has reputedly said: 'Hollywood can keep the Oscars. The only award I really care about is having a kid of my own.' There is a no more Yin statement than that. He's Rectangle/Taurus's ideal all right.

IN STYLE

Rectangle/Taurus is not over-concerned with clothes or how she looks. You couldn't accuse the Queen, Glenda Jackson, Shirley MacLaine or Barbra Streisand of being snappy dressers. Practicality, value for money, and quiet good taste are the hallmarks of her look. Her sensual side likes clothes which *feel* good, a good heavy silk, for instance, and fine jerseys like cashmere, but she cannot be bothered with expending much thought and effort on thinking out the best look for herself, or working out which accessories go best with which outfits. There is no great pleasure in the whole experimental business of putting garments together and creating different looks.

Rectangle/Taurus often has quite a strong and sturdy body which looks best in unfussy, classic clothes of fine quality. With a Rectangle body shape, a woman's hips and shoulders are similar in width and she does not have a marked waist. (Princess Diana, Vanessa Redgrave and Glenn Close are slim versions of this type, Victoria Wood, Cilla Black and Jennifer Saunders the more generous examples). Unlike the Pear and Hourglass, Rectangle/Taurus's hips are not curvy but straight. Also, when she puts on weight she becomes 'deeper' rather than wider, putting weight on the front of her body – on her tummy, spare tyre and bust – and becoming more of a cube than a rectangle. Her legs remain slim however heavy she gets. For more specific information, see In Style on page 41.

Style Treat

Although a knee-length, straight skirt in a good quality material like wool or cotton gabardine looks terrific on this shape, Rectangle/Taurus can get into a bit of a rut with her clothes. So it would be a treat for her if she pushed the boat out a little and bought a pair of really smart business-like shorts. Worn with a medium heel and good quality tights they look great with her business jackets and no-nonsense Rectangle/Taurus will really appreciate the freedom of movement – and the comfort – that such shorts will provide.

As with her skirts, they should be in a good quality wool or cotton gabardine, anything softer crumples and loses the flattering tailored shape. For smartness they should be straight and slim, with the hem – with or without a turn-up – ending just above or on the knee. They don't come cheaply, however, and as someone who appreciates a bargain, Rectangle/Taurus could do no better than to track down a beautiful pair of shorts at the next sale time.

IN HEALTH

Strong and robust with an excellent constitution, Rectangle/Taurus will only encounter real health problems if she overdoes things – food, drink and work being the most likely candidates. She has great powers of endurance and her body can put up with a lot of abuse, but when it gives up she can be slow to recuperate. So it's worth looking after herself along the way.

Traditionally, the weakspots of this combination are the throat, the voice-box and thyroid. Some Rectangle/Taurus also have bad backs. Perhaps loosening up a bit and carrying a little less of the world's weight on her shoulders might help that. Prone to constipation, the wrong food (particularly mis-combining, see below) and not enough exercise can cause Rectangle/Taurus trouble. But this is easily prevented by sensible eating. As she gets older, added weight might also cause her some problems, which is a pity because she loves food and is often a fine cook.

Putting on weight will not be a problem when she is young. Bel's research with volunteer dieters for her book *The Body Breakthrough* showed that the Rectangle body shape tended to stay slim when young, but the pounds may begin to pile on a bit in her middle years. This body type has a robust constitution, and she has an athletic body with a strength and solidity about it which is mirrored in the constancy of her energy flow.

When overweight, this type becomes the classic 'apple' shape, mentioned in the scientific papers in this book's introduction. These point out that case histories of tens of thousands of women have shown that this shape is less protected than the Pear and Hourglass from male type diseases, like arteriosclerosis and diabetes. Rectangle/Taurus, whose busy life may lead to irregular scrappy meals and snatched periods of exercise and not enough rest, really needs exercise and a well-balanced diet for the sake of her health as well as any vanity about her looks. For more specific information on diet and exercise, see In Health on page 43.

CELEBRITY RECTANGLE/TAURUS

Glenda Jackson exhibits the down-to-earth, no-nonsense elements in this combination perfectly. She is as honest as they come. It's not just her face which is free from artifice of any kind, her character too is thoroughly good-hearted and strong. She also embodies the virtues of perserverance and unflashy endeavour, which characterizes Rectangle/Taurus so well. Her most notable feature, perhaps, is her quite beautiful speaking voice, deep and expressive.

Given her unstarry looks and nature, it is all the more remarkable that she made such a success of her acting career before turning to the more serious and worthy second career as a Member of Parliament. Despite being well cast as Gudrun in Russell's *Women in Love* with some of the bull-headedness and lack of judgement of her Rectangle/Taurus nature, Glenda Jackson chose some awkward films to follow, such as *The Music Lovers* and *The Romantic Englishwoman*. She gave up film making with some relief in the late eighties when she decided to put her deeply held socialist convictions to use and concentrated on politics. She is as honest and unvarnished in her opinion as ever.

RECTANGLE/TAURUS PROFILE

Sally is a solid rock of a personality. She is the assistant to a very dynamic, workaholic, fellow Taurus and they make a superb team. While her boss is dashing off to conferences, international meetings, or sales conventions, Sally holds the fort back at headquarters, calmly dealing with everything from major political crises to the stationery ordering. She has been with the company for 15 years (Taureans often need a bomb under them to persuade them to change jobs!) – was one of the founding members in fact – but underestimates her value to the firm. 'I do sometimes feel that my work is taken for granted, it would be nice to be offered some sort of share scheme or bonus scheme as a way of rewarding effort and success, but I like the work and wouldn't want to change really.'

All around her, more pushy personalities demand better status and rewards and some get what they ask for, others move on, but Sally is as dependable and rock-like as ever, just grumbling occasionally, 'I like to have a moan sometimes, but I know my own worth and that's what matters most anyway.'

She is a handsome woman and her style of dressing is well coordinated and understated. She always looks nice and rather classic. She went to a style consultant who suggested she try some more imaginative colour combinations, but Sally feels happiest in the goldeny, muted shades of autumn and continues to buy mostly these colours. She does have a particular penchant for cashmere though, 'It's the feel of it as much as anything. I know it's horribly expensive but I go at January sale time and buy one or two jerseys in wonderful colours and that sets me up for the year. I feel so good wearing cashmere – although I look better in the

double-knit weight rather than the very lightweight ones. That is my greatest luxury – but I think worth every penny!'

She has not married but has a long-term man friend who is a tenor in the same choir that she sings with. She goes off once a week to rehearsals and sees him that night and then at the weekend. 'He's really very understanding and gives me a lot of support. It could be more exciting I suppose, but I feel secure with him. We'll move into a house together next year when his mother goes to live in sheltered accommodation. At the moment he lives at home with her and I wouldn't want to take that responsibility on. I have a full life of my own anyway, with my own friends, the choir and then a pottery class I do every Saturday morning – I'm making myself a set of plates for the house Will and I will buy together. They're a bit heavy, and not at all perfect, but they are all individual and I've enjoyed making them. They're a bit like my proxy family, I suppose.'

IN HOPE

Rectangle/Taurus is someone you can always rely on and trust with your life. She is the rock among shifting sands, she is the cliff against which waves crash, she endures when others break down, crack up, freak out. Her winning streak is her perserverance and belief in herself. She will continue against all odds, when weaker souls or those of lesser faith have fallen back. She's never going to be there first but she'll be there in the end – and that's long before the majority – for most don't manage to last the course.

Remember what perserverance and self-belief did for that great fellow Taurean, Fred Astaire. The studio report on him after his first screen test said: 'Can't act. Can't sing. Can dance a little.' They didn't realize what bull-headed determination can achieve.

RECTANGLE
GEMINI

(Yang/Yang)

MOTTO:

Variety is the spice of life

IN LIFE

Rectangle/Gemini is more focused than most Geminis. The Rectangle body type brings a practical, down-to-earth element to this most airy of signs. The Yang body type has a no-nonsense approach, a self-centredness and ambition which can help changeable temperaments channel their energies more effectively. Certainly, Rectangle/Gemini is more able to concentrate on her career, for instance, than the Pear and Hourglass versions of this type, whose Yin disposition brings a confusing mix of intuition and over-concern for others to this intellectual Yang sign.

As an air sign, Gemini is most concerned with ideas, gaining information and disseminating it. She is often a great talker and needs space and air in which to think and breathe – and socialize. Variety, truly, is the fuel which keeps her going, but Rectangle/Gemini is lucky to have this body type to root her a little more securely to earth, and give her the drive to achieve. Her talents lead her into all areas of communication, such as television, radio, newspaper journalism, the law (particularly the Bar) and teaching. These professions are bursting at the seams with Geminis, and among the women it is Rectangle/Geminis who predominate.

Rectangle/Gemini is at her best in situations where she can be emotionally detached, can stand back, observe, make intellectual connections and then talk or write about what she has seen. She is thrilled by ideas, less comfortable with the feeling, suffering human beings who may contribute to them. For instance, going as a journalist into a war zone, Rectangle/Gemini is protected from

entering into the suffering of the people by her intellectual detachment and the armour of her job – she is there to report fairly and honestly the situation on the ground. She is not a feeler, and this is her strength in allowing her to do work like this. It can be a weakness though in other areas of her life.

This combination can have trouble with the emotional side of her life. Her uneasiness can express itself in all sorts of ways: in finding it difficult to write with emotional depth and passion; in being unable to really sympathize with the feelings of others; in thinking herself inadequate in close, intimate relationships in her own life. She approaches emotion warily and can try to explain, or analyse it away – or in a real panic will attempt to run from it in a feverish round of work and socializing and quick, superficial relationships.

The Yang body type aspect in this combination doesn't really help Rectangle/Gemini to better integrate her emotional life. It certainly gives her greater strength, but it is an influence also which separates rather than increases the sympathetic feelings and understanding of others. She is better at impressing herself upon the world, rather than finding her place in the world: she is assertive rather than responsive. So Rectangle/Gemini has to guard against denying the feeling side of herself because it seems easier than just letting it out. Chilliness, nerviness or an empty sentimentality are all possible results of this suppression.

In the external world of work and friendship, however, Rectangle/Gemini is a star. Spontaneous, a wonderful talker, deft, witty, informative, she can be an excellent improviser and makes a first rate debater and barrister. This facility with language and love of society, means she is in great demand at parties, charming, amusing and never dull. She needs people, and to make connections with them, if only on an intellectual level. She is drawn to societies and clubs and classes where like minds gather and ideas are discussed. She is not likely to be the quiet one at the back, though, for in working or intellectual circles she has an easy confidence which launches her into new situations and discussions with little hesitation.

The changeableness of Gemini is less marked with Rectangle/Gemini than with the Yin body shape Geminis. The practical, more solid qualities of the Yang body type make their mark. This is all to the good and produces a combination which can really get things achieved, rather than just talk brilliantly about what she will do some day. It's quite interesting to compare the Yin body type Geminis (like Helena Bonham-Carter, Naomi Campbell, Joan Collins, Marilyn Monroe, Isabella Rossellini,

Brooke Shields) with the Rectangle/Geminis like Linda Bellingham, Judy Garland, Steffi Graf and Peggy Lee for you can see that they are a more heavyweight, focused collection of women. Their careers have had ups and downs, but fewer of the complete reversals and emotional vicissitudes which characterize the lives of the more female body shaped Geminis, where so often their feeling side becomes a central and problematic thing in their lives.

IN WORK

Here Rectangle/Gemini is in her element. She may think she prefers to lie around in a hammock in the sun, but if she had that she wouldn't want it for long. This woman needs to get things done. She is ambitious and enjoys the variety and intellectual challenges of projects to be started, reports to be written, meetings to be held, people to be seen. She is particularly good in areas of work where people and ideas come together. The Yang body type gives her a greater staying power and focused ambition than might be the case with Pear/ and Hourglass/Geminis who are aware of wider possibilities in life and are less driven by worldly success.

The immediately obvious work for Rectangle/Gemini is in the related media, and Rectangle/Gemini would make an excellent print, radio or television journalist. She dislikes routine and general drudgery, and journalism offers one of the most varied jobs she could do, never knowing from one day to the next what she may be asked to cover. She is good in any situation where she has to enter a situation cold, knowing no one: her ability to talk to anyone, her curiosity about life and people, carries her through. Rectangle/Gemini is also good at thinking on her feet and being able to improvise when things don't go strictly to plan. This gift can be of greatest use during a live broadcast when something untoward happens and the poor journalist is left ad libbing. It is also one of the most important abilities to have when interviewing difficult subjects.

Writing books and publishing – dealing with language generally – all come under this combination's umbrella. The dissemination of information and ideas is very close to Rectangle/Gemini's heart and if she isn't writing the books, articles and programmes herself then she's just as likely to be publishing or publicizing them. If communication is the name of the game then you cannot do much better than employ a Rectangle/Gemini to do the communicating.

The law, particularly the Bar, is also a traditional focus for Gemini talents and Rectangle/Gemini, particularly, has all the

qualities of ambition and toughness to compete in what is still an old boy's network of nepotism and preferment. She is more prepared for the sacrifices of her personal life than the Pear/ and Hourglass/Geminis are likely to be. She will also take rejection and failure less personally and is more single-minded and less concerned with how she appears to others and whether she is liked or not. Her ability to talk fluently and well, to remain emotionally detached from her client and the case, and to think fast on her feet, are all great assets in the art of being a barrister.

All the qualities mentioned before also make Rectangle/Gemini a talented saleswoman. She has the gift of the gab, is not easily put off by the evident lack of interest in her prospective customer and doesn't take refusal to buy personally. Her capacity to deal with a wide range of strangers from every sort of background is also a help. And, of course, she would never get bored – as long as there were enough people passing and products to sell.

Teaching and the dramatic arts are professions to which Rectangle/Geminis are drawn. Again it is that skill at communicating ideas which make them so good here, but as the administrative burdens increase on teachers generally, Rectangle/Gemini is likely to find herself getting restless and resentful. She joined the profession to teach, not to do dull administration in some dingy office. Rectangle/Geminis don't tend to hang about moaning if things are not to their liking; they are much more likely to up sticks and try something quite different, if need be, on the other side of town.

Ideal Fantasy Job

Chief profile writer for one of the leading Sunday newspapers. This would strike a Rectangle/Gemini as the sort of ideal combination of all her needs, requiring most of her particular areas of expertise. She would be high profile and highly paid (appeals particularly to the Rectangle aspect) and such a job would give her a great deal of autonomy: she could chose pretty much who she wanted to interview. Also, her fame would open all sorts of doors which would otherwise be closed to her.

IN LOVE

Where work and career is a natural stage for Rectangle/Gemini, so love and intimate relationships is rather more bundled away backstage. Gemini does not express her emotions easily as she prefers to deal in the realm of reason, analysis and ideas. She will talk endlessly about feelings, if you ask her to, but she is much more cautious about actually *feeling* them. The Rectangle Yang body type also removes her further from the sympathetic, other-orientated attitude to life. Intimate relationships can worry her and are certainly not her main motivation in life.

Rectangle/Gemini needs light and air and space and nothing will send her running for the door quicker than a possessive, erotically-charged encounter with a passionate and jealous man. Give her light flirtation and romantic courtship with lots of talk and theatre-going and nights on the town, give her dinner parties and soirées, give her avant garde art festivals and sitting up late talking philosophy in bars. But don't make her claustrophobic with your sexual demands or emotional expectations.

Rectangle/Gemini is unlikely to settle to one relationship early in life. There is far too much to do and to experience for that – mainly the non-erotic: travel, meeting different people, trying a variety of jobs, seeking to know something more about herself. The sort of man for her is going to be a lovely, caring Yin man, someone who is not embarrassed by his feeling side and who can help her explore her own with more confidence. Yang men with Yang women cause all sorts of problems, not least the clash of egos and a general competitivenes with each other. Neither is very good at nurturing the other.

There is a reason, for instance, why Marilyn Monroe, an Hourglass/Gemini (therefore a Yin type of woman) fell in love with Joe diMaggio, the playwright Arthur Miller, and JF Kennedy (all thoroughly Yang kinds of bloke). The sexual electricity was there all right, but there was a complementary balance to the whole relationship, difficult and unsuccessful as they turned out to be. Any of those Yang blokes with a Rectangle/Gemini would be disastrous from the start. (JFK married a Triangle/Leo, one of the most Yang combinations, and that *was* a disaster from the start.)

Yang people can sometimes be very insensitive towards more emotional people and Rectangle/Gemini is someone who finds it hard to feel things with her heart which she does not already understand with her mind. If she has no children, for instance, don't expect her to be able to appreciate even a part of the agony of a mother whose child dies before her.

This does mean, however, that she brings a practical, light-hearted approach to areas where there is often too much heaviness and introspection. Marriage break-up and divorce will be seen by her as the opening of new doors and the beginning again of more possibilities. She may not be able to share your suffering but she will charm you and make you laugh. Although you may

not choose to discuss your deepest feelings with a Rectangle/Gemini friend, you will certainly ring her up if you need to be cheered up, or entertained.

Just as early coupledom does not hold much attraction for her, so full-time family life strikes her as too much like drudgery and self-sacrifice to be much fun. Rectangle/Gemini is not well-equipped for dealing sympathetically with non-verbal relationships and so while her children are babies she can feel very inadequate and rather alarmed. She's frustrated by what she sees as a one-way flow in the relationship. She's driven up the wall by the lack of other adult companionship and conversation. Although she is a much happier and better mother when her children start to talk properly and respond to conversation, Rectangle/Gemini is likely to have returned to work, at least part-time, by the time this transition happens.

Rectangle/Gemini can put off having children for so long that she ends up not having them at all – if this happens she is unlikely to be as devastated by the lack of children in her life than are most women in this situation. She takes a cool, philosophical view of most things and, especially if her own career is going well and she's feeling fulfilled, she will make the most of things as they stand. If she has a family she is likely to be a lively mother, full of fun – if rather highly strung and overwrought at times – who has distinct academic aspirations for her children. She is not interested in upward social mobility, like a Rectangle/Capricorn mother for instance, but in extending her children's chances of excelling academically, for the sake of their education and future prospects.

All Rectangle- and Triangle-type mothers are better having some interests outside the home into which their formidable energies and ambitions can be channelled, otherwise everyone in the family suffers. Rectangle/Gemini will have a wide range of interests which she will fight to keep up even after maternity has ambushed her. There will be evening classes, and art classes at the weekend. Creative writing courses in the summer holidays are no problem for she will go off for a week without a qualm, knowing that her wonderful, kind, Yin, 'new man' husband is holding the fort and the babies – and far more patiently probably than she.

Ideal Fantasy Lover

Well no unreconstructed old ravers for Rectangle/Gemini. It has to be a man who has intelligence to match her own and an unselfish caring nature, a Yin male to complement her Yang female. There are few actors more handsome and there are even fewer as selfless and kind as Pierce Brosnan, star of *The*

Lawnmower Man. He turned down all work for a year to help his wife Cassandra in her fight against ovarian cancer. She said that his presence by her side made her believe that miracles could happen. He explained that his career didn't matter if only he could see his wife get better. Tragically, she died at the end of 1991 and he is left bringing up their young son Sean.

There is a sweetness in his temperament which Rectangle/Gemini would find utterly irresistible, and his uninhibited emotional side will help her feel cared for, and more at home in the feeling part of her own nature. In return, she would be able to help galvanize his career, reading scripts with him, discussing parts and generally looking at all the possibilities. A match to cross-fertilize both lives.

IN STYLE

Gemini is a star sign of many faces: changeable, whimsical, loving variety. She often looks younger, and behaves much younger, than her years. However, Rectangle/Gemini isn't terribly interested in spending time, thought or money in putting her wardrobe together, but she does want to make the most of her looks (as long as it's quick) and likes to keep her clothes individual and youthful.

There is nothing heavy, or overtly flashy about Rectangle/Gemini's natural style. A Principal Boy look if she's slim is one of the most flattering to this body type and temperament. But she is likely to have a few clothes that she can put together in various combinations to achieve the kind of surprise and variety which expresses her character best. Dashes of colour, nothing in a style that is too restricting or formal, and clothes which have pockets are a must. Rectangle/Gemini has a mind that is always working, curious about most things, she will have lots of bits and pieces to carry around – a pen, possibly a penknife, keys, money, a half-read paperback, a list of characters in a play, a piece of fossil picked up on a walk, perhaps even a mobile phone. She doesn't like to be weighed down with handbags and briefcases and more often than not uses her coat and jackets pockets instead. For more specific information, see In Style on page 41.

Style Treat

The best way to have a number of different looks with the minimum of fuss, cost or effort is to buy a really good quality blazer style jacket in a neutral colour that suits her colouring and will go with a variety of outfits and looks. Colours for

Rectangle/Gemini to consider are charcoal or pewter if she has dark colouring, or mid-grey or taupe if her colouring is lighter.

The style of the jacket should follow the pointers above. Then she can put it to good use to get a number of looks out of it. Worn over a crisp shirt with a narrow, kneelength skirt gives her a smart, conventional work outfit; worn with a longer, narrow skirt and a silk blouse in a glowing colour, she has a more informal and individual work look. For the gangster look, she could try wearing the jacket over a shirt with a scarf tied like a tie, pushing up the sleeves of the jacket and turning up the collar. The whole outfit could be pulled together with a pair of tailored trousers or a long, narrow skirt.

A jacket like this could also be worn over leggings, with ankle boots, or over jeans and a T-shirt for a breezy, boyish look. For something more glamorous at night, she can use the jacket again by wearing it over a silk satin blouse and shiny ski-pants, and dress it up with a good piece of costume jewellery in the shape of a geometrical brooch, or a pair of dangly earrings and an important looking necklace. The possibilities are endless and should give the Rectangle/ Gemini some fun working out a different look every day of the week if she wants. All that matters is that she finds a good quality jacket that really suits her in all respects – style, colour, fabric, scale.

IN HEALTH

Traditionally, Gemini rules over the nervous system and respiratory system. It is in these areas that Rectangle/Gemini needs to watch her health. Certainly, if she doesn't make an effort to slow down sometimes and take time off, she can become very frazzled and overwrought. Stress and fatigue need to be guarded against, although the Rectangle body type brings a greater constitutional robustness to this combination.

The hands and arms are also ruled over by this sign, and Rectangle/Gemini is likely to have expressive hands, and be dexterous and good at doing things with them. Arthritis is a possible problem and a good diet generally is important for her general health.

Putting on weight will not be a problem when Rectangle/ Gemini is young. Bel Hislop's research with volunteer dieters for her book *The Body Breakthrough* showed that the Rectangle body shape tended to stay slim when young, but the pounds may begin to pile on a bit in her middle years. This body type has a particularly robust constitution. She has an athletic body with a strength and solidity about it which is mirrored in the constancy of her energy flow.

When overweight, this type becomes the classic 'apple' shape, mentioned in the scientific papers in this book's introduction. These point out that case histories of tens of thousands of women have shown that this shape is less protected than the Pear and Hourglass from male type diseases, like arteriosclerosis and diabetes. Rectangle/Gemini, whose busy life may lead to irregular scrappy meals and snatched periods of exercise and not enough rest, needs exercise and a well-balanced diet for the sake of her health as well as any vanity about her looks. For more specific information on diet and exercise, see In Health on page 43.

RECTANGLE/GEMINI CELEBRITY

Steffi Graf is someone who is an extreme example of the sportiness of this body type's physique. Whether a Rectangle type is a sportswoman of Steffi's class or working in an office and barely managing more than a few games of tennis every summer, she has the same basic shape – broad shoulders, not much waist, straight hips and strong lean legs. If Steffi was to put on weight it would collect in the torso area, predominantly on the front – face, chest, spare tyre and tummy. But while Steffi is young and fit, she has all the physical advantages of her body type, great strength in the top half of her body, and hips and legs built for speed. The disposition that comes with this body type gives her greater mental focus and a good deal of ambition too. Without these attributes she would never have made the world-class champion she is.

Her Gemini side is also evident in her friendliness and general sociability. She's well-liked in a world where there are many who are neither liked nor likeable. She plays straightforwardly both on and off the court. Her weakness is her emotions, however, and she cannot deal very well with life in general when they rear their head. She was extremely upset by all the publicity surrounding her father's mistress, and her play was adversely affected. Like so many Rectangle/Geminis she would prefer to keep this problematic feeling side of her nature in constant abeyance. It throws her completely when she can no longer keep her emotions in check.

RECTANGLE/GEMINI PROFILE

Mel is personnel officer in a company in Bristol. She has been concentrating on working her way up in the company and puts

her private life a long way second to work. 'I just find it more rewarding to put all my energies into work at the moment. I know where I stand I suppose, whereas with relationships I never know where I am. I'm constantly taken by surprise – and it's usually nasty surprises. So at the moment I'm not bothering to look for anyone and I'm just doing what I know I can do well – working on my career.'

She is very close to her sister who also works in Bristol and they do quite a lot of things together during their time off. 'We have got interested in learning to glide and so we go off most weekends, to the airfield near here. I love the feeling of space and freedom – and all that air when you're up in an aeroplane. To be in a glider which has no engine, and just to have the sound of rushing air, is really exhilarating. When I come down to earth I am still high as a kite.'

Mel is in her early thirties and doesn't want to think about whether she will settle down and have children. 'I still feel there's so much more to do and experience. I'm afraid of being constrained I suppose. I know I'm no longer young in conventional terms but I feel so young – and look quite young – so I can't take seriously this idea that I might want to enter the grown-up world one day and be responsible for anyone other than myself.'

She is very good at her job, interested in people and able to find them the jobs and courses that make the most of their individual abilites. She is also much liked about the company, she's cheery and full of fun, game for anything – and has an excellent sense of humour. 'Yes, I think of myself as a typical Gemini – and being really quite ambitious and sporty too I fit the Rectangle description well. I certainly think of myself as a bit of a cube on legs!'

IN HOPE

Rectangle/Gemini is able to do so many things. She has the sort of curiosity for life which hoovers up information and then reprocesses it to enlighten and entertain. If she can also approach her emotional life with the same sort of confidence, she can see that her way of making relationships – with lots of space and air between the protagonists – can be just as successful as those made by more passionate combinations. She needs to recognize who she is and what she needs, not try to act out some other ideal which she has in her head.

When Ian Fleming (a Gemini, of course) was asked what made him start to write the James Bond books, he replied that it had been quite simply to take his mind off 'the shock of getting married at the age of forty-three'. Only a Gemini could have made that remark: the implication that he could turn his hand casually to anything – and make it into a spectacular success; the flipness towards, and fear of, marriage, the greatest emotional commitment most of us ever make; and the quirky sense of humour which nevertheless carries a kernel of truth. If Rectangle/Gemini can turn all these qualities into a similarly remarkable success, then she's laughing all the way.

RECTANGLE
CANCER

(Yang/Yin+)

MOTTO:

You've got to kiss a lot of frogs to find your prince

IN LIFE

Here we have a complicated mix of energies. The body type is Yang, out-going, ambitious, executive in the world, basically self-promoting and matter-of-fact. Yet here it is combined with a Yin+ star sign, a water sign, one of the most sensitive and feeling of the zodiac. Yang with Yin+ spells strength with sensitivity, extroversion with reclusiveness, imagination with practicality, a drive for power with a hidden, crabways approach to the world. Rectangle/Cancer has two distinct faces, the public one of down-to-earth energy and self-promotion in the outside world, and the inner one which is super-sensitive, moody and in desperate need of security and understanding.

Princess Diana and her stepgrandmother Barbara Cartland are Rectangle/Cancers and there is in both great determination and strength. The Yang body type gives a desire for success and fame and the Cancer star sign provides an exceptional ability in manipulating the media and public opinion.

The inner self is only shown to those closest to her. She guards her feelings from others, but is compassionate and intuitive about the suffering and thoughts of everyone she comes into contact with. Her family and home are the sources of much of her emotional security, they are also the arenas where her melancholy and moodiness are played out. Rectangle/Cancer's outward appearance and manner, her crablike protective shell – together with her strong, broad-shouldered Yang body type – hide from the outside world the turmoil of her feelings within. Worry and apprehension can make her ill. Cancer finds it hard to be optimistic

about life and can have a fearful, sorrowful side which the no-nonsense, extrovert qualities of the Rectangle body type does something to mitigate.

Cancer's feelings are easily hurt, she readily sheds a tear. This is less the case with a Rectangle/Cancer who, though still sensitive to criticism or rejection, is more likely to direct her hurt outwards, and express it with a tantrum or an ultimatum. She can surprise people who only know her as kind and compassionate with just how determined and steely she can be when her mind is made up.

Cancer is the star sign which represents the mother and here is a woman who likes to be needed, who wants to be valued for her maternal qualities, as well as her womanly ones. With an outgoing Yang body type, however, Rectangle/Cancer is more likely to want to express this maternal quality on a public stage than her Pear/ and Hourglass/Cancer sisters who are more content to express their motherliness within the family and at home. This woman can set out to become a mother of the nation, or even mother on a global scale. Rose Kennedy, for a while the mother figure for America, is a Rectangle/Cancer – and of course Barbara Cartland is the matriarch of romance and advice, and Princess Diana, Britain's own Mother Teresa.

Another dominant quality of this combination is her love of tradition, the nostalgic and imaginative connections she makes with the past, and her reluctance to clear out all the baggage, both real and metaphorical, from that past. She will have a loft full of baby clothes and photographs and momentoes. Scrap books can be for her an art form which suffuse her with memories everytime she opens one. She keeps up with family, even distant members, and knows where they all belong on the family tree.

Rectangle/Cancer is a woman who is very aware of the continuity of things and values the national and family history which has produced her, and the lineage which she hands on to her children and to their heirs to come. Cancer is said to be manipulative, which is true in the sense that she is instinctive in her reading of emotional situations and atmospheres and isn't above using subtle emotional blackmail to get her own way. This is less subtle and more transparent when employed by the Rectangle/Cancer, but her will is steelier and she is less easily deflected than the Yin body types who have this star sign.

There can be a distinct egocentricity too in this character. The negative side of this complex combination can throw up a defensive, insecure, devious and irritable personality who is always needing affection and reassurance, and slipping easily into

depression and moodiness. The Rectangle body type increases the egocentricity but energizes the over-anxious, melancholic side of Cancer. This means Rectangle/Cancer spends less time in the doldrums but more time demanding something be done about her needs, and hopefully doing something herself to right her own world.

When each contrary aspect of this personality is working to complement the other then there is a remarkable and happy marriage of feeling and action. Rectangle/Cancer is capable of achieving great things for her family and friends and, more specifically, for humanity at large. She is more likely than most to gain celebrity along the way. Helen Keller and Emmeline Pankhurst were Rectangle/Cancers and, in the male version of mothers-of-their-country, there are Dr Barnado, Virgin's Richard Branson, Julius Caesar, Nelson Mandela and Henry Vlll!

IN WORK

With the dynamism of this Yang body type united with the ultra female, caring, intuitive side of this star sign, Rectangle/Cancer is tailormade to succeed in all humanitarian concerns. She genuinely cares for the people being helped by aid organizations, charities, hospitals and hospices, and she is very effective at mobilizing funds and support for this kind of work. Her Rectangle body type gives her a greater detachment from suffering than would otherwise be the case, and she can therefore channel her energies into real areas of help, rather than being engulfed in despair at the inhumanity and suffering of individuals.

Cancer is ruled by the Moon and this traditionally gives Cancerians a real talent for publicity, and for understanding the responses of large groups of people. The Yang body type of this combination adds a need for success and fame and gives the strength of character and ambition to be able to deal with it. Rectangle/Cancer might well find herself in a high profile job and – contrary to her expectations – thoroughly enjoying the limelight and able to use it to her advantage, and to the advantage of her cause.

Rectangle/Cancer also has a canny business brain and can be well suited in work which requires the implementation of strategic policies or the investment and management of money. Cancer is again great at conserving things and has a nose for money. Rectangle/Cancer could be extremely successful as a fund manager investing other people's money in the Stock Exchange, for instance. Her strong instincts, aligned with an astute financial brain, means she can read successfully the movements of such an

institution which runs much more on group dynamics and emotion than on rational systems.

Her appreciation of history and tradition also steers Rectangle/Cancer into professions which deal with the past. Teaching history is an obvious one, but heraldry, and the restoration of buildings, gardens and works of art are all other fruitful areas in which she can work happily. Her love of collecting and her inability to throw anything away, combined with the love of the past, can mean she ends up working with collecting, identifying and selling of antiques and old books.

Running a restaurant or a hotel is another possibility, as Cancer often makes a wonderful cook and the Rectangle body type makes for an excellent manager. She can appear a little bossy at times but her genuine hospitality and caring side wins her more friends than enemies. This caring side may also express itself directly in professions like nursing, but Rectangle/Cancer is just as likely to end up on the administrative side, or even become spokeswoman on national committees representing the rights of hospitals and their staff.

Cancer/Rectangle is not as modest, nor as shy as she may at first appear. Her Yang body shape gives her a much more determined disposition, driving her to achieve and make some sort of mark for herself in the world. She will work one to one with people who need help, and she will be able to call on her dual strengths of energy and compassion. But she is just as capable in running organizations and will find, particularly as she gets older and gains in confidence and self-knowledge, that she wants positions which give her more executive power.

Ideal Fantasy Job

Mother Teresa's sainthood. This extraordinary woman exhibits an extreme of the best qualities which Rectangle/Cancer can bring to a job – to life itself. She has infinite compassion for the people in her care and yet she is detached enough, and energetic enough, to continue her work in dire physical circumstances and despite the apparently overwhelming magnitude of her task. She is modest and tireless in her work, and yet she is not averse to publicity, and is perhaps the most famous and best-loved woman in the world. She is a modern day saint, and Rectangle/Cancer could not do better than that.

IN LOVE

Things can get complicated in this area of Rectangle/Cancer's life. She has this deeply sensitive, emotional side and yet has a Yang

body type which makes her strong, quite detached and tough at times. This Rectangle body type means that she is most attracted to a Yin, caring, sort of man – but not too much so because her own Cancerian nature makes her more sensitive herself than the average Rectangle. She may find that she gives out mixed messages and in the process confuses both herself and any man who is interested in her. The body type predominates and so it could be a bit of a mistake if her emotional, sensitive star sign attracted a really Yang bloke – sparks would soon fly and mutual competitiveness would threaten to ruin the mix. Princess Diana, for instance, is much better off with someone like Prince Charles, or James Gilby of 'squidgy-tape' fame – or Nigel Havers, than a Yang man like Prince Philip, Sean Connery or Mel Gibson.

Sex, for Rectangle/Cancer, may be less important in itself than warmth and closeness and cuddling. Her body type makes her matter-of-fact and not very sensually-driven, her star sign makes her romantic and sensitive to atmospheres and moods; neither influences make for an unihibited orgiastic abandonment to sensation. Love and caring come into the equation, as well as how tired she is and whether she's going to have to get up early in the morning.

Love and family life really matters to Rectangle/Cancer. However hard she works, her home is always centrally important to her and her security is rooted in the people closest to her. She expresses her maternal nature in a variety of ways. Women with Yang body types often become very frustrated and restless if they are at home playing mum full-time and so, although she may not elect to look after her children entirely herself, she will be very fussy indeed about who she leaves in charge of these precious babies. For her, their emotional welfare is even more important than how well they are fed and the sorts of toys they have to play with. Rectangle/Cancer does find it hard to drag herself away from the nursery and particularly if a child is ill or unhappy she is unlikely to be able to leave her. Her sympathies are readily engaged by suffering children, particularly her own.

Emotional possessiveness is one of the qualities which Rectangle/Cancer brings to her most intimate relationships. She finds it almost impossible to let people she loves go, even though she may appreciate intellectually that children need to be encouraged to become independent, and old lovers perhaps need to get on with the rest of their lives. Rectangle/Cancer is likely to be too busy to be able to really put the drag-nets on everyone she loves, but she will still have her grown-up children moving back after college and showing little inclination to find their own accommodation.

And old flames will continue to take her out to dinner 20 years on.

Rectangle/Cancer is a marvellous mum and friend to whoever comes into her orbit. But she can be a bit of an emotional blackmailer if she doesn't get what she wants or feels she isn't appreciated enough. The best thing for her is to have all sorts of outside interests, as well as her work, to properly utilize her undoubted energies and ambitions. When women who need a larger stage than their own imaginations and their own four walls are confined in domesticity, then their frustrations can be vented on their family or themselves. Rectangle/Cancer is particularly prone to pyschosomatic illness and collapse, and so she has to be careful not to bottle up her feelings, and to do something about finding outlets for her needs. If she doesn't, she may turn to trying to realize her own ambitions through her children. The stage mother is too often a frustrated Rectangle/Cancer.

Ideal Fantasy Lover

Divine, delicious, full of Irish good looks and charm, but this actor, whose first part was Sir Gawain in *Excalibur*, is as gentle and kindly as they come. Liam Neeson won an Evening Standard award for his part in *Lamb* and has gone on to parts in *Husbands and Wives* and Spielberg's *Schindler's List*. He has escorted a number of striking actresses, more often than not going in for long relationships. The first was Helen Mirren (Rectangle/Leo) then Barbra Streisand (Rectangle/Taurus), Julia Roberts (Pear/Scorpio) and Sinead O'Connor (Triangle/Sagittarius), and he only has kind words to say about each – and they no doubt about him too.

This sort of balanced, Yin guy would make a Rectangle/Cancer very happy. He would nurture her when things got too overwrought in her life, and he would admire her for her drive and ambition, while he was content to watch the waves come in.

The ultimate nice guy ambition has to be his: 'I love women, all shapes, sizes and ages, and if I'm remembered by anybody, a girlfriend or anybody else, I hope they'll say that I never trod on a single person . . . it could be a better world if only we were nicer to each other.'

IN STYLE

Rectangle/Cancer brings some confusion to the area of her clothes too. She finds it very hard to be ruthless with her wardrobe and tends to hang on to individual clothes long beyond their natural or stylish life. She always thinks they might come back

into fashion again, or she could give them to her daughters when they're old enough. Her daughters haven't got the heart to tell her she'll have to wait a very long time indeed because they wouldn't be seen dead in them.

She longs to be classic and chic, but finds it rather a hard thing to achieve. Few Rectangle/Cancers are as much of a clothes horse as Princess Diana, but even she took some time to get her look together – making more than a few bloomers along the way – but now has managed to find the right look for her shape and her job. The Rectangle part of this equation is not over-bothered with all the thought and experimentation that goes into getting together an integrated wardrobe, and an attractive, individual way of dressing that expresses her own personality while being appropriate for the occasion.

Rectangle types prefer dressing to be speedy, comfortable, informal, even casual – and once she's dressed she doesn't want to bother with making sure folds stay folded, blouses don't gape and skirts don't ride up or blow open in the breeze. The Cancer element, however, adds a certain love of romance and nostalgia for the past and so, although constrained by her more Yang shape and the tailored clothes which suit her better, she is likely to indulge in a bit of whimsy now and again.

Rectangle/Cancer, therefore, may be drawn to a nice mumsie cardigan, which sabotages the crisper angularity of the skirt she's wearing; she may fall in love with a frou-frou hat which would look more becoming on a Pear or Hourglass type. She is likely to have a full bosom (à la Camilla Parker Bowles, another Rectangle/Cancer) and likes to make something of her cleavage, in and out of evening wear. In fact, she is likely to put on weight with advancing years – as Barbara Cartland memorably said; 'You have to decide – face or figure as you get older – I decided face'!

More specific information on style is given on page 41. However, although the Cancer side of this combination adds a softer element to the Rectangle body type, the body type predominates visually and so she should dress to the principles outlined on page 42 and should try and restrain her impulses towards frills and furbelows. She can indulge herself, however, with a lacy blouse, for instance – but in a stiffish, substantial lace – or softer colours generally, or add a feather to her chic, angular hat. And she can always go to town on madly romantic underwear – although to suit her body shape best that too should be geometrical in line rather than too frilly and gathered. But she may not care!

Style Treat

The Rectangle body shape looks terrific in a suit which is the right fit, style and colour. Following the guidelines above, look for a jacket and skirt – knee-length is probably still the smartest and most versatile length – which makes you feel a million dollars. To get the most wear out of it choose a neutral colour, like pewter or charcoal, or mid-grey, taupe or mid-navy. The jacket should fit really well: check across the shoulders, ensure that it isn't too waisted, and that it has straight lapels and hem.

Try it with a variety of blouses and T-shirts underneath. Try with the jacket open and sleeves pushed up, collar turned up, try it buttoned up with some more formal jewellery on the lapel. You can wear the jacket over other toning skirts and trousers – or possibly over your jeans for a really casual look. Experiment, and to ring the changes possibly buy a couple more tops in stronger, toning colours which flatter your skin tone. Turn out your jewellery box and try a variety of necklaces, earrings and brooches just to explore the variety of looks you can achieve.

IN HEALTH

Highly emotional but not very good at expressing these feelings, Rectangle/Cancer can make herself ill through emotional tension. This is a combination with very strong powers of recovery but she has to realize when she is running her health down with the unexpressed resentments and unhappiness in her life. Therapy can be a useful treatment for some of her physical ailments. Cancer traditionally rules the breasts, chest, oesophagus and stomach. Indigestion, ulcers and general circulation problems can cause some trouble.

Putting on weight is not so much a problem for Rectangle/Cancer when young. Bel's research with volunteer dieters for her book *The Body Breakthrough* showed that the Rectangle body shape tended to stay slim when young, but the pounds may begin to pile on a bit in her middle years. This body type has a particularly robust constitution. She has an athletic body with a strength and solidity about it which is mirrored in the constancy of her energy flow.

When overweight, this type becomes the classic 'apple' shape, mentioned in the scientific papers in this book's introduction. These point out that case histories of tens of thousands of women have shown that this shape is less protected than the Pear and Hourglass from male type diseases, like arteriosclerosis and diabetes. Rectangle/Cancer, whose busy life may lead to irregular scrappy meals and snatched periods of exercise and not enough

rest, needs exercise and a well-balanced diet for the sake of her health as well as any vanity about her looks. For more specific information on diet and exercise, see In Health on page 43.

CELEBRITY RECTANGLE/CANCER

Princess Diana is the most famous of all the Rectangle/Cancers and she exhibits so many of this type's characteristics. The shyness and lack of confidence of her early days reflected the traumatic effect that her parents' broken marriage and the disappearance of her mother must have had on this most sensitive, home and mother-centred star sign. Not well-educated and sheltered from ordinary life, this girl grew up reading romantic novels, like those written by her future stepgrandmother, Barbara Cartland. She believed that a girl had only to marry her prince for her to live happily ever after.

When she is hurt or things don't go her way, the Cancerian has a disconcerting habit of disappearing, in spirit if not in actuality. As Diana's unhappiness in her marriage took hold of her, her bulimia was the way she chose to 'dissolve like a Disprin and disappear'. While she was immersed in this emotional trauma she managed to present her outward shell as smiling and pretty much in control. This is the protective shell of the crab coming into play. But Princess Diana is also a Rectangle body type, and this too provides her with her shield. Naturally robust, athletic, and down-to-earth, this body type came to her aid by allowing her to soldier on and keep the real truth from showing.

The Cancer's need for emotional control, both over herself and those around her, combines in Princess Diana with the Rectangle's need to be in charge, to be in the public eye, to win. This is where she is most formidable. She can manipulate the public's response to her brilliantly, and she is extremely tenacious and determined to win. She is naturally a much more competitive character than her Yin/Scorpio husband, and much more adept with public opinion. She also has an emotional strength of true compassion for others which she will continue to express with her family, and particularly out in the world – thanks to the robust, ambitious and out-going temperament which comes with her Yang body type.

RECTANGLE/CANCER PROFILE

Jenny works in public relations handling actresses who are on the way up in their career and need careful publicity advice. She is extrovert and full of energy, but also sensitive to her clients' needs and very good at reassuring their fragile egos. 'I like working so closely with young aspiring people. It's really creative helping someone plan their career, choose which parts to try for and then work out how best to put themselves over at the audition. I like the mother/agony aunt side of the job too. I always end up hearing about their domestic and emotional problems, and not having any children myself I suppose I get some of the pleasures of being a mother without any of the responsibilities.'

She aims to start her own agency, once she has learnt all there is to learn from where she is. 'As I've got older [now 38] I've realized just how ambitious I really am. When I was young I thought that all I wanted was to get married and have children and live happily ever after. But that didn't happen. And looking back I can see that if I'd really wanted it to happen, then I'd have married young and had my children. But now, as I put that dream further behind me, there is a kind of thrill in realizing that my life is mine to do with as I will. And that I can make a real go of this job.'

She works late, sees a man friend twice a week, spends a lot of time planning what sort of agency she wants to make hers, and when she can goes to sales to add to her collection of silver tea caddies. 'It's funny how when you stop hoping some prince will ride over the hill and whisk you away, you really begin to put all that wasted creative energy elsewhere. Mine has gone into my job, my house – which I love – my friends, my extended family, my hobbies and my cats. Once I stopped mourning not having a conventional domestic set-up with husband and two kids, I realized I have a wonderful life.'

IN HOPE

Cancer is ruled by the Moon, a mysterious globe of reflected light whose influence is felt by all. Moonlight is romance, maternity, femininity, imagination. But there is a dark side to the moon, from where the fears and fantasies and self-destructive impulses which can haunt this personality arise. Rectangle/Cancer is touched by all these influences. The Yang body type brings it's own stabilizing, earth-bound strength which can harness the fluidity of this star sign and help her to make her mark in the world. But the dark side of the moon has to be acknowledged. There is an old Ethiopian proverb, 'He who conceals his disease cannot expect to be cured' and just as surely Rectangle/Cancer can only succeed in the world if she allows her turbulent emotions, and irrational fears, to come into the healing light.

RECTANGLE
LEO

(Yang/Yang+)

MOTTO:
Lights, Music, Action!

IN LIFE

Here we have a real powerhouse, flamboyant, big hearted, energetic, magnanimous, but to more sensitive souls this double-Yang woman can seem a little overbearing, bossy even. There is no ambivalence for her, she is an energetic, go-getting body shape with a sun sign to match. Leo, ruled by the sun, thinks it rules the world and this combination makes that almost possible – well, ruling the Parent/Teachers Association or keeping unruly members of Parliament in order at least. Leo/Rectangle needs to be appreciated, and noticed: no hiding her light under bushels for this one. The Bible says that the meek shall inherit the earth, but Leo/Rectangle won't wait to inherit, she's set on earning it for herself.

Leo loves all the good press that surrounds her star sign. She really likes to think of herself as ruled by the sun, the giver of warmth, the recipient of adoration from all quarters. And who can blame her. It's a seductive biography. And all of it is in part true. She is larger than life and twice as handsome. She is blessed with a big mouth, heart and ego. But there is much less said about the insecurity at the centre of Leo's character which makes her feel that this is all the greatest *act* of her life and she's not really like this at all.

It is interesting how relatively few actors and actresses are Leos. Superficially it would seem to be the perfect career for this personality which loves the stage, the limelight, the applause. But a prominent Rectangle/Leo explained that Leos are so busy acting in their everyday life that they have no real need to take this up as a profession. Perhaps there's some truth in that. Perhaps they are too busy strutting the stage of life and partaking of real power to bother with the pretend sort.

Fidel Castro, Mussolini and Napoleon, for instance, had a much greater stage of operations than the Theatre Royal. Of course, the sign is bursting at the seams with film *directors*, but that is power of a different order from that enjoyed by a mere actor – after all, who bosses whom about? Alfred Hitchcock, John Huston, Stanley Kubrick, Cecil B. de Mille, Roman Polanski are a formidable band – and no one could ever accuse any one of them of being democratic, collaborative, and sensitive artists.

So Rectangle/Leo is not a subtle, shy or self-effacing woman. She may feel these things at times but there is no way that she will show them, even to herself. She needs to be the centre of attention, to be admired and looked up to, and who is going to look up to someone who reveals that she is sometimes frightened, sometimes fails, and is occasionally (only occasionally) disinclined to sparkle on every social occasion? She has a vision of herself as heroic and she is continually living out this dream. It means she is often baffled with how mean and small-minded other people can be, for Rectangle/Leo sees the world in very simple primary colours, where there are good people, coloured in in yellow and lovely glowing red, and bad people, coloured in in black and purple, and they live in a world coloured blue for the sea and sky and green for the fields.

Rectangle/Leo goes in for great broad brush strokes which means she has the energy and vision for ambitious projects, she will enthuse those she needs to work for her, she will achieve what she sets out to, but she is confused and alarmed by the subtleties, the depths and undercurrents of human interraction. She is so simple and noble in her approach to the world and she thinks that everyone else should be too. Above all she needs to be somebody special in that world, and she will be very unhappy indeed, and somewhat dangerous, if she is severely constrained by circumstances and convention so that she cannot find a platform of sorts for herself to star on.

Competitiveness is an inevitable part of this need to be special – it's no good if there are lots of other people who are special too. Both the Yang body type and Leo star sign bring an ambition to make a great splash in the world, to be pointed out, idolized and admired. Madonna and Mick Jagger couldn't be any other sign but Leo. This is a royal sign, the sign of the archetypal queen, and who best to embody that than the Queen Mother, Jackie Kennedy Onassis, and the Princesses Anne and Margaret, both of whom

secretly believe they would make better monarchs than their elder siblings, the constitutional (but not astrological) heirs to the throne.

Both the Rectangle aspect of this combination and the ultra Yang fire sign makes for a degree of egocentricity. Rectangle/Leo is not very sensitive to the feelings of others because she is so centred in herself and the task of projecting that self on the world. When it is pointed out to her that she has ridden roughshod over someone else, her warm heart is immediately contrite and she is quick to make amends. She doesn't like to think of herself as anything less than wonderful. And for most of the time that is just what she is. Her family and friends are quite prepared to play the adoring subjects and forgive her autocratic lapses, just because she is such good value the rest of the time.

IN WORK

Rectangles are the organizers and showwomen of the world. They have prodigious energy and enthusiasm, they have broad backs and readily load their own burden and the burdens of others onto their shoulders. However, they have to be careful that they don't overdo things and take some holiday just to get away from it all. But when a Rectangle is allied with the sybaritic, sometimes lazy, lion we have a slightly different scenario. The Leo/Rectangle can work non-stop as long as the enthusiasm carries her, but she will suddenly flop and have to lie under a tree for a few days to recover. Above all, she needs to feel appreciated and rewarded.

This woman wants fame and fortune – and lots of executive power, and given the right impetus and a bit of will-power she is capable of earning it. She can be the powerhouse in a team situation but is inclined to take over and become bossy. The Women's Institute, Salvation Army, the Monarchy are run by Rectangular women, add a bit of Leo and you get more queening it, more generosity, more laughs.

This woman needs a career but it has to have some glamour. She's not keen to do too much menial work and does not care to be taken for granted. Loving to lay down the law, the legal profession attracts her but as a barrister on stage – or better still a judge. Never a mere clerk beavering away in the back, unless it's very much a short term expedience to get her somewhere better fast.

Anything to do with showbusiness or public life is a great attraction, Leo/Rectangle loves to be on stage, although it's usually a bigger and more important stage than one made of floorboards and plaster. With her body type, the Leo/Rectangle can be very good at sport when young (and still slim) with plenty of ambition to win – although anything that demands too much tedious training she's not likely to stick at.

Business, particularly where she can extend her largesse to grateful clients, is another fruitful area for her talents. Big boardrooms, teams of willing helpers to take the mundane tasks off her shoulders, leisurely lunches and meetings with other top flight executives: all is the stuff of which her fanatasies are made. Sometimes she lacks the application and sheer focused drive to get there, but she can dream.

Given all these qualities, Rectangle/Leo is a gifted publicist and is drawn to the whole area of publicity, advertising and public relations. Her slightly over-the-top behaviour is perfectly at home in these professions. Nothing makes a personality like this more unhappy, surly even, than being forced to work in dead-end, low status jobs in seedy surroundings with unprepossessing people. Don't forget that this woman is royalty – because she won't!

Ideal Fantasy Job

There is nothing more theatrical or glamorous in the world of entertainment than opera and so the fantasy job for Rectangle/Leo has to be Director of The Royal Opera House, Convent Garden. This is a tailormade job for her, meeting the rich and the famous, raising money on a grand scale from the most glamorous corporate clients, deciding on the musical programmes, meeting the stars. A grand office full of fine pictures and furnishing, a clothes allowance to allow her to look the part on all occasions, a team of devoted workers to do the administrative detail which she would leave in her grand wake as she jetted off to Sydney, Milan or New York.

Wining, dining, wheeling, dealing, negotiating vast grants and sponsorships, presiding over magnificent productions, making and breaking the grandest careers. All that power to produce pleasure and excellence and admiration, and all in her hands. Oh, the sound of thunderous applause can be heard in her dreams!

IN LOVE

The Rectangle/Leo is a bit of a challenge to a mere mortal. She definitely wants her man to love, cherish and *worship*. Nothing can turn her into a scowling, dangerous old lion more quickly

than too many dirty dishes and not enough praise, sprinkled with judicious bunches of flowers, chockies and well-chosen (and expensive) little gifts. If she gets what she needs, she's a generous, purring creature who will do anything for those she loves. But where to find this paragon of manhood? He can't be too Yang and macho because then he clashes with her will and energy, he has to have style and a whiff of grandeur (a title or small fortune would do), above all he has got to be caring and respectful. He has to be Yin, Yin, Yin, and it won't worry her one bit if he earns less and has a lower status job than hers. It is she who does the shining.

The emotional side of life, however, can cause Rectangle/Leo some trouble. Warm-hearted as she undoubtedly is, she is a woman who is more at home with action than with intimacy and feeling. She does not like to have to operate in areas where she isn't entirely at ease and in charge, and this aspect of life is too complicated and mysterious for her straightforward soul. She can easily go over the top in panic, throwing caution to the winds, heading for the hills with or without her lover, still expecting in old age that her prince will come.

Ever the optimist and fantasist, even in her middle years, Rectangle/Leo is quite capable of imagining she's met the love of her life after only one visit to the opera and an undistinguished candlelit meal afterwards. So much of her life is lived out in theatrical fantasy, it can be difficult for ordinary human beings to know quite where they stand with her, or what she really wants from them. But in the end this woman is rooted in good sense by the fact that Leo is a fixed sign and resistant to change, and the Rectangle body shape is basically a down-to-earth, practical influence which vetoes many of the more madcap schemes.

As a mother, the Rectangle/Leo is energetic and loyal. She expects her children to be a credit to her as far as looks, manners and academic achievement go. However, as long as she has enough going on in her own life into which her excess energy can be channelled she is not too awkward if her children don't quite live up to these high ideals. She will support them in whatever they wish to do – as long as it's not too inferior – and although she errs on the bossy side, her children never doubt that she loves them.

However, this is a woman who should most definitely go out to work. Her home and family are never going to provide a wide enough stage for her to be happy and fully herself. She will act the devoted mother for a while when they are babies, but very soon the routine palls, and the lack of positive feedback demoralizes her. Her family would get awfully tired of always having to tell her how wonderful she is, even though they secretly think it's so.

Ideal Fantasy Lover

The young Laurence Olivier, emperor of stage and screen, electrifying in his performances, breathtakingly beautiful in his close-ups and oozing regality and style. A Yin male, he would be happy to be told what to do by this extra-Yang female. He would value her advice on his career, her efficient management of his life, and her toughness in dealing with importunate members of the public. Eventually ennobled, of course this would mean he would make Rectangle/Leo a Lady – never a disadvantage to this starry type, she would order new cheque books immediately! There might be a little bit of a scuffle over who gets to be in the limelight most of the time, but certainly Rectangle/Leo would be happy to let him hog the mirror – she's nothing like as vain as he.

IN STYLE

This woman will find it hard to blush unseen. She is not an English rose. Here is a big personality, in an athletic body which can get more top-heavy and solid with age. Bold dressing suits this combination; animal prints, gold lamé, leather, fur. She is practical and boyish when young and looks wonderful in sporty clothes or the Principal Boy look – leggings, boots and a neat straight jacket. As she gets older, she may tend towards a more glamorous image, although she's never going to be as interested in the sensual detail of clothing and dressing as is a Pear or Hourglass, for instance. She is into action rather than reflection and is more likely to be late for a meeting and throw on a selection of clothes which might or might not go together.

For an occasion the Rectangle/Leo really enjoys dressing up. Quieter dressers may say she's over the top, but this woman is not shy at turning heads and stopping conversations in their tracks. This is not your quiet stay-at-home pussycat. For more specific information, see In Style on page 41.

Style Treat

Rectangle/Leo works hard and plays hard – she also doesn't need much encouragement to indulge her lazy side. The best treat for this woman who loves the sun, and really *needs* to feel the rays of her great ruler, is a sun lounger. Ideally, it should be one of the more comfortable padded kinds, covered in an animal print, with a table on the side stocked with delicious fruit cocktails and a pile of glossy magazines.

To complete the treat, she could well buy herself lots of expensive suntan lotions and sunblocks (no sunbathing the face

past 25), and a lovely young man to massage them in. Finally, she needs a pair of filmstar-large, dark glasses. These should have square-ish frames, rather than round: for the right effect think – famous filmstar trying to conceal identity but really saying look at me!

IN HEALTH

The heart is the part of the body ruled by Leo and it gives a general vitality and strength to her whole constitution. Back and chest complaints are her areas of weakness but she has great powers of recovery and is unlikely to succumb to chronic diseases, going more for sudden fevers and collapses, from which she soon gets back to normal.

Rectangles have robust constitutions and healthy appetites, Leos ditto. This is of little consequence when they are young because this is an extremely energetic combination and as a girl the Rectangle/Leo is likely to be sporty and to burn up a good deal of energy. But as she gets older and does less exercise, but her appetite remains hearty, the weight can begin to accumulate – on the tummy, spare tyre, upper hips, shoulders and face. When Philip Larkin wrote 'their beauty has thickened' he surely was talking of Rectangle women whose pattern of putting weight on their upper bodies can give this coarsening effect.

Indeed, when overweight, this type becomes the classic 'apple' shape, mentioned in the scientific papers in this book's introduction. These point out that case histories of tens of thousands of women have shown that this shape is less protected than the Pear and Hourglass from male type diseases, like arteriosclerosis and diabetes. Rectangle/Leo, whose busy life may lead to irregular scrappy meals and snatched periods of exercise and not enough rest, needs exercise and a well-balanced diet for the sake of her health as well as any vanity about her looks. For more specific information on diet and exercise, see In Health on page 43.

CELEBRITY RECTANGLE/LEO

Helen Mirren has always been an actress with terrific presence and largeness of character, both on and off the stage or screen. She has all the forcefulness of the Rectangle/Leo, and admits to her ambition and toughness. Lacking in false vanity (as befits a Rectangle), but not lacking in pride (as befits a Leo), she is matter-of-fact about displaying her naked body in parts where this is

required and burst to public notice when she was 19 and appeared naked on the stage of The Royal Shakespeare Company.

She is an acclaimed actress although she has never made it really big in Hollywood and has been angered by the decision not to allow her to play the part she has made her own in the film version of *Prime Suspect*. Like many Rectangle and Triangle types, she took some time to come into her own and admits 'I didn't truthfully find any real satisfaction in life until I was in my late thirties.'

She has never married but has a long-standing relationship with an American film director. This involves long periods apart and does not include marriage and children. But an independent life suits her: 'I have never ironed a man's shirt, for example, although I don't mind doing *some* of the housework.'

RECTANGLE/LEO PROFILE

Belinda runs a very successful West End agency helping both male and female clients with their personal style, presentation and career and life choices. 'I started just with the style and personal presentation side of this work, and that is important enough. When you consider how many judgements we make about someone before she even opens her mouth, it's crucial to look attractive and right for whatever situation she's in. But then I realized that much deeper personality traits were involved, as well as individual's hopes and aims in their lives, and so I brought in therapists as well to help clients sort out their focus and how to achieve what they really wanted.'

She is a tall, extremely attractive woman in her late forties, and has been a model, a public relations assistant, a teacher and involved in local government. Leo is the sign of the teenager, when life lies before one full of possibilites, and energy and enthusiasm is at its peak. However old she gets, Rectangle/Leo always retains an element of this teenage optimism and naivety. Belinda admits, for instance, to still believing her prince will come – or at least the opportunity for her to play the princess might still arrive out of the blue: 'Sometimes walking down the street, I will notice someone look at me with a stab of recognition or admiration and my heart will miss a beat as I think – it's ridiculous I know – but I think, "Perhaps, he's a film director and he'll stop me and tell me I'm just the person he's been looking for to play the lead in his latest movie" ! '

Belinda has been married twice and has two lovely grown-up children who look on her with a mixture of love and exasperation.

'I've only just realized that I'm not very easy to live with. I have such swings of energy and mood – one moment things are marvellous and the next I'm in despair. I'm also not very good at dealing with strong emotion, in myself or others. I tend to want to run away from it, or put it in a box and pretend it isn't there. Of course, when it catches me up I go completely over the top. I do have a very melodramatic streak. My husband can disappear to the office for an hour and I get myself convinced that he's being held hostage by a gang of desperados and I'll have to go charging in to the rescue. Or that he's had a car crash and is lying in a pool of blood in the road. Life is never on an even keel, which is how I like it I suppose, but it can be difficult for more phlegmatic individuals who have to live with me.'

Her style has evolved from jeans and a shirt when she was young to a smart collection of suits and tops which she mixes and matches successfully. She doesn't care to spend ages over selecting her clothes and prefers a slightly slapdash approach, relying on a good range of individual designer jewellery which adds interest and focus to her more classic jackets and tops.

'I am very happy with most aspects of my life. Of course, I'd like to be richer and more famous, I'd love to appear on stage at Convent Garden singing *Aida*. Actually I do have one real fantasy which I daren't even admit it's so over-the-top: I'd love to do a video singing "Barcelona", with myself taking the Freddy Mercury part and this male friend of mine (another show-off Leo) taking the part of Montserrat Caballé (a magnificent Rectangle/Aries). If I could manage that – with all the fireworks, lights, huge crowds, the roar of applause and the utterly excessive music – I'd die happy.'

IN HOPE

What hope can there be for Rectangle/Leo? She is larger than life and can be twice as maddening. She lives 90 minutes to the hour and then goes to sleep for a week, she demands all the limelight and then sulks when someone else sidles in beside her, she extends her generosity and largesse to her audience and then snaps the head off her nearest and dearest: she is queen and despot rolled into one. But thank heavens she hasn't learnt the dinosaurs' eloquent lesson – some bigness is good, an over abundance of bigness is not necessarily better!

RECTANGLE
VIRGO

(Yang/Yin)

MOTTO:

Don't put all your eggs in one basket

IN LIFE

Sweetness and strength characterize this combination of influences. Work, and practical caring for others is how Rectangle/Virgo is likely to express her personality best. She sees herself as unselfish, serving the interests of others at home and in her work, but the Yang body type means that she knows the boundaries within which she is willing to help. She can be very determined about just how far her unselfishness goes and she is seldom undermined by hardluck stories or appeals to her emotions.

Virgo is an earth sign and the Rectangle body type is equally down-to-earth, but more energetic and self-centred. Consequently, Rectangle/Virgo is not overflowing with sympathy and fellow-feeling, rather she is likely to want to roll up her sleeves and get on with some tangible way of helping. If a friend's mother has just died, for instance, she is not at ease dealing with the immediate outflowing of passion and grief. She is much happier organizing the funeral arrangements for her, or taking over the catering, or just working away in the background, making meals, producing cups of tea at the right moment and answering the door to callers.

Rectangle/Virgo is really kind in a practical way, and genuine and supportive to her friends. She likes to bring out the best in people, to educate them, help them to organize their lives and fit the pieces together. She hates waste and disorganization, in all areas of life, from the material through to the spiritual. Systems, whether internal or external, matter.

This combination finds it hard just to let life unfold while she enjoys the passing show. She wants to know just where she is

going, how things fit together, where everything belongs. A Rectangle/Virgo child will ask her mother's visitor as she arrives – with great seriousness, 'When are you going?' not because she is rude or wants the visitor to go, but just because she likes to have a determined pattern to her life and needs to know how external influences fit into it.

Virgos have a dull press from many astrological books who make them out to be the nags and nit-pickers of the zodiac. This is to misunderstand them sorely for there are much deeper and more creative springs which sometimes produce these less attractive traits. Virgo has a finely discriminating mind, she notices the subtlest changes in everything, from the weather, to the smell of her loved one, to the shift in attitude of the government to private education. She likes to fit all these influences and observations together into a complete system. Rectangle/Virgo is even more distinctly interested in fitting things to the pattern she's already imposed on her experience of life. Everything has a use and that use has to be found.

Rectangle/Virgo is fortunate in having a real ability to work, to stick at things even when success or recognition is slow to come. A fire sign like Aries will look at her with complete incomprehension, how can she stay in such a dull and unrewarding job for all these years? But Aries doesn't understand the deeper processes at work, the slow accretion of experience and confidence, the slow-burning ambition which does not need recognition now – or preferably yesterday, if you're Aries. For make no mistake, the Rectangle element in this combination adds much more worldly ambition than would usually be the case with a quiet, self-contained Virgo temperament.

She not only observes, discovers, synthesizes and puts into rightful places, she also communicates. And this is Rectangle/Virgo's other great strength. She is intelligent and articulate, although not such a chatter-box as Gemini, the other sign which, like Virgo, is ruled by Mercury, planet of communication. Rectangle/Virgo wants to communicate what she discovers and sees, she wants to explain the way the world works, explain where everything belongs in the jigsaw puzzle of life. It is not surprising how many are famous writers. Virgos all, but most have the extra drive for fame and fortune that comes with being a Rectangle/Virgo: AS Byatt, Agatha Christie, Shirley Conran, Lady Antonia Fraser, Jessica Mitford, Edith Sitwell, to name but a few.

The Virgo character is one who loves being highly skilled at intricate puzzles and nice theories. Agatha Christie's biographer described the way she worked with admirable Rectangle/Virgo thoroughness and detachment: 'Each of her characters is surveyed, analyzed, dissected as murderer-potential without an ounce of involvement. And it is because the non-involvement is total that the puzzle remains paramount, stands at the centre of the reader's interest loud and crystal clear.'

Rectangle/Virgo finds it impossible merely to enjoy herself and waste a little time, to kick off her shoes, loll on the sofa with a magazine and just while away a few hours. She drives herself and others with the need to get things done, to put things in their place, to find useful things to do with her life and her time. In a social situation she is more often than not making herself busy by passing round the crisps, or sitting observing and being critical (not necessarily adversely) of all the other guests disporting themselves in various stages of ridiculousness. She has a resistance to throwing herself into the melée and enjoying herself along with the rest.

When she can be encouraged to relax this watchful, critical faculty, when she can be persuaded to stop being useful all the time, she has an earthy sexuality which can take her and her loved one by surprise. She may still object to his smelly feet, and wish he wouldn't sing out of tune, or crease her clothes with his firm embrace, but there is a real flesh and blood woman beneath all that business and fuss.

IN WORK

Rectangle/Virgo thinks she was made for work. If she's not putting her back to the wheel in a conventional job, then she is committing all her dogged energy to the gardening, the laundry, her childcare, party-giving and organizing of the neighbourhood jumble sale. She is in her element running organizations. Not necessarily in high profile, glitzy professions, and she would never demand more than her fair share of the limelight or recognition, but definitely be in charge.

Rectangle/Virgo has a marvellous discriminatory mind and eye for detail. She excels at intricate tasks where observation, comparisons and evaluation are involved. The whole financial world in its many manifestations appeals to her. She could be financial director of a company, or an accountant, auditor or tax adviser. Gambling is not her metier and so stockbroking is less likely to attract. But the Yang body type makes her more ambitious to be at the head of things, in charge of teams, getting some public recognition. Although Rectangle/Virgo has no pretensions,

does not expect the world to owe her a living and is more prepared than most to work her way up from the bottom, she won't be quite so content to beaver away in some back room for years to come.

She is someone who is very good with her hands. She can mend and make things and enjoys the constructive creativity of making useful things, like pottery, jewellery, or clothes – or restoring things and making them useful again, like clocks or old mechanical toys.

Writing and communication in all media are also areas where her intelligence and articulacy are put to successful use. Radio, television, publishing in all its activities and guises. Rectangle/Virgo would make an excellent managing editor of a book publishing firm, with her love of detail, her fine judgement, her unflagging energy to do the best for each author and each book, and her single-mindedness which can make her stand her ground and push through what she thinks is right. Newspaper offices are full of Virgos, although it is the Yang body-shaped women, the Rectangle and Triangle, who more easily compete in masculine preserves for greater editorial space, better conditions and pay, and bigger bylines.

Rectangle/Virgo is quietly ambitious. The ambition and competitiveness which the Yang body type brings to this combination is much tempered by the more subtle, self-effacing and self-contained Virgo star sign. Virgo is a Yin influence and brings with it a concern for others. But behind that sweetness and genuine helpfulness is someone with a steely backbone who wants to succeeed, to be better than her rivals, someone who needs to have that superiority achnowledged publically. She will choose areas of work where there is a career ladder, and although it may be slow in coming, she is determined that she will climb that ladder to the top if possible.

Teaching and nursing are the conventional professions of service, and are the careers traditionally suggested for the dedicated Virgo. And it is true that many find real fulfilment here, making a significant difference to the lives of many others. Rectangle/Virgo, however, enjoys the executive positions and will end up on the committees and as team leader – or matron. She likes being in charge and is prone to think her way is always the best way of doing anything. She is often right, of course, but she does fall down in areas where imagination, ability to take risks and spirit of the enterprise are needed.

She is not a radical in any way. She is frightened by change and the disorder and breaking down of systems which may result.

She does not have flair or charisma and is not successful at rallying a tide of support; she is not the passionate orator who can call on reserves of emotional energy and the primitive collective unconscious. Her medium is the rational mind and the material world.

Ideal Fantasy Job

Chief Librarian at the new British Library. This is a wonderful job for Rectangle/Virgo because she is brilliant with systems, and running this will be akin to controlling an army, keeping track of all the millions of books and other printed matter in her control. Books and the written word is also her greatest area of concern and here she would be surrounded by them every day of her working life, with access to anything ever published in any language the world over. Heady stuff.

Rectangle/Virgo is good as a head of a team. She can be a bit of a stickler for detail and a slave driver, but would never expect more from anyone else than she gives herself. Finally, her need for some public acknowledgement would be satisfied – and more. She would be interviewed, introduced to everyone from royalty downwards, and her name would be known among the great and the good. The perfect job indeed.

IN LOVE

By its very nature love does not conform to expectations or fit into any pre-ordained pattern, and Rectangle/Virgo can find this resistance to categorization difficult to cope with. The discrimination which makes her such a good editor, and observer and commentator on human nature, also means she can be highly critical in her relationships. When it comes to marriage, she is unlikely to rush in. She is picky and quite capable of drawing up a list of qualities the chosen male ought to have, and those he ought definitely not to have – and then tick them off with each new candidate.

Consequently, if she does marry it will be late, and then only because she has learnt that mere mortals have imperfection built in with their mortality. She will, with some disappointment, accept that lover X is the best she's going to get. This woman is nothing if not realistic. Rose-tinted spectacles were not handed out to her as she left the nursery.

There is a definite emotional self-containment about Rectangle/Virgo. She is not someone who feels she's only half living if she is without a partnership. Even in a relationship, there is a

part of her which is private and solitary to which she retreats at times. She is not likely to tell her husband that she couldn't live without him – except in jest. Because she is herself so practical and capable, and emotionally self-contained, nothing becomes so life-and-death important.

However, when she finally makes her choice, Rectangle/Virgo may still appear to the world to be terribly well-behaved and modest, even prim and proper, but this is to forget that Virgo is an earth sign and has, under that perfectionist façade, an earthy sexuality and an affectionate supportiveness which can make her a most satisfactory partner in marriage. She is fastidious, she is maddeningly organized, she is not easily seduced into anything risky, outrageous or downright good fun. She can be so *worthy*, but her good earth qualities of reliability, good-heartedness, honesty, practicality and willingness to care for others, makes her a great friend and partner – as long as that critical eye can be directed into her work and the external world.

As a mother, all the above good qualities make for a happy and secure family. However Rectangle/Virgo's critical side, and her Yang body type ambition, can be very destructive for the self-esteem of her children if she expresses these two abrasive qualities in her relationship with them, and her expectations of how they will live their lives. The slave-driving side which can drive her team mad at work, will do greater damage if unchecked at home. All it needs is a little more tolerance of diversity and individuality – and acknowledgement of the fact that not everyone is going to be like her and value the things she does.

This is the real weak link in many earth sign people (Taurus, Virgo, Capricorn) particularly with the Yang body shapes (Rectangle and Triangle): they do not have much imagination about or sympathy with other people's feelings, ideas and dreams. They tend to think only their way is right.

The debate between motherhood and career is more clear cut for a Rectangle/Virgo than for many women. Work does matter very much to this woman, and she is likely to want to continue it in some way once she has had her children and been at home a little time. But it does not have to be work with a high profile, out on the public stage. She could well run a business from home (and she would be breathtakingly efficient at keeping home life and work separate), and she would be very happy with job-share or working part-time – as long as it had some proper status and rewards. She would always expect to be back full-time, if not almost immediately, then within a few years. This woman is happiest keeping very busy and working her way to the top.

Rectangle/Virgo can sometimes overrate the material aspects of motherhood, the providing of balanced meals and clean clothes, of a secure home and good education, at the expense of the less obvious, emotional elements; a parent always willing to listen, who is on your side come what may, who thinks you are the bee's knees, and tells you so. Someone who puts you first before her boss, her work, her company pension.

Ideal Fantasy Lover

A Rectangle/Virgo is attracted to a caring, sensitive man with a romantic heart. If that man also has a voice which can charm birds from trees and make the angels weep, she might even abandon her orderly life and follow his music, as mesmerized as the rest. Luciano Pavarotti would sing Rectangle/Virgo out of any tizz, she would not be miserable for long with this glorious lyric tenor steaming up her bathroom.

The only opera singer to have topped the pop charts, with his recording of 'Nessun Dorma', adopted as the theme for the World Cup, Pavarotti is world famous and loved by everyone from princesses to the woman in the street. He cares terribly about his size and a Rectangle/Virgo would be sensitive and firm enough to help him cut back on the pasta and pass on the third and fourth helpings of zabaglione. In return, he would banish her anxieties in his bear hug embrace and lift her spirits with song.

IN STYLE

It may be too predictable to say it but it happens to be true, Rectangle/Virgo is going to be a neat dresser. You will not find remnants of her breakfast on her spotless, freshly laundered blouse, or cat's hair on her coat. Neither will she have a great snaking ladder up her leg. Should she ladder a stocking while out, she, more than any other woman, is likely to be carrying a spare in her handbag.

This handbag can achieve an inflated importance, filled as it often is with every essential for any emergency: needle and cotton, a packet of gold safety pins, a couple of clean handkerchiefs, a packet of tissues, a paperback book for reading at odd moments, even a piece of needlepoint for same purpose, a muesli snack bar, breath freshening tablets, a travel toothbrush and paste, her first aid handbook, a donor card, and then of course a lipstick and comb. (She tends to keep make-up to a minimum, nothing usually, but a slick of lipstick and a bit of powder for special occasions.)

Her clear-skinned good looks are best served by classic cut, well made clothes in natural colours. Her Yin star sign gives her an occasional yen for feminine gathered dresses or frilly underwear but she is sensible enough to know what suits her, and it is her Rectangle body type which largely dictates that. She hates waste and naturally will not tend to be a big spender on clothes. Nor will she have cupboards full of them like some of her Yin body type friends. For more specific information, see In Style on page 41.

Style Treat

A good haircut. Just as straight clothes suit Rectangle type women best, so do short, chic geometric hairstyles. Think how much slimmer, chic-er and prettier Princess Diana looked when she had her long bob cut into her short, upswept style.

Unstructured, wavy, romantic hair which suits her curvy Pear and Hourglass friends can look untidy and frumpish on a Rectangle/Virgo. Virgos hate to look untidy, and frumpy for that matter. But if she has naturally curly hair then it is most flattering for her to have it cut in an angular style – either short and a bit spiky, or a jaw-length bob with a straight clubbed line at the back. Finding the right stylist for a good haircut is essential. If you aren't happy with your current hairdresser, look at other women you know and see who has a particularly good cut. Ask who does her hair and go to see him or her. The best hairdresser isn't necessarily the most expensive, or the one who brooks no discussion, insisting on imposing a certain style on you. Nor is he or she the one who just attempts to do what the client wants, without any experimentation and discussion. The best stylists will look at the texture and quality of your hair, will take into account the shape of your head and face, your height and way of life. They will discuss the pros and cons and how to maintain the sort of style they suggest, and will only go ahead when you both are happy with the decision.

IN HEALTH

Rectangle/Virgo might have been occasionally accused of hypochondria (Rectangle/Virgo Agatha Christie had a whole room in her house set by for medicines!). Usually so sensible and down-to-earth, health is an area where she can be vulnerable to irrational fears. The trouble is she knows all the symptoms of most of the terrible diseases, she has that sort of mind which picks up these random facts and stores them under, Beware. Actually, she has great stamina and endurance, but she has a sensitive nervous system which can wreak revenge for a stressful, over-worked life by attacking the digestive system. There is always an anxious worrier lurking behind this practical exterior, and she needs to take steps to face her anxieties and calm her fears in order to keep in the peak of fitness.

Rectangles have robust constitutions and healthy appetites, but Rectangle/Virgo is more discriminating over food, and less likely to just enjoy feasting out of sheer exuberance, like Rectangle/Leo for instance. When she is young the Rectangle/Virgo is likely to be quite sporty and to burn up a good deal of energy. But as she gets older and does less exercise, but her appetite remains quite hearty, the weight can begin to accumulate – on the tummy, spare tyre, upper hips, shoulders and face. When Philip Larkin wrote 'their beauty has thickened' he surely was talking of Rectangle women whose pattern of putting weight on their upper bodies can give this coarsening effect.

Indeed, when overweight, this type becomes the classic 'apple' shape, mentioned in the scientific papers in this book's introduction. These point out that case histories of tens of thousands of women have shown that this shape is less protected than the Pear and Hourglass from male type diseases, like arteriosclerosis and diabetes. Rectangle/Virgo, whose busy life may lead to irregular scrappy meals and snatched periods of exercise and not enough rest, needs exercise and a well-balanced diet for the sake of her health as well as any vanity about her looks. For more specific information on diet and exercise, see In Health on page 43.

RECTANGLE/VIRGO CELEBRITY PROFILE

Superwoman Shirley Conran personifies Rectangle/Virgo. With her three marriages, two children, succesful career in journalism and then five *Superwoman* books and four blockbuster novels, she is someone who exhibits an extraordinary capacity for hard work. Discipline and research are the keys to her success. She will work seven days a week from 9am to 6pm when she's in the middle of a book and will often produce 400,000 words which then have to be edited down. All her books, she argues, are feminist tracts: 'Women's vulnerable point has always been to hand responsibility for their lives to a man'. She also thinks that independence and therefore money is important. 'The importance of money is played down to women – but if it's so unimportant why have men got it all?'

RECTANGLE/VIRGO PROFILE

Rectangle and Triangle body types, the Yang women, can be more influenced by the male members of their family than their Yin sisters would be. Often there is a closer identification with the masculine temperament. Jane, a Rectangle/Virgo in her thirties, felt very oppressed by her grandfather's disapproving presence in the household while she was growing up. He had wanted her to be a boy, to carry on his name and to make his mark in life, where he himself felt he had failed.

Jane loved him and wanted to please him, but never could and so retreated into work and eating as her solace and armour. 'When he died about five years ago, I was amazed at what a weight slipped from my shoulders. My friends even noticed how I walked better. And I began to lose actual pounds too. And was not so narrowly focused on work and achievement. I think I started to have some fun for the first time in my life.'

As a lecturer, married to another lecturer, and with two daughters, she realized that she had terrific academic aspirations for her children and was in danger of doing to them what was done to her, 'I suddenly caught myself driving them to achieve better and better results at school, and showing my disapproval if they didn't, or if they scrimped homework to go out with their friends and enjoy themselves. I had to really go against the grain and try and get off their backs a bit.'

She has always worked full-time, but had the holidays with her children. 'I think I would have gone up the wall, and sent them up the wall too, if I'd been home looking after them without a job outside to go to. I do agree that children need great security and continuity in who cares for them, and I've always been over-conscientious about who I hire. Also I have a very good, sympathetic husband, who is around for them a lot and in some ways is a good deal more nurturing of babies and young children than I seem to be. I am naturally ambitious, and wanted to get on, and I realized that I would be a better mother going out to work and getting satisfaction there.'

However, since the oppressive influence of her grandfather has gone, Jane admits to taking her foot off the accelerator slightly, and enjoying the view more along the way. 'Certainly my husband and children have benefitted from my not being so single-minded – and so tired. Life is more fun for us all, I think!'

IN HOPE

A surprising aspect of Virgo is her sense of humour, often hidden. It is likely to be expressed more as a wry, ironic thing than a great belly laugh, but it is one of the attractive elements in a personality that can too often seem lost behind a wall of over-work and obsessive attention to form and detail. Humour, with Rectangle/Virgo, is more often than not an expression of something sad, or painful, 'emotional chaos remembered in tranquility' as the great humorist James Thurber chose to put it. But this is the sign of a touchingly valiant heart. And who is more valiant and touching than the genius Peter Sellers, a true Virgo, whose humour was built entirely on extraordinary perceptiveness and personal suffering?

RECTANGLE

LIBRA

(Yang/Yang)

MOTTO:

Four be the things I'd be better without – Love, curiosity, freckles and doubt

IN LIFE

For all her good looks and charm, there is nothing soft and feeling-centred about this double Yang combination. Rectangle/Libra has a cool, steely mind and knows precisely what she is doing, and where she is going. Betty Boothroyd (Speaker of the House of Commons), Judith Chalmers, Jackie Collins, Angie Dickinson, Linda MacCartney, Martina Navratilova, Anneka Rice and Angela Rippon are all Rectangle/Libras and there is a similar sense of power uniting them all. No one could remotely think of them as soft, gentle, nurturing women. (Whereas Brigitte Bardot, Catherine Deneuve, Anna Ford and Patricia Hodge, all Librans with Yin body types, have a distinctly softer, more mysterious, more female feel.)

Good looking, organized, determined and socially adept, she can deal with most situations, but Rectangle/Libra is happiest in the centre of things. She is a great strategist and can see both sides of every question. She has the particular talent of being able to achieve what she wants while causing the minimum of offence. Her diplomatic instinct, her awareness of alternative ideas, rather than feelings, which permeate every situation involving others, means she knows just what to say – and what to leave unsaid until a later date.

Although Libra has a reputation for indecisiveness, for never being able to come down on one side of the fence or the other, Rectangle/Libra can be more decisive than most. She has a clear, unclouded intellect and an unflinching eye for what is and has to be done. The danger arrives when her life gets out of balance – then she can veer from one extreme to the other, and start doing and saying things which seem completely at odds with her usually cool, detached and sociable self.

As an air sign, she is much more at home in the world of the intellect and ideas and is ill at ease with passionate emotions and profound and obscured depths of feeling. Her Yang body type increases her desire to express her ambitions and ideas outwardly, to promote herself and her vision. But it also increases her alienation from the feeling side of life. When this incomprehensible part of human nature forces itself into her life, she is frightened and confused by how irrational the world of the emotions can be.

Rectangle/Libra has an ideal view of the world where harmony, truth and beauty reign and she finds it very hard to confront the inevitable feelings in herself and others which do not conform to this ideal. She will repress her emotions to avoid facing these unhappy truths. In this way she can appear to be rather superficial, her manner running the gamut from light and flirtatious banter to slightly chilly but perfectly charming aloofness. This overweening pleasantness makes her a tremendous hostess. The Rectangle element in the combination adds energy and extraversion which means she is able to entertain on a large scale and in a grand manner. A wonderful harmoniser and flatterer, Rectangle/Libra knows just when to step in, and just who to introduce to whom, and exactly which guests should be kept from making fools/party-poopers/drunken pigs of themselves.

However, repressed feeling will find it's way out – and in unexpected and inconvenient ways. Rectangle/Libra can be rather taken by surprise by a sudden surge of bad feeling which makes her say something destructive and bitchy to someone's face, or an unexpected excess of bloody-mindedness which finds her arguing doggedly from an impossible position, long after she would naturally have made a gracious apology and backed down.

But Rectangle/Libra is an attractive, popular and ambitious woman who has all the abilities to go far in whatever arena in life she may choose. She is ultimately interested in fairness, balance and harmony. She tends to prefer compromise to battle, to achieving things instead of sticking doggedly to principle. She can be accused of hypocrisy, of sailing with whatever wind blows, but it is more that she is diplomatic and does not hold any opinion as a life and death matter. She prefers spreading sweetness and light to rocking the boat just for the sake of a bit of principle.

She is very concerned with the aesthetics of things and people. The beauty of something or someone is almost a sign of their

innate goodness. Her own looks matter to her very much in a coolly detached and critical way. She recognizes that they are an important part of her armoury in getting what she wants in this world. She certainly knows how to make the best of what she has and she is not a woman to ignore the artificial aids of the make-up bag, bleach bottle or even the surgeon's knife. She also recognizes the absolute importance of image and visible status. No thrift shop dressing for her, or being seen around town in a beat-up old jalopy (unless it's distinguished and chic, like an old Lagonda or Golf cabriole). From the pushchair to the glossy BMW/Mercedes/Porsche/Bentley, Rectangle/Libra has always been a winner – and been seen to be one.

IN WORK

Rectangle/Libra is particularly well-suited to work which involves her mediating with the public. She has such a gift in social situations she can usually find the right thing to say to the right person at precisely the right time. Her sense of justice and innate need to balance things up, makes her particularly successful in the law. Being a barrister or a judge is slightly more preferable to being a solicitor, although a solicitor who takes on civil rights cases, perhaps, or has a high profile position putting right miscarriages of justice would be good too. She is clear-thinking, detached and articulate and can be very impressive with complicated briefs, where an element of arbitration is called for. She would always prefer to get a satisfactory compromise than go in for a bloody fight where both protagonists risk suffering and loss.

Politics is also a natural home for Rectangle/Libra for virtually the same reasons as those given above. She likes to be on the side of the underdog, but has not got much taste for the dirty play or rough and tumble of so much of political life. She is tough enough to get there, but may not choose to stay too long.

Rectangle/Libra's strong aesthetic sense also leads her into any of the arts, either as a practising artist or as an agent or entrepreneur. The Rectangle body shape means this woman is good at organization and business and would run an art gallery or artists' agency with efficiency and flair.

Libra is the sign of relationship, but it is relationship in a broader and more detached sense than is usually meant by that word. She is not so keen on the close intimacy of one to one relationships so much as the looser connections with friends, work colleagues, clients, the public at large. This can mean that Rectangle/Libra makes a natural celebrity, because then she is able to appear to be in love with everyone in her audience, without it progressing to any sort of imperfect reality, as it does in real life. This facility to relate to her audience through the television set, or cinema screen, is a great asset and explains why so many Rectangle/Libras are up there on the screen.

Rectangle/Libra will not be happy working in dingy, unglamorous conditions for long. She likes to be surrounded by attractive things in harmonious arrangement. Above all, she likes to be appreciated and to be able to have a few status symbols to underline her natural value and taste. A company car of a classy make will be very much to her liking. A clothes allowance suits her fine. She will always be a credit to whomever she works for or with. She is less likely to live up to the description 'lazy Libra' than many of her sign and there will never be any reason to warn Rectangle/Libra about anti-social habits or personal hygiene!

Ideal Fantasy Job

Super-trouper film star. This combination's qualities make for a natural actress with a great rapport with her audience. She can give the impression that she is in love with every one of them, because her nature is such that to her, love is more a fantasy and a stylization, than a less than perfect reality. Rectangle/Libra has the looks and the potential to have a love affair with the camera. She also has the toughness, which many of the Yin body type actresses lack, to set her goal and work towards it, making what sacrifices are necessary along the way. And these sacrifices are usually personal – privacy and family life. Her more detached emotional nature means she can use her talents to promote her career, without being hi-jacked by falling in love with an unsuitable man, having moral qualms about playing certain parts, or a self-protectiveness about what she is required to do in the film and in promoting it afterwards. She is a professional to her toes.

IN LOVE

Love is on every Libra's agenda and yet it can cause her much trouble, because so often she prefers all the romance, the courtship, the stylized rituals to the real thing. Rectangle/Libra is even more this way inclined. She does not welcome a surprise roll in the hay. She would not be swooning over a Laurencian Mellors-style bloke with dirt in his fingernails, rough, workers' clothes and even rougher talk.

She works in the realm of ideas and has an idealized view of love which involves quite a lot of admiration from the adoring

one, a great deal of conversation, some romantic wooing with candle-light and flirtatious talk, and then a soft-focus coupling with not too many details filled in. She can see the attraction of those novels which leave their lovers at the bedroom door with the discreet implication of three short dots...

Rectangle/Libra enjoys the romance of the chase and the pleasures of courtship, but it is really the joys of companionship which are her longtime goal. Rectangle/Libra enjoys partnerships of all kinds, she likes to have somebody to do things with, to share with, but she is not good in passionate, possessive relationships. She has to maintain some space and air. The sort of man who will make her dream of coupledom will be a sensitive, handsome, Yin sort of man to complement her own good looks, determination and Yang kind of woman. She prefers the effete Lord to the primitively sexual gamekeeper, the kind sympathetic companion to the wild-at-heart lover.

The juggling of marriage and children with career does cause her some heartache as she is so keen to be perfect at everything she does. Because she is intelligent and reads a good deal, she knows about the research which shows small babies need bonding, continuity, security and responsive mothers or mother substitutes. She is determined to be the very best of mothers to any children she may have. But she also knows that she needs to have her work and status in the world at large. She needs to maintain balance in order to keep happy and functioning and it is in this area that she can sometimes feel she is in danger of having all the spinning plates crash to her feet at once.

Rectangle/Libra is not very good with very small, demanding children and enjoys much more being with them when they are older and companionable, can carry on conversations and be independent and good fun. A Rectangle/Libra mother wants above all to be *friends* with her children, and that is what she often truly is. She is reasonable and fair in her treatment of their wishes and rights and, when she is happy and in balance herself, she is a harmonizing influence in the home. More intense and emotional characters might long for her to be less rational and more passionate about the world – and themselves. She does love her children deeply, but is unlikely to do the big matriarch bit; my children before anything, loyal to death. Her children's only disadvantage, however, may be in growing up thinking that everyone conducts themselves as reasonably.

Her house is likely to be well furnished in a conventional but attractive way. It will always be light and airy, and a pleasant and peaceful place to be. Rectangle/Libra will have loads of friends

who she will entertain to dinners and Sunday barbeques, always the perfect hostess with an unerring sense of which of her friends will mix best, what kinds of food to provide, and what sort of entertainment or conversation to encourage. A capable and charming person, she does make life a little more fun and a lot more pleasant.

Ideal Fantasy Lover

Daniel Day-Lewis has everything most Rectangle/Libra women would want in their dreams. He is highly cultured and well educated, the son of the Poet Laureat Cecil Day Lewis. He has absolutely drop-dead good looks – lean, dark, with an aquiline, refined face and smouldering eyes. Above all, he has a sensitive and idiosyncratic personality and great acting ability which has allowed him to turn in scorching performances in very different roles. Most notably, perhaps, he was Christy Brown in *My Left Foot* (for which he won his Oscar), and most romantically, Hawk-eye in *The Last of the Mohicans*.

Stylishness, status, refinement and good looks in a man are all important to Rectangle/Libra women. She can be instantly put off by coarseness or vulgarity: form matters more than substance. Luckily, Daniel Day-Lewis has both the perfect form and pretty substantial substance.

IN STYLE

Rectangle/Libra is always beautifully turned out. It is rare, if not unheard of, to see her with dirty hair or food-spattered cardigan – even if she has the excuse of being in the middle of feeding the baby his first solids. Rectangle body types are not very interested in the whole creative complexity of putting looks together, experimenting with different garments, colours, accessories. But Libra brings a great aesthetic sense to this personality combination and so Rectangle/Libra is likely to care very much how she looks, but not want to spend a lot of time and speculation achieving that look.

She is quite happy to be business-like about getting her style together. She recognizes instinctively how important it is, in every walk of life, to look one's best, to attract people and influence them. She is likely to go to a style consultant, for instance, listen to her advice, accept the good sense of her reasoning and the system of individual colour and style, then go and buy a few carefully chosen, designer clothes (this is important to her if she can afford it) which she can cleverly mix and match to provide a

whole wardrobe of outfits. She is at her best in simple, tailored clothes in fantastic, luxury fabrics. Everything must look classy and expensive. For more specific information, see In Style on page 41.

Style Treat

An evening outfit. Evening clothes are not easy for the Rectangle shape. Whereas curvy Pear- and Hourglass-type women can easily put together a romantic evening look – soft, feminine, fitted top and flowing skirt cinched at the waist with a belt – Rectangle-type women need to go for a chic, sophisticated or dramatic look. The most versatile outfit is an evening jacket with trousers or a narrow skirt.

The style of this jacket should be similar to her business style, ie straight or slightly fitted line, straight line at the hem, angular lapels or V-necked. She should choose a crisp, rich fabric like a heavyweight ribbed silk, silk gabardine, lamé, beaded or sequinned work on a stiff base fabric. If her finances cannot run to an evening jacket then a silk satin blouse will be just as glamorous. This shiny fabric is ideal for straight body lines, looking crisp and expensive, but she should make sure that its hem is straight, not shirt-tailed. She could add a waistcoat, with tailored trousers or smart leggings and – *voilà* – a great Principal-boy look.

It is important to check that the colour of the garment you are buying suits you well. Take it into daylight, hold it under your chin and look at what it does to your skin, eyes and hair. If wearing it intensifies and enlivens your colouring then that is a colour that is right for your skin tones. If you look washed out or sallow, or your hair loses colour and dark rings seem to appear under your eyes, then you are getting it wrong. This sounds a lot of trouble to go to, but it is worth it for it enhances the pleasure you will get every time you wear it.

IN HEALTH

Rectangle/Libra is extremely healthy if she manages to lead a sensible life.

Balance is what she continually strives for: her career and home life in harmony; her need to be liked in balance with her necessary detachment; a network of friends and loved ones in balance with her need for space and air to breathe. If too many demands crowd in on her then she can sucumb to illness. Her particular vulnerabilities are the kidneys, with a possibility of hypertension and headaches. She is also vulnerable to mental problems like claustrophobia. She is best advised to make sure she gets good food, some exercise and lots of sleep, even when life seems too hectic.

Rectangles types generally have robust constitutions and healthy appetites. As a girl, the Rectangle/Libra is likely to be sporty and to burn up a good deal of energy. But as she gets older and does less exercise, but her appetite remains, the weight can begin to accumulate – on the tummy, spare tyre, upper hips, shoulders and face. When Philip Larkin wrote 'their beauty has thickened' he surely was talking of Rectangle women whose pattern of putting weight on their upper bodies can give this coarsening effect.

Indeed, when overweight, this type becomes the classic 'apple' shape, mentioned in the scientific papers in this book's introduction. These point out that case histories of tens of thousands of women have shown that this shape is less protected than the Pear and Hourglass from male type diseases, like arteriosclerosis and diabetes. Rectangle/Libra, whose busy life may lead to irregular scrappy meals and snatched periods of exercise and not enough rest, needs exercise and a well-balanced diet for the sake of her health as well as any vanity about her looks. For more specific information on diet and exercise, see In Health on page 43.

CELEBRITY RECTANGLE/LIBRA

Susan Sarandon has just the sort of angular beauty which characterizes the Rectangle/Libra woman, it is not a look of soft femininity which is epitomized by Geena Davis (Hourglass/Aquarius), for instance, her co-star in *Thelma and Louise*. There is a sort of masculine beauty to her tall frame with the dramatic face with that comic roll in her eyes. She is a great and gutsy actress who has played a number of different roles, bringing to all her thoughtful depth of characterization. As befits her Rectangle/Libra sign, she is an actress with brains and a good deal of Yang energy, which was used to brilliant effect in *Thelma and Louise*.

Her own life has not been such plain sailing. When her marriage broke up in the seventies she had a painful mental breakdown but struggled back to greater strength and stardom, and now lives happily with the actor Tim Robbins. The last ten years have seen her life in much greater balance and some of her best work has been done as a result. Nearing fifty, there is no reason why she shouldn't go on getting better and better.

RECTANGLE/LIBRA PROFILE

Gina runs a dress shop in Yorkshire which is well-known for the quality of the designer clothes she sells and the warmth and good advice that she offers her customers. 'I love helping people choose just the right outfit. It's really rewarding to see a woman stand in front of a mirror and look at herself, for the first time, wearing some really beautiful and flattering garment and see how it changes her view of herself. She becomes beautiful. Clothes do matter. They are not trivial, they can really be a powerful therapy from the outside in. I've seen women walk out of this shop who will never think of themselves again as plain, or uninteresting, or unlovable, just because they have seen how transforming the right clothes can be. It's a great job and I love it.'

She has a particularly good eye for the sort of clothes which her clients will buy, and as they are expensive she cannot afford to make mistakes – and can't afford to let her customers make expensive mistakes either. 'The only reason we're such a success is because no woman leaves this shop with a garment that isn't absolutely right for her shape, her colouring and the occasions she wishes to wear it at.' Her shop is not just a place to go to buy clothes but it is somewhere a woman will drop by at, see what's new, perhaps try on something, discuss what she might need for a wedding or party that is coming up, and get advice on how best to make the most of her looks and the clothes she already has.

When she was young, Gina had always loved making the most of the few clothes she had, and realized early on how important looks and image were in this world. The obvious thing to do when she found herself in a different area with two small children and desperate for some sort of outside work was to open a shop in the nearby town. 'I was at home virtually full-time with my two daughters for the first three years but I really needed some outside stimulation and was actually getting very depressed. So I had to do something.'

Enormous energy, great discipline and an instinct for what to buy, which hasn't let her down so far, has brought her a thriving business. 'I've worked hard, but I've also been lucky. The best thing is the rapport I have with my staff and my customers – in fact they're much more than customers, they're friends. I feel really proud when I see one of my friends walking down the street or at a party, looking wonderful and wearing something she's bought from my shop, with the benefit of my advice. That to me is being creative.'

IN HOPE

Rectangle/Libra has such an array of talents and personal charm that she can really achieve anything she puts her mind to. Her only problem is this striving for perfection in all things. It can be the motor of her success if she directs this outward, and puts her considerable energies into law reform, or costume designing or politics or whatever strikes her as the right arena for her vision. But it can be truly destructive if it's focused on her friends and family – and herself. It is sometimes hard for her to deal with the mundane realities of life, to allow the less than pleasant things to exist alongside the good. Rectangle/Libra too easily can seem like the peacock, whose breathtakingly beautiful plumage is acclaimed by all, whose exotic form is celebrated, while all he sees is the ugliness of his feet.

RECTANGLE
SCORPIO

(Yang/Yin+)

MOTTO:
Strength in adversity

IN LIFE

This is not an easy combination of energies but it is an immensely rewarding one, if Rectangle/Scorpio finds the place where she can best express her qualities of emotional depth, creative intuition and determined ambition. She is a powerhouse, although – unlike Rectangle/Leo – it is a hidden power and far from obvious. You will not find her entering a room full of strangers, all her guns blazing. She has a watchful presence and only when she has sussed out the landscape will you see her open up and extend her friendship, sociableness and understanding. Nothing much passes her by. She notices, understands and remembers.

If you look at a list of famous Rectangle/Scorpios: Roseanne Barr, Jodie Foster, Elizabeth Frink, Whoopi Goldberg, Mahalia Jackson, Billie Jean King, Tatum O'Neal, Stephanie Powers, Joan Sutherland, what you have is an overwhelming sense of power. All these women mean serious business. They might go about that business with kindness and humour but there is no getting away from the intensity of the impression they make on the world.

So we are talking power and ambition and terrific emotional resources which make Rectangle/Scorpio someone to be reckoned with. Scorpio has a great understanding of suffering and great compassion for those who suffer; she can be an artist with great emotional force. In this combination, with the ambition and more straightforward energy of her Yang body shape, she can express this emotional depth through her art, her work generally, and take it into the world.

There is a conflict for her, however, in the Yin+ of her Scorpio star sign, a water sign, and the Yang of her body type. One is characterized by intense feeling and hidden sensitivity and receptivenesss, and the other is to do with a much more outgoing flow of energy, a desire to make a mark on the world – with competitiveness and ambition. How is she to integrate this female feeling side with this masculine outrushing energy?

Work is one of the areas where these two powerful aspects can be united and when that happens great things can be achieved by Rectangle/Scorpio. It is even possible that she can change the world for the better. There is something about Scorpio that is intrinsically to do with death and regeneration. The phoenix arising from the ashes is a powerful symbol of what this sign is capable of doing. Transformation of herself and others is one of the great motivations in her life, and that transformation can take many paths, from healing wounds to teaching others and spiritual exploration. Nothing Rectangle/Scorpio does or feels is ever trivial or superficial. She cares deeply about everything and will take on causes and organize crusades. Charles de Gaulle, Billy Graham, Martin Luther, Nehru, St Augustine and Trotsky were all Scorpios and all driven by a spiritual vision of something larger than themselves, for which they would sacrifice themselves if necessary.

Rectangle/Scorpio really doesn't much care what people think of her. This is one of her particular strengths, but it sometimes does not win her friends in professions where flattery and compromise are endemic. She is little affected by others' flattery of her and is incapable of insincerely praising them, even if it may be expedient for her to do so. When she genuinely likes something she will be generous and profound in her comments, and with her friends she is loyal unto death. But as long as she is pursuing what she feels is right (and with that intensity of feeling and accurate intuition she follows the feeling more than the thinking) then nobody else's opinion matters very much.

Seeking always the intimate, passionate relationship, Rectangle/Scorpio is not so good at having relationships with a large, unintimate public. Unlike Libra who is happier with the crowd, Scorpio longs for the intensity of one to one relationships. She is a private individual who keeps her deepest thoughts to herself and does not care for even small details of her personal life to be known by the public at large. There is always a secret life with Rectangle/Scorpio, not necessarily sinister, but an alternative private self who can be different from her everyday self. This might explain why so many Scorpios choose acting as a career. She can

live out on stage or screen her secret self. Or can keep her own non-actressy self as that private other person.

With the simple energy and ambition of her Yang body type and the depth and intensity of her Yin+ star sign, Rectangle/Scorpio is an unusual combination of sweetness and strength. Nothing will defeat her. Tell her something is impossible and you know that she will manage it somehow. Tell her something is forbidden and she will explore it, tell her something is a secret and she will have to know.

IN WORK

Healing and the arts, and sometimes the two together, are the obvious areas for Rectangle/Scorpio's significant gifts. It is the Scorpio intensity of feeling and intuition and natural identification with suffering that makes her a natural healer in any manifestation. She might choose orthodox medicine, where the single-mindedness of character given her by her Rectangle body type will help her overcome prejudice and deal with gruelling long hours and demoralizing lack of resources. Surgery is a traditional area for Scorpio who, according to the old books, has an affinity for metal and the cutting edge.

The well-developed spiritual side of Scorpio might well lead Rectangle/Scorpio more towards the forms of healing which consider the human being as both a body and a soul, anything from acupuncture and homoeopathy through to faith healing. Psychoanalysis and therapy are also areas where Rectangle/Scorpio can flourish, and really make a difference to the lives of others. Her interest in investigation, integration and transformation all come together in helping others to shine some light on their hidden selves and the wounds through which energy bleeds.

To be a practising artist is to choose one of the most difficult areas in which to make a living. Anything difficult attracts Rectangle/Scorpio like St George to the dragon. This is, in fact, a very good combination for an artist to have, because the emotional depth and soul of the Scorpio is given, as an arrow head, the Yang energy of the Rectangle body type which helps make a necessary impact on the world.

All the determination, perserverance, self-discipline and vision naturally assigned to Scorpio is doubled up by the influence of this body type. And self-promotion, self-centredness and ambition is thrown in for good measure. Yang/Scorpio Picasso was a genius, but he was also a brilliant self-publicist, and it was that as much as his brilliant work which sprang him to such extraordinary pre-eminence.

Rectangle/Scorpio is dynamic, creative and thorough in everything she does. She has obvious authority and is a great strategist, but she can be veiled about her real ambitions and competitiveness. Rectangle/Scorpio has a Yang body type which makes her need to make her mark on the world, and get some praise and favourable response back. If she can't do something really well, she is disinclined to even try – 'good enough' is not a phrase that easily springs to her lips. She wants to be the best, or at least the best that she can be. There is nothing lazy or half-hearted about Rectangle/Scorpio. Neither does she stand on her dignity and refuse to do menial, unpleasant or dirty tasks. If they have to be done she will do them; she is not someone who thinks of society as divided up into them and us.

Research of all kinds is also a fruitful area for Rectangle/Scorpio. She is less likely than her Hourglass or Pear sister Scorpios to be happy beavering away on her own in a library for months on end, she needs a bit more contact with the world than that. But scientific research, or journalism uncovering some story where might has overcome right, would suit her very well indeed. She is resouceful enough and self-contained and tough enough to be a foreign correspondent for a news gathering medium. She is also adventurous enough to take an aid job overseas, working with impoverished people, nursing them, or teaching them how to make their land productive or lobbying for them in the corridors of power at the UN.

She is ever practical and supportive of others. She is clearly able to be a good team player and can let others take the lead but will not be patient for long if they are weak, ineffective or fluff their responsibilities. She does not suffer fools gladly and in extremis is quite capable of organizing a palace coup. Rectangle/Scorpio is only interested in dealing with the truth and feels demeaned by the generalized compromise, glossing and euphemism that characterizes so much of public life.

Ideal Fantasy Job

Rectangle/Scorpio's vision, courage, energy and powers of transformation are badly needed in the public sector and she would be a wow as Chair of an organization restoring historic buildings. She has a particular love of old structures, and especially old ruins which she finds full of the spirit of those who have gone before. She has all the Yang energy and drive that any man would have, but has the added qualities of sensitivity and imagination

which so many Yang men, who have been in executive positions of power all their lives, sorely lack.

She would not be content just with running the place, she would particularly want to be involved with the restoration ensuring that the work is in keeping with their period and the uses to which they would be put. The research and uncovering of historic information and past lives will fascinate her as much as anything. She can preside over a phoenix truly rising from the ashes.

IN LOVE

You would not know it to see her in everyday action, but this woman's feelings run very deep and only in matters of love and betrayal are they likely to make their presence known. Most of the time she goes about her self-contained way, efficient, cheerful, affectionate and controlled. She is the last person to let her feelings hang out all over the place. She is unlikely to ring up even a good friend in the heat of the moment and rant and rage about the dastardly behaviour of a loved one. Rather, she will seek her friend's advice in calm recollection and sit there serene and smiling as if nothing too terrible had happened at all. But back at the ranch, the errant lover might be lying down with an ice pack trying to recover his courage and self-esteem, having had her hurt and fury explode on him like a nuclear bomb.

Rectangle/Scorpio needs to explain how deeply she feels about certain things – well most things – and not expect other people in her life to have anything like her radar perception about these matters. She is such a master at veiling her feelings most of the time, she cannot expect anyone else to intuit their extent. All this makes her a challenging woman to love. She will be passionate and faithful and open up to her man a whole world of feeling and awareness he may never have known existed. But she is not happy being dominated or patronized. And if he betrays her love and commitment he has a force of nature to deal with which, like a tidal wave or a flood, can be a frightening and dangerous thing.

The sort of man for Rectangle/Scorpio is strong but sensitive, leaning more to the Yin side of the scale so that he complements her Yang self. Anyone too Yang would clash with her need to be in control, her desire to be out in the world, her need to come home to a sweet and nurturing individual. But he has to be confident and sure of himself not to be overwhelmed by this most determined and energetic woman.

The balancing of career and children is a particularly complicated debate for Rectangle/Scorpio. She has this deeply feeling,

intuitive side which makes her identify strongly with the weak and suffering, and she will want to extend all her sensitive care to her own children. But she also has this Yang side which really *needs* to be out in the world in some way, working on her own life which is separate from her life as wife and mother.

She will not be a mother who will be happy handing over the full-time daily care of her children to someone else, but she will be champing at the bit to fulfil her own ambitions. The only happy compromise (and Scorpio isn't happy usually with compromise) is to work part-time while they are really young and vulnerable. And then go great guns when they are older and can articulate better their needs and fears. A passionate woman anyway, Rectangle/Scorpio feels most passionately of all about her children.

She is the kind of mother her children know they can always rely on. She is neither squeamish nor cowardly. She will go into battle if she has to. There is nothing soppy and coochie-coo about her, but her children know she will love them with an unconditional love to the end of her days. She extends the same loyalty to her friends, but whereas she expects very little from her children she does expect a reciprocal loyalty from others outside the charmed circle of her immediate family.

Ideal Fantasy Lover

For a clever, sexy, Rectangle/Scorpio who could be better than clever, sexy, supercilious Alan Rickman, who completely stole the show as the evil, deranged Sheriff of Nottingham in Kevin Costner's *Robin Hood: Prince of Thieves*? Tall and sneeringly good-looking he was a natural for Vicomte de Valmont in *Les Liasons Dangereuses* which he played to acclaim in London and on Broadway. As the ghostly lover in *Truly, Madly, Deeply*, his quirky sense of humour made him a whole new band of fans. He is a Yin male and therefore so complementary to this Yang female who has the strength and mystery to keep him intrigued.

IN STYLE

This woman is a most distinctive personality and this shows in the way she dresses. Sometimes she does not care one bit and will pull on an old pullover and a pair of baggy-kneed leggings, but other times she will look quite wonderful in an eclectic collection of clothes which only someone like her would wear. One day she might sling an Army surplus leather waistcoat over her best designer silk shirt and jodhpurs and then finish the whole thing

off with a dressage hat. Or she has a beautiful velvet twenties'-style dress of her grandmother's which she wears with black tights and high-heeled ankle boots. You will never find Rectangle/Scorpio dressing in a conventional way, and even if she is forced to wear a uniform there will be something quirky and individual about it. Wild earrings, the skirt narrowed and hem turned up, whatever.

Rectangle/Scorpio appreciates the luxurious feel and look of well-made designer clothes and would buy them if and when she can afford to, but she is not a flashy dresser and is not drawn to label dressing or obvious displays of wealth. Rectangle types generally do not like spending for ever traipsing round the shops or putting time and effort into thinking up stunning combinations of clothes. They would rather simplify the whole thing to a few good quality clothes which she can put together in a number of different ways with the minimum of fuss and effort. The Scorpio side brings in the need for distinctive touches. It is in the area of jewellery that Rectangle/Scorpio can choose to express her style, going for a one-off designer piece, or even turning to making something herself. She has the ingenuity and flair. For more specific information, see In Style on page 41.

Style Treat

Silk satin underwear. Silk satin is a flattering fabric for Rectangle type bodies. Rectangle/Scorpio needs to take care with her choice of colour – it's important even with underwear. Black may have a sexy reputation but it's not a colour that suits everyone. If she has dark colouring, fine, but for medium to light colouring, soft white, ivory or lighter colours will be more flattering, as well as more universally useful.

Women with straight hips are more flattered by sporty underwear. Rectangle types are practical women who like to be comfortable. Cotton, no frills, high-cut legs. Those high-cut sporty underpants are comfortable and sexy on her straight-limbed body. Any lace insets should be stiffish rather than flimsy. This is one body shape which an all in one body doesn't generally flatter.

This body type often has big, rather low breasts. A good quality underwired bra will be comfortable and give good support. If she feels like a bit of lace, keep it to a half cup. She should make sure she is measured by a competent assistant before she buys a bra. Apparently, the majority of women think they are a 36B and they are not. Rectangle types are particularly prone to fluctuations in bust size with weight gain and loss registering

immediately in the torso area. The right bra size makes all the difference in the world in terms of comfort and appearance.

IN HEALTH

Rectangle/Scorpio combines two robust influences to produce a constitution which rarely succumbs to illness. She has great recuperative powers if she makes sure that she gets plenty of rest. Her commonest problems are to do with the nose and throat and the reproductive system. Tension can cause breakdowns in her health and it is important that she finds an outlet for some of the intense feelings which sometimes overcome her. Meditation and other reflective, creative pursuits, like painting or weaving, can do much to channel these feelings out of the body.

As Rectangles have robust constitutions and healthy appetites this can cause Rectangle/Scorpio some problems when she gets older. This is an energetic combination and as a girl the Rectangle/Scorpio is likely to be quite sporty and to burn up a good deal of energy. But as she gets older and does less exercise, but her appetite remains hearty, the weight can begin to accumulate – on the tummy, spare tyre, upper hips, shoulders and face. When Philip Larkin wrote 'their beauty has thickened' he surely was talking of Rectangle women whose pattern of putting weight on their upper bodies can give this coarsening effect.

Indeed, when overweight, this type becomes the classic 'apple' shape, mentioned in the scientific papers in this book's introduction. These point out that case histories of tens of thousands of women have shown that this shape is less protected than the Pear and Hourglass from male type diseases, like arteriosclerosis and diabetes. Rectangle/Scorpio, whose busy life may lead to irregular scrappy meals and snatched periods of exercise and not enough rest, needs exercise and a well-balanced diet for the sake of her health as well as any vanity about her looks. For more specific information on diet and exercise, see In Health on page 43.

CELEBRITY RECTANGLE/SCORPIO

Jodie Foster shows all the indomitable qualities of this combination: enormous emotional power, tenacity and sensitivity. She is a film star who does not behave in a starry way and who can summon up great emotional resources for her roles. The harder they are, the more she excels, particularly in parts which convey a world of pain and rejection that seem to be beyond acting. She

started her career as a child actress in the Disney fold. She took time out and went to Yale to study for a degree. She then moved her flagging career into the really big time with scorching performances in *The Accused* and *The Silence of the Lambs*. For both films she won Oscars.

She is a no frills personality and a no frills actress, who says she doesn't like to be treated with kid gloves. She admits to being bossy and is proud to be called a feminist, although she is more into the humanist side where she allows that both women *and* men need to have their rights respected.

Now into her thirties it was inevitable that such a capable and authoritative personality should want to have some of the control herself, and so she made her directorial debut, as well as starred, in *Little Man Tate*. This was an intelligent, funny and touching picture where her part as the single mother of a highly gifted seven-year-old had some resonances with her own mother's position bringing Jodie up alone. It is always interesting to see what forces she taps in her own deep and multilayered character. With little vanity, and great support of her fellow actors, she brings hard work, no nonsense and surprising emotional power to everything she does.

RECTANGLE/SCORPIO PROFILE

Sam was reading History of Art at university when she realized that she didn't want to make this her career. 'I was really drawn to alternative people with political views. A completely different world, a different way of thinking and living. I became part of the squatting scene but soon found that was too extreme. Then I got interested in healing, particularly acupuncture. It was much more intuitive than herbalism, for instance. Ever since I was a child I thought that there was one big secret that was being kept from me. And acupuncture seemed to be part of this secret.'

Sam trained to be an acupuncturist and knows that working at this even through all the difficulties, all the time learning more, changing herself in the process, is what really matters. 'Sometimes I'm so scared by how difficult my patients are but I know there is no way I'd give it up. It's such a challenge and I'm continually changing and growing.'

She realizes how important it is to make her mark on the world and get some glory back. She used to not enter into anything that she couldn't excel at, but has learnt to be less demanding of herself: 'I have to be busy all the time. I definitely want to be as good an acupuncturist as I can – I used to want to be the best in the world, but have learnt to take things one day at a time.'

Sam is in her late twenties and one day having children will be a central part of her life, but not yet. She wants to get better established so she can continue giving treatments soon after having her babies, 'I never want to be someone who gives her whole life to her children. I would hate to look back on my life and feel I had wasted my talents.'

She has a strong spiritual nature but, brought up a Catholic, she is drawn much more to the Tibetan Buddhist philosophy: 'To be loving and dedicated and mindful of others' is what she tries to follow in her life. But she also recognizes that what she has to do is also important, and that sometimes this involves a necessary focus, even selfishness, in order to do it.

IN HOPE

Rectangle/Scorpio is the sort of woman who can help build empires or start new faiths, so it is not surprising that when she is constrained by the narrower confines of a suburban life, for instance, she can be frustrated by a sense of her greater destiny. Passion, however, is an absolute necessity of her life – and to think that just means love for her man and children is to misunderstand the extent and depth of her feelings for everything important in her life. The great Russian novelist Dostoevsky, a Scorpio himself, expressed a simple truth which all other Scorpios will recognize: 'With love one can live even without happiness.'

RECTANGLE
SAGITTARIUS

(Yang/Yang+)

MOTTO:

Nothing ventured, nothing gained

IN LIFE

Energetic, light-hearted, embarking on a quest, this woman is a traveller *par excellence*, through the medium of both her body and mind. She is forever seeking something which appears to be just over the next brilliant horizon. This is a double Yang combination of outflowing energy, action and verve. No one could expect this personality to be deeply sensitive to the feelings of others or reflective on the effects of her actions. Always curious, always on the move, she is much more interested in anticipation of the quest and in the journey itself, than in the eventual arrival. Metaphorically, at least, as long as there is always a horizon to travel towards, there is no real need for a home.

Now most Rectangle/Sagittarius women only manage to travel in the literal sense on their holidays for two weeks of the year (but you can be sure she's keener on the far-away, exotic places than on a package holiday to Benidorm). But even if she is stuck in one country for 50 weeks of the year, she will be travelling in her head, exploring new avenues of thought, setting out on local crusades against pollution or political corruption. She will be restless and unhappy if she's cooped up indoors at some routine job which does not use her intelligence or give her any scope for variety and getting out and about. With Sagittarius being a mutable sign, unlike the fixed signs of a Scorpio or Leo, for instance, Rectangle/Sagittarius does not stick at anything which is not to her liking.

This is a character which can suffer from the feeling that she's missing something, that there's a party going on to which she isn't

invited. The vulnerable side of Rectangle/Sagittarius is this sense that there is so much that is new and different in the world, all waiting to be experienced; it can drive her into frantic socializing, or headlong attempts to be at the hippest places with the trendiest people, or, sometimes even, general promiscuity of behaviour and feelings.

But she is born with a lucky streak. More often than not, she emerges unscathed and sometimes much enriched by her headlong rushing in where wise women never go. Her sense of humour too, often wacky and sometimes completely foot-in-mouth, can stand her in excellent stead. Who bears the Rectangle/Sagittarius Bette Midler any grudges, even though she has said and done some outrageous things? This combination produces a personality who operates sometimes with a too brutal honesty, or exhibits gob-smacking insensitivity by blurting out necessary truths – but at the wrong time and in completely the wrong place. There is no malice, however, in her. She is a large, generous spirit.

She is an open breezy character who can be less discreet than is good for her career. Her frankness and candour can take people aback. At the office party, she can congratulate her boss, for instance, on how nice she's looking and then enquire if her new suit is the one that had been in the window of the shop for larger ladies, reduced by 75 per cent? Rectangle/Sagittarius is genuinely interested to know these things, but cannot understand why the boss is looking less than friendly. She is generous and sincere, but she can cut a swathe through a group of people with her ill-judged comments which leave more sensitive souls reeling.

Boredom can also cause Rectangle/Sagittarius problems and then goaded beyond endurance by the mindless routine of a job, or the mundanity of her life, she can start to throw tantrums, or crockery, or just suddenly veer off course into the wide blue yonder. In many ways she is much keener on friendship than on one-to-one passionate involvement. She needs so much open country to gallop over and fresh air to breathe that she bridles at any attempts to rein her in. She likes to think that the world is full of possibilities, and finds it hard to consider any future ones being closed down for the sake of those currently on offer.

She is a truth-seeker, searching for the secret of life itself. This is where Sagittarius's reputation for being interested in religion and the spiritual life comes from, expressed in anything from a feeling of connectedness to the universe to a full-blown acceptance of a complete belief system.

As a mutable fire sign, Sagittarius can be rather erratic in how she expresses her energy and adventurousness. She can have a

terrific enthusiasm for a person or an idea one day and then have veered off onto a completely different tack by the end of the week, almost forgetting the original interest in the process. This can be disconcerting for more fixed temperaments and can be the cause of misunderstandings when Rectangle/Sagittarius may be accused of fickleness, lack of feeling and general unreliability. In such situations her saving grace is always her downright honesty. Unlike other mutable signs, she is incapable of stretching the truth, promising things she cannot deliver, or pretending the situation is other than it is. Hard as such honesty can be to live with, it does mean that you do know where you are with a Rectangle/Sagittarius, even if it is changing all the while!

IN WORK

Nothing monotonous, anything with horizons. The wide world is her concern and her playground, and ideally Rectangle/Sagittarius needs a job which allows her some travelling – in mind if not in body. Intellectual study and teaching is a natural for this combination. She is interested in languages, naturally, but also the larger systems of our culture, the law, theology and philosophy. Anthropology attracts, too, because it involves the exploration of alien peoples and distant lives – as well as field trips to exotic and sometimes dangerous places. This woman is excited by change and challenge – articles in the newspaper on how to take the unexpected and the dangerous out of travel are greeted with incomprehension and contempt.

With her athletic body shape and competitive nature, Rectangle/Sagittarius is often a very good sportswoman, and some may choose to make that a career. Chris Evert is a Rectangle/Sagittarius with all the qualities of straightforward good nature and honesty which one could expect from this combination of Yang qualities.

If not choosing to play sport as a career, Rectangle/Sagittarius would make an excellent sports instructor or administrator of any kind. Running the local sports centre, or teaching various sports, sitting on committees which promote sport or introduce certain games into other countries, lobbying for more resources; all this would benefit from her energy, enthusiasm and expertise.

Although the intellectual life has a real attraction for her, she is better off not being completely desk-bound. An editor in a publishing house would be very suitable, as long as there were occasional trips to New York and Europe to refresh the Sagittarius's need for variety and excitement, and the Rectangle's need for a wider stage on which to strut her stuff (with just a little praise as well).

It does seem too obvious, but exploration, travelling, and travel writing are areas where this character excels. The more difficult and challenging, the better. Amy Johnson, lone transatlantic pilot, was a Rectangle/Sagittarius and Dervla Murphy, the fearless traveller and writer is another.

Animals and the outdoors also hold enormous appeal. Anything to do with horses suits this centaur symbol, half-woman, half-horse. But other animals from exotic zoo species to the humbler farmyard and pet end of the animal spectrum, all draw her interest and concern. Working as a vet would strike many a Rectangle/Sagittarius as a great job with its continual variety and challenge – as well as the ethical advantage that a vet helps to mitigate some of the terrible suffering of animals in this exploitative world.

Ideal Fantasy Job

Presenter of a travel programme on television. This would combine so many of Rectangle/Sagittarius's many talents. She would be intellectually satisfied by attempting to provide a show that addressed much deeper issues than just where to go to get the cheapest alcohol and the most sun in the shortest possible time. Work on such a programme is full of surprises, challenge, hectic schedules and quick-thinking trouble-shooting – and all this gets her adrenalin going and ensures she is never bored. There is also the travel!

IN LOVE

'I'm not in love . . . but I'm open to persuasion/East or West, where's the best/For romancing?' sings Rectangle/Sagittarius Joan Armatrading and that just about sums it up. Falling in love, turning it into husband and baby, two-up-two-down-love, is not this woman's first priority. Love and marriage, in their more orthodox manifestations, can cause this combination some trouble. Both her body type and star sign make it unlikely that she will rush headlong into marriage – unless it's in flight from something else. She may decide to get married young as the only obvious means of escape from her narrow horizons and stultifying life, but it is unlikely to be passion for the man, and an overwhelming desire to be a couple with a joint future and family together, which will propel her to the church or registry office.

Young Rectangle/Sagittarius is more likely to be found working her way around the globe, or at least doing summer waitressing

back home so that she can set off to explore some unknown part of the world in her next holidays. She will take a long time to settle down with one job, one home, one man. She will be in love, perhaps many times, along the way, but it seldom gets really intense and demanding and seldom is allowed to get in the way of the more important things, like work and friendship and exploration of every wonderful possibility which might come her way.

Rectangle/Sagittarius can find it difficult to identify with her body, to really inhabit it – with all its foibles, inadequacies and limitations. This woman finds it hard to accept limitation generally, her mind and ideas are always running ahead of her and it can be a shock to her that her body has needs too. Allied to this is an uneasiness about her femaleness. It's not that Rectangle/Sagittarius feels she's more male than female but that she doesn't really feel in her body at all. Sometimes it's as if she is disembodied mind or pure energy, and she can feel rather dislocated from her physical nature.

The man who may finally capture her heart will have to be an intuitive, nurturing Yin kind of man. The sort who will keep the home fires burning for her when she's off on her wanderings, and when he occasionally goes with her, he'll make sure there's enough bandages in the first aid kit and cotton socks in the rucksack. He will soothe her nerves when she returns home having battled for some improvement in the services at work, or taken on the government over the inequality in women's pay, and he is completely unchauvinist about sharing the household chores.

This combination of Rectangle/Sagittarius is a double Yang woman, and any equally Yang man will mean a clash of ego and competitive energies – with nobody doing much nurturing of anyone else, or the relationship. They will both want to be out in the world slaying dragons and neither will be a true prop or support to the other.

She's great as a real pal to her men and women friends alike. Not at all happy playing the sex kitten, her flirtatiousness is more likely to take the form of a joke at the pub and a hearty slap on the back. A more feline femininity is not her style. Similarly, she is not one to sit chatting to her women friends for hours over love lives and the mysterious movements of the human heart. Get up and go is her motto, and that is what she prefers to most things.

As a mother, Rectangle/Sagittarius is wonderfuly adventurous, not bothered by convention and unlikely to hang over her children, breathing down their necks. Her aspirations for them will be intellectual rather than social or material. She would not care too much what jobs they did as long as they were interesting people with something to say. She also needs to be relatively detached from the everyday care of her children. Ideally, she retains her job and manages to run both sides of her life, but if she is full-time at home she will not stop going out and travelling and pursuing her disparate interests. Baby and then toddler will come with her, whether it's out to the jazz café for a bit of alternative life, or on a plane to Ecuador. She is not likely to allow her style to be cramped by the fact that she has a small person along who needs care and attention. The children of a Rectangle/Sagittarius mother will never be bored by her, will probably be very proud indeed of her, but the more Yin ones may long sometimes for a little more time with her, and a little more sympathy and emotional understanding. But if she has married that good Yin man, then their dad will provide the emotional intuition which mum might be too busy or not tuned-in enough to provide.

Ideal Fantasy Lover

Richard E. Grant is an intriguing actor who has brains and a powerful social conscience – all absolute necessities for Rectangle/Sagittarius. Oh, and he's also a quirkily good-looking, tall, lanky, *kindly*, kind of guy, who is not in thrall to his own ego. He came to wacky prominence with his performance of the self-absorbed and druggy scrounger, Withnail of *Withnail and I* and a few films followed. However, following his role as the hustling screen writer in *The Player* more offers of work than he can do have come his way. Rectangle/Sagittarius would always be kept on her toes by such a man with a range of interests almost to rival her own.

IN STYLE

Sporty, freedom-loving, informal, all-natural. These are words which could describe Rectangle/Sagittarius quite well and certainly describe her style of clothes. She is not going to spend hours putting things together, savouring the pleasures of the cloth or the beauty of the garment, like her Yin sister might. She wants to look striking and lovely, it's true, but in a split second – and then she must above all feel comfortable, and not have to look in the mirror again until she goes to bed that evening. No fuss, she likes chic and unstructured clothes, and good natural fabrics like heavy linen, cotton, wool and silk. For more specific information, see In Style on page 41.

Style Treat

Because Rectangle/Sagittarius cannot be bothered with spending hours over sorting out her look, and yet she likes to look distinctive and individual, a super piece of jewellery which makes a bit of a statement can be her short cut to distinction. This can be a necklace or a brooch, evening earrings or a bracelet – whatever she chooses should be dramatic and unusual. Bold, ethnic jewellery would fit the bill very well because of Sagittarius's love of travel and the out-of-the-ordinary. A stylized African face as a brooch, primitive tribal bangles or bracelets in rough-hewn metals or woods, striking necklaces of trade beads, amber, non-precious stones, carved wood, coloured beans and seeds. Of course, as a traveller, at best, she should buy this treat in its country of origin, and be forever reminded of the journey. Otherwise, bought in this country from a shop specializing in ethnic jewellery, the piece can offer a promise of a journey to come.

When choosing shape or pattern, Rectangle/Sagittarius should bear in mind that having a straight body type requires a straight line in clothes and jewellery, nothing too curvy or flowery in shape. For advice on choosing the right colour and the scale of jewellery, see page 43. However small she is, though, the Rectangle/Sagittarius should never go for anything too delicate and tiny – this is a robust body type and an outgoing star sign so anything too discreet will be lost on her. Rectangle/Sagittarius should tend to go bigger rather than smaller.

IN HEALTH

Recklessness leading to accidents, lack of everyday care for herself and driving herself too much are the main reasons for any undermining of her usually excellent health. There can be something rather gauche and clumsy about Rectangle/Sagittarius; she can fall off horses more readily than most, trip down stairs or slip on the tennis court. Of course, it's not just clumsiness and carelessness, this woman is more sporty and active than most and is easily egged on to do foolhardy things by an appeal to her competitive streak – especially by men she wishes to impress!

Otherwise, overindulgence of food and drink can take its toll, especially when she's young and thinks she can match the men drink for drink – something no woman's liver can manage for physiological reasons. Liver disorders, stomach upsets, gall bladder trouble and rheumatism are possible areas of weakness, but otherwise Rectangle/Sagittarius has a terrific constitution with good powers of recovery.

There can be some downside to this, though. Rectangles have robust constitutions and healthy appetites, Sagittarians tend to too. This is of little consequence when they are young because this is an extremely energetic combination and as a girl the Rectangle/Sagittarius is likely to be sporty and to burn up a good deal of energy. But as she gets older and does less exercise, but her appetite remains hearty, the weight can begin to accumulate – on the tummy, spare tyre, upper hips, shoulders and face. When Philip Larkin wrote 'their beauty has thickened' he surely was talking of Rectangle women whose pattern of putting weight on their upper bodies can give this coarsening effect.

Indeed, when overweight, this type becomes the classic 'apple' shape, mentioned in the scientific papers in this book's introduction. These point out that case histories of tens of thousands of women have shown that this shape is less protected than the Pear and Hourglass from male type diseases, like arteriosclerosis and diabetes. Rectangle/Sagittarius, whose busy life may lead to irregular scrappy meals and snatched periods of exercise and not enough rest, needs exercise and a well-balanced diet for the sake of her health as well as any vanity about her looks. For more specific information, on diet and exercise, see In Health on page 43.

CELEBRITY RECTANGLE/SAGITTARIUS

If you consider that Jane Fonda, Bette Midler and Tina Turner are all Rectangle/Sagittarius you can appreciate the powerhouse of energy that this combination can produce. Bette Midler is the boldest and brassiest (and some would say the most difficult) of over-the-top performers, she is a tiny powerpack of anger, ambition and wild humour. She was nominated for an Oscar for her perfomance as a distraught, strung-out Janis Joplin figure in *The Rose* and is at her best playing larger than life personalities, although she herself is deceptively small – and bosomy. 'I have more than one person in this body. One is very bawdy and one of them is demure and very thin and duchess-like'.

She is unorthodox in everything she does, falls out with the rich and powerful and has been known to behave very badly on and off stage. Having signed a lucrative deal with Disney, she then bad-mouths the films they make and fights their rigid views on what vehicle is best for her. Her career and reputation has been a roller-coaster, but personally she seems to be settled at last; well into middle-age she has a happy marriage and a young daughter Sophie, whom she tries to protect from the raunchiness

of her own performances and personality. One feels this particular ambition is doomed to failure.

RECTANGLE/SAGITTARIUS PROFILE

Maya is an Australian who at 19 left Adelaide to travel the world and then stopped off in England and never returned. 'In Australia I felt so cut off from the rest of the world. When I got to Europe it was as if I was at last at the centre of a great interconnected culture, with roots stretching back for thousands of years and a feeling that I was looking up into the branches of a great tree which had grown in the meantime. I really liked that feeling of connectedness – although I missed the weather.'

She married in her late twenties, because it seemed easier for all sorts of practical reasons like visas and accommodation. But she lived with Malcolm happily, 'We were both rather detached about it, more like two batchelors, then he left after five years, when he found someone who had really fallen madly in love with him.' Maya seems perfectly happy living in a small flat, writing a newsletter for a press syndication back in Australia, and travelling when she can and sometimes writing pieces on the places she has seen. This just about pays her bills.

'Money has never been part of the equation for me. Above anything else, I've realized I have to have freedom. Variety in my work – if it's also worthwhile and interesting then that's a bonus, but above all I have to have freedom, to be able to go at the drop of a hat, to not have to worry about responsibilites, contracts, fear of losing job or money. No thanks! I'd rather be poor anyday.'

Maya is slim and blonde and looks marvellous in the jeans and cotton pique shirt which is an outfit she is rarely without: 'I dress this up with a pair of super Maori earrings and a Navajo silver belt or down with a bandana and a scarf tied as a belt. I really feel that just by changing my accessories I can go from working in the communal gardens out the back, clearing leaves say, straight to the theatre, perhaps just pausing to wash my hands and change my shoes. Ever since I was a little girl I've known that I looked better in boy's clothes and it used to mortify me that I had to wear silly skirts and short socks while my brother could roar around in shorts and a bare chest.'

IN HOPE

Rectangle/Sagittarius will always be poised for flight, if only in the mind. She needs to feel that the horizon is still there, even

though she may be grounded for the time being with work or children, or the demands of her material life. Love and friendship she may have in plenty, but still she hears the train in the distance:

> 'My heart is warm with the friends I make,
> And better friends I'll not be knowing;
> Yet there isn't a train I wouldn't take,
> No matter where it's going.'

They must have been written by a Rectangle/Sagittarius gazing towards the blue line on the horizon.

RECTANGLE
CAPRICORN

(Yang/Yin)

MOTTO:

She who would eat the fruit must climb the tree

IN LIFE

Power, effort, achievement, these are the predominant characteristics of this combination, not that you would necessarily recognize it when you first meet this quietly-spoken, serious-minded woman. There is nothing flashy and look-at-me about Rectangle/Capricorn. She knows what has to be done and just gets on and does it. She has a tremendous capacity for hard work, but doesn't make a great song and dance about the fact that she has toiled solidly for two months without a break to get a report out/study for an exam/finish decorating the house.

She likes to be in positions where she can advance herself in life. Rectangle/Capricorn is not happy in some hippy organization where power is shared. She likes hierarchies, she likes to know where she stands and where she's climbing next on her path ever on towards her goal. Onwards and upwards. To some Rectangle/Capricorns life is a deadly serious game of snakes and ladders, which she envisages herself negotiating with great conscientiousness and tenacity. There is no burning urgency, she is happy enough to climb a rung at a time – and she is not too proud to haul herself up by her bootstraps if need be. She is canny and careful enough to know which are rungs and which are just diversions, or empty spaces – or, worse still, snakes which will tumble her down to the bottom again.

Rectangle/Capricorn doesn't often make strategic mistakes. She sets her sights and usually reaches them, while all around her others are rushing into things, falling out of them, panicking because they've lost their way, heart or ambition – and generally making a pig's ear of it. The woman in the corner with an air of quiet concentration, who keeps her head when all about are losing theirs, is Rectangle/Capricorn.

There is a sense of rootedness and solidity about this character. Rectangle/Capricorn is enigmatic; so much of her depth is hidden beneath a rather melancholic and distinctly serious persona. If you consider the great Capricorn actresses, like Capucine, Marlene Dietrich, Faye Dunaway, Ava Gardner, Diane Keaton, Jane Lapotaire and Maggie Smith, there is this overwhelming strength about them all, but also a poignant melancholy – even when they are being funny. Of course, this star sign produces great beauties with prominent bone structure (Capricorn rules the skin and bones) but they are not ebullient women who one would take out for a drink and a laugh.

She is a serious woman, who takes life seriously and needs to have goals to aim for otherwise she falls prey to that old Saturnian depression. But it is wrong to think that it is only success and mastery in the material world that matters to her. Rectangle/Capricorn knows she has this slow-burning power, she knows she is not easy to fathom, she is aware how much more subtle are her ways of operating than most of those around her: she intends to not only master the code of the social and professional world in which she lives but also crack the master code of life, to determine what we are here for.

Rectangle/Capricorn finds it hard not to be in control both in her professional life and at home. She needs power and a place to express that power, something worthwhile to work towards and appreciation of her efforts. She is not lightweight in her character or ambitions. But as she grows older, and having achieved some of her goals, a greater peace will descend on her and she will be less driven and grow more light-hearted. She will even seem to grow more youthful as her friends grow older and more set in their ways.

It is an extraordinary thing about Capricorn. When she's young she can seem old before her time. When she's a teenager, she is ill at ease fooling around with the gang; she feels somehow isolated and out of place. But then as she grows into middle-age, the reverse process begins to happen. Just as all those goodtime Leos and Sagittarians, who had had such a wild time as youngsters, start to get more sedate and crotchety in their old age so Rectangle/Capricorn starts to become brighter and springier and more full of fun than she has ever been before.

Her place in society really matters to her and she is careful to dress and behave in the manner befitting her appropriate

station in life. Her house and car, and the clothes she wears, are not just an expression of her personality and taste but an indication of her status in the world. Her family also matter to her, the family from which she is descended as well as her children. She will feel a strong brew of love and duty and likes to think of herself as a responsible person. There is something good and wise about Rectangle/Capricorn and when she finds the right stage out in the world for all that dedication and hard work, she is one of the strongest, kindest and most indomitable of characters.

IN WORK

This woman has to work. Rectangle/Capricorn has two powerful influences, her Rectangle body type and her star sign, propelling her towards a job where her need for power and influence can be satisfied. This is not an obvious, over-bearing kind of character but her presence will be powerful with a sense of authority about her. Her love of structure and hierarchy makes the Civil Service a place where she can excel and be happy in her work. One big system itself, there are clear pathways to success for those who want to take them. Everyone knows their place and their job and there is a civilized atmosphere of tolerance and support in most levels in most of the departments.

Surprisingly, the Civil Service is also very good at employing women who want to spend more time with their children in part-time capacities, offering some opportunities to job-share. The best news about these arrangements for any Rectangle/Capricorn is that working part-time or job-sharing doesn't significantly slow down a woman's progress in her rise to the top jobs. Also good news for a woman who plans for her old age and is concerned with security – Civil Service pensions are still most generous indeed.

Rectangle/Capricorn is often blessed with tremendous concentration and so can excel at jobs which require study and taking exams – or in fact comparing facts or figures and drawing relevant conclusions. The law or medicine attract her. She can cope with the amount of learning but also likes the status of the professions. In fact, working on legislation is one area of fruitful endeavour and Rectangle/Capricorn can bring quite a zeal to her work in making life better organized for society generally, and altogether a little fairer.

The countryside and the buildings in it have their attraction too. Estate management, the restoring of old buildings and the building of new all suit a personality which loves permanence and order and restoring the status quo. Architecture is an obvious profession for Rectangle/Capricorn to pursue if her love of building and structure and form is expressed in brick and stone and wood.

Whatever she turns her hand to she will stick at and make work if she possibly can. Rectangle/Capricorn is never one to give up when the going gets tough. She likes working through the pain barrier; the achievement seems all the greater because of it. Comfort and ease are not words which find top billing in her vocabulary. More like effort and success. And she will make it.

Ideal Fantasy Job

The writer of a social diary in an up-market monthly magazine. Rectangle/Capricorn would be brilliant at this job, researching and writing up the diary, having done the rounds of various society weddings, balls, polo matches, coming-out dances, elegant soirées, ambassadors' dos. You have to know intimately the endless social hierarchies, both overt and covert; who takes precedence over who, what everyone's correct title is, whom they're currently married to, whom they may be seeing – but can't be mentioned.

Knowing everything, but being the sole arbiter as to what is mentioned in your influential diary, courted by everyone, all gives Rectangle/Capricorn terrific power. She also needs amazing stamina for all that standing around, smiling and chatting and downing glasses of champagne. Rectangle/Capricorn is more than up to the job. (And she might even land one of the landed gentry!)

IN LOVE

Rectangle/Capricorn has built a few defences against love. Running out of control, throwing caution to the winds, being deaf and blind to reason – all are alien experiences to her temperament and ones she does not want to encourage or give in to. Relationships are not easy for her. There is something quite self-contained about her emotions; she is on her way and her blinkers are down while she plods up that rocky path. Being both a cautious old Capricorn and a Yang Rectangle body type, love is not the first thing on her agenda and she is unlikely to rush into marriage. If she does marry young, however, it will be for security and safety rather than as a result of a wild passion or irresistible instinct. When she marries later, she will have surveyed the scene and will make her choice with good sense, considering all the qualities necessary in a husband and father. The old clichéd advice, that

one can just as readily fall in love with the conductor as with the first violinist, would not fall on stony ground with a Rectangle/Capricorn looking for a mate.

Nevertheless, she is capable of great passion and more than a little romance when she feels sure enough to let her defences down. Although embarrassed by emotional outbursts in herself, she finds it quite refreshing and a relief too to be with others who can express their emotions more easily and uninhibitedly. The kind of man for her is a caring Yin male with marked intelligence and, ideally, a good career and from a good family. She will be a most loyal and faithful spouse, hard-working and efficient rather than sexy and exuberant, and will always rise to the occasion, seldom letting herself or her partner down.

She brings the same loyalty and love to her children and although she is not naturally a cuddly, demonstrative woman, they – like her husband – know that when the chips are down family matters. Sometimes they may feel, however, that Family matters to her more than the individuals within it. Rectangle/Capricorn may not be the kind of mother who says she will love anyone come hell or high water, only as long as that person does not bring her or the family into disrepute or disgrace. Badly behaved, recalcitrant teens may find themselves being banned from the house until they reform. This woman is not soft or over-sympathetic to what she considers eccentricities, bloody-mindedness or weakness.

It is much better for everyone concerned if a Rectangle/Capricorn mother manages to keep her work, or study, going at least part-time. She needs to express herself on that outside stage, she needs to retain that sense of climbing ever upwards. Stuck at home, without that outlet for her own ambitions, she might well end up breathing down her children's necks, driving them to succeed in her stead.

Ideal Fantasy Lover

Cheers star Woody Harrelson has many of the caring, easily affectionate qualities which Rectangle/Capricorn would find irresistible. His little-boy lost charm, his willingness to talk about love, has all the attraction for her of opposites. A long relationship with Glenn Close (Rectangle/Pisces), 14 years his senior, which is now over, taught him a lot about life and love: 'Before I was careless and destructive. Now I've made room for love.'

His quirky sense of humour and willingness to let his woman be in charge would suit Rectangle/Capricorn to a T. She'll loosen up a bit herself and begin to see the pleasures in spontaneity.

IN STYLE

Clothes and accessories are very important to Rectangle/Capricorn, not so much as an expression of her own personality or for the sensual pleasure of the colour and cloth – as they more often are for the Yin body types – but as a necessary armour and flag of her personal status in the world. Ideally, she would like classy, understated designer clothes which she wouldn't have to fuss with or worry about. They would be her highly attractive uniform which she would only have to throw on to know she was dressed appropriately for any occasion.

Neither fussy nor flashy clothes are her style. But good quality, understated elegance most definitely is. Her Rectangle body type means she is basically a no-nonsense, practical kind of woman who wants to be comfortable at all times. Her Capricornian side makes her very partial to good leather clothes and accessories. A pair of straight cut leather trousers, a good leather jacket, fine quality shoes, all interest her, and suit her body type/star sign personality. For more specific information, see In Style on page 41.

Style Treat

A classy coat dress. Dresses that suit the Rectangle body shape are very difficult to find, and a coat dress is smart, versatile and the most flattering. She should look for one which is wedge-shaped, ie broad at the shoulders and tapering to the hem, or cut in a straight line from the shoulders with a little shaping at the waist in the form of straight darts. Anything more curvy just emphasizes the Rectangle's solidity at the waist.

The colour is important. Something neutral is most versatile, eg stone, taupe, pewter, navy, grey or black, but Rectangle/Capricorn must make sure it is a flattering shade for her own colouring. It is important to check that the colour of the garment you are buying suits you well. Take it into daylight, hold it under your chin and look at what it does to your skin, eyes and hair. If wearing it intensifies and enlivens your colouring then that is a colour that is right for your skin tones. If you look washed out or sallow, or your hair loses colour and dark rings seem to appear under your eyes, then you are getting it wrong. This sounds a lot of trouble to go to, but it is worth it for it enhances the pleasure you will get every time you wear it.

Choice of material also matters. She must look for a dress in a crisp, tightly woven fabric – wool gabardine, for instance, for winter or cotton gabardine for summer. In terms of style, she

should go for single or double-breasted buttoning, with a sharp jacket-type collar and lapels, or a plain V-type neckline. A round neckline will not look smart enough on the Rectangle shape, unless it's a high neckline.

Because a dress has more limited uses than a suit or jacket, it is important to ring the changes with accessories. She can wear a suitable jacket over the dress for a super smart suit effect, or she can use jewellery. Keeping everything on the angular side, brooches, necklaces, earrings can all be used to dress her look up, or with ethnic jewellery to make it more informal. A scarf in a flattering colour and tied neatly at the neck and tucked into the front of the dress gives another variation. The coat dress can become a most useful and attractive garment in any Rectangle body type's wardrobe.

IN HEALTH

Capricorn traditionally rules the skin and bones of the body, and if there are any weaknesses to this generally strong physique they will possibly be in the areas of arthritis, tendonitis, toothache and skin complaints. There is a natural melancholy traditionally attached to Capricorn's ruler, Saturn, and Rectangle/Capricorn may feel occasionally that there is a dark cloud over her head. This can be one of the reasons why she works so hard, and does not allow herself much time off for contemplation, or plain wasting time. It is most important that she tries to strive for balance, play as well as work, love as well as duty.

Rectangles have robust constitutions and healthy appetites, and Capricorns eat to live, rather than live to eat. When she is young Rectangle/Capricorn is likely to be quite sporty and to burn up a good deal of energy. But as she gets older and does less exercise, the weight can begin to accumulate – on the tummy, spare tyre, upper hips, shoulders and face. When Philip Larkin wrote 'their beauty has thickened' he surely was talking of Rectangle women whose pattern of putting weight on their upper bodies can give this coarsening effect.

Indeed, when overweight, this type becomes the classic 'apple' shape, mentioned in the scientific papers in this book's introduction. These point out that case histories of tens of thousands of women have shown that this shape is less protected than the Pear and Hourglass from male type diseases, like arteriosclerosis and diabetes. Rectangle/Capricorn, whose busy life may lead to irregular scrappy meals and snatched periods of exercise and not enough rest, needs exercise and a well-balanced diet for the sake

of her health as well as any vanity about her looks. For more specific information on diet and exercise, see In Health on page 43.

RECTANGLE/CAPRICORN CELEBRITY

Shirley Bassey is a wonderful trouper displaying all the staying power and quietly tenacious ambition of this combination. Born in Wales to a seaman father, she began singing in local working men's clubs when she was sixteen. She was never afraid of hard work and willing to slog from the bottom to the top. Her big booming voice and melodramatic delivery worked wonders on show-stopping film and show tunes like 'As long as he needs me' and suitably, 'Climb every mountain' and 'What kind of fool am I?' to which the only answer can be 'No fool at all'. Her greatest hits perhaps were the two Bond theme songs, 'Goldfinger' and 'Diamonds are forever'.

In true Rectangle/Capricorn manner, Shirley Bassey seems to get younger and more glamorous as she grows through her fifties. Terrifically self-disciplined, she spends two hours a day working out in the gym before a big tour. Forty years in showbusiness, she is still a star, still loving work, but her personal life has had some terrible tragedies. Her first husband committed suicide, and her daughter, more recently, was found dead in a Welsh river. But Shirley recognizes how hungry she was for success, particularly in her younger days. She has a terrific strength that drives her through.

RECTANGLE/CAPRICORN PROFILE

June has her own company running personal development courses for individuals and companies. She trained as a counsellor and then started her own business and worked flat out for five years to establish it. She has two teenage children and a domesticated, kindly husband who was willing to take on a good deal of the domestic responsibilities while she established her company. 'I couldn't have done it without Bill's support. As it was, I think my children felt I was never around and when I was I was so distracted with other things. I tend to get really concentrated on one thing at a time and am not good at diversifying. They went by the board, I'm afraid, for a few years. But Bill was a wonderful parent for them, and always available to discuss their worries at school and so on.'

She never really stopped work, even when she had her babies. There was always studying to be done, with a book propped up

while she was breastfeeding. 'I was not your usual young mother, popping in to see other mums and have a cup of tea and compare notes. I was always aware of how much I wanted to do. I know that I irritated a few of my friends in the area by turning up for the occasional cup of tea and talk, but I always insisted on bringing my darning, so that I wasn't wasting time. Looking back now, I can see why they might have felt that I never had time just to be friendly. But it was difficult to feel so driven and to know that time was passing, rather unproductively it seemed to me then. Quite soon I was back into full-time work and I think I was happier not having to split myself in two and always feeling guilty.'

June was diagnosed as having ME, the post viral syndrome which leaves its sufferers exhausted by the slightest physical effort. 'I was horrified at what happened to me. I had taken for granted all my life that I could push myself to achieve anything I wanted. Tiredness didn't really rear its head. But I realize now, I never listened long enough to my body to ever *let* it raise its head. I think I was chronically tired, but never let up until my body took things into its own hands and forced me to slow down.'

It has been the worst year of her life as she has been forced to rest and has had to hand her business over to someone else to run: 'I have been into the slough of despond and back. But it taught me some useful lessons. I know how much my work means to me. I would die if I couldn't work. I almost felt I was dying at times, when I had to watch someone else take over my company and not necessarily run things like I wanted.

'But I also realized how rewarding my children are now that they are almost grown up. They are such good company, and although I know I couldn't have spent more time with them when they were younger, because I was building up the business, I think I'll make an effort not to be so single-minded and workaholic again – and to do more fun things with them, and enjoy their last few years at home, before they go.'

IN HOPE

The Rectangle/Capricorn woman can do most things and achieve what she wants in the end, but the costs along the way need to be recognized, even if she feels they are worth paying. One involves the difference between stability and stagnation. Rectangle/Capricorn will always be concerned with security and stability and that is partly what makes her such a good and reliable friend and colleague. But she can become so averse to spontaneity or risk

that she loses out on some real excitement and genuine progress – both professional and personal – along the way.

The other cost she may be unwillingly paying is in the area of her emotional life. In the end, the feelings of those close to her matter far more than her reputation. They may not matter more than her success, but what is worth the sacrifice for the sake of reputation? Oscar Wilde, who experienced this from the other side, offers his own brand of philosophic wisdom, 'One can survive anything nowadays, except death, and live down anything except a good reputation.' True a hundred years ago when he wrote it, it must be all the more true now when no one resigns from public office any more and life goes on regardless.

RECTANGLE
AQUARIUS

(Yang/Yang)

MOTTO:
It takes all sorts to make a world

IN LIFE

Strong, determined, cool and sometimes distinctly wacky, Rectangle/Aquarius knows what she wants in life, and it's not likely to be what other people want. She is unconventional and does not conform to her parents', schoolteachers' or the world's expectations one little bit. She will always go her own way, so much so that some people might even accuse her of being perverse just to make a point, or to stand out even more distinctly from the crowd. This is a balanced combination of double Yang, not as strongly masculine as the fire signs who are combined with a Yang body type, but nevertheless clear-sighted and untroubled by unruly emotions. Intellectually she may at times suffer from lack of confidence and confusion, but she is seldom disconcerted emotionally. She is prone to repress her feelings and pretend they don't exist. She likes to maintain a detachment and coolness, does not court intimacy and is better relating to the crowd.

Highly individualistic, madly unconventional, what other sign houses such off-the-wall personalities as Zsa Zsa Gabor, Germaine Greer, Barry Humphries, John McEnroe, Yoko Ono and Vanessa Redgrave? Colette, James Joyce, Gertrude Stein and Virginia Woolf, all truly experimental writers whose work broke with centuries of literary tradition are also Aquarians, as did the poetry of Lord Byron and the bizarre works of William Burroughs.

At heart, they are all pioneers and have their eyes set on the intellectual horizons of the future, on new ideas, a new order of things, a fairer and better world for all humanity. They're not so likely to get down to doing the boring, nitty-gritty of lobbying for change (they'd rather lob a bomb being more naturally anarchists than democrats) but they will talk and dream and argue and write until the cows come home. Unfairness upsets Rectangle/Aquarius. Freedom and human rights are her concern and, believing passionately in freedom, she can get very dogmatic, even overbearing on the subject, stubbornly insisting on her interpretation of events.

Rectangle/Aquarius is a complex and enigmatic character. Not at ease emotionally, she can nevertheless show deep care for someone in trouble, which she will express in practical ways, or by talking things through rather than offering a physical embrace. Sincerity of feeling is one of her virtues. She may not express much but what she does say or show is true. There will be few declarations of undying love, but she only says what she means, and anyway who could ever know that they would love someone for ever? Loyalty is also a strong suit, tending to stick with her decisions to love, honour and – well not obey exactly, but – respect.

Rectangle/Aquarius is a cerebral woman, who lives much more comfortably in the airy realm of ideas and ideals than in the murky half-hidden underworld of the emotions and the soul. She can be embarrassed by romantic effusions and will try to reason out of existence anything she can't understand. Irrationality irritates and alarms her. She likes to sort everything out in her mind and has all the answers. With a real talent for analysis, she is brilliant at understanding those things which can be measured and quantified, and which respond to the laws of logic. But she is less confident in the intuitive, emotional reaches of the human character.

Here is a woman who always has a cause for which she is prepared to be self-sacrificing. She is, for example, likely to be involved in the feminist movement in some way, if only by discussion and example. It is not surprising that two of the most influential feminists of this century – Betty Friedan and Germaine Greer – are both Rectangle/Aquarius. Both are radical thinkers, both better with theories about human beings than with managing intimate relationships with one or two. Neither are much concerned with what others think of them, and both adore the limelight and generating controversy. Both are dogmatic and idealistic and not in the least embarrassed by the fact that there have been some fundamental shifts over the years in their ideologies. And both are *always right*. This makes for great intellectual fireworks, much valuable disruption of the status quo, and a

great deal of intentional (and unintentional) mirth. Rectangle/ Aquarius is great value. But there are no modest, shrinking violets here.

She has a large view of humanity and much prefers dealing with people in the abstract, or in a more detached way, than in intimate one to one relationships. Her caring is humanitarian more than personal. A Pear/ or Hourglass/Aquarian manages more successfully to unite the thinking side of this air star sign with the feeling side of the Yin body type, but here, with a double Yang, the thinking, cerebral side dominates. Together with the drive, self-centredness and worldly ambition of the Rectangle body type, this combination can succeed at anything she puts her mind to.

IN WORK

Teaching, in all its myriad forms, is the most obvious place for this talented woman to put her energies. It is as a professor or lecturer that she will be able to electrify her students with her intellectual energy and open-mindedness. As a teacher of secondary children she will inspire them with the possibilites of their lives and the pleasures of widening their intellectual horizons. She is less likely to want to teach really young children who need more patience and nurturing care than intellectual muscle. But vocational teaching too, as nursing tutor or as a professional mentor, like a solicitor or barrister with her pupil, all suits her character and talents really well.

Rectangle/Aquarius's humanitarian side leads her into work with aid organizations abroad, or with social services and charity work in her own country. She is good at dealing with the grass roots problems, the needy and suffering people, because she does not get deeply drawn in emotionally, and so does not succumb to the compassion fatigue and despair that more feeling-dominated characters might feel when confronted with the massive suffering of victims of civil war or famine. The practical side of this combination wastes no time with sympathy and tears and just rolls up her sleeves and gets on with what has to be done. There will be some colleagues who will find her matter-of-factness in certain heart-breaking situations rather shocking, but it is women like this who actually get things done, and perhaps manage to change sytems permanently and for the better.

Science and invention is also an area of traditional concern for this modern, forward-looking sign. Rectangle/Aquarius not only thinks up the ideal world, she works towards it in medical

research, laboratory work, working with telecommunications, space and technology. She is not held back by traditions, prejudices and outmoded ways of thinking and working.

Exploration of the human mind through psychology and psycho-analysis also has its attractions, and Rectangle/Aquarius is likely to be gifted at all the theoretical, ideological foundations of principle and thought in the field. But she will be less easy with the intuitive, emotional side of this work. Her brusque no-nonsense side can be unnecessarily tough on those who are less capable themselves, and those too with more sensitive feelings.

Rectangle/Aquarius can also turn to radio and television where she will promote her ideas, making programmes or working out broadcasting policy. She is capable on the technical side and could well be a camerawoman or editor. Good in a team, she is not good, however, at being told what to do. She may be difficult and perverse and go her own way when she feels too restricted by others' more conventional ideas, or overbearing tactics. Rectangle/Aquarius will sooner walk out of a project or a job than be made to do anything of which she doesn't approve or see the point. But she won't indulge in backbiting and politicking. She's straightforward, can in fact be brutally frank, and although you may not really understand her, you always know where you are with her. She lets you have it straight.

Ideal Fantasy Job

Pilot of a rescue helicopter. Rectangle/Aquarius has just the right kind of mind to make an excellent pilot, and being a helicopter pilot, particularly involved in sea or mountain rescue takes even greater skills. She can combine the practical robustness from the Rectangle body type and fine analytical reasoning and good hand/eye co-ordination from the Aquarius star sign. She is also very unlikely to panic. In moments of extreme tension, her brain can operate in an almost computer-like mode which makes the necessary calculations and helps her navigate through any hairy situation. Rectangle/Aquarius would also enjoy being the lone woman in a team of men, with all the strong but un-intimate bonds which working together in dangerous situations forge.

IN LOVE

This woman is strong, straightforward and lacking in feminine wiles. She knows what she wants and she is not afraid to get it. She does not operate any oblique strategy or courtship game. If she likes a man, she will tell him so. And the kind of man she goes

for likes this forthrightness in his women. She is double Yang and is most attracted to a Yin man, kind, sympathetic, affectionate – someone who provides all the feeling side which she can find so difficult sometimes to express.

But her unconventionality will express itself in her choice of partner. She is not likely to go for the traditional good catch; his family status, education and what he earns is of no interest to her whatsoever. She'll leave the Eton-educated stockbrokers and solicitors to her Capricorn and Leo cousins, she'll go for the (just about) reformed jailbird, the juggling busker, the singer in the band. The free spirit of the man matters more than his adeptness at social chit-chat in a Surrey drawing room.

But actually, love and marriage are likely to rate just about on a par with friendship. Rectangle/Aquarius is at her best relating to a group of friends. She is the centre of things, the live wire, the initiator of good ideas and the cultivator of a circle of like-minded friends to rap with and go on adventures. Settling down with one person and spending most of your free time with him can seem a rather limiting thing to do. When Rectangle/Aquarius finally makes the leap of commitment, she is quite capable of inviting a few friends along on her honeymoon, and will certainly strive to keep the old relationships up once she is married.

In the abstract, a mother caring full-time for her children may strike her as the right and good thing to do, but when it comes to the practical reality when she has her own children on her knee, she will be up the wall before too long with the claustrophobia of continual responsibility and emotional demand, with too little time to think her own thoughts. This woman needs personal space and an outside arena to explore; a larger world to belong to and in which to be influential. She will probably feel she has to work, part-time at least, to be happy and herself – and as good a mum as possible for her children.

They will never be bored with their Rectangle/Aquarius mother. When they are young and want conformist parents, they may be rather embarrassed by her unconventional get-ups and behaviour, by her disregard for the neighbours approval, and her own dogmatic and forcefully held opinions. But as they grow older they will take pride in this individualist who is always so much more interesting to talk to than any of the other mums they know, even if they wish that sometimes she would be home baking brownies on an Aga when they come home from school.

Although Rectangle/Aquarius may find it hard to commit herself, and may bolt a few times before she gets to that place in

life, once she makes her mind up she doesn't easily give up. As a fixed sign, Aquarius can bring great tenacity and loyalty to everything she does. She may dream of escape, but is more likely to escape through the mind than by packing up her bags and going walkabout.

Ideal Fantasy Lover

The gorgeous Irish actor Gabriel Byrne would fit the bill wonderfully well. Good looking with his blue-eyed, black-haired Celtic colouring, he is highly intelligent and worked as an archaeologist after obtaining his degree at Trinity College Dublin. This intellectual side is so necessary to Rectangle/Aquarius as it allows her to have someone to bounce ideas around with. Gabriel Byrne has added class to a number of movies including *Defence of the Realm* and *Julia and Julia*, and he met his future wife Ellen Barkin in *Siesta*.

To have a man like this waiting for you with his feet up by the fire might make Rectangle/Aquarius think it was just about worthwhile swopping the nomadic life with friends for home, cocoa and a cuddle.

IN STYLE

In one word, eclectic. Rectangle/Aquarius may be wearing the finest, most understated designer clothes, or just a pair of jeans and a white T-shirt, and whatever extreme she is in, she will look different from the rest. This woman likes to stand out, she is different and likes her clothes to signal that, even if it's just a subtle alteration or addition to what may seem a conventional uniform, it will separate her out from the crowd.

On the whole, the Rectangle body type is practical about clothes. She does not like spending endless time and trouble putting together a look, but she is realistic enough to know that how she looks matters and affects how she is treated in the outside world. The Aquarius part of this equation adds a much more devil-may-care attitude. She also can't really be bothered with spending too much thought and energy on something so unimportant, compared to the real concerns in the world. But she does need to carry her strong non-conformity and individuality into her dress. So the jeans might be worn with an old gamekeeper's waistcoat, and the designer gear might have the added surprise of a studded black leather belt. For more specific information, see In Style on page 41.

Style Treat

A pair of cowboy boots. These are just the thing for this action woman who likes something unusual and stylish but never at the expense of comfort or practicality. Not only will she get years of comfortable mileage out of them, in all weathers, they also give her get-up a personal signature every time she wears them – just the sort of distinction Rectangle/Aquarius values. This woman is unworried by fashion, so it won't concern her if fashion dictats decree cowboys are dead. She'll go on wearing them just the same.

She should buy genuine Texas boots if she can – they are more rugged than fashionable copies. Made in stiff, double thickness leather, they have a masculine feel to them, which suits all Rectangle-type women. Worn with jeans, a checked shirt and a waistcoat or jacket is the timeless and flattering casual look. But with either casual or smart clothes, a good pair of well worn, well dubbined cowboy boots cannot be beat.

IN HEALTH

Good, but some risk of nervous exhaustion from too much work and anxiety and not enough fertilizing from the emotional side. This is a healthy, long-lived combination. Traditionally, Aquarius rules the ankles and the circulatory system so varicose veins, ankle injuries and minor circulatory problems, like cold hands and feet may prove troublesome, but otherwise Rectangle/Aquarius has good powers of recovery. Being such a forward-looking personality and ruled by Uranus, the planet of electricity, sudden changes and magical transformations, she may be a particularly suitable patient for alternative methods of healing. Miracles can happen.

Rectangles have robust constitutions and healthy appetites, Aquarius less so. Rectangle/Aquarius is intellectually energetic and, as a girl, quite physically active. She is likely to burn up a good deal of energy when young. But as she gets older and does less exercise, the weight can begin to accumulate – on the tummy, spare tyre, upper hips, shoulders and face. When Philip Larkin wrote 'their beauty has thickened' he surely was talking of Rectangle women whose pattern of putting weight on their upper bodies can give this coarsening effect. However, the Aquarius element in this combination helps her retain a transparency and lightness in her face.

When overweight, this type becomes the classic 'apple' shape, mentioned in the scientific papers in this book's introduction. These point out that case histories of tens of thousands of women have shown that this shape is less protected than the Pear and Hourglass from male type diseases, like arteriosclerosis and diabetes. Rectangle/Aquarius, whose busy life may lead to irregular scrappy meals and snatched periods of exercise and not enough rest, needs exercise and a well-balanced diet for the sake of her health as well as any vanity about her looks. For more specific information on diet and exercise, see In Health on page 43.

CELEBRITY RECTANGLE/AQUARIUS

Vanessa Redgrave is an extraordinary personality and an actress of terrific range and power. But despite her undoubted genius, Hollywood has never been comfortable with her distinctive character and radical political beliefs, nor has she been comfortable with the superficiality and glitz of that world.

Always the Aquarian, Vanessa Redgrave remains an earnest seeker after truth, but somehow remaining on the cerebral plain and removed from earthy reality she remains faithful to an increasingly redundant and ridiculous dogmatic Marxism. Rectangle/Aquarius is never one to follow fashion, or be concerned with the opinions of others, but this stance seems particularly perverse even for this combination.

Her personal life has been as unconventional as her working life with a marriage to Tony Richardson producing her two actress daughters, Joely and Natasha, and then a long passionate involvement with Franco Nero. She allows only the most limited of interviews and manages to keep her private life largely to herself, but her political views have in some sense limited her creative genius in alienating certain influential people. She is drawn also to politically correct movies which sometimes do not allow her brilliance its full head.

She did win an Oscar, however, for her radiant performance in *Julia* where she played a mysterious saviour of Jews in Nazi Germany. At the awards ceremony she lectured the assembled glittering company (and Hollywood is largely built on and maintained by Jewish talents and wealth) on the evils of Zionism and the rightness of the Palestinian cause. She has always had an unerring instinct for picking exactly the wrong place and the wrong time. But being a Rectangle/Aquarius truth matters much more than good manners, good sense or expedience. She is one of the greatest actresses of her generation and quite obviously a true original whose integrity is unimpeached. The gods handed everything out to her at her birth, beauty, genius, intelligence,

tenacity, loyalty, hard work, a brilliant destiny – but they forgot a sense of humour.

RECTANGLE/AQUARIUS PROFILE

Susie works as the managing director of her own import company in London and lives with her husband, David, and baby son in a village in Sussex. She commutes to work every day and leaves David behind to look after the baby and household. 'He's a househusband' she says with a laugh, 'his day starts at about six when he brings me a cup of tea in bed. Then he deals with Sam, the baby, while I get dressed.'

She enjoys her job immensely. There are always new problems to deal with and new products to consider, and this continual variety, together with a few trips to her suppliers abroad every year, keep her on the go and interested. 'I like the challenge of having to think on my toes. I'll be on the phone to Hong Kong and have to make split second decisions on whether I'm going to commit £100,000 to some consignment or other. I really get a buzz from that. And from visiting our suppliers in exotic places.'

There was never any discussion of her giving up her work when Sam came along. But David was feeling unhappy with the fact his career was stagnating, and he was much more stressed by the commuting, so they decided to reverse roles. He stayed at home and both are happier. 'He does everything around the house. And he's also rather good at do-it-yourself. But I won't let him wash my good clothes because I don't trust him not to mix the wrong colours together.'

Susie worked right up to the last week of her pregnancy and was back at her desk a month later. 'It may sound awful, but I don't feel any wrench at leaving the baby every morning. I know he's well looked after by his dad, better looked after in many ways than by me if I had decided to stay home instead. He's much more patient and caring. It works quite well.'

She was not in the least worried by the responses of her friends. 'Some were shocked, and quite a few felt sorry for David, but I pointed out that no one feels sorry for a woman in the same position. I think it's rather narrow-minded to think that there are things women do better or more happily than men, just because they're women – and vice versa.'

IN HOPE

The actress, Mrs Patrick Campbell, who captured many men's hearts including George Bernard Shaw's, displayed Rectangle/

Aquarius's eccentricity and strength to the ultimate degree. She cared little for what people thought of her, could be terribly rude to their faces and then kind when she needed to. A friend recalled one of many extraordinary incidents in her life: 'A taxicab driver once demurred at transporting her and a disagreeable pooch named "Moonbeam", but she swept into the vehicle commanding, "The Empire Theatre, my man, and no nonsense." The dog, never housebroken, misbehaved en route, and the driver gave Mrs Campbell a furious I-told-you-so look as she descended. "Don't blame Moonbeam," she informed him loftily. "*I* did it." '

With such magnificent sang-froid no wonder there are so many successful and individualist Rectangle/Aquarians in this world. And so much amazed entertainment for the rest of us too!

RECTANGLE

PISCES

(Yang/Yin+)

MOTTO:

Sweetness out of strength

IN LIFE

Rectangle/Pisces doesn't know if she is coming or going. Is she a drivingly successful career woman (her body type makes her tend that way) or is she the ultimate imaginative, caring, feminine woman, as suggested by her star sign? Well, the answer is both, but with a bias towards her Yang body type. So she has a life that is outwardly directed, aims at worldly success, but with this emotional depth and subtlety which can sometimes sabotage the single-mindedness of her body type's ambition. Properly integrated, these two opposing qualities give heart to her energy and ambition, and add toughness and energy to her sweet nature. But when they are working in opposition, the Piscean feeling side can undermine the straightforwardly practical and ambitious Rectangle side, and make her feel defensive and so her natural forthrightness can come over as being plain tough.

This is an intriguing combination which it is sometimes difficult for even Rectangle/Pisces herself to fathom. The last sign of the zodiac is the most evolved and spiritual stage of human experience, the most complex of all the star signs to live with and to understand. Combined with the Yin body types, Pisces expresses herself in an emotional, intuitive, nurturing way. Delicate, imaginative and empathic to an almost psychic degree, she sees success in personal terms of making others happy and evolving herself into greater goodness and creativity. This is a sign with extraordinary creative resources.

But the Rectangle body type brings greater robustness, self-centredness and desire for a more public success. This means

Rectangle/Pisces suffers less for others and can channel her energies better into areas which will produce something tangible and good for herself. But she can also be more confused as to where her energies should be going and guilt creeps up on her with the fear that she rations her feeling side and refuses to sacrifice herself to the needs of those she loves.

She needs to accept that her body type is the predominant influence and, because she has such a sensitive and caring overlay from her star sign, she finds it much harder to express this single-mindedness and sense of purpose than a Rectangle/Aries might for instance. Rectangle/Pisces will always have a struggle, but it is her deeper feeling side, her more complex nature that gives her the potential to be both a subtle and a successful operator in her career, both a beloved friend, wife and mother and a determined, business-like manager of life and work. It is this determination allied with profundity of feeling which makes her such an intriguing and rewarding personality and, if she's an artist, then such a powerful and poignant one. Vera Lyn, Liza Minelli and Nina Simone are all Rectangle/Pisces singers and they all have managed, in their quite different ways, to express profound emotion through their music, and to evoke passionate responses in their listeners. They are not just great belters out of good songs.

Pisces is a star sign whose imagination can be boundless. Here with the practical energy and ambition of the Rectangle body type, Rectangle/Pisces stands a chance of putting some of those extraordinary dreams she may have into action. Procrastination, lethargy and occasional failures of the spirit can haunt other Pisces natures, but this one is more likely to be able to deal with the harsh realities of life, and make things happen. It is in the realm of this dark night of the soul that the robust Rectangle type energy comes to Pisces' aid. This Yang influence will provide the optimism and energy that means Rectangle/Pisces can turn from the dark to the light, bringing some of that profound inspiration and understanding with her. It is the Piscean inspiration which can make her an artist, and the Rectangle type practicality and ambition which can help her translate this into substance and success.

Pisces people traditionally are meant to be particularly susceptible to drink and drugs. This is not to say that they necessarily take these things to excess, but just that they are likely to be more adversely affected by them when they do drink or take drugs. Elizabeth Taylor, an Hourglass/Pisces, is the most famous case in point where at times in her life her health has been almost

destroyed by drink, and then the prescription drugs she was too freely given for her various illnesses and injuries, like her persistent back trouble. Rectangle/Pisces is more likely to use alcohol as a way of winding down after a stressful time at work and she needs to be aware that too much of a good thing can do her a great deal of harm.

More subtle and sympathetic than any other Rectangle body type, more dynamic than most Pisces (although not always more driving than the Triangle/Pisces), Rectangle/Pisces can make friends and influence people, and change the world for the better too.

IN WORK

Music and dancing is something Rectangle/Pisces really enjoys and may well be good enough at to make her career. Even if she doesn't make it to the *corps de ballet* or becomes a star like Sylvie Guillem, she could well teach dance or be part of a professional choir, or a singer of any kind of music from folk to rock to opera. To any of these activities, whether her work or her hobby, she will bring a little bit of extra emotional zest.

Writing is another area where Rectangle/Pisces' imaginative force can find real expression. Her body type's ambition and drive helps manage the dogged work and unrewarding slog which is necessary to bring these creative dreams to the light of day. There will always be a few 'which got away', but Rectangle/Pisces will manage to net quite a few more, biggish fish which give her a sense of achievement and worth. She may sacrifice something of her visionary nature for a more practical approach, but probably she will have few regrets.

Film and theatre, with its dealing in imagination and illusion, exerts its fascination over this personality. Running pub theatres, writing plays, being in charge of the camera or lighting in a film crew, editing, producing, directing – anything behind the scenes Rectangle/Pisces is highly capable of doing. She is also just as likely to pound the boards, or take to the silver screen, where she has a particular dreamy presence. This is not a hard-edged woman, although she may be quite tough enough to survive in a tough business.

Nursing and voluntary service is also an area where both the practical and compassionate sides of this combination are called for. As a healer, she is more drawn to the alternative wing, where her intuition and recognition of people's spiritual natures is more closely involved in the healing process. Rectangle/Pisces may even find herself with a spiritual vocation, and now that women can become priests in the Anglican church, there are likely to be more Rectangle/Pisces queueing up for the job.

Business is always an area where Rectangle type women can excel. Although they are keen on promotion and improving their personal standing in the company, they are usually good team workers and seldom let their private lives get in the way. Rectangle/Pisces brings to such work an extra dimension of feeling and intuition, but she is also less likely to be single-mindedly ambitious, willing to sacrifice her personal life for her work. She will struggle to combine her own ambitions and her family's needs, recognizing how important her work is but trying to be two places at once, two people at once. Being something of an idealist, Rectangle/Pisces may well think she fails at both.

Ideal Fantasy Job

Lady Bountiful – or failing that, a *caring* tycoon businesswoman, like Anita Roddick of Body Shop fame. This kind of job combines beautifully the two aspects of Rectangle/Pisces' character. Her body type's need to be in the limelight, properly appreciated and rewarded, and her star sign's need to be generous and imaginatively nurturing of others. Ecological concerns would be in the forefront of the company's practices. Like Anita Roddick, a Rectangle/Pisces can show the business world that a remarkably successful company can be built on unlikely foundations – that a woman's alternative, nurturing view of the world can make as much hard cash for investors as the more traditional exploitative attitudes which generally characterize successful business.

IN LOVE

The problems of mixed messages and opposing energies, which can make life difficult for Rectangle/Pisces, can also make love appear at times to be nothing but a vale of tears. Pisces has an eager, soft heart and longs for love, but her Rectangle side gives the impression that she is matter-of-fact, tough-minded and unromantic. She has two sides to her nature, and sometimes it is hard for her to show her vulnerability and need for affection and gentle handling. She attracts Yin men, emotional and sympathetic themselves they look to her to be strong. In her out-going Yang mode she is, but then they are disconcerted by this unexpected vulnerability in her, this sudden collapse of confidence, which sometimes rears its complicated head.

Relationship is so important to Rectangle/Pisces that she can give the impression sometimes of being rather promiscuous with

her affections, but that is to misunderstand her real need for connection and her adaptable, fluid character. Admittedly, the Rectangle body type characteristics make her slightly more aware of her own boundaries, less self-sacrificing, less willing to put others before herself. But she is still an impressionable, empathic personality who falls in love easily and sometimes tries to disguise the sensitivity and depth of her feelings by a feigned detachment and coolness. She can be attracted to everybody, her imagination is free-ranging, and although she may remain faithful in deed, her feelings can be engaged elsewhere, if only in her dreams. Nobody can own this woman's fantasies and they encompass all her hopes and speculations about life, lovers, her work, her future.

Friends also matter, and to these, Rectangle/Pisces shows her understanding, sympathetic face. Some people are born listeners and sympathetic spirits, others are better at encouraging their friends to get up and go, energizing them with their unsentimental view of life. Rectangle/Pisces has both qualities and is sensitive enough to know when each approach is likely to be most beneficial. She is willing both to listen and to urge action when necessary.

As a mother she combines these two aspects to perfection. She is sensitive and affectionate, imaginative about her children's points of view and always willing to hear them out. But she is also quite dynamic and will not put up with their wingeing for long, much preferring to get them to grab their bat and ball and head for the nearest park, with her leading the expedition if need be. She is good at encouraging her children's independence, partly because she cannot do with having them relying on her for everything. Being a Rectangle, she is likely to want to have work to do outside her domestic life. She needs the wider stage, the continuity in her career, the independence. But her Pisces nature will make it hard for her to leave her children when they are young and so she may compromize by working at home, or working part-time until they are at full-time school.

Pisces do have an otherworldly side which makes them seem rather mysterious and unknowable – and fascinating too. Rectangle/Pisces brings a greater capability and practicality. But she can also, at a moment's notice, slip away from everyday reality into some private dream. Much loved by friends and family alike, she runs a hospitable home, with good food, comfortable furniture, games and lots of music. Even when her children have officially fled the coop, they will find ways of creeping back 'Just for a week or so Mum, while the damp's being treated in my flat'.

Husbands too find it hard to leave. Although she may drive him mad, there is a sweetness in her strength and a steeliness to her softness from which it is very hard to turn away.

Ideal Fantasy Lover

Gary Lineker, the nicest, kindliest, sweetest footballer in the world – with the most magnificent thighs! His personal qualities were all the more enhanced as far as his fans were concerned by his honest, emotional responses to his son George's birth and then the terrible news that he had leukemia, now in remission. Imported by the Japanese to give their football a much-needed lift, and to teach them something about his impeccable good manners and saintly morals, he conducts himself with composure and dignity and is kind to everyone.

Rectangle/Pisces would appreciate the goodness of his nature (he's a Scorpio and a Yin male and so well-suited to her on all counts) as well as his hardworking, unegotistical side. He would support her with all her wild schemes – and would have the emotional depth to appreciate her intensity of feeling and need for love and tender care.

IN STYLE

Rectangle/Pisces is likely to show some of the ambivalence of her character in her way of dressing. The Rectangle body type requires a more structured, angular way of dressing and the Pisces side wants to be sexier and more romantic, a look which isn't very flattering to the more masculine lines of the Rectangle body.

Rectangle types like clothes certainly, but don't want to be bothered with spending hours over choosing them and putting outfits together. They recognize how important it is to wear the right clothes for the right occasion, but they would ideally go to one place and buy what they need for the season and not have to think about it all again. Pisces, however, is a different matter. She has an ability to express many facets of her personality through her clothes, and is adaptable and imaginative. She wants to add something quirky and individual to the classic, clean lines which she knows suits her body type, but doesn't quite satisfy her fantasy side. Accessories are probably the way that she can express this other part of herself, and it is here where her imaginative Pisces nature can take flight. Hats, gloves, a striking necklace or designer earrings. All can add the distinctiveness and mystery which this character likes to express, but she should keep them generally unfussy and geometrical to suit her physical self best. For more specific information, see In Style on page 41.

Style Treat

A hat makes a great style treat for Rectangle/Pisces. Apart from Ascot, weddings and funerals, not many women wear hats any more, which is a pity because they can be so much fun and can be the brilliant finishing touch to any outfit. They are practical too – always a plus for Rectangle-type women – because in the right hat you can go striding out, come rain come shine, without having to bother with an umbrella.

As with all things, she has to take care when choosing her hat. No flowers, please, neither floppy bows, organza or net, no squidgy, floppy, romantic little numbers. Instead she should go for more masculine-looking hats with clean, straighter lines, like a boater. Alternatively, a trilby, sombrero, fedora or panama all have the right line, although the width of brim will be governed by her height and bone structure – particularly the size of her face. If she is tall and has big bones then a hat with a large brim is fine. If she is not particularly tall or big-boned then a more moderate sized brim is more flattering. If she is a petite woman (under 157cm [5ft 3in] tall) with small bones (wrist less than 14cm [5 1/2in]) she would be better sticking with a trilby-type hat or a pillbox style.

Her best bet for versatility is to choose a neutral colour – black, brown, navy, taupe or stone – but making sure that it is a flattering tone for her own colouring. It is important to check that the colour of the garment you are buying suits you well. Take it into daylight, hold it under your chin and look at what it does to your skin, eyes and hair. If wearing it intensifies and enlivens your colouring then that is a colour that is right for your skin tones. If you look washed out or sallow, or your hair loses colour and dark rings seem to appear under your eyes, then you are getting it wrong. This sounds a lot of trouble to go to, but it is worth it for it enhances the pleasure you will get every time you wear it.

The creative Pisces in her might well want to jazz the hat up a bit, or match it to her outfit. Stiff ribbon, like petersham is perfect and can be used to make a hatband or a geometric bow. Straight feathers (not floppy ostrich!), or fans of fabric – again echoing that geometric look – are also good trimmings for a hat to suit a Rectangle/Pisces woman wanting to make a statement.

IN HEALTH

Rectangle/Pisces has a robust body type with a highly sensitive star sign. This means that it is essential that she gets enough rest and does not continue in stressful situations for prolonged periods of time. The lymphatic system, the circulation generally and the feet specifically are all sensitive areas. There will be periods of faintheartedness, when the enormity of all she has to do, or the weight of suffering in the world, overwhelm her spirit. Affection and warmth, both human and physical, are needed then.

Rectangles have robust constitutions and healthy appetites, Pisces are sensual eaters. When Rectangle/Pisces is young she can be pretty energetic, even sporty, and is likely to burn up a good deal of energy. But as she gets older and does less exercise, but her appetite remains, the weight can begin to accumulate – on the tummy, spare tyre, upper hips, shoulders and face. When Philip Larkin wrote 'their beauty has thickened' he surely was talking of Rectangle women whose pattern of putting weight on their upper bodies can give this coarsening effect.

Indeed, when overweight, this type becomes the classic 'apple' shape, mentioned in the scientific papers in this book's introduction. These point out that case histories of tens of thousands of women have shown that this shape is less protected than the Pear and Hourglass from male type diseases, like arteriosclerosis and diabetes. Rectangle/Pisces, whose busy life may lead to irregular scrappy meals and snatched periods of exercise and not enough rest, needs exercise and a well-balanced diet for the sake of her health as well as any vanity about her looks. For more specific information on diet and exercise, see In Health on page 43.

RECTANGLE/PISCES CELEBRITY

Liza Minnelli has all the strengths and weaknesses of this combination. A sensitive child, she was the daughter of Judy Garland and Vincente Minnelli and did not have a childhood which made for security and easy happiness. During her days of greatest stardom, drugs and drink became a real problem for her until the mid-eighties when she gave up on her addictions. She has since realized that she is actually allergic to drink and cannot touch the stuff. She believes in God, 'The human spirit is amazing. I'm not a religious person but a spiritual one. I believe in God helping through other people.'

Liza's huge, soulful eyes are very typically Piscean and her emotional sensitivity brings great affecting power to her singing. She also loves dancing (this sign is full of dancers) and the whole stardom thing she manages with affection and some humour. Three marriages have failed and she is sad that she has had no children, but enjoys playing aunt to her half-sister Lorna Luft's two children. She admits that her friends matter enormously to

her, that they and family have helped her pull through the drink and drugs and the deaths of those close to her. But her work is what she feels she is here for, 'the thing that I love most'.

RECTANGLE/PISCES PROFILE

'I came from the sort of family which strongly disapproved of working mothers, so I stayed home although I did not really enjoy bringing up three children and not using my brains.' Catherine still regrets not keeping some sort of work going for herself during those early child-rearing days so that she could pick up the threads of her career again when her children were at school. 'I encourage my children to do something besides child-rearing – I still feel that I have missed out on an important part of life, not having a proper job, with the independence and sense of achievement and comradeship which that brings.'

Catherine likes feeling stretched intellectually and has decided in her middle age to do an Open University course. 'This has made such a difference to my confidence and self-esteem. I wake up excited because I have something important to do, that doesn't just revolve around the housework and getting the meals. I'm really looking forward to the summer school when I will meet other students, of all ages and from every kind of life. Perhaps I'm a late developer, and there is still time for me to find myself a career which will use all my energies and talents!'

She longs to be able to dress romantically, in slinky, sexy clothes, 'But as a Rectangle shape I know that more classic lines suit me better, but I do add jewellery, or a hat sometimes just to look more individual. I'm very sensitive to criticism so try to look nice at all times. I'm also a great day dreamer and still think that one day there might be a knock at my door and a prince on a white steed will be there, impatient to whisk me off to his far off land. So I always make sure I'm wearing a bit of lipstick and mascara, just in case!'

IN HOPE

The kind, imaginative heart of this Pisces woman beats in a robust, Rectangle body shape, a body made for action and ambitious forays into the world. The empathic, ever-changing nature of her Pisces temperament is given structure and focus by this masculine body, which dispositionally adds a personality less concerned with others. Rectangle/Pisces can achieve anything she decides to do, particularly when it involves her feeling, intuitive

side, energized by her Yang body type. The famous Pisces poet, Elizabeth Barrett Browning, recognized the power of feeling in her own life and the lives of others: 'Whoso loves/Believes the impossible.' The same is true for the integrated Rectangle/Pisces.

gains weight on
face and shoulder

looks top-heavy
when weight
is gained

gains weigh
above th
hip bone
tummy, ches
spare tyre
upper arms
and upper hips

has straight
hips which
get boxy when
overweight

gains weight
on inner thigh

has lean lower leg

TRIANGLE

ARIES

(Yang+/Yang+)

MOTTO:

Cry 'Havoc' and let loose the dogs of war OR
I want it now!

IN LIFE

This combination of double Yang+ produces the most forceful character of the whole 48 body shape star signs. This woman would be at her best marshalling armies, running the country – or at the very least – in charge of a large listed company. She has to have power and the space to exercise it. The extreme Yang body shape adds extra ambition, and a certain ruthlessness, to an already energetic and forthright personality.

Aries is a cardinal fire sign and so is brilliant at initiating things. Full of energy and enthusiasm, she has great executive power – for as long as she doesn't lose interest. She is also highly competitive and has to be first in everything she undertakes. The Triangle body type is just as competitive, brilliantly focused on self and not much deflected by the feelings and demands of others. When you consider these famous Triangle/Aries you can see the special strength of will and determination which has got them to the top. Joan Crawford, Bette Davis, Ali MacGraw and Gabriela Sabatini are all this combination and none has the look or feel of gentleness or femininity in the conventional sense of the word.

This is a character who is full of vitality and optimism. Nothing gets her down for long, but the full extent of her strength of mind and ambition may not be clear to her until she is well into adulthood. She may veil it from herself and from others, afraid to seem too overbearing, too unfeminine. But it is important that Triangle/Aries recognizes her true strengths and finds the right platform for them, then she is less likely to come over as being so

tough. She needs to bear in mind, though, that when she is in full flight she can seem rather intimidating to more subtle, feeling, imaginative individuals – both men and women – who don't see life in terms of such red-and-black boldness, where action matters more than thought and feeling.

The Triangle/Aries kind of determination and need for power is difficult for a woman to express in a culture where women are still meant to be the nurturing, sympathetic and kindly sex, while men are admired for their ambitiousness and single-minded pursuit of fame and fortune. Just as there are women *and* men who are basically Yin, there are men *and* women who are basically Yang, more concerned with impressing themselves and their ideas on the world. They are the movers and shakers in life, who change things and inspire others. In the personal realm, this body type brings energy and ego into the equation.

In the case of Triangle/Aries, she is the woman who has all the qualities to succeed, particularly in careers traditionally dominated by men and male values. Action is her strongest suit. She does not rely on her intuition to work out strategies, she does not want to bother with research and deep analytic thought. Naturally someone who takes immediate and energetic action, she wants to do it NOW and the devil take the consequences. Her weaknesses are the very reverse of these strengths – lack of sensitivity to the feelings of others, little foresight or insight into the effects of her actions, a headstrong nature that refuses to wait, to listen or to learn.

Ruled by Mars, the god of war, this combination produces a fighter who has courage and pugnacity to spare. She loves a challenge – some might even say she prefers a fight. She is unlikely to take the way of conciliation if she feels she has been wronged. Her fire sign energy is uncomplicated and up front, but her Triangle body type can make her veil the full impact of her will, for fear of being too transparently ambitious or powerful. Opinionated, Triangle/Aries does not waste time pulling her punches or sweetening the pill. She says what she thinks, and it may sometimes sound pretty brash and brutal. You do know, however, just where she stands – most of the time. It is only in the area of her own personal ambitions that she may rein herself back a little, just so that she doesn't alienate her supporters, or completely steamroller the opposition.

Her self-confidence is high, particularly in areas to do with work and travel. She knows where she's going and although she may not have worked out the ten-year-plan, she certainly knows what she's going to do to get there in the next half-hour. But in the areas of love and relationships she is less sure, less confident, more confused. There is something quite isolated sometimes about the Triangle-type woman. She sets herself apart, is not a natural team player and always likes to be in charge. She may have a wide circle of friends but is not naturally intimate with them and her ambition can set her apart from the social herd where friendships, having fun and wasting time reading the paper and chatting are all parts of the daily round. This woman is more serious and focused than any of the other body types. As far as career and material achievement goes, she is also quite willing to make the personal sacrifices to ensure she goes much farther.

IN WORK

Triangle/Aries is interested in anything which gives her the chance of getting to the top and being in charge. She doesn't mind starting at the bottom, as long as there is a ladder and she can climb it three rungs at a time. Once she has discovered her ambition and focused it on the right career, once the bit is securely between her teeth, she is unlikely to be deflected by love affairs coming or going, by marriage, childbearing, childrearing, and all the other emotional vicissitudes which affect most women's and many men's lives. This woman means business, and without a doubt would swop the rose-covered cottage and rocking the baby's cradle, for a fast car, a high profile job and lots of measureable success and professional esteem.

She has the body type and natural competitiveness and assertiveness to make a world class athlete. Gabriela Sabatini is a perfect example of a Triangle/Aries who has got to the top and intends to stay there as long as she can.

Any business, particularly if it involves challenges and risks, will also appeal to Triangle/Aries and she will strive to climb the executive ladder. She has the dedication and focus to get to the top. She is not good in groups or team situations, preferring to work by herself, for herself. The really high risk, stressful areas of commodity broking and futures, for instance, also attract this kind of temperament which thrives on adrenalin and adventure – the individual pitted against the odds.

Science and engineering also attract their fair share of Triangle/Aries. Machinery can fascinate her and she is likely to want to know how most things work. She is also probably a very good driver and not averse to going to car maintenance classes to be able to sort out any failures in her own car.

Brilliant in any emergency, practical and cool-headed and quick to act, Triangle/Aries with her leadership potential would

make a terrific General, Chief of Police or head of the emergency services. She is also very happy in masculine environments, like being part of the ambulance or fire brigade, where she can readily become one of the boys.

Gifted as a promoter or salesperson, Triangle/Aries can persuade most people with her natural enthusiasm and boundless energy. It is a job that allows her to work on her own, monitoring her own performance through her sales and returns, and this all suits her fine. She knows what has to be done and will do it, without fuss or squeamishness. Her only problems can come from being too focused, blinkered even, so that nothing else matters in her life. Then as she slips into workaholism, she becomes out of balance and becomes increasingly alienated from other people.

Ideal Fantasy Job

Head of a venture capital company investing in quoted and unquoted companies. Triangle/Aries would love the gambling side of this job, and the creativity and unadulterated power involved in being able to sign over millions to a company who wants to expand, or a brilliant entrepreneur who wants some financial backing for a company he or she wants to start up. This is real grown up Monopoly and the risks and rewards are great, and women are a rarity so high up. Triangle/Aries would make it a dazzling First. The only place she wants to be!

IN LOVE

This causes Triangle/Aries some trouble. Aries is traditionally the fool who rushes in where wise women never go, and there certainly is a headstrong side to this combination. She has a volatile energy which extends to her emotions. Brilliant at starting things, not so good on the long haul, particularly when life gets boring or difficult. But the Triangle side of the equation is a perfectionist and basically a loner who finds real intimacy and sharing hard to handle. Research among Bel's clients shows that Triangle types tend to put off marriage and childbearing until later, some never choosing these experiences at all. An overwhelming number put their work at the centre of their lives, and those few who make their marriage or children central (for a time anyway) consider being a wife and mother as work which has to be done to the utmost point of perfection too. These are hard people to live with, and hard for themselves to live with too.

If she does have children, she will be an active and adventurous mother, much better at taking them on expeditions or ski-ing holidays, than sitting curled up cosily by the fire. Everything she does has to be done to the best of her ability, and if she should decide to channel her powerful energies into her Mother-Earth or Supportive-Wife roles then she will do that to the best of her abilites too, but at a cost to herself and sometimes to everyone else involved. She will be in charge of a busy, well-run household where she is at her absolute best when in the middle of a huge party she has organized herself.

The best place for all this energy and ambition, however, is outside in the world where Triangle/Aries can operate from her own powerbase and leave her domestic life to others who enjoy it more and are less exacting in their demands. The kind of man to whom she is attracted is the Yin, sensitive soul who is perfectly happy to leave the conquering of corporate dragons to his wife while he gets on with gentler pursuits. He will be the nurturer in their relationship. He is the one who will listen to their children and allow them to be, without any preconceived ideas of what or how they should be.

She is not likely to have a band of really close women friends. She gets on better with men and sees no real point in intimate chats with the girls about men, life and the universe. She wants to concentrate on serious things, work and sport, and rather than talk about them she prefers to get on with the doing.

Ideal Fantasy Lover

Television personality Jonathan Ross has all the sweetness of nature and sense of humour to keep a Triangle/Aries woman happy. His high profile job might mean she feels in some competition with him in her own demanding job, but his laid back character and enthusiasm generally will be a tonic for her when she comes home tired out from the office/gambling den/battlefield.

He admits that as a student at university he always preferred to amuse people and make friends than to work really hard. And although he works hard to research his shows, he is still in the business of amusing people and making friends. Being a Yin man, he probably gets more pleasure from his clothes and from looking good than a Triangle/Aries woman does, and he would be perfectly happy looking after the baby. The perfect man for an intelligent, hard-driving, successful woman to come home to for a laugh.

IN STYLE

Triangle/Aries recognizes how important her clothes and the way she looks is to her job and to how successful she is in the world.

Being a double Yang+ personality, she does not get enormous pleasure from experimenting with various garments and outfits, feeling the cloth, comparing the colours and textures, trying different accessories and combinations. She wants instant results. Ideally she would like to be able to walk into a shop and buy her whole wardrobe in one fell swoop, everything worked out to mix and match, all good quality, practical, highly suitable for her work, and *smart*. Preferring casual clothes to any other look, above all Triangle/Aries has to feel comfortable, and cannot bear to wear any clothes which restrict movement or need fussing and adjustment every time she stands up or sits down.

The style of clothes that really flatter Triangle/Aries are determined by her body type. The Triangle shape has broader shoulders than hips and more of a marked waist than the Rectangle. She falls into two basic types, the small boned, boyish figure like Mia Farrow who probably rarely, if ever, puts on weight and the more muscular, athletic looking type, like Princess Stephanie of Monaco, Jamie Lee Curtis and Anjelica Huston, who can get heavy in the upper torso area, but keeps her inverted triangle shape with straight hips and lean lower legs. When thin, this shape is the classic fashion model shape with coat-hanger shoulders, next-to-nothing-hips and long lean legs.

If Triangle/Aries has got very heavy she may prefer to dress in jackets and tops which are straight, rather than emphasizing her waist which might have given up the fight a bit. Long jackets, tunics or crisp men's style shirts (but with straight hems, not shirt-tails) over lean trousers or skirts will continue to look very flattering even on the large Triangle body types.

Some women with this body type try to counteract their broad-shouldered look by wearing flimsy, ultra-feminine clothes – think of Diane Keaton (a Triangle/Aquarius) in *Annie Hall*. Those soft, drifty clothes on the angular Diane make her look a bit like Little Orphan Annie, rather gawky and fey. This suited the character very well in the film, but for Triangle/Aries, wanting to be taken seriously in the real world, it can be a counter-productive look. Her femininity is best expressed with clothes that have simple geometric lines, certainly angled to the waist if she likes, but it's better to avoid soft fabrics, gathers and bows. For more specific information, see In Style on page 49.

Style Treat

Any Triangle/Aries worth her salt has got her business wardrobe sorted out early on in her career – she's ambitious and needs no encouragement to spend money on quality clothes because she recognizes already how important is image in reflecting her success.

A real style treat for her would be a swimming costume, an aerobics outfit or a tracksuit – and the best running shoes that money can buy. This would be a timely reminder to her that working 12 hours a day and not doing any exercise is bad for her state of mind and body. A Triangle body shape positively needs to exercise; she is likely to put on weight if she doesn't and risks having all those beautiful clothes staying in her wardrobe because they don't fit any more. It is important to check that the colour of the garment you are buying suits you well. Take it into daylight, hold it under your chin and look at what it does to your skin, eyes and hair. If wearing it intensifies and enlivens your colouring then that is a colour that is right for your skin tones. If you look washed out or sallow, or your hair loses colour and dark rings seem to appear under your eyes, then you are getting it wrong. This sounds a lot of trouble to go to, but it is worth it for it enhances the pleasure you will get every time you wear it.

If swimming is her choice of sport, then it is best to go for a proper sports costume which are made for serious swimming and suit the Triangle shape. She should choose a solid plain colour, or if she prefers a pattern keep it straight and geometrical. She should use the same guidelines for choosing an aerobics outfit – going for a body and leggings, or cycle-type shorts in a good quality, heavyweight lycra fabric. Tracksuits are a great style for all Triangle body types – she could try a good red one, a favourite colour for fiery Aries.

Even with tracksuits, the most flattering are those made in a crisp, tightly woven fabric. When choosing running shoes, ideally she should go to a shop where the assistants know what they are talking about and can give genuine advice on the choice of shoe. Quality and price are governed by the sort of distances she will be running – the greater the distance, and the harder the surface, the greater the shock absorbency needed.

And then, Rectangle/Aries should get out there and do it. She will find that exercise gives her more energy and greater stamina – all of this rewards her many times over in terms of the time taken out to do it.

IN HEALTH

Triangle/Aries has a strong and vital constitution and any illness she suffers from is more likely to be swift and intense in duration rather than chronic. She has great powers of recovery, but her

weakest points are the head and the adrenal glands. Headaches, hay fever and sinusitis are possible problem areas – the best preventative is working some relaxation into her life. This combination thrives on stress, but too much over a prolonged period takes its toll. Exercise is one of the best ways of alleviating any anxieties and maintaining the Triangle/Aries health and vitality.

To keep healthy, it is worth looking at the whole area of diet and exercise, too. The Triangle type is likely to have been slim as a teenager, athletic, and with a big appetite. In adulthood, the demands of a family and career can mean she does less exercise, eats the wrong things at wrong times, still has an unrestrained appetite and can then start putting on weight. Triangle/Aries, however, is very organized and disciplined and when she decides to do something about her shape she works out a routine and readily sticks to it.

Triangle/Aries positively *needs* regular, energetic exercise and can get depressed if she isn't doing enough. In Bel's questionnaire, 75 per cent of the Triangle types said they recognized that they needed to exercise *and* diet if they were to lose weight – and it was energetic exercise which they favoured: a much higher proportion than the other body types (for instance, only 30 per cent of the Pear types thought exercise important). For more specific information on diet and exercise, see In Health on page 50.

TRIANGLE/ARIES CELEBRITY

It is no coincidence that there were two Queens of Hollywood in the forties and fifties, Bette Davis and Joan Crawford, who were both Triangle/Aries and both loathed each other. This combination has all the will and energy to achieve prominence in even the most difficult and competitive fields. Bette Davis was described as 'being charged with power which can find no ordinary outlet.' and her husband is quoted as saying, 'Whatever Bette had chosen to do in life she would have had to be the top or she couldn't have endured it.'

Joan Crawford too was an image of will in action and had the necessary ruthlessness to remain a Hollywood star most of her life, against some long odds. A contemporary described her: 'She is much given to good works once they have been glamourized, and would not step on the hands of another girl grasping at a straw except under exceptional circumstances. Nobody with a life such as that lived by the Queen of Hollywood today would do anything differently.'

There are many more benign Triangle/Aries stars, and one of them is the Australian model/actress, Elle Macpherson, nicknamed 'The Body'. Incredibly disciplined she does at least 500 sit-ups a day for starters. She then runs up and down four flights of stairs five times before breakfast which consists of one piece of toast 'just so I can swallow my vitamin pill'. Discipline is the word she uses most in her conversation.

More than a model now, she has become a personality and also a filmstar, co-starring in *Sirens*, but her insecurities remain. She doesn't particularly like her body, she says, she fears people think she is unintelligent and can only talk about modelling. She looks forward to having children and hopes to end up the matriarch of the family.

TRIANGLE/ARIES PROFILE

Clare is nearly 30 and admits to being very ambitious. She took time out to travel the world, ran her own financial company for a while, and is now financial controller in the London office of a top European company, 'But I intend to be running this place before two years is out.' She works extremely hard and long hours, quite prepared to do what's necessary to get what she wants. Complaint and excuses are alien to her nature. However, she does strike her colleagues as rather alienated and tough: 'I am very forthright and outspoken, but people labelled me "tough" and so I thought it better to rein myself in a bit and hide the full force of my personality. I don't want to jeopardize my promotion prospects.'

She is interested in clothes in so far as they are part of her professional life and signify her status. Clare is business-like about this. She does not like wearing make-up, for instance, but is prepared to consider it if it adds credibility and professionalism to her appearance. 'Actually my man is more interested in clothes than I am – in the pleasure of putting things together and experimenting with colour and so on.'

In her family there is a history of heart trouble and she went to her doctor recently, complaining of certain symptoms which worried her, and was given a cardiogram which reassured her. Her work is highly stressful, which she enjoys, but she realized she ought to be careful. Although she is only a few pounds overweight, her Triangle body type is one of the 'android' shapes which the scientific papers (see Introduction) show to be less protected by their female hormones and therefore more prone to heart attacks than the 'gynoid' shapes – the Pear and Hourglass body types.

She is wonderfully frank and straightforward in her manner and gives the impression of great executive energy and confidence. 'I think I'd eventually like to have children, but I know that my career will always be of paramount importance, so I would want to continue with working full-time. I'd be a better mum anyway, if I was fulfilled elsewhere, instead of frustrated at home and focusing all my energies on the poor kids.'

IN HOPE

When Triangle/Aries recognizes her strengths and isn't afraid of using them she is a happy and successful woman, with the world before her. She may not be at her best in teams, or playing happy families, nor is she likely to make love the centre of her life, but she is one of the real achievers in this world. There is an old Chinese proverb, 'The key to success isn't much good until one discovers the right lock in which to use it.' Triangle/Aries might not find that right lock first time, but her great strength is her enthusiasm to go on trying. And even if it takes ten tries and twenty years, she will find it – and turn the key.

TRIANGLE
TAURUS

(Yang+/Yin)

MOTTO:

I used to be conceited – but now I'm absolutely perfect!

IN LIFE

This woman has terrific powers of endurance. She has great, unflagging executive energy and can work until she drops. She is always right and always has the last word – often with good reason for she is rooted in reality and recognizes how things really are, stripped of romance, aspiration, and all those fuzzy emotional bits which confuse and entertain everyone else. She has great persistence and will set her sights and work solidly and undistractedly towards them. There is some danger that Taurus, being a fixed sign anyway, combined with the strength of the Triangle body type may get too blinkered and focused – and fail to recognize when it might be better to abandon a sinking ship or change tack half way. Sometimes it takes a bomb to shift her from her set path.

Triangle/Taurus likes power, although this will not be obvious to the passing show. There is nothing flashy and upfront about this kind of woman but she is really good at drawing power to herself and conserving it for when and where it's needed. Security matters very much to this personality. She recognizes how important money is, for instance, for it buys security, comfort, power. The fact it buys freedom too isn't of so much interest to her because she is a natural worker, she doesn't mind constraints, and anyway wouldn't care to lie for long in a hammock eating lotus flowers. Triangle/Taurus is quite capable of managing her own portfolio of stocks and shares and making her monetary resources grow, to provide her with more and more protection from the unpredictable world outside.

As an earth sign, Taurus is a Yin sign, receptive, synthesizing and transforming. However, in this combination she has an extreme Yang body type which adds a dynamic ambition, and the will and energy to achieve. Taurus is an innately conservative character, valuing home and hearth, the land and its traditions. She loves beauty in her surroundings and the good things of life, like food and music and art. She is drawn to nature and the countryside. Her placidity is energized by her Triangle body shape which gives her the drive not just to enjoy, but to conserve, build and achieve. Her natural tenacity is given bulldog jaws: Triangle/Taurus finds it almost impossible to give anything up.

This combination is invincible in anything to do with the material world, with things that can be held and seen and measured. She has all the right ideas about how to develop a business or reclaim some land or turn a £1,000 investment into a two comma figure. But she lacks imagination and inspiration and can be rather dogged and literal in her interpretation of things. She is honest and loyal to a fault but misreads people's motives because she is so lacking in subtlety and guile herself. A clever, intuitive operator can run rings round her, although there will be few who can outlast her in powerful resistance during any stand-off.

Triangle/Taurus is also blind to the feelings of others. She can be oblivious to what her actions mean to the personal lives of those who work for her or her company. She thinks that her values and priorities are shared by everyone, and an alternative approach to life, which may not value security, home and status, leaves her bemused. She is in no way an entrepreneur, flair and risk-taking is better left to the Rectangle/ and Triangle/Aries who thrives on her adrenalin rush.

Triangle/Taurus is as rooted as a tree and as obstinate as a bull, and no amount of goading or enthusiasm will get her to change her mind if it's already made up. Reliable, trustworthy, matter-of-fact, conscientious and often almost omniscient, this confidence and fixity is one of her great strengths – and like all strengths it has a weakness too. She can miss so much else in life; the fun, fantasy and ecstatic love, a sense of adventure, fascination with the unknown – many things which the other combinations would love to share with her. But Triangle/Taurus likes her life simple and black and white. The fuzzy edges worry her, the grey bits don't improve the picture.

This simplistic view of life has its dark side. Triangle/Taurus needs to guard against a dogmatism that runs to fanaticism. It is expressed as an intolerance of the viewpoints of others, an inability to accept that there are a whole range of truths and different ways of living, which are just as valid as her own. She does believe that her way is the right way. This gives her admirable determination and an ability to perservere beyond the endurance of virtually everyone else. It gives her staying power and the potential for terrific success. But it can mean she crushes a few more sensitive souls in the process – although she may consider that a price worth paying. After all, she would point out rationally that no one ever achieved anything great in the real world by being over-concerned about the feeling or welfare of others.

IN WORK

The steady power and application that Triangle/Taurus can bring to any job means she is made for success. She is not going to impress everyone immediately with her razzle-dazzle smile and her effervescent energy, she is not going to make wild promises she will never keep. But she will move into a new organization with efficiency and good sense. She'll immediately know where the structural weaknesses are, she will have sussed out the weak links in the management chain and, most importantly, she will also have seen where her route to the top lies. Because, make no mistake, Triangle/Taurus may be quiet and deliberate in her actions but she definitely knows what's what and where she's going – and set-backs only ever make her determined never to give up.

The business world is a natural place for Triangle/Taurus to make her mark. She is good at dealing with facts and figures and is a hard and conscientious worker. Her division in any company will be run with far greater efficiency and productivity than the average, and she will expect from the rest of the staff the same sort of loyalty and dedication which she puts in. Work is an important and serious part of life and she cannot understand those who consider it either just a necessary evil, or something that requires the minimum effort you can get away with. The comradeship on the shop or office floor is something else she does not care to share. She is happier working on her projects at her own pace, not as part of a team. Best of all she likes being in charge. However, her perfectionism can make her an exacting boss.

Triangle/Taurus can also excel in the financial world. Anything from working in a bank to being the financial director of one of the top FOOTSIE companies. She has a healthy respect for money and likes conserving it and making it grow. This is one of the ways her creative conservatism is expressed. She hates to see any resources wasted and money is perhaps the most flexible and

attractive of all the resources available to her. She will be a stickler for the accounting of every expenditure. Cher is a Triangle/Taurus and she has been very careful to conserve the vast fortune she has earned, and actually increase it over the years through judicious management and thriftiness.

There'll be no slipping creative expenses slips past this Triangle/Taurus's nose. But, with her interest in money and her ability to get the good jobs and great salaries, she is likely to manage to accrue quite a tidy little sum for herself. Not that she is going to blow it on a lipstick-pink Porsche, but she will want a reliable car and a comfortable house – and a nice security blanket in the bank.

Taurus is traditionally blessed with the most beautiful voice. This can be evident in either her singing or speaking voice, and she can be tempted to make the stage her a career. A Triangle/Taurus has all the necessary drive to make a success of this most precarious of professions. She will not lack confidence or ambition, and the inevitable disappointments and set-backs only make her more determined to succeed. Triangle/Taurus is most unlikely to be just a four-day-wonder. She is the type who may start slowly then build her reputation and manage to keep her show on the road long after others have put the old thing up on blocks and pensioned off the horses.

There is a love of beauty and glamour in some Taureans which can make Triangle/Taurus look to the more glitzy areas of artistic work, to dress designing, for instance, and art collecting and dealing. Always appreciating things of beauty which can be seen or touched, rather than the nebulous ones of fantasy and the imagination, she can turn her sensual appreciation to financial advantage in the fields of art dealing. Again, she would be wonderfully business-like, even in an arty profession, and there would be no dangerous buying on whim or for sentimental reasons. Everything has to have a sound financial basis. This is what makes her such a success. (A list of the richest people in Britain has more Taureans than any other sign.)

There is another type of Taurus who is back-to-nature and down-to-earth. When this character is allied to the Triangle body type it produces an immensely strong, hard-working farmer or forester or environmentalist who will work alongside the men, doing whatever hard physical labour is necessary. She can express her indomitable nature so well when she's really up against the elements – or circumstances. Enduring the exhaustion and hardships of this sort of life and coming through to something better provides a real sense of achievement for her. At home, her belief in the natural way of life can be translated literally into feeding the family only on whole foods, for instance – no sugar or processed food, no imported foods out of season, no caffeine, nicotine – and certainly no television. She can turn her own austere side, her lack of tolerance for the points of view of others, and her sense of always being right, into a minor domestic tyranny. But it's all for everyone's good, of course. Whatever she chooses to do, she causes ripples of amazement at what she thinks she can get away with, and admiration at what she does.

Ideal Fantasy Job

Governor of the Bank of England. There has never been a woman governor and Triangle/Taurus is the one to make a new precedent. She has all the qualities of character to make an excellent one. Honest, trustworthy, ambitious, brilliant at conserving reputations, traditions and money. She is not a reformer, values the status quo and enjoys hierarchies, as long as she is somewhere near the top. Here she would be the boss, and that would be the crowning achievement to all those decades of dedicated work.

IN LOVE

Taurus is known as the sign with the earthiest sexuality. Some Triangle types don't really indulge in sex much for its own sake – as a release from tension, yes, or as part of being the good wife or lover, but they are generally not relaxed enough to be spontaneously sensual and erotic. In this combination, the sexual energies may be slightly at odds, with sometimes the Taurus in ascendancy, making her amorous and sybaritic, and other times the Triangle type being far too busy to take time out for such pleasure – unless it's good for her work! Anyway, work will always be central on Triangle/Taurus's agenda and when love comes along it may be shifted slightly to one side, but not for long.

The man who may manage that temporary shift will be a good Yin man, much more laid back and less ambitious than his Triangle/Taurus woman. She doesn't want to have to be competitive with him, and is happy to have the more high-powered job. He is happy to have a tough woman who pushes the outside world about a bit and comes home to him for a little love and tender care. She's good at focusing her energies, usually on work, and he's good at taking everyone's interests into account, sympathizing with the children and possibly enjoying the cooking and entertaining.

Triangle/Taurus may feel when she has children that she wants to stay at home and look after them. In Taurus there is a home-loving Yin personality who is patient with small children and animals. But the extreme Yang body type gives her a much greater ambition, a need to have a larger stage than the four walls of her home, a bigger audience than two sweet children. Those who do stay home, put all their drive and perfectionism into their children's upbringing – and it can be rather overwhelming for them and frustrating for her. 'Everything I do I want to do perfectly' is a sentiment that comes up time and again in the questionnaires from Triangle types.

There is something very emotionally self-contained about Triangle/Taurus. She does not need to have a close relationship in order to function. This means she is never completely blown off course by a love affair arriving in her life, or coming to an end. She never gives herself up to love completely. And it can be hard to make really close friends. Intimacy, and talking about feelings does not come easily to Triangle/Taurus. She has a competitiveness too which can intrude in her relationships with women who are as successful as she is, but those friends she does have know how loyal and consistent she is and that, however busy she is, she will always be there in any crisis.

Ideal Fantasy Lover

Despite his posturing as a Rambo-esque tough guy, despite the body-building and monosyllabic grunts, Sylvester Stallone is a soft-hearted, Yin kind of guy who goes for the extreme Yang kind of woman. His current girlfriend, Jennifer Flavin, said he had always been a caring New Man type but had been so hurt by his marriage to Brigitte Nielsen (another Yang+ Triangle type) that he had retreated into a self-protective shell. As a Cancerian anyway, Stallone tends to hide his sensitive inner self inside the tough old crab's shell and all his butch-boy films have been an attempt to prove that he's not what he really is. Triangle/Taurus would appreciate this kind, gentle side (she'd appreciate the multi-millions too and show him the best investments for his loot) and her solid, confident reliability would encourage him to come out of his shell and be more himself.

IN STYLE

Taureans like luxury and comfort and their clothes will reflect this. Triangle types recognize how important clothes are in one's whole presentation, how much it matters to be attractive and dressed appropriately for the work one does. She will quote the statistics which say that when one meets someone for the first time it is how we look which is overwhelmingly important in determining how that person rates us. For that first crucial minute we are judged almost entirely on appearance: our body language and the way we are dressed.

So Triangle/Taurus will buy herself good-looking, good quality clothes which are comfortable to wear. She has a soft spot for silk and cashmere, because they feel so good, and Taureans are a tactile bunch of people. But she tends to be rather conservative and could be encouraged to step out of character a little with a brightly coloured blouse, under her suit, or some striking designer jewellery.

The style of clothes that really flatter Triangle/Taurus are determined by her body type. The Triangle shape has broader shoulders than hips and more of a marked waist than the Rectangle. She falls into two basic types, the small boned, boyish figure like Mia Farrow who probably rarely, if ever, puts on weight and the more muscular, athletic looking type, like Princess Stephanie of Monaco, Jamie Lee Curtis and Anjelica Huston, who can get heavy in the upper torso area, but keeps her inverted triangle shape with straight hips and lean lower legs. When thin, this shape is the classic fashion model shape with coat-hanger shoulders, next-to-nothing-hips and long lean legs.

Some women with this body type try to counteract their broad-shouldered look by wearing flimsy, ultra-feminine clothes – think of Diane Keaton (a Triangle/Aquarius) in *Annie Hall*. Those soft, drifty clothes on the angular Diane make her look a bit like Little Orphan Annie, rather gawky and fey. This suited the character very well in the film, but for Triangle/Taurus, wanting to be taken seriously in the real world, it can be a counter-productive look. Her femininity is best expressed with clothes that have simple geometric lines, certainly angled to the waist if she likes, but it's better to avoid soft fabrics, gathers and bows. For more specific information, see In Style on page 49.

Style Treat

You can't go far wrong with a beautiful suit. Taureans like comfortable and practical clothes and prefer not to spend too much money on them – unless there is a compelling reason to do so. A really good reason, which Triangle/Taurus will appreciate, is that a good quality suit makes her look and feel entirely credible. In terms of getting value for money, the higher the price often the better the quality – and the more wear there is to be got

from the garment before it starts to look tired. Really good quality fabrics don't crease as much, keep their finish and maintain the structure of the garment too – no sagging and bagging.

The secret of a suit's long life, however, isn't just to do with quality, the colour and style is important too. The greatest versatility comes from a suit in a neutral colour so that it goes with a variety of different coloured blouses, tops and accessories. The best colours are black, navy, taupe, stone, pewter, charcoal, beige, olive green. A suit in one of these colours is less of a statement than, say, a red suit which, however gorgeous, is more of an occasional suit and not one to wear continually. Separating the skirt and jacket and wearing them with different garments also adds to its versatility. It is important to check that the colour of the garment you are buying suits you well. Take it into daylight, hold it under your chin and look at what it does to your skin, eyes and hair. If wearing it intensifies and enlivens your colouring then that is a colour that is right for your skin tones. If you look washed out or sallow, or your hair loses colour and dark rings seem to appear under your eyes, then you are getting it wrong. This sounds a lot of trouble to go to, but it is worth it for it enhances the pleasure you will get every time you wear it. The line of the skirt and jacket is just as important, as outlined above.

Skirts can be tricky for this body shape. Straight skirts are best, but care should be taken that seams again are straight and not curved – particularly when softer, tulip skirts and wraparounds are in fashion. If necessary buy a straightish skirt and have the seams altered to straighten up the line.

IN HEALTH

Overwork is the only real problem for Triangle/Taurus. She can get so focused on work that she doesn't allow any time for sport or exercise (which she needs). Basically, she has a terrifically strong constitution which rarely lets her down, but if she does exhaust herself, it will take a long time for her to build back her legendary stamina. So it is worthwhile for Triangle/Taurus to make some time for relaxation and pleasure.

To keep healthy, it is worth looking at the whole area of diet and exercise, too. The Triangle type is likely to have been slim as a teenager, athletic, and with a big appetite. In adulthood, the demands of a family and career can mean she does less exercise, eats the wrong things at wrong times, still has an unrestrained appetite and can then start putting on weight. Triangle/Taurus, however, is very organized and disciplined and when she decides to do something about her shape she works out a routine and readily sticks to it.

Triangle/Taurus positively *needs* regular, energetic exercise and can get depressed if she isn't doing enough. In Bel's questionnaire, 75 per cent of the Triangle types said they recognized that they needed to exercise *and* diet if they were to lose weight – and it was energetic exercise which they favoured: a much higher proportion than the other body types (for instance, only 30 per cent of the Pear types thought exercise important). For more specific information on diet and exercise, see In Health on page 50.

TRIANGLE/TAURUS CELEBRITY

Cher is a textbook case Triangle/Taurus in full flight. She has all the terrific perserverance, endurance and belief in self which gets her every drop of stardom and success she could ever have wanted. Starting life as a backing singer, then the wife of Sonny Bono with their hit single 'I got You Babe', she didn't really register as an actress until she was 36 when she was in a Broadway play *Come Back to the Five and Dime, Jimmy Dean, Jimmy Dean* and then chosen to play her part in Robert Altman's screen version.

She quickly submitted herself to extensive cosmetic surgery to produce a flawless but less interesting version of herself, but she was always prepared to do whatever seemed to be necessary to get where she wanted. She could turn in some powerful performances (in *Mask*, *Moonstruck* and *Suspect*) which relied less on her physical beauty than on her force of character. But this need for power made her insist on having control over everything in the film *Mermaids*, from wardrobe, to co-stars, to director. This much-hyped film promptly belly-flopped, her least memorable film to date.

The trauma of working on it left Cher with a fatigue syndrome – one of the last resorts for a body who has been pushed too far, a common problem for Triangle/Taurus. But her belief in herself carries her on. One of her friends says 'She is so intricate and precise. Her mind never stops. Cher's a perfectionist. She never stops re-creating herself.' Never known for much awareness of self or others, much-dated Cher once stated, 'I could write what I know about men on the head of a pin – and still have room for the Yellow Pages'.

She shows the true professionalism and focused ambition of a typical Triangle/Taurus when, asked to explain what it's like to be her, she says she's too busy *being* Cher, it's difficult sometimes 'But it's a good job'!

TRIANGLE/TAURUS PROFILE

Lisa is 29 and has three children who she looks after full-time at home. 'I'm a perfectionist – the house has to be just how I want it. I feel restricted by the children, but accept it won't last for ever. I do a lot with the children – I want them all to do well. When the children are in school I want to work part-time, but I also plan to go to night school to get an education – my husband doesn't think I'm very bright but one day I'll prove him wrong. I'm quite competitive with him, perhaps because we're both perfectionists.'

Lisa had worked before she had children, as a domestic in a retirement home. Her potential was recognized and she was offered a job working with a team of auxiliary nurses, 'But I didn't want to be part of a team, I prefer being independent, so I turned down the job and continued with the cleaning one.'

While she was single she felt equal to any man and confident about her work and how to handle her relationships: 'I could be quite ruthless – people who knew me thought I didn't have any feelings because when I'd had enough of a bloke that was it, I'd pack his bags and he'd have to go. I had one long-term on-off relationship and friends asked this man "Why do you put up with her, the way she treats you?" He was really soft and I walked all over him.'

Then when Lisa was 24 she decided that she would like to have a baby, 'But I didn't see the father as part of the scheme. He had visions of us all being a happy family and he actively being a dad. But I didn't want that so I made his life hell until he moved out. He had begged me to let my daughter have his name and I had relented but, within a week of his going, I had her name changed to mine. He was very upset, but we are good friends now.'

She has since married, had her next two children, and has really helped her husband gain confidence. With her encouragement, he has got himself a good job. For the time being, her energies and ambitions are focused on him, the children and the home but she does think about the future. 'I will have a career – perhaps helping my husband with his own business. At the moment I only think in terms of, when the children start school . . . when we have a nicer house . . . getting the garden nice – I just want to make my own little world better for the time being.'

IN HOPE

Triangle/Taurus can be so busy building her life or career, working away with her head down, concentrating on the task in hand, that she risks not noticing the small movements of the human heart. It is her own feelings that she ignores as much as those of others. And it might be worth becoming a litle more aware of this other side of life where things are not as cut and dried as she might hope. Allowing feelings more credit, she will then fertilize what can seem an otherwise rather arid approach to life, relationships and the universe.

Bertrand Russell, the great philosopher and mathematician, and himself a Taurus, wrote in his maturity, 'We know too much and feel too little. At least we feel too little of those creative emotions from which a good life springs.' Triangle/Taurus can attempt to redress the balance a little.

TRIANGLE
GEMINI

(Yang+/Yang)

MOTTO:
Time and tide waits for no woman

IN LIFE

This woman is an arch communicator, endlessly curious and fascinated by ideas. She lives in the present, processing ideas at a great rate, gleaning new information, comparing it with old, moving on all the time to the new enthusiasm, the next novel experience, and wanting above all to communicate it to others. Triangle/Gemini is more focused than the other body type Geminis, more ambitious, more likely to succeed. Gemini has too often been accused of being superficial and butterfly-brained, but it is more her appreciation of variety and the broad sweep of information which leads her to flit from idea to idea rather than seek knowledge in depth.

Triangle/Gemini is interested in people, but from a distance, as a species worth investigation. She is able to talk to anyone for a short while, and is good at finding out interesting snippets of fact about almost everyone she comes up against. With her way with words and her light touch, she can appear flirtatious, although it seldom means anything more than that she enjoys the playful use of words, and experiments in seeing just how many people she can charm at one time. Ideas are her currency not emotions, unless these emotions are expressed in words and then there is all the fun of analysis and comparison, with little emotional involvement. Heavy-duty passion leaves Triangle/Gemini distinctly uneasy and looking wild-eyed for the door.

The feeling side of life is a bit of a mystery to her. She is an air sign, cool, cerebral and detached, and allied to a Yang+ body type which is itself rather self-centred so that Triangle/Gemini can seem rather coldly detached from her own emotions and the affections and suffering of others. Like all powerful characteristics, this is both her strength and her weakness. She can operate most efficiently in difficult situations, for instance, reporting brilliantly on what is happening at the front in a war zone, neither devastated nor distracted by the suffering of the individuals caught up in the holocaust. She can do what has to be done cleanly and effectively, without the confusion of feeling and concern for others.

But it also means that she is disconnected at times from the very springs which make us human. She can feel isolated and alienated from the warm intimacy of passionate relationships, shut out, she fears, from the acceptance of an unconditional love which encompasses everything. Triangle/Gemini is always standing back, making notes, analysing, her mind always absolutely in gear, her heart never quite engaged. This combination wishes she could explain and understand the emotions in the same systematic way as she can the process of a logical argument or the recipe of a soufflé. Most times she does not know what she feels about things or people: she knows what she thinks, but her feelings can be obscure to her, and therefore something frightening that she tries to ignore, denigrate or explain away.

It is sometimes quite hard for Triangle/Gemini to grow up, in the sense of taking responsibility, understanding her own motives better and making commitments to people and work. She can remain eternally childlike, with all the good and bad characteristics that implies. Ever enthusiastic and curious, she is never dull. There is always something interesting for her to talk about and she loves sharing her latest findings or thoughts; she is a great guest and keeps the conversation flowing and the men energized by her flirting. But, she is also the little girl who flits and flirts and makes out she needs someone to watch over her, never properly acknowledging her own power and ambition. Triangle/Gemini can masquerade as the sweet little thing when really she has a cool toughness which can be ruthless, quite disregarding the feelings or interests of others.

She has a fidgety side which is most noticeable when she loses interest or hasn't got enough to do. Boredom is one of her bugbears and it can cause trouble for her in jobs as well as relationships. The telephone is her favourite tool of communication, and, as a relief from the sudden tediousness of life, she is capable of ringing up all her friends in succession, for an enlivening gossip that keeps the dreaded ennui at bay.

IN WORK

Triangle/Gemini is driven by the need for knowledge, variety, stimulation and space to breathe. She can be the most cultured woman, with wide interests and an admirable ability to talk, or write, amusingly and informatively on virtually anything. Being a Triangle body type she is likely to want to exercise this talent on a larger stage or screen, she has the energy and ambition to be successful, even famous, and she will not balk at the sacrifices of her personal life that that may involve.

The most obvious place for Triangle/Gemini to express love of communicating information has to be in the media. Her wide interests and lively manner would be just the thing for a journalist or reporter on a newspaper, radio or television. She is particularly good at bright, clever pieces that don't go into too much detail and depth. With her Yang+ body type she has enough energy and courage to report from the front lines in difficult and dangerous situations. She can be rational and disinterested, her loyalty being to the facts of the situation and the brief of her job.

Triangle/Gemini is less flippertygibbet than many Geminis and she will be more likely to stick at a job and work her way into a position of power and influence. At her best in charge of her own projects, rather than having to be a member of a team who closely work together, sharing responsibility and information, she is very likely to start her own business. Of terrific advantage to her in any entrepreneurial ventures is the fact that she is an extremely articulate and persuasive talker and could probably persuade her bank manager to lend her money to raise the Titanic, if she should so wish. She has not got the dogged determination and sheer power of a Triangle/Taurus or /Capricorn, for instance, but she has flair and focus and should make a success of anything she undertakes, within her own areas of interest and expertise.

Teaching in all its guises is another area where Triangle/Gemini can excel. She is gifted at imparting her enthusiasm to her students, although she is not so talented when it comes to giving them pastoral advice. She is more likely to want to be in charge, and so might be drawn to the administrative areas of university or school life. She might even run a language or tutorial college.

Similarly, advertising is a profesion where Triangle/Gemini would feel very much at home. Most likely to thrive on the copywriting or account executive side, she would find the variety of the work, the demand for facility with language and novel ideas, and an ability to explain products and advertising campaigns with great plausibility, all made the most of her talents. She would never be bored and would have the potential to go far, fast. Triangle/Gemini can put the same talents to excellent use in marketing and public relations where a lively and light touch with the public is a great asset. Charming, light-hearted, entertaining, she can make anything sound a must.

Acting also appeals to Geminis who are so used to living with their own multiple personalities that they are relieved sometimes to have to pretend to be someone entirely different – and sometimes more substantial than they themselves feel. Triangle body types have the focus and emotional toughness to make their way in this most ruthless of professions.

Ideal Fantasy Job

The editor of a daily newspaper is a job that many Triangle/Geminis would die for. She enjoys reading intelligent, well-informed editorial; light-hearted, celebrity-centred features – a good gossip column – and she will be excellent at providing the right leadership for a newspaper providing this combination of information and entertainment.

Triangle/Gemini will be great at coming up with ideas, enthusing her staff, judging the popular taste of her readers. She will have all the clarity of thought to see through reforms and won't be swayed by sentimental appeals to her emotions. She's tough but she rules with a light hand and some humour. She doesn't want her colleagues' love – but she would certainly get their respect.

IN LOVE

Triangle/Gemini finds the pursuit more fun and much more entertaining than the consummation, and certainly much more fun than cosy married life. Love is not number one on her agenda. In fact, passionate, soul-matey, hand-in-glove sort of love probably heads her list of things to avoid. She loves space and distance, and that is particularly true in her emotional life. She is not happy if she feels tied down by commitments or responsibility.

Intellectual companionship, someone to go to parties with (although not to stay with once she's there), or someone to talk through new ideas or flirt with is more her style. Triangle/Gemini does not like it when the talk stops and the feeling starts. She is puzzled and embarrassed by her own emotions when they arise, and doesn't really know how to deal with the emotions of others. Sympathetic imagination is not one of her talents and she has

little access to anyone else's feelings, and certainly is quite in the dark about any experiences which she has not been through herself.

It will take her a long time to settle down with one person, and she may never be quite committed to monogamy for life. She is so variable – life is so various and full of novelty and opportunity. Being emotionally detached, she is not very aware that there are other more feeling-orientated people who do make commitments and who are really hurt by love being treated as if it is no more profound than a contractual arrangement which can be cancelled when it is no longer cost effective, or if something more up-to-the minute comes along.

Triangle/Gemini will choose a Yin man, who offers to the relationship the nurturing, emotional side which she finds so difficult to express herself. More the Jason Donovans and Daniel Day-Lewises of this world than the Sean Connerys and Mickey Rourkes. She is not likely to take to motherhood and babies with enormous alacrity. Much better with children once they can communicate properly, Triangle/Gemini finds the continual need for care, unselfish love and tactile, instinctual, non-verbal communication so necessary with small babies almost impossible to administer on a full-time basis.

If she decides to have children, she can find the very physicality of childbirth and the messiness of dealing with small children very hard to bear. Here is a woman who will probably feel much better back at work, leaving a full-time nanny, or her caring man, to do the 24-hour nurturing back home. Triangle/Gemini will come into her own once her children have reached the age of reason. Then she will enjoy talking to them, find them delightful companions with their curiosity and fresh view of life. Their education will also be of particular interest and importance to her. She means them to do well.

The house may not be a comfortable doss for all the teens in the neighbourhood, with mum producing mounds of pasta from a steaming kitchen, but there will be space and airiness and lots of books and a generally enlightened regime. Triangle/Gemini mum might be considered by her teenage children to be rather neurotic and a stickler for tidiness and rules, but they will have learnt young that they can get round her by putting forward an articulate argument for why they think they should be allowed to stay out late/leave their motorcycle bits all over the bedroom carpet/have their girlfriend stayover/not go on the annual family holiday. She may not be the most sympathetic of mothers, she may not be the most passionate or loyal, but she is wonderfully reasonable and incapable of emotional blackmail and heavy guilt-trips. She will tell it like it is, coolly, matter-of-factly.

Triangle/Gemini has loads of acquaintances, enjoys the company of men, but is not one to have intimate women friends with whom she can sit and rap for hours on the secrets of the heart. She would rather be talking about work, or the latest film/theatre/book she's seen or read. Competitive, even in her social and domestic life, she finds it hard to let her hair down and just slouch around having a relaxing time. She always has to be doing something, or at least thinking something out.

Many Triangle/Gemini women can give the impression of being highly-strung and rather emotionally repressed. All this, and her general restlessness and lack of serenity are part of her fear of her inner self, whose feelings she is so disturbed by and unfamiliar with. She would rather skate hectically over the surface brightness of life and hope that by ignoring her emotions they might eventually go away.

Ideal Fantasy Lover

Michael Bolton. Despite the raunchy, hardman reputation of so many men in his profession, the soul superstar is a caring, fatherly type of man who, although divorced, has two of his teenage daughters living with him and is very concerned for their happiness and welfare. He worries about being away from them and rushes back from venues, 'Not having as much time to just relax with the kids is pretty brutal sometimes'. But he extends this paternal side of his character to the other musicians on the road with him, 'I care about their financial well-being, their personal well-being and their personal lives.'

He would be a man to give Triangle/Gemini all the space she needs, but he would add spice and variety, and the feeling Yin side which so complements the self-motivated, driven characteristics of her extreme Yang combination.

IN STYLE

Triangle/Gemini isn't really interested in clothes. She knows that they are an important uniform for what she wants to do in life, good quality clothes appropriate to her job matter. Personally, she is happier in comfortable, casual clothes which don't restrict her fast-moving lifestyle. She has so many moods that she has no one way of dressing by which her friends can identify her. She is not likely to go for great dramatic statements or romantic frocks, but will be quirky and amusing in her choices

of combinations of clothes. And everything has to be chosen quickly.

Triangle/Gemini gets no particular pleasure from shopping. Lingering over the glory of fabric or cut of various garments, experimenting with the best way to wear certain outfits, all bore her. She wants what is necessary to keep warm, look good and dress appropriately for whatever job she does, especially as she has no wish to have to think about her clothes again once she has put them on. Trouble-free and practical and individual is all she asks from her wardrobe.

The style of clothes that really flatter Triangle/Gemini are determined by her body type. The Triangle shape has broader shoulders than hips and more of a marked waist than the Rectangle. She falls into two basic types, the small boned, boyish figure like Mia Farrow who probably rarely, if ever, puts on weight and the more muscular, athletic looking type, like Princess Stephanie of Monaco, Jamie Lee Curtis and Anjelica Huston, who can get heavy in the upper torso area, but keeps her inverted triangle shape with straight hips and lean lower legs. When thin, this shape is the classic fashion model shape with coat-hanger shoulders, next-to-nothing-hips and long lean legs.

Some women with this body type try to counteract their broad-shouldered look by wearing flimsy, ultra-feminine clothes – think of Diane Keaton (a Triangle/Aquarius) in *Annie Hall*. Those soft, drifty clothes on the angular Diane make her look a bit like Little Orphan Annie, rather gawky and fey. This suited the character very well in the film, but for Triangle/Gemini, wanting to be taken seriously in the real world, it can be a counter-productive look. Her femininity is best expressed with clothes that have simple geometric lines, certainly angled to the waist if she likes, but it's better to avoid soft fabrics, gathers and bows. For more specific information, see In Style on page 49.

Style Treat

Choice of underwear is not easy for the Triangle-type figure. However much Triangle/Gemini might dream of ultra-feminine, lacy or frilly little numbers, these are not really flattering enough for her. Sporty underwear looks much better on the Triangle type, but that doesn't mean it can't be sexy. Sexy for Triangle/Gemini means sporty, high-cut knickers, or short boxers, or triangular bikinis. The point is to keep the same angularity, which is so much more flattering a line in clothes for this body type.

She can buy lacy garments but it has to be lace which is not flimsy or frilly. Satin actually looks better on her, but for real flattery it is worth her choosing garments which have angular, rather than curvy, necklines and leg-lines.

A pretty underwired satin bra will give good support to the Triangle/Gemini figure which can be heavy in the bust. Another alternative is the crossed-back sporty bra. A satin all-in-one can be very flattering, but she should make sure again that any lace inserts are angular and made of substantial, quality lace. If she really wants to spoil herself, Triangle/Gemini should look at Calvin Klein – that label does a mean line in underwear ideal for this sporty shape.

IN HEALTH

Stress and fatigue are the main problem areas for Triangle/Gemini. This is a nervous, highly strung star sign allied to a driven, ambitious, hard-working body type, which also adds the extra stress of being a perfectionist. She has to be best at everything she does and so puts herself under more strain than most.

The nervous system and lungs are both traditionally ruled by Gemini and so asthma and breathing sensitivities in general are something to beware of, especially as these ailments are significantly affected by the emotions and tension generally. Triangle/Gemini has a dislike of self-analysis and will always prefer to rush on to the next relationship/project/idea rather than look beneath the surface at what is really going on and causing upset and failure in her life. A little more time off from the rush of work and life, perhaps some meditation, and an occasional foray into the emotional side of her personality might help keep her healthy and happier.

To keep healthy, it is worth looking at the whole area of diet and exercise, too. The Triangle type is likely to have been slim as a teenager, athletic, and with a big appetite. In adulthood, the demands of a family and career can mean she does less exercise, eats the wrong things at wrong times, still has an unrestrained appetite and can then start putting on weight. Triangle/Gemini, however, is very organized and disciplined and when she decides to do something about her shape she works out a routine and readily sticks to it.

Triangle/Gemini positively *needs* regular, energetic exercise and can get depressed if she isn't doing enough. In Bel's questionnaire, 75 per cent of the Triangle types said they recognized that they needed to exercise *and* diet if they were to lose weight – and it was energetic exercise which they favoured: a much higher proportion than the other body types (for instance, only 30 per cent

of the Pear types thought exercise important). For more specific information on diet and exercise, see In Health on page 50.

TRIANGLE/GEMINI CELEBRITY

Annette Bening, Mrs Warren Beatty, is the one woman who could reel in this fabled Lothario. In fact, her own mega-fame rests almost solely on her success in bringing to an end his 54 years of famous and frenetic batchelorhood. Having achieved some critical accalim in films like *Postcards from the Edge* and *The Grifters*, Annette met Warren Beatty when she was cast in his film *Bugsy*. She then became pregnant by him and it was this which catapulted her into big-time gossip and Hollywood celebrity status.

This woman knows precisely what she is doing, and is unlikely to let anything like a pregnancy happen to her by chance. Certainly, Warren Beatty seemed at last to be ready for fatherhood and domesticity and, prompted by the pregnancy, decided to hang up his gun – and proposed. Annette, more than 20 years his junior, may not be so keen to stay just sweet Mrs Beatty for long, however. Her career matters just as much and although her pregnancy meant giving up the part of Catwoman in *Batman* 2 to Michelle Pfeiffer she is determined to be back and making up for lost time.

TRIANGLE/GEMINI PROFILE

'I've always wanted to be a writer, ever since I was little and got carried away by Enid Blyton's Famous Five adventures. It struck me as the perfect thing – to be able to make up your own friends and adventures and bring them alive in the pages of a book. I always preferred fictional friends anyway. They were easier to handle, and make do what you wanted.' Maysie is a writer living in London who turns her hand to journalism, playwriting, novels: whatever she can earn a living from. 'Money isn't my main motivation, the interest of the job matters most I suppose, and also that I can work alone, not under the rules or timetable of anyone else.'

Maysie is dedicated to her work and will set herself deadlines and work towards them with a focus which her other writer acquaintances find admirable. 'I feel pursued by time. I want to be successful, and I reckon that will only happen if I put in the effort required. I don't waste time on other things which don't help me get better and move towards my goal. For instance, I will read other novels to see if I can pick up any tricks of the trade, I go to the theatre to keep up with the new plays. I do love variety, but I'm not your typical Gemini, flitting, butterfly-like from flower to flower. I have much more single-mindedness than that – perhaps I get it from my body shape as you suggest.'

She is in her late thirties and has never married, or even had a live-in lover. She prefers her own company and the sense of privacy which having her flat to herself gives her. 'I sometimes think it would be nice to have someone at home, cooking me a meal, wanting to hear about my day – particularly when things haven't gone well. I'd like a sympathetic ear sometimes. But I think personal relationships are very difficult, and the older I get, the more difficult they seem. I think I like things too much my way. I'm a bit of a perfectionist and also not very good with having someone in my space for long. I'm probably very difficult to live with. I'm so intolerant, and easily thrown when things go wrong.'

Children have never fitted into her life's plan and she says she is perfectly happy to accept that she will never have them now. 'There's some relief when you realize that either you are too old, or that circumstances make it an impossibility. By making this decision, instead of always having a bit of my mind wondering whether it was something I should do, I have felt all this creative energy flow back into my hands. It's very exciting. I only have myself now to think about, and my work is top priority and so I can focus on that totally. I really feel nothing now can stop me. I shall be famous – perhaps even rich – and happy I hope!'

IN HOPE

Triangle/Gemini can take some time to really come into her own. She is a woman with great strength of mind and a mission to use it, preferably on a public stage, out in the world. Her emotions are a less well-developed part of her character and she can get involved in complicated relationships where she feels fearfully at sea when the temperature starts to rise and feelings start to flow. Her instinct is to try and pretend nothing is happening or to cut loose and run.

'These boots were made for walking/And that's just what they'll do/One of these days these boots are gonna walk away from you' was the song which made Nancy Sinatra (a Triangle/Gemini) famous and that is precisely the sort of reaction which other Triangle/Geminis have when the going gets tough – and emotional. But rather than walk, Triangle/Gemini might try staying,

and discovering something important about herself. Facing up to these unfamiliar, irrational sides of human nature make her a more profound and interesting person in the process, a stronger one too. After all, no one can create experience in their minds, it's something which has to be entered into and gone through.

TRIANGLE
CANCER

(Yang+/Yin+)

MOTTO:

A bird in the hand is worth two in the bush

IN LIFE

Here is one of the most difficult combinations of opposites for any woman to integrate into one personality. Cancer represents the great maternal principle being receptive, intuitive, nurturing, retentive. And this extreme Yin+ is overlaid on the most masculine body type with its powerful character traits of self-centredness, interest in impressing that self on the outside world and with the necessary focused ambition to achieve it. How Triangle/Cancer manifests this is through a powerful mothering of people, jobs, the world.

Esther Rantzen is a Triangle/Cancer who came late to personal motherhood (many Triangle types do) and then took on the causes of children, and the world of the family in general, but in a detached, dynamic, effective but impersonal way. Triangle/Cancer is the archetypal Jewish Momma, she has to be in control, she has to know everything that's going on – and *always* knows best. The creative side of this is her bringing to birth of ideas and projects, and the personalities and talents of others.

Cancer is a water sign and therefore emotional, subtle, and highly sensitive. In this combination she gains a great deal of power and ambition and her highly developed intuition can make her able to get others to do what she wants at work and at home. She has the ability to be an awesome wheeler-dealer on the highest levels, to set her sights and then in the most secretive and oblique way to achieve them.

Her sensitivity is well-hidden inside that crab-like shell, but with a Triangle body shape it is given more shell than most, is

more self-protective and less concerned with others than the Cancerian with the Yin body types. She might expose her powerful feelings, and surprise everybody with this unaccustomed expression, and then she'll scuttle back into her protective shell, and be quite unknowable, unreachable and apparently invulnerable. Even surrounded by friends, family and acquaintances, there can be something quite mysterious and isolated about Triangle/Cancer, a feeling that her real self and most of her feelings are hidden from everyone, even those closest to her.

Triangle/Cancer needs to be needed. She wants to be the indispensible kingpin at work, the centre of the family at home. And she has the capacity to be both these things. She is terrifically hard-working, astute, never lets anything pass her by, and knows everything that's going on. She can take these qualities too far and be very bad at delegating (only she knows how to do anything properly) and will interfere unapologetically in other people's business. She can also be an arch emotional blackmailer, although it will be done so subtly that most simpler souls won't realize what magic it was that made them decide that they would volunteer to work the next three week-ends in a row, or accept a drop in pay, or write that report for her in 24 hours flat.

Family is terrifically important to Triangle/Cancer, more the sense of belonging and continuity than the actual hands-on mothering, worrying about nappies and baby food and getting up at night. Her own mother and the family she grew up in will exert their influences throughout her life. She will look back, either in great nostalgia for that lost world, which remains vividly with her still, or in hurt that it wasn't as nurturing and close to the ideal as she wanted it to be.

She is a master of disguise. This strong self-protective impulse means she veils from the world her true feelings, the depth of her ambition, her need for control, and her inability to let things and people go. Triangle/Cancer will more likely as not be the one who asks a boyfriend to leave when she's had enough, but she will find it very hard to actually physically let him go. She will hope that she is left with some vestige of the relationship, that he will remain attached to her in some emotional way. Even though she does not want him in any real sense, she wants to think that he goes on wanting her and will never be able to cut that umbilical cord. If, on the other hand, a man who she wants does not concur with her demands and needs, and himself decides to walk away, she can bring herself almost to nervous disintegration in her despair at being thwarted, at being forced to release something she wants – at her own terrible vulnerability which she hates to have so exposed.

This is a complicated and powerful combination and Triangle/Cancer must feel at times she is riding a schizophrenic horse, sometimes a Lippizaner, perfectly in control, reined in, focused, working harder than anyone else, achieving everything she wants – and then suddenly being thrown by a bucking bronco, hair flying, everything hanging out all over the place, her emotions in turmoil. This woman hates revealing herself. Her counter-reaction is to withdraw into her controlled persona. Then she becomes in danger of becoming a workaholic, so single-mindedly can she throw herself into her work, so perfectionist is she in her demands on her self.

Triangle/Cancer is protective of those she loves. She is good at understanding human motivation and longing, she recognizes the deep influences that the past and family have on people. She wants to help and make things better. But the shadow side of this is the desire to control, is the fact that this love can come with a price attached, which may remain hidden – even to the giver – until she realizes she wants some recognition, or favour in return. How can her teenage children want to move out of home, when she's given them so much? How can her protege at work move on to a better job after all the help she's been given? Then it may be that Triangle/Cancer finds to her horror that she feels resentful and ungenerous, and even wishes to somehow get her own back, but in the most oblique and unstraightforward way.

She is never quite what she seems. She is constitutionally incapable of meeting anything head on, with absolute candour. So, bad atmospheres, back-biting and what can only be described as sulky withdrawal are her way of showing disapproval, and it is very disconcerting to more up-front personalities. But once the area of complaint has been cleared up there is no one more supportive and understanding, no one who would fight as hard for what she believes in, no one more loyal in the end.

IN WORK

Triangle/Cancer is an imaginative, creative combination. She can tap into her deep emotions and the images of the unconscious. Her Yang+ body type gives her all the power and drive necessary to make a career in the difficult artistic fields of acting and writing. The need to disguise her deeper self means Triangle/Cancer is naturally adept at being other than herself. Her complexity of character and feeling provides the creative resources for her art.

Cancerian writers include Barbara Cartland, Monica Dickens, Iris Murdoch, George Sand and Mary Wesley. Again it is the

imaginative force of this sign, together with her endurance and capacity for hard work, which helps Triangle/Cancer carve herself a profession in this over-subscribed field. The Cancerian author Laurie Lee, who wrote *Cider with Rosie*, exhibited all the classic traits of the secretive old crab: 'He is amiably secretive, a born burrower. His cottage has no telephone . . . To make contact you send a telegram and await his answering call. His cottage is his bolt hole. [Like the crab with his shell] Books to be autographed are passed over the garden wall.'

The 'born burrower' aspect of Triangle/Cancer can also be expressed in a love of research and history. This woman is imaginatively drawn to the past, both recent or personal history or the very distant past, and she is an excellent investigator and scholar. She likes her own company and enjoys working alone and would be happy beavering away for years on some manuscript, or ancient site – as long as there was a good possibility that she would gain some recognition from her labours. The Cancer side of this combination can certainly be shy and self-effacing but the more powerful influence is the Triangle body type and that gives a healthy regard for publicity, recognition and power.

Triangle/Cancer is good at managing money, both her own and other people's. It's an expression of that conservative, retentive side of her which hates to see resources wasted and which drives her to save carrier bags and energetically recycle bottles, paper and tins. Triangle/Cancer is also interested in security and conserving money as one of the important ways of gaining a sense of safety and continuity. This combination would make a very good bank manager, investment adviser or top flight accountant. She is not, however, one of life's gamblers and so is unlikely to be happy in any of the riskier financial ventures.

The Triangle body type with its Yang+ energy and drive can help the Cancerian side of this personality to achieve anything she sets her mind to. Her determination and tenacity can be alarming. For instance, she may be an excellent cook, but Triangle/Cancer is not going to be satisfied running an informal catering service for her friends' weddings and parties. She will work every hour of the day and night to invest in a restaurant and to make it the best of its kind.

Her talent for antiques and old books will not express itself in having a charming small shop in a provincial town where she is known and loved by everyone, and makes just enough to get by: Triangle/Cancer will be much happier running a smart gallery in London where people with serious money buy, or working her way up the hierarchy in one of the great fine art auction houses.

Her Yang+ side means hard work, palpable achievement. She may join a television company as a trainee straight out of university and while most of her fellow trainees are thinking how nice it would be to become an assistant producer on some sports/arts/drama programme, Triangle/Cancer is quietly deciding that it's managing director for her. Quietly, secretively, she sets her sights. No one would guess to look at her just what her feelings and ambitions were. But she gains strategic points by keeping them hidden. And Triangle/Cancer is the ultimate tactitian.

Ideal Fantasy Job

Managing director of a television company. Triangle/Cancer would bring efficiency, cost cutting, and common sense to the job. She hates waste and doesn't see much point in perks and material evidence of status, although she'd see to it that the canteen served delicious food and she'd expect everyone, from top executives to the cleaners to eat there. Terrifically hard-working, she would look to her employees to put in as much energy and commitment as she does.

She would also bring an inspired creativity, a lack of pomposity and a willingness to have a wider kind of voice heard. Unlike Mrs Thatcher, another driven Triangle type, she would not deny that she was a woman, but she would think that women had as much chance of getting and doing as any man. Triangle/Cancer takes it for granted that intellectually and in strength of character she is streets ahead of the opposite sex.

IN LOVE

Love and belonging matters enormously to Cancer, but the Triangle type in this equation tends to push this need to one side while she gets on with work and life. Triangle/Cancer is good at hiding her deepest feelings and emotional needs and she can go for years giving the impression that her studying, her work, her life in the outside world is all she wants. But when love does rear its head, and sometimes take her by surprise, she can go overboard and lose all the control. Everything she does she takes to the limit. So when she does allow herself to fall in love then she has to have him, and nothing else will do.

Friends will watch in amazement and some alarm, as Triangle/Cancer, usually so cool and collected, plots how she is going to get a friend of a friend to ask the focus of her passions to lunch, just when she is due to return a book she has borrowed, and then be invited to stay on too. She will map his way to work

and plan how she can accidentally on purpose cross his path and end up in the cafe nearby, and talk over a coffee and croissant. She will buy herself new clothes (not something she has much thought or time for generally) and go on a diet. All because she has set her sights on something and cannot rest until she has achieved her goal: making him love her too.

Triangle/Cancer's true love is slow to be given, she has to feel she can really trust someone before she allows herself that kind of vulnerability. When she does commit herself, her feelings are more likely to be expressed as a rather motherly concern and control, helping her partner to find his way in the world, supporting him, advising him, sorting him out. She is not entirely straightforward, although the Yang body types tend to be more up-front than the Yin are. Anyone who has Triangle/Cancer as a friend or lover has to be good at reading the signs. She won't be baring all, for just anyone to see.

The kind of man who will make her feel secure enough to open up a little and commit her heart will be a sensitive, caring Yin kind of man who is perfectly happy for her to be the powerhouse in the outside world. He may well have a high profile job too, but he will be less single-minded in his ambitions, more interested in the human relationships along the way.

Triangle/Cancer may well come late to motherhood. Her career is of central importance to her and this, allied to her natural conservatism and lack of trust in the emotional area of life, means she does not rush into commitment and a full domestic life, as many of her more Yin friends and sisters might. If she does have children, Triangle/Cancer is more likely to want to continue with her career than stay at home full-time. However, because she finds it very hard to delegate she will be closely involved with the bringing up of her children. She would try every possibility to keep her own career going, and yet remain the central person in her children's lives. She is always on the verge of exhausting herself through overwork, and she stands a chance of over-reaching herself trying to be superwoman in the office and at home.

Ideal Fantasy Lover

Tim Robbins, the tall, crumply-faced, tousled actor who, almost against his will, has sprung to fame and glory would be a wonderful complementary force to Triangle/Cancer. He played the central figure, the thrusting young studio executive, in *The Player* and then moved on to even greater acclaim as the director and star of *Bob Roberts*.

He is highly intelligent, thoughtful and generally laid back about his film career, determined to keep his personal life with Susan Sarandon and their sons as normal as possible, and to be able to continue his diversified working life. His brother recognizes how relaxed he is about the phenomenal strides his career has taken, 'Tim never went into acting to be a star . . . He wasn't looking for stardom, and therefore it came to him.' This is just the sort of well-balanced Yin man who makes a natural partner for a Yang woman like Triangle/Cancer.

IN STYLE

Triangle/Cancer is not a flamboyant dresser, she does not want to make great statements that cry 'Look at me!'. However, she gets very attached to certain garments which have good associations for her. She likes things to be familiar and isn't very concerned with being up-to-the-minute. Fine quality clothes are appreciated by Triangle/Cancer but above all she likes them to be comfortable, going for separates and a generally casual look.

The style of clothes that really flatter Triangle/Cancer are determined by her body type. The Triangle shape has broader shoulders than hips and more of a marked waist than the Rectangle. She falls into two basic types, the small boned, boyish figure like Mia Farrow who probably rarely, if ever, puts on weight and the more muscular, athletic looking type, like Princess Stephanie of Monaco, Jamie Lee Curtis and Anjelica Huston, who can get heavy in the upper torso area, but keeps her inverted triangle shape with straight hips and lean lower legs. When thin, this shape is the classic fashion model shape with coat-hanger shoulders, next-to-nothing-hips and long lean legs.

Some women with this body type try to counteract their broad-shouldered look by wearing flimsy, ultra-feminine clothes – think of Diane Keaton (a Triangle/Aquarius) in *Annie Hall*. Those soft, drifty clothes on the angular Diane make her look a bit like Little Orphan Annie, rather gawky and fey. This suited the character very well in the film, but for Triangle/Cancer, wanting to be taken seriously in the real world, it can be a counter-productive look. Her femininity is best expressed with clothes that have simple geometric lines, certainly angled to the waist if she likes, but it's better to avoid soft fabrics, gathers and bows. For more specific information, see In Style on page 49.

Style Treat

Cancerians love jewellery and have great collections of earrings, necklaces, brooches and rings. It doesn't have to be the real thing, but a Triangle/Cancer will prefer to have a few less pieces than her Hourglass- and Pear-type sisters, and go for better quality instead. It is important for her to remember that her jewellery follows the same lines as her body and clothes. Therefore a Triangle type is best suited by jewellery which is angular, with predominantly straight lines. Chain links should be flat rather than curvy and necklaces with round beads are not becoming. Brooches and earrings look better if they are unfussy and geometric. Squares, diamond-shapes, rectangles, triangles and variations of these look really classy on this type – regardless of the cost of the piece – whereas curved shapes, however expensive the jewellery, can look just plain cheap.

For business wear Triangle/Cancer should avoid long, dangly earrings. Instead she can choose simple geometric shapes, preferably in silver or gold colour. Choice of colour depends on her own colouring – for advice on choosing, see page 50. Earrings can be worn with a complementary brooch or necklace, but for business she should resist wearing all three together.

Lots of Triangle-type women are petite (157cm [5ft 3in] and under) and if Triangle/Cancer is this scale she must beware of wearing jewellery that is too big for her height and bone structure. Dangly earrings, even for evening, can be a problem on a petite woman, for they overwhelm a small face too easily. Most of the time, clip-on or stud type earrings have a lighter, more elevating effect. Again, choose geometric shapes, but earrings such as this can be more colourful or glittery – diamond-studded (real or diamante) or with other gem-like stones.

The taller Triangle/Cancer can wear larger-scale jewellery for day and night, and go to town with dangly earrings for evening but, again, she should make sure that there is an overall geometric look to them, rather than intricate and romantic.

IN HEALTH

The Triangle/Cancer takes criticism personally and is a natural worrier. Poor at delegating, she too easily takes on more and more work and adds to her stress levels. She can seem obsessive and uncooperative to others because of this need to do everything herself. So her health weaknesses are often stress-related, things like ulcers and digestive upsets. Psychsomatic symptoms are prevalent in this combination, but her general powers of recovery are strong.

To keep healthy, it is worth looking at the whole area of diet and exercise, too. The Triangle type is likely to have been slim as a teenager, athletic, and with a big appetite. In adulthood, the demands of a family and career can mean she does less exercise, eats the wrong things at wrong times, still has an unrestrained appetite and can then start putting on weight. Triangle/Cancer, however, is very organized and disciplined and when she decides to do something about her shape she works out a routine and readily sticks to it.

Although the Cancer side of this disposition may hate the idea, her body type demands exercise for general well-being. Triangle/Cancer positively *needs* regular, energetic exercise and can get depressed if she isn't doing enough. In Bel's questionnaire, 75 per cent of the Triangle types said they recognized that they needed to exercise *and* diet if they were to lose weight – and it was energetic exercise which they favoured: a much higher proportion than the other body types (for instance, only 30 per cent of the Pear types thought exercise important). For more specific information on diet and exercise, see In Health on page 50.

TRIANGLE/CANCER CELEBRITY

Anjelica Huston is a striking, classy and intelligent actress, and a woman who has much more to her than that. Tall and big-boned, she has a masculine authoritative presence in life and on screen. As the daughter of director John Huston, she was given a birthright to Hollywood but came late to film with her first real part as the lion-tamer in *The Postman Always Rings Twice*, a film she made when she was thirty. Parts in *Prizzi's Honour*, *Crimes and Misdemeanours* and *The Grifters* then followed.

In true Triangle/Cancer style, her past is of enormous importance to her. She grew up in Ireland and looks back to that period still as an idyllic interlude in her life from which she draws some of her creative energies. At 42 she was still unmarried, although she had a much-publicized 17-year liaison with Jack Nicolson, who finally deserted her for one of his young women, when she became pregnant. An old childhood friend describes her as being an amalgam of four personalities, the Beauty, the Wit, the Drama Queen and the Self-Mocking Loon. There are great emotional depths and hurts which she rarely shows anyone, but the individuality and ambition burn on and will take her to greater achievements as one of the most original and powerful actresses in Hollywood.

TRIANGLE/CANCER PROFILE

Teresa is an estate agent dealing with farms in the West Country. 'I was born and raised on a farm and loved working with the animals. From the age of about six I was going everywhere with my dad helping him with lambing, feeding the pigs, just anything. He said I was as good as any son would have been. I was strong too and by the time I was about 11 I felt I was the equal of any of my male cousins – more equal than the two who lived in London and didn't know how to drive a tractor, let alone had the strength to pitchfork bales of hay.'

Teresa loves being out and about with her job and works extremely hard. She wants to end up running her section before she's 30 and is determined to be better than the two men in the office. 'It really helps that I have been a farmer and understand the mentality of the farmer, as well as all the processes and terms of reference. Although farmers are still predominantly men, and they tend to be a conservative chauvinistic breed, I think they are beginning to realize that I really know what I'm talking about and are actually asking that I deal with their properties now.'

Her personal life comes a poor second to her work. She is concentrating on that at the moment but would like one day to be married and have children, 'I barely have time and energy to spare. As well as my job, I'm also renovating a cottage in the village. I really like that too. Restoring things. I don't want to settle down 'til I'm well into my thirties, I think I'm a late developer emotionally. I wasn't interested in boys at all until I was about 18, long after most of my friends had fallen madly in love at least four times already. I don't know if I'll ever fall madly in love: I don't think I'd want to. Whenever my feelings have got the better of me, it's been a bit of a disaster. A part of me longs for someone special who loves me. But, I hate being so out of control.'

IN HOPE

Triangle/Cancer is a powerful combination of opposites, which can sometimes appear to be pulling in contrary directions causing confusion and grief. Perhaps, the answer to this dichotomy of head and heart, ambition and privacy, Yang energy and intuitive Yin feeling, is to be a little less afraid of the mystery, the inexplicable and uncontrollable aspects of human nature. Being a little less blinkered in her ambitions and a little easier on herself might increase her pleasures in the day. The great prophet Rabindranath Tagore turned his thoughts to this problem, 'Let the dead have the immortality of fame, but the living the immortality of love', was the answer he came up with.

TRIANGLE

LEO

(Yang+/Yang+)

MOTTO:

A cat in gloves catches no mice

IN LIFE

Power and ego rule this combination. There are no pussycats here, and certainly no one wearing gloves. This double Yang+ personality demands attention and is determined and ambitious enough to get just what she wants. Unlike Rectangle/Leo, who is uncomplicatedly exuberant about her desire for fame and fortune, Triangle/Leo, aware of the force of her power, veils it with more sophistication. But her body type is even more Yang and her will is even more driven and determined. If this is not harnessed by her concentrating on a demanding career with a great deal of scope for her ambition, then she can be utterly overwhelming to more sensitive, reflective souls – and possibly destructive to herself.

These women are not natural team players. They are, however, wonderful if they are the leader of a team, where their pride of place is secure and everyone else rallies round. She is generous and magnanimous when things go well. But she is not that keen on working to bring benefit or acclaim to others. Her name has to be up there leading the credits. The confidence and energy that she exudes is terrifically attractive, but it hides a much greater insecurity within. All Leos are actors in life: their home, workplace, the restaurant and party, all are but stages on which they live out the fantasy of themselves as the princess (and then the queen), the entertainer, the wit, the philospher or saviour. They play these thrilling roles but always with an unease that perhaps they are not as superhuman as they believe, not above the usual run of humanity – not, after all, almost divine.

But Triangle/Leo is not all sound and fury signifying nothing. She is not just an actress in life. Her star sign gives her a big heart and a largeness of character which, although at times may be just a weeny bit egocentric, even a teeny bit autocratic and overbearing, is never, ever, mean or petty. A genuine appeal to her feelings will get her off her high horse and kneeling on the ground beside you. She may not stay there long, and will spring back into the saddle and gallop off as soon as she can, but her genuine warmth of feeling will bubble up when she realizes that help is needed. (You may need a megaphone, or a mallet, to get the message across, but when it registers she will be there.)

There is something naturally sunny and open about Triangle/Leo. As a young woman she will be sporty and energetic, one of the boys, finding more to interest her in daredevil activity and adventures than sitting around experimenting with make-up and talking about love. She is naturally competitive and needs to win, to be the best at anything she does. She is unlikely to perservere at things in which she cannot excel. She does not want to just play the game, do her best, be good enough. She has to be the best. This can make it hard for her to share things with her friends if she feels that it might lose her her competitive edge. When a student, her Leo side might be happy to pass on copies of her English notes, for instance, to a clever friend who has lost hers, but the ultra-competitive, individualist, Triangle side might find reasons not to be there when the friend came round to collect them.

Triangle/Leo will never be able to pass through a crowd unseen. Not that she would want to. This woman is likely to draw people's attention wherever she is. She cares about the image she gives to the world. She wants it to be sophisticated, dignified and classy. Jacqueline Kennedy Onassis is a Triangle/Leo who is intensely self-aware, never caught off guard – and never made to look a fool. Along with the desire for public recognition comes an awareness of the public's expectations. In her own mind, Triangle/Leo is never off duty, she is playing the part even when she is slopping around at home on a Sunday – what if her prince might chose that day to come?

IN WORK

The best work for Triangle/Leo has to be a job with a view (upwards), and a stage and lots of limelight *en suite*. There is no way that this woman will be happy working in the wings, unless it's a necessary (and temporary) part of the upward climb. This

is the combination which produces politicians, lawyers and businesswomen. The Triangle body type gives the luxury-seeking, fun-loving Leo the kind of dedication to hard work and solid ambition which will get her to the top of her professions. Leos with other less driven body types can spend time dreaming about glory, but will find there are always more interesting things to do than the hard old slog necessary to get there.

The Triangle/Leo is well-equipped for professions where she has to compete with men, using male rules. She has the toughness to endure the competition, and actually thrive on it, and has the good humour and warmth to make herself rather likeable, even while she's carving up the opposition. Brilliant on the marketing and publicity side, she excels where she has to impress people and make a plausible case for a product, argument or client.

Law-giving is a traditional Leo trait – some would change that to laying down the law, a related talent of hers – but making and upholding the law is something particularly suited to Triangle/Leo. This embraces politics, whether she works with local government, sits in Parliament or is head of policy making think tanks or pressure groups which lobby for the law to be changed. More directly, it also includes the legal profession, particularly the jobs of barristers and judges, where Triangle/Leo will feel really at home with all the ceremony, dressing up and the ancient hierarchy which shows her the direct way to the top. The respect, honour and pageantry is all a big attraction to this show-woman. One of the most senior women judges, the Rt Hon. Lord Justice Butler-Sloss is one such Leo who has made it.

There are fewer actresses in Leo than in any other sign: she is not very good at putting herself in another's shoes. Her ego can get in the way of her portraying someone outside her own experience. Susan George and Shelley Winters (Rectangle/Leo both), Melanie Griffiths (Hourglass/Leo) and Madonna and Mae West (Triangle/Leo both) are great at being themselves but rather lacking in the imaginative sympathy and sensitivity to bring to life an independent character.

One of the things Triangle/Leo would do best of all is be queen. Jackie Kennedy managed it brilliantly for a while as uncrowned queen of the American People, Coco Chanel, another Triangle/Leo and queen of couturiers managed it for longer, Whitney Houston is determined to make herself both beauty queen and queen of soul, and of course the old queens of Hype and Hollywood, Mae West and Madonna, have no pretenders to their thrones. Triangle/Leos all, they are not easy to upstage.

Ideal Fantasy Job

Lord Chancellor. This job combines most of the qualities any Triangle/Leo could wish for. It offers her the opportunity to be centre stage during a great show of pageantry and power in the opening of Parliament. All eyes would swivel her way as she processed. It involves some hobnobbing with real royalty, and genuine collaboration with the great and the not so good in the land. It is the position of greatest moral authority in the government and – not a minor point – she would be paid more than even the Prime Minister. She is ultimately responsible for seeing that justice is done.

The costume is rather impressive too, all that dressing up in luxurious robes and christmas tree trimmings, which carry with them ancient rituals and traditions, has its charm. But above all, should Triangle/Leo attain this position other than in her dreams, her fame would be assured for the rest of her life.

IN LOVE

Ah love! All Leos love the idea of love, the excitement of those first few feverish weeks of pursuit, near-capitulation, escape, pursuit...and then surrender. However, with Triangle/Leo, a double Yang+ woman, the pursuit is more likely to be on her side, and the surrender belong to her sweet-natured Yin man, although both will be careful to make it look as if it is the more conventional way round. Love is another area where the self-dramatization of this combination can take over. Robert Graves and Shelley, two great poets who wrote miraculous love poems, were both Leos, and both in thrall to the romance of the feeling – and less good at dealing with the reality.

Triangle/Leo too is quick to fall in love, and quick to find the whole thing loses its excitment rather fast and becomes something of a drag – and that she would rather be working. Warm-hearted as she is, she is the least spontaneous of all the Leo body types, and is most likely to fall in love with someone who will enhance her position in this world. She will not go home to mum and announce, for instance, that she is throwing in her lot with the out-of-work juggler she met on the bus. She will make her choice, when she makes her choice, with her brain very much in gear. What's the point of falling in love with the gamekeeper, when she could just as easily fall in love with the squire?

Status matters, although of all the Leos Triangle/Leo is most likely to want to make that status for herself. It will be she who wants to be the managing director, and her man's status is consequently not so important. Although he'd better look good on her arm! There is the accessory side of things to consider. The best man for this doubly Yang+ woman is a good, sensitive, caring man who is not going to compete with her. Another Yang like her would only mean there would be a horrid clash of egos, and someone would get hurt. But Yang with Yin works much better, with the Yin partner sensitive to and supportive of the Yang, who is out in the world fighting battles, conquering mountains and generally seeking fame or fortune in the process.

Motherhood will attract her, in the end. She's good with children and has a good deal of the playful, energetic child in her. But she does have a great deal to do, she feels, before she turns her attention to that. Staying at home, caring for tiny, vulnerable babies, selflesly giving up her sleep, her interests, her own self, is not for Triangle/Leo. She can manage it picturesquely for a bit, playing the adorable new mother, the superwoman, but the reality soon palls and she really is much more sensible to don the power suit, pick up the briefcase and go back to work in the world. Her sort of power and desire for attention and influence has to have a larger stage than the domestic hearth. She can be positively dangerous if she decides to make her life's work being a mother and wife. Both her husband and her children, by the time they can talk, will be begging her to go back to the boardroom, courthouse, catwalk, factory floor – or wherever she best struts her stuff – and let them get on with their lives, their way, without being pushed about, cross-examined and told what to do and how to do it. Sublimated ambition can wreak havoc on the home front.

Triangle/Leo is a great party-giver and party-goer. She knows just how to create the right atmosphere, although she isn't very sympathetic to shyer guests who don't, in her opinion, pull their weight properly and enter into the spirit of things. She doesn't see any reason why anyone should not want to be entertaining, and play their part. Her house is likely to be as large and luxurious as she can afford. This, along with her family, her clothes and her car, are all part of the statement she is making about her own status in the eyes of the world. She feels she lives a public life with all eyes upon her (and for many Triangle/Leos this is literally right) and so her decisions are public ones. There is a danger that the private self almost disappears from view.

Ideal Fantasy Lover

Money, status, a title, breeding, Triangle/Leo couldn't do much better than the Duke of Westminster. He is a deeply Yin man who

loves his children and has decided not to send his small children away to boarding school because it was such a nightmare for him – against generations of family and class tradition.

In the 1992 *Sunday Times* Top 400 guide to the wealthiest people in Britain he was second only to the Queen, with his interest valued conservatively at £3,500 million. The 1993 guide saw his 300 acres of Mayfair devalued and his own rating drop to seventh, but he still found the money to buy a £650,000 executive jet for commuting to London. This, of course, would be the ultimate accessory for a Triangle/Leo. Yin-type men are much more suitable mates for the Yang+ Triangle woman and the Duke, with his inherited wealth rather than self-made millions, is one of the few seriously rich Yin men. He's also quite good-looking – for an aristo – and this is an important plus for a discerning Triangle/Leo.

IN STYLE

Glamour, style, drama, these are what Triangle/Leo likes to express with the clothes she wears. She likes them to be conspicuously wealthy too. There is no real or false modesty here. With her basically athletic figure and Yang+ personality she tends to prefer smart casual clothes, built for comfort and speed. But she recognizes more than most that she has to have the right uniform for the job and the status she wants to broadcast to the world. This is where the luxurious, stylish clothes come into the picture.

Triangle/Leo is not someone who wants to spend hours shopping or poring over the beauty of a garment's design or the quality of the cloth. She doesn't particularly enjoy the whole creative business of putting clothes together and trying different looks and accessories, as her more Yin friends do. Instead, she likes the idea of going out and buying the clothes she needs with the minimum of fuss and then not having to think of them again. Just wear them, know she looks a million dollars, and forget them.

The style of clothes that really flatter Triangle/Leo are determined by her body type. The Triangle shape has broader shoulders than hips and more of a marked waist than the Rectangle. She falls into two basic types, the small boned, boyish figure like Mia Farrow who probably rarely, if ever, puts on weight and the more muscular, athletic looking type, like Princess Stephanie of Monaco, Jamie Lee Curtis and Anjelica Huston, who can get heavy in the upper torso area, but keeps her inverted triangle shape with straight hips and lean lower legs. When thin, this shape is the classic fashion model shape with coat-hanger shoulders, next-to-nothing-hips and long lean legs.

Some women with this body type try to counteract their broad-shouldered look by wearing flimsy, ultra-feminine clothes – think of Diane Keaton (a Triangle/Aquarius) in *Annie Hall*. Those soft, drifty clothes on the angular Diane make her look a bit like Little Orphan Annie, rather gawky and fey. This suited the character very well in the film, but for Triangle/Leo, wanting to be taken seriously in the real world, it can be a counter-productive look. Her femininity is best expressed with clothes that have simple geometric lines, certainly angled to the waist if she likes, but it's better to avoid soft fabrics, gathers and bows. For more specific information, see In Style on page 49.

Style Treat

A really good geometric haircut. Leo's mane is her crowning glory but Triangle/Leo needs to tame that mane – no Pre-Raphaelite mass of tumbling curls for her – her glory will be in the classiness of the cut.

Just as clothes for a Triangle type need to be angular and chic, so too does her hair style. Straight and swingy, or short and sharp is the look for her. Soft, wavy, romantic hair just looks dull and untidy on this woman – and at odds with her broad-shouldered frame. Jamie Lee Curtis is a classic example of a Triangle-type woman who looks wonderful in her short spiky haircuts. But when she appeared in a long blonde, wavy wig in the court scene in *A Fish Called Wanda*, she looked more like a man in drag.

If Rectangle/Leo has naturally curly hair, however, it will look much more flattering if she wears it short and spiky, or if she wants it longer then with a straight blunt cut at the bottom. She must think geometric. It is also worth while treating herself to a good cut with a really good stylist who will take into consideration the weight and wave of her own hair and the shape of her face.

If she is petite (below 157cm [5ft 3in]) she will always look better with a short, crisp hairstyle. Long hair or hair that is very full will tend to overwhelm her and spoil the balance of her head to body proportions. A tall Triangle/Leo can wear her hair long – particularly if it is straight – but career women should be aware that long hair is not really appropriate in business and anything longer than shoulder length needs to be clipped back – perhaps with a large Rectangle-shaped hair slide – or neatly worn up. Finding the right stylist for a good haircut is essential. If you

aren't happy with your current hairdresser, look at other women you know and see who has a particularly good cut. Ask who does her hair and go to see him or her. The best hairdresser isn't necessarily the most expensive, or the one who brooks no discussion, insisting on imposing a certain style on you. Nor is he or she the one who just attempts to do what the client wants, without any experimentation and discussion. The best stylists will look at the texture and quality of your hair, will take into account the shape of your head and face, your height and way of life. They will discuss the pros and cons and how to maintain the sort of style they suggest, and will only go ahead when you both are happy with the decision.

IN HEALTH

Triangle/Leo has a basically robust constitution. Anything that might go wrong with her health is likely to be acute and quickly over. Long, lingering diseases are not her style. But sudden fevers and seizures, from which she recovers fast might be more likely. Leo is ruled by the sun which corresponds to the heart in the human body. Because of the latest research (see Introduction) which shows that when top-heavy women (Triangles and Rectangles) put on weight they are more prone to heart attacks and vascular problems than bottom-heavy women (Hourglasses and Pears) it makes real sense for Triangle/Leo to take care with her weight as she gets older, and to do some serious exercising.

To keep healthy, it is worth looking at the whole area of diet and exercise, too. The Triangle type is likely to have been slim as a teenager, athletic, and with a big appetite. In adulthood, the demands of a family and career can mean she does less exercise, eats the wrong things at wrong times, still has an unrestrained appetite and can then start putting on weight. Triangle/Leo, however, is very organized and disciplined and when she decides to do something about her shape she works out a routine and readily sticks to it.

Triangle/Leo positively *needs* regular, energetic exercise and can get depressed (or neurotic) if she isn't doing enough. In Bel's questionnaire, 75 per cent of the Triangle types said they recognized that they needed to exercise *and* diet if they were to lose weight – and it was energetic exercise which they favoured: a much higher proportion than the other body types (for instance, only 30 per cent of the Pear types thought exercise important). For more information on diet and exercise, see In Health on page 50.

CELEBRITY TRIANGLE/LEO

Both Madonna and Mae West are Triangle/Leos and they share the stage as examples of power and ego taken to global excess. In their own times, both were the most well-known women in the world, and both have aroused powerful emotions of admiration and vilification. They have lost their own personalities in the drive for fame and glory, and the transformation of self that this has involved, until they appear like glittering carapaces around an empty shell. Both also have such a strong element of camp parody that they appear to be female impersonators rather than real women who feel and bleed.

Madonna was determined to be a star from the moment she could dream. One of eight children born to a poor immigrant family in Michigan, as a Triangle/Leo with all that natural ambition and drive for fame, there was no way that this young woman was going to settle for a life like her mother's. Brilliant at self-publicity, it was the pop videos with her scantily clad in nothing more than underwear and sporting a large crucifix which courted her first rush of notoriety.

Subsequently she has shocked and surprised through her costumes, hair colour changes, and outrageous look-at-me behaviour. Underneath all this is a canny young woman who is nobody's fool. But her disastrous marriage to wild boy Sean Penn, her self-publicized lesbian flings, her search to adopt a perfect girl baby, are all part of the great publicity machine which chews people up and spits them out – and is in danger of doing the same to Madonna herself.

Mae West was an even cleverer operator, although she was just as capable of terrific lapses in judgement and taste – for instance the grotesque *Myra Breckinridge* which she appeared in when she was 84 trying to be forty-four. She did, however, have the tenacity to hang onto stardom until her death at nearly ninety.

She was not so much a great actress as a great star: her one-liners are more memorable now than her films, with 'Come up and see me sometime' entering every book of quotations imaginable. 'When I'm good, I'm very very good, but when I'm bad I'm better'; 'Is that a gun in your pocket or are you just pleased to see me?' and then the incomparable, 'Sometimes it seems to me I've known so many men that the FBI ought to come to me first to compare the fingerprints'. In fact, there was very little evidence that Mae West got much involved with any man, let alone the hundreds she would have the world believe. But that

was all part of her own mythology, something that she needed to promote and have us believe.

There is, however, one line which no one would dispute she meant and by which she lived her life: 'Too much of a good thing is . . . wonderful!'

TRIANGLE/LEO PROFILE

Kate is 25 and a fashion model. 'When I was little I thought I was a re-incarnation of a princess. From quite a young age I had a big ambition to be a recognized figure – someone people would look up to and admire – preferably in a creative area.'

She sees modelling as simply a means to an end, giving her the chance to travel, to have fun while she works out what she really wants to do. 'The good money is important, but it's for spending now. I feel I don't need to put money by for the future because I'll always be doing something that makes money. Money is particularly important because it does make life easier and brings joy. It saves you from struggling just to survive.'

Work is a central part of Kate's life and she realized this early on: 'I couldn't survive not working. I need to keep my mind active and be busy doing things. I think I'll continue modelling for another six months and then I'm ready to move on. I think everyone should do something for the world they live in, so I might work for an organization like Greenpeace – not inside doing administrative stuff but out, travelling the world, perhaps, doing grand deeds to save nature and mankind.'

She also thinks that she would enjoy working in public relations. It's something she's really good at: 'I can work in a group, it's fun working in a team, but I do prefer to be the boss. I think this is definitely the Leo side of me, but there is the other side which likes to go off and do my own thing. And that's really important.'

When it comes to love Kate is still working things out: 'The beginnings of relationships are really exciting and it is then that they matter most. But it's difficult to say whether work or relationships matter more, but after a while . . . well, a girl has to work! When I do settle down I will want to earn my own money but also want a bloke who can keep me in comfort.'

'I definitely want children one day but in the very, very distant future. I think I'd want someone in to help with housework and looking after them, but feel now that I would want to be around. I don't want someone else moulding my children. I also think they should be given all the opportunities and openings they need so

that they can find out what they are best at, and yes, I'd certainly be ambitious for them.'

IN HOPE

'Fame is the spur' is the famous line from Milton which expresses much of what drives Triangle/Leo on. Even if that fame is just to be found among her schoolfriends or the local community fete, she needs to stand out from the crowd, to be one among many. But the following line in the poem which outlines the sacrifices which have to be made, 'To scorn delights and live laborious days' is where she and Milton part company. Triangle/Leo may well dream of world dominion, BUT she is saved from absolute megalomania by her need for fun and an appreciation of the easy life (although harder working than any of the other Leo body types). Fame *is* the spur, but not to the extent that Triangle/Leo has to scorn too many delights, or make her days too overburdened with hard labour.

Part of the theatricality of her character means she truly believes she'll win the pools one day/be plucked from a crowd by a film director to star in his next film/that her prince will finally come. She feels she is so special she is sure that magical things will happen. And who's to say she's wrong – after all, wishing is more than halfway to having.

TRIANGLE
VIRGO

(Yang+/Yin)

MOTTO:
Genius is an infinite capacity for taking pains

IN LIFE

Subtlety and obsessiveness characterize Triangle/Virgo's way of operating. She need not be the obsessively tidy housewife to which popular astrology sometimes relegates the good Virgo, she might even live in a bit of a pigsty – although that's pretty unlikely – but she will have the kind of mind which grades and refines and categorizes every aspect of life. She likes to know precisely where she is and where she's going. She does not like surprises and cannot live her life hand-to-mouth, day-to-day. She believes that life has a pattern or a code, however intricate, and that she needs to find out exactly what it is in order to truly understand and thereby to feel secure.

Triangle/Virgo is a sensitive, highly-strung individual whose scrupulous, gentle and kindly star sign is combined with a Yang+ body type which confers a powerful will and drive to achieve. She may sometimes feel she is caught between two warring sides of her personality, the Yin need for privacy and the Yang desire for recognition, the need to be of service to others and the Yang need to promote herself. Both the Virgo and the Triangle dispositions come together, though, in a perfectionism and need for control, of herself and others.

The Triangle body type also adds to Virgo's already well-developed capacity for hard work. This combination produces someone who will work without complaint on the most gruelling mental tasks, although her body type gives her the strength and physical robustness to work just as hard at sport, labouring or gardening. She does not shirk or rest and is never easy on herself, or others. To leave a task half done or, worse still, badly done goes completely against the grain. She can become quite nervous, even neurotic, in her drive to do things properly, perfectly.

Emotions, like all other aspects of her life, need to be clear cut and in their place. She is not happy with misty romanticism, intuitive feeling, with poetic outpouring and irrational longings. She can be very scathing of those who do deal in dreams and have a more ecstatic approach to life and love. Triangle/Virgo can be in danger of being so rational and critical of everything and everyone that she discards anything which does not come up to her high standards of verity, or usefulness.

Knowledge, however, is something she will seek out and respect. This sign is full of writers and Triangle/Virgo will probably be a scholar and reader, trying to improve her understanding of all that she surveys. The more information she has to fit into the giant jigsaw of life, the nearer she comes to cracking the code. She is someone who always knows best. This told-you-so side comes as much from her fear of what she doesn't know, a fear of the chaos beyond the small bright light which is her own mind shining in the blankness of the unknown universe.

Rather than be excited by the great mystery of life, as a romantic water star sign might be, Triangle/Virgo desperately seeks to broaden that circle of light until she can no longer see the darkness that surrounds it. She would rather stick with what is safe and familiar than risk venturing into that unknown, in the leap of faith that could lead to knowing infinitely more, on a different plane altogether. Venturing in hope strikes her as a foolish stance. Building on what she has is much more her style, and – to be sure – she has the willpower and strength of mind, the sheer intelligence and capacity for work, which can build her a powerful edifice on solid foundations.

There is something solitary too about Triangle/Virgo. She is happy with her own company, her own thoughts. She has a self-containment which makes for great inner strength, but also denies a whole range of human experience and feelings. She has friends, family, but there is always an unknowable, unreachable side which is private and hers alone.

IN WORK

Triangle/Virgo is made for work. She would not be happy for long, lolling in a hammock on a tropical beach, spitting melon seeds into the sand. Lazy-bones is not the first epithet that will spring to her friends' lips when they are asked on *This is Your*

Life to celebrate her life's work. Give her a task, however difficult, and she will complete it, probably superbly well, even if it means her going without sleep for a week. She gets great pleasure from doing things well. Wherever she turns her finely-honed talents she will succeed.

Communication is the most obvious choice. Writing books, reporting, lecturing, teaching, broadcasting, all involve dissemination of knowledge and at this Triangle/Virgo excels. She is particulary drawn to the written word. Her fine discriminating mind makes her fascinated by words and the complex combinations which produce either sentences of factual reportage or lines of melting poetry. She is also a critic – literary, theatrical, art, culinary, whatever – of great discernment, wielding an unsparing scalpel.

If Triangle/Virgo should decide to channel her prodigious energies into writing she has an impressive array of writers to inspire her who have shown their endurance in producing epic quantities of fine literature; Dante, Goethe, William Golding, Dr Johnson, DH Lawrence, JB Priestley, Tolstoy and HG Wells are all Virgos who have never shirked the sheer hard work involved in heavyweight literary production. On the more popular side, Shirley Conran, a Yang/Virgo, has never stopped being superwoman in whatever guise – now as popular novelist. Agatha Christie, Lady Longford and her daughter Lady Antonia Fraser and Fay Weldon (also Yang/Virgos) have all produced quantities of work too. The occasional slim volume is not Virgo's way.

Scholarship and teaching are also areas where Triangle/Virgo's skills can be well expressed. Although she may at first seem shy and self-effacing, the Triangle body shape gives her a natural force of character which cannot be ignored or overlooked. Her love of learning and articulate expression of ideas can make her an excellent teacher, but a stickler for accuracy and hard on any woolly thinking. This woman likes dealing with facts and logic, not vague feelings and intuitive speculation. She will accept anything that a student can back up with argument, but is not happy with subjective judgements and artistic interpretations.

She is discriminating in all that word's good and bad aspects. Triangle/Virgo can tell in an instant the kind of accent someone has, she recognizes a line from the play she did for an English examination, even if it was 40 years ago, she remembers conversations word for word, complete with inflexions. These fine critical faculties make her excellent in editorial jobs or anything requiring weighing of evidence and drawing conclusions such as report writing or policy making.

Triangle/Virgo can also be very skilled with her hands and may well go into craftwork where she is making intricate things, or mending precious objects, or perhaps restoring paintings. Her fine discrimination can be expressed visually as well and so she may be gifted at seeing the almost imperceptible graduations of colour – and being able to match them – which is a necessary skill in any restoration work. Her Triangle body type makes her even more of a perfectionist, and determined to be the best in her field. Her competitiveness burns brightly, even if she is just on a country bicycle ride with a friend. She likes to be first.

Ideal Fantasy Job

Chief crossword compiler for a national newspaper. The Triangle/Virgo mind is uniquely skilled at all word games and a crossword is the greatest intellectual wordgame of all. Who better to have the chief's job compiling the most fiendishly clever of all crosswords than her?

IN LOVE

Triangle/Virgo is essentially an impersonal combination. Virgo has a natural reserve and lack of ease with intimacy and the Triangle body type increases her sense of isolation and aloofness. She cares about people but it is hard for her to come across as warm and sympathetic. Too readily she can seem cool and clinical, and her genuine interest in others interpreted as critical.

Love anyway is a problem for Triangle/Virgo. The necessary giving up of control, venturing into the unknown is always something that she shies away from. As an intellectual star sign ruled by Mercury, the planet of communication, she is wooed through her mind. Talk will be the foreplay which will best catch her interest and warm her heart. And talk about her work too, for Triangle/Virgo will place her work very much at the centre of her life and can even identify herself almost solely with it. A man needs to be sympathetic to this in order to get behind her self-contained defences.

Triangle/Virgo will never be swept away on a tide of passion, and when she falls in love she will be above all practical and sensible in her choice. She might toy with a completely unsuitable boy for a while, but when it comes to serious decisions in anything from men to clothing, she will always choose the sane over the zany, the plain over the fancy, the good solid value over risk and excitment.

Her Yang+ body type means that a Yin man, caring, imaginative, in touch with his feelings, is the best partner for her. He might

give her the confidence to let some of her deep-rooted feelings out in return, for Triangle/Virgo can be a generous lover if she can hang up the critic's hat and put her competitive, workaholic side to sleep.

The debate about children and family life versus work will raise its head at some stage, later rather than sooner, and Triangle/ Virgo might have some difficulty in deciding if she really wants to confuse matters with the arrival of little demanding creatures who distinctly resist control. Work matters very much to her, she wants to carve a niche for herself and be the best in her particular field of skill or expertise. So she is unlikely to want to give up work permanently.

But she will be very particular about who looks after her children, should she decide to risk having any. Triangle/Virgo could never be an informal, lackadaisical mother, and she wouldn't want to employ anyone who would treat her children with an easy affection but lack of self-discipline and control. If she could afford it, the fully trained, even properly uniformed, nanny might seem to her the perfect solution. Then at least she'd be certain that they were brought up with proper manners and speaking well.

Triangle/Virgo can drive herself relentlessly and is a candidate for overwork and exhaustion. She allows herself so little time out for relaxation and fun and games. If she is a mother and a full-time worker, particularly in a demanding position, she is going to want to be perfect at both jobs and – given her natural obsessiveness and highly critical approach to herself and others – is bound to fail.

Her children will be beautifully provided for, well-turned out and mannerly, but they might long for a little letting down of hair back home at the ranch. Their hard-working mother is rather distracted and highly strung when it comes to trying to get her to listen to their day at school or offer a sympathetic shoulder to cry on. She is going to expect high academic achievements too, and will not look kindly on general slackness of ambition, goofing off, and sloppy work. This is a mother who installs domestic work rotas, reward and punishment systems and strict curfews. The only chance for her children of a more chaotic, child-centred regime is if they have a sweet, easy-going Yin father who will be more sympathetic to their points of view, and not so good at enforcing regulations.

Ideal Fantasy Lover

Jason Donovan and/or Phillip Schofield, his friend and substitute in the hit production of *Joseph and the Technicolored Dreamcoat*.

Both these men are sweety-pies of the first water, genuinely nice and kind and very, very Yin. Jason Donovan made his name in *Neighbours* which gave him a passionate following of fans and Phillip Schofield came to stardom through being a DJ and a television presenter and took over the role of Joseph from Jason. Both men would be supportive of Triangle/Virgo, and would help her relax and take life with a good few pinches of salt, and a lot more laughter. Humour is the levening agent in what can become for her a rather grim cycle of work, and more work.

IN STYLE

This woman is a paragon of neatness, chicness and understatement. She does not go for dressy clothes, for gold-embossed, gonged and tasselled, flashy, Versace clothes. She is classic and classy in her taste, always preferring the cool and coordinated to the brash. She does not want people to notice what she wears and comment on how expensively she dresses. (She's not profligate with money and so this is unlikely to be true.) The workmanship of the garments matter to her. A poorly sewn seam, a crooked hem, buttons which don't fit the button-holes, all irritate her greatly and immediately spoil a garment for her.

Her sense of colour too is likely to be subdued and classic. Navy, oatmeal, grey, black, taupe and cream are among her favourites. Cecil Beaton wrote a description in his 1946 diary of seeing Greta Garbo, the ultimate Triangle/Virgo type, 'No shadow of the conventional New York woman of fashion hovered near her; the hat could have belonged to a tinker engraved by Callot; and her skirt was that of a highwayman. In her all-greys she looked like a Mantegna. Although she exuded no impression of luxury one knew her to be a person of most sifted quality.' It is her very lack of flash and unnecessary detail which can make Triangle/Virgo look distinguished.

The style of clothes that really flatter Triangle/Virgo are determined by her body type. The Triangle shape has broader shoulders than hips and more of a marked waist than the Rectangle. She falls into two basic types, the small boned, boyish figure like Mia Farrow who probably rarely, if ever, puts on weight and the more muscular, athletic looking type, like Princess Stephanie of Monaco, Jamie Lee Curtis and Anjelica Huston, who can get heavy in the upper torso area, but keeps her inverted triangle shape with straight hips and lean lower legs. When thin, this shape is the classic fashion model shape with coat-hanger shoulders, next-to-nothing-hips and long lean legs.

Some women with this body type try to counteract their broad-shouldered look by wearing flimsy, ultra-feminine clothes – think of Diane Keaton (a Triangle/Aquarius) in *Annie Hall*. Those soft, drifty clothes on the angular Diane make her look a bit like Little Orphan Annie, rather gawky and fey. This suited the character very well in the film, but for Triangle/Virgo, wanting to be taken seriously in the real world, it can be a counter-productive look. Her femininity is best expressed with clothes that have simple geometric lines, certainly angled to the waist if she likes, but it's better to avoid soft fabrics, gathers and bows. For more information, see In Style on page 49.

Style Treat

This most dextrous and verbal of women would be happiest with a super little lap-top computer on which she could work as she travelled. Prone to workaholicism, Triangle/Virgo would be delighted to be able to utilize any spare moment of her time. There is no snoozing on airplanes, or watching second rate movies while swigging duty-free champagne: there is no lazy flicking through magazines on the train. While executive Triangle/Virgo is on the move she is hammering out the next report or proposal on the lovely little magic box on her knee. For modern women, this neat box of tricks has taken the place of the vanity case.

IN HEALTH

Nervous tension, and all the pyschosomatic illnesses that are associated with stress, are what can cause Triangle/Virgo trouble. Digestive upsets, exhaustion, ME, can be her body's last ditch attempt to get her to slow down a bit and learn how to relax. This is actually a robust body type with good powers of recovery. But Virgo anyway is known as the great hypochondriac – or rather most health conscious – member of the zodiac and the obsessiveness of the Triangle body type tends to make this even more the case.

To keep healthy, it is worth looking at the whole area of diet and exercise, too. The Triangle type is likely to have been slim as a teenager, athletic, and with a big appetite. In adulthood, the demands of a family and career can mean she does less exercise, eats the wrong things at wrong times, still has an unrestrained appetite and can then start putting on weight. Triangle/Virgo, however, is very organized and disciplined and when she decides to do something about her shape she works out a routine and readily sticks to it.

Triangle/Virgo positively *needs* regular, energetic exercise and can get depressed if she isn't doing enough. In Bel's questionnaire, 75 per cent of the Triangle types said they recognized that they needed to exercise *and* diet if they were to lose weight – and it was energetic exercise which they favoured: a much higher proportion than the other body types (for instance, only 30 per cent of the Pear types thought exercise important). For more specific information on diet and exercise, see In Health on page 50.

CELEBRITY TRIANGLE/VIRGO

Greta Garbo was an enigma while she lived and remains one now she is dead. She was a screen legend whose name has passed into common usage. She is the standard against which all other screen actresses are measured. But her personality and private life remain as mysterious as ever. Even before she went into permanent retreat, at the age of 36 and still at the height of her career, she was known for her reclusiveness, the aloofness of her temperament, her demand for 'closed' sets while working, her melancholy.

Her extraordinary beauty was only part of her mystique. The rest has something to do with her remote and utterly impenetrable character. Numerous people would approach, tentatively knock, and get no answer. No one has ever understood her, or even understood the material aspects of her life. Why did she quit so young? Why did she never marry? Why live alone, and apparently unhappy for nearly 50 years? She was a remarkable Triangle/Virgo who, nevertheless, had never managed to integrate her stardom, and the inevitability of having to have a public face, with her own intensely private, self-protective self.

TRIANGLE/VIRGO PROFILE

Frances is an academic in her mid-thirties. She is not married and has always enjoyed her work. 'Having status is important to me. It makes me feel good to work in a high status job. But I only realized recently how important working for a high status organization is for me. I went into academic work from business because I wanted more freedom to pursue other interests, but I realize that where I work now is not very high status. But when I feel put down or unappreciated by others I hang onto the fact that for one day a week I work for a man who is very high profile. This fact impresses my colleagues and students and it helps me keep up my self-esteem.'

She comes from a line of strong women who always worked, even when it was not the usual thing for married women and mothers to do so. Frances was always brought up to feel she had equal opportunities alongside her brothers. 'When I was young – eight years old I think – my dad asked me what I wanted to do when I grew up and I said "I want to go to Manchester Business School – after university." '

She felt she had some important things to do which having children would inhibit. 'However I have achieved most things now so would consider having kids. But I'd want the same status, with part-time work if possible. I do, however, have a fear of losing my self in having children.'

IN HOPE

Humour, a wider perspective, and time off from the routine of life, these are the Triangle/Virgo's essentials – to allow herself a bit more fun. Life is too short for it all to be serious. Although not a natural comedienne herself, Garbo and her myth could cause others some merriment. David Niven remembered an occasion when Garbo was unwillingly teamed with one of the Marx Brothers; 'Garbo had an icy look in her eyes when anyone sought to impose on her as Groucho Marx discovered one day. He saw a well-known figure approaching in slacks and floppy hat, waylaid her, bent down in his famous crouch and peered up under the brim. Two prisms of Baltic blue stared down at him and he backed away muttering "Pardon me, ma'am. I thought you were a guy I knew in Pittsburgh." ' Perhaps Triangle/Virgo could do with a Groucho in her life? But if a similar confrontation happened to her, let's hope she would have linked her arm in his and gone off with him, both doing his silly walk.

TRIANGLE

LIBRA

(Yang+/Yang)

MOTTO:

Where there's a will there's a way

IN LIFE

Perfectionism and a cool, emotionally detached intellect are what makes this woman a formidable force. She has the energy and ambition of her double Yang personality and the unsentimental ability to do what has to be done. Libra is traditionally known for her beauty and charm, and these attributes she undoubtedly has, never more pronounced than in the remarkable number of famous Yin body type Libras – the Hourglass/Libra actresses and personalities which start with the immortal Brigitte Bardot, through Julie Andrews and Catherine Deneuve and on to Anna Ford. The Triangle/Libra, however, is a different kind of charmer altogether. There is nothing soft and kittenish about her. She has beauty, she has social grace, but she is steely cool when it comes to knowing what she wants and getting what she needs.

Triangle/Libra is a dedicated worker. She is clever and there is nothing that she cannot do once she puts her mind to it. She is nothing like as frivolous and light-hearted as traditional astrology would claim. The Yang+ body type adds real heavyweight ambition to the airy lightness of the Libra star sign. She wants everything she does to be to the best of her ability, and when her competitive spirit is up, to best everyone else's ability too. Always seeking balance in her nature and in her life, she is thrown off-centre by failure or criticism. She wants to be liked, she wants to be good, she needs to be top.

Life is certainly more fun when a Triangle/Libra is around. She is cultured and talkative and has opinions on everything under the sun. She can, in fact, be terrifically opinionated even

about things she has no real experience of. One of Bel's Triangle/Libra clients ended up telling her how to run her business, even though she was an actress and hadn't done a day's work in any business in her life. She is full of good ideas but sometimes rather insensitive in the way she dogmatically puts them across.

Libra has an undoubted concern with outward appearance and needs to have beautiful things about her, to be beautiful herself. With the tendency for Triangle/Libra to turn rather obsessional, this concern with the appearance of things can be taken to the extremes of anxious self-regard, when she feels dissatisfied with her body and unattractive if any small thing is not quite right. That bit of extra weight on her tummy, that unexpected spot, can send her into a decline.

She loves the idea of courtship and romance – it is always the *idea* and the ideal that is so attractive, and the reality can be a different matter. This need for everything, including herself, to be so perfect can readily trap her in her own ego, with the world a reflecting mirror. She can easily feel disconnected from the human race. When she is anxious or unhappy, Triangle/Libra can become narcissistic, where no one except herself really exists emotionally. Creative work is her absolute need, especially that which allows her a platform in the world and involves other people. She is someone who needs to relate to others, not intimately, not passionately, but intellectually, in harmony and friendship. But she will always hold herself a little apart. This separateness is the legacy of the Yang+ body type, whose own sense of difference and competitiveness prevents her forgetting herself enough to truly unite with others in common humanity.

An over-riding sense of fairness is a great Triangle/Libra strength and it is one of the ways in which she can use her own desire for prominence and influence to do some good in the world. She hates inequality and unfairness – it's all part of that trying to balance the scales. Although she is willing to argue, even fight, for the ideal of equality, the Triangle/Libra character also has a powerful dose of the diplomat. She is not going to rush in, both pistols blazing, determined to right a wrong. She is more likely to want to approach the whole problem through negotiation, even flattery if need be.

It is in this conciliatory mode that she comes under greatest fire from bolder, more openly combative characters for being superficial, for sitting on the fence, betraying principles, for being weak-willed and lily-livered, even downright dishonest. She may, in fact, end up with an even more satisfactory outcome than does the gun-toting approach, it is just a matter of style, and

Triangle/Libra doesn't see any reason to make enemies if talking will serve the same ends.

IN WORK

Charm, diplomacy, physical attractiveness and ambition all combine in Triangle/Libra to produce a personality who can succeed at anything she does. She often has an excellent brain, unclouded by emotion and personal considerations. She has a capacity for dedicated work – in spurts – with some good times in between: she has a social adeptness which allows her to move in all strata of society without making waves.

Politics is an obvious arena for these talents. Speaker Betty Boothroyd, Edwina Currie, Melina Mercouri and Emma Nicholson are all Libras with Yang body types (mostly Rectangles) apart from the most famous – and toughest – of them all, the Triangle/Libra Mrs Thatcher.

The law is also a natural place for Triangle/Libra because of her real concern for justice. The fact that she can administer it dispassionately makes her more likely to go further than most other women in this male-dominated profession where her good, logical mind is appreciated. To succeed in male-dominated professions, where the rules and traditions have been made for men by men, a woman has to be more intelligent, more determined, more ambitious and tougher than the average man. Triangle/Libra can be just that and she will get as far as she possibly can in whatever branch of the profession she chooses. Her general air of lightness and attractiveness, and her flirtatiousness and pleasure in having a bevy of admiring male colleagues will help her too. She will not come over as a battle-axe, or a ball-breaker, although she may strike some colleagues as a pretty cool fish.

Other intellectual areas like teaching appeal too, but at the higher levels, or in administrative positions where there is some chance of wielding power and influence. Philosophical discussions, critical assessments, all suit her kind of analytical brain. Triangle/Libra can see all sides of an argument and although she is opinionated and can be fiercely emphatic she is always open to argument. She does not go in for irrational, feeling-driven opinions, like 'I loathe all Germans, they have a cruel and porky look' or 'It doesn't matter that I never have the car serviced, I just know I'll never have a car crash, it's not in my karma.'

The arts are also a natural place for the aesthetically minded Triangle/Libra. Most obvious would be the arts which are more intellectual, particularly writing and critical appraisal. One

Triangle/Libra writer was the brilliant Katherine Mansfield who died at 35 of TB. 'What was unusual about [her] – genius apart – was the persistence within her of the schoolgirl; theatrical, passionate in her wishes, surgically inquisitive, ruthlessly self-regarding in her decisions.' She cared about her work more than anything, and this is a characteristic of Triangle/Libra. Work matters for its creative outlet, its opportunity for her to impress herself on the world, to make money, have fine things, be acclaimed.

Acting also is a Libran pursuit, but it seems it is pursued more by the Hourglass/Libras than by other body types. There are only three prominent Triangle/Libras – Angie Dickinson, Britt Ekland and Sigourney Weaver – and only one of them has much real ability. But poetry and music too, involving a basic appreciation of all levels of harmony and balance, are areas where she can be really creative.

Ideal Fantasy Job

Television chat show hostess. As far as the arts and media are concerned, television presenting and chat show hosting is perhaps the place where Triangle/Libra is at her very best. She has every necessary quality – good to look at, charming, articulate and happy with the prominence involved in being the one who fronts a team. She is not one to shun the limelight either, handling most on-camera situations with coolness and grace.

Triangle/Libra, like all Libras, cares about her looks and enjoys good clothes. This would be a great opportunity to have some stunning outfits sent in to try, and to have the company foot some of her inordinate bills. A dream job.

IN LOVE

In the world of the emotions Triangle/Libra is often quite at sea. Her need to keep everything on an even keel, and *nice*, is too easily thwarted when she moves into the realm of the heart. She can be reliant on her friends to protect her from the realities of life where emotions, particularly, are often far from harmonious, pleasant and civilized. She is not a deeply feeling person and the passions aroused in others can baffle and disconcert her. She is much happier with charming company than with wild desire, profound love or heart-stopping ecstacy. But when she sets her heart on someone or something, she is as determined and obsessive about getting what she wants as anyone could be.

Friends matter to all Libras. It's the relating that she enjoys, but with Triangle/Libra there is less ease with intimate relationships, more need to be separate, a greater sense of competitiveness. Because work and success matter so much to this body type, friends can become useful connections, connections can be part of her power-broking. She is great at putting people together, because she enjoys their company as well as values their influence. Triangle/Libra has an attractiveness about her which draws attention and admiration. She is witty and flirtatious and enjoys having a band of adoring young men hanging on her every word. She is extremely loyal to her partners but can treat sex in a traditionally 'masculine' way, with some emotional detachment which can mean that she is not necessarily faithful – and that fact doesn't necessarily mean very much. 'It's not love, and it doesn't change the fantastic relationship I have with my husband – in fact it's something quite separate' was how one client explained this to Bel.

It is all tied up with the need for romance, the love of courtship, ritual, the pursuit, being desired. Romance is something that survives in the imagination, and evaporates pretty fast among the dirty laundry and everyday familiarity. Facing up to the lack of perfection in all human beings, and especially in all man/woman relationships, can be a painful and demoralizing thing for Triangle/Libra. So she may try to pretend she's still in a world of courtly love.

The kind of man for her double Yang+ personality is a real Yin man, caring, emotionally in touch, intuitive – and someone who is not going to be in competition with her. The writer Katherine Mansfield knew which sort of man to go for: 'Comfortable, if masterful adult men are to be found convincingly in her stories. None played a part in her life. She had a predilection for "boyish" lovers . . .' Yang women should leave the masterful men to their Yin sisters, Triangle/Libra needs her man to be nurturing, while she goes out and gets her name put up in lights. It might be that he has his name in lights too, but he will not be the sort of Yang, driven, ambitious personality she is. And he'll have to look good – he is an accessory of sorts on her elegant arm. And ideally have a good deal of money to help provide the stylish house, the good furniture and glamorous lifestyle – although Triangle/Libra is well-equipped to provide all that for herself.

The bearing and caring for children can cause 'huge conflicts', as one client admitted. Triangle/Libra wants to do everything perfectly – and that means mothering as well. Being a part-time mother with a part-time job suits many women who are realistic about what's possible and are happy enough to be 'good enough' at both jobs. But for Triangle/Libra it is almost the

worst scenario because then she knows she is doing neither job to the absolute best of her ability – and the lack of challenge and status in most part-time jobs is hard for her to bear. Working full-time means that she at least continues with her central concern, her career and the promotion of herself in the outside world. But then she can fear she's really failing to give her children the absolute best. It is hard being so demanding on herself, but she is more likely to plump for the full-time career and hand the children over to a well-vetted, highly caring full-time nurturer – or her husband.

Her house will be elegant, attractive, artistic and warm. Nothing too outrageous, but airy and light. Triangle/Libra is a terrific hostess. She knows just who to invite, how to mix them, what food to serve. She has a fine and aesthetic discrimination and a drive to harmonize and balance things, she is charming and gracious and always has something interesting to talk about. She will be attentive in every way to her guests. However, Triangle/Libra is too much of a perfectionist to take it all in her stride with casualness and ease. She wants it to be as good as possible, and that involves a great deal of thought and effort. Not very good at delegating – and then letting someone else get on with the job their way – she either has to do everything herself, or hangs over someone else's shoulder telling them how best to proceed.

Her children will find her a stimulating, honest and fair mother who doesn't submit them to emotional blackmail – but may just resort to benign dictatorship. She likes having things done her way and is wonderfully cooperative and appreciative as long as everyone falls in line, but does not tolerate mutiny or criticism.

Ideal Fantasy Lover

John Travolta is the perfect sweet-natured, sweet-faced guy for this super-cool Libra. He was sprung to phenomenal fame with his performance in *Saturday Night Fever* but after Grease a series of flops followed. (Someone with the discernment of Triangle/Libra might have knocked some sense into him and helped him choose a few more winners.) However, it was the soft-hearted comedy *Look Who's Talking* which returned him to great box office success and showed he could be affecting, and funny, as well as dance up a storm.

Triangle/Libra is likely to be quite a fancy dancer herself, so she couldn't wish for a better partner. He'd also make a terrific father, on the evidence of *Look Who's Talking* where he co-stars with a wise-cracking baby – and would be quite some accessory to wear on her arm!

IN STYLE

Triangle/Libra looks good whatever she's wearing. Appearances matter to her and she has innate style. Her love of balance and harmony is reflected in her choice of clothes. She doesn't go for any excess or vulgarity. Coolness, coordination, classic lines and classy styles are her natural choice. The more arty Rectangle/Triangles might experiment a bit with wilder accessories or an unusual colour combination, but on the whole this woman is not going to be a zany dresser. Status matters to her too, and she likes the idea of wearing really expensive clothes. If the cognoscenti recognize the fact that they're expensive and exclusive all the better. There is a part of her which thinks you are what you wear. And she is cool and classy.

The style of clothes that really flatter Triangle/Libra are determined by her body type. The Triangle shape has broader shoulders than hips and more of a marked waist than the Rectangle. She falls into two basic types, the small boned, boyish figure like Mia Farrow who probably rarely, if ever, puts on weight and the more muscular, athletic looking type, like Princess Stephanie of Monaco, Jamie Lee Curtis and Anjelica Huston, who can get heavy in the upper torso area, but keeps her inverted triangle shape with straight hips and lean lower legs. When thin, this shape is the classic fashion model shape with coat-hanger shoulders, next-to-nothing-hips and long lean legs.

Some women with this body type try to counteract their broad-shouldered look by wearing flimsy, ultra-feminine clothes – think of Diane Keaton (a Triangle/Aquarius) in *Annie Hall*. Those soft, drifty clothes on the angular Diane make her look a bit like Little Orphan Annie, rather gawky and fey. This suited the character very well in the film, but for Triangle/Libra, wanting to be taken seriously in the real world, it can be a counterproductive look. Her femininity is best expressed with clothes that have simple geometric lines, certainly angled to the waist if she likes, but it's better to avoid soft fabrics, gathers and bows. For more specific information, see In Style on page 49.

Style Treat

A good quality handbag – and Triangle/Librans love quality – will last for years, but care should be taken with choice of style, scale and colour. All accessories for the Triangle type should follow the same line as her body and clothes. The most flattering shape of bag is geometric – square, rectangle, triangle – and should be made in stiff leather or patent. Square buckles, straight

seams or panels, mock-croc, snakeskin or lizard patterning give reinforcement to the geometric look of this most important accessory. Because Triangle/Libran prefers a classy, understated look, she should choose a bag in a neutral colour – brown, taupe, pewter, navy or black – to give the greatest versatility. It is important to check that the colour of the garment you are buying suits you well. Take it into daylight, hold it under your chin and look at what it does to your skin, eyes and hair. If wearing it intensifies and enlivens your colouring then that is a colour that is right for your skin tones. If you look washed out or sallow, or your hair loses colour and dark rings seem to appear under your eyes, then you are getting it wrong. This sounds a lot of trouble to go to, but it is worth it for it enhances the pleasure you will get every time you wear it.

Finally, consideration needs to be given to scale. If Triangle/Libra is petite she should choose a small to medium size handbag, whereas the taller Triangle type needs a large size handbag.

Since her career is such an important part of Triangle/Libra's life and as she likes to have the right accessories for the job, and everything as beautiful and chic as possible, it's worth her while choosing her briefcase carefully. This is her most important – and probably most expensive – accessory. She is best with a rigid-framed type in stiff, shiny leather. The soft leathers and unstructured cases just don't look chic enough for this body type. Colour again should be chosen with the same considerations as for the handbag. If she doesn't want to look overwhelmed by the size, petite Triangle/Libra should choose a slim, small-scale briefcase. A final consideration, for business it is best to carry either a handbag or a briefcase, rather than both at once as this gives a cluttered, unprofessional look.

IN HEALTH

It may be a bore but once again balance is the key to Triangle/Libra's health. She should be strong and robust, but she can become anxious due to her competitiveness and perfectionism which can cause nervous exhaustion, cystitis, kidney trouble and hypertension. She also needs to have lots of air and can be prone to claustrophobia.

To keep healthy, it is worth looking at the whole area of diet and exercise, too. The Triangle type is likely to have been slim as a teenager, athletic, and with a big appetite. In adulthood, the demands of a family and career can mean she does less exercise, eats the wrong things at wrong times, still has an unrestrained appetite and can then start putting on weight. Triangle/Libra, however, is very organized and disciplined and when she decides to do something about her shape she works out a routine and readily sticks to it.

Triangle/Libra positively *needs* regular, energetic exercise and can get depressed if she isn't doing enough. In Bel's questionnaire, 75 per cent of the Triangle types said they recognized that they needed to exercise *and* diet if they were to lose weight – and it was energetic exercise which they favoured: a much higher proportion than the other body types (for instance, only 30 per cent of the Pear types thought exercise important). For more specific information on diet and exercise, see In Health on page 50.

CELEBRITY TRIANGLE/LIBRA

Sigourney Weaver is a tall, handsome woman who excels at playing tough, cool women in nasty situations. She became best known internationally as the astronaut Ripley in *Alien* and then went on to feature in *Working Girl* and *Gorillas in the Mist*. Now well into her forties she is showing no signs of loosing her grip on any big Yang heroine part Hollywood might have up for grabs.

In her private life she has followed the pattern of Yang women being attracted to Yin men. She made the first move and asked a handsome man working behind the bar at a small theatre festival in Massachusetts to dance. She has since married him, a tall, gentle, fringe theatre director who is five years her junior and happy to cook and look after their young daughter Charlotte when he's not working. He's not phased by the fact that his wife brings home the bacon, £3.3 million worth of bacon for her last movie, 'we're not conspicuous spenders, there's not a lot of toys that I want to have.'

TRIANGLE/LIBRA PROFILE

Fiona is a journalist, married with two children, and running her work from an office at home. She is very successful but has taken some time to recognize where she wants to channel her energies and ambitions. 'Work is very important to me. When I was young I wasn't very focused. I was a late developer. But now I feel I'm coming into my own.'

She had known since she was about 13 that she wanted to be a journalist but was lacking in confidence and so did not choose that career straight away. 'I wanted children too but I always knew that I would have to continue working as I wouldn't be

happy not working. I was lucky. I could have my cake and eat it too because my mother helped with the children. This gave me enough of a safety valve to survive.'

It gave her a sense of freedom, she says, but acknowledges too how difficult it is for a woman working from home: 'You don't have a career structure in the same way as when you go out to work. I feel quite cross about this – I sit on panels with City blokes who are paid fat salaries and are all paid to be there and I'm not. Yet I come up with better ideas than theirs. But you can't have it all. It was my decision to work freelance although I may not have realized exactly what I would be missing.'

Fiona had been all set to go back to work after the birth of her first baby. She had a very senior job where she was boss, with lots of power and control, which mattered to her. But a series of domestic crises forced her to reconsider leaving the house and baby in someone else's charge. 'But in my first two years as a mother I wrote my first two books. But I was also quite ill for years – permanently depressed for years. But that isn't the case any more.'

She now feels she has sorted out her work so that it suits her needs as well as possible. 'Now only sometimes do I feel I'm not in control of my work, and being out of control irritates me. The basic difference between a career and having children is that a career gives definite, tangible success in terms of status, power and money. But children are difficult. Success is not so tangible. Teenagers are such a problem that you more often than not wonder where you've failed!'

IN HOPE

In the *Odyssey* Homer writes, 'We cannot all hope to combine the pleasing qualities of good looks, brains and eloquence.' But, of course, this is just what Triangle/Libra does manage to combine so pleasingly. The crack in her armour, however, is her drive for perfectionism. She makes life hard for herself and for those closest to her by this fear that nothing is ever quite good enough, the concern that she will never be the best. But it is only in her faults and her failing that she allows other people to come closer and identify with her, that she manages to make real connections, real friends, true relationships. And this, rather than an abstract perfection, is what makes Triangle/Libra so Homerically pleasing – even perfect!

TRIANGLE

SCORPIO

(Yang+/Yin+)

MOTTO:

Strength in adversity

IN LIFE

Emotional intensity, force of character and the will to achieve, characterize this extraordinary combination of opposing forces. Scorpio, as a water sign, is to do with profundity of emotion, depth of intuition and terrific collected power. It is a Yin+ star sign, allied with the ultra Yang Triangle body type which itself gives executive energy, desire for worldly achievement, and single-mindedness of purpose. Triangle/Scorpio is a powerhouse of passion and will. There is also nothing conventional about this woman, nor does she care. Of all the 48 combinations, Triangle/Scorpio cares least of all what others may think of her, she has her own path to tread and it will never be a path that many have trod before her.

But she has a difficult tiger to ride. Underneath the tough exterior and the indomitable will, which can bring her whatever she needs in life, is a sensitive heart needing to make human connections. She is unhappy if she has to exist self-contained and alone. Her emotional nature adds depth and fascination to a character who hides her deepest self, and yet is driven to express that self. Externally Triangle/Scorpio is dynamic, opinionated, enormously determined, even obsessive. She is intolerant of weakness, laziness and indecisiveness in others: with so much get-up-and-go herself, she cannot understand that some people are shyer, slower, more concerned with the opinions or feelings of others, less certain that they are always right.

But to her friends and family, or anyone in trouble, she is loyal and caring and will do what she can to help. That help is much

more likely to involve action than receptive sympathy (that she'll leave to her Yin Scorpio sisters) but she will go to great efforts to fight injustices, change circumstances, move things on. Triangle/Scorpio can lose patience, however, if the friend in need does not start to pull herself together and *do* something to improve her situation. She is not a saint – and doesn't ever pretend to be one.

Triangle/Scorpio is in no way an easy-going, laid back kind of woman. Whenever she's around life seems more interesting, sometimes more dangerous. She can laugh at herself, it's true, and knows how to have a good time. Sometimes wildly wacky, she is at heart serious, powerful (although she's good at hiding just how powerful) and never rests in her quest to improve herself – and others too! She is in the business of transformation, and that is an eternally difficult task and makes her restless, questing.

Although this sign produces some of the most beautiful actresses (Grace Kelly, Vivien Leigh, Demi Moore, Julia Roberts, Jaclyn Smith), Triangle/Scorpio does not have to be beautiful to be noticed. She may be small, she may not necessarily be very striking-looking at first glance, but she will never be overlooked. There is an energy, a mysterious force of character that emanates from her, and she probably has the legendary Scorpio's eagle-eyes which can speak volumes – as well as transfix her prey with their unswerving gaze.

She does not care for spontaneous living. She is much happier knowing just where she stands, and where everyone else stands in relation to her. Above all, she needs to be in control, both of herself and life around her, which includes those who come into her orbit. This can produce the greatest friction, for she finds it very hard to let others do things their way, to move out of her sphere of influence. It is particularly hard to get her to change a little in order to meet them just a bit of the way. Everything is done to her very high and demanding standards and she cannot necessarily see that there are other standards that may be just as valid, and which her colleague or lover believes in, just as strongly – well *almost* as strongly. There are few characters who feel so passionately about everything as does Triangle/Scorpio.

Her Yang+ body type means that she has little patience with self-analysis and reflection. Fascinated by human behaviour as Scorpio is, Triangle/Scorpio doesn't often stop long enough to wonder why she does or feels certain things. She externalizes. Rather than stop long enough to hold the mirror up to herself, she rushes on in her own world of great extremes, of black and white, them and us, good and bad. Grey areas don't interest her, neither do excuses. She is sceptical of flattery and gush and soft, liberal views. As she sees it, it is all to do with getting on with the hand that life has dealt you. It is up to each individual to make the most of their cards; what's the point in sitting there moaning because you haven't got a trump? This is what you've got and only you can play this hand. She has little patience with the weak and inadequate.

The painter Georgia O'Keeffe is one of these remarkable Triangle/Scorpio individualists. She explained once that when she moved from New York to the desert of New Mexico she wanted to begin painting the monumental landscapes there. She looked for someone to show her how, 'But no one could show me how to paint landscape. They could show me how to paint *their* landscape, but I had to find out for myself how to paint *my* landscape.' That is Triangle/Scorpio to a T. Scorpios Picasso and Rodin were two other great individualist artists, indifferent to the world's opinion of them or to generally accepted models of behaviour. Solitary, unique, courageous, Triangle/Scorpio doesn't mind what others think and just goes her own way without fuss.

IN WORK

Triangle/Scorpio is better working on her own, as a freelancer or consultant, or if she's in a team she's happiest as boss. She is not an easy boss because she expects as much from her employees as she puts in herself. She sees through every trick in the book and is intolerant of laziness, sloppiness, dishonesty and complaint. Not naturally blabbermouths or sharers, she plays her hand close to her chest and keeps others guessing as to what she's up to. Her great redeeming feature, however, is the fact that she does not particularly value status, unless it's necessary for her progress upwards to at least acknowledge it. Neither is she interested in hierarchies, except in so far as they point the way for her ambitions. Having the biggest office, the most expensive car in the garage and the best perks are not what she's about. Her superiority is internal and she does not have to wear badges to proclaim it.

The law really is a good place for her to exercise her strong sense of justice, but it is as a barrister or judge that she is happiest, ploughing her own furrow, and making her own decisions. She is very good at being decisive and acting on her decisions. It is only one step sideways into politics, and that is a natural move too for Triangle/Scorpio to make. The admirable, and alarming, Indira Gandhi, Prime Minister of India until her assassination in 1984, showed both sides of this complex combination

: a ruthless natural autocrat and a composed, courageous and courteous mother of her country.

Triangle/Scorpio also has the emotional power and strength of purpose to make her career as an artist in any field, but her voice will always be a strong one; there is nothing frivolous and soft about these Rectangle/ and Triangle/Scorpios – Roseanne Barr, Jodie Foster, Dame Elizabeth Frink, Whoopi Goldberg, Jamie Lee Curtis, Mahalia Jackson, Demi Moore, Georgia O'Keefe, Joan Plowright (Lady Olivier) and Dame Joan Sutherland.

It is in the area of artistic expression that the two contrary forces in this character, the Yin+ feeling, intuitive side, and the Yang+ side, driven, ambitious and self-orientated, can come together in powerful creativity. The Triangle body shape gives her the focus and toughness to drive her ambitions through any amount of competition and opposition. The Scorpio adds the emotional and spiritual force of understanding, sensitivity and ability to transform and be transformed. Triangle/Scorpio has not only the will to succeed, she has the strong sense of her own individuality which makes her such a distinctive artist, unconcerned with fashions or trends.

Her organizational skills are phenomenal. Triangle/Scorpio could really run a whole army with the most amazing efficiency and precision. This ability needs to be put to good use, however, otherwise it can turn her into a bit of a domestic tyrant. Running a public company is just where she belongs, but she more than many women feels the injustice of the kinds of predudices that women come up against. Because her nature and ambitions tend towards the traditionally masculine, she is more exposed to the glass ceilings – or sometimes the glass door – which greets women in certain walks of life.

Detection and research is another area of traditional Scorpio talent. Certainly if there was more opportunity to be a Private Eye, then Triangle/Scorpio would make a particularly good one. She is gifted at uncovering mysteries (while keeping her own intact), excellent at research, and her Triangle body shape makes her particularly courageous and unsentimental. She is able to do what necessarily has to be done, and is unsqueamish about the doing.

Journalism and biography also use this ability of hers for research and endurance. There is a Triangle/Scorpio absolutely dominating the glossy and cut-throat world of fashion magazines – Anna Wintour, who went from editor of *British Vogue* to the even more powerful and prestigious post as editor of *American Vogue*, and queen bee of the powerful Conde Nast empire.

Medicine is another profession for Triangle/Scorpio. She has the extra Yang drive to succeed where other women have found it hard to make inroads – areas like heart or brain surgery – all the higher kudos, higher paid specialities which have been largely kept by men for themselves. When Triangle/Scorpio has come into herself, and it may take some time for this is a strong and difficult character to live with, then there is nothing which she cannot achieve.

Ideal Fantasy Job

Artist – with a cult following. Triangle/Scorpio particularly likes metal and monumentality and so she is perhaps best fitted to be a sculptor, but any artist who can pursue her own ideas, without interference from outside, would suit this highly creative and individual character very well. A Triangle/Scorpio artist with a real cult following is Georgia O'Keefe. As far as her art was concerned, she pursued an individual, largely figurative line, with her stylized, erotically-charged flower paintings, and her geometrical New York cityscapes and desert landscapes. She set out to make herself an icon and succeeded brilliantly, enhancing her reputation as an artist and her way of living in the process. But she was only ever interested in herself. No life could be so well-suited to a Triangle/Scorpio – entirely her own person, working alone, world-famous, influential and admired – and therefore free to go on living just as she pleased.

IN LOVE

Usually an area of emotional turmoil and high drama – but then that's how Triangle/Scorpio likes it best. She is never happier than when up against it in some way. Challenge and excitement energize her, familiarity and contentment get her down. She feels passionately about life and love. But her Yang+ body type means she has a healthy respect for her own interests and is less likely to sacrifice herself on the alter of someone else's ambitions or desire. She needs to make deep connections with others and is naturally loyal and committed, but she is also very aware of her own boundaries and can be tough-minded and matter-of-fact in saying 'This far and no further'. She is not going to submerge her personality and aspirations for long.

She can get moody and resentful, however, when she feels that her loyalty and commitment are not returned in kind, and in fact it is very hard for other less intense personalities to offer the same degree of intensity in return. The sort of man for Triangle/Scorpio

has to be Yin. She couldn't bear to have to relinquish control, or even share it, with a Yang bloke, with what would seem to her to be his overbearing manner and macho posturing. If anyone's going to do the bossing about it's going to be her. She'll do it more subtly than a Triangle/Leo might for instance, but she's just as likely to get her own way.

The ultra-Yang body type of Triangle/Scorpio makes her the least intuitive combination of an otherwise very intuitive star sign. This means she has the powerful feelings but can sometimes misunderstand them and throw herself into completely the wrong situations, with some pretty explosive results. Her lack of interest in introspection, results in her feeling sometimes she is in the grip of forces which she cannot properly understand – let alone find how to harness them for creative rather than destructive purpose. She is not at ease sitting around with a load of women friends rapping about the movements of her heart, or soul. She is serious and she is a woman who acts rather than emotes or sympathizes.

Triangle/Scorpio needs a gentle, soft-hearted soul who welcomes her organizing abilities, her confidence and dynamic approach to life. He is not in competition with her, and is happy for her to gallop out to see off dragons – or tilt at windmills – while he gets on with quieter, more internal pursuits, like thinking, doing the gardening or playing with his children.

Triangle/Scorpio will probably want to have children. But she will not relish the idea of giving up work – and the excitement and influence which comes with operating in the world outside – to care for them full-time. She is passionate and loyal towards them, but is bored by the minutiae of domestic life. As she'll candidly admit, she is not very good at having to think of the needs of others 24 hours of the day. She is happier continuing her career and sharing the care of her children with their father or a paid help.

She is unorthodox and goes her own way in work and life. Her house can be anything from the most conservative and spotlessly clean abode to a zany, eclectic collection of things bought on the spur of the moment, or dragged back on camels from far flung lands. She is not a social climber, she is not particularly concerned with displaying status, but because she is pragmatic rather than romantic she is aware of the hard realities of life. She will play whatever game is necessary to get on, as long as her personal honesty and integrity remain unbreached. So her children will not have great expectations put upon them, other than a certain independence and mannerliness, a sense that they should fulfil some of their potential. This is not a mother-hen sort of mother, they are kicked out of the nest pretty smartish, although there is always some corner of the nest to which to return.

Ideal Fantasy Lover

Jeremy Irons is tall, broodingly sensitive and sexy. This man can match the tortured depths of Triangle/Scorpio and not be too phased by her bossiness. Starting his film career with romantic roles as Charles Ryder in a television adaptation of *Brideshead Revisited* and then opposite Meryl Streep in *The French Lieutenant's Woman*, he showed his more tortured side as a saintly Jesuit in *The Mission*, more than holding his own against the powerful (and overwhelmingly Yang) Robert de Niro.

IN STYLE

Triangle/Scorpio will one day pay as litle attention as possible to her clothes, throwing on an old pair of jeans and a man's shirt, and then she'll turn up dressed to the nines. Dramatic, theatrical and sexy is her preferred mode of dressing when she can be bothered. She likes provoking strong reactions in people. She hates looking too classically understated and will add some distinctive touch to an outfit if she feels it's erring too far to the conventional.

Yang women generally are not thrilled by the whole palaver of clothes. The feel of the fabric, the experimentation with colour and different looks and accessories bores them after about five minutes. If they could have a marvellous coordinating wardrobe, bought for them twice a year, and then didn't have to think about clothes again they would be happy. But Triangle/Scorpio is realistic enough to know how important are looks and clothes if one wants to get on in the world, be attractive and yet get taken seriously.

When she can bring herself to buy some clothes, it helps to know some pointers. The style of clothes that really flatter Triangle/Scorpio are determined by her body type. The Triangle shape has broader shoulders than hips and more of a marked waist than the Rectangle. She falls into two basic types, the small boned, boyish figure like Mia Farrow who probably rarely, if ever, puts on weight and the more muscular, athletic looking type, like Princess Stephanie of Monaco, Jamie Lee Curtis and Anjelica Huston, who can get heavy in the upper torso area, but keeps her inverted triangle shape with straight hips and lean lower legs. When thin, this shape is the classic fashion model shape with coat-hanger shoulders, next-to-nothing-hips and long lean legs.

Some women with this body type try to counteract their broad-shouldered look by wearing flimsy, ultra-feminine clothes – think of Diane Keaton (a Triangle/Aquarius) in *Annie Hall.* Those soft, drifty clothes on the angular Diane make her look a bit like Little Orphan Annie, rather gawky and fey. This suited the character very well in the film, but for Triangle/Scorpio, wanting to be taken seriously in the real world, it can be a counter-productive look. Her femininity is best expressed with clothes that have simple geometric lines, certainly angled to the waist if she likes, but it's better to avoid soft fabrics, gathers and bows. For more specific information, see In Style on page 49.

Style Treat

Evening clothes are tricky for all Triangle types. Frills, flounces, bare shoulders with a scooped neckline, cinched waistlines and full skirts just do not flatter her shape. Instead, Triangle/Scorpio should choose simple, geometric lines – like a sheath dress in a rich, crisp fabric like silk gabardine, lame or beaded and sequinned work on a strong base fabric.

Another good idea for Triangle/Scorpio, who tends to be ingenious and likes adapting things to suit her character, is to customize a plain, business-type jacket. She can take a jacket which she might have tired of, or which itself is tired with slightly fraying edges perhaps, and edge it with metallic braiding or trim. This emphasizes the geometric look of lapels and hem which is so flattering to a Triangle shape. For a full military look, she could splash out on some really classy metal buttons in the same colour as the trim, to make a really flashy but becoming evening jacket.

Petite Triangle types should stick to one row of braid and small to medium size buttons, but the taller Triangle types can go the whole works, a double row of braid, tasselled epaulettes even, with medium to large buttons. The colour choice of the metal is important – for advice on choosing gold or silver, see page 50.

This glamorous, individual and chic garment can then be teamed with a narrow skirt or trousers for an individual and flattering evening look which will take Triangle/Scorpio to anything from a cocktail party to the opera or a club.

IN HEALTH

Triangle/Scorpio is seldom ill. She has a robust constitution and terrific powers of endurance. Suppressing her emotions and tension generally can cause her some trouble, however. She is not a laid back character and feels everything deeply. She loves and loathes things, rarely equivocates. 'Either will do, I really don't mind' are not words she'll use about decisions. So all this emotional energy has to find creative outlet otherwise it can bank up, causing outbreaks of stress-related illness, like exhaustion, allergic reactions or aches and pains. Traditionally, it is her reproductive system which might cause some health problems. The best preventative is living as healthily as possible and finding time for exercise, relaxation and counting of blessings.

To keep healthy, it is worth looking at the whole area of diet and exercise, too. The Triangle type is likely to have been slim as a teenager, athletic, and with a big appetite. In adulthood, the demands of a family and career can mean she does less exercise, eats the wrong things at wrong times, still has an unrestrained appetite and can then start putting on weight. Triangle/Scorpio, however, is very organized and disciplined and when she decides to do something about her shape she works out a routine and readily sticks to it.

Triangle/Scorpio positively *needs* regular, energetic exercise and can get depressed if she isn't doing enough. In Bel's questionnaire, 75 per cent of the Triangle types said they recognized that they needed to exercise *and* diet if they were to lose weight – and it was energetic exercise which they favoured: a much higher proportion than the other body types (for instance, only 30 per cent of the Pear types thought exercise important). For more specific information on diet and exercise, see In Health on page 50.

TRIANGLE/SCORPIO CELEBRITY

The actress Demi Moore has shown just how far and how fast ambition, business acumen and a formidably focused will can take someone. She was just one other good-looking actress with talent until she was cast opposite Patrick Swayze in *Ghost*, where the touching and sentimental plot line, her beauty and nudity sprang her to wider notice. Soon afterwards, she etched herself on everyone's eyeballs and memory with her sensational appearance – beautiful, naked and nine months pregnant – on the cover of *Vanity Fair*. She was married to one of the princes of Hollywood, Bruce Willis – and that had brought its own rewards in terms of fame – but by posing for that photograph Demi swung the celebrity spotlight firmly back on herself. As a publicity stunt it was inspired.

She has a terrifying reputation for being so tough, for going for the big money that equals if not challenges the male star's

fees, for knowing just where she's going and refusing to compromize on any small detail – like the size of her limousine or the availability of the executive jet.

To be fair, she is behaving no worse from a business point of view than tough old hands like the ultra-Yang Sean Connery, who is known for his steely negotiating. She wants to be a star and she will do whatever has to be done. She also doesn't much care what people say about her personally, which is another strength in a bitchy town. She is tough and capable of anything which involves her indomitable will. While she was a young actress (and part of the Brat Pack), trying to make it in Hollywood, she was abusing drugs and alcohol until she was bawled out on a film and threatened with being fired. 'In 24 hours this young woman turned her life around.' her director recalled, 'It was an extraordinary, mature step in a very fragile life.' The only thing he got wrong is Demi's fragility. As a Triangle/Scorpio she is innately powerful, full of doubts maybe, tortured with a childhood which didn't have enough love, perhaps, but as a person this woman is not a delicate, fragile little flower.

TRIANGLE/SCORPIO PROFILE

Anastasia is a copywriter in a large advertising agency. She is beautiful and naturally very blonde, with two grown-up daughters. 'One of my main problems that I've had to overcome is being blonde. It doesn't matter so much now that I'm older, but when I was young everyone thought I was pretty and sweet – and just a bimbo. I don't think I'd ever call myself sweet. In fact, I'd rather be a man. They have things handed to them on a plate. In my business I meet so many men in middle management who are really *stupid*. They enter a career and there's a ladder for them already in place, however mediocre they are. You have to be so much better than that to get anywhere as a woman. Just look at our language, if you're a man then you're dynamic, but the same behaviour in a woman is labelled aggressive.'

She feels the same double-standards exist in relationships and parenthood. 'Women have to put 80 per cent into their relationships while men can get away with only about 20 per cent. When I wanted to go to university full time when my children were small, I had a great deal of opposition. My own mother said, if I didn't want to look after my children why did I have them? Women aren't allowed to be single-minded in the same way men are. But I didn't like being at home with small children. I loathed small children.'

In fact, she's been a marvellous mother whose daughters know they can turn to her for anything – and who get on really well with each other too. But Anastasia feels that when she was a child she didn't fit in anywhere, 'I was a round peg in a square hole. There was this feeling, "oh dear, she's not a boy, what a shame" because my father, a really old-fashioned Mr Barrett of Wimpole Street type of man, had a business which he wanted to pass on to a son.' Actually she'd be terrific at running any company, far better than most men.

Ana characterizes her best qualities as being her organizational ability, her honesty and foresight. She can plan ahead and is at her best in emergencies. If she'd been educated with the thought that women could do more than get married and have children she would have made a great barrister. She can argue the hindlegs off a stuffed elephant and gets incensed by the stupidity of so many people in power. Injustice gets her writing to newspapers. She is also so terrifyingly decisive, quick-witted and punctual, that those who aren't quite so well-endowed with these qualities quail as she greets them, quietly breathing fire through her nostrils.

'I'd have done a darn sight more with my life if I hadn't got so emotionally involved with my men. I remember as a teenager turning down a chance to go and study at the Lycee Francais in Paris because I wouldn't leave my boyfriend of the moment. But I always felt I needed all the love I could get, but then resented that that stopped me pursuing my own interests wholeheartedly.' She has a great deal of energy which she recognizes can be used positively or negatively. Her frustrations with being at home with small children, having a husband who was working so hard he was rarely at home and did very little to help, made her ready to fall into the arms of another man. Deciding to go on with her education was a result of realizing she would continue to express her energy destructively if she didn't start doing something constructive instead.

IN HOPE

It is hard in a male-dominated culture to be a woman with this force of character and unwillingness to play the soft, sweet womanly role. Triangle/Scorpio is at her best in a position of power, where she can be most truly herself, not worrying about whether her boss can take her level of competence and ambition without feeling threatened and ending up firing her. She is at her best too in relationships where passion, honesty and forthrightness is seen

as a strength and not an undermining influence. It's perhaps interesting to look to Demi Moore one last time and director Alan Rudolph's assessment of this singular personality, 'What she wants, she gets. She has an opinion on everything and she lets you know it. She's very, very smart. She's like a beautiful ballerina who can also kick-box'.

TRIANGLE

SAGITTARIUS

(Yang+/Yang)

MOTTO:

She travels fastest who travels alone

IN LIFE

This is a combination of Yang qualities which makes for an adventurous, lively and ambitious character who will never stay still for long. She has a questing mind and an athletic body which loves movement and travel. Challenge and exploration, both physical and intellectual, are what make her tick. She cannot be caged in either a routine job or a life without a view. Her imagination and energy is larger than life: with inflated ideas and the confidence to try and put them into practice. Triangle/Sagittarius can sometimes get carried away with her own imagination as to how her plans should work, or how the latest project she has thought out will come off. There is nothing slow and plodding and down-to-earth about her. She has big plans and bigger dreams, but unlike Rectangle/Sagittarius who expresses them freely and exuberantly, Triangle/Sagittarius veils the true extent of her ambitions from others – and sometimes from herself.

The last of the fire signs, Sagittarius is intuitive and optimistic, with her eyes set on a distant horizon. Her Triangle body shape, however, makes her more focused on her homeland, more ambitious for material success and tangible achievement. But she will be left standing in the starting blocks when it comes to the really ambitious achievers, like Triangle/Taurus and Triangle/Capricorn. Triangle /Sagittarius is too easily distracted by interesting ideas, and new avenues which need to be explored, to ever be able to drive along a straight, undiverting single track, and keep her eyes on the road.

She is an optimist, but also an opportunist, and is never slow to see openings and possibilities which will bring her closer to her

goal. Or just give her the chance of getting out of a dead-end she may currently be in. Triangle/Sagittarius sees no reason why she should continue one path when it has ceased to be interesting or useful to her. One of her great strengths, as well as weaknesses, is her ability to kick up her heels and head for the hills when things lose their lustre. She does not sit around moaning and making herself and everyone else miserable, but neither does she stick at things through loyalty to others, or a sense that good will prevail. She does not even allow herself to find out if in fact the most valuable things in life are those for which you have to struggle.

This double Yang combination is not naturally at ease with passionate feelings and psychological introspection. If she's forced to confront them she can misunderstand her feelings and mistime her responses to others. She feels happier with a group than with intimate tête-à-têtes, more relaxed with friends than with lovers – and happy to turn lovers into friends. Hurt feelings, intense suffering or ecstatic desire are areas of human experience she would rather avoid.

Triangle/Sagittarius has an air of self-sufficiency, a feeling that sometimes her mind is elsewhere, on larger issues than the everyday. She needs to understand life, not her own personal life so much as the great mystery of the universe and the networks of human life within it. She might well have a strong religious sense, which need not be orthodox in any way, but which allows for a connectedness between mankind and something larger. This is what gives her the horizons towards which she travels, either in the physical world, or more likely in her philosophy. This is why she cannot live without a view, but why she also cannot live with hand-in-glove intimacy and closeness. Familiarity is her dread and claustrophobia her fear.

This woman is opinionated. She has thought about many things and pursues knowledge with alacrity. But she is a mutable sign and so she does not become obstinately fixed. She does not hold her opinions for all time, although she may express them very emphatically while she has them. She can be rather overkeen to impress with her knowledge, or her fashionable insights into the latest literary novel, newest celebrity author, the hottest critical judgements in town. But she is always fundamentally honest, and her bluff can be called when she will admit she is a terrible groupie for the latest enthusiasms.

Triangle/Sagittarius enjoys risk. This can take the form of going in for sports or activities which involve physical danger, like off-piste skiing or bungee-jumping, motorbike racing or travelling alone into uncharted seas/jungles/war zones. But for other Triangle/Sagittarius it might be expressed more internally, courting that adrenalin buzz by gambling, playing the more risky side of the stock market, or having unsuitable affairs. Harebreadth escapes exhilarate her. She loves excitement, adventure, challenge, danger, pitting herself against some other force, be it elemental or man-made. The word alone is important because above all this combination is an individualist. Deep down, she is happiest working, dreaming, questing for the holy grail, or the secret of life. Or just the answer to which turning she takes next, on her own.

Triangle/Sagittarius can sometimes be very disconnected from her own physical body and her feelings. She hates constraint and the limits of the body will exasperate her. Illness or being physically unfit can really undermine her confidence and optimism. She doesn't necessarily identify closely with her body and can be careless and abusive towards it, working too hard, ignoring exhaustion, or smoking or drinking too much.

She can also be blind to her own emotions, ignoring for years, for instance, her resentment of her elder brother whom she felt got all the attention, and then be mortified and uncomprehending when some overwhelming feeling of explosive anger towards him comes up and strikes her in the face. This blindness is extended to the feelings of others, and Triangle/Sagittarius can say things which hurt terribly, but are more just an expression of her own honest views blurted out without any concept of their effect on the listener. She is never malicious, she is a much larger character than that. But her lack of self-reflection means she can be taken aback at her own feelings of competiveness and need for attention – that she is not as noble and cerebral as she would like to think she is.

IN WORK

Anything where she can be in charge of her own division or department, anything with a challenge, and a future, which demands energy, enterprise and vision. Triangle/Sagittarius is quick thinking and fast working, she doesn't hang around long if she feels she's not appreciated or the job's going nowhere. She is not very materially minded and is more likely to take on an interesting job than a job which just pays a lot of money – unless she's saving for some greater plan, in which case it's a means to an end. Status and recognition, however, do matter to her. Hence her need to be head of a team or working on her own.

Any areas of work which involve ideas appeal to her. She can make an inspired teacher or lecturer, able to pass on her vision of

the world of knowledge as something enriching that goes far beyond tests and exams. Writing and publishing books also comes in here, as part of the dissemination of knowledge, the making of connections with other minds and other ideas.

Ruled by Jupiter, the planet of temporal and spiritual law-giving, Sagittarians traditionally are meant to be drawn into work with the church and the law. Triangle/Sagittarius has the ambition and drive to compete in these male-dominated bastions – and win. She could make a barrister, a judge or a vicar and be as successful and well-regarded as anyone, male or female.

She has a great sense of humour and some acting ability, and could choose to strut her stuff on the stage or screen. Triangle/Sagittarius's need for variety and individual challenge is well-served by these worlds where there is no real sense of predictability or continuity. She will never know what job is around the corner, what break may be about to happen, what near-disaster may befall – from which, of course, she will extract herself in the nick of time.

Triangle/Sagittarius has the physical build and the necessary mental will to win which makes a good sportswoman. She loves the outdoors and would be happy training and competing. Because Sagittarius is symbolized by a centaur/archer, horses are meant to be the beasts with which she traditionally identifies. Riding in all it's manifestations from cattle driving to dressage, from pony clubs to point-to-point, are where she will be found.

The other obvious place for a typical Triangle/Sagittarius is up an impenetrable river, deep in a rainforest or trekking across a remote desert. She has the desire and the nature to lead her into such adventures. Her love of the unknown, of discovery, her need for excitement, for being unique and individual, carries her into situations of which other more cautious combinations would only ever dream. She also has the acuteness to write about her experiences and make them into a best-selling book (although her love of truth will prevent her from the embroidery and artistic licence which enlivens so many of these travel narratives).

Ideal Fantasy Job

For many Triangle/Sagittarians the perfect fantasy job would indeed be to be a lone traveller through an ancient land. Her natural singularity would respond to the sense of being one of the first, if not the first, traveller into an area of the world unfrequented by mankind. Her body type gives her great strength and her disposition is one which can endure physical hardship and deprivation. She may long for a hot shower and clean sheets on her bed, but would be quite happy to put these basics off until her mission was done. Neither would she be phased by creepy crawlies and other beasties who come out to torment her in the heat of the night.

Always one to make the most of every situation, Triangle/Sagittarius would be busy scribbling a diary as raw material for a book, while the mosquitos whined overhead and the grasses rustled with mysterious movement.

IN LOVE

Being in love is not Triangle/Sagittarius's forte. Both star sign and body type make her ill-at-ease in emotionally charged situations. The *idea* is wonderful, romance and pursuit after all is a challenge, can be dangerous and gets the adrenalin rushing. But the reality of the everyday is harder for this mutable personality to deal with. Her work and dreams are in her control and are hers alone. She is happier in these areas of life where the mind largely rules. When the heart starts upsetting things, and resisting control, trouble starts. And trouble for Triangle/Sagittarius takes the form of having to think about settling down, having children, and the inevitable closing off of opportunities that these decisions imply.

Sagittarius is a notorious bachelor girl, but no one more so than Triangle/Sagittarius. It is very hard indeed for her to say 'I do'. She'd much rather say, 'I will for now/maybe/so far so good'. 'Nothing lasts for ever' is a cliche which strikes Triangle/Sagittarius's heart with joy. Unlike more security-minded and emotionally orientated combinations, she is excited by the prospect of change, for it means new horizons, more excitement – progress.

Triangle/Sagittarius is a truthful character who does not indulge in trickery and subterfuge, but her very honesty can cause great hurt in personal relationships. She will not be particularly adept at sugaring the pill. And will tell you straight out that, for instance, she thinks your feet are the ugliest she has ever seen, or she loathes your family and wouldn't want to have any children if there was the slightest chance they'd look like your mother. When it comes to breaking off a relationship, there is little beating about the bush. She will say 'I don't love you anymore' as if she's reporting on nothing more momentous than the latest cricket scores, and county cricket at that!

Her sort of man is not going to be another Yang like her. Two Yangs together make for competitiveness and power play until

one of them is defeated. And that is not a happy situation. They can only survive if they are pals rather than lovers, and if she doesn't want a passionate love affair that might be an answer. But it may not be the answer for him. Anyway, if it's love that she's after, then a caring, imaginative, other-orientated Yin man can share her dreams, and support her tentative emotional life with his much more confident feeling self.

Marriage and children can cause her problems for the reasons given above. 'Freedom . . . freedom . . . perhaps it is just another word for nothing left to lose?' but Triangle/Sagittarius likes that state too much to give it up lightly. She is not naturally domestic or maternal, in the nurturing sense of the word. Her way of mothering is active and adventurous. She would have no qualms about setting off for a transcontinental trek with baby strapped to (Yin husband's) back. She will tell her children wonderful stories and encourage them to try anything and go anywhere. She will be far from a clinging, over-protective mum and will enjoy her children more as they grow older, making them into friends rather than continuing the parent/child relationship.

Triangle/Sagittarius needs to make her moves on the larger stage and she is not happy looking after her children full-time. Her restlessness and often unacknowledged ambition would soon have her climbing the walls with frustration. It is better for her and her children to have that energy expressed positively in her career, and for her to share some of the daily care of her children with a nurturing, patient father or grandmother, or a paid mother's help.

As a wife and mother, she will not be conventional. She may be too much on the move and too focused on her own horizons to be always there for others, but Triangle/Sagittarius is great fun with those she knows and loves – and her optimism and energy mean life is never predictable or flat when she's around.

Ideal Fantasy Lover

Triangle/Sagittarius is a vivid, powerful woman with a great sense of humour and a tendency to clumsiness in action, and foot-in-mouth speech. Cuddly Dudley Moore would appreciate all these aspects of her character, including the fact that she probably towers over his 155cm (5ft 2in) frame. He is also clever enough for this woman whose love of the quest includes a philosophical journey. His first claim to fame was as a musician playing jazz, and musical pastiches in revues while still at Oxford University. He then became the shorter half of the comedy duo on the television series *Not only...but Also*; and then he decided to try his luck in Hollywood, where he has remained.

The film that really made his name was *10*, in which he was cast as the improbable lover of the voluptuous Bo Derek (another Triangle type, but a Scorpio this time). This pattern of sweet, touching Dudley lusting after great Amazonian beauties seems to have been acted out in his life, with him photographed on the arm of a series of tall, bold women.

Alongside his film career, rather languishing lately (Triangle/Sagittarius could ginger that up), Dudley Moore has managed to keep his music going. He may be small, but life with Dudley would never be predictable, and would never be dull.

IN STYLE

Triangle/Sagittarius does not care too much for clothes. She hasn't got the time to really work out a good working wardrobe, can't be bothered with spending hours shopping and fiddling about putting outfits together. She recognizes that a successful working woman has to take into account the whole business of image and clothes, but basically she wishes she didn't have to bother. Her preferences are for casual, comfortable clothes, preferably wonderfully well-cut and in good fabrics.

Triangle/Sagittarius is not happy in anything that feels restricting. She has to be able to move with ease, and move fast if need be. She is practical and when she's buying a new garment rather than concentrating on the aesthetics, she'll consider how big pockets are and whether a jacket is waterproof. She has an outdoorsy look to her and favours clothes which imply action, riding boots, jodphurs, jeans, flying jackets, big fishermen's sweaters and sailing anoraks, deck shoes. She is also fond of ethnic clothes and accessories which evoke the mystery and exoticism of distant lands and unknown peoples.

When she gets round to buying herself some new clothes it helps cut down the time and effort if she remembers a few pointers. The style of clothes that really flatter Triangle/Sagittarius are determined by her body type. The Triangle shape has broader shoulders than hips and more of a marked waist than the Rectangle. She falls into two basic types, the small boned, boyish figure like Mia Farrow who probably rarely, if ever, puts on weight and the more muscular, athletic looking type, like Princess Stephanie of Monaco, Jamie Lee Curtis and Anjelica Huston, who can get heavy in the upper torso area, but keeps her inverted triangle shape with straight hips and lean lower legs. When thin, this shape is the classic fashion model shape with coat-hanger shoulders, next-to-nothing-hips and long lean legs.

Some women with this body type try to counteract their broad-shouldered look by wearing flimsy, ultra-feminine clothes – think of Diane Keaton (a Triangle/Aquarius) in *Annie Hall*. Those soft, drifty clothes on the angular Diane make her look a bit like Little Orphan Annie, rather gawky and fey. This suited the character very well in the film, but for Triangle/Sagittarius, wanting to be taken seriously in the real world, it can be a counter-productive look. Her femininity is best expressed with clothes that have simple geometric lines, certainly angled to the waist if she likes, but it's better to avoid soft fabrics, gathers and bows. For more specific information, see In Style on page 49.

Style Treat

Hats aren't worn enough these days and Triangle/Sagittarius is just the person to redress the balance. Masculine and jaunty hats for casual everyday wear, like a baseball cap, a costermonger's cloth cap, a beret – perhaps in red or yellow, since Sagittarius likes these fiery colours. These hats also give the impression of action sports and the outdoors.

For more formal dressing, masculine style hats still fit the bill – sombreros, trilbys, fedoras or panamas. If she is a petite Triangle type then she'll need to be careful of brim size. She should go for the smaller ones otherwise she will be overwhelmed by the scale. Another good option for a petite Triangle/Sagittarius is the pill-box – or fez, if she wants something redolent of foreign lands.

If she wants greater versatility than red and yellow offer, for instance, then she should go for a neutral colour. It is important to check that the colour of the garment you are buying suits you well. Take it into daylight, hold it under your chin and look at what it does to your skin, eyes and hair. If wearing it intensifies and enlivens your colouring then that is a colour that is right for your skin tones. If you look washed out or sallow, or your hair loses colour and dark rings seem to appear under your eyes, then you are getting it wrong. This sounds a lot of trouble to go to, but it is worth it for it enhances the pleasure you will get every time you wear it. For a formal occasion, she can match her neutral hat to her outfit by repeating its colour in a hatband using a stiff ribbon like petersham. To make it more dressy she could add a crisp, geometric looking bow to the band.

IN HEALTH

Excessive eating and drinking can wreak havoc on this naturally robust constitution. Triangle types often try to relieve the stress of their high-powered jobs through drink, and Triangle/Sagittarius is particularly prone to this. Sagittarius's ruler Jupiter rules the liver and gall bladder and both these poor overworked organs will complain if abused. Reckless thrill-seeking is another danger area for this combination – limbs broken on ski slopes, legs strained on gruelling climbs. Triangle/Sagittarius has to listen to her body sometimes and give it a rest and a bit of respect. She is exhausted by boredom as much as overwork, and so needs to walk the middle ground between always rushing on to the next excitement and staying in some stagnant, unsatisfactory status quo.

To keep healthy, it is worth looking at the whole area of diet and exercise, too. The Triangle type is likely to have been slim as a teenager, athletic, and with a big appetite. In adulthood, the demands of a family and career can mean she does less exercise, eats the wrong things at wrong times, still has an unrestrained appetite and can then start putting on weight. Triangle/Sagittarius, however, is very organized and disciplined and when she decides to do something about her shape she works out a routine and readily sticks to it.

Triangle/Sagittarius positively *needs* regular, energetic exercise and can get depressed if she isn't doing enough. In Bel's questionnaire, 75 per cent of the Triangle types said they recognized that they needed to exercise *and* diet if they were to lose weight – and it was energetic exercise which they favoured: a much higher proportion that the other body types (for instance, only 30 per cent of the Pear types thought exercise important). For more specific information on diet and exercise, see In Health on page 50.

TRIANGLE/SAGITTARIUS CELEBRITY

Sinead O'Connor is a Triangle/Sagittarius who, typically, lives dangerously on the edge. She seems to have had a troubled childhood which spreads its tentacles into her young adulthood. She first made an impact with her pure voice and her extraordinary, otherworldly beauty, appearing with a shaved head and wide staring eyes. But since her early success she has had trouble dealing with the demands of celebrity, it would seem of life itself. She has made aggressive political statements in quite the wrong places (a rock concert in the US in celebration of Bob Dylan, for instance, where she was booed off stage by an incomprehending and outraged audience) and yet seems to have also a childlike vulnerability.

She espouses very right-on views, but somehow mis-manages her proselytising and causes not righteous recognition but cringing embarrassment instead. The latest episode involved her failing to turn up for a charity concert in Ireland and then taking a full-page advertisement in the *Irish Times* to publish her self-justifying apologia, thus increasing the embarrassment quotient (as some Triangle/Sagittarius are apt to do). 'My name is Sinead O'Connor. I am learning to love myself, I am deserving . . . I deserve not to be hurt. My name is Sinead O'Connor. I am a woman. I have something to offer.' and on and on it went.

Here is an example of a very extreme Triangle/Sagittarius woman who lives out her life too much in the public eye, getting so out of touch with herself and the effect she has on others that she doesn't know quite when to stop.

TRIANGLE/SAGITTARIUS PROFILE

Sarah is in the middle of an executive programme at the London Business School. She has been sent on this high-powered nine-month course by her bosses, bankers at an investment bank where she works in corporate finance. 'I enjoy a challenging job, but I need to help keep my naturally positive outlook on life and to reduce my levels of stress so I chant daily, which seems to help.'

The course has made her question a lot of her pre-conceived ideas about herself and her ambitions. 'We do all sorts of sophisticated personality and aptitude tests and I was surprised to see that I am not a natural team player, but much more someone who has her own ideas and likes to follow them through. It made me think of how I'd been shocked by my reaction when a promotion went to a colleague – who was also a friend. I'd been really upset that it hadn't come to me and it took me months to come to terms with it. It was only then that I realized just how ambitious – and competitive – I really am'

She has also questioned how satisfactory her current work really is to her. 'I sometimes feel dealing with the world of finance suppresses creativity and is a strange way to earn a living. However, I do love the travelling and the meeting with people from all over the world, making relationships with them.'

Her real love though is speech, verbal communication and words in general and if she ever turned her back on high finance and the perks of foreign travel then, 'I would love to work as a speech therapist – to help someone communicate would be a great gift and enormously satisfying.'

She hasn't had children yet, but feels she would want to have some input into their upbringing because the early years are so precious and formative, but she knows she would need some kind of job as well, 'which would fulfil a need to communicate with the outside world' but she fears that women with children so easily lose out to men, and she is not happy to give up her career path, her independence or her status.

IN HOPE

Triangle/Sagittarius does not choose a safe and predictable path through the woods. She is easily deflected into other turnings, drawn towards a different grail. And all the while she finds that the horizon changes as she travels – where, she wonders, does she really want to be? What is all this questing for? The great mystic and poet William Blake was a Sagittarius. He understood the question and simple is his answer:

'To see a World in a Grain of Sand
And a Heaven in a Wild Flower,
Hold Infinity in the palm of your hand
And Eternity in an hour.'

TRIANGLE
CAPRICORN

(Yang+/Yin)

MOTTO:

Talk quietly and carry a big stick

IN LIFE

Can she be determined! Not that anyone would know it, except herself and perhaps those closest to her. Triangle/Capricorn is one subtle operator, capable of being tough when she has to be. She has the qualities necessary to change the world. Just think of the strength and steeliness of figures such as Marlene Dietrich (a classic Capricorn/Triangle), Onassis, Stalin and Mao Tse-Tung (all of them are the most Yang male versions of the sign) and the indomitable Joan of Arc! In the power stakes, Triangle/Capricorn has got rather a lot to live up to – or live down.

Her indomitable strength comes from two sources. The Capricorn side of her is an earth sign, powerful with great endurance and an ability to get where she wants to, which is to the top. She doesn't mind how long or how hard she has to toil. She is undeflected in her aim, but she *will* get there through a combination of hard slog, patience and will power. As a Yin sign she has great internal resources; she doesn't allow all that collected energy to rush out and be squandered. She conserves and concentrates. This retentive powerhouse of Capricorn is then united with the ultra Yang body type of the Triangle, which brings a different kind of power and focus.

Ambition, competitiveness, drive, and energy are the passwords here. With this combination, Triangle/Capricorn can seem like a submarine, sometimes sleekly visible, often enigmatically submerged, her hull impenetrable, her movement largely hidden, her goal known only to herself. But the power of her as she drives silently through the deepest oceans is undeniable, at times awesome.

When Triangle/Capricorn allows her self-protective public face to relax, she reveals the funny, intelligent, self-aware individual who has a mysterious inner self which can be fascinating to less complex characters. Deep down, behind all that hard work and serious purpose, there is a seeker after the arcane mysteries of life itself. She wants, above all, to be master of herself and of her world. And that requires watchfulness, diligence, application and control. She never wastes time. She is not good at taking time off and will always fill her hours with something useful to do. She won't just slump in a chair with a drink after a hard day's work. She'll have letters to write, or the ironing to do. She is happiest when she is busiest.

Triangle/Capricorn is far from being lighthearted and superficial. Down to earth, she values the traditional and hierarchical. This has led Capricornians to be accused of snobbery and social climbing. There is certainly an element of understanding where power is vested and how much more satisfactory it is to be one of the privileged in society, rather than the outsider. This makes her aware and respectful of rank, even if it is in an alternative society, like the theatre, for instance – where the importance of ranking on the billboard, and size of dressing room matters.

When you first meet her, or before you properly know her, Triangle/Capricorn can appear shy and wary. She is summing up the situation, she is not one to rush in to anything, arms waving, friendship offering. Particularly as a young person she can feel out of step with everyone else. Old before her time, she can be as ill at ease with the grown-ups as with her contemporaries. Both the Triangle type and Capricorn star sign are late developers. It might take time for her to come into her own, recognizing the ambitions and needs which drive her, for they are not what is conventionally expected of young women.

They are likely only to know exactly where they are going once they have reached their maturity – but then there is no stopping them. This combination has a double dose of this characteristic, and so suffers even greater isolation and a sense of being misunderstood as she works out the sentence of youth. But then, as her twenties fade, the engine of her ambition and focused aspirations roars into life. It is then that she begins to power forward, the nuclear submarine who makes few waves but silent, steady progress – and leaves the flashier speedboats, the elegant yachts and the risk-loving wind-surfers behind.

This woman means business and there is nothing that can stop her once she has set herself her target. She doesn't mind much if she's not liked, but she wants to be admired and respected. She

has staying power and endurance, and it may take her some time. But what she wants, she gets, and she wants to win.

Joan Baez, Marlene Dietrich, Faye Dunaway, Annie Lennox, Dolly Parton and Maggie Smith are all Triangle/Capricorns and all exhibit tremendous staying power. They either manage brilliant comebacks, or they never go away, and virtually die on stage. The society photographer, designer and social climber, Cecil Beaton, an ever-youthful, ever-enduring Capricorn himself, wrote in his diary of Marlene's will to endure: "It is entirely due to her perserverance that she is not just another old, discarded film star. She magnetizes her audience and mesmerizes them (and herself) into believing in her. The old trouper never changes her tricks because she knows they work, and because she invented them.'

IN WORK

Work is central to Triangle/Capricorn's life, and even if she won the jackpot on the Pools she would be unlikely to take off for the nearest tropical isle to while away the rest of her days. She likes the challenge, the overcoming of obstacles, seeing her plans unfold and her goals eventually come to her. All her successes will be well-earned and a just reward.

She can be a good member of a team, will take orders from others, and work diligently and hard for a joint cause, as long as there is mutual respect. But, she is always aware that she is on the way up, that this subordinate position will not be for ever, or even for very long. It is just one of the means along the way. She is discreet and quietly gets on with her work.

Triangle/Capricorn is likely to be very well-organized and will expect the same levels of discipline and organization from others. She is not profligate with praise, and when she says 'well done', you know that you've come near to performing a miracle. But she is kind and ready with help and advice when anyone asks for help.

Triangle/Capricorn will not be an indulgent boss. But she is extremely fair and kind to anyone in trouble. Horribly punctual and hardworking, it is hard for her employees to cut corners themselves with the occasional long lunch hour.

Business is an obvious area for her to make her mark. She likes the existence of career structures where there are ladders to climb and titles and status along the way to mark her ascent. She has an astute and logical mind which can plan ahead and account for every eventuality, from the amount of stationery which will be

needed to the projected dividends for investors during the next three years. Security matters to her, as does a good pension for that old age: in Capricorn's back-to-front ageing process, she may seem older when she is young, but she is certainly younger and more full of life than all her contemporaries when she is old.

The Civil Service is another good employer for Triangle/Capricorn. She is not put off by bureaucracy and can deal happily with the structure and hierarchy of a department. The pensions are still excellent and there is less discrimination against women than in many careers. She can go far and fast if she plays the game to the rules and work there can be very rewarding for the right Triangle/Capricorn.

Architecture and art and design are also areas where Triangle/Capricorn can excel for she appreciates structure expressed through line and colour. An important part of her creative drive is her natural desire to be highly skilled at whatever she undertakes. She also has all the dogged determination and ability to work on through all sorts of difficulties that will stand her in good stead in these professions where so many talented people fall by the wayside through becoming disheartened and discouraged. Triangle/Capricorn seems to thrive on hardship and is not likely to give up for want of appreciation or success. If she has her eye on her future goal, she will stick at it until she gets there.

Science and engineering has the attraction for Triangle/Capricorn of being thoroughly real and tangible. She likes dealing with the visible, measureable, malleable. She likes seeing a positive outcome for her work too. To know that you are responsible for making life a little better or easier for some people appeals to her more than just being creative for the sake of her own creativity.

For the same reasons, working on the land appeals to her. She is interested in horticulture and landscape gardening, estate management and forestry and wildlife conservation. All these activities are to do with tangible things, which she can watch grow and change and increase. They are jobs which allow her to work on her own, setting up her own systems and working to her own exacting standards.

Government in all its guises, from school governor through chair of the local conservative party to local and national government, is another place for Triangle/Capricorn to end up. She has a natural authority and an interest in the structure of society and improving the efficiency of social systems and the lot of people generally. She has all the perserverance, ambition and toughness to penetrate and then excel in masculine preserves. There is nothing that she cannot do.

Ideal Fantasy Job

Triangle/Capricorn really should be running the country. Prime minister has to be top job for her, something which would stretch every one of her talents to the full. She has an essential grasp of reality. There would be no romantic dreams fuelling her leadership. It would be all to do with building from solid foundations, emphasizing discipline, good budgeting, and fair but unsentimental welfare. She is not a character who is seduced by short-term rewards, she is quite capable of working towards long-term goals, sacrificing some of her own interests and comfort in the meantime. She would expect the same sort of acceptance of present privation in order to effect a common future good.

Above all, Triangle/Capricorn has the capacity for phenomenal hard work and would set out to master all the areas of expertise which fell within her brief. She may not be loved as prime minister, but she would be respected and admired for her strength of character and unwavering purpose. Her own willingness to shoulder sacrifice and austerity would make her able to ask sincerely for the cooperation of the country. And she would get it.

IN LOVE

Love is not what makes Triangle/Capricorn's world go round. Work is, and love comes in a good second. Relationships for her are possibly difficult. They don't conform to reason, and chaos and unreason unsettle her own carefully crafted equilibrium. She finds it very hard to relinquish control. It is almost impossible for her to abandon herself to anyone or anything. In fact, as an earth sign, Triangle/Capricorn has a healthy sexual nature when she finally allows it to surface, but the vagaries of love, the unpredictability of feelings, all make her wary of this world where angels fear to tread.

Her recognition of the value of security and status means that when, and if, she marries she will be aware of aspects of her choice which are not just to do with his character and lovability quotient. His status, both social and financial, come into the equation. When wild, passionate love is not your driving criterion, these practical considerations hold sway.

Family also matters. Both her family and the family she will be joining. She believes that you owe a duty to your family not to bring them into disrepute, not to embarrass or humiliate them through your actions, and if not actually to love them then certainly to respect them and do your best by them. Triangle/

Capricorn will sometimes remain in a loveless marriage long after others would have stormed out heartbroken. But she will renegotiate the boundaries and continue her independent life within the shell of her marriage rather than upset the children or in-laws, the neighbours or the status-quo.

There are quite a few Triangle/Capricorns who choose to remain single, ploughing on self-contained through the sea of life, maintaining her singular course. But the man for her will always be Yin; caring, emotionally sympathetic, less driven and competitive. He will provide the nurturing side to her life which too quickly can become emotionally arid, dominated as it often is by work and her own quiet but steady ambition to get on in the world.

She is seldom in a hurry to have children, but is proud of them and interested in them when they come along. Triangle/Capricorn is unlikely to want to stay at home full-time to care for them, although if she does elect to do this, or is forced to by circumstances, then she makes it into a job which she does as efficiently and skilfully as possible. She is a well-organized and responsible mother. She will insist on her children learning good manners and knowing how to behave in company. She is not a great advocate of child-centred learning and undisciplined free-expression. Triangle/Capricorn is much more likely to send her children to traditional schools where the foundations of knowledge and learning are laid down early and strongly.

As a mother she's always busy, and quick to offer practical solutions to every upset, even when it is emotional and needs just a bit of sympathy. She is tough-minded herself and not very tolerant of others who view life in a less clear cut way. But she is enormously reliable, strong and reassuring in that strength. Although she can have moments of black despair and inevitable feelings of inadequacy, Triangle/Capricorn gives those whom she loves a sense of utter loyalty and solidity. She will always be there for them.

Ideal Fantasy Lover

Has he got status? Is he rich? Is he someone who'd look good on your arm? Yes, Yes, Yes. Warren Beatty is many a Triangle/Capricorn's dream man, or as like him as possible. He may be old, but that's never been a bar to sensible Capricorn who has always appreciated older men anyway. He may have been a Don Juan to a ridiculous extreme, but Triangle/Capricorn likes a challenge and is firm enough to handle even a rattlesnake who's got his tail up. Getting Warren to heel would be chicken feed.

His fame rests more on his looks and his extravangant reputation as a ladies' man than on his films. But Beatty is much more than a good-looking stud. He is mega-rich, largely through his astute commercial and artistic sense. He produced *Bonnie and Clyde*, *Shampoo*, *Reds* and *Bugsy* which made him a a good few bucks.

But underneath all this charm, womanising and money-making is a rather soft Yin man (much softer than his Yang sister Shirley Maclaine) who is relieved to be caught and grounded by a young actress, Annette Bening, who got pregnant and pushed him into parental responsibility for the first time in his mid-fifties. Only a determined Triangle type could have manoeuvred him into what was best for himself – and her. And Annette, as a Triangle/Gemini, was well-equipped for the rescue.

Triangle/Capricorn would be even better equipped, having a much more powerful and resolute character which no amount of misbehaviour from Beatty would undermine. She would not only keep him home nights, she'd also be able to advise him on some of his future film choices, either as actor or producer.

IN STYLE

Good quality clothes are important to Triangle/Capricorn. She is not a flashy dresser, she does not want to draw attention to herself, or risk looking odd, amusing or zany. Although she is happier in casual, comfortable clothes, she does recognize that dressing appropriately for the job or the occasion is courteous and good form, and she will not turn up at a wedding in black, or leave off her hat if she is invited to one of the Queen's garden parties. Classy, well-made clothes in good fabrics and well put together is her natural preference. Nothing too bright in colour or fussy in detail.

Clothes are an extension of oneself, another layer of protection, and they reveal a good deal about us. Triangle/Capricorn, when she's not too busy to think about them, knows what she wants her clothes to say – and if they make any statement at all they will make it in a well-bred voice – here is a successful, attractive, classy woman, who can take on anything, and make it work.

The style of clothes that really flatter Triangle/Capricorn are determined by her body type. The Triangle shape has broader shoulders than hips and more of a marked waist than the Rectangle. She falls into two basic types, the small boned, boyish figure like Mia Farrow who probably rarely, if ever, puts on weight and the more muscular, athletic looking type, like Princess

Stephanie of Monaco, Jamie Lee Curtis and Anjelica Huston, who can get heavy in the upper torso area, but keeps her inverted triangle shape with straight hips and lean lower legs. When thin, this shape is the classic fashion model shape with coat-hanger shoulders, next-to-nothing-hips and long lean legs.

Some women with this body type try to counteract their broad-shouldered look by wearing flimsy, ultra-feminine clothes – think of Diane Keaton (a Triangle/Aquarius) in *Annie Hall*. Those soft, drifty clothes on the angular Diane make her look a bit like Little Orphan Annie, rather gawky and fey. This suited the character very well in the film, but for Triangle/Capricorn, wanting to be taken seriously in the real world, it can be a counter-productive look. Her femininity is best expressed with clothes that have simple geometric lines, certainly angled to the waist if she likes, but it's better to avoid soft fabrics, gathers and bows. For more specific information, see In Style on page 49.

Style Treat

Capricorn traditionally is meant to be drawn to leather, and certainly she likes good shoes. As her style treat for business she could choose a really classy leather court shoe or pump with pointed or chisel toe. Rounded toes do not look smart on any Triangle-type woman. A neutral colour – black, brown, navy, grey, pewter, olive or taupe – will be most practical and versatile because it will go with everything. Triangle/Capricorn needs to look at her business wardrobe to find which neutral works best. Black and navy are popular but are not the best choice for everyone. If her own colouring is medium to light then some of the other neutrals will work better. Patterns like moc croc or snakeskin reinforce the geometric feel to shoes and boots.

For casual wear Triangle/Capricorn might choose square-toed and heeled boots, eg Chelsea boots, or lace-ups. Again they are much more smart for a Triangle type if they are in a stiff, strong leather than in soft leather or suede. The more masculine type shoes also flatter her casual look, and many a young Triangle type will be happy to wear DMs – boots or shoes – or even motorbike boots – all of which give a marvellous androgynous look like that favoured by that well-known Triangle/Capricorn, Annie Lennox of Eurythmics fame.

IN HEALTH

One of the great benefits of being a Triangle/Capricorn is that her health tends to get better with age. Traditionally, Capricorn is

associated with the skin and bones and the connecting ligaments and joints. Skin ailments, arthritis and sprained muscles might cause some trouble, but generally this is a robust constitution, although the Triangle body type is more prone to heart and arterial diseases if she gets too heavy (see Introduction).

To keep healthy, it is worth looking at the whole area of diet and exercise, too. The Triangle type is likely to have been slim as a teenager, athletic, and with a big appetite. In adulthood, the demands of a family and career can mean she does less exercise, eats the wrong things at wrong times, still has an unrestrained appetite and can then start putting on weight. Triangle/Capricorn, however, is very organized and disciplined and when she decides to do something about her shape she works out a routine and readily sticks to it.

Triangle/Capricorn positively *needs* regular, energetic exercise and can get depressed if she isn't doing enough. In Bel's questionnaire, 75 per cent of the Triangle types said they recognized that they needed to exercise *and* diet if they were to lose weight – and it was energetic exercise which they favoured: a much higher proportion than the other body types (for instance, only 30 per cent of the Pear types thought exercise important). For more specific information on diet and exercise, see In Health on page 50.

CELEBRITY TRIANGLE/CAPRICORN

Marlene Dietrich is one of those icons whose face and voice has entered the cultural inheritance of this century. She is a Triangle/Capricorn with all the perfectionism, incredible staying power and will to succeed. With the help of the film director Joseph von Sternberg, she turned herself from a plump German stage actress into the most glamorous screen personality, whose versions of 'Lili Marlene', 'The World was Young' and 'Where Have all the Flowers Gone?' have become definitive.

For 50 years she went on producing the minutely rehearsed and manipulated magic on screen and stage. It was feathers, sequins and paste which made the Dietrich look immortal, but it was indomitable will and gruelling hard work which made *her* immortal. Her military precision was impressive. She directed the spotlight operators exactly, 'One, two, three, *then* shine the spot'. And there suddenly in the white light was her look of surprise that she was somehow caught off guard, and yes, even more surprisingly, there was an audience in front of her clapping and stamping before she'd even sung a note.

Nothing ever caught her off guard and she had no life other than her life as a celebrity, continually on stage. There were no happy marriages and just one sadly neglected child, who nevertheless seems to have been just another aspect of the Dietrich ego: 'My mother was convinced she alone had conceived me.' But difficult and complex as her character was, she exerted an extraordinary individual influence that lasted half a century, and will continue well into the next. She achieved what she set out to do.

TRIANGLE/CAPRICORN PROFILE

Stella is a Californian, working as an osteopath in France. She is keen to get more skilled at what she does, she likes the idea of improving and progressing: 'I have a very strong will, I suppose that makes me ambitious. When I set my mind on something I want, I almost *always* get it. I feel having a career is very important, but it is really important that it is a career that I enjoy. I am much happier inside myself when I am busy. I can get quite depressed if I haven't got enough to do. I am much happier when I am active.'

She is interested in what she sees as the two sides of her character. Of her star sign she says: 'I think I am quite a typical Capricorn, down-to-earth, stubborn, career-minded. I do have conflicts with myself sometimes. Essentially I am a Yin type of person, shy, quiet, down to earth, easy going. But underneath there is a strong driving force that is very Yang. I am not easily pushed around. And if I set my mind on something I do everything I can to get it.' This Yang side comes from her Triangle body type, a shape Stella is happy to be. 'I like the shape of my body, especially when I work out and am in good shape. Then I look very athletic and strong. And having broad shoulders means I never have to wear shoulder pads!'

In her early thirties, Stella has no children yet, 'I would like to have some in the future. My fantasy is to be able to work from home and have my partner or someone else look after them while I am working. I don't want to work more than four days a week, and then I'd have some time to look after my children. But I know I will feel the need to work once I have children – I am not the sort of person who could just be with my kids all day without climbing the walls.' She is concerned sometimes that her own strength of will has somehow emasculated her partner.

The complexity of Stella's character intrigues her friends. Like all Triangle/Capricorns she is much more determined and steely than she seems. 'My friends often say that they are surprised by

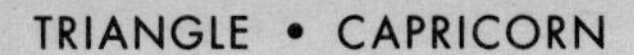

me, because at first I come across as being shy, quiet, almost weak. One friend described me as having a surprisingly quiet strength. And that makes sense to me. I may appear a bit absent-minded, but I know *exactly* what I'm doing and where I'm going.'

IN HOPE

The admirable Thomas Jefferson, one of the founders of modern America (surprisingly an Aries not a Capricorn), had this archetypal Capricornian advice to give his wife in a letter: 'Determine never to be idle. No person will have occasion to complain of the want of time who never loses any. It is wonderful how much may be done if we are always doing.' He was founding a new nation, a job which is rarely available these days, even to an ambitious Triangle/Capricorn, but even so Tri/Cap lives out this Jeffersonian philosophy in everything she does. And she is just as likely to reap her just rewards for hard labour, for her enduring sense of the long-term goal, and the distant prize.

TRIANGLE
AQUARIUS

(Yang+/Yang)

MOTTO:

The end justifies the means

IN LIFE

This combination produces one of the most individual personalities in all 48 body star sign types. Powerful and self-centred, she is nevertheless completely herself, a one-off. Laura Dern, Mia Farrow, Zsa Zsa Gabor, Eartha Kitt and Princess Stephanie of Monaco are all individualist Triangle/Aquarians who go their own way with little concern for the opinion of others. Muriel Spark and Virginia Woolf are both Triangle/Aquarian writers, as is the explorer and writer Freya Stark. All had most distinctive voices and a pioneering zeal to live and write as they choose. Driven by the head rather than the heart, this combination is concerned with ideals, theories, and impressing herself and her ideas upon a (sometimes) reluctant world. She may not be easy to live with but she is always honest and continually coming up with something interesting to think about and argue through.

At heart she is a pioneer, someone who is intellectually and emotionally independent, an eternal outsider whose mission is to live as freely as she can – and upset a few conventions and status quos along the way. Freedom, equality, friendship is her cry and she has a genuine concern at the unfairnesses of society and the corruption of those in power. Some of the most extreme characters belong here, but unlike Rectangle/Aquarius, who tends to let it all hang out, Triangle/Aquarius is less abandoned in her pursuit of truth at all costs. Her idealism, however, risks becoming fanaticism, her concern about humanity at large means she can be detached and unfeeling about the suffering of individuals under her nose.

Inventive and creative, Triangle/Aquarius has a brain that is fast-moving and penetrating. She is most at home in reason and will endlessly discuss ideas and plans of action. She is sometimes not so good at putting these plans *into* action, preferring to confine her dynamism to talk. For dynamic she is, and when she does get the idea on the road she can work wonders in changing the outmoded, teaching the new, energizing the tired and jaded.

Another area where there can be all talk and little action is the whole realm of the emotions. This is where Triangle/Aquarius can feel all at sea. She is afraid of irrational, unreasonable, murky areas of the human psyche. She attempts to deny or argue these inconvenient things away. She'll do so to her own feelings, she'll be inclined to do the same to her partner's and children's feelings. She thinks she can't cope with this mysterious aspect of human behaviour in her usual ultra-capable way, and because she hates to fail, she denigrates and denies – and then gets taken by nasty surprise. For suppressed emotion will always find a way to escape.

'The dragon-green, the luminous, the dark, the serpent-haunted sea' in which her water sign sisters, Cancer, Scorpio and Pisces – whose currency is feeling – are so at home, frightens the life out of Triangle/Aquarius. She is not very good in the realm of the personal. And being a Triangle/Aquarius she is only interested in areas where she can be very good, if not the best. This can make things even more difficult for her because it makes it tempting for her to withdraw increasingly from the personal and concentrate more on the universal, on the public at large, on her career and her position in the world where she has control. She also has the focus, the ambition and the vision to excel.

There is something quite edgy and isolated about the typical Triangle/Aquarius. She is not usually at the centre of a group of women friends: she is more of a pal to men, but feels some disdain for much of their cavorting and posturings. She is a bit of a loner, double Yang herself and not at ease with cosy domesticity or emotional intimacy. She lives in the mind and wants to make her mark on the world. Whatever she does, however, she will do with dedication. If she has to care for her sick mother, for instance, she may be driven almost to distraction by the demands put upon her, and by her own claustrophobia. She will do what she has to do to the best of her ability, but dreaming always of release.

She is the first to admit that she is not one of nature's nurturing women, that she is not deeply sympathetic to the suffering of others, although she is moved by the inhumanity of man to man on a broader scale. But she is a strong and loyal woman who does not buckle under pressure, and takes pride in her ability to transcend difficulties through willpower and hard work. She is remarkable too. A woman before her time, she finds it quite difficult sometimes to live in a world where powerful, radical, unorthodox women are not treated with much understanding or sympathy. Where her individuality is seen as eccentricity and her unconventionality interpreted as threat.

Tallulah Bankhead, one of the most famous pioneering film actresses, was described by someone who knew her: 'She was an open, wayward, free, cosmopolitan, liberated, sensuous human being. In thus systematically invading her own privacy she was the first of the modern personalities.' Those adjectives could as readily describe any Triangle/Aquarius, someone who believes that every woman is the architect of her own fortune.

IN WORK

Triangle/Aquarius is not a comfortable, submissive employee. She always knows best, and although she may learn not to make this fact obvious to all, she will never be a compliant, obedient little helpmeet. She is great if she is allowed to do things her way, and is appreciated for her vision and hard work, but she can be explosive and rebellious if she feels unfairly constrained or blamed. She is more likely to walk out than stay and work out a compromise.

If she is boss she will be fair, and concerned with improving conditions for all her workers. But she won't be very sympathetic over her staff's emotional gripes and general slackness and lack of drive. She is impatient with those who have a slower way of thinking and working, but she is not a heavy disapproving type of personality. Any complaints will be dealt with rationally and out in the open.

Work is a central importance in her life. She may not recognize it until later in life, but Triangle/Aquarius is an ambitious and determined woman who really needs to express her talents and energies in the outside world. She is a singular individual and needs to be noticed and rewarded with some public recognition, however localized that may be. She is not happy being the support staff in the wings. She is much keener to be on the stage of life, with some of the spotlight at least trained her way.

Anything where she can pass on her ideas and participate in the ideas of others attracts her greatly. Teaching is an immediate area for this kind of intellectual to express herself. She will never be dull. No lecture will ever be just a churning out of the previous

years' leavings. Triangle/Aquarius never stops thinking and so there will always be some up-to-the-minute thoughts and ideas to share with her students.

Television and radio are another way of spreading the idea. As a Triangle type, she likes being the presenter, the spokesperson, rather than one of a team. And she is good under pressure, cool and contained when everyone else starts to boil over. If not in front of the microphone or camera, Triangle/Aquarius is just as adept at directing or producing the programmes. She has all the necessary ideas and the drive to get things done.

Brilliant as the regional organizer or chair of any charity, she can bring her organizational abilities to bear on some of the humanitarian issues that concern her most. She is a natural protester, never happy just to accept the party line or status quo on any issue. But she is good too at understanding how best to plan any kind of opposition. Far from being a hot-headed activist who rushes in without thinking through a proper strategy, she coolly works it out and then imposes it charmingly on the rest of the organization.

Science and technology have a fascination for Triangle/Aquarius. She is intrigued by new inventions, by the future and the unknown. Flying, space travel and the latest gadgetry in telecommunications and computers give her a thrill. She is likely to be skilled in all these areas, her logical brain good at understanding complex patterns and intricate systems. Astrology and astronomy are other related systems which catch her interest. Again, she is best working on her own as a consultant, or teacher.

Ideal Fantasy Job

Chief construction engineer. Triangle/Aquarius could then be responsible for building a beautiful suspension bridge with all the soaring qualities of one of the great Isambard Kingdom Brunel's bridges, but with the lightness that now can be achieved with the new technologies and materials which combine strength with fineness. A bridge is a good metaphor for what Triangle/Aquarius attempts to do in her life; using the medium of the strong but airy idea she tries to connect people and countries in an elegant construction of logical argument and explanation. It would also be a monument to her talents and aspirations for generations to come.

IN LOVE

Triangle/Aquarius combines two Yang influences, both of which shy away from easy expression of their own emotions and responsiveness to the emotions of others. Much happier with the impersonal, she is not naturally passionate, and intense feelings, possessiveness and jealousy make her run a mile. She likes everything to be light and open and free. Is much happier with a friend for a lover, to whom she will be loyal and faithful, if not in every conventional sense.

Triangle/Aquarius is much more likely to be attracted to a man through the mind than through the loins. She will want lots of fascinating talk, is great at the theory of love and sex and not necessarily so keen on the practice. She is likely to be experimental in a cool and scientific way, and knows just where love and desire belong in the priorities of her life. She is not going to kick over the traces and give up everything for the sake of a smouldering look and a passionate embrace. She might throw up everything for someone who could talk up a storm, but basically Triangle/Aquarius is a reasonable woman for whom work and a life in her control matters most.

The kind of man to suit this double Yang woman is a Yin man. He will be a man for whom feelings are not a mysterious and alarming land, a man who can bring the emotional and sympathetic into Triangle/Aquarius's over controlled, cerebral life. If he's easy-going and laid back then all the better.

Children are likely to be a problem that she puts off for some time. Not overly maternal, she will not feel the pull of biology until she is in her late thirties, if at all. Triangle/Aquarius would not necessarily choose to stay at home and look after her children herself, but if she had to do it full-time she would treat it like a job that she did as well as any other job she turned her hand to. This woman prides herself on her ability to do anything well.

She may well be an impatient and not very sympathetic mother, but she would be always interesting, and able to encourage independence in her children. Triangle/Aquarius is also always wanting to improve herself, through education or getting experience of different kinds of work. One of Bel's clients admitted, 'I need a career as I have always been competitive, and above all want my kids to be as proud of me (in my career) as they would be of their father.' She would not be the kind of mother who invests everything in her children and finds it impossible to let them go. Cool and detached, Triangle/Aquarius provides an intellectually free environment in which they can grow. They may miss a certain cosy warmth, but they would probably get that from their Yin father anyway, and look more to their mother for the intellectual interest and energy.

Although Triangle/Aquarius does not go in for intimate friendships she does like having a circle of friends to do things with. She is active rather than passive and is likely to take the initiative in most of their arrangements. She is great fun, full of life and fizzing with ideas. Although she may not be loud and obvious, her power is evident and draws admirers to her. Seemingly aloof at first, she warms up when she relaxes and starts to talk. She enjoys being the mentor to others, the queen bee in the hive.

Ideal Fantasy Lover

Nicholas Cage is a distinctly Yin and broodingly self-aware man, he has gone on the record as saying he'd die for the love of his life. He is a kind, caring Yin guy who would bring a ray of sunshine and laughter into the hard-working life of a Triangle/Aquarius.

He established himself with films like *Peggy Sue Got Married*, *Moonstruck*, and *Wild at Heart*. Good looking, big-headed, a little bit crazy and an attention seeker *par excellence*, he would happily take some of the emotional burdens off Triangle/Aquarius's shoulders.

IN STYLE

Aquarians have a desire to look different from everyone else. One of Bel's clients expressed it this way, 'I like to be the best dressed person around (not in terms of designer clothes) but enough to be noticed for originality and a "quiet" presence. I hate looking like any other Indian girl with long permed hair! Something has to be different!' Triangle/Aquarius will never be a slave to fashion, and will always have her own distinctive look, even if it's natural grunge born of not caring one jot how she looks. Dressing so that she stands out from the crowd reflects the fact that she thinks and feels – and often acts – differently from everyone else in the group. But dressing differently also separates her from others, and enhances her isolation. This is the impersonal part of the Triangle/Aquarian saying don't identify with me, don't think you know me, I don't belong to any identifiable group.

Within these criteria, Triangle/Aquarius can dress in a variety of ways, there is no one way which characterizes her, except that she is unlikely to go for anything overly romantic or fussy in detail. Assymetric lines, geometric patterns, something rather futuristic, can have its appeal. Not a stickler for natural fabrics, she is just as happy with modern easy care fabrics which are so practical to wash and keep crease-free.

Although Triangle/Aquarius has not often got the time or patience for serious clothes shopping, she recognizes that how she looks and what she wears matters if she wants to get on in the world. The same client uses her clothes to get more notice taken of her opinions at work, 'If my voice isn't audible at work, then for a while I'll power dress.' She recognizes how eloquent one's clothes are about ourselves and our aspirations. It is worth her knowing a few of the pointers which make shopping easier, quicker, more effective, and with less likelihood of making expensive mistakes.

The style of clothes that really flatter Triangle/Aquarius are determined by her body type. The Triangle shape has broader shoulders than hips and more of a marked waist than the Rectangle. She falls into two basic types, the small boned, boyish figure like Mia Farrow who probably rarely, if ever, puts on weight and the more muscular, athletic looking type, like Princess Stephanie of Monaco, Jamie Lee Curtis and Anjelica Huston, who can get heavy in the upper torso area, but keeps her inverted triangle shape with straight hips and lean lower legs. When thin, this shape is the classic fashion model shape with coat-hanger shoulders, next-to-nothing-hips and long lean legs.

Some women with this body type try to counteract their broad-shouldered look by wearing flimsy, ultra-feminine clothes – think of Diane Keaton (a Triangle/Aquarius) in *Annie Hall*. Those soft, drifty clothes on the angular Diane make her look a bit like Little Orphan Annie, rather gawky and fey. This suited the character very well in the film, but for Triangle/Aquarius, wanting to be taken seriously in the real world, it can be a counter-productive look. Her femininity is best expressed with clothes that have simple geometric lines, certainly angled to the waist if she likes, but it's better to avoid soft fabrics, gathers and bows. For more specific information, see In Style on page 49.

Style Treat

Because leather is a crisp, shiny fabric it really suits Rectangle and Triangle type women. Leather trousers are a particularly good investment for any Triangle/Aquarius because, unworried by fashion fads, she will go on wearing hers for years. A good pair will also give her a distinctive look and suit her desire to stand out from the crowd.

A tailored, straight or tapered line is best, with little or no pleating at the waist. Proper fit is important – a comfortably loose fit is better than anything too tight, since any clothes that fit too tightly will make her look larger than she is and cause unsightly 'seating' however good the quality of the leather. A

neutral colour will give her the most versatility – black, navy, pewter, taupe, olive – but she should make sure that the colour she chooses goes with most of the tops in her wardrobe.

The great thing about leather trousers is that they can be dressed up or down. With a jacket and smart shirt or blouse, or with an elegant sweater, both accessorized with a classy necklace and earrings she has a cool, sophisticated look. With bomber jacket, T-shirt or casual sweater and chunky boots for footwear she's got the androgynous, tom boy look that suits her shape so well.

Petite Triangle types should be careful about scale. It's not enough to find trousers that fit at the top and then simply have 15cm (6in) chopped off the bottom. Triangle/Aquarius needs to check that the trouser rise (length from waist to crutch) is correct, that the zip does not look too long in relation to her body length and, finally, that the weight of the leather isn't too much for her petiteness, overwhelming her small frame. A fine quality, light-weight leather is more flattering on a small lightly-boned woman. If all these details are correct then she must check that if those 15cm (6in) are chopped off each leg are the trousers going to be too wide at the bottom? (This will certainly be the case if they have a tapered leg.) She has to enquire whether they can then be re-tapered as well as shortened. It is not easy being a petite size, a fact she is reminded of every time she tries to buy clothes.

IN HEALTH

A computer-fast brain and a high level of nervous tension can cause a Triangle/Aquarius to become stressed if she is frustrated in her job or life because she can't get her ideas taken seriously, or if she doesn't make enough time for relaxation and unwinding. She can have erratic fluctuations in her health and well-being, but usually is strong and recovers fast from any illness. Ankles and circulation are problem areas, but long walks in the country, lots of good air, good food and enough sleep, cure most of Triangle/Aquarius complaints.

To keep healthy, it is worth looking at the whole area of diet and exercise, too. The Triangle type is likely to have been slim as a teenager, athletic, and with a big appetite. In adulthood, the demands of a family and career can mean she does less exercise, eats the wrong things at wrong times, still has an unrestrained appetite and can then start putting on weight. Triangle/Aquarius, however, is very organized and disciplined and when she decides to do something about her shape she works out a routine and readily sticks to it.

Triangle/Aquarius positively *needs* regular, energetic exercise and can get depressed if she isn't doing enough. In Bel's questionnaire, 75 per cent of the Triangle types said they recognized that they needed to exercise *and* diet if they were to lose weight – and it was energetic exercise which they favoured: a much higher proportion than the other body types (for instance, only 30 per cent of the Pear types thought exercise important). For more specific information on diet and exercise, see In Health on page 50.

TRIANGLE/AQUARIUS CELEBRITY

Princess Stephanie of Monaco looks the archetypal Triangle/Aquarius: tall, broad-shouldered, narrow-hipped with fair hair and blue eyes. She is at her best in casual, sporty clothes which show off her long, tanned legs. She can look terribly trussed-up and uncomfortable in more feminine, frilly clothes.

Princess Stephanie has lived a life that is as unorthodox as a princess's life can be. Fast motor bikes, unsuitable boys, and wild professional ventures which career off the track as soon as they're started. She crashed a motorbike going the wrong way up a one way street, she coolly foiled an armed mugging by suggesting they all repair to the palace to discuss things with Prince Rainier – and this with a gun to her head. She is headstrong, foolhardy and does not care much what people say about her.

She was with her mother when Princess Grace's car ran off the road and she was killed. Her mother's favourite daughter, this traumatic event seems not to have calmed her down. Stephanie has continued on her accident-prone way, trying to make a career as a swimsuit designer, a singer, a model, a promoter of her own perfume, and all the time there were the succession of failed relationships with brat-pack boys or father-figure men. 'I have always wanted to lead an independent life, to have a career, just all the things that women want.'

Then, to really rub home her Triangle/Aquarius rebel side, which so exasperates her tired father and the conventional burghers of Monaco, she fell in love with her bodyguard, a man from very much the wrong side of town, and became an unmarried mother without any attempt to cover it up with a hasty marriage. She seems happy at last but this kind of explosive, erratic temperament will cause ripples again before too long.

TRIANGLE/AQUARIUS PROFILE

Diana is in her early fifties, the generation who still thought careers were until you got married. She is a top personnel trainer

running courses for employees of large companies. 'I see my life as three distinct stages. The first stage I did a job which my parents suggested, a civil service job. Then I got married and had my kids – this was a job and I did it. But now, I have really come into my own, I have lost all the nervousness I used to have, and I do a job that is really for me. I knew from the beginning I would get to the top. I wanted to be the very best there was. I have to achieve for myself and am better working on my own.'

Looking after her children took up the middle part of Diana's life, and she did that job to the best of her ability: 'It was important to make a good job of it – to do all the things mothers do. Although I felt devoted to them and only worked part-time, I didn't feel fulfilled and never felt good at it. When they were in bed, then I felt like a caged tiger. I didn't think "God, this is awful" at the time, but when I got out I was free. It was a prison sentence, you got on and did it. I don't like to fail so I worked hard at being a good mother, but I thought I was abnormal because other women seemed to do it so much more easily. I had a friend with children of a similar age and she seemed so suited to motherhood. She obviously found it fulfilling and even managed to have coffee mornings and other social events that I never felt I'd manage to do. Unless it's perfect, I can't do it.'

Diana is now at the top of her profession, every ounce of creative energy goes into her work and she is exhilarated by what she does. 'I don't care what anyone else thinks of me. I have few friends – they are limited to those whom I feel I can trust and could turn to in a crisis and they would be there for me.' At last she has things in her control and is doing something which she can do perfectly, or almost perfectly, 'I have really come into my own.'

IN HOPE

Triangle/Aquarius is a truly individual personality, someone who isn't easily categorized, or made to conform to any type. She stands out from the crowd and she stands alone. She has a singularity which is a part of her forward looking nature. She naturally belongs to the future, is drawn forwards into the unknown and most truly understands what Andre Gide wrote in his journal, 'Whoever starts out toward the unknown must consent to venture alone.'

TRIANGLE
PISCES

(Yang+/Yin+)

MOTTO:

The iron hand in the silken glove, or is it: The silken hand in the iron glove?

IN LIFE

Here is an extraordinary combination of extremes. The body type is ultra-Yang, robust, competitive, and self-promoting, but it is teamed with this ultra-Yin star sign, sensitive, imaginative, and highly emotional in its influence. There will be conflict at times between the Triangle aspect which wants to go out and conquer the world and the more retiring, more caring, emotionally indecisive Pisces.

There may well be some confusion and mixed messages – a kittenish, soft-spoken persona hiding a steely claw of determination. Or a tough, dynamic manner covering up a sensitive emotional core. Not only may the Triangle/Pisces confuse others with this double message, but she may well be confused herself as to how best to express herself in the world. When the straightforward, hard-hitting Triangle meets the oblique, subtle Pisces, subterfuge and pretence are a risk. The Triangle characteristics are the stronger, so Triangle/Pisces can put away that kittenish play and admit she's really the cat who wants the cream, but can purr sweetly when she's asking.

This is a very creative combination with the imaginative, visionary side of the true artist coming from Pisces and the drive and ambition to achieve coming from her Triangle body type. The writer/poet and creator of a great garden, Vita Sackville-West, was a Triangle/Pisces and she magnificently combined energy and drive with sensitivity and vision. She was a romantic woman in an androgynous body; a combination of the two

extremes of Yin and Yang. A contemporary described her as looking like Lady Chatterley from the waist up and more like her gamekeeper Mellors from the waist down (a reference to her long, lean legs which she often preferred to encase in plus fours with kneelength laced boots).

This is the last of the 12 star signs and the most evolved and otherworldly of them all. There is a wisdom and mysticism in this personality, an awareness of something of the secret of life which makes her a gifted synthesizer and interpreter, someone who can bring the transcendent into everyday life. It is a distinctly unselfcentred influence, her boundaries are not clearly defined and she is open to influence from everything and everyone with whom she comes into contact. She feels for the world. But the Triangle body shape is the complete opposite in that it *is* self-centred, it has very strong boundaries which can sometimes seem impenetrable. This can be a most positive advantage to the fluid Pisces, where it can harness and focus all those flowing energies. It can make her more self-interested. Less saintly, for sure, but more successful in a worldly sense.

But the polarities do not influence each other happily if they have not been properly integrated. The wilder sides of the Piscean nature, the propensity to escape reality through drink, drugs and dreaming can then predominate. The romanticism which keeps her feet off the ground, never allowing her to commit to anything concrete, can become obsessional and seriously destructive. This can be united to no good effect in a self-centred personality who isolates herself from real life and true intimacy with others, and wastes her energy on fantasy. She can become the misunderstood genius who never writes that definitive novel, or makes it as a great singer. Or who puts life off while she waits for the call from Hollywood that never comes.

This is a combination with such gifts and energy, and anyone blessed with it needs to recognize the forces with which she has to deal. The Yang drive and focus can really get things done, but it also constrains Pisces' natural emotional openness and sensitivity to others. Triangle/Pisces then becomes more earthed and self-contained, but less intuitive and responsive – to both the good and bad in people and the world. Triangle/Pisces can be so genuinely kind to people in need. She can be also detached and self-protective. She can swing from one extreme to the other, or with the practical help of her Yang+ body type she can learn how to harness all the best in her nature and focus her dreams on real achievement and true goals.

IN WORK

Triangle body shape women need to work and be in positions of authority. They are not natural team players at their best in the supportive role. But that said, the Pisces overlay is a much more sympathetic element and Triangle/Pisces may well be a benign dictator, concerned about the welfare of her colleagues and staff, sweet to pets and children. She can seem such a kind and malleable personality, willing to help out, reasonable to a remarkable degree. But push her too far, take advantage of her just once too often, and you'll soon see the hidden strength within that silken glove. When it comes to the bottom line, no one is going to take advantage of her for long.

Triangle/Pisces would be very happy running some artistic concern, an art gallery or craft store; she'd make a brilliant businesswoman/designer. There is a talented artist in many Pisces. For most, however, the dreams are powerful, but she lacks the down-to-earth drive that is necessary to get anywhere in a commercial hard-headed and stony-hearted world. Luckily, Triangle/Pisces has just the drive and ambition and necessary self-centredness to see her vision to completion, to go and promote herself if need be, to refuse to take no for an answer. She has the tenacity to make it as an artist on her own, or as a business woman in the arts field.

Acting and film also attract the Triangle/Pisces. The artistry and ability to deal with fantasy and illusion comes from the Pisces element; the toughness and the necessary single-mindedness to succeed in such a ruthless and competitive place as Hollywood, for instance, is provided by the ultra-Yang body type. Efficient, hard-working and more intuitive and emotional than the average Triangle type, Triangle/Pisces will go far if she can admit without embarrassment the extent of her need to be in the limelight and to run the show.

Music and dancing is also a fruitful place for this most talented of women. Ballet is dominated by Piscean mega-stars – from the immortal Nijinsky and his successor, Nureyev, through to the dazzling (and difficult) prima ballerina Sylvie Guillem (Triangle/Pisces), and the equally starry Leslie Collier and Antoinette Sibley. The strong body and the absolute iron determination and discipline that ballet at this level demands is all to be found in a Triangle/Pisces. The world of singing is similarly littered with Pisceans. The greatest tenor, Caruso is joined by Kiri te Kanawa (Hourglass/Pisces), Nat King Cole and Nina Simone (Rectangle/Pisces) – all singers with quite remarkable powers to

touch the soul. The Triangle/Pisces Elaine Paige, who was moving and memorable in *Evita* and *Cats* is another powerful singer. Triangle/Pisces may not decide to make music or dancing her career, but she is very likely to want to do one or the other as a hobby.

The altruistic side of Pisces combined with the ambition and dynamism of the Triangle type might take her into the healing arts, but more on the administrative side. She could run a hospital with a great combination of compassion and businesslike verve, perhaps, or go and do overseas service where her Yang side would protect her from compassion fatigue.

Her religious side can take any form from an orthodox belief in one of the Western churches to the practice of Buddhism, pantheism or even more subjective mysticism. Triangle/Pisces may choose to become a priest, and she has the determination to fight for her vocation against a wall of prejudice. Or she may prefer to journey on alone, researching, thinking, writing books or reaching people through other media. She has a force of character and conviction which can carry her message to others, although she's better dealing with the abstract than with the reality of fallible, needy people, each demanding some sort of relationship with her.

Ideal Fantasy Job

Running MGM film studios. Nothing could combine better these two apparently opposing energies in Triangle/Pisces than a hard-driving, monstrously difficult job managing the ultimate Dream Machine. Triangle/Pisces has the vision to know what will be box-office hit material. She has an uncanny direct line into the workings of the collective unconscious, but she is much more than the poet that that implies. Her Triangle body type gives her the necessary ruthlessness in action to keep such a giant corporation full of overwheening egos in operation (and in credit).

IN LOVE

Here may lurk some real problems for a Triangle/Pisces who has not sorted out the conflicts in her character. Pisces brings the most subtle sexuality and seductive qualities to this character, mysterious, allusive, infinitely feminine. BUT, the underlying personality is a broad-shouldered Yang of a woman, who has all the delicacy of feeling of a Sherman tank.

How to integrate these two contradictory energies? With difficulty. When she is younger or less secure, Triangle/Pisces may

imagine herself a little woman who just wants a nice big man to look after her, and her kittenish, play-acting self (Triangle type Dolly Parton, at her most 'little ole me' is one of these) may attract some poor, big, simple soul. But the truth of the matter will emerge with the Triangle/Pisces' growing independence and confidence. She has a formidable will. She's the great big strong one and she'll only clash horribly with a similarly Yang bloke.

Ideally she needs a kind, sympathetic man who will support her emotionally while she carves her career for herself. Her emotional side will be well-hidden, but it is there and she is liable to sudden emotional collapses into lack of confidence, into a neediness for lots of love and tender care. These unexpected fissures in her otherwise pretty impermeable character can cause her and those closest to her some confusion. But they are only the feeling Yin+ side demanding a little recognition from the driven, work-and-success-orientated Yang+ side, which tends to predominate in this combination.

Triangle/Pisces can also deal with these conflicts by becoming suddenly evasive and slipping out of sight or reach, either by shutting herself off emotionally, or by actually disappearing for a few days. Nothing is quite predictable about this woman. She will be some tough cookie most of the time, confident and ambitious, carving her way through corporate life, but then can amaze all, not least herself, with the softness of her heart or sensitivity of her response to someone who needs help.

Children, however, will not necessarily be a central part of her plan. Triangle-type women often come late to motherhood, and sometimes don't choose it at all. They certainly don't wish to stay home and mind the baby full time but are efficient, active and exciting mothers to the offspring they do have.

Triangle/Pisces, with her strong Yin+ influence from her Pisces side, will be more attracted to the idea of motherhood than most Triangle types. But she is still not likely to be entirely fulfilled by it as a full-time job, unless she really goes the whole hog and has four or five children – or more – and turns the whole enterprise into a career. These women have executive energy and a need for power and so won't waste time sitting on the sofa crooning over little babies when they could be building an empire elsewhere. A few might choose to make their empire centred on home and family, but it can be difficult having such a powerful personality focusing all her energy on the vulnerable emerging selves of small children. An outside platform for the Triangle/Pisces ambition might be healthier for all concerned.

Imaginative, full of energy, and sometimes remarkably wise about people and life, Triangle/Pisces makes a rewarding mother

and friend. She has to guard against using her deep Pisces emotions, combined with her will to power, as a powerful tool in the murky waters of emotional blackmail, but the sensitivities she does have enrich her own personality and the relationships she makes.

Ideal Fantasy Lover

Triangle/Pisces needs someone who is sympathetic to the polarities in her character, the Yang+ driven body type and the emotional, imaginative Yin+ star sign. Prince Charles is a man who has been forced to pretend he is as Yang as his father, when all the time he is a sensitive Yin male who has learnt to be self-protective and invulnerable. More interested in his organic gardening and farming at his country house than reviewing regiments and strutting about in ceremonial dress, he will find in Triangle/Pisces a dynamic Yang woman who will help energize him in his difficult role in life. But her Pisces side will also understand his deep but hidden emotional nature. It would be a passionate and well-balanced combination – and Triangle/Pisces would thrive in the limelight as a royal consort, and look wonderful in all those designer clothes!

IN STYLE

Pisces is a mutable sign and even Triangle/Pisces, the most powerful of all the Pisces, still has that ability to change how she looks from one day to the next. She can assume the character of the clothes she wears: casual and sporty in jeans and shirt one day, and knock-em-dead sultry in floor-length black satin crepe the next. Although there's something theatrical about her, she tends to walk the middle ground with most of her dressing.

Most Yang women aren't terribly concerned with the shopping and experimentation involved in putting looks together, they are more practical in their approach and prefer to have standby garments which they feel good in and can rely on. There is a romantic *manque* also in some Triangle/Pisces – despite their broad-shouldered, angular physique, they hanker at times after the drifty moon-maiden look. It doesn't suit them, even if they're very thin, but they can indulge that side of themselves with quirky, individual, designer jewellery, or an imaginative hat. But they should keep to angular masculine shapes, rather than anything too floppy, beribboned and bowed.

The style of clothes that really flatter Triangle/Pisces are determined by her body type. The Triangle shape has broader

shoulders than hips and more of a marked waist than the Rectangle. She falls into two basic types, the small boned, boyish figure like Mia Farrow who probably rarely, if ever, puts on weight and the more muscular, athletic looking type, like Princess Stephanie of Monaco, Jamie Lee Curtis and Anjelica Huston, who can get heavy in the upper torso area, but keeps her inverted triangle shape with straight hips and lean lower legs. When thin, this shape is the classic fashion model shape with coat-hanger shoulders, next-to-nothing-hips and long lean legs.

Some women with this body type try to counteract their broad-shouldered look by wearing flimsy, ultra-feminine clothes – think of Diane Keaton (a Triangle/Aquarius) in *Annie Hall*. Those soft, drifty clothes on the angular Diane make her look a bit like Little Orphan Annie, rather gawky and fey. This suited the character very well in the film, but for Triangle/Pisces, wanting to be taken seriously in the real world, it can be a counterproductive look. Her femininity is best expressed with clothes that have simple geometric lines, certainly angled to the waist if she likes, but it's better to avoid soft fabrics, gathers and bows. For more specific information, see In Style on page 49.

Style Treat

A watch can be a real treat as a status symbol or a piece of fashion fun. Triangle/Pisces won't be as corporate business orientated as some of the other Triangle types but she will nevertheless appreciate the status that a well-chosen watch can give. Since a good watch will give a lifetime, and more, good use it really is an accessory worth investing in and as such it is worth choosing the shape, scale and colour with care. Watches for the Triangle type are better if their faces are square or rectangular. For advice on scale and whether to choose gold or silver, see page 50.

If Triangle/Pisces prefers to make her treat a fun or fashion watch then she can take all these points into consideration, but since she has a quirky sense of fun anyway may well choose to ignore them. For an individual, zany look, Triangle/Pisces can get away with over-the-top accessories – but pint-sized women should resist gallon-sized watches and earrings if she doesn't want to look like Minnie Mouse!

IN HEALTH

Triangle/Pisces is subject to stress, and is hypersensitive to those social antidotes to stress, alcohol and cigarettes. She has a hard time sometimes uniting the extreme feeling Yin side with her

driving, self-centred Yang side and when they are in confusion she can too easily turn to drink and drugs for escape. Much better to tackle the symptom and try and integrate her needs and wishes through meditation and holistic treatments, to which Triangle/ Pisces responds well.

Her feet and the lymphatic system are traditionally areas of weakness for Pisces, but the Triangle body type brings a physical robustness and strength, and a quick recovery time when any illness does strike.

To keep healthy, it is worth looking at the whole area of diet and exercise, too. The Triangle type is likely to have been slim as a teenager, athletic, and with a big appetite. In adulthood, the demands of a family and career can mean she does less exercise, eats the wrong things at wrong times, still has an unrestrained appetite and can then start putting on weight. Triangle/Pisces, however, is very organized and disciplined and when she decides to do something about her shape she works out a routine and readily sticks to it.

Triangle/Pisces positively *needs* regular, energetic exercise and can get depressed if she isn't doing enough. In Bel's questionnaire, 75 per cent of the Triangle types said they recognized that they needed to exercise *and* diet if they were to lose weight – and it was energetic exercise which they favoured: a much higher proportion than the other body types (for instance, only 30 per cent of the Pear types thought exercise important). For more specific information on diet and exercise see In Health on page 50.

CELEBRITY TRIANGLE/PISCES

Ursula Andress is an individualistic Triangle/Pisces. Work has always been central to her life, and she says she is not afraid of any sort of work, however hard: 'I never wanted to be kept by any man and I have never made an exception to my rule'. A long relationship with the Svengali of Triangle-type actresses, John Derek [(went from Ursula (Triangle/Pisces) to Linda Evans (Triangle/ Scorpio) to Bo Derek (another Triangle/Scorpio)] ended when Ursula met Jean Paul Belmondo and entered into a tempestuous relationship, where she played more the admonishing parent to a difficult but delightful child.

Although she admits to being such a powerful character, she has a Piscean propensity to give everything up for love. But it is always she who does the leaving. Then at 42 she got pregnant, had her first child and decided to give Hollywood up to look after him. Again she was 100 per cent emphatic about this, rather too intensely so: 'Yes, I totally gave up my career for my son. I breastfed him and took care of him from day one, never leaving him for a moment . . . Since he was born I've tried to be father and mother to him.' Solitary, individual, very much her own woman, she has now decided as she approaches 60, that she is going back to her career. What she wants, Triangle/Pisces will get, and so will Ursula Andress, the woman who once played *She*.

TRIANGLE/PISCES PROFILE

Isabel works in a music company promoting new singers and bands. She is in her early thirties and full of life and energy, swimming every morning before work. 'Other people think I'm really together and tough, but I don't feel this about myself. I don't feel that I'm attractive or that my body is good.' She is actually very attractive and looks great in the clothes she wears with a very individual sense of style.

'I wouldn't say I'm particularly ambitious – although I am at the moment because I want to make a career change. But I do drive myself and I am hard on myself too. I need to exercise or I would climb the wall. People are always telling me "Slow down" '

Isabel is really friendly in the changing rooms at the local swimming baths where she swims most mornings. Unlike most of the other swimmers, she talks to everyone and knows their names. 'I care very much about other people and wish I didn't – you can't expect anything back. I feel highly sensitive to people and feel their pain. I don't like anyone to be sad – even strangers. I wish I could be more focused on myself.'

She is emphatic about not wanting children: '*Anything* is more important than kids! I definitely don't want children, so much so that I was sterilized at the age of twenty seven. However, I do love other people's kids and have a strong mothering instinct for kids and men.'

'I've had some pretty disastrous relationships with men and a year ago decided they weren't worth the effort so I gave up on them. Now, to my great surprise, a man who has been a friend for ages is starting to be more than that. And, so far, things are going well. This relationship is different. In the past I've always done the mothering, the giving and, if I've dared to show my vulnerable side, the man in my life has been horrified. They were only interested in my strength and what I could give to them. But this guy, well, it's more equal. He doesn't seem to mind my needy, weaker side – says he likes that I'm vulnerable sometimes. And it's nice – I don't have to be strong all the time. Perhaps it's true

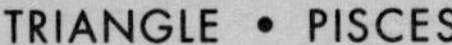

that you have to give something up, let it go, before you can truly have it.'

IN HOPE

This combination of extremes, Yang+ with Yin+, has the potential for great things. For creativity energized by single-mindedness of purpose, for dreams rooted in real life. Triangle/Pisces can be an enigma to herself and those who know and love her because she can express the toughness and the sweetness, the iron claw in the velvet glove, and it is always hard to predict which side is going to prevail.

But in the searching for self and the secret of life, Triangle/Pisces never loses her sense of humour. She is also not one to be pompous and self-important – but can be taken unawares by self-pity. One side of her agrees with the old French proverb, which likens life to an onion, which you peel crying. But in her wiser, more mystical self, she understands what Nabokov means: 'Human life is but a series of footnotes to a vast obscure unfinished manuscript.' And Triangle/Pisces has a clearer view of it than most.